D1420737

AA

ILLUSTRATED GUIDE TO FRANCE

With **MICHELIN**® *Maps*

Published by The Automobile Association
Fanum House, Basingstoke, Hampshire RG21 2EA

Project editor: Rebecca King
Copy editor: Richard Dawes
Editorial contributors:
Paul Atterbury (The North, The Loire)
Keith Howell (Paris and the Ile de France)
John Lloyd (Burgundy, The Rhône Valley)
Robin Neillands (Brittany, Normandy)
Tony Oliver (Auvergne and Languedoc, Provence and the Côte d'Azur)
Ian Powys (Alsace and Lorraine, Franche-Comté)
Mary Ratcliffe (The Atlantic Coast, Périgord and Quercy)
Kev Reynolds (The Pyrenees)
Richard Sales (Auvergne and Languedoc, Provence and the Côte d'Azur)
Melissa Shales (Berry and Limousin)
John White (The Alps)

Published by The Automobile Association, Fanum House, Basingstoke, Hampshire RG21 2EA

Mapping reproduced with the permission of Michelin from the 1:200 000 map series, sheets 51-90 and the 1:1 000 000 map sheet 989.

Key maps and regional maps produced by The Automobile Association

A catalogue record for this book is available from the British Library.

ISBN 07495 0500 1

Typesetting by Avonset Ltd., Midsomer Norton
Colour reproduction by Scantrans Pte Ltd., Singapore
Printed and bound in Italy by Amilcare Pizzi s.p.a.

Pages two and three: a rural scene in Burgundy
Pages ten and eleven: a boulangerie in Dieppe

CONTENTS

REGIONS AND DÉPARTEMENTS

In this book France has been divided into 16 regions as numbered and colour-coded on the map opposite. Individual maps of these regions appear at the beginning of each section.

The map also shows the *départements* into which France is divided. Each *département* has a standard number, as shown on the map and in the key, which for postal purposes replaces its name. These numbers also form part of the registration number of French cars, thus indicating the *département* in which the car was registered. The *départements* are listed here alphabetically under the regional headings of the book.

1 BRITTANY (Bretagne)
Côtes-du-Nord 22
Finistère 29
Ille-et-Vilaine 35
Morbihan 56

2 NORMANDY (Normandie)
Calvados 14
Eure 27
Manche 50
Orne 61
Seine-Maritime 76

3 THE NORTH (Nord)
Aisne 02
Ardennes 08
Aube 10
Marne 51
Marne(Haute-) 52
Nord 59
Oise 60
Pas-de-Calais 62
Somme 80

4 ALSACE AND LORRAINE (Alsace et Lorraine)
Meurthe-et-Moselle 54
Meuse 55
Moselle 57
Rhin (Bas-) 67
Rhin (Haut-) 68
Vosges 88

5 THE LOIRE (Loire)
Cher 18 (part)
Eure-et-Loir 28
Indre 36 (part)
Indre-et-Loire 37
Loir-et-Cher 41
Loire-Atlantique 44
Loiret 45
Maine-et-Loire 49
Mayenne 53
Sarthe 72
Sèvres (Deux-) 79 (part)
Vienne 86 (part)

6 PARIS AND THE ILE DE FRANCE (Paris et Ile de France)
Essonne 91
Hauts-de-Seine 92
Paris 75
Seine-et-Marne 77
Yvelines 78
Seine-St-Denis 93
Val-de-Marne 94
Val-d'Oise 95

7 BURGUNDY (Bourgogne)
Côte-d'Or 21
Nièvre 58
Saône-et-Loire 71
Yonne 89

8 FRANCHE-COMTÉ (Franche-Comté)
Belfort (Territoire-de-) 90
Doubs 25
Jura 39
Saône (Haute-) 70

9 THE ATLANTIC COAST (Côte Atlantique)
Charente 16
Charente-Maritime 17
Gironde 33
Landes 40
Sèvres (Deux-) 79 (part)
Vendée 85
Vienne 86 (part)

10 BERRY AND LIMOUSIN (Berry et Limousin)
Cher 18 (part)
Creuse 23
Indre 36 (part)
Vienne (Haute-) 87

11 AUVERGNE AND LANGUEDOC (Auvergne et Languedoc)
Allier 03
Ardèche 07 (part)
Aveyron 12 (part)
Cantal 15
Gard 30 (part)
Hérault 34
Loire (Haute-) 43
Lozère 48
Puy-de-Dôme 63
Tarn 81

12 THE RHÔNE VALLEY (Vallée du Rhône)
Ain 01 (part)
Ardèche 07 (part)
Drôme 26 (part)
Isère 38 (part)
Loire 42
Rhône 69

13 THE ALPS (Alpes)
Ain 01 (part)
Alpes (Hautes-) 05
Drôme 26 (part)
Isère 38 (part)
Savoie 73
Savoie (Haut-) 74

14 PÉRIGORD AND QUERCY (Périgord et Quercy)
Aveyron 12 (part)
Corrèze 19
Dordogne 24
Lot 46
Lot-et-Garonne 47
Tarn-et-Garonne 82

15 THE PYRENEES (Pyrénées)
Ariège 09
Aude 11
Garonne (Haute-) 31
Gers 32
Pyrénées-Atlantiques 64
Pyrénées (Hautes-) 65
Pyrénées Orientales 66

16 PROVENCE AND THE CÔTE D'AZUR (Provence et Côte d'Azur)
Alpes-de-Haute-Provence 04
Alpes Maritimes 06
Bouches-du-Rhône 13
Drôme 26 (part)
Gard 30 (part)
Var 83
Vaucluse 84

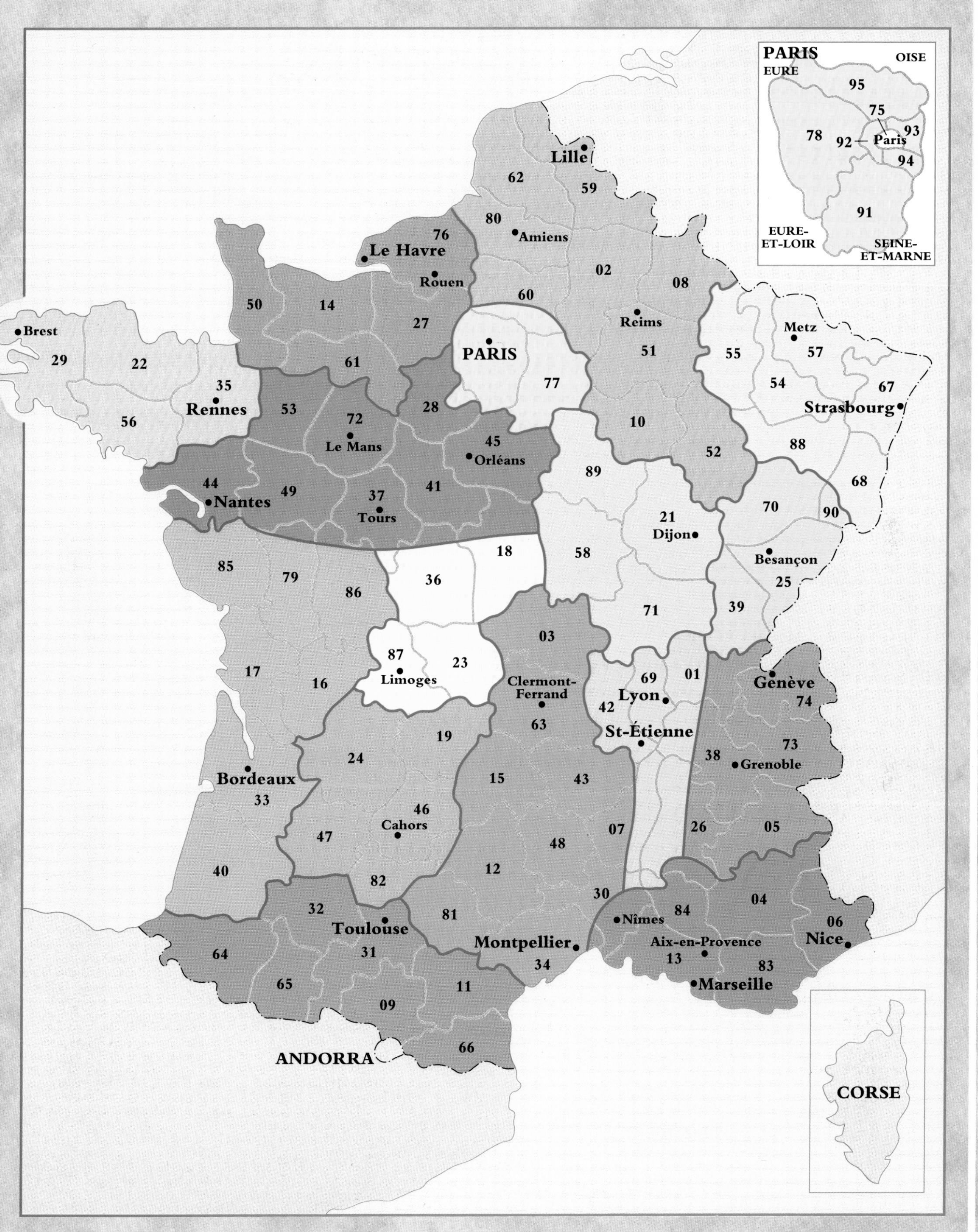
PARIS
EURE
OISE
95
75
93
78
92
Paris
94
91
EURE-ET-LOIR
SEINE-ET-MARNE
Lille
62
59
80
Amiens
76
Le Havre
Rouen
02
08
60
50
14
27
Reims
Brest
29
22
PARIS
51
55
Metz
57
61
35
77
54
67
Rennes
53
28
Strasbourg
56
72
Le Mans
10
45
Orléans
52
88
89
44
Nantes
49
37
Tours
41
68
70
90
21
Dijon
85
18
58
79
36
Besançon
25
86
71
39
03
87
Limoges
23
17
16
Clermont-Ferrand
69
01
Genève
74
Lyon
42
63
St-Étienne
19
73
24
38
Grenoble
Bordeaux
15
43
33
46
Cahors
47
07
26
05
48
40
12
82
30
04
32
Toulouse
81
Nîmes
84
06
Nice
Aix-en-Provence
64
31
Montpellier
13
34
83
Marseille
65
11
09
66
ANDORRA
CORSE

ABOUT THIS BOOK

Each of the 16 regions into which France has been divided opens with an introduction and a map showing the extent of the region. Within each of these sections there is a selection of some of the best areas the region has to offer and these, illustrated with Michelin mapping, are laid out as illustrated below.

Interspersed with these pages are features which examine in detail subjects, ranging from churches to mountaineering, that are particularly associated with the regions.

Location maps pinpoint the area covered by each extract of Michelin mapping.

A short introduction captures the flavour of each selected area and highlights its distinguishing characteristics.

Listed alphabetically, these places fall within the map extract shown. They range from large cities to natural features.

Within each region various areas of particular interest have been selected and these are illustrated with extracts of Michelin mapping. The majority of these extracts are at a scale of 1:200 000, but those extracts on pages 42, 50, 118, 172 and 242 are at a scale of 1:1000 000. Legends for mapping are shown opposite.

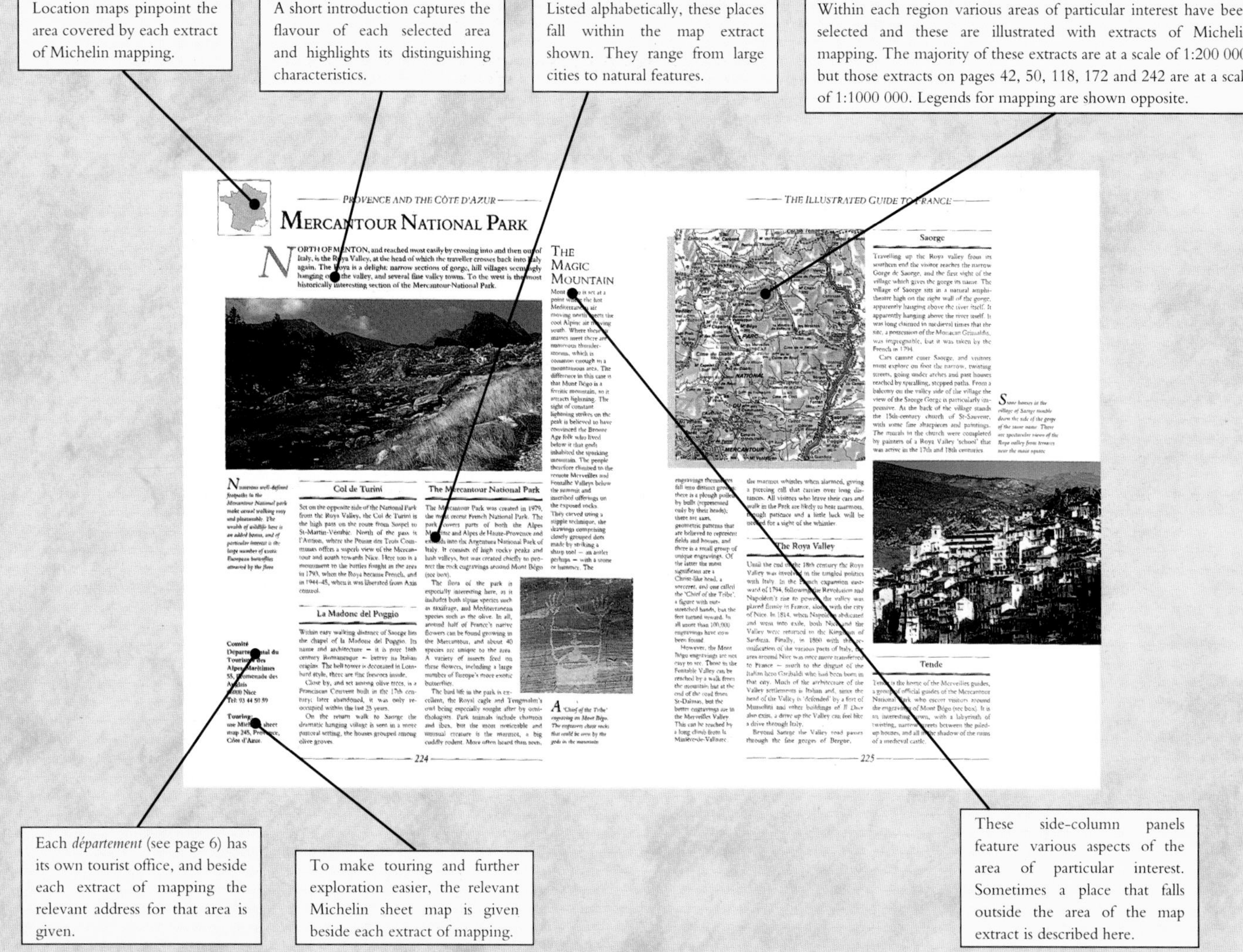

Each *département* (see page 6) has its own tourist office, and beside each extract of mapping the relevant address for that area is given.

To make touring and further exploration easier, the relevant Michelin sheet map is given beside each extract of mapping.

These side-column panels feature various aspects of the area of particular interest. Sometimes a place that falls outside the area of the map extract is described here.

INTERNATIONAL DISTINGUISHING SIGNS

The following signs are used on the regional maps, which appear at the beginning of each section, to indicate adjacent countries.

B	Belgium	CH	Switzerland
D	Federal Republic of Germany	E	Spain
L	Luxemburg	I	Italy

Motorways - Roads

Motorways : dual carriageway, single carriageway
Dual carriageway with motorway characteristics (no at grade junctions)
Numbered junctions : complete, limited
Major road
Secondary road network
Road : surfaced, unsurfaced or of doubtful quality
Cycle track - Cart track, footpath
Motorway, road under construction
(where available : with scheduled opening date)

Road width

Dual carriageway
Four lanes
Three lanes
Two wide lanes
Two lanes
One lane
One narrow lane

Obstacles

1:20 to 1:12 — 1:11 to 1:8 — + 1:7
Gradient (ascent in the direction of the arrow)
Pass and its height in metres above sea level — 1250
Difficult or dangerous stretch of road
Level crossing, railway passing under road, over road
Headroom (given when less than 4.50 m)
Car ferry (Michelin Red Guide France gives the phone numbers of main ferries)
Ferry (pedestrians and cycles only)
Load limit of a bridge, of a car ferry (given when less than 19 t)
Drawbridge or swing bridge - Toll barrier
Load limit of a national or secondary road
One-way road
Road subject to restrictions (closed at certain times, tidal traffic flow,...)
Prohibited road

Distances

Total distances — 15 — 17 — 11
Intermediary distances — 7 8 toll section — 12 5 free section — 6 5 on other roads

Accommodation

The information below corresponds with the selections given in the various Michelin Guides.

Red frame : towns having a plan in the Michelin Red Guides « Hotels and Restaurants »
Red underlining : towns or places mentioned in the Michelin Red Guides — St Jean
Camping sites listed in the Michelin Guide « Camping Caravaning »
Secluded hotel or restaurant

Tourist information

Most of these sights are described in the Michelin Green Guides

Viewing table
Panoramic view
Viewpoint
Scenic route
Ecclesiastical building
Castle
Ruins
Megalithic monument
Lighthouse
Windmill
Cave
Other place of interest

Stadium
Golf course
Racecourse
Riding
Bathing
Swimming pool
Sailing
Country park
Cable-car, chairlift
Mountain refuge hut
Long distance footpath — GR
Gliding airfield - Parachuting

Railway, station
Tourist train
Mountain airfield
Airfield
Airport
Communications tower or mast
Emergency telephone
National boundary
Customs post
Oil or gas well
Quarry
Mine
Overhead conveyor
Factory or power station
Dam
Lighthouse
Windmill
Water tower
Hospital
Church or chapel
Cemetery - Wayside cross
Castle
Fort
Ruins
Statue or building — Mon!
Cave
Forester's lodge — MF
Forest or wood
State forest

Seat of local government : Prefecture.. P , Sub-prefecture.. SP , Canton.. © — Altitude..(340)

UN PAIN POUR
30 Sortes
PLAISIR DE LA CHASSE

A Journey Through France

France is the heart of Europe, and in terms of its landscape, architecture, culture and history it is incomparable, without rival in the wealth and diversity of its appeal. Just across the Channel, and increasingly accessible, there is another world, full of secret delights waiting to be discovered and whose pleasures are a constant temptation to the senses. It is a world of space, light and colour, to be enjoyed in haste or at leisure, and made memorable by its contrasts. In France there is room still for both the traditional and the modern and for a way of life that reflects both the pace of change and the impact of centuries of civilisation.

This book is a guide to the best of France, a region by region exploration of the familiar and the unfamiliar by writers and photographers united by their love of the country, and by their intimate knowledge of their chosen areas. Together, they bring to life the distinctive qualities of a country remarkable for its variety in a book designed to please both the casual visitor and the dedicated traveller.

France is a country for all tastes and all times, always responsive to visitors' expectations and demands. This book will make easier the appreciation and enjoyment of a country whose essential differences are part of its widespread appeal.

Paul Atterbury

BRITTANY

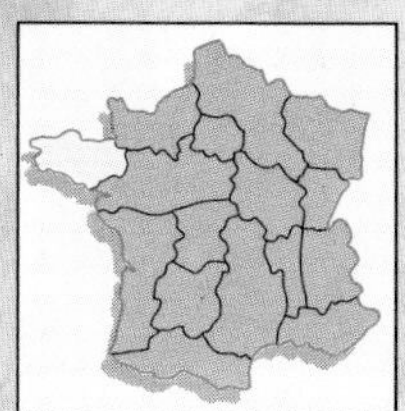

BRITTANY IS NOT LIKE OTHER parts of France. Brittany is Celtic, outward-looking, defiant, a wolf's head snapping and snarling at the green waves of the Atlantic. It is a place where the people sing their own songs, speak their own tongue and maintain their own ways in spite of the eroding influences that come in across the River Couesnon.

That Brittany remains so different from other parts of France is hardly surprising because it became part of France late. The first dynastic link came in 1491 when the Duchess Anne – that same duchess who is commemorated in the names of restaurants and cafés all over Brittany – married Charles VIII of France. To maintain the link when he died in 1498 she then married his successor, Louis XII, but it was her daughter Claude who married François I and finally ceded the Duchy to the French Crown, although that was not until 1532.

Brittany is a place of magic and myth. King Arthur's wizard, Merlin, lives on in Brittany, trapped inside a stone in the Forêt de Brocéliande, which some call the Forêt de Paimpont, and if you pour water on his stone it rains. Processions of local people go to the stone in times of drought and pour on the water, and it usually rains. In a nearby castle Lancelot of the Lake was born.

Those who prefer a legendary character who actually lived need look no further than Dinan, home of the good knight and sometime Constable of France, Bertrand du Guesclin, whose body may lie with the kings in St-Denis but whose heart is safe in Dinan. For something rather more curious, visitors can splash across at low tide from St Malo to the Ile du Grand Bé, and visit the grave of the writer Chateaubriand, all alone on the rock, facing out to sea.

Brittany is full of such fabled characters and living legends. It boasts over 7000 saints, most of whom no foreigner has ever heard of, though some, such as St Yves, are world-famous. To their shrines go the pilgrimage processions, the Breton *pardons*, to their glory and memory stand the great calvaries and the *enclos paroissiaux* (parish closes) of Finistère. Brittany has menhirs, including lines of these megaliths at Carnac, great castles such as Josselin and walled towns such as Vannes, Vitré and St Malo, the city of the Corsairs, and many more pretty places.

The coastline is long, rugged and full of sandy beaches and rocky coves, with offshore islands where sea birds gather. And for something different yet again, there is the Morbihan, the wonderful Little Sea of Brittany (*Mor* meaning sea and *bihan*, small). The Bretons prize both the coast, Armorica, the Country of the Sea, and the Argoat, the Country of Wood, with its tracery of footpaths, canals and winding country roads. Brittany is not a place to rush around in, but one where wise visitors take their time, exploring this Celtic province at a gentle pace.

If there is a snag with Brittany – and every honest guidebook finds at least one – it is that this is not the place to visit if you hate seafood. Here it is excellent.

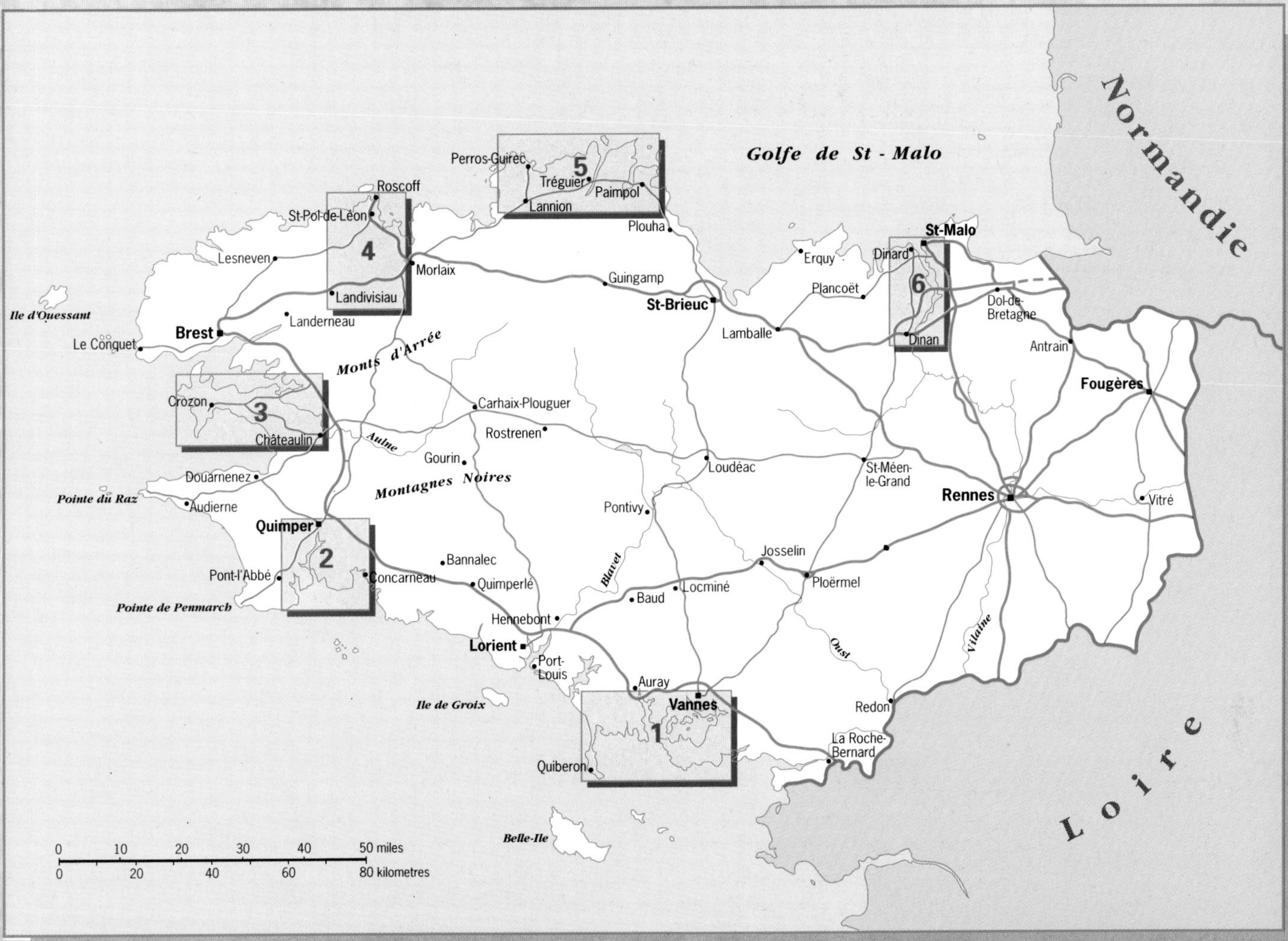

Golfe de St - Malo
Normandie
Loire
Ile d'Ouessant
Le Conquet
Brest
Lesneven
Landerneau
St-Pol-de-Léon
Roscoff
4
Landivisiau
Morlaix
Perros-Guirec
5
Tréguier
Paimpol
Lannion
Plouha
Guingamp
St-Brieuc
Erquy
Plancoët
Dinard
St-Malo
6
Dinan
Dol-de-Bretagne
Lamballe
Antrain
Fougères
Monts d'Arrée
Crozon
3
Châteaulin
Aulne
Carhaix-Plouguer
Rostrenen
Gourin
Montagnes Noires
Douarnenez
Pointe du Raz
Audierne
Quimper
2
Pont-l'Abbé
Pointe de Penmarch
Concarneau
Bannalec
Quimperlé
Hennebont
Lorient
Port-Louis
Ile de Groix
Blavet
Pontivy
Loudéac
St-Méen-le-Grand
Rennes
Vitré
Baud
Locminé
Josselin
Ploërmel
Oust
Vilaine
Auray
Vannes
1
Quiberon
Belle-Ile
Redon
La Roche-Bernard
0 10 20 30 40 50 miles
0 20 40 60 80 kilometres

Traditional Breton costumes (right)

Finistère, in the north-west, has a dramatic rocky coast (below right)

Standing stones are a common sight in Brittany. Around Carnac (above) there are more than 5000

Pilgrimage processions, or pardons, *take place throughout Brittany. Those saints who have a shrine – there are many in the region – are traditionally celebrated in these annual events*

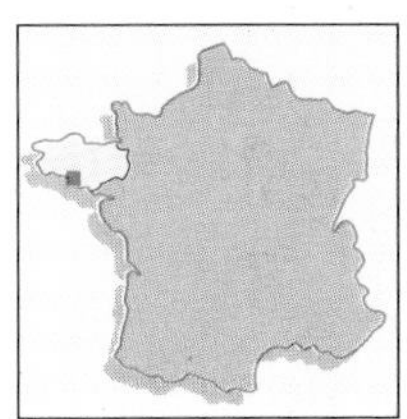

The Morbihan Gulf and the Megaliths of Carnac

THE SOUTHERN DÉPARTEMENT of Brittany, Morbihan, is full of interest. It contains historic towns such as Vannes and Auray, the famous menhirs or standing stones of Carnac and the long Quiberon peninsula. All these places and many others worth visiting lie on or around the shores of the Morbihan. This great tidal gulf, crammed with islands, is a paradise for yachtsmen and sea birds.

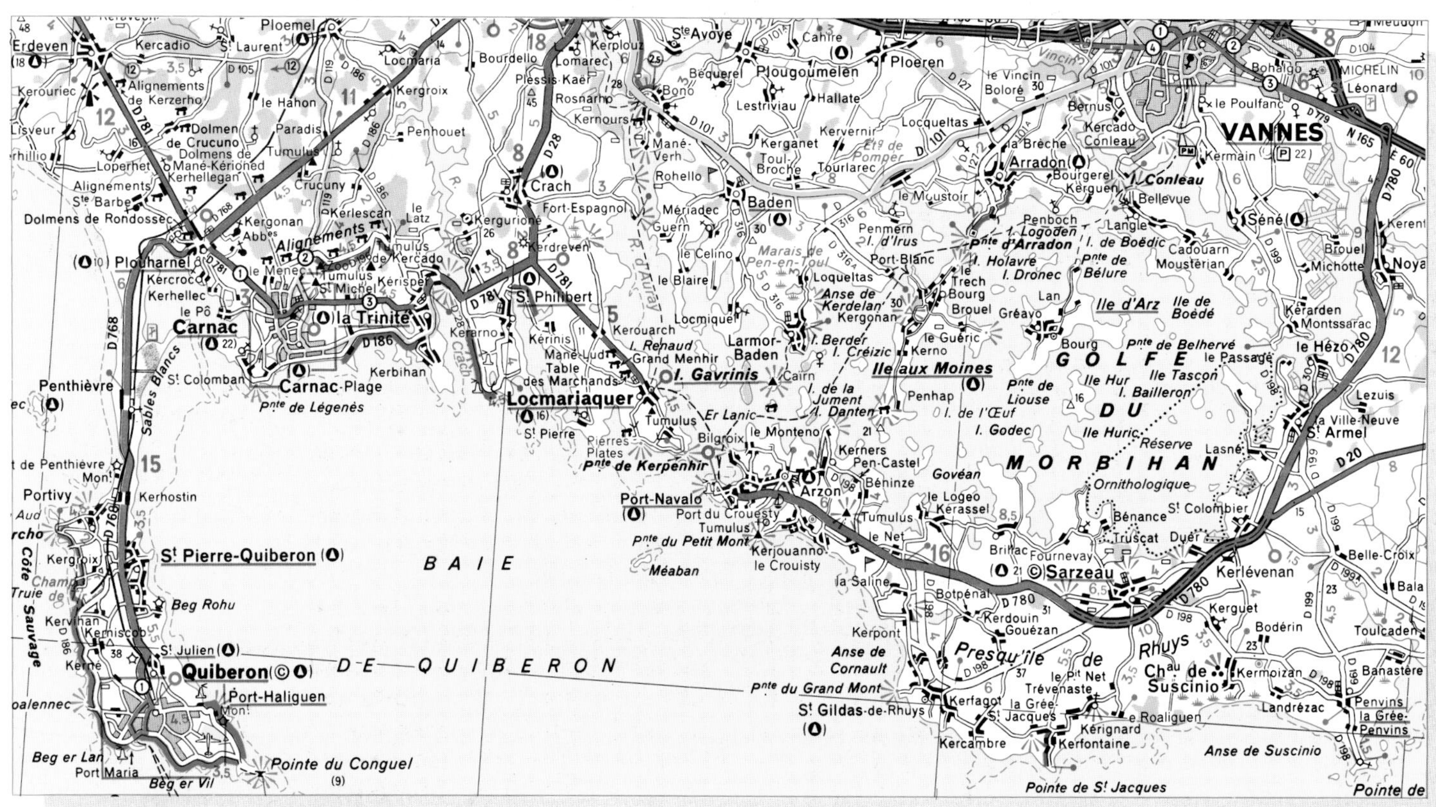

Standing stones such as these at Carnac may have indicated the direction of the sunrise at the solstices and the equinox, so playing a part in sun worship

Carnac

The standing stones of Carnac are said to form part of a prehistoric solar observatory arranged in long lines, one of which, the Alignements du Ménec, is nearly 1.5km long. The sight of these long lines of standing stones is curiously impressive. The story of what their purpose may be and how they were preserved is told in Carnac's Musée Miln-Le Rouzic.

Locmariaquer

This village overlooks the narrow gap through which the Atlantic pours into the Morbihan gulf, and is another prehistoric sight, famous for the great dolmens and menhirs that lie in and around the village in considerable numbers. The largest and most impressive of all are the shattered Grand Menhir, which was over 20m tall, and the great flat Table des Marchands, which seals a huge tumulus. Boats of the Vedettes Vertes fleet stop here on their cruise around the gulf.

Golfe Du Morbihan

The Morbihan, or 'little sea', of Brittany, is one of the great attractions of the province. This is not simply because of the beauty of the gulf itself, a maze of sandbanks and green islands flooded twice a day by the Atlantic, and studded with the sails of cruising yachts, but also because of the interesting and historic places that lie around the shore.

The gulf is some 20km wide and about 15km in length, running inland from the

Comité Départemental du Tourisme du Morbihan
Hôtel du Département
Rue Saint-Tropez - BP 400
56009 Vannes Cedex
Tel: 97 54 06 56

Touring:
use Michelin sheet map 230, Bretagne

Quiberon harbour is used by both sardine fishermen and pleasure boats since, like many fishing ports in Brittany, the town is also a popular tourist resort

Megaliths

Brittany is full of prehistoric sites, and menhirs, or standing stones, appear all over the province. There is a particularly splendid specimen at St Duzec, near Perros-Guirec, and more at St Pierre-Quiberon in the Morbihan, close to the great number of large dolmens at Locmariaquer. These great flat stones cover grave-pits that date back to the early Celtic period, long before the coming of the Romans who invaded this part of Gaul in the 1st century BC. Splendid as these are, no megalithic site in Europe can rival the standing stones of Carnac. The word 'megalith' means 'large stone', and there are more than 5000 megaliths around Carnac, most of them arranged in long lines – a feature that adds to the great mystery surrounding their transportation and erection. The manpower required must have been immense. But what are they for?

The Musée Miln-Le Rouzic in Carnac, founded by a Scot in 1881, gives a good account of the Carnac megaliths and their construction and contains a great number of prehistoric artefacts.

narrow channel between Locmariaquer and Port-Navalo to the walled city of Vannes. About 40 of the gulf's many islands are inhabited. The largest of these is the Ile aux Moines, which, as the name indicates, was once inhabited by a community of monks. The climate of this island is a certain attraction, for it is mild and mellow and permits palm trees and exotic flowers such as mimosa and camellias to flourish among the small walled gardens. The Ile aux Moines can be visited by taking one of the Vedettes Vertes ferries that ply around the gulf from Vannes.

The Ile d'Arz, just to the east of the Ile aux Moines, is somewhat smaller but still inhabited and noted for its megalithic tombs, which are quite common in and around the gulf.

Quiberon

Set at the far end of a long peninsula, the town of Quiberon is a sardine fishing port and tourist resort, the point of departure for visitors sailing to Belle-Ile. The Quiberon peninsula is flanked by wide beaches popular with devotees of sand yachting, and the Côte Sauvage is the name given to the peninsula's wild west coast.

Places to visit here include the beautiful village of Port Maria at the southern end of the Côte Sauvage, and if time permits, Belle-Ile, an hour away by ferry. Belle-Ile once belonged to Nicolas Fouquet, finance minister to Louis XIV, and was captured briefly by the British in 1761. The main town, Le Palais, is most attractive. The island's west coast is, like that of the Quiberon peninsula, known as the Côte Sauvage.

St Gildas-de-Rhuys

The village here grew up around the monastery founded by St Gildas-de-Rhuys in the 6th century, which became famous after Abélard, a noted scholar and the lover of Héloïse, became the abbot here at the end of the 11th century.

Visitors to St Gildas can see the much-restored abbey church, built in the 11th century, which still holds the tomb of St Gildas and a reliquary containing his arms and legs. The abbey is set in a beautiful spot near the sea and the great ducal castle of Suscinio, which was besieged and taken by Bertrand du Guesclin in 1373. The repairs he made to the breach can still be seen in the curtain wall. Close to Suscinio is the town of Sarzeau, now a resort and once the home of Le Sage, the author of *Gil Blas*.

Vannes

Walled Vannes is a splendid example of a medieval town, and with the walls still standing above formal gardens the setting is quite beautiful.

The streets of Vannes are narrow and winding, and lead to the Cathédrale St-Pierre, which holds the tomb of St Vincent Ferrier, who died in Vannes in 1419. The town has a great many old houses, with some very fine examples in Rue de la Monnaie, one of which bears two gargoyles known locally as Vannes and his Wife.

A good number of robust town houses, some of which have been turned into shops, survive in the old quarter of Vannes

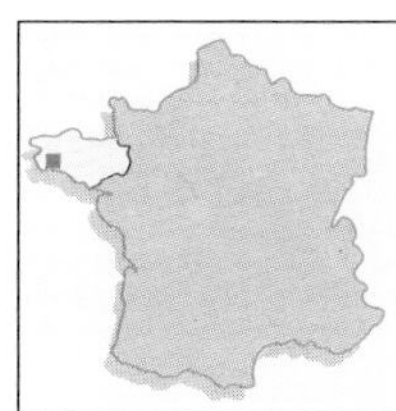

QUIMPER AND THE COAST OF CORNOUAILLE

THE SOUTHERN PART of the *département* of Finistère, Cornouaille is the old heart of Brittany, a place of legend and folklore. Part of this area, around Pont-l'Abbé, is the Bigouden district, a place where the Breton language is still spoken and where visitors are most likely to see people wearing traditional costume.

Bénodet

Bénodet is the archetypal modern seaside resort. It has beaches and a marina, a conference centre, a casino and many hotels, restaurants and discothèques.

Essential sights include the lighthouse – the Phare de la Pyramide – which is open to visitors, and there are various corniches that also give fine views over the sea and the harbour. The church of St Thomas dates from the 13th century and is dedicated to the English martyr St Thomas à Becket. There is a bridge across the Odet and a ferry to the village of Ste Marine, and boats go upstream to Quimper.

Built between the mid-13th and the early 16th centuries, Quimper's striking cathedral is considered to be the most complete Gothic cathedral in Brittany. Its twin spires were added much later, in 1856

Concarneau

Concarneau is one of the major fishing ports of Brittany and a particularly attractive one, with a medieval quarter – the *ville close* – a colourful fishing fleet and an annual festival. This takes place on the third Sunday in August, when the blue nets of the fleet are hung up with bunting and most of the fishermen don traditional costume.

Sights to see in Concarneau include the daily fish auction, where a great number and variety of fish, especially tunny, are sold. The *ville close* occupies an island in the middle of the port and a walk around its ramparts is the best way to look at the new town on the mainland and the fishing fleet in the harbour.

There is a shellwork craft centre, a fishing museum and the Marinarium.

Fouesnant

This pretty village stands in rich farming country, surrounded by apple and cherry orchards, the former for the production of Breton *cidre-bouché*, for which the village is famous. The villagers usually wear traditional dress and always do so for the *pardon* of St Anne, which takes place on the nearest Sunday to the 26 July. Local costume is also worn by the figures depicted in the carvings on the monument outside the 12th-century church.

Loctudy

The tiny seaport of Loctudy lies at the mouth of the Pont-l'Abbé estuary and was once one of the main fishing ports for the Bigouden district. The setting and the small houses and cottages around the harbour are the chief attractions but the church is said to be the finest Romanesque church in all Brittany and is worth seeing for this reason alone. From the harbour it is possible to take a boat to Ile-Tudy, a pretty fishing port well off the tourist track.

COIFFES

Breton *coiffes*, attractive lace head-dresses, were once an everyday feature of Breton women's dress but are rarely seen today except at *pardons*, at weddings in Finistère and, from time to time, in church and at markets. The *coiffe* is the most distinctive item of traditional Breton apparel but the full costume includes a black dress and a fine lace apron, which, like the *coiffe*, varies in style from place to place. The men have their own costume – rather less distinctive, again in black but with an embroidered waistcoat and a beribboned felt hat – but it is usually the ladies' *coiffes* that steal the show.

Of the several different regional styles of Breton *coiffe*, the most famous is the tall 'Bigouden' *coiffe* from the country around Pont-l'Abbé. There is a good display of *coiffes* in the museum at Quimper.

THE BRETON LANGUAGE

Breton is a Celtic tongue and those who speak Welsh, Cornish or Gaelic, especially Irish Gaelic, can understand it, at least to a certain degree. Undermined for many years by French, Breton is now undergoing a revival, and is taught again in many schools in Brittany, especially in Finistère, where visitors may sometimes hear it spoken in village markets. Visitors will soon pick up a few Breton words, realising that *ker* means place or village, *lann* means church, *plou* means parish and *aber* means estuary.

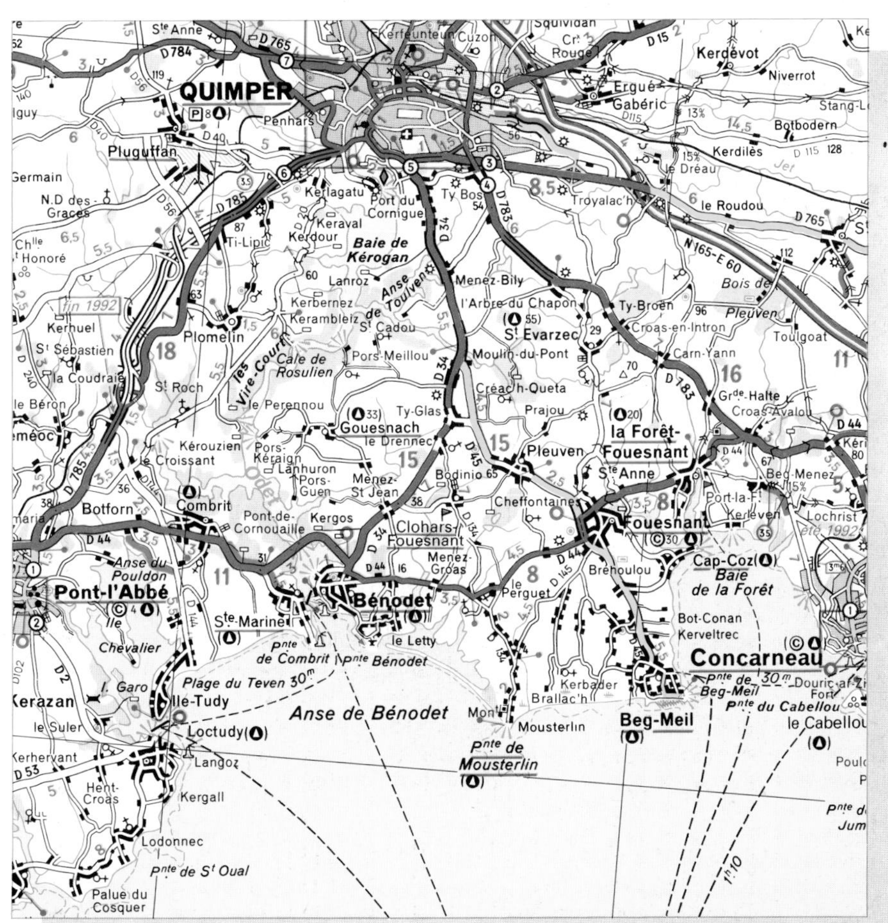

Comité Départemental du Tourisme du Finistère
11, Rue Théodore-le-Hars - BP 125
29104 Quimper Cedex
Tel: 98 53 09 00

Touring:
use Michelin sheet map 230, Bretagne

Pont-l'Abbé

Pont-l'Abbé is the capital of the *pays Bigouden,* the part of Brittany that has most retained its old customs, costumes and traditions. It stands at the head of a wide estuary and takes its name from the bridge that was built here in the Middle Ages by monks from Loctudy. Sights to see include the good possibility of a lace coiffe, especially on Sunday outside the abbey church of Notre-Dame-des-Carmes. They are sure to be worn for the town *pardon,* which takes place on the first Sunday after 15 July. Alternatively, *coiffes* can be inspected in the Bigouden museum in the castle.

Cornouaille's attachment to its roots can be seen in the manufacture and sale of traditional artefacts such as these plates

SEAWEED

Brittany is an agricultural and fishing province, the sea and land producing many valuable cash crops. Among the less familiar harvests is that of seaweed, which is dredged from estuaries, stacked in great piles in the fields and burnt to provide a rich fertiliser. A side benefit is that the constant dredging for seaweed helps to keep the estuaries open and small boats' propellers free of weed. Seaweed is also processed and used in a range of products, from cosmetics to iodine.

Quimper

Set astride the River Odet, Quimper is the capital of Cornouaille. The town hosts an annual international folk-music festival, the Festival de Cornouaille, which attracts performers from all over the world but in particular from the Celtic fringes in Wales, Cornwall and Ireland.

The cathedral is dedicated to a Breton saint, St Corentin, and bears between the two towers the equestrian statue of King Gradlon, ruler of the legendary city of Y's. When Y's was destroyed in a flood, the king came to live in Quimper, where St Corentin looked after him. St Corentin lived on a miraculous fish: he ate half of it every day, throwing the other half into the Odet, where it regrew the missing half, ready to be caught and half-eaten again next day – a reliable if monotonous diet.

The Musée des Beaux-Arts in the town hall has an extensive art collection and the Musée Départemental Breton explains Breton life and the traditions of Finistère. The town has attractive public gardens and good walks along the Odet and up to Mont Frugy.

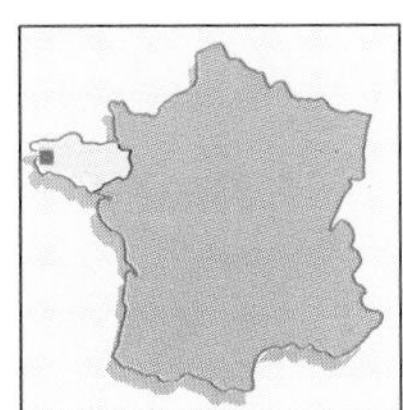

The West Coast and the Crozon Peninsula

THE CROZON PENINSULA rolls out westwards between the jaws of Brittany like a great lolling tongue lapping at the chill green waters of the Atlantic. Although most of the peninsula is a summer resort, it is a place to visit out of season, when the great gales come booming in from the sea, pounding the coast until the air is full of salt sea spray. The hinterland is the Argoat, the old forested heart of Brittany.

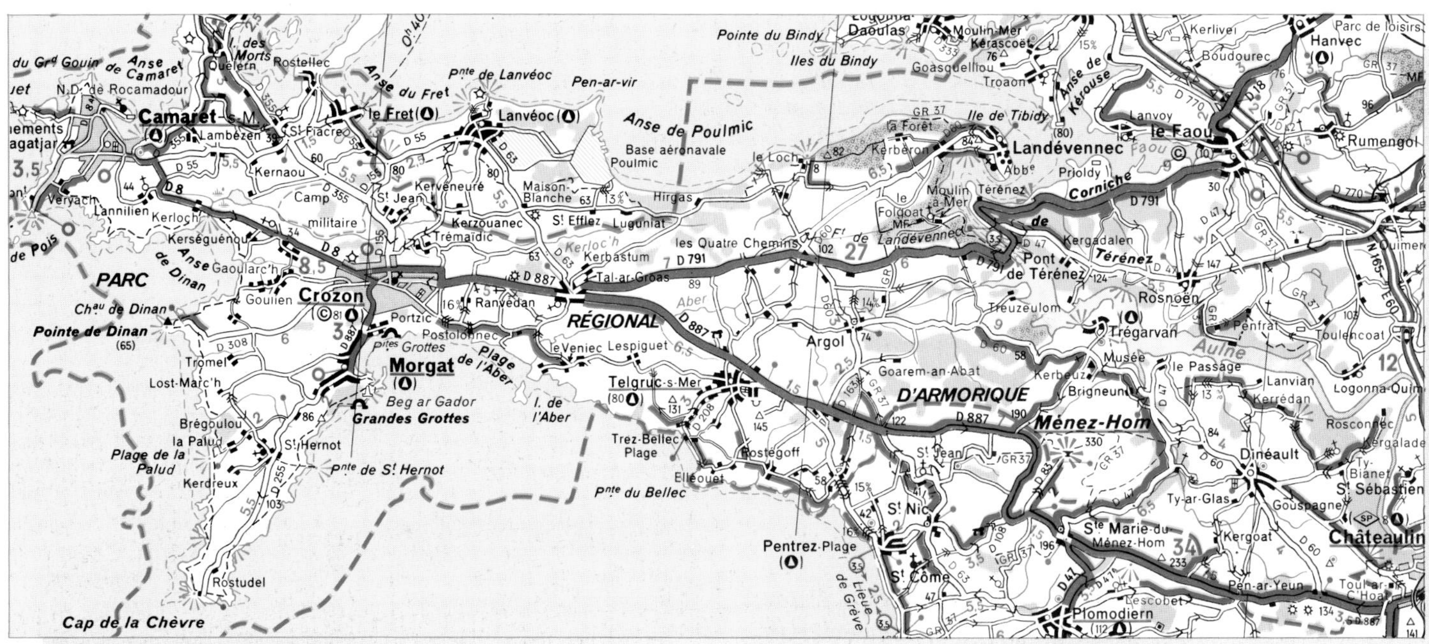

Comité Départemental du Tourisme du Finistère
11, Rue Théodore-le-Hars - BP 125
29104 Quimper Cedex
Tel: 98 53 09 00

Touring:
use Michelin sheet map 230, Bretagne

Camaret-sur-Mer

Camaret is the foremost lobster port of France, but most of these succulent spiny delights vanish soon after landing *en route* for the restaurants of Paris, Nice, London or New York. Even so, the restaurants of Camaret can provide delicious meals and the port itself is pretty. So is the coast on either side, but particularly that to the north, up to the Pointe des Espagnols and the Brest Roads. The American inventor Robert Fulton used the waters off Camaret for his first experiments with his submarine in 1801, during the Napoleonic Wars. Propelled by oars and without a periscope, the submarine unsuccessfully attempted to sink a British frigate in the bay, but Fulton and his gallant crew eventually surfaced and survived.

Apart from the fishing, Camaret is a seaside resort and local sights include the Château Vauban, built to protect Brest in the 17th century, and the chapel of Notre-Dame at the end of the Sillon dyke.

The many opportunities to dine on delicious lobsters and langoustines do much to make Camaret-sur-Mer a popular tourist centre. But it is also a town with a history, for in 1694 the Château Vauban played a significant part in seeing off an attack on the port by a combined British and Dutch fleet

BRETON *PARDONS*

Pardons or pilgrimage processions to the shrine of the local saint are a feature of Breton life and no visitor should miss the chance to see one. Brittany has a great number of saints and all those with a shrine have a *pardon* at least once a year, a celebration and thanks offering from the local people. The pilgrims wear traditional costumes, including *coiffes,* and carry religious banners, while the service at the shrine includes flowers, hymns and candles.

Pardons can be quite jolly affairs, for the procession and service are usually followed by a fair with folk dancing and singing. The most famous *pardons* in Brittany are the one at Ste Anne-d'Auray, on 16 July or the following Sunday, and the one to the chapel at Ste Anne-la-Palud, near Locronan in Finistère on the first Sunday in September. Lawyers come from all over the world to attend the *pardon* of St Yves, their patron saint on 19 May, a ceremony that involves crawling on one's knees beneath a tomb in the churchyard in Minihy-Tréguier.

Châteaulin

This little town on the River Aulne is noted in Brittany for its salmon fishing. Much of the river is tidal and Châteaulin has quays, but the tide subsides before getting this far inland. The best fishing takes place between Châteaulin and the village of Châteauneuf-du-Faou, some 25km upstream. The setting of Châteaulin, a wooded river valley, is most attractive and the town is a good excursion centre. A little way to the west Ménez-Hom rises against the sky, a great bulk of moorland. At its foot is the small chapel of Ste-Marie-du-Ménez-Hom, from where a footpath leads up to the top of the hill. There is a statue of King Gradlon of Y's in the calvary at Argol, and 7km away, in the village of Cast, there is one to St Hubert, the patron saint of hunters.

Crozon

Crozon is the small town that gave its name to the entire peninsula. It is a tourist centre crammed with visitors from Easter to October, although almost empty in winter. The church was built in 1900 and contains a tablet recording the fate of the Theban Legion, who underwent a mass conversion to Christianity and were crucified, all 10,000 of them, on Mount Ararat. Places to visit around Crozon include the beaches at Kerloch and Cap de la Chèvre to the south. Another good excursion is to Pointe Dinan, to watch the waves coming in during a gale. The 'Dinan castle' referred to on maps is simply a large rock joined to the mainland by a natural rock bridge.

Le Faou

This village at the head of the Faou estuary lies on the main road that leads round from Brest on to the Crozon peninsula. Apart from the old houses and the riverside church, it is chiefly notable as a tourist centre for the Argoat and the area around the Brest Roads. A few kilometres to the north lies Daoulas, a small town with a very old *enclos paroissial* (parish close) and calvary. Another excursion from Le Faou is the ride round the Corniche de Térénez.

There are many excellent viewpoints along the Crozon peninsula, but in places the combination of a rocky coastline and strong currents restricts bathing

Morgat

Morgat is the main seaside resort on the south shore of the Crozon peninsula, looking out to the bay of Douarnenez. Like most of the villages on the coast of Brittany, it is also a fishing port and a yachting centre with a large marina, harbour and good beach. The great attraction of Morgat is the caves that stud the surrounding cliffs. Some are of a considerable size, while others are very colourful, with different kinds of rock, and one, the Chambre du Diable, leads out to the cliff top. Some of the caves can be reached at high tide on boat trips from the mole in Morgat.

Castles and Fortresses of Inland Brittany

ALTHOUGH BRITTANY has many coastal castles – at the Fort de la Latte and the Tour Solidor near St Malo, at Suscinio in the south, at Dinan above the Rance – the most splendid examples of medieval military architecture in the province lie inland. Their purpose was both to defend the hinterland from ravaging armies and to protect Brittany's land frontiers from its most implacable foe, France.

Fortunately, these castles had to be maintained and repaired even after the advent of the cannon, and when the final conquest came, it was through marriage rather than the use of the *ultimo ratio regis*, 'the king's last argument' – artillery. As a result they survived the blast of war and even the hand of Cardinal Richelieu, who destroyed many strongholds of the turbulent, provincial French nobility. Many are still in good condition.

Josselin

The castle at Josselin was and remains the home of the dukes of Rohan, one of the oldest and proudest of the Breton noble families. 'King I am not, Prince I would not stoop to be, I am the Duke of Rohan', proclaims one of the family mottoes.

The present castle dates from the late 15th century, when it replaced the one dismantled by the Duke of Brittany. The original castle was the property of the Constable of France, Olivier de Clisson, husband of Marguerite de Rohan. It was from here that Beaumanoir led out the garrison to fight the mainly English garrison of Ploërmel at the Mi-Voie oak, in that murderous tournament of 1351 known as the Battle of the Thirty. The garrison of Josselin triumphed, though not without loss. This battle, fought in a time of truce between France and England, features in Froissart's *Chronicles of the Hundred Years War* and the surviving participants were greatly honoured in the years that followed. The site of the battle is still marked, 5km to the east of the castle, beside the road to Ploërmel.

The present castle has witch's-hat towers and crenellated walls, a small park, thousands of books and much fine furniture in the library, and shows every sign of constant care. The main building was restored as living quarters in the last century and is covered with extremely elaborate carvings and tracery. The castle is open to visitors and one tower can be climbed, the top offering great views over the town and the valley of the Oust.

Apart from the castle, visitors to Josselin can also explore the small and delightful town that surrounds it and visit the Basilique de Notre-Dame-du-Roncier – Our Lady of the Brambles – a much-venerated local shrine. This is the site of a great annual *pardon* on 8 September, and the place where the knights of Josselin prayed before marching out to give battle at the Mi-Voie oak.

Vitré

Over in the east, in the *département* of Ille-et-Vilaine, the visitor will come to a fine frontier castle at Vitré. Essentially a fortified town, Vitré is probably the best preserved medieval town in Brittany, with lots of old houses set about narrow streets and small squares on the way up to the castle. The castle was the seat of the La Trémoille family, who feature frequently in the medieval chronicles and who rebuilt and expanded the castle constantly during the Middle Ages and the Wars of Religion. The present building, triangular with turrets at each corner and curtain walls between, is set behind a large, cobbled forecourt, and overlooks the River Vilaine. The castle is now owned by the municipality and contains the council offices and a fine musuem that records the troubled history of this frontier town and has, among other treasures, Aubusson tapestries and fine furniture.

The best view of the castle is either from the forecourt, Place du Château, or from the road north of the town. Vitré itself is well worth exploring, with its many picturesque corners, especially along Rue d'Embas and Rue Poterie.

Fougères

North of Vitré, the traveller will soon come to another frontier town and castle, at Fougères. This is a very fine castle with all the traditional accoutrements: towers, battlement, a moat and three lines of curtain walls. Furthermore, it has been very well preserved. The castle occupies a loop in the River Nançon, which serves it in the office of a moat, and can be viewed either close to the walls or from the Jardin Public in the town.

Five towers stud the outer curtain wall, which has musket loops as well as arrow slits, and gun platforms for cannon. The Tour Mélusine is the most splendid of these towers, with walls 3.5m thick. The castle is open to visitors and also contains a shoe museum (Fougères was noted for the skill of its cordwainers from the Middle Ages until the 1920s.) There are also displays of local costume. The castle gives visitors a great feeling of the Middle Ages, in a setting of considerable beauty.

Fougères itself contains an interesting old quarter around Place du Marchix, and was the place where the Chouan rebellion of 1793-1804 began and flourished until it was put down with great brutality by French troops.

Combourg

The final example from a wide choice is the castle of Combourg, just south of St Malo. This is a real medieval castle, built and rebuilt between the 11th and 15th centuries, and belonging for a time to Bertrand du Guesclin. It was refurbished in the 18th century by the Chateaubriand family, of whom the most famous scion is the 19th-century writer François-René de Chateaubriand, who spent part of his childhood here and whose writing seems to have been influenced by the gloomy atmosphere that still hangs about this grim fortress.

The building does not contribute to levity. The castle is a real *château-fort*, and parts of it are said to be haunted. Although there are pleasant views from the battlements, the castle interior is particularly sombre. Open to the public, it contains a museum devoted to Chateaubriand's life and work and the tour includes a visit to the Tour du Chat, where the author had his bedroom. Chateaubriand was born in St Malo and after his death in 1848 was buried on the small island of Grand Bé. The tower gets its name from the spectre of a former lord of Combourg who was said to haunt the tower in the guise of a black cat.

Vitré's castle (above) was rebuilt in the 14th and 15th centuries

The castle at Combourg (below) has its origins in the 11th century

The fortress of Fougères (left) was of great strategic importance, being near Brittany's border with Normandy

Owned by the Rohan family since the 15th century, Josselin castle (above) holds some fine family portraits

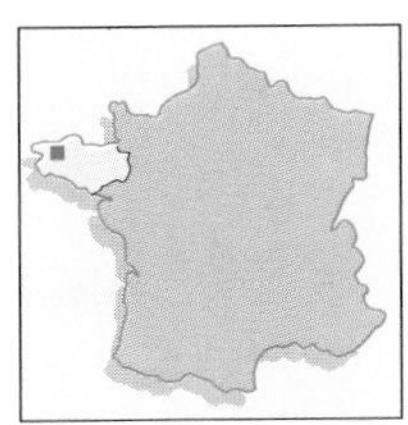

Roscoff and the Parish Closes of Finistère

ALTHOUGH THEY APPEAR on most of the posters and postcards, the calvaries and *enclos paroissiaux*, parish closes, of Brittany are by no means as common as the visitor might suppose. The best of all the Breton calvaries are found in three small villages in Finistère, just south of the ferry port at Roscoff. These are St Thégonnec, Guimiliau, and Lampaul-Guimiliau.

For centuries Roscoff, among other Breton ports, traded with Brittany's Celtic neighbours in south-west England and Ireland. Now Roscoff is best known as a ferry port and quiet resort

Carantec

Carantec is well known in western Brittany for its *pardon* or pilgrimage procession to the shrine of Notre-Dame de Callot, which takes place on the offshore island of Callot every year on the first Sunday after 15 August. Visitors are drawn to Carantec by the beaches, which are large and safe and very popular. Like most coastal villages, Carantec was once a fishing port, but is now a quiet and pleasant holiday resort well off the main tourist route.

Places to visit locally include the Chaise du Curé, a splendid viewpoint on the nearby headland.

Lampaul-Guimiliau

One of three great parish closes in this corner of Brittany, that of Lampaul-Guimiliau is especially notable for the church. This dates from the early period of parish close building, the mid-16th century, and contains a remarkable rood beam supporting a crucified Christ and life-size figures of the Virgin and St John. The calvary is well carved but has been damaged while the ossuary, or charnel-house, which contained the bones retrieved from the cemetery, dates from the end of the 17th century and has various statues.

A little east of the village lies Guimiliau, which has yet another fine calvary, the largest in the area with 200 carefully carved figures.

Landivisiau

The town is famous for its cattle fairs, which bring farmers and stockmen from all parts of France, but it has further attractions, including an interesting church dedicated to St Thivisiau, one of the more obscure of the Breton saints, of which there are many –

Parish Closes

The Bretons are a devoutly Catholic people, a fact evidenced in stone by the *enclos paroissiaux*, parish closes, of Finistère. These were built at the end of the 16th and beginning of the 17th centuries in reaffirmation of Catholic beliefs after the Reformation.
The true parish close contains three elements: the church, the ossuary or charnel-house, which contained the bones of parishioners exhumed from the graveyard to make room for their descendants, and the famous carved calvary, or crucifixion.

Apart from the well-known calvaries of Finistère, there is a splendid one at Pleyben (below), near Douarnenez, a fine, well-carved example at Plougastel-Daoulas, and many others dotted about the Breton countryside.

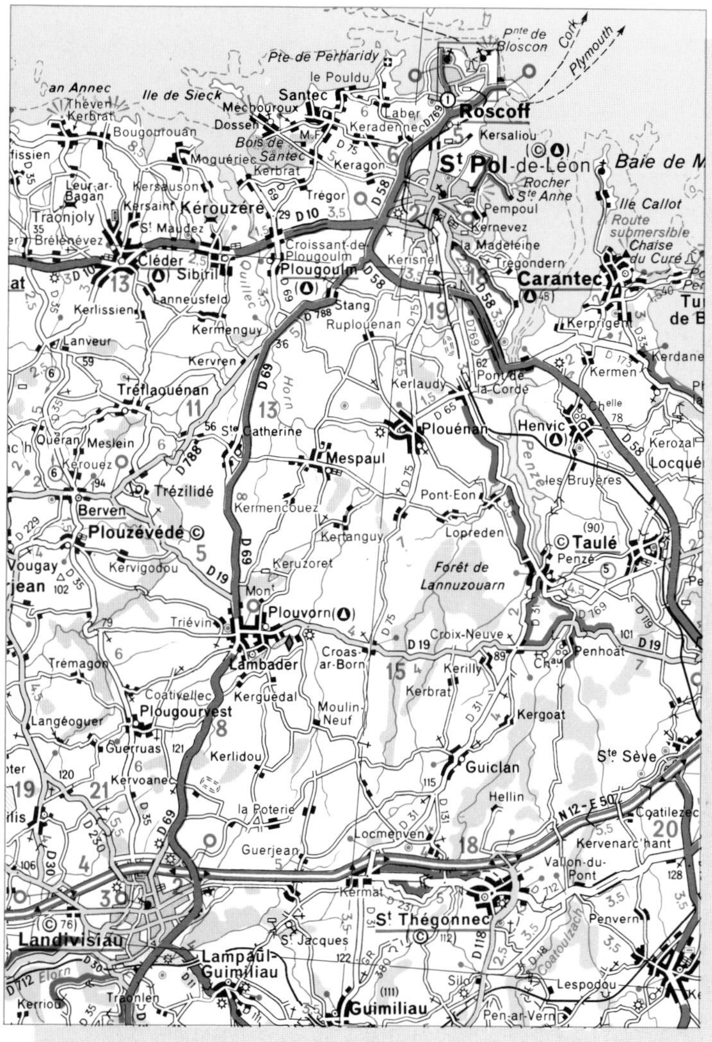

Comité Départemental du Tourisme du Finistère
11, Rue Théodore-le-Hars - BP 125
29104 Quimper Cedex
Tel: 98 53 09 00

Touring:
use Michelin sheet map 230, Bretagne

7777 by some estimates.

Eight kilometres north of Landivisiau at Lambader, lies the rebuilt 15th-century chapel of Notre Dame, which contains a number of late-medieval relics in an attractive setting.

Roscoff

Pretty Roscoff is much more than a ferry port. It has historic roots and a great reputation as a centre for thalassotherapy, the treatment of ailments by sea water. Roscoff is also a fishing port famous for shellfish and crustaceans, and local farmers come here to auction their crops. Sights to see in the town include the old streets and quays around the harbour, the harbour itself and the Channel fish that are on display at the Charles Pérez aquarium.

There are several good restaurants and hotels, and Notre-Dame-de-Kroaz-Batz has a most curious open belfry rather like a gigantic calvary. A good view of the town, the harbour and the surrounding seascapes can be had from the Chapelle de Ste-Barbe on the eastern side of the harbour and there are daily excursions to the Ile de Batz, a small and treeless island just offshore, where the locals make a living from small market gardens or by collecting and burning seaweed for fertiliser.

St Pol-de-Léon

The modern *département* of Finistère is divided into two historic parts: the southern, Cornouaille, and the northern, Léon. St Pol-de-Léon has one of the finest churches in Léon, a former cathedral with soaring Gothic architecture, which is not often found in rural Brittany. Curious features include a lepers' door and two fine towers, as well as a Roman stone coffin that serves as a stoup for holy water.

Churches are so common in Brittany that the visitor can afford to be selective but the Chapelle du Kreisker in St Pol-de-Léon must be seen, if only for its magnificent belfry. This late-14th to 15th-century chapel was once the town hall, but is now open to the public and gives magnificent views over the surrounding countryside from the top of the tower. From the town there are good walks into the surrounding countryside and along the coast, and an excellent excursion to the castle at Kérouzéré, 8km to the west, a *château-fort* with witch's-hat towers and machicolated walls. The rooms of the castle are still furnished, and although parts of it were destroyed in the 16th century, Kérouzéré remains a splendid example of a medieval fortress.

St Thégonnec

St Thégonnec is hardly more than a hamlet, yet it draws visitors from all over the world to see its splendid and intact parish close and calvary. The buildings are in silvery Breton granite, which in part accounts for their splendid state of preservation. The calvary, which dates from 1610, has been wonderfully carved with details from the life of St Thégonnec. In the church is a Tree of Jesse that traces Christ's ancestry.

There are comfortable walks from the village to the two other famous *parish-clos* of Léon at Guimiliau and Lampaul-Guimiliau.

Breton Food

Seafood is the staple fare of the region. Lobster, langoustines, crab, mussels, sea perch, sole, oysters – the list is long and the portions tend to be large. The seafood platter of St Malo, the *assiette de fruits de mer*, might consist of a whole crab, a pair of lobster claws, 12 oysters, several langoustines and handfuls of assorted shellfish.

The Breton version of bouillabaisse, or seafish stew, is *cotriade*, of which the best example can be found at Lomener, a fishing village near Lorient. Cancale is famous for oysters, and that classic dish, *homard à l'Américaine*, is always called in Brittany by its correct name, *homard à l'Armoricaine*.

Apart from seafood, Brittany produces good lamb, first-class vegetables and a range of puddings including *far*, a local speciality. The region is also well known for its crêpes or *galettes*, which are savoury pancakes made with buckwheat flour.

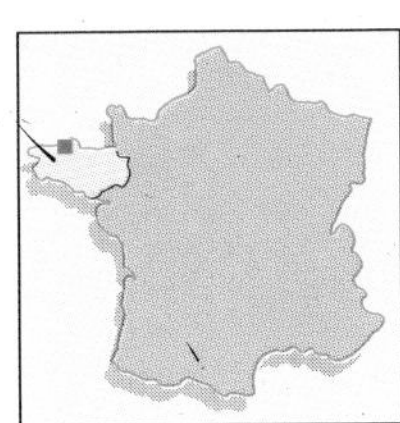

The Rose Granite Coast

BRITTANY'S JAGGED, ROCKY, island-littered north shore is one of the most beautiful and interesting parts of its coastline. Much of the attraction comes from the curious red rocks that give this region its popular and evocative name, the Rose Granite (Granit Rose) coast, for they are indeed red, often very large, and smoothly rounded by the relentless scouring action of the sea.

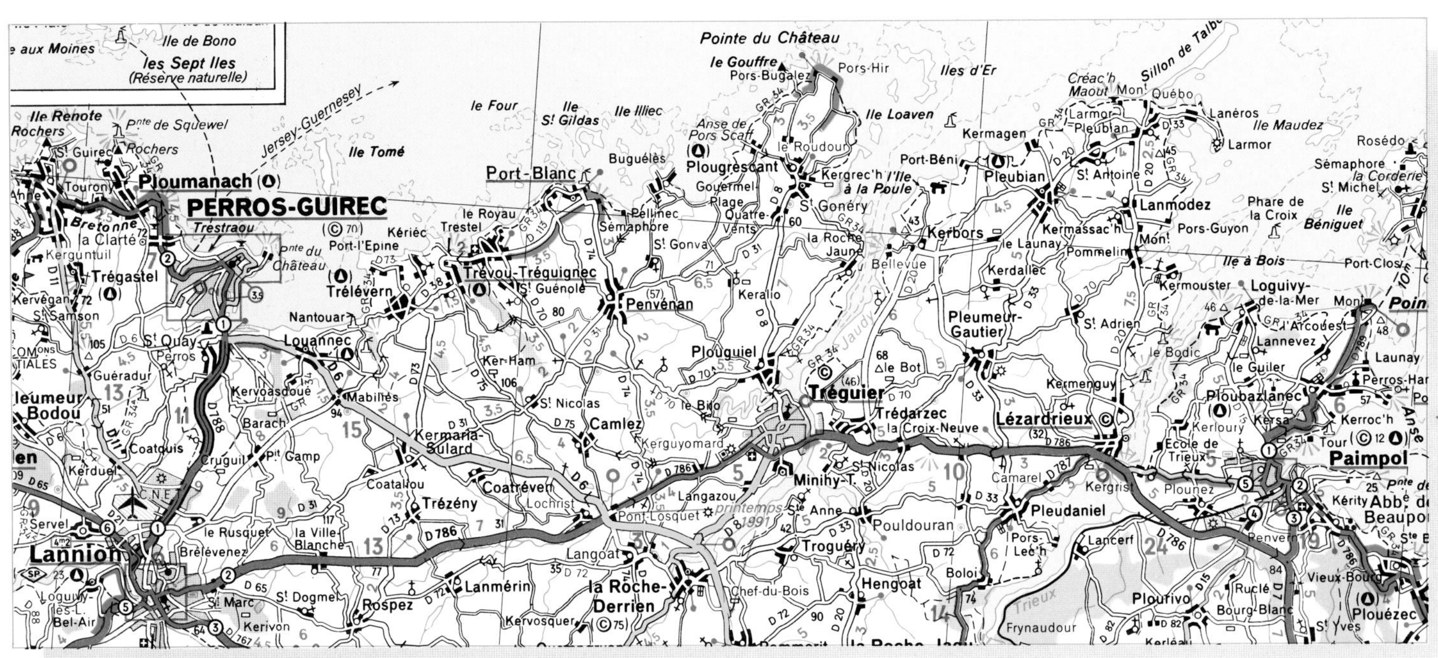

Lannion has many houses evoking the Brittany of the late Middle Ages. Some are half-timbered, others are slate-faced and all have slate roofs

Lannion

Set on either side of the River Léguer some way inland from the sea, Lannion is a typical Breton town. This is a place to park the car and walk along the river and around the town centre. The church that dominates the town, the Église de Brélévenez, was built in the 12th century by the Knights Templars, but was rebuilt after the Order was supressed in the 14th century.

There are good views of the town and river from the bridges, but Lannion is also a good excursion centre. Places to visit locally include the château at Kergrist, which displays architecture from every period from the Middle Ages to the 18th century; the Chapelle des Sept-Saints, with a crypt dedicated to the cult of the Seven Sleepers of Ephesus, 10km to the south of Lannion; the chapel at Kerfons; and to the west of Lannion the village of Trédrez, where St Yves, one of the few Breton saints to win an international reputation, as the patron saint of lawyers, was the rector.

Lézardrieux

This small town is the gateway to a part of the Rose Granite Coast known as the Presqu'île Sauvage. This runs west to the town of Tréguier and north to the real peninsula of the Sillon de Talbert, a dyke that juts out into the sea. Lézardrieux has an old mill and lots of pretty houses around an 18th-century church, but is best known as a touring centre for the Presqu'île Sauvage.

Comité Départemental du Tourisme de l'Ain
34, Rue du Général-Delestraint - BP 78
01002 Bourg-en-Bresse Cedex
Tel: 74 21 95 00

Touring:
use Michelin sheet map 230, Bretagne

Parks and Nature Reserves

Brittany has several nature reserves on the coast and offshore islands and the very large Parc Régional d'Armorique. This runs inland from the Crozon peninsula to Huelgoat and takes in a wide and varied cross-section of the Breton countryside, forest and moorland, valley and coast.

The region offers plenty of good walks, some waymarked by the local people, others on the Breton section of the nationwide network known as the Grande Randonnée.

The Réserve du Cap Sizun is a bird sanctuary on the coast of Finistère, a nesting place for a great variety of gulls, cormorants and petrels, which gather on the high cliffs and are best seen from mid-March to early August. When in this area do not neglect to visit Pointe du Raz and the town of Locronan.

On the north coast the Sept Iles off Perros-Guirec contain the Réserve Chappelier, which is known for puffins, oyster-catchers and gannets. Landing is forbidden in the nesting period between March and the end of July.

Paimpol

The harbour at Paimpol was once full of trawlers that made a good if hard living off the Newfoundland Banks, but that trade has almost entirely fallen away. Fortunately, Paimpol has the compensations of beauty and a good location. These have given it a fresh lease of life as a yachting centre, a market town for local farmers and a tourist resort.

Places to visit include the Musée de la Mer, which has interesting displays on the port's colourful past, Pointe de Guilben, and Place du Martray in the town centre, with its beautiful houses, one of them the home of Loti when he was writing his novel *Pêcheur d'Islande*. Like most Breton ports, Paimpol has a *pardon*, in December.

Paimpol is close to the Goëlo country, with its yellow gorse, and various other interesting excursions are possible. The ruins of the 13th-century Abbaye de Beauport, destroyed after the Revolution, are very evocative, as is the Croix des Veuves, near Perros-Hamon, where the fishermen's wives waited to catch their first sight of the returning fleet.

In the little fishing village of Port-Blanc, east of Perros-Guirec, you can see the unusual sight of a tiny chapel perched on a rock by the shore

Perros-Guirec

If the Rose Granite Coast can be said to have a first-rate tourist resort it is probably Perros-Guirec, which has the prime advantage of a delightful setting between two fine sandy beaches on a headland overlooking a magnificent, sheltered harbour. The harbour still has colourful fishing boats and in summer many yachts, while the town, apart from an abundance of agreeable houses, has a part Romanesque, part Gothic church.

Three kilometres to the west of the town lies the Chapelle de Notre-Dame-de-la-Clarté, built in fulfilment of a vow in the 16th century. East of Perros-Guirec, travellers should visit the little village of Port-Blanc, which has a tiny chapel perched on a rock just offshore – a most unusual sight. There are boat trips to the Sept Iles, now a nature reserve famous for gannets, kittiwakes and puffins. Most boats also stop at the Ile aux Moines, Monks' Island.

Tréguier

A fine little town on the banks of the Rivers Guindy and Jaudy, Tréguier is famous as the home of famous men. The writer Ernest Renan (1823-92), who is little known outside France and perhaps not as well known as he deserves to be within it, was born in Tréguier and the town celebrates the fact with a statue and by preserving his house. The other famous son, St Yves, is celebrated not only as the cause of the largest of all the Breton *pardons* but also as the patron saint of lawyers.

Yves Hélori was born near Tréguier in 1253, studied law in Paris and then took holy orders. He was soon regarded as a saint because, when arguing cases in the local courts, he refused all bribes, demanded the truth and declined to favour the rich.

Tréguier has a magnificent medieval gateway by the river and several half-timbered buildings. The Cathédrale St-Tugdual is held to be one of the finest in Brittany, part Romanesque, part Gothic, with lots of memorials, including the Chapelle du Duc Jean V and votive offerings to St Yves, plus a good treasury.

The timbers of some of Tréguier's well-preserved medieval houses are picked out in strong colours

There are a number of good excursions and these should include a visit to the nearby castle of La Roche-Jagu and to Minihy-Tréguier, less than 1km from Tréguier. St Yves was born in this village and here his *pardon* takes place on 19 May each year.

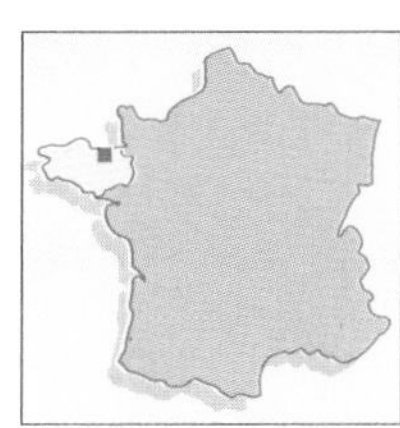

Three Historic Towns on the River Rance

THE RIVER RANCE and its estuary connect three of the most historic, varied and interesting towns in Brittany. St Malo, a walled town, is a major port, yachting centre and holiday resort. Dinard, just across the estuary, is quite different: evoking the early 20th century, full of hotels, a pleasure ground for the idle rich, while Dinan, which lies up river, is purely medieval.

Dinan

A fortress, a stronghold for the medieval dukes of Brittany, Dinan remains medieval, full of sloping, cobbled streets and leaning half-timbered buildings, many of them hung with painted shop signs. The Rue du Jerzual is one of the most photographed streets in Brittany, cobbled and sloping down steeply to the banks of the Rance, which almost encircles the hill on which the town stands. There is a late-medieval clock tower, donated to the town by the Duchess Anne. It can be climbed and the view from the top extends far beyond the river and over the surrounding countryside. There are some well-preserved timber-framed buildings, set in the narrow ways around the old centre, Place des Merciers.

Like many medieval towns, Dinan is a place to explore on foot, well supplied with parks, little squares and gardens. Set above the Rance is a small park known as the Jardin Anglais, behind which lies the Basilique St-Sauveur, which contains the tomb chest holding the heart of Dinan's favourite and most famous son, the good knight of Charles V, Bertrand du Guesclin.

Other sights to see in Dinan include the Hôtel Keratry in Rue de Lèhon, which now contains the Tourist Office. A town walk, for which the Tourist Office can provide a map, takes in all the main sights. These include the school where Chateaubriand was educated, the Basilique St-Sauveur and the ducal castle, which was thrown up hurriedly between 1382 and 1387. The Duchess Anne sheltered here in 1507, and the Tour de l'Horloge was presented to the townspeople in gratitude for their hospitality. Parts of the castle are open to visitors and contain a museum of Breton life and furnishings, while the former quarters of du Guesclin are devoted to displays illustrating the history of the town.

Dinan's position on the River Rance and near the coast gave it strategic value during the Middle Ages. Today much of the town's medieval heart remains intact

The Rance Dam

The road from St Malo to Dinan follows the course of the River Rance and crosses the top of the great Rance dam, the Usine Marémotrice. This is a large construction, 800m long, cleverly built to exploit the great tides of the Brittany coast, which surge up the narrow Rance valley and drive turbines at the installation. The dam then contains the sea water and lets it out gradually, back through the turbines at low tide, to maintain a continuous flow of power into the national electricity grid. There is a good view over the valley from a viewing platform on the dam, and a lock enables small vessels to travel from St Malo to Dinan.

Comité Départemental du Tourisme de l'Ain
34, Rue du Général-Delestraint - BP 78
01002 Bourg-en-Bresse Cedex
Tel: 74 21 95 00

Touring:
use Michelin sheet map 230, Bretagne

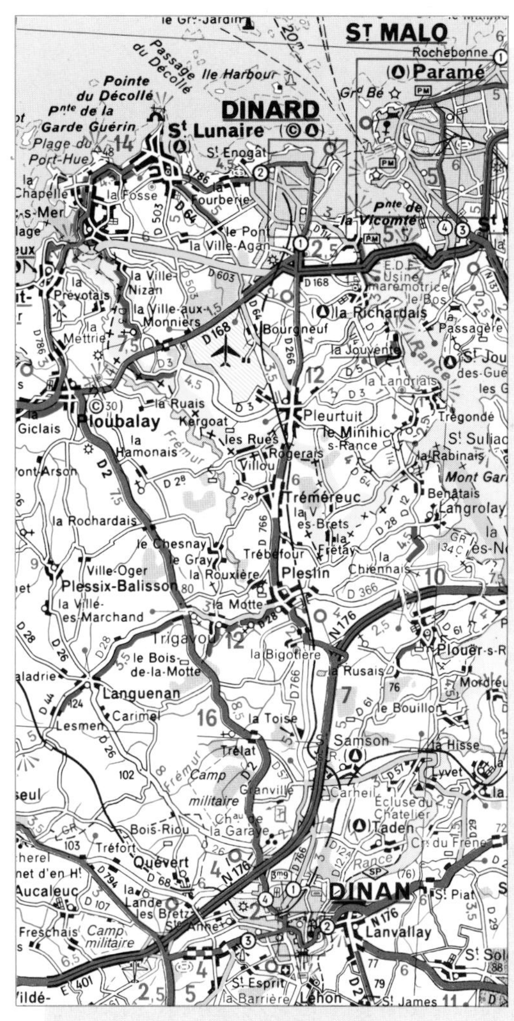

Dinard

Dinard, in contrast, is a fairly modern town and resort, developed over the past century on the site of the old fishing harbour. It is an international rather than a French or Breton resort, and attracted the smart set in great numbers between the wars.

The resort has a number of fine hotels and good beaches as well as a selection of promenades and parks where the rich folk could mix and mingle while enjoying the crisp Channel air.

Modern attractions include a combined natural history and marine museum, with an assortment of Channel fish, and the Pointe Vicomte, which offers great views across the harbour to the walls of St Malo. Also recommended is a cruise up the Rance to inspect the tidal dam and power plant.

St Malo

Many visitors enter Brittany by St Malo, an ancient and very fine seaport still enjoying a thriving trade as a yachting centre and port for Channel ferries as well as cargo ships and fishing boats.

The great interest for visitors is the old town, which lies inside the walls – the Intra-Muros. This is the site of old St Malo, but what we see today is largely a reconstruction, for the original city was severely shelled and bombed when it was besieged in 1944. Fortunately, the people of St Malo not only rebuilt but also restored the town. It has been marvellously recreated and stands again as a great memorial and credit to the Malouins.

Just offshore and in reach at low tide lies the Ile du Grand Bé, where the writer François-René de Chateaubriand (1768-1848) elected to be buried. St Malo is also protected by a castle, now the town hall and museum. There are many hotels and restaurants and the town as a whole is well worth at least a day's visit.

Outside the Intra-Muros lie the town beaches, great swathes of sand at low tide, and the modern resorts of Rothéneuf and Paramé, which are now suburbs of St Malo. Other places to visit close to St Malo include the great castle at Fort la Latte, which lies on Cap Fréhel to the west, and the oyster port at Cancale to the east, which has restaurants famous for their seafood.

Tragic Lovers

The tale of Abélard and Héloïse is one of the world's great tragic love stories. Abélard was a Breton, born at La Palet near Nantes, and the most famous teacher of his day. Canon Fulbert of Notre-Dame invited Abélard to give lessons to his daughter Héloïse. When he discovered that his daughter had become pregnant by Abélard he hired thugs to beat and castrate Abélard, and sent Héloïse to a nunnery after she had given birth to a son.

Following his unhappy time at St Gildas-de-Rhuys, where he spent some months in fear of his life from the enmity of the monks, Abélard retired to Cluny and the protection of the Cluniac Order. He corresponded with Héloïse for the rest of his life, though they never met again.

At the height of its elegance in the 1920s and 30s, Dinard is nowadays a busy tourist resort blessed with a mild climate

St Malo's mainly 14th- and 15th-century castle protected the coastal town from sea and land attack during Brittany's turbulent history

NORMANDY

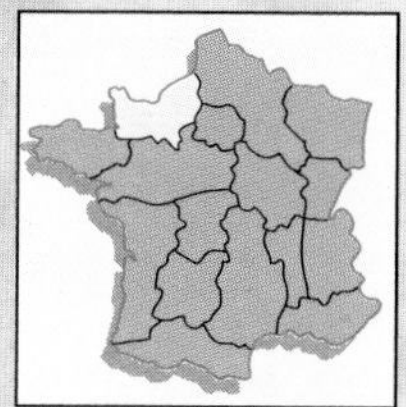

A GIFT TO THE VIKINGS FROM THE King of France, later the vigorous heart of the Norman empire, then the great dukedom of the English kings and now a lush and prosperous modern province, Normandy is one of the most historic and interesting parts of France.

Because they are already well known and must be visited in the course of travel, certain famous places, such as Rouen, Caen and Falaise, are not covered in detail, though they appear when the castles, abbeys and history of Normandy are dealt with. Many of the places covered are no less worth visiting for being less famous: the Vexin, the resorts of the Côte Fleurie, the hills of the Suisse Normande, the chalk plateau of the Caux, the Seine valley. These are all worth exploring and have sights no traveller should miss. Besides, as the visitor travels from one to the other, the whole marvellous panoply of Normandy will unfold.

That Normandy has remained so beautiful and unspoiled is itself a minor marvel. This part of France has many times felt the heavy hand of war since Charles the Simple met Rollo the Viking on the banks of the River Epte in 911 and gave all the land between the Vexin and the sea to this fierce sea-rover in return for his allegiance and in hope of peace. So the Northmen gained their richest prize. Conflict continued: throughout the Middle Ages and the 16th-century Wars of Religion, right down to recent times.

It is a great tribute to the determination of the Norman people that the province today bears few marks of that terrible time apart from a great number of cemeteries and a coast and hinterland studded with memorials. The towns were rebuilt, the scars were painted over, and the Normans returned to their traditional pursuits of farming and fishing.

Apart from a long coast, a green hinterland and a good number of fine towns and cities, all offering a great deal to see and do, Normandy can boast one of the great cuisines of France. This reputation is based on that superb fresh produce that both the sea and land of Normandy provide in such profusion: the sole of Dieppe, the cream and butter of the Auge and the Cotentin, a score of local dishes, and the cheeses, Livarot, Pont-l'Évêque or, perhaps best known of all, the Camembert of Vimoutiers. In addition to all these the area prides itself on its cider and calvados, the two great drinks of Normandy.

Normandy can also offer something for the mind and soul, for this is a province beloved of artists and writers. Courbet, Flaubert, Monet, Bonington, de Tocqueville – these and a score more found a home and inspiration here and a visitor would have to be lacking in soul indeed not to discover something worth seeing in this fascinating corner of France.

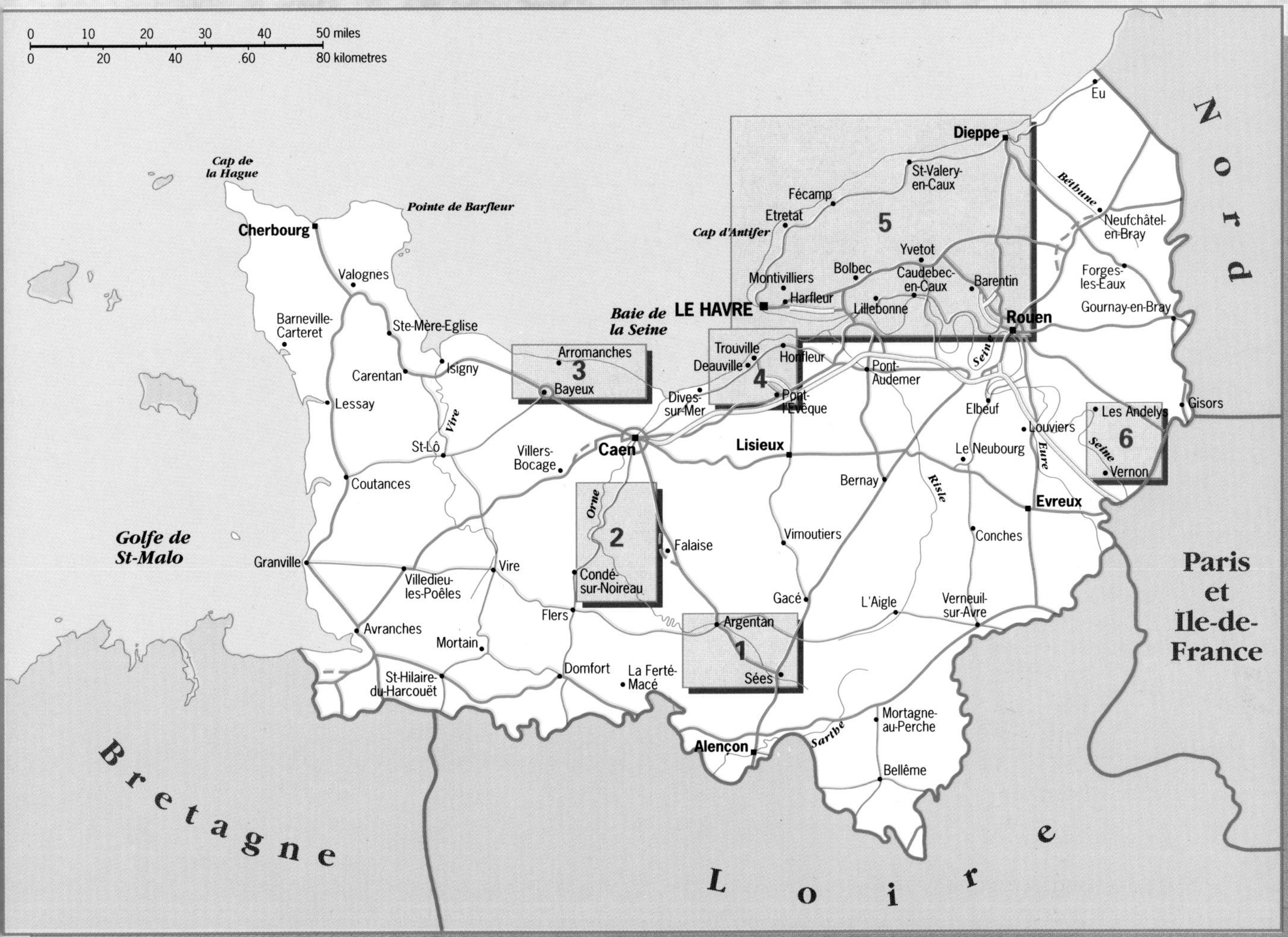

FEATURES

Honfleur, with its medieval quarter, is among the most attractive of Normandy's coastal towns. The port, where yachts have now largely replaced small fishing boats, was in the 18th century the principal port for the fur trade between France and Canada

Shellfish (right) are one of the gastronomic delights of Normandy. Other local fruits of the sea include sole, turbot and sea perch. Agriculture, the area's other major industry, is sustained by farmers like this (far right)

Mont St Michel

MONT ST MICHEL IS SAID TO BE the most beautiful and spectacular tourist site in France. No one who has seen it rearing out of the golden sand in the vast bay of Mont St Michel, a cone of rock topped by a great Gothic church, is likely to disagree.

Beautiful as it is, visitors will enjoy and appreciate Mont St Michel far more if they visit it outside the summer months, and in particular not in July or August, when the narrow main street is solid with tourists.

The first church, an oratory, was built on this 82-m rock as long ago as 708, when the Archangel Michael appeared to Aubert, Bishop of Avranches. The Archangel gave his name to the rock before striding on to fight the Devil on the top of Mont Dol, just south of the bay. This oratory was succeeded in turn by a Carolingian church, parts of which still remain in the abbey crypt, and then by a Romanesque building that was finished at the end of the 11th century, only to be destroyed by fire in 1203.

Fortified Site

Most of the present building dates from the Gothic period, being built between the 13th and 16th centuries, a time of almost continual conflict in France, which accounts for the fact that much of the site is fortified. The shrine of St Michel, which lies in the small chapel of St Pierre, to the left of the Grande Rue, drew pilgrims from all over Europe, even at the height of the Hundred Years War (1337-1453) and pilgrim badges can still be purchased from the tourist office just inside the main gate. This, the Porte du Roi, was the strong point in the lower bastion, and was guarded by cannon. These came into use towards the end of the 14th century, and Mont St Michel possesses some early and very rare examples of the 'hooped' cannon, which are set on plinths and can be viewed just inside the outer walls.

Grande Rue

The Grande Rue is the main thoroughfare of Mont St Michel, and the first notable sight inside the gate is the Mère Poulard restaurant, famous in France for the production of large, feathery omelettes, the great gastronomic attraction of Mont St Michel. After that, small restaurants and tourist shops filled with souvenirs and postcards and suchlike follow one another in relentless succession up the steep hill.

The first building worthy of attention as you climb the hill is the parish church, which, though dedicated to St Peter, contains a statue of St Michael, covered with silver. Pilgrim banners hang from the roof and votive offerings cover the walls. This church is an early foundation dating from the 11th century, and the apse spans the narrow side street. Near here is a medieval house said to have been built by Bertrand du Guesclin for his wife, Tiphaine, when she was sheltering on the Mont and Bertrand was soldiering in Spain. Bertrand was Captain of the Mont in the mid-1360s and much of the furniture is said to have belonged to him. Another old building is notable for its curious name: La Maison de la Truie-qui-file, the House of the Spinning Sow.

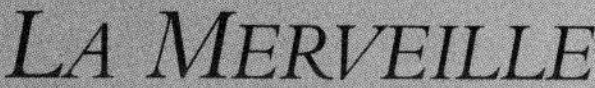

La Merveille

Everything described above is a prelude to the great attraction of Mont St Michel: La Merveille, the Marvel, the great Gothic church and abbey buildings that occupy much of the top of the Mont. These were built between 1211 and 1229 and are a mixture of religious and military buildings but in a harmonious and pleasing style. The eastern half was the monks' quarters and contains the refectory, the guest hall and the almonry. The western half contains the garrison's quarters and Salle des Chevaliers, the Knight's Hall, which was built for the Military Order of St Michael by King Louis XI in 1469, as well as the cloisters, which are in exemplary Gothic style, and open to the sky.

What makes La Merveille so marvellous is the purity of line in the architecture, probably because the buildings went up so

quickly, in under 18 years, and therefore retain a continuity of construction not spoiled by later alteration and repair.

Always a great church, the abbey has also been a fortress and, in the early years of the last century, a prison. One relic of this last function is a huge wheel, rather like a treadmill, which half a dozen prisoners operated to haul provisions up to the cell level. After the abbey had been decades in decline from the 1660s, the last monks were driven out at the Revolution, and the abbey, by now in urgent need of restoration, came into the hands of the state in 1874.

SECULAR ARCHITECTURE

Apart from the great church and the abbey buildings, the other great attraction of the Mont is that it is a treasure house of secular architecture, especially of buildings from the medieval period. Space is too precious to permit the establishment of large modern hotels and most of the buildings that cram the rock date from the 15th and 16th centuries, still lived in and cared for by local families, who exist by catering in various ways for the million or so visitors who come here each year. Apart from the church and abbey there is an historical museum and a maritime museum, and a lot to see along the network of narrow streets and cobbled alleyways.

It would be quite easy to spend a full day exploring the Mont and the buildings of La Merveille, finding something new to enjoy around every quiet corner. But surprisingly few tourists ever go all the way to the top, or stay long if they get there, and visitors in the winter months may have the place almost to themselves. This is the time to climb to the top platform and watch the tide come booming in across the sands. The tide around the Mont is one of the highest in western Europe, at over 13m, and with the wind behind it is said to come in at the speed of a galloping horse. Walkers on the sands should be aware of this fact and exercise care, especially when the tide is on the turn.

Once down from the heights of the Mont and back across the causeway connecting it to the mainland, visitors should look back for another view of this remarkable and beautiful sight, and take note also of the River Cousenon, which flows into the sea beside the causeway and has played its part in the long history of the Mont. By long tradition the Cousenon marks the boundary between Normandy and Brittany, and when a violent storm and flood switched the river's flow from east of the Mont to west of it, the ownership of the Mont transferred from Brittany to Normandy where, storms notwithstanding, it looks set to remain.

Proud on its rock surrounded by sea, Mont St Michel (left) is one of the finest sights in France

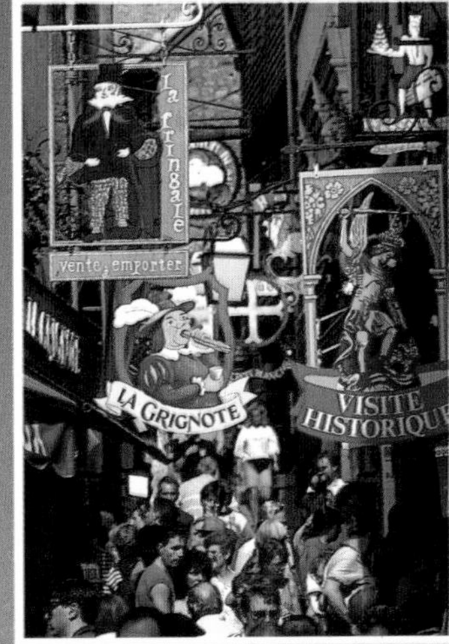

Mont St Michel is busy all summer

The cloisters of Mont St Michel's abbey (above) and the abbey church (below)

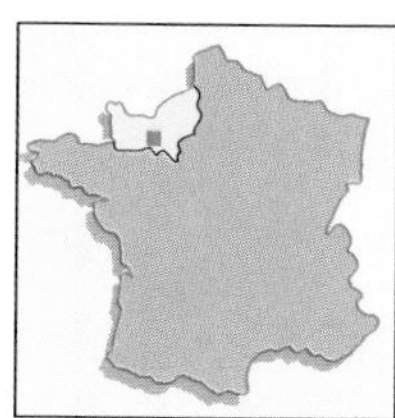

The Perche Country and the Écouves Forest

THE SOUTHERN FRONTIER OF NORMANDY is marked by two great forests, the Forêt des Andaines and the Forêt d'Écouves. Large parts of these are contained within the boundaries of the great Parc Régional Normandie-Maine, which straddles the province from Mortain as far east as Alençon. This rolling landscape is horse-breeding country where the famous Haras du Pin, the French national stud, can be seen.

Argentan

Argentan stands on a small hill above the Orne, a commanding site that inevitably attracted attention in the fighting of 1944, when much of the town was severely damaged by shell fire. The Église St-Germain was hit but, like the rest of the town, has now been carefully repaired and stands intact. The lacemaking industry here was established in the 17th century by Colbert and examples of the famous Argentan lace stitch, the *point d'Argentan*, can be inspected in the Benedictine abbey, which is actually a nunnery, the nuns owning the exclusive right to this intricate stitch.

Other historic sites in Argentan include the castle from where Thomas à Becket's four assassins set out for Canterbury and the stained glass in the Église St-Martin which dates from the 15th and 16th centuries. For an evening stroll, try the banks of the Orne just outside the town.

The moated brick-built château near Carrouges dates mainly from the 15th and 17th centuries, but the gatehouse was constructed in the 16th

Carrouges

The centre of Carrouges is set around a small square, a maze of little streets and leaning buildings – a typical small town of the French countryside. The great attraction lies just outside the town, at the gatehouse and château. This is now in the hands of the state, and part of it contains the Maison du Parc, a visitors' centre for the Parc Régional Normandie-Maine.

The gardens contain a splendid selection of apple and pear trees, and many of the varieties are no longer grown commercially. The brick gatehouse with its slender, witch's-hat towers is particularly fine, while the château contains much fine furniture, including the bed in which Louis XI slept when he visited Carrouges in 1473.

Écouché

The first sight to greet the visitor to Écouché is a World War II tank mounted on a plinth, a memorial to the men of the French 2nd Armoured Division, which marched across here in 1944 and took the town of Alençon from the Germans after a stiff fight at Écouché. The rest of this otherwise pleasant little town has a somewhat unfinished air. The late-Gothic church was never completed, even after two centuries of effort, and the 13th-century nave has never been restored since being damaged in 1944.

Haras du Pin

Set in splendid buildings amid lush green fields the national stud-farm (*haras*) at Le Pin has a long history. It was established in 1665 by Colbert, Finance minister to Louis XIV, to improve the stock of French horses and in particular to provide breeding stallions for the cavalry. Even the gardens and buildings here are splendid, the former the work of Le Nôtre, the latter attributed to Hardouin-

A gilt horse's head looks down on visitors to the national stud-farm at Le Pin. Apart from its breeding role, Haras du Pin offers courses in all aspects of equestrianism and trains grooms and stable lads

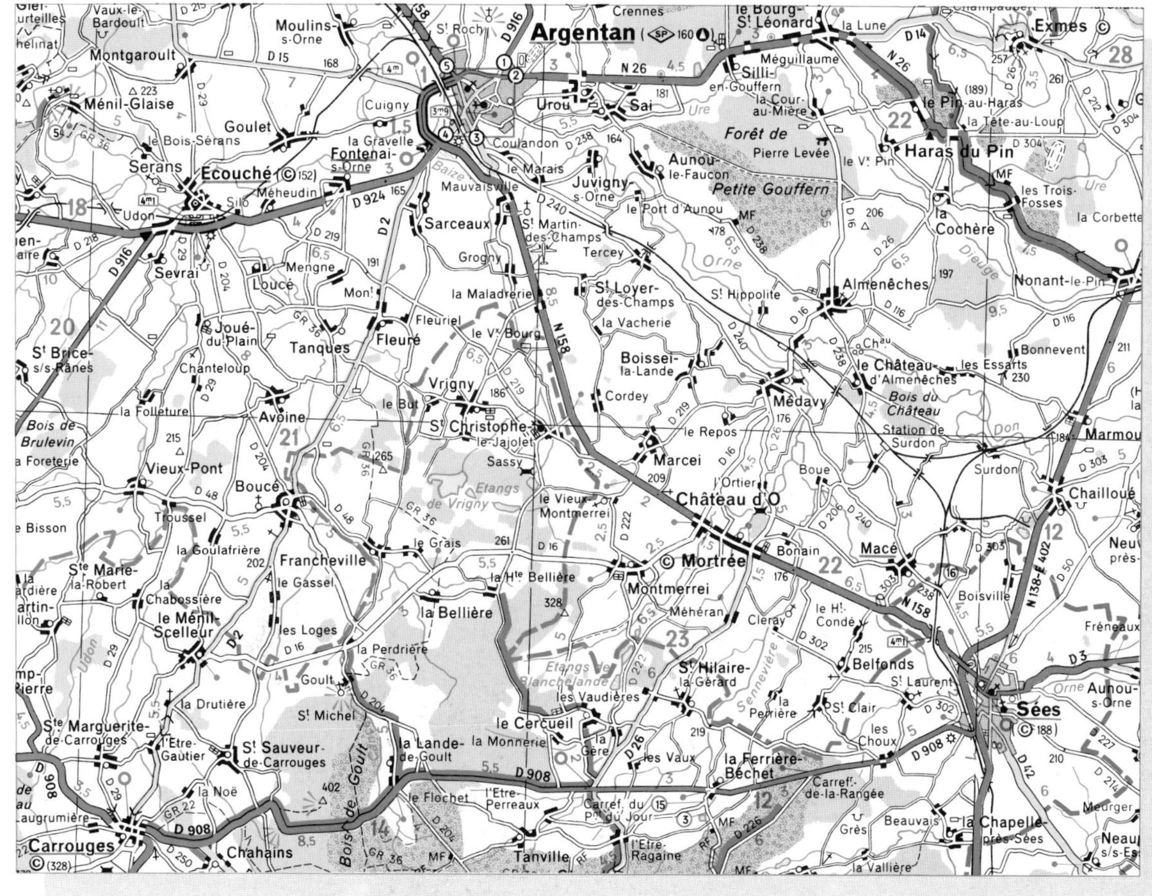

Comité Départemental du Tourisme de l'Orne
88, Rue Saint-Blaise - BP 50
61002 Alençon Cedex
Tel: 33 28 88 71

Touring:
use Michelin sheet map 231, Normandie

Mansart, and in this setting the work of breeding horses and teaching horsemanship continues.

A little to the north of Le Pin stands another splendid pile, the 17th-century château of Le Bourg-St-Léonard. This is a most elegant building and contains a great deal of the original Louis XV tapestries and woodwork as well as much 18th-century furniture.

St Christophe-le-Jajolet

The church in this little village in the Orne is dedicated to St Christopher, the patron saint of travellers, and celebrates the fact in uncompromising fashion. The church door shows St Christopher standing guard over an aircraft, a car and the passengers, and there is an imposing statue of the saint in the grounds. This church has become a pilgrimage centre for modern travellers, especially on the feast days of St Christopher. These are the last Sunday in July and the first Sunday in October. A visit should also be made to the nearby Château de Sassy, which is surrounded by beautiful gardens.

Sées

Sées is a rather splendid market town, with a fine Norman-Gothic cathedral that contains the venerated statue of Notre Dame de Sées. Visitors should also note the column at the south end of the choir, which is carved with over 30 heads, some of them grimacing at the congregation, and the fine 13th-century stained-glass windows.

Not far away, on the far side of the River Orne, which runs through the town, stands the market hall.

Norman Dukes

Normandy is the land of the Northmen, the Vikings, who started ravaging the coast of France in 800, coming south from Denmark, or Frisia, in their longships. By 820 they had made their way up the Seine valley and started to settle, and by 885 they had laid siege to Paris. Finally, in 911, Charles the Simple, King of France, met the leader of the Northmen, Rollo the Viking, and concluded the Treaty of St-Clair-sur-Epte, by which Rollo became a Christian and a vassal of the French Crown. Thus began the dukedom of Normandy, which was to exercise great power in Europe over the following three centuries.

Not far from Sées is the handsome Château d'O. This consists of three pavilions, each in a different style: Gothic, Renaissance and 18th-century

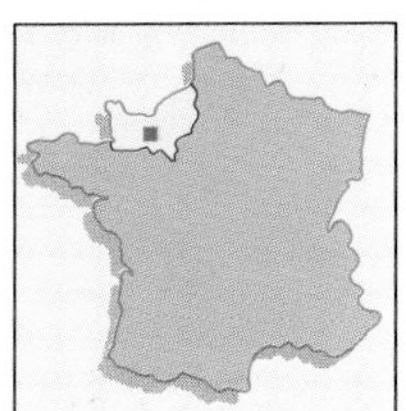

THE ORNE VALLEY AND THE SUISSE NORMANDE

THE RIVER ORNE is one of the great rivers of Normandy, flowing across the province to empty into the sea at Ouistreham, north of Caen. Caen, ancient capital of the Norman dukes, is the true gateway to the Orne valley, which lies to the south of the city – a fine place for walking and water sports, well supplied with good small hotels, a delightful area to wander in, on foot or by car.

A couple of kilometres south-east of Clécy the impressive La Lande viaduct bridges the Orne. The stretch of river below the viaduct is particularly well suited to water sports

Clécy

A small town that claims to be the 'capital of the Suisse Normande', Clécy clings to the side of the Orne valley in the very heart of the Suisse Normande. Lying at the heart of this region of hills and rivers, Clécy has long been a favourite centre for walkers and water-sports enthusiasts. Canoeists test their skill in the fast water by the Vey bridge and in the waters below the La Lande viaduct, overlooked by the towering rock face of the Rochers des Parcs, a favourite place for rock climbers.

Clécy lies on the GR36, one of the great footpaths of the Grande Randonnée, which runs from Ouistreham to the Pyrenees, but there are many short walks around Clécy, to the Pain de Sucre and over the Rochers de la Houle, and many of these walks have been waymarked by the local tourist board.

The town has several good hotels, and a museum of Norman life and crafts in the 16th-century Manoir de Placy near the Orne, as well as a model railway museum. Clécy is also an excellent base for visitors to the Suisse Normande, Falaise, Caen and the D-Day Coast.

Pont-d'Ouilly

This little riverside town, situated at the confluence of the Orne and the Noireau, is a good touring centre, very popular with day-walkers, who can ramble out from here along the river to the great viewpoint of the Roche d'Oëtre, which overlooks the River Rouvre. The path from Pont-d'Ouilly follows the route of the GR36, and is therefore waymarked with the red-and-white GR signs, cutting round the great loop made by the Orne, the Méandre de Rouvrou, before climbing up to the high belvedere of the Roche d'Oëtre. *Do not let small children run about here, for the drop to the Rouvre valley is both steep and unguarded.*

The impressive Roche d'Oëtre is the closest thing the Suisse Normande has to a mountain

CALVADOS

The bright red cider apples that glow in the Norman orchards supply the juice for the two great native drinks of Normandy, cider and calvados (apple brandy). These two drinks form a part of any traditional Norman meal. The cider apples produce a potent, fermented apple juice, which wise visitors and many Normans prefer to dilute with water. Calvados is drunk as an aperitif or a digestive, *'un calva'*, or as *'le trou normand'*, between courses to create space for more of that rich Norman food. Those who do not care for strong liquor between courses may prefer to take their calva in a sorbet. A good calvados, kept in the cask for 10 or 12 years, is the perfect digestive. *Pommeau* is another local liqueur. People interested in distilling should visit the Maison de la Pomme et de la Poire at Barenton near Mortain.

The sad state of the ruined château at Thury-Harcourt is compensated to some extent by its park, which offers 4km of attractive walks along the tree-lined banks of the Orne

Comité Départemental du Tourisme du Calvados
Place du Canada
14000 Caen
Tel: 31 86 53 30

Touring:
use Michelin sheet map 231, Normandie

Putanges-Pont-Écrepin

Like most of the other small towns of the Suisse Normande, Putanges-Pont-Écrepin is best regarded as an excursion centre. It stands at the southern end of the Suisse Normande, and straddles the river, the last place of any size before the hills give way to the flatter country of southern Normandy and the Sarthe.

Suisse Normande

The Suisse Normande is a surprising area to find in Normandy, set as it is within a few minutes' drive of the *bocage* (open woodland country) and the Caen plain. A jumble of forested hills, streams and rivers, it is very beautiful, especially in the late spring and autumn, when the yellow gorse and broom are flaring on the hills. The region is small, some 60km from north to south, between Thury-Harcourt and Putanges-Pont-Écrepin, and about 24km from west to east.

The hills of the Suisse Normande give drama to the countryside, even though they are not very high: the Rochers de la Houle rise to 258m and the Pain de Sucre near Clécy to 205m. Although close to several large towns and cities – Caen, Bayeux, Mortain and Falaise – the Suisse Normande remains very rural and quite unspoiled, with only a few villages providing accommodation and refreshment for the thousands of visitors who pass through here every year.

Thury-Harcourt

Known as 'the gate to the Suisse Normande', Thury-Harcourt stands at the northern end of the Orne valley, a few kilometres south of Caen. At one time this was mining country – the last mine closed in 1967 – and the scars left by the old iron workings can still be seen on the hillsides.

Thury-Harcourt was severely damaged in 1944, the château of the dukes of Harcourt being burned by the Germans on the night before they left the town. The park of the château is now open to visitors and offers good, gentle strolls to the banks of the Orne. Thury-Harcourt also has a good number of hotels and some very agreeable restaurants. There is a pleasant, early-medieval church, with a 13th-century façade, and a number of hotels that cater in particular for walkers and fishermen. From Thury-Harcourt there are good walks in all directions, and slightly longer tours by car will take the visitor to William the Conqueror's birthplace at Falaise, to the heights of Mont Pinçon, a moorland much fought over in 1944, and the Chapelle St-Joseph, where a viewing platform offers sweeping views over the Orne valley and the surrounding hills.

FOOTPATHS

Normandy is great walking country, seamed with footpaths. Every town, and nearly every village, boasts a waymarked network of local trails, details of which can be obtained from the local tourist office. Some of the best walking in Normandy can be found in the north of the Cotentin, in the Suisse Normande and in the forests of Orne and Seine-Maritime.

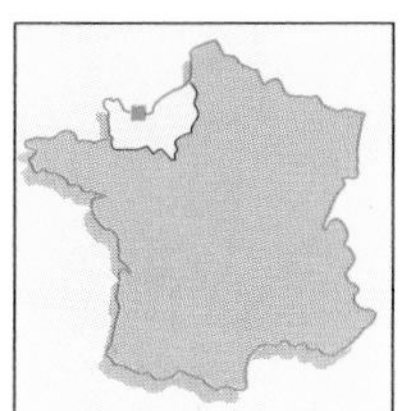

The D-day Coast and the Bessin

THE CALVADOS COAST OF NORMANDY is a place where wide, sandy beaches, studded with small seaside resorts, fade away west of the River Orne into tall chalk cliffs. Behind the beaches lies open farming country, pleasant rather than striking, which soon gives way to the fields of the Normandy *bocage*.

In June 1944, off Arromanches, the British created a huge artificial harbour. By August, having briefly been of great strategic importance, the harbour was no longer needed, largely because Cherbourg was once more in use. The full story of the Normandy Landing is told in the town's Musée du Débarquement

Arromanches-les-Bains

Until 6 June 1944, Arromanches-les-Bains was a small, undistinguished seaside resort with a short promenade and a few hotels. Then came the Invasion. Arromanches was the site of the British artificial harbour, codenamed 'Mulberry', used by the Allies until a major port could be captured and made serviceable. When fully operational, this Mulberry – there was another in the Cotentin – could land 9000 tons of military stores every day. The caissons of Mulberry still lie offshore.

Bayeux

Bayeux is a very old town with roots predating the Normans and the Franks. Captured on the evening of D-Day by troops of the British 50th Division, it was spared the bombardment and street fighting that wrecked so many Norman cities in 1944. The city also contains what is arguably the most interesting relic in France: the famous *Tapisserie de la Reine Mathilde*, the Bayeux Tapestry.

Housed in the Centre Guillaume le Conquérant, close to the cathedral, the tapestry – actually an embroidery – recounts in muted colours all the events of 1066 and the Battle of Hastings. King Harold is depicted with the arrow in his eye. The work, 70m in length, is Saxon and was probably commissioned in England soon after Hastings by Bishop Odon of Bayeux.

The old parts of Bayeux around the cathedral are well worth exploring, and there are many fine medieval houses along Rue St Malo and Rue Franche, and especially along the Quai de l'Aure, from where there is a photogenic view of the old water-mill. There are several museums, including the Musée Baron Gérard in Place des Tribunaux, which contains Italian and Flemish paintings of the 16th and 17th centuries as well as displays of local crafts and porcelain.

Notre-Dame in Bayeaux (right) is an outstanding example of the Norman Gothic Cathedral. The tower and the crypt remain of an 11th-century building, but most of the rest dates from the 13th century

The Hôtel du Doyen houses the Bayeux lace workshop, where this local craft is being revived, and a museum of religious art, while on the outskirts of the town lies the Mémorial de la Bataille de Normandie, which commemorates the fighting that took place around here between 7 June and 22 August 1944.

D-DAY

The D-Day Invasion of 5-6 June 1944 took place along an 80-km front around the bay of the Seine, between what is now Utah Beach in the eastern Cotentin, and the Caen canal, east of what is now Sword Beach. American, British, Canadian and French forces took part, and they were opposed by strong and well-entrenched German forces. The invasion began shortly after midnight on 5 June, when parachute and glider forces of the American 88th and 101st Airborne and the British 6th Airborne Division landed in the Cotentin and astride the Orne at Bénouville to seal the flanks for the seaborne assault.

The latter began at dawn, when troops of the American 4th Division landed on Utah Beach and continued to the east as the tide rose. The American 1st Infantry was checked and badly mauled, losing 3000 men on the beach, before getting ashore at Omaha. Further east the Canadian and British Infantry, supported by tanks and Commando units, went ashore and seized all the objectives by the end of the day. The 6th Airborne and 1st

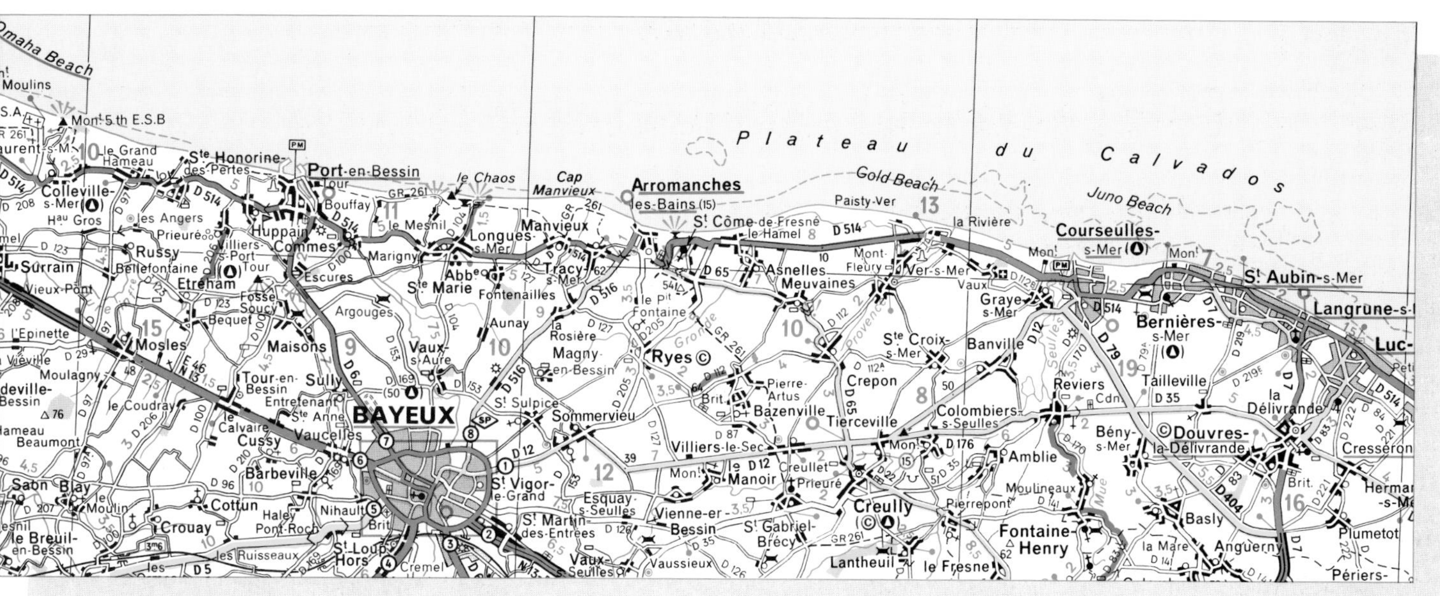

Commando Brigade held Ranville, the British 50th Division took Bayeux, the Commandos and Americans seized all the vital objectives, and by nightfall on D-Day the 4th US Infantry had linked up with the US Parachute Divisions. By midnight the Allied armies were fully ashore, although there was much bitter fighting ahead. Eleven months later, on 8 May 1945 (VE Day), World War II in Europe ended in an Allied victory.

Courseulles-sur-Mer

A seaside resort and a yachting centre, the little port of Courseulles is best known locally for the quality of its oysters and as a place where local fishermen come to buy their boats. Courseulles has a thriving boat-building industry, specialising in trawlers. The D-Day landings are commemorated by one of the rare D-D (duplex-drive) swimming tanks, dredged from the sea years after the war and now mounted in the town centre as a memorial to the Canadian troops who captured this town in 1944.

Creully

Creully is a small, engaging town in the valley of the meandering River Seulles. A straggling place with a long main street, the town is dominated by the walls and towers of a very fine 12th-century castle. This contains an exhibition of radio equipment dating from World War II. Also notable is the Grange aux Dîmes, a huge tithe barn just outside Creully.

Plages du Débarquement (D-Day Beaches)

There are five D-Day beaches around the bay of the Seine, each remembered by its codename. Apart from Utah, an American beach in the Cotentin, this area contains, from west to east, first Omaha, where the American infantry divisions lost over 3000 men before midday. Many of the fallen of Omaha lie in the American military cemetery at St Laurent, just above the beach. East of here, after Port-en-Bessin, is Gold Beach, where the British 50th Division came ashore and moved swiftly to take Bayeux. Then comes Juno, the Canadian beach around St Aubin, where 48 (Royal Marine) Commando had a very rough reception before capturing the strong point at Langrune, and finally, just west of Ouistreham, the British Sword Beach.

Though most of the Atlantic Wall fortifications have gone, the D-Day Coast is littered with memorials to the fighting.

Port-en-Bessin

Tucked into a niche in the cliffs, this little fishing port of the Bessin had a brief moment of fame in 1944 when it marked the line between the invading American and British forces, and was the landing point for the cross-Channel petrol pipeline code-named PLUTO (Pipe Line Under The Ocean), which delivered much-needed petrol to the Allied tanks and trucks. As well as a good beach, the town has a large fishing fleet and therefore a fascinating harbour, full of life, especially when the boats come in with their catch.

St Laurent-sur-Mer

A small village set above and behind the low cliffs and sand dunes that mark out the wide strand of bloody Omaha Beach, St Laurent was captured by the US 1st Infantry Division on the night of 6-7 June 1944. Here they brought in their dead and here many of them still lie, in this vast but beautiful plot above the sea. Other memorials, to 1st Infantry ('The Big Red One'), 29th Infantry and other American units, can be found on the beach below.

Comité Départemental du Tourisme du Calvados
Place du Canada
14000 Caen
Tel: 31 86 53 30

Touring:
use Michelin sheet map 231, Normandie

A long-abandoned gun emplacement speaks eloquently of the conflict witnessed by Utah Beach, north-east of Carentan, during the Allied invasion of June 1944

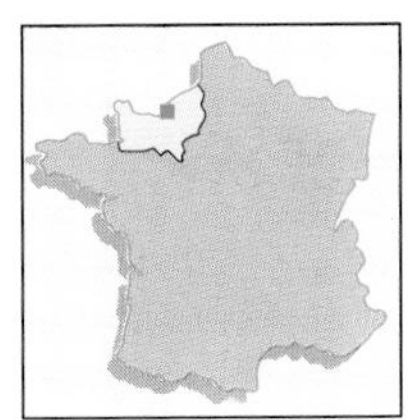

The Côte Fleurie and the Pays d'Auge

THE CALVADOS COAST changes as it runs north and east from the Orne towards the mouth of the Seine. The resorts become fashionable, and in the countryside gardens and orchards replace the great fields of the Caen plain. Behind the coast lie woods and orchards through which the River Touques meanders towards the sea, across the rich farmland of the Auge.

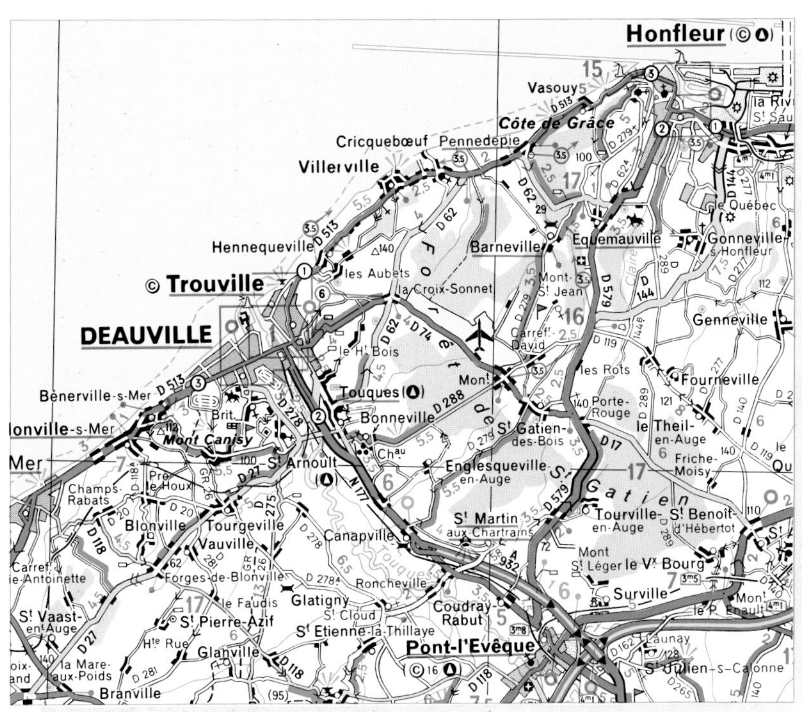

Comité Départemental du Tourisme du Calvados
Place du Canada
14000 Caen
Tel: 31 86 53 30

Touring:
use Michelin sheet map 231, Normandie

Blonville-sur-Mer

Pretty Blonville, best known for its long, sandy beach, is a place of refuge when the summer crowds take over the even longer strand and streets of Villers-sur-Mer, a couple of kilometres to the west. The beach runs up to the foot of Mont Canisy, the highest hill hereabouts at just 112m, but worth climbing for the coastal views. Notre-Dame chapel has modern Biblical frescos.

Deauville

By common agreement among those who know the Côte Fleurie – The Floral Coast – pretty, fashionable, lively Deauville is the Queen of the Coast, and not just because of her size. Indeed, with a resident population of under 5000, Deauville is not very large, but it possesses all the requirements of a top-quality resort: first-class hotels, a casino, the beach, two race courses, a great marina crammed with expensive yachts (some of which occasionally go to sea), and the affection of a large and elegant clientele.

Since the last war Deauville has expanded. Many of the fine old buildings have fallen to the spreading growths of later development, while others, once the palaces of the nobility, have become fashionable hotels. The marina, Port Deauville, opened in 1973 and has since become a haven for yachtsmen, the harbour bustling with craft throughout the summer. With two race courses, one at La Touques for flat racing and another at Clairefontaine for jumps, the horse is king, and the sport commands the close attention of the smart set.

Off the Planches are the fine hotels and the best restaurants, and these ensure patronage of the Casino and the gardens of the Terrasse de Deauville. Sport is ever more popular, with tennis, golf, riding, sailing, and swimming in a covered and heated pool, all competing for attention.

Honfleur

Set at the foot of the Côte de Grâce, Honfleur, like Deauville, was once a fishing port, but they have little else in common. The fishermen remain at Honfleur, though the more profitable yachting trade has largely driven them, at least in the summer months, from the picturesque Vieux Bassin in the town centre. Honfleur is a medieval port and town, and much of the Middle Ages remains in the old buildings and narrow streets, in the

Writers

If Normandy attracted artists, it gave birth and inspiration to writers. Perhaps the most famous of these, and certainly the most widely read, was Gustave Flaubert who, in *Madame Bovary*, created an unmatched tragic character. Flaubert came from Rouen, which also numbers Corneille and Fontenelle among its native sons.
Other writers who have found inspiration in Normandy include Guy de Maupassant, and André Maurois. In Villequier there is a Victor Hugo museum.

Honfleur's Chapelle de Notre-Dame-de-Grâce, built in the early 17th century, enjoys an attractive position flanked by trees

There is much to see in Honfleur, so it is well worth a full day. However, since parking is limited it is best to walk. Any tour should begin in the Vieux Port (above) and include the Lieutenance, where the town's governor once lived. In a square close by stands the Église Ste-Catherine, and the streets surrounding the square will delight the eye

CHEESE

The fat Norman cattle, grazing belly-deep in the lush grass, provide the basic ingredient for that rich cream and cheese which, with calvados, underpin Norman cuisine. Normandy has some notable local butter, such as that from Isigny, but Norman cheeses are world-famous. Pont-l'Évêque is said to be the oldest Norman cheese, dating back to the 13th century, and Livarot is another survivor from the medieval period, while Petite Suisse from the Bray region dates from 1850. Camembert is even more recent and attributed to Marie Harel, a dairymaid from Vimoutiers, who is said to have obtained the recipe from a priest she sheltered during the Revolution. Vimoutiers has a museum showing the original process.

tall houses that surround the Vieux Port, and perhaps most of all, in the Église Ste-Catherine, built in the 15th century entirely of wood by the local fishermen and shipwrights to celebrate the end of the Hundred Years War.

Commerce plays a part in the life of Honfleur, but without damaging the charm of a place so beautiful that artists continue to flock here, as they have done since the middle of the last century, when the Normandy coast became popular with the painters of Paris. Stroll around the Vieux Port today and you will find artists at their easels, like Corot, Boudin, Bonington and others before them. A good selection of the work of the Honfleur School can be found at the Musée Eugène Boudin.

Pont-l'Évêque

In 1944 the retreating Germans and the advancing British both took their toll of Pont-l'Évêque, which has very few old buildings left and is now mostly famous for its cheese. Places worth inspecting include the Église St-Michel, an example of the Flamboyant Gothic style, though the stained-glass windows are post-war, and some of the remaining houses along Rue St-Michel. Today, Pont-l'Évêque is most useful and notable as a base for exploring the surrounding countryside. Worth a special mention is the attractively situated village of St André-d'Hébertot. You should also try the restaurants of the Auge, which have produced some of the outstanding dishes of the rich Norman cuisine.

Trouville

Set on the right bank of the Touques, just opposite Deauville, Trouville has a very good beach and, like Deauville, a boardwalk behind it, but is much less frenetic and fashionable. Many people feel that while Deauville has the reputation, Trouville has the charm. There is the Musée Montebello, which contains an exhibition devoted to the history of sea bathing, a casino and an aquarium, many good hotels and fine views along the Côte Fleurie from the corniche road.

Villerville

Those who like a quiet little seaside resort may find the village of Villerville ideal, with its peaceful setting between the sea and meadows and woodland. This resort is not yet developed apart from a number of cottages, and some parts of it are very old indeed. The belfry of the church is Romanesque, while the church at Cricqueboeuf, which is practically a suburb, dates from the 12th century and is so picturesque that it may well be familiar from its frequent appearance on travel posters.

Churches and Abbeys

NORMANDY POSSESSES a rich heritage of secular and ecclesiastical buildings, some of them dating, at least in part, from before the year 1000. Norman churches are built in a variety of architectural styles. The Romanesque, otherwise known as Norman, flourished in Normandy until the middle of the 12th century, only giving way gradually to the exoticism of Gothic, which arrived from the Ile de France. This, to reflect the strong character of Norman life, evolved at first in a distinctive local way, which is called Norman Gothic.

Norman religious life, thought and architecture always stayed close to the central body of the Church. Indeed, Normandy has a rightful claim to the title of the great engine of Western Christendom during the early Middle Ages, producing many learned clerics and powerful archbishops. As Normandy was always a wealthy province, the Norman dukes and nobles were able to endow rich abbeys and construct fine cathedrals, as well as supporting a quantity of smaller but very beautiful churches.

Any selection of Norman churches, abbeys and cathedrals is inevitably subjective, though some are so outstanding as to be beyond argument. This selection not only represents the best but also provides a varied sample of Norman churches of every style from the Romanesque to the Flamboyant Gothic, from every period from the 10th the 18th century, and from all over the region.

Lessay

To begin with one of the finest religious buildings in the region, there is that jewel of the Romanesque, Lessay, a Benedictine abbey in the Cotentin. Lessay is interesting for a reason other than beauty, for it was completely shattered in the fighting of 1944 and has been wonderfully restored by the local people, who even gathered up the shards of stone to piece it together again.

The abbey was founded in 1056, the apse and chancel being completed by 1098 and the nave a few years later. The present church, which took ten years to restore, has stained-glass windows that were not in the original structure, but otherwise this Romanesque gem is much as it was at the end of the 11th century. The baptistry chapel is later, from the 15th century. It is the abbey's exterior that commands attention, presenting the finest example of the pure Romanesque to be found in all of Normandy.

Coutances

Another church of particular note in the Cotentin is the Norman-Gothic cathedral of Coutances. The nave was endowed by one of William the Conqueror's knights, Geoffroy de Montbray, in 1056, but his church provided only the foundations for the present cathedral, which dates from 1218, though the original Romanesque towers, with much Norman Gothic, are to be found in the present façade. Otherwise this is a good example of the Gothic, with flying buttresses to support the walls, rose windows and, from the 14th century, wide aisles that gave crowds of pilgrims access to the image of Notre Dame de Coutances, a statue that survived the heavy bombing of the town in 1944.

The cathedral at Coutances is held to be the best product of the 13th-century fusion of Gothic and traditional Norman styles

Jumièges

On the other side of the province, on the banks of the Seine, stands a very notable relic of Norman religious life, the great Gothic ruined abbey at Jumièges. The original abbey dated from the 7th century but was burnt by the Northmen and the present foundation was the gift of William Longsword, Duke of Normandy, son of Rollo the Viking, the buildings being consecrated in 1067 in the presence of his descendant, William the Conqueror. Jumièges flourished until the Revolution, when the community was dispersed and the buildings sold for their supply of dressed stone. Shattered and despoiled, Jumièges was given to the nation in 1852 and remains one of the most beautiful and evocative ruins in Normandy, if not the whole of France. The outlines of many of the buildings survive, and several arches still stand, together with most of the nave. There is an excellent view of the abbey from the steps inside the main gate, and the 17th-century abbey lodgings are still intact.

The abbey church of St-Georges at St Martin-de-Boscherville, just to the west of Rouen, was saved from similar destruction by becoming the local parish church at the Revolution. Much smaller than Jumièges, St-Georges is of similar date, being erected from 1080 and completed in 1125. The speed of construction gives it great unity of line. There is Norman carving on the main door, a plain façade, and Gothic work in the nave, all of which add variety to a pleasing whole.

The abbey at Hambye in the lush valley of the Sienne, south-east of Coutances, is a vast, immensely imposing ruin, parts of which date from the 13th and 14th centuries, as well as from the original foundation of 1145-1200. There is rich carving from the 16th century and tapestries from the 17th in the refectory, as well as beautiful cloisters. Many of the abbey buildings are open to view.

ST WANDRILLE

Returning to the Seine valley, St Wandrille is well worth a visit because here Benedictine monasticism still lives. The original abbey of St Wandrille dates from the 7th century, though the surviving ruins are from the Norman construction of the 10th century and much of it from much later still, for example the 13th-century chancel and the 14th-century nave. Visitors and pilgrims still come here, to see the medieval statue of Notre Dame de Fontenelle, or the shrine in the church that contains the abbey's principal relic, the head of St Wandrille.

Benedictine monks still occupy part of St Wandrille's abbey

A secluded location lends charm to the ruins of the 7th-century Benedictine abbey of Jumièges

CAEN AND ROUEN

The final selection of Norman churches must be drawn from those available in the two great cities of Normandy, Caen and Rouen, both of which are crammed with churches built at various times since the founding of the dukedom. The two abbey churches of Caen, the Abbaye aux Hommes and the Abbaye aux Dames, were built by William the Conqueror and his wife Matilda as their penance for having married within the bounds of consanguinity: they were cousins.

William's foundation centres on the Église St-Étienne, which was begun in 1067 and completed in the 13th century. The mixture of styles works very well and since the church escaped destruction when Caen was embattled in 1944, the church and surrounding abbey buildings remain a fine example of medieval church architecture. The Conqueror's tomb is before the high altar, but his bones were dug up and thrown into the Orne at the Revolution, only a femur surviving to be reinterred a few years ago. The monastery buildings are now used as the town hall, but most of the old monastic quarters remain and can be visited on conducted tours.

Matilda's Abbaye aux Dames also has a great church, which dates from 1062 and is dedicated to the Trinity. Matilda's bones were left undisturbed at the Revolution and still lie under a black marble slab before the high altar. The nave is Romanesque, the transept Gothic, the spires much later, having replaced the original towers in the 18th century. Here, too, the buildings that once sheltered the nuns have been taken over for use as offices, in this instance by the Regional Council, but guided tours of the nunnery are still available.

Unlike Caen, the glories of Rouen rest chiefly on the churches and on the Cathédrale. The city's great cathedral of Notre-Dame is a marvellous example of the Gothic, having been built when the style was at its purest, between the 13th and 15th centuries. One of the cathedral's most curious features is the Tour de Beurre, built from the donations made by those gourmets of Rouen who wished to continue eating butter during the abstinence of Lent. The 12th-century Tour St-Romain is the earliest of all the spires of this soaring edifice, but the whole cathedral takes at least a morning to see properly.

When the cathedral has been explored, several churches remain, all worth inspection. St-Maclou is in the Flamboyant Gothic style, and dates from the latter half of the 15th century. The Hundred Years War delayed the completion of the other Gothic masterpiece of Rouen, St-Ouen, begun in 1318 but not completed until the following century. Particularly fine are the chancel and the nave. Finally, St-Godard is notable for its marvellous stained-glass windows.

Caen's Abbaye aux Hommes was begun in the 11th century by William the Conqueror

These Norman churches, abbeys and cathedrals, and scores more like them, can certainly be enjoyed separately. However they are worth exploring in a systematic way, for then they present a story in stone, vividly recounting Normandy's long and glorious history.

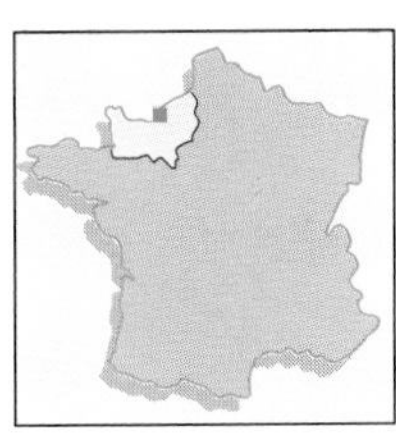

The Côte d'Albâtre and the Caux Country

THE *DÉPARTEMENT* OF SEINE-MARITIME, which runs from north of the Seine up the Channel Coast, offers a variety of scenery, from the high chalk cliffs along the Channel Coast to great forests, including those in the Parc Régional de la Brotonne. All this area, which marks the northern frontier with Picardy, is threaded with streams and rivers and dotted with small towns, the most beautiful of which are a string of resorts between Fécamp and Dieppe.

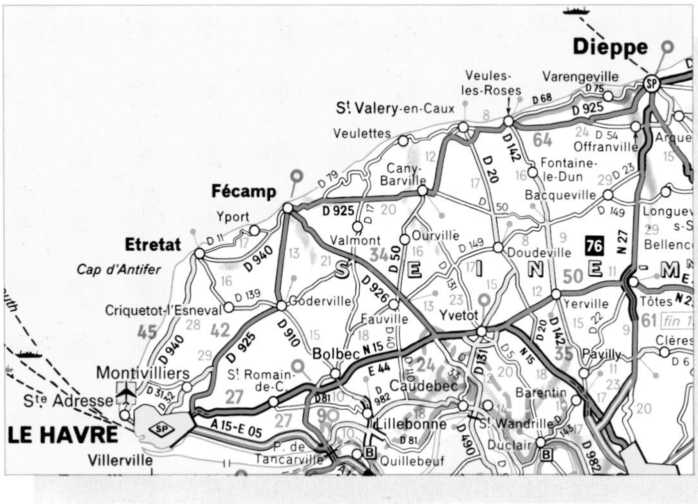

Caudebec-en-Caux

One of the main towns along the lower Seine, between Rouen and the sea, Caudebec dates back to the 11th century, when it was founded by monks from the monastery at St Wandrille. Many medieval buildings remain, notably the Église Notre-Dame, which was built from 1425, and around Place du Marché, where the Saturday market dates back to 1390. The so-called Maison des Templiers is certainly 13th-century, but there is no record that the Knights Templars ever had a *commanderie* in Caudebec. Various sections of the ramparts remain, including two towers, the town prison and two chapels. Equally interesting and of more recent date is the Musée de la Marine de Seine, which describes river trade and navigation over the past three centuries. Caudebec is also a good touring centre, the south bank being served by two new and imposing bridges, the Pont de Brotonne, which lies just to the east, and further downstream the great Pont de Tancarville.

Cany-Barville

Set astride the River Durdent, this little town has several churches and a splendid late-16th-century château surrounded by a moat fed by the river. The setting is extremely picturesque: a quiet, green valley off the usual tourist track.

Dieppe Fishing

Although there are a good number of fishing ports in Normandy, with fleets at Port-en-Bessin, Fécamp, Trouville, Honfleur and Barneville-Carteret, none of them is so active or so successful as Dieppe.
The fishermen tend to live in the old quarter of the town, on the right bank of the river, and their huge fleet of trawlers is still active, but has abandoned the 'Grand Banks' for the more lucrative trade in local cold-water fish: turbot, sea perch, sole, the ingredients of *sole dieppoise*. There is a daily fish market and a number of good seafood restaurants along the Quai Henri IV and the quays of the Port de Pêche.

Comité Départemental du Tourisme de Seine-Maritime
2 *bis*, Rue du Petit-Salut - BP 680
76008 Rouen Cedex
Tel: 35 88 61 32

Touring:
use Michelin sheet map 916, Francia

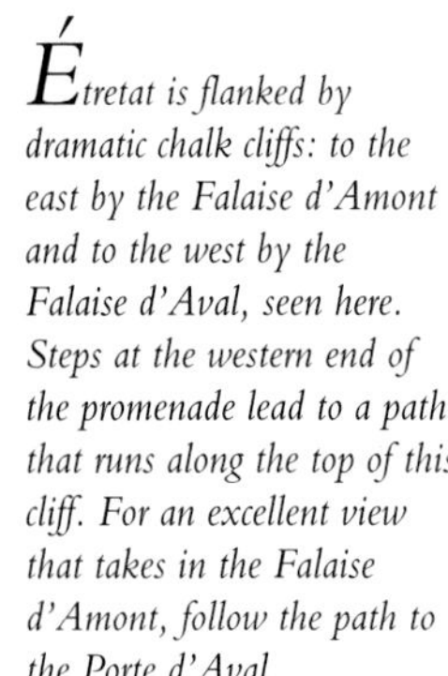

Étretat is flanked by dramatic chalk cliffs: to the east by the Falaise d'Amont and to the west by the Falaise d'Aval, seen here. Steps at the western end of the promenade lead to a path that runs along the top of this cliff. For an excellent view that takes in the Falaise d'Amont, follow the path to the Porte d'Aval

Dieppe

This busy, pretty port, set in the high cliffs of the Côte d'Albâtre, the Alabaster Coast, is the oldest seaside resort in France. Dieppe is also a major fishing port and has a ferry terminal offering easy access to the Pays de Caux and the Seine valley, though the ferry terminal is to move along the coast within the next few years.

The seafront of Dieppe is set behind a long shingle beach, site of the famous Dieppe Raid of August 1942, when Canadian troops and British Commandos attempted a surprise attack on the town and were driven off with great loss, over 5000 men being killed or taken prisoner on the beaches. The town beach is now backed by a wide promenade and behind this is a line of hotels.

The fishing port of Dieppe remains active, for commercial fishing plays an important part in the local economy. Dieppe is also a major Channel ferry port, with the benefit of a deep-water harbour

Ivory Carving

Scrimshaw, the carving of ivory by seamen, has a tradition that goes back to the earliest days of seafaring. Given the great number of seafarers who lived in or sailed from the port, it is not surprising that Dieppe became a centre for the ivory trade. However, the quality of the work far exceeds that produced out of boredom by simple sailor folk. Dieppe's ivory carvers were artists, and their work was profitable enough to support over 300 of them in the middle to late years of the 17th century. The Musée de Dieppe, in the château above the seafront, has an extensive collection of Dieppe ivory carving and a reproduction of a carver's workshop.

Étretat

Although Étretat is a pleasant resort, full of good hotels and seafood restaurants, the great attraction here is not the town or the pebble beach, but the high chalk cliffs flanking it. These have been worn into curious shapes by the constant action of the sea, and here and there great holes have been worn in the chalk to create arches. The most striking is the pierced Falaise d'Aval, to the west of the town. Just out to sea stands a solitary pillar of chalk, L'Aiguille, Needle Rock, which rises 70m out of the water. A good view of these chalk formations can be had from the cliffs to the south of the town. For a look at the resort, go the other way, to the seaman's chapel of Notre-Dame-de-la-Garde, and the museum and monument to two French transatlantic flyers, Nungesser and Coli.

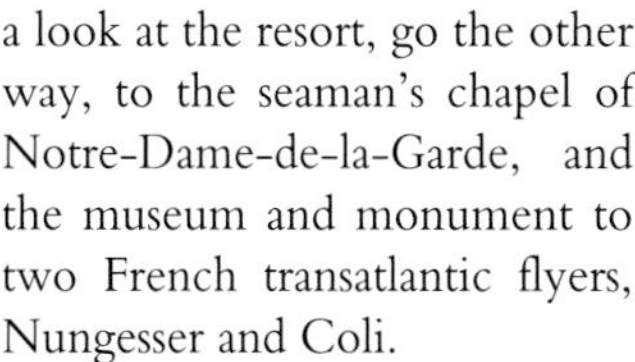

Sights to see in the town include the covered market and parts of the church of Notre Dame.

Fécamp

A thriving fishing port, Fécamp is best known to visitors for two historic reasons. The first is as a shrine that has held, since the 7th century, the Precious Blood. This relic led to the creation of the Benedictine monastery by Count Richard at the start of the 11th century. The monastery provided the town's second claim to fame when, in 1510, a monk of the abbey used the aromatic herbs of the Pays de Caux to create a liqueur that is still known as Benedictine. Only parts of the abbey remain but the Benedictine distillery is still in working order and can be visited. So, too, can the Precious Blood, which is kept in La Trinité church and is the object of a pilgrimage on the Tuesday and Thursday following Trinity Sunday.

There are good restaurants overlooking the harbour, and a large marina. Six kilometres to the south lies the Château de Bailleul, a splendid 16th-century château.

Yvetot

Set in a breezy corner of the Caux plateau, Yvetot is a market town for the surrounding countryside, and a good touring centre. In the town itself the great attraction is the stained glass by Ingrand in the modern Église St-Pierre. This church was built in 1956 and is a very interesting example of contemporary religious architecture. Other sights worth seeing locally are the Musée de la Nature set in an old Caux farmhouse with displays of local wildlife, and the great oak outside the church at Allouville-Bellefosse south-west of Yvetot, which is said to be one of the oldest trees in France. Two chapels have been built inside the trunk.

A famous liqueur, enjoyed all over the world, is produced in Fécamp. Visitors to the town should see both the distillery and the Musée de la Bénédictine

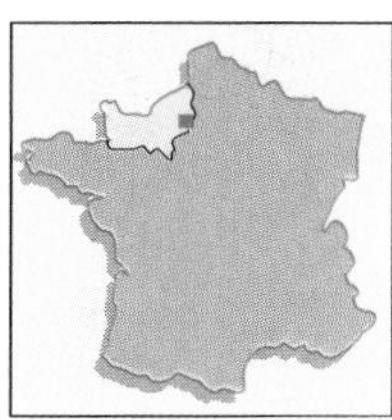

The Seine Valley and the Vexin

THE SEINE is one of the most beautiful and historic rivers of France, and nowhere more so than here, along the short stretch that flows between Vernon and Les Andelys, a place where kings and painters and poets have lived. Apart from Monet's garden at Giverny and the ruin of Richard Lionheart's castle at Les Andelys, the great attraction in this part of Normandy is the countryside itself, the Vexin, a farming area full of pretty, little-visited villages.

Comité Départemental du Tourisme de l'Eure
35, Rue du Docteur-Oursel - BP 187
27001 Évreux Cedex
Tel: 32 38 21 61

Touring:
use Michelin sheet map 237, Ile-de-France

Les Andelys

The pleasant riverside town of Les Andelys is divided into two parts. By the river, where the bank is well supplied with restaurants and hotels, lies Le Petit Andely, while a little to the east but connected by a long avenue lies Le Grand Andely, the original site of the town. The whole is overlooked by the massive keep and walls of Richard Lionheart's 12th-century Château Gaillard.

Le Grand Andely grew up on the site of a 6th-century monastery founded by Queen Clothilde, who, in addition to being the wife of King Clovis, was a saint. In the town visitors can still see the fountain where she performed the useful miracle of turning water into wine.

The town is watered along the line of Avenue de la République by the River Gambon. Apart from a plentiful supply of flower-beds and a glorious setting by the river, there are two fine churches: the Gothic Église St-Sauveur dates from the 12th and 13th centuries, while the Église Notre-Dame in Le Grand Andely is in the later Flamboyant Gothic style, with some good stained glass and a 16th-century entombment.

Château Gaillard

Richard I, King of England and Duke of Normandy, called Lionheart, leader of the Third Crusade and the greatest soldier of his day, built the Château Gaillard as the key in the lock of the Norman Vexin and to defy his rival, Philippe-Auguste of France. The castle was also a gesture of defiance and for that reason called the 'Gaillard', or Saucy, Castle.

In 1203 Philippe-Auguste laid siege to Château Gaillard. When a French soldier climbed into the inner castle via the latrines and let down the drawbridge the castle fell to an assault, after a seige of just eight months.

It remained a fortress until dismantled in the 16th century on the orders of Cardinal Richelieu. Much of the dressed stone was used to build the houses of Les Andelys, but what remains is enough to present an evocative and romantic spectacle of the Middle Ages.

Gasny

Little Gasny, in the valley of the Epte, grew up around a priory founded in 660 by two saintly clerics, St Nicaise and St Ouen, who both became Bishops of Rouen. Their foundation was destroyed by the Northmen and eventually replaced by the present Église St-Martin, a 16th-century building, while the 15th-century Chapelle de Mesnil-Milon is now a barn.

Artists and Musicians

Normandy has always attracted painters, who are drawn to the province by the clear Atlantic light and the variety of subjects. Claude Monet, who lived at Giverny, was born in Le Havre, as was Raoul Dufy, and in the latter half of the 19th century the province began to attract Impressionists such as Sisley, Renoir, Boudin and Pissarro. Before them had come the English landscape and seascape artist Richard Bonington, who came to Normandy at the end of the Napoleonic Wars, and Corot, who painted scenes of Rouen, Dieppe, Le Havre and Honfleur. The latter, a beautiful, evocative port, has been featured in the work of early-20th-century artists such as Vallotton, while Deauville inspired Van Dongen. Even today, a tall water-tower outside Dieppe supports a painting by Vasarely, and the port has inspired artists such as Seurat. The many museums and art galleries to be found in Normandy contain numerous examples of work inspired by the local countryside and towns.

The redoubt of Richard Lionheart's Château Gaillard, overlooking the Seine, has kept only one of its five towers, but the main fort is more intact

Giverny

The small village of Giverny chiefly attracts visitors because of its connection with the Impressionist painter Claude Monet, who lived here from 1883 until his death in 1926. His house is now a museum to the artist's life and work, and the garden where, among other works, he painted his famous

Monet's Japanese-style garden at Giverny inspired some of his most popular paintings

Les Nymphéas is very much as he left it, full of flowers and ponds with water-lilies in season, having been restored to its original state in 1966. Many of Monet's paintings are on display in the house.

Vallée de la Seine

The Seine is one of the great rivers of France, 776km long, of which the last 100km flows through Normandy, from Vernon to the sea. This is the most beautiful and interesting part of the entire river, and today, below Rouen, ocean-going ships forge upstream to Rouen docks. This lower part of the river is the place of the *mascaret*, the great Seine tidal bore that once swamped the riverside villages but rarely occurs nowadays. The river varies: parts of it, such as the section between Giverny and Pont-de-l'Arche, are slow and meandering, making great sweeping loops.

Vernon

Vernon is a pleasant residential town of straight streets and fine houses, a popular place where people stay while visiting nearby Giverny. Within the town itself there are medieval houses along Rue Carnot, and a fine selection of paintings by Monet and other Impressionists in the A-G Poulain Museum. Close by stands the keep of the old castle, built by Philippe-Auguste to command the old bridge, the piles of which are visible from the castle roof and the present road bridge.

Places worth seeing near by include the Château des Tourelles, across the river, and the 18th-century Château de Bizy.

CASTLES

There are so many castles in Normandy that a selection is inevitable here, but not to be missed are Falaise, birthplace of William the Conqueror; Caen, the great stronghold of the dukes of Normandy; Richard Lionheart's Château Gaillard in the Seine valley; the almost intact 14th-century *château-fort* at Bricquebec, which is now an hotel; the imposing ruins of the castle at Arques-la-Bataille near Dieppe, which defied Henry V on his march to Agincourt; and the classic 15th-century castle at Lassay.

THE NORTH

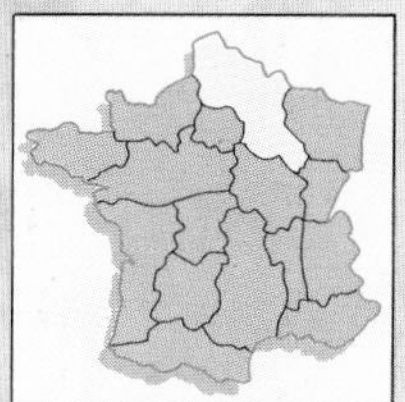

MANY PEOPLE SIMPLY HURRY through the North of France on their way to other parts of the country, yet there are few regions that are so rich in history and architecture, or possess so varied a landscape. The coastline to the west is marked by dramatic cliffs and miles of sandy beaches, while inland the open countryside is broken by pockets of woodland and pleasant hidden river valleys. It is a well-developed landscape largely given over to the cultivation of cereals, sugar beet, hops and root vegetables, and in the south-east to the extensive vineyards of the Champagne region. To the west, on the low-lying estuarine marshlands that were formerly part of the sea, there are large flocks of the famous *pré-salé*, or salt-marsh sheep.

Composed largely of the old kingdoms of Artois, Picardy, Flanders and Champagne, the North retains a strong feeling of independence. Because the frontiers of France were established only relatively recently in the regions external influences remain strong. Since the Middle Ages, the English, Dutch, Flemish, Spanish and Germans have battled with the French for possession of these territories and have all left their mark on a landscape that has long been a battleground. Elements as diverse as Flemish architecture, beer, windmills and a distinctive regional folklore reflect the lasting impact of these cultures.

The Romans were the first to invade, and were followed by many others, the most recent being the Germans in 1940. The slaughter at Crécy (1346) and Agincourt (1415) was echoed centuries later on the Somme and the Marne, World War I having a major impact on the region, with vast areas being totally destroyed. The sombre legacy can be seen in the hundreds of military cemeteries and war memorials that litter the North of France. The best of these are masterpieces of 20th-century architecture, continuing a strong tradition of fine building in the region.

This area was the cradle of the Gothic style, which attained its peak in the great cathedrals of Amiens, Beauvais and Reims. After the Gothic came the northern Renaissance, with its emphasis on decorative brickwork, followed by the classical style of the 17th and 18th centuries. Abbeys and cathedrals apart, a number of buildings emerged to characterise the North: notably the towering belfries, the great town halls and the châteaux and citadels designed by Vauban in the late 17th century. In the 20th century art deco and Modernism have made their impact.

The eastern part of the region has long been industrial, the textile trade having been important since Roman times. Later came coal, and related chemical and heavy industries, all of which have inevitably left their mark. The landscape is divided by a complex network of canals and navigable rivers whose leisure potential in the post-industrial age is just being realised. Even in the heart of the industrial region there are pretty villages remarkable buildings and attractive countryside, just waiting to be discovered.

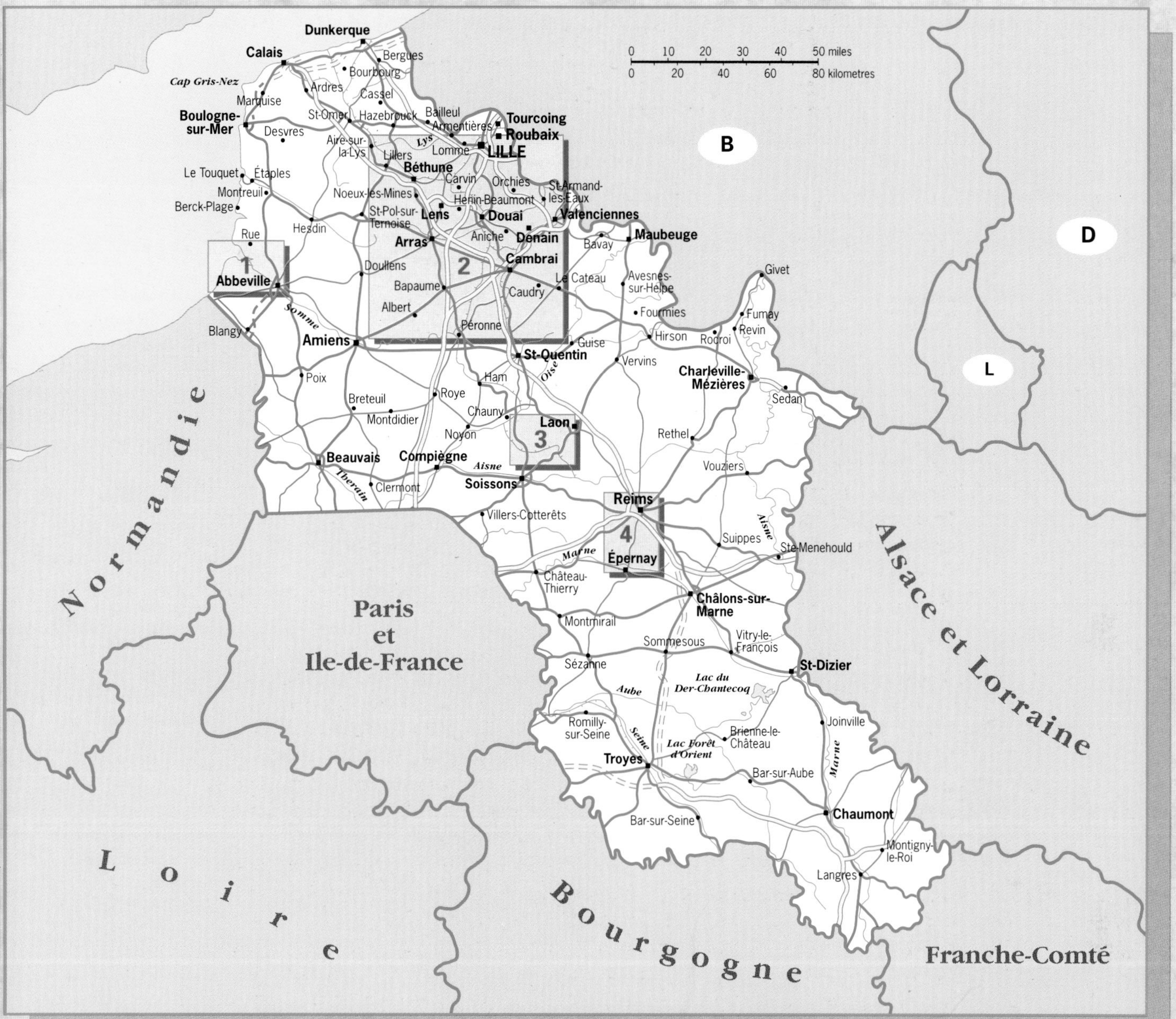

Coal mining (right above) and the production of steel, textiles and chemicals make a major contribution to the regional and national economies. Smaller but established since the 18th century is the North's ceramics industry (right below)

Rodin's imposing Burghers of Calais *stands in front of the city's early-20th-century town hall*

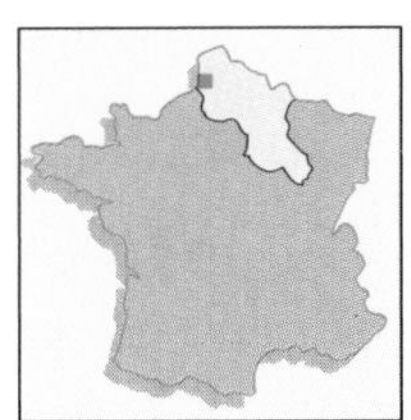

The Bay of the Somme

THE BAY OF THE SOMME is a distinctive region of low-lying salt-marsh and remote coastal scenery, famous throughout Europe for its bird life. Today, it is an area of old-fashioned towns and quiet resorts, yet within it are great cathedrals and abbeys, among other echoes of past glories and medieval might.

Comité Départemental du Tourisme de la Somme
21, Rue Ernest-Cauvin
80000 Amiens
Tel: 22 92 26 39

Touring:
use Michelin sheet map 236, Nord/ Flandres-Artois/ Picardie

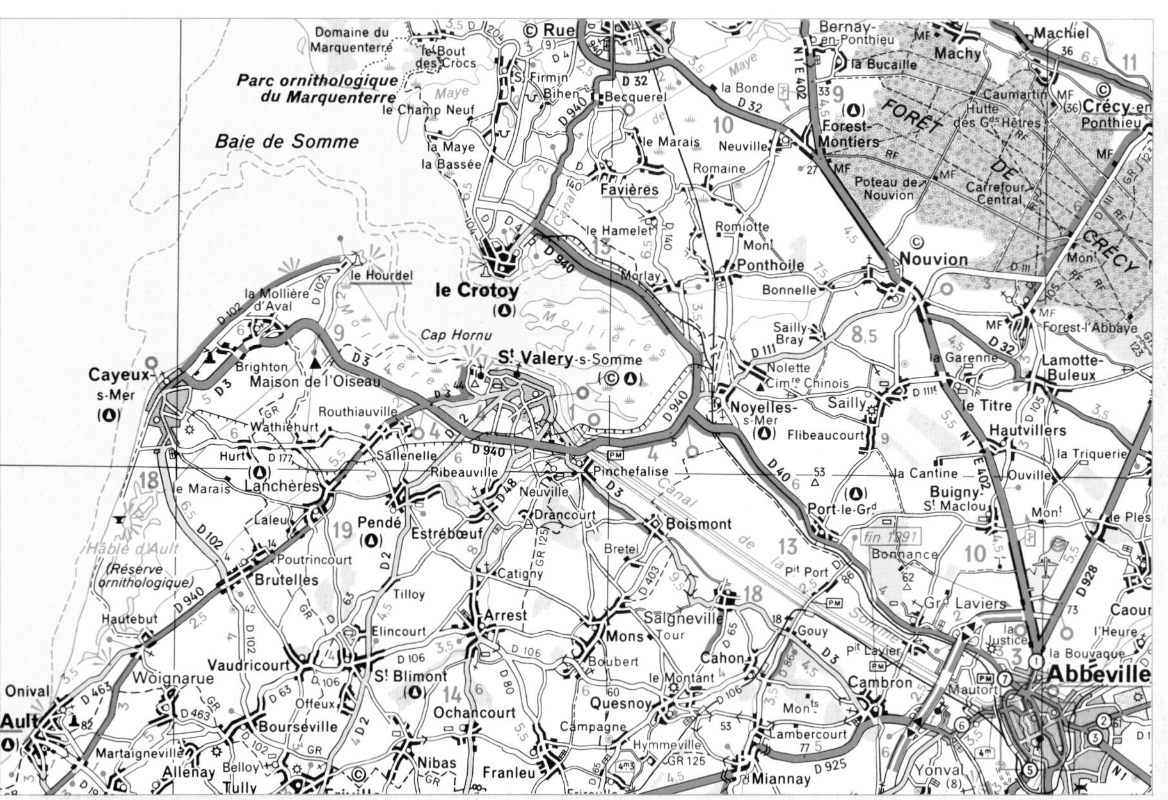

Birds

The bay of the Somme is internationally famous for its bird life, and over three-quarters of all Europe's known species are recorded here. Large areas of the remote salt-marsh of the tidal estuary have been turned into wildlife reserves, and species that formerly fell in thousands to the guns of sportsmen are now carefully protected. A mecca for serious ornithologists, the region also caters excellently today for the less specialised tastes of the casual visitor. To the south is the Maison de l'Oiseau, a living museum that celebrates the bird life and the distinctive environment of the region, while to the north is the huge expanse of the Parc de Marquenterre, a reserve where both local and migratory birds can be observed from a range of carefully planned trails. Both have cafeterias and souvenir shops with ample parking, and there is a picnic area in the Parc de Marquenterre.

The neo-Gothic railway station at Abbeville, a town that suffered massive destruction during World War II

Abbeville

The English owned Abbeville for two centuries from 1272, and in 1514 Henry VIII's sister Mary Tudor was married here to Louis XII. The great Gothic cathedral of St-Vulfran, begun in 1488 and left unfinished 50 years later, once towered over a network of narrow streets of timber-framed houses, but much of the medieval old town was destroyed by the Germans in one devastating air raid in May 1940. Notable survivors are the 17th- and 18th-century mansions with their grand gateways, built by the local textile barons of that era, splendid houses that ornament the streets of the town's compact centre. Abbeville's long history of manufacturing textiles continues, and this is still the town's most important industry. Also striking are the 13th-century belfry, now part of the local museum, and the decorative façade of the 1912 Flemish-style railway station, a period piece of great charm. The canalised Somme runs through Abbeville, and its old quays and locks, rarely busy today, add a distinctly Dutch flavour.

Ault-Onival

This small resort with its decidedly old-fashioned atmosphere is best known for the dramatic views of the cliffs that stretch westwards towards Le Tréport and the Normandy borders, perspectives familiar to painters as diverse as Cotman and Delacroix. At the town's centre is the large 15th-century church, with its unusual chequer-board flint and pebble decoration. Notable also are the tile panels and ceramic house name plaques with their strong *fin de siècle* flavour. These are a feature of the many holiday and retirement homes built in this area during the years that preceded and followed those of World War I.

In the Middle Ages Le Crotoy was rather more grand, boasting a château that guarded the Somme estuary. Here, in 1430, Joan of Arc was briefly held prisoner on her way to her trial in Rouen

Le Crotoy

Isolated in the salt-marshes with wonderful views over the estuary of the Somme, Le Crotoy claims to have the only south-facing beach on the north coast. A popular resort since the 19th century and famous for its seafood, which helped to attract writers and artists such as Jules Verne, Colette, Toulouse-Lautrec and Seurat, the town is little more than an old-fashioned, but still busy, fishing port. In the Middle Ages it was rather more, boasting a grand château to guard the Somme's entry. Here, in 1430, Joan of Arc was held prisoner on her way to her trial at Rouen. She is commemorated by the square that bears her name.

Chemin de Fer de la Baie de Somme

A memorable way to travel either from St Valery-sur-Somme to the resort of Cayeux, or from St Valery round the bay of the Somme to Le Crotoy, is on the narrow-gauge steam railway, a rare survivor from the time when little lines such as this were the backbone of rural France. Elderly, panting locomotives haul iron-verandahed wooden carriages on a slow, rocking journey across the salt-marshes, giving wonderful views over the distinctive landscape of the bay. A short walk from the intermediate station at Noyelles-sur-Mer, a village in fact now well inland, leads to a remarkable World War I Chinese cemetery, set in empty fields. Trains run at weekends and some weekdays during the holiday season, and the journey starts on St Valery's old quay.

Scenic trips by steam train to Cayeux and Le Crotoy begin at St Valery's old quay

Crécy-en-Ponthieu

In 1346 a small English army under the command of Edward III defeated a much larger French force in a muddy field near Crécy, thanks largely to the devastating fire of the English archers. Over 20,000 French soldiers, 1300 knights and 11 princes died that day, and English dominance over a large part of France was assured. During the battle Edward used a windmill as his look-out, and the site of this, long since disappeared, is marked by a viewing platform with descriptive panels, and there is a large car park nearby, off the D111.

Rue

Centuries ago Rue was a busy seaport, but today this appealing little town is 8km from the sea. Unexpectedly grand buildings contrast with the quiet shops and cafés of the market square. The best of these is the extravagant Flamboyant Gothic Chapelle du St-Esprit, built originally to celebrate a wooden crucifix, perhaps the True Cross, which was washed up on a nearby shore in the 12th century, having been thrown into the sea by Crusaders in the Holy Land. Much simpler is the wooden roof of the chapel of the 16th-century hospice close by, carved with hunting scenes. Also worth a visit is the belfry with its four grand turrets. This now houses a small museum devoted to the local pioneers of aviation, the Caudron brothers.

St Valery-sur-Somme

It was from St Valery that William set off in 1066 with his 400 ships to conquer England. Nothing remains from that eventful time, but today St Valery is a jolly little seaport at the mouth of the Somme, with brightly painted old houses lining the quay and looking over fishing boats and yachts to Le Crotoy, far away across the sandbanks and marshlands of the bay. To the west is the beach, and nearby are grand *fin de siècle* mansions that reveal the town's former glory.

Fortified walls and gateways reflect the former strategic importance of medieval St Valery

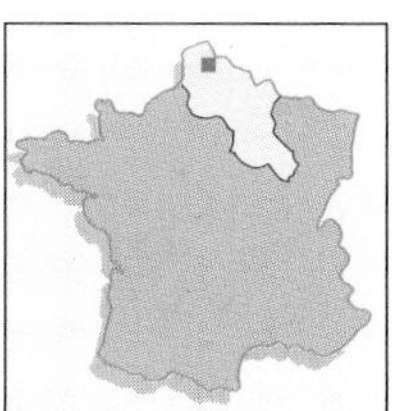

THE HEART OF THE NORTH

THIS REGION OF VARIED LANDSCAPE has been marked by centuries of exploitation. Well watered by the Lys, the Escaut and the Scarpe, the area is a major producer of cereals, sugar beet and hops. The underground coal seams have encouraged industry for many centuries but the wealth of the region came initially from textiles. Directly attributable to this wealth are a number of fine towns with excellent Renaissance and 17th- and 18th-century architecture.

Arras

Famed in the Middle Ages for its tapestries, which carried the town's name far and wide, Arras is a remarkable monument to the influence of the Flemish style in the North of France. At its heart are two great arcaded squares framed by handsome 17th-century town houses enriched with a wide diversity of architectural detail in brick and stone. In one is the town hall, marked by its 80-m belfry, and richly ornamented in a 15th-century Flemish Gothic style, a precise replica of the original, which was destroyed during World War I. These magnificent squares, seen at their best on market days and without equal in France, set the tone for a fine town, the capital of Artois, whose assets include the excellent Musée des Beaux-Arts, a grand late-18th-century cathedral built on the site of a former Benedictine abbey and a wealth of other interesting 18th-century buildings. Away from the centre is Vauban's massive citadel of 1670, still in military use and with its moats partly filled with water. Nearby is the British military cemetery and memorial. Arras is a town full of tradition and history, with a compact centre that is easy to explore on foot.

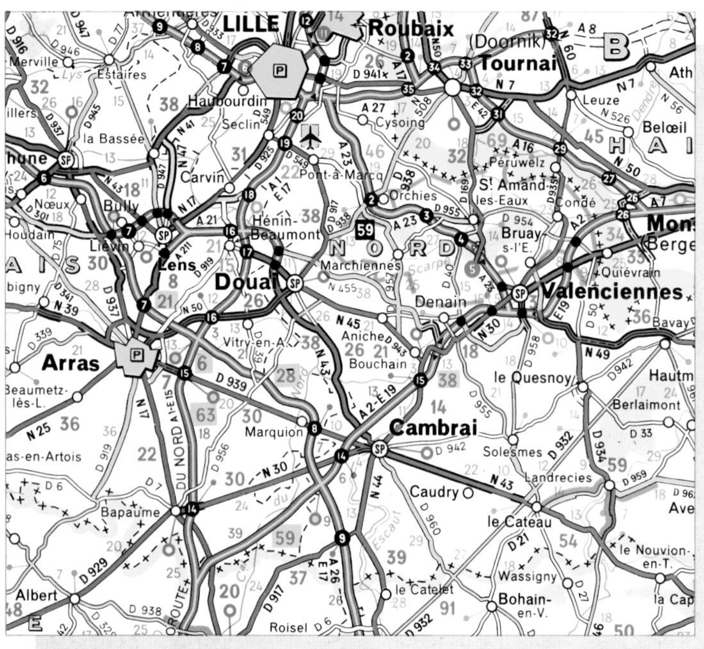

Comité Départemental du Tourisme du Pas-de-Calais
24, Rue Desille
62204 Boulogne-sur-Mer Cedex
Tel: 21 83 32 59

Touring:
use Michelin sheet map 916, Francia

Cambrai

A famous name in the annals of World War I, Cambrai is a traditional Flemish town long associated with the textile trade. The fine linen known as cambric takes its name from the town. Despite wartime destruction, Cambrai still has great character, with old cobbled streets lined with 17th- and 18th-century houses, pleasantly old-world shops, handsome squares and a huge public garden filled with sculpture and laid out around Vauban's 17th-century citadel.

The town is notable for its churches, which include the 18th-century cathedral, a fine example of northern classicism containing a striking memorial by David d'Angers to the local writer Fénelon, the Jesuit chapel of 1694 and, best of all, St-Géry with its high tower, built between 1698 and 1745. Inside is a splendidly lively Baroque rood-screen in contrasting marbles, sculpted by the locally born Marsy brothers. Another building in the classical style, but more restrained, is the town hall, with its tall belfry, whose animated figures, Martin and Martine, strike the hours.

The belfry of Cambrai's classical town hall, built in 1786, has the unusual feature of a pair of bronze figures from about 1510. Two metres tall and dressed in Moorish style, they announce the time by striking the bell with their mallets

Douai

Despite the proximity of the coalfields Douai is still an elegant, predominantly 18th-century town. There are plenty of fine façades and terraces in the old streets; particularly attractive are those flanking the old quays of the Scarpe on its course through the town centre. At the heart of Douai is the large main square, dominated by the town

Canada's national war memorial honours the 60,000 Canadian soldiers killed in the battle for Vimy Ridge in 1917

WAR MEMORIALS

Traditionally a battleground since Roman times, the North of France is marked, above all, by the scars of World War I – and by monuments to that conflict. Among the many memorials designed by the British architect Sir Edwin Lutyens, that at Thiepval stands out. It is a magnificent and powerfully complex composition of pierced arches carrying the names of 73,357 soldiers killed in the Somme who have no known grave. Also impressive are the huge American cemetery and memorial at Bony and Bellicourt, and Sir Herbert Baker's South African memorial at Delville Wood. Set high on a crest across the valley from Vimy Ridge is the French national memorial and cemetery, commemorating the dead of the battles of 1915. The cemetery, which mixes traditional and revivalist architectural styles, is immense. There are literally hundreds of lesser memorials and cemeteries, many of which have some artistic or architectural quality.

hall, the latter dating in part from the 15th century, and the famous belfry with its carillon of 62 bells that plays tunes every quarter of an hour. Douai is a centre of the French legal profession, maintaining the tradition established by Louis XIV when he made the town the seat of the local Flemish government that held power through much of the 18th century. The Palais de Justice, a handsome building of 1762, still stands by the Scarpe, and the chamber where the parliament sat can be visited. The painter Jean Bellegambe was born in Douai in 1470 and work by him is included in the interesting collections in the municipal museum, pleasantly housed in a former monastery.

Lille

A massive urban conglomeration devoted to the production of textiles, chemicals, beer and machinery, Lille is nonetheless a city of considerable style and elegance, with much to appeal to the visitor. It is a lively city that has preserved its links with its proud past while meeting very successfully the demands of modern urban life. A new underground railway network and new motorways have left intact the old heart of the city, where it is still a pleasure to explore streets lined with 17th- and 18th-century houses and an enticing variety of traditional shops and cafés. The city has its own opera house and its own orchestra, numerous theatres, one of the best provincial museums in France, a contemporary arts museum and France's largest bookshop.

A comic figure entrusted with an important role near the opera house in the heart of Lille

Lille's first great period of expansion was in the 17th century, and dating from this time are the Flemish Baroque Vieille Bourse, on the main square in the city centre, the Porte de Paris, a triumphal arch dedicated to the glory of Louis XIV, and the huge Citadelle, the finest and the best preserved of all Vauban's fortifications. Other buildings echo the city's growth in the 18th and 19th centuries, notably the churches and the merchants' houses, but it was in the present century that some of Lille's most exciting buildings were put up. These include the new Bourse, with its tall belfry, the opera house, the eccentric art nouveau Maison Coilliot with its tiled façade, designed by Guimard, the architect of the Paris Métro and, above all, the art deco town hall with its 104-m tower. The best time to visit Lille is in early September, when a huge fair takes over the old quarter.

NORTHERN GOTHIC

A BATTLEGROUND FOR CENTURIES, the North of France has nonetheless preserved intact the prime examples of the region's greatest gift to the cultural development of Europe, the Gothic church. While the cradle of the style was certainly in the Ile de France, it was in the North, and above all in Picardy, that it reached its maturity. It was also in this region that the Gothic style achieved its aim of maximum lightness combined with a remarkable delicacy of structure, a final flowering of art and technology before the all-conquering classicism of the Renaissance replaced the Gothic as the Christian style *par excellence.*

The great abbeys, cathedrals and churches of the North give ample opportunity for visitors to explore and enjoy the style in all its diversity, by studying the buildings that echo the three main periods of Gothic.

The first of these was the transition in the 12th century from the Romanesque style of the Normans to the initial flowering of Gothic, epitomised by Laon cathedral; the second was the 13th- and 14th-century development of mature Gothic, known in France as the Rayonnant style, and illustrated by Beauvais cathedral; and finally came the High Gothic, or Flamboyant, style of the 15th and 16th centuries, as at St Riquier.

TRANSITIONAL GOTHIC

Although the identities of the architects of many medieval buildings remain unknown to this day, some of the names of these master builders have been passed down by history. A key figure was Villard de Honnécourt, who was born near Cambrai and whose work at Laon, at the abbey of Vaucelles, at St Quentin and elsewhere was instrumental in marking the transition from the massive style and rounded arches of the Romanesque period to a far lighter and more daring structure based on the pointed arch, notably in the form of vaulting.

The 12th-13th-century Noyon cathedral (above)
Laon's Notre-Dame cathedral (above right and right)

Laon's cathedral is the finest example of this style because its period of building was relatively short and it was not greatly altered during later ages. As a consequence, the primitive Gothic elements in its structure are still clearly apparent. The four-tier elevation of its nave walls, a major indication of the overriding desire for light and lightness, is also seen in Noyon cathedral, completed at the end of the 13th century. Similar in style is the cathedral at Soissons, whose nave and choir were built at the same time, yet both cathedrals still contain obvious Romanesque features.

The basilicas at St Omer and St Quentin also have interesting 12th- and 13th-century transitional work, but in both the impact has been lessened by later developments.

RAYONNANT GOTHIC

In the 13th and 14th centuries church builders were inspired by the pursuit of lightness. This was the great age of rose windows and walls pierced by soaring openings in delicate vertical Gothic, all intended to project light into the massive interiors. The primary monument to this period is Amiens cathedral, the largest, and to many eyes, the best cathedral

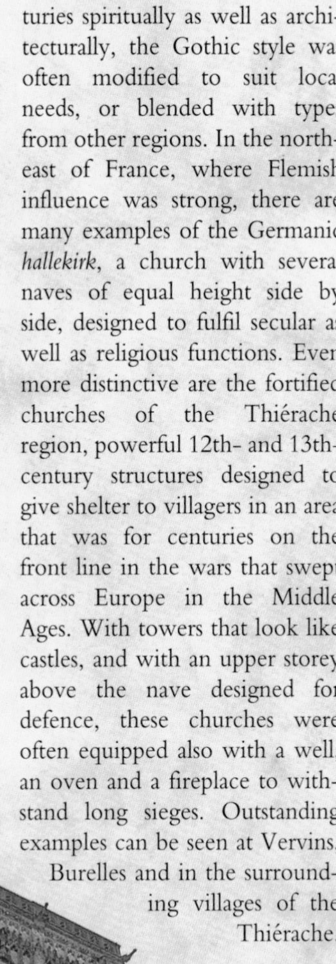

The Cathédrale Notre-Dame at Amiens (above and left), largely completed in 50 years

in France, a building whose finest qualities are its scale and its stylistic unity. Work on the cathedral started in 1220 and was virtually complete 50 years later, with only the towers and the west front belonging to a later period.

Even more ambitious was Beauvais, begun in 1247 but never taken beyond a choir and transept. Yet the space inside is immense, a daring mass of delicate Gothic columns and vaulting, soaring to 50m. This building fulfilled the dreams of the Gothic architect, with walls reduced to a minium and so pierced with tracery that the windows seem to float in space, and with stability maintained apparently by faith, but actually by flying buttresses on the exterior. Two further excellent examples of the Rayonnant Gothic style can be seen at St Omer and St Quentin.

FLAMBOYANT GOTHIC

The structural revolutions of the 13th and 14th centuries were exploited much more decoratively during the Flamboyant period, with ornamentation in carved stone achieving the delicacy of lacework. The strong vertical emphasis of the Rayonnant period was often lost in a mass of applied ornament and in many cases the aim seemed to be to achieve a decorative effect for its own sake. Typical examples of Flamboyant Gothic are the façade of St-Vulfran, in Abbeville, and the Chapelle du St-Esprit in Rue, but the most impressive in the region is the abbey church of St Riquier, which was almost entirely rebuilt in this style in the 15th and 16th centuries. Flamboyant elements can often be found in lesser churches, in the details of façades and porches and applied to tombs.

OTHER STYLES

While dominant for several centuries spiritually as well as architecturally, the Gothic style was often modified to suit local needs, or blended with types from other regions. In the north-east of France, where Flemish influence was strong, there are many examples of the Germanic *hallekirk*, a church with several naves of equal height side by side, designed to fulfil secular as well as religious functions. Even more distinctive are the fortified churches of the Thiérache region, powerful 12th- and 13th-century structures designed to give shelter to villagers in an area that was for centuries on the front line in the wars that swept across Europe in the Middle Ages. With towers that look like castles, and with an upper storey above the nave designed for defence, these churches were often equipped also with a well, an oven and a fireplace to withstand long sieges. Outstanding examples can be seen at Vervins, Burelles and in the surrounding villages of the Thiérache.

St Riquier's abbey church (below), which was destroyed and rebuilt several times, is the finest example of Flamboyant Gothic

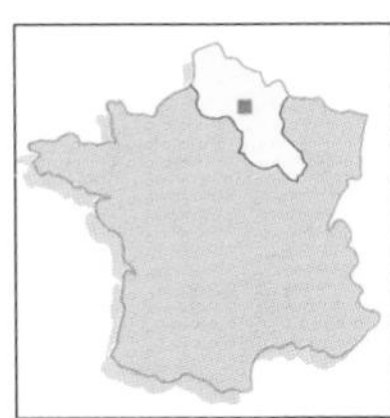

IN THE FORESTS OF ST GOBAIN

THIS IS A REGION OF forest, woodland and attractive farmland, intersected by small rivers. Hidden in this landscape are old abbeys and small villages with Romanesque and early Gothic churches, buildings whose quality reflects the former importance of Laon as the capital of France.

Brancourt-en-Laonnois

This farming village has a remarkable church, from the 1920s, distinguished by its unusual details and by its pierced spire, supported by powerful Expressionist angels. Inside there is dynamic stained glass of the same period. Across the road is a contrast in the form of an old-fashioned *charcuterie*, whose decorative façade features fine ironwork and interesting lettering.

Coucy-le-Château Auffrique

Formerly a fortified town, Coucy stands high above the valley of the Ailette, a commanding position underlining the power enjoyed by the château that was built here early in the 13th century. A massive structure erected by Enguerrand III, the self-styled 'Sire de Coucy' and claimant to the throne of France, it surrounded the village with its fortified wall and 28 towers. The keep, 54m high and with walls up to 7m thick, was its centre, but more domestic living quarters were added in the 15th century. Today much of the château has to be conjectured from the model in the local museum or the old photographs in the hotel, for most of it, including the keep, was blown up by the Germans in 1917. Two of the town gates survive, and walking along the remaining sections of the wall gives a good idea of the layout of the site, and ample opportunity to enjoy the fine views.

The unconventional design of the church at Brancourt-en-Laonnois comes as quite a surprise in a largely traditional region

Laon

A remarkable city in many ways, Laon was, from the 8th to the 10th century, the capital of France and the residence of the Capetian kings, direct descendants of Charlemagne. Previously Laon had been a Roman city, the Romans being among several cultures to make the most of its extraordinary setting. Laon is perched high up on an isolated block of Tertiary limestone, overlooking a vast plain, and protected by the steep cliffs that surround it. The same physical features have continued to protect the city, and so Laon today is still virtually medieval in structure. At its heart is Notre-Dame, one of the finest cathedrals in France and one of the earliest in Gothic style. Its splendid façade and four towers, two of which rise to 52m, are covered in sculpture and architectural detail that mark the transition from Romanesque to Gothic.

Around the cathedral is the old heart of Laon, still retaining an air of detachment from the main town to the west, old streets ranged around the Église St-Martin, another remarkable early Gothic structure. To the east of the cathedral is the citadel, whose fortifications date back to the 16th century. Also to be seen are fine episcopal buildings, a Romanesque Knights Templars' chapel, old city gates, and a wealth of medieval, Renaissance and later buildings lining the narrow streets. Later developments are all below, in the plain, and the newer section, including the railway station, is linked to the old city by an excellent cable railway, a continuous service of modern driverless carriages that makes access very easy. Laon is a good place to explore on foot with sudden views at every turn.

As befits a town with an illustrious history, Laon has a particularly handsome cathedral, despite the fact that of the seven towers originally planned, only four were completed

Prémontré

Founded in the early 12th century by St Norbert, Prémontré became the mother abbey for the order that carried the founder's name, the Norbertins, who were closely associated with St Augustine in their beliefs and dress. The huge abbey was entirely rebuilt in the 18th century, and stands today, a series of grand classical buildings in golden stone, ranged round a formal

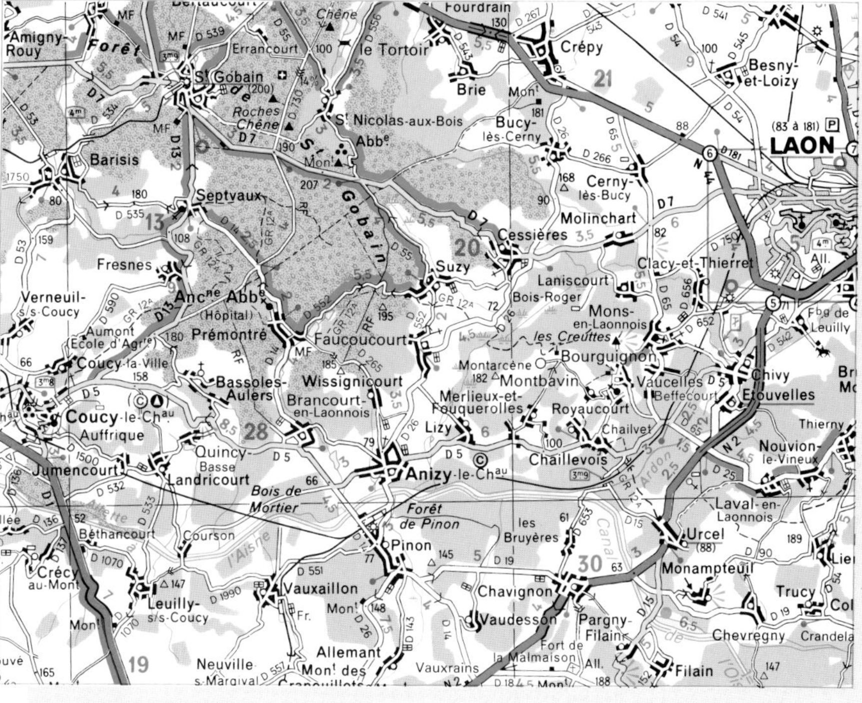

A Nation of Giants

Picardy has always been a strongly independent region, half French and half Flemish, with its own way of life, its own gastronomy and, originally, its own language. Illustrative of this independent spirit are the lively local fairs, a distinctive feature of which are the giants that are processed around the town, huge figures carried by several men. Originally made of straw and basketwork, these are now constructed of more lasting materials, in a range of sizes up to 7.5m in height. Generally in marital pairs, and sometimes accompanied by their children, the giants represent figures from myth, legend and history, popular local heroes and warriors, and local trades such as fishermen, miners, farmers and shoemakers. Some of the giants are on display all year in the local town hall.

garden, rich in carved detail and fine ironwork. The buildings now house a psychiatric hospital, but the exteriors can be visited, along with the magnificent central staircase.

St Gobain

Set high on a promontory above the surrounding forest, this small town developed originally as a pilgrimage site for the Irish hermit, St Gobain. Today it is better known for its glass works, which was founded by Louis XIV in 1692 and became quickly well known thanks to new methods of making large, flat sheets of glass suitable for mirrors. Expansion in the 18th and 19th centuries turned the St Gobain works into a centre for the glass trade, and it is still one of the most important in France. Little remains of the original factory, built on the site of the old château, but a fine 18th-century monumental gateway guards the entrance. All around St Gobain lies extensive natural woodland.

St Nicolas-aux-Bois

Hidden in a secret wooded valley in the St Gobain forest, the remains of this 15th-century Benedictine abbey are now part of a private house, visible from the road. The site is surrounded by lakes and by the remains of the moat, still filled with water. Standing in romantic isolation in the middle of a field, at the edge of the woods, there is a ruined Gothic gateway that nowadays leads nowhere.

Comité Départemental du Tourisme de l'Aisne
1, Rue Saint-Martin
BP 116
02006 Laon Cedex
Tel: 23 20 45 54

Touring:
use Michelin sheet map 236, Nord/Flandres-Artois/Picardie

The abbey of St Nicholas-aux-Bois lies in a secluded spot, with a tranquil lake in front and woodland behind

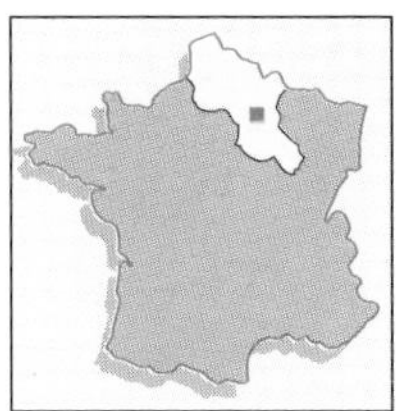

AROUND THE VINEYARDS OF CHAMPAGNE

THE GENTLE HILLS OF THE MARNE VALLEY are dedicated entirely to the champagne industry. Vines stretch in regimented lines to the horizon, a sea of green and gold broken only by the sturdy towers of village churches. At the heart of the region is the dense natural woodland of the Montagne de Reims.

Chapelle St-Lié

Hidden in a clearing that was once a Roman sacred wood and surrounded by trees is a simple stone chapel dedicated to St Lié, a 5th-century hermit. Dating largely from the 12th and 13th centuries, the chapel stands quite alone with its graveyard. Set into a niche is a statue of the Virgin and nearby is a wrought-iron cross bearing the tools of the Passion and surmounted by a cockerel. From here there is a magnificent view over a landscape of vines and pockets of woodland punctuated by the towers of the 11th- and 12th-century churches of Ville-Dommange and Sacy.

Épernay

After Reims, Épernay is the major centre for the production of Champagne, and much of the town is devoted to this industry. It is a pleasant place without being in any way remarkable and the main feature of interest is the champagne houses, with most of the major names in grand mansions flanking the broad Avenue de la Champagne, which climbs away from the town centre. Behind these mansions, some of which date back to the 18th century, are the caves and cellars in which the wine is manufactured and stored. Among the leading names represented here are Moët et Chandon, Mercier and de Castellane, all of whose facilities can be visited. The architectural styles of the champagne houses are interestingly varied, ranging from 18th-century classical to 19th-century eccentric, and notable on some of the latter are decorative panels of richly coloured ceramic tiles.

Ay

Spread over the sheltered, south-facing slopes of the Marne valley, the vineyards of Ay have been famous since Roman times. The local wine found favour with such illustrious figures as François I and Henry VIII of England. Today this small town is still totally devoted to the production of wine. Best known among its many producers is Gosset, active in the town since 1584 and the oldest champagne house in the region.

Another producer is based in the château at Mareuil, just to the east along the Marne valley, a fine 18th-century building overlooking the river.

Comité Départemental du Tourisme de la Marne
2 *bis*, boulevard Vaubécourt
51000 Châlons-sur-Marne
Tel: 26 68 37 52

Touring:
use Michelin sheet map 241, Champagne/ Ardennes

SCHOOL OF REIMS

Ninth-century Reims was the centre of a thriving intellectual and artistic life that found its most lasting memorial in the style of manuscript illumination associated with the abbeys of the region. The creative centre for this new style was the abbey of Hautvillers, and between 820 and 830 the monks working in the scriptorium produced a series of revolutionary manuscripts. Supreme among them is the Utrecht Psalter, whose frenetic style of illumination was echoed by other manuscripts.

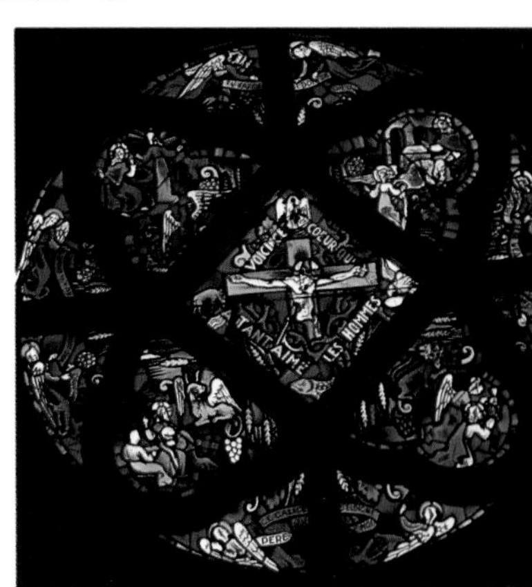

Visitors to Épernay who want to see something of the town besides the champagne houses should visit the Église Notre-Dame, which has some beautiful 16th-century stained-glass windows

CHAMPAGNE

Reims, Épernay and the villages that surround the woods of the Montagne de Reims are encircled by vines that extend in every direction over the soft hills of the Marne valley. These vines grow the grapes used in the making of champagne, the sparkling wine that has changed the face, and the fame, of the region over the last two centuries. The process of making sparkling wine was developed in the late 17th century by the monk Dom Pérignon, but the region had been known for its wines since before Roman times. Some of these wines had a natural effervescence, but it was the development of the double fermentation technique that inspired the creation of the true champagne. The industry began in the 18th century but it was not until around the turn of that century that the manufacture of champagne achieved anything like its present significance. Many of the most famous champagne houses were established during this period, perfecting the complex techniques of blending and manufacture that have made champagne so famous throughout the world. Much imitated but never equalled, the sparkling wines of the Champagne region have a unique quality that is jealously guarded by its manufacturers in order to preserve the integrity of a product vital to the local economy. Many leading champagne houses, in Reims and Épernay, can be visited and *dégustation* (sampling) is possible in many of the small villages.

Vineyards dedicated to the production of champagne, such as these at Hautvillers, extend in every direction over the gentle hills of the Marne valley

Fort de la Pompelle

Built in 1880 on a natural outcrop of rock, the Pompelle fort was designed to guard the eastern approaches to Reims. Although it was briefly captured by the Germans during their rapid advance in September 1914, it soon returned to French hands, to become a symbol of French resistance throughout the battles of Champagne and the Marne. Preserved much as it was at the end of the war, the fort is accessible to visitors and contains displays telling the history of World War I, and a collection of German helmets.

Hautvillers

This pretty village on the south-facing slopes of the Marne is well known for its traditional houses with their decorative wrought-iron signs as well as for its vineyards, which, like those at neighbouring Ay and Avenay-Val-d'Or, produce the best wine of the region. At one end of the village is the abbey, founded in 660 by St Nivard. At the peak of its fame in the 9th century, Hautvillers played a leading part in the development of the richly coloured style of manuscript illumination associated particularly with the Reims region during the Carolingian Renaissance.

Parc Régional de la Montagne de Reims

The Park is famous for its oaks, chestnuts, deer and wild boar. At the eastern edge are the famous Faux de Verzy, an extraordinary group of beech trees whose twisted and distorted trunks and branches are the result of some local genetic variation. Nearby, on one of the highest points of the Montagne de Reims, is the Mont Sinaï observation point, offering magnificent views westwards and northwards towards Reims.

To the north is Verzenay, one of several villages in a sea of vines. Its most famous feature is a windmill set dramatically on the crest of a ridge, an unexpected feature in a countryside devoted entirely to the vine. From the winding road below the mill there are excellent views over the rolling fields towards Reims.

Reims

The champagne capital of France, Reims has been a city of major importance since the Roman period, when it had a population of 80,000. However, the city was completely destroyed by the invading Vandals in 406. This pattern has been followed in subsequent centuries, with the city's strategic position in a low-lying valley ensuring repeated assaults and destruction, the most recent of which was during World War I when over three-quarters of the centre was demolished. For the Romans, Reims was a major textile centre, and the textile trade remained important until the 18th century, when champagne began to take over. Many of the great champagne houses are in the city, including Pommery, Taittinger, Veuve Clicquot, Mumm and Piper Heidsieck.

Even older than the cathedral is the 11th-century Basilique St-Remi, whose simple but powerful Romanesque style is in marked contrast to the cathedral's bold Gothic. Notable in both is the wealth of stained glass.

The greatest glory of Reims is the Cathédrale Notre-Dame. Planned as the largest church in Christendom, it was built largely in the 13th century and miraculously spared from destruction in World War I. The exterior is dazzling, the interior an eloquent expression of the Gothic desire for lightness. In front stands a statue of Joan of Arc

ALSACE AND LORRAINE

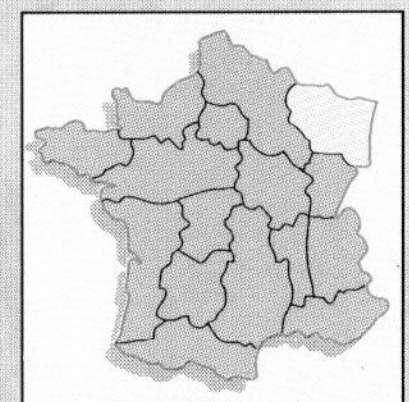

ALSACE-LORRAINE DOES NOT exist. The linking of the two names reflects only the administration of the two regions as the German imperial territory of Elsass-Lothringen, from 1871 to 1918.

Each has its own varied landscapes, character, architecture and treasures. This eastern flank of France has not always basked in the peace enjoyed by today's tourists. For a thousand years this was the frontier of the Holy Roman Empire. Its towns and villages still have their Porte de France, the start of the road leading west to whatever part of today's France was not at that time being disputed between Gauls, Romans, Englishmen, Burgundians, Swedes, Spaniards and others.

The constant passage of armies, bringing famine, plague and destruction, has, however, similarly tempered the inhabitants of both regions. The Alsatian dialect, still widely used every day in Alsace's two *départements,* Haut-Rhin and Bas-Rhin, and to a lesser extent in Lorraine, is the prime example of a determination that the individuality and character of both cultures should survive.

The fertile Plain of Alsace leads from the Rhine, through vine-covered slopes with half-timbered houses and red sandstone churches, many still fortified, clustered together in medieval walled villages. Narrow streets, each a potential stage set for *Faust,* wrought-iron shop signs, *winstubs* (winebars), *flammekeuche* (pizza) and *kougelhopf* (cake), *choucroute* (sauerkraut) in the north, fried carp in the south – here the *gens de l'intérieur,* as French travellers from the rest of France are called, can go abroad without crossing any national border.

To the east the rounded summits of the Vosges rise to 1424m at Grand Ballon. Cross-country skiers and summer walkers can follow well-signposted paths along hilltop or valley, and in spring the meadows are full of wild daffodils and orchids. Here the land slopes down to the plateau and the River Meuse, which for the most part marks the western limit of Lorraine.

Lorraine has as many attractions as Alsace, but is almost three times as big, so the tourist has to travel further to find them. Three *départements* – Meuse, Meurthe et Moselle and Vosges – never formed part of Elsass-Lothringen and remain much more French than the rest of the province. There is Celtic Lorraine, its sacred springs and hilltops beloved of Roman and Christian. There is the Lorraine of Joan of Arc, of Stanislas, last Duke of Lorraine and inspirer of the magnificent architecture of Nancy and Lunéville. It was to Nancy that the inhabitants of Alsace, between 1871 and 1920, would make their annual visit to take part in Bastille Day festivities. A further attraction is the Parc Régional de Lorraine.

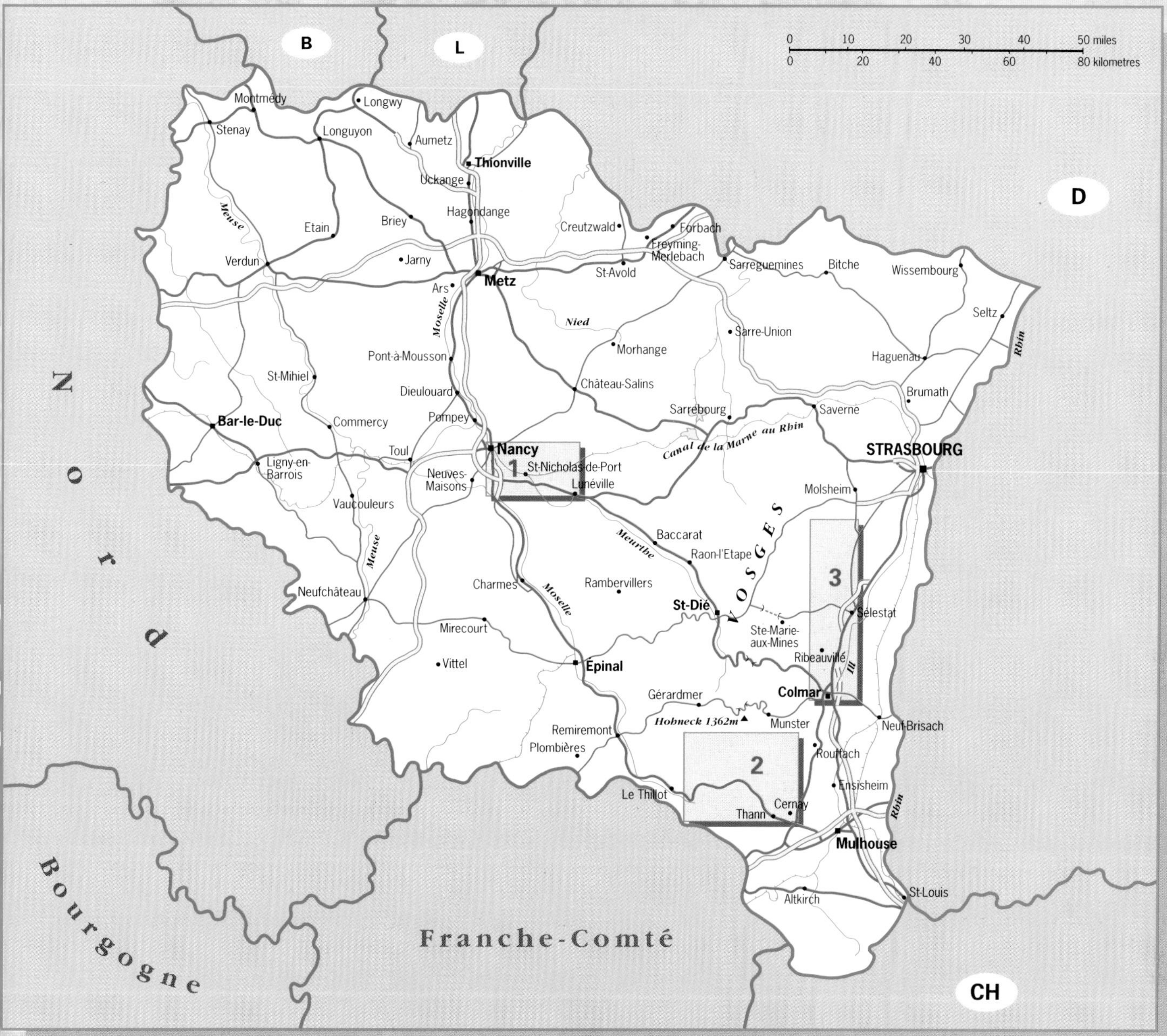

Colmar (right) is a small town which retains a pleasingly human scale. Many of the houses have a friendly look, with their window-boxes and their extensive use of wood and coloured tiles

Some local grapes (below) produce red wine

The wrought-iron shop signs in many of the medieval towns remind the visitor of the region's strong links with its past

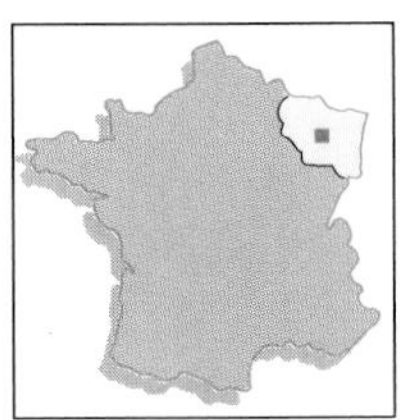

NANCY TO LUNÉVILLE

ALTHOUGH WE ARE HERE CONCERNED with the less well-known wonders to be discovered by the venturesome and enquiring traveller, no guide book should ignore the 18th-century architectural splendours of Nancy and Lunéville. In between, along a road and river both dedicated to industry and commerce, is the Gothic basilica of St Nicolas-de-Port. It is for these three gems, not for its natural beauties, that this area is best known.

LIVERDUN

Dun was the Celtic word for a hilltop fort and a bend in the Moselle encircles this hilltop village 4km north-west of Nancy. The road leads up past 13th-century walls and through the 16th-century 'Porte Haute'.

In the 13th-century church is the tomb of St Euchaire, martyred in nearby Pompey in 362. He is depicted lying in full episcopal robes, his crozier beneath his left arm, and his head, still wearing its mitre, cradled on his chest.

There are unusual 14th-century memorial inscriptions deeply carved into the pillars of the nave and chapels. Each inscription has a delicately wrought hand, in elegant ruffed sleeve, its finger pointing down towards the tomb in the floor.

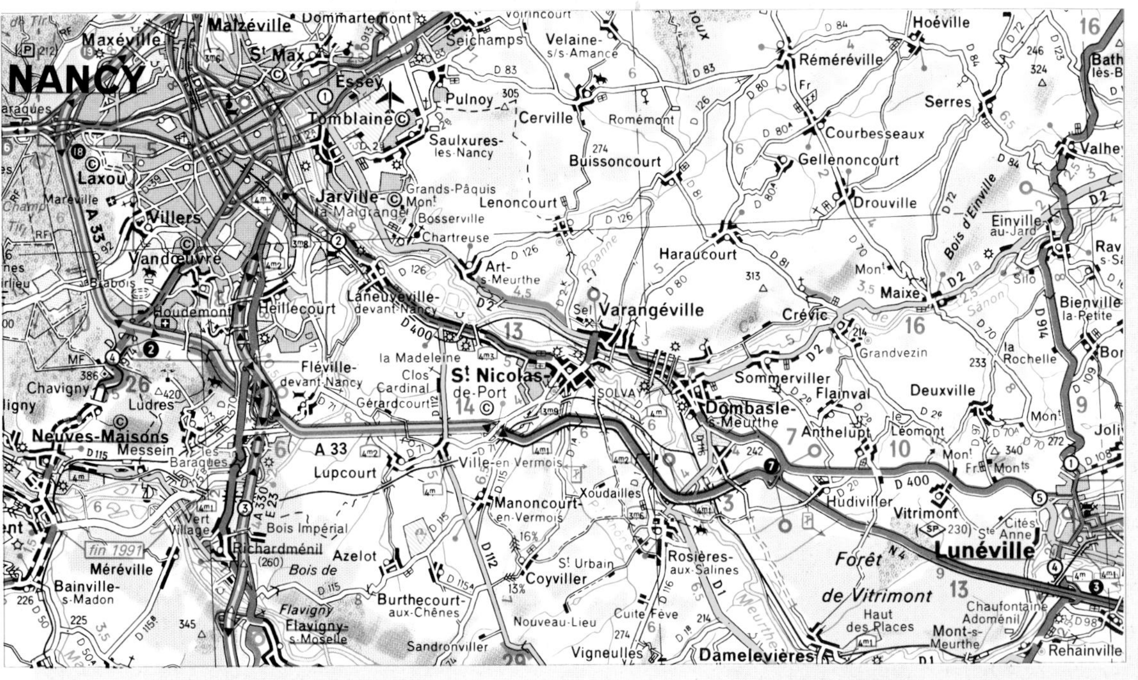

Comité Départemental du Tourisme de Meurthe-et-Moselle
3, Rue Mably - BP 65
54062 Nancy Cedex
Tel: 83 35 56 56

Touring:
use Michelin sheet map 242, Alsace et Lorraine

Lunéville

Léopold, Duke of Lorraine, during the first quarter of the 18th century laid out and built much of the château. He laid out the park and planned the wide streets in respectful admiration for the Versailles of Louis XIV.

Stanislas Leszczynski, deposed King of Poland, was made Duke of Lorraine, placed here by his father-in-law, Louis XV. He acted as governor, to accustom the people to French rule, since the duchy would revert to France on his death.

An easygoing man who loved good living and beauty, he was popular and attracted a dazzling court, both here and at Nancy. He chose good architects to enlarge the château and initiated the porcelain factory, many fine examples from which can be seen in the château's museum. Particularly splendid are the set of vessels made for the hospital pharmacy.

The life-size automata that Stanislas commissioned for the Parc des Bosquets were destroyed in the Revolution but the pools and parterres, fountains and statues are as they were. In the museum a painting gives an idea of the park as Stanislas knew it.

Also worth seeing in Luneville is the Église St-Jacques. Built between 1730 and 1747, the church has impressive baroque woodwork and an ornate clock.

The approach to the huge château at Lunéville, built between 1702 and 1712 and known at one time as 'Petit Versailles'

The heart of Nancy remains a virtually intact example of 18th-century urban planning. The driving force behind the town's redevelopment, among the most ambitious in France during that century, was Stanislas Leszczynski, Duke of Lorraine

Nancy

Nancy lay between Burgundy and Flanders and was coveted by the dukes of Burgundy. Here before the walls of Nancy, on 5 January 1477, Charles le Téméraire, last of the Valois dukes of Burgundy, was slain. The victorious René II and later dukes of Lorraine came into their own and made Nancy a capital worthy of them.

But it is 18th-century Nancy, Place Stanislas and its surroundings, that attracts today's tourists. Laid out by Stanislas Leszczynski, the centre of Nancy was ten years in the building and finished in 1760. Symmetry reigns supreme, with fountains, statues and nymphs and wondrous wrought-iron work – a fitting setting for both the statue of Stanislas and the town hall. The nearby Musée des Beaux-Arts displays European painting from the 14th to 20th centuries.

In the Musée de l'École de Nancy are many of the extraordinary creations in glass of Émile Gallé. He founded the 'École de Nancy', leading the reaction against slavish copies of 'classical' art. In the Musée Historique Lorrain, in Grande-Rue, can be seen the whole story of Lorraine from the Middle Ages to World War I. There are Books of Hours, sculpture, tapestries and in particular much of the work of Jacques Callot, who was an early 'war artist', recording, for Cardinal Richelieu, many sieges and battles.

The Musée des Beaux-Arts, in Place Stanilslas in the centre of Nancy, has a fine collection of paintings spanning seven centuries

St Nicolas-de-Port

When Islam threatened the shrine of St Nicholas – patron saint of Russia, Greece and New York – Italian sailors took his body to Bari. Crusaders from the village of Port managed to acquire a finger joint, for which the earliest shrine was built. In 1429 Joan of Arc came here to pray for the success of her mission.

After his defeat of Charles le Téméraire, René II, ruler of an independent dukedom at last, decided on a fitting tribute. The first stone of this Gothic masterpiece was laid in 1481 and the towers were completed by 1560. The whole building was virtually destroyed by fire in 1635, during the Thirty Years War. These three dates are commemorated in the west window, where such stained glass as was saved has been incorporated under the vivid red rose design.

In a niche of the centre doorway is a representation of the miracle of St Nicholas – the bringing back to life of three youngsters, pickled in brine as potential material for sausages by an unscrupulous butcher. This is believed to be by Claude, brother of the Lorraine sculptor Ligier Richier.

On entering the basilica, the immediate impression is of height and light. Newly cleaned pale stonework soars up 28m to the tallest vault in France. Old frescos on the pillars have been refurbished.

Spas of Lorraine

Vittel and Contrexéville are two names nowadays closely associated with slimming and healthy living. But they are only two of the many springs exploited since the days of the Romans and earlier. Plombières-les-Bains, with slightly radioactive waters, was appreciated by Roman gourmets, who came to treat their digestive problems and rheumatism. Bains-les-Bains could hardly have assumed a prouder name. Much of its charm lies in its peaceful setting on the banks of the Bagnerot amid beech and oak. The waters here help those suffering from typically 20th-century ailments: hypertension, heart disease and arthritis.

A hundred years ago Vittel was an agricultural village, with springs known to the Romans but abandoned after they left. Now it is the most important of the spas, an airport at Mirecourt and road and rail bringing in over 7000 '*curistes*' each year, seeking help with kidney and nutritional problems.

The waters of Contrexéville are used only for drinking today.

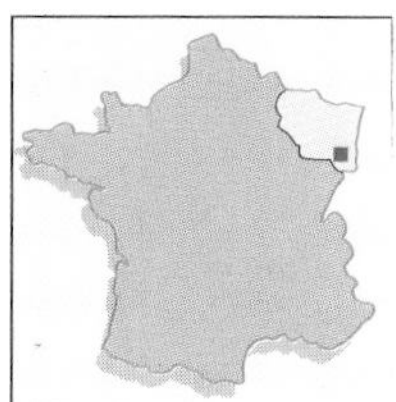

The Stronghold of the Vosges

ROMANESQUE RATHER THAN THE FLAMBOYANT Gothic of the Alps, the Vosges rise up from the Lorraine plateau to the west, through green meadows and peaceful and pastoral scenery. Viewed from the east, however, they are a bastion, crowned by hill forts and castles, from which generations of sentinels have watched the Rhine and the Black Forest beyond, whence invaders have come.

Grand Ballon rises from the main chain of the Vosges and is the highest peak in the whole range

Ballons d'Alsace

As the crow flies, the three highest summits at the southern end of the Vosges lie within 15km of the central resort of Markstein. By road the circuit is considerably longer. The highest, Grand Ballon (1424m), is topped by an orientation table and the monument to the 'Blue Devils' – the Chasseurs Alpins. From both the Petit Ballon (1267m) and the Ballon d'Alsace to the south (1250m), there are equally breathtaking views.

The summit of Grand Ballon offers views of the southern Vosges and the Black Forest. On a clear day, the Jura and the Alps can be seen

Guebwiller

At the entrance to the Lauch valley – known as Florival to its inhabitants – Guebwiller owes its existence and its walls to the monks who came here from Murbach. Cars are forbidden in many of the most picturesque spots in the local forest. Notre-Dame is one of the largest 18th-century churches in Alsace. The gradual transformation of style towards neo-classicism is well represented.

Le Markstein and Jungfraukopf

In this centre for both downhill and cross-country skiing in winter, many of the *pistes* serve also as summer rambles. By some of the ski lifts are wildly convoluted plastic channels, which when packed with snow become bob-sleigh runs. The enthusiast can hire mountain bikes and there are many signposted routes available for all levels of competence. All around are launching spots for hang-gliders, often to be seen sailing past below as you admire the view from one of the many belvederes.

From Le Markstein the D27 winds its way down to Lac Wildenstein and right round the lake, which has a ruined castle at one end. There are many spots at which to stop, admire the scenery, have a picnic, or watch local sub-aqua club members in action. Perhaps they should try Lac de la Lauch on the other side of the Route des Crêtes, for it is said that Attila lost a wagon load of treasure in the lake that was here before the present dam was built. The white bulls that pulled it are said to sometimes rise up from the lake at full moon, their horns hung with pearls and jewels.

Murbach

The road up the valley effectively ends at nearby Belchenthal, but in a wooded valley, in the shadow of the Grand Ballon, the two towers of the abbey of Murbach rise impressively above the trees. Irish Benedictines founded the original abbey in 727. By 925 their work in clearing the forest, bringing prosperity and the word of God, had made

Munster Cheese

Tradition says that Munster cheese has been made in Alsace since the arrival of a group of Irish monks in the 7th century. True, cheese has long been made as a convenient way of preserving milk for consumption, and Munster can certainly trace its origins back 600 years.

By the 17th century, Lorraine herders had long been bringing their cattle up into the high pastures in Alsace in summer and they grazed them well down from the tops – in what was then the Holy Roman Empire and no longer the fief of the dukes of Lorraine. The consequent intricate legal disputes, beloved of the jurists of the day, took time to settle, but it was finally agreed that the rent should be the production of cheeses on 23 June.

Thus did the Holy Roman Empire collect its rent, and an annual fête has grown up around this arrangement, at Gérardmer. There are many varieties of Munster, for milk is collected from over 5000 farms, 500 of which make their own cheeses.

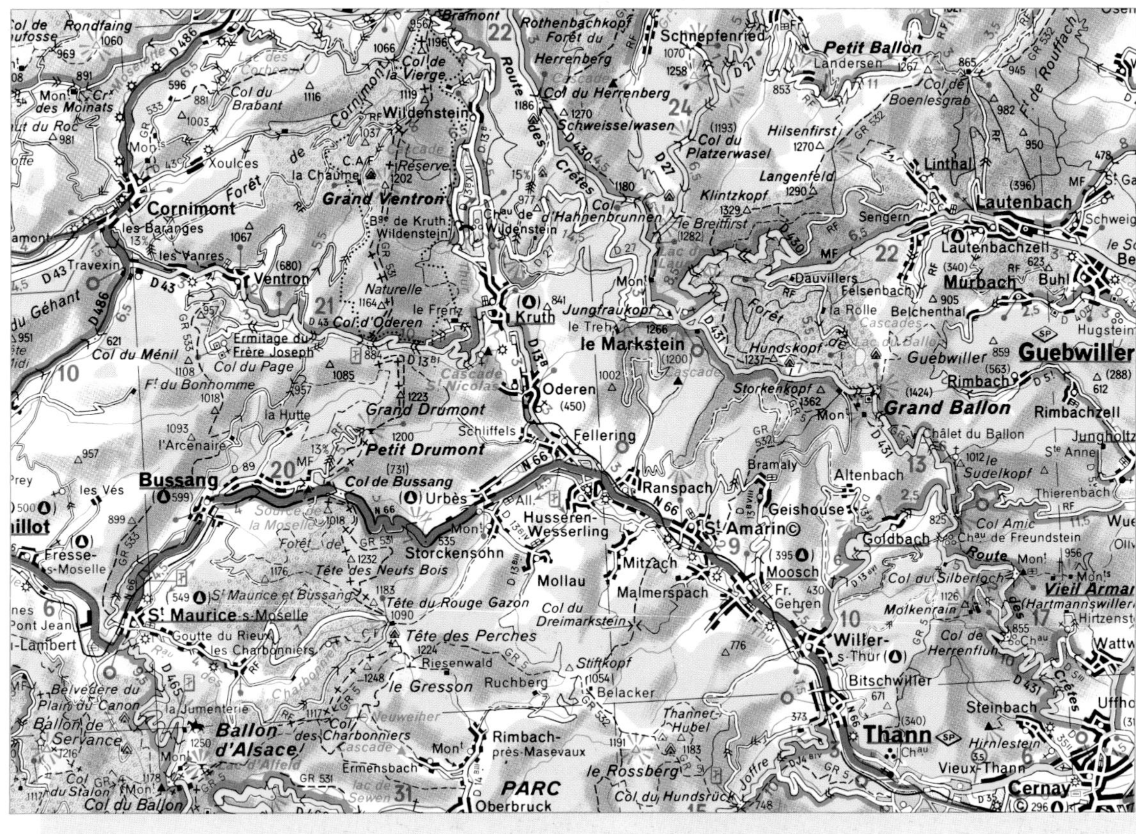

Association Départementale du Tourisme du Haut-Rhin
Hôtel du Département
68006 Colmar
Tel: 89 23 21 11 -
89 22 68 00

Touring:
use Michelin sheet map 242, Alsace et Lorraine

the abbey so wealthy that Attila came to plunder its treasures. It attained its greatest influence in the 11th and 12th centuries, when its library contained over 300 volumes, including copies of works by Charlemagne himself. Only the transept and choir remain of what was one of the flowers of Romanesque architecture in the Rhine Valley style. The abbey having been destroyed in 1444, and again during the Peasants' War (1524-5) and the Thirty Years War (1618-48), the community moved to nearby Guebwiller, where they founded a vast complex. This was sacked by the locals in 1789 and only the Notre-Dame church remains.

Thann, situated at the entrance to the Thur valley, was at one time on an important trade route between Italy and the Netherlands

Thann

Legend has it that Bishop Thiébaut, who died in Italy in 1160, had promised his ring to his servant. Trying to loosen the ring, the servant inadvertently pulled off the bishop's thumb. On his way back home with the relic, he stopped overnight by the river crossing at Thann. His pinewood staff took root and three bright lights hovered over the pine trees, attracting the attention of the Count of Ferrette in his castle of Engelbourg nearby. The count took them as a divine sign and promised to build a chapel on the site.

Thann is still surrounded by pine forests (*Tannenbäume* in German) and on 30 June every year, the eve of the anniversary of the miracle, the town reaffirms the legend of its origins, burning three pine trees in the square in front of the church. By 1287 this Flamboyant Gothic church dedicated to St Thiébaut was attracting many pilgrims. The lace-like stone tracery of its 76-m spire makes it one of the most beautiful in Alsace. The church, finished around 1423, suffered badly during World War II, but the beauty of the original has been retained in the restoration.

The exquisite carved-oak stalls and misericords are incontestably the finest in Alsace. Among the figures and caricatures are a scholar and a fiddler and a quaint gentleman in 15th-century spectacles. Of the castle on the Engelbourg the most remarkable relic is the base of a tower, blown up by incompetent sappers in the 1670s. It stands, like a huge doughnut, overlooking the town.

Viel Armand

The area around Thann, German territory at the start of World War I, was reclaimed by French forces on 7 August 1914. For months they battled against the Germans, well supplied by train from Mulhouse, to hold these commanding heights. After a year the sacrifices were finally seen as futile, but only after over 30,000 men had died. The hilltop mausoleum, rows of crosses looking out over the plain with the tricolour for ever flying above, is a place for reflection.

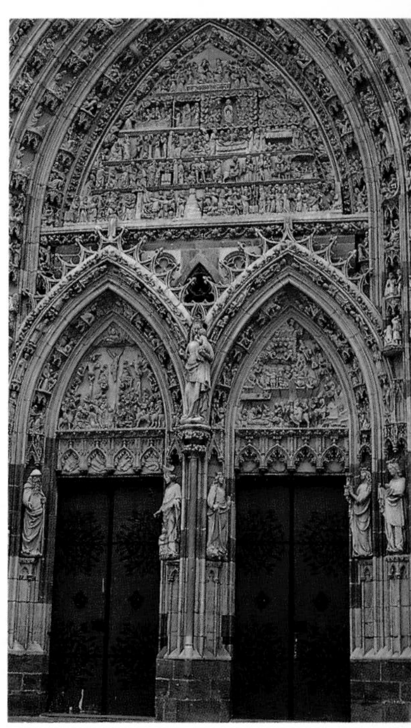

The main doors of Thann's Flamboyant Gothic church, built between the 14th century and the beginning of the 16th

CASTLES OF ALSACE

THIS HAS ALWAYS BEEN a frontier land. Along the Route du Vin every rocky crag and spur overlooking colourful villages and their vineyards has its castle. These face east, whence the invader has usually come, guarding river crossings and the entrance to valleys up into the Vosges. Whether supporters or opponents of the Holy Roman Emperor, local rulers needed the safety of their clifftop eyries. Many of the ruins romantically silhouetted on their hilltops have been there since the 12th century. Most were occupied until the 16th century and played some part in the dark days of the Thirty Years War.

CINQ CHÂTEAUX

Along the Fecht valley from Colmar to Munster is 'La Route des Cinq Châteaux', but this is only the start of a road with dozens of châteaux. Above Éguisheim are three ruined keeps of the summer homes of the counts of Éguisheim. A short car journey up a forest road and, after parking by a small snack bar, a ten-minute climb, will reward the visitor with a glorious view out across the Plain of Alsace. Built in the 11th century, abandoned in 1646, after the 'Guerre des Six Oboles', the keeps have received much repair work since 1966 to make them into a more attractive tourist site. Most has been done to the central Wahlenbourg tower. The paths, however, are still somewhat uneven and not for those who have any difficulty in walking or scrambling over rocky outcrops.

About 4km along the road is Hohlandsbourg, to which access can be gained by a footpath. Built in 1279, it is another excellent example of military architecture during the Middle Ages in Alsace. Only two years later the local Colmar garrison occupied it, having turned out Provost Sigrist, who had been dismissed by his Habsburg overlord. It remained a Habsburg fief, and artillery bastions were added by Count Schwendi in 1563 and the castle was slighted and abandoned in 1637.

The road dips down into the valley towards Pflixbourg, with a lovely view down to the right. Pflixbourg, or Bliksberg (hilltop viewpoint), is well named. It was the 12th-century residence of the Sire de Ribeaupierre, the Emperor's representative in Alsace. The path from the car park climbs up to the knoll where the castle stands.

The circular keep has walls at least 3m thick, with only 4m of space within. The 'Witch's Eye' on the Engelbourg above Thann is the base of a destroyed keep and is of similar proportions.

Fleckenstein's watch-tower was carved out of red sandstone

FLECKENSTEIN

There has been a stronghold here since the 11th century. It is, however, by no means the only one in this border region – Falkenstein, Arnsberg, Hohenbourg, Weglenburg, Wasigenstein are all as menacing and inaccessible.

Fleckenstein, though, is the most impressive and only a short walk from a car park. It stands on a sheer rock 40m above the forest. The Great Hall has gone, destroyed by Louis XIV's troops in 1680. But they could not destroy the chambers and passages carved from the living rock nor the separate watch-tower.

FERRETTE

Down on the Swiss frontier near Basle is this hilltop fortress, home of the once powerful Counts of Ferrette, a title still held by the Grimaldis, the ruling family of Monaco. Built about 1125, it stands on a spur dominating the little town below. News of revolution reached the village from Paris on 23 July 1789 and the population spent two happy days and nights sacking and burning the castle. The blue, white and red of the tricolour of France now flies over the ruin of Ferrette.

HAUT-KOENIGSBOURG

Of all the castles in Alsace, Haut-Koenigsbourg, restored to a romantic semblance of its former power and glory, must be seen to be believed. Its fairy-tale roof rises from the forest above Sélestat. Viollet-le-Duc, restorer of Carcassonne and Pierrefonds and cathedrals and churches all across France, cast longing eyes at the ruins in the 1890s. But Alsace was German territory and the impoverished citizens of Sélestat offered their ruin to the Kaiser. He engaged Bodo Ebhardt, whose work has been the subject of controversy every since. Ebhardt studied every castle along the Vosges, talked with historians and read widely before starting work. The castle was too ruinous to be rebuilt as it was, so Ebhardt created his idea of a medieval stronghold. It is saved from banality by the use of superb materials and workmanship. Casemates and bastions, murder holes and battlements, drawbridge and keep, are all in the solid sandstone of the Vosges. If they still look a little new, perhaps we should bear in mind that the original castle did too, at least for a few generations after it was first built.

Kaysersberg

The bailey walls, which were joined to those of the town in 1223, still surround a grim tower guarding Kaysersberg. The bridge across the river was fortified in 1514 and an oratory chapel built on it.

Kintzheim

A square inner bailey is surrounded by a polygonal outer wall, with bastions. Not much remains of this 13th-century castle, bought as a defence by the citizens of Sélestat in 1428 and finally destroyed by Swedish troops in 1632.

La Petite Pierre

Built on the escarpment overlooking the valley, the castle itself, much altered since its foundation in the 13th century, is now headquarters of the Parc Régional des Vosges du Nord. Tucked away in what was once the 17th-century artillery captain's quarters, is a tiny museum devoted to the typically Alsatian delicacy, the *Springerle*, an aniseed-flavoured biscuit made in intricately carved wooden moulds.

Ribeauvillé

Three castles overlook the town. The largest, a fine example of a medieval stronghold in Alsace, is St Ulrich, or Grand Ribeaupierre. This 11th-century keep had a Great Hall added a century later and further improvements had made it a splendid residence, on its rocky spur overlooking Ribeauvillé, by the 16th century. But the attractions and comforts of life in the town were beginning to outweigh the disadvantages of life on a rocky outcrop and the seigneur's family finally abandoned their eyries.

Mont Sainte Odile

The 10km-long Cyclopean 'Pagan Wall' that surrounds the hill on which the convent stands, is witness to probably 3000 years during which the site has been, as well as a fortress, a place of reverence for many religions. St Odile, patron saint of Alsace, was the daughter of a 7th-century duke and founded a convent on this crag. It was destroyed by fire and rebuilt in 1687. There is a terrace right around the convent buildings, giving magnificent views across the plain below, with occasional Mirage jet fighters flying past beneath one's feet. The Chapelle des Larmes, out on the point of the spur, was built over the cemetery of the Convent and several rock-cut tombs survive.

With a million visitors a year, Mont Saint Odile is the most visited site in Alsace after Haut-Koenigsbourg.

The castle at Kaysersberg (above) afforded protection from the warring dukes of Lorraine

The Chapelle des Larmes at Mont Sainte Odile (below) is dramatically sited on a spur of rock

Haut-Koenigsbourg (above), rebuilt this century, is the epitome of the Alsatian castle, with its commanding position and pointed towers

A 'Pagan Wall' (below) encircles the hill on which stands the convent of Mont Saint Odile

Ottrott

Castles abound here. Twin strongholds separated by a moated ditch overlook Ottrott, bearing witness to a family quarrel that lasted three centuries. Birkenfels was built to protect the abbey at Hohenbourg, as was Rathsamhausen with its surviving tall square keep and two towers. Lutzelbourg was the home until the end of the 14th century of the family from which came several abbesses of the nearby Mont Sainte Odile convent. Ottrott has other claims to fame. It produces the only red wine in Alsace and there is a little steam train – 1906 vintage – that carries passengers the 8km to Rosheim. Here, sitting cross-legged on the roof of the 12th-century church, is an enigmatic statue. Is it a begging bowl he holds? Or could it be a cup of the good red wine?

Saverne

The Château des Rohan is more like one of the châteaux along the Loire than any hilltop feudal stronghold. From the 13th century the Bishops of Strasbourg had a residence here and the prince-bishops of the Rohan family held court here from 1704 to 1790, rebuilding in neoclassical style the façade along the Marne–Rhine canal.

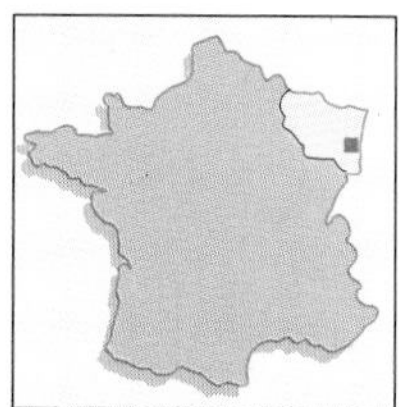

STORKS OVER THE WINE ROAD

TAKE THE BYWAYS, enjoy the views, stop for a glass of wine at a roadside stall made from a huge wine barrel. On one side castles dot the hilltops and vines cover the lower slopes; on the other the fertile Alsatian plain stretches down to the Rhine. With luck, thanks to the rescue programme at Hunawihr, you will see storks flying again over the Route du Vin.

The castle and church of Éguisheim (above)

Ribeauvillé (below)

Barr

Winding streets between the overhanging roofs of half-timbered houses make up characteristic Barr, a small town with tanneries and an excellent selection of good wines. The Folie Marco, built in 1763, now houses a collection of furniture, pottery and objects of local interest. Among the latter are the old man-hauled sledges on which felled timber was brought down log tracks from the forest.

Dambach-la-Ville

All householders decorate their house fronts and window-boxes in the summertime, to maintain Dambach's reputation as the prettiest of the *villages fleuris* on the route du Vin. But it could be that the excellence of the local wines has more than a little to do with the influx of visitors. A forest road leads off the D203 up to the St-Sébastien chapel, with its Baroque carved wooden high altar. Further on – a couple of hours' return walk – the view from the Château de Bernstein on its granite spur amply repays the climb.

Éguisheim

An octagonal basin, filled with lazy carp, surrounds the fountain in front of the castle where, in 1002, Bruno d'Éguisheim was born. He became the only Pope from Alsace, Léon IX. Here is a village in which the visitor can really walk around in circles, for at least seven of the narrow streets follow the concentric pattern employed for over 1200 years, each time the village needed to grow. Walk around in circles, too, in the vineyards around Eguisheim. You will find Sylvaner, Pinot, Tokay, Muscat, Riesling and Gewürztraminer, apart from the rarer Auxerrois, as well as the whole range of Alsatian wines.

Haut-Koenigsbourg

'*Ich habe es nicht gewollt.*' Do the Kaiser's words, on the fire-screen in the Great Hall, inscribed when he last visited, in April 1918, refer to his not having wished for World War I – or to the 'restoration' of this medieval castle? The subject of furious dispute among purists – 'pretentious', 'a pastiche', 'without soul' – the workmanship and quality of materials used are, however, above reproach. In ruins since the Thirty Years War, Haut-Koenigsbourg was presented to Wilhelm II by the deferential (but very hard up) citizens of Sélestat in 1900 and virtually rebuilt in 15th-century style.

On its 757-m crag, Haut-Koenigsbourg dominates the very heart of Alsace, and is the most visited tourist spot in the whole region.

WINES OF ALSACE

Unlike other French wines, those of Alsace tell you from which variety of grape they are pressed – Riesling, Muscat, Sylvaner, Gewürztraminer, Tokay and Pinot Blanc and Noir. A Tokay or a Riesling may come from

anywhere along the 120-km Route du Vin, though individual villages have their own reputation for high-quality wine from particular grapes.

The vineyards are sheltered by the Vosges from westerly winds and enjoy a warm, dry climate with low rainfall. A wide range of soil types mean there is always one best suited to a specific grape. Sylvaner is the most widely grown *cépage*, doing best in the light,

Association Départementale du Tourisme du Haut-Rhin
Hôtel du Département
68006 Colmar
Tel: 89 23 21 11 - 89 22 68 00

Touring:
use Michelin sheet map 242, Alsace et Lorraine

sandy soils around Barr and Rouffach. It produces a light, often slightly sparkling wine. Pinot Blanc, also known as Klevner, accounts for about 10 per cent of the area under vines. Only about one per cent of the area grows Pinot Noir, which gives the only rosé to light red wine in Alsace. Riesling is the favourite, growing best around Riquewihr, Ribeauvillé and Dambach. One of the older grape varieties grown here, it produces a wine well suited to *choucroute*. Muscat is another old-established variety, producing a dry white wine unlike the sweeter Muscat varieties grown in warmer southern vineyards. Tokay came, as its name suggests, from Hungary in the 16th century and produces a rich wine, excellently suited to foie gras and blue cheeses.

Gewürztraminer has a splendid bouquet, well suited to both cheeses and some of the rich Alsatian desserts.

Chasselas Blanc, grown principally in Haut-Rhin, is a pale, almost greenish-yellow wine, often the house wine in the grey and blue *pichets* of Betschdorf pottery.

Hunawihr

Hunawihr has two assets not possessed by other equally picturesque villages along the Route du Vin: its fortified church and its stork-breeding centre. The 14th-century church tower is more castle keep than belfry. Its defensive wall, with six towers, dates from two centuries earlier.

Kintzheim

The ruins of this 15th-century castle hold a collection of many different species of birds of prey, including condors and vultures. Demonstrations of their flying and hunting skills are a part of the visit.

Ribeauvillé

Ribeauvillé is justly famous for its fine Riesling, but much of its attraction lies in its flower-decked houses, oriel windows, turrets, hidden courtyards and balconies. The tradition of the Ribeauvillé 'Pfiffertag' draws large crowds to the town. A medieval seigneur tossed some coins to a piper who had broken his fife and had no way to earn his living. Tradition says 'a purse of gold', but then tradition often exaggerates! The piper and his friends paraded to the castle to thank their seigneur – and a parade is still held on 8 September each year. The Renaissance fountain in front of the town hall runs with free wine all day. Of the many ornately carved house façades, a particularly fine one is that of the 'Pfifferhüs', now a *winstub*, where the procession usually ends the day.

Riquewihr

The Dolder and Obertor fortified gateways, a double row of ancient town walls, cobbled streets, the Sinnbrunnen fountain, 16th- and 17th-century half-timbered houses with intricately carved corner posts, oriel windows and lintels, courtyards hidden behind high doorways, old wine presses and a Renaissance château (rather incongruously now housing a postal museum) – all add up to what is frequently called 'the pearl of the vineyards'. Riquewihr lives up to its reputation as a tourist attraction. In summer it can be crowded, but out of season it is a living open-air museum with a great deal to interest the visitor.

Storks

Symbol of Alsace for generations, the stork population had dropped from over 170 pairs in 1948 to just five pairs by 1976. It was decided to set up the Centre for the Reintroduction of Storks at Hunawihr. Here the eggs are incubated and the young storks raised, by hand and in semi-captivity for three years, until they lose all instinct to migrate. Storks did not fly to West Africa for the sunshine – they can withstand cold quite well. It was the lack of food, partly caused by the disappearance of the local wetlands, that drove them south each winter.

They suffered, also, from senseless slaughter, both in flight and in Africa. By 1988 there were over 60 pairs, part hand-raised, part wild,

breeding and remaining for the winters in the surrounding villages. The nest sites on many a house and church roof are gradually being recolonised. The local people rejoice to see flights of storks over their beloved Alsace again.

STRASBOURG AND COLMAR

STRASBOURG AND COLMAR – two jewels in the crown of Alsace, both of equal brilliance, architecturally, culturally and historically. Each has its winding streets and multicoloured half-timbered houses, its river and its famous sons. Strasbourg now hosts the Council of Europe but Colmar has retained its quiet charm at the heart of the Route du Vin.

STRASBOURG

'City of the Crossroads' – Hansi and Schweitzer, Gutenberg and Goethe, Maison Kammerzell and Vauban stonework, canals and cathedral, the Council of Europe, *winstubs* and *choucroute* – Strasbourg, part of France since 1648, has so much to offer and much is already well known. Petite France, all geraniums and tourists by day, is a different place in the dusk and dawn mists. Here, near water, lived the tanners, exercising their trade far away from – and hopefully downwind of – the houses of the good citizens.

A good way to gain your own first impressions of Strasbourg is to climb the 365 steps to the top of the tower of Notre-Dame and see the city spread out 66m below. A less strenuous way is by boat. Strasbourg, with its canals and the River Ill, is ideally suited to such indolence. An hour's trip from the Palais Rohan will take you through 1000 years of history: past the old mills, covered bridges and fortified towers of Petite France; along the line of the old ramparts to the Palais de l'Europe, home of the Council of Europe and the European Parliament, passing the old harbour and the Krutenau before returning. Strasbourg has a proud history, but is also proud of the part it plays in today and tomorrow.

A Bronze Age trade centre became Roman Argentoratum, sacked by Attila the Hun in 451. A Frankish city was built along the Ill half a century later. When the wooden church that Clovis had built here in 510 burned down, Bishop Wernher began, in 1015, the construction of the magnificent cathedral that is so much a part of city life today.

For lovers of symmetry, it is perhaps a pity that Jean Hültz's steeple, completed in 1439, was not matched on the south tower, but the tracery is none the less magnificent standing on its own. Visit the Musée de l'Oeuvre Notre-Dame. Two gable ends, a courtyard and a hexagonal tower enclose a *courtil*, a tiny jewel of a garden such as can be seen in the background of so many medieval paintings of the Virgin. It was laid out between 1240 and 1268 by Albert le Grand, teacher of St Thomas Aquinas. This museum of medieval and Renaissance Alsatian art now houses many of the original statues from the exterior of the cathedral, the replicas now in place being better able to withstand erosion and pollution.

Church and *Synagogue*, dating from 1230, are typically idealised medieval sculptures. Just 30 years later the power of the merchants was overriding that of the bishops. The difference can be seen in the *Wise Virgins* and *Foolish Virgins* on the south doorway.

There is nothing idealised here – these are the folk who were to be seen in Strasbourg's streets and alleyways: stolid, down-to-earth young women and the conniving Tempter with his apple – the serpents and toads crawling up the back of his robe being added

Petite France, the old quarter of Strasbourg (left), which surrounds the cathedral of Notre-Dame (inset), considered to be among the finest Gothic cathedrals in France

An ornate clock on Strasbourg's Notre-Dame (above), which was begun in 1015 in the Romanesque style and completed in the Gothic around 1440

French and German influences meet in typically Alsatian Colmar (right)

for salutary effect. Perched on the western façade of the cathedral, at home amid the saints and prophets, a stork, symbol of Alsace, watches over the city.

The pulpit, finished by Hans Hammer in 1486, is a masterpiece of intricate Flamboyant Gothic tracery. Followers of Geiler of Kaysersberg, already preaching sermons denouncing the iniquities of the Church, became so numerous that he was allowed to preach in the nave. Here they placed the pulpit they ordered for him. Geiler's little dog would accompany his master to the cathedral, but slept peacefully through his three-hour sermons. Hammer has carved him as he must often have seen him: asleep at the top of the pulpit steps.

You should not miss St-Thomas, the 'Protestant Cathedral', with the magnificent tomb of Marshal Maurice de Saxe (1696-1750). Illegitimate son of a King of Poland, Marshal of France, Louis XV's Commander in Flanders, capturer of Prague, victor of Fontenoy, but 'bastard, a Protestant and a foreigner', he could not rest in the cathedral. Allegory is everywhere in Pigalle's work.

As the Marshal steps down to his tomb, a weeping 'France' holds his hand, trying to push away Death, who is raising the coffin lid. The lion, leopard and eagle of the countries Saxe had conquered lie amid fallen banners.

Colmar

Colmar, a quarter the size of Strasbourg, heart of the Route du Vin and the Alsace wine industry, has never lost its importance as a centre of art and culture. Its pattern of winding streets and multicoloured, half-timbered houses retains a warm, human dimension. Most of its historic heart is now a pedestrian zone, adding greatly to its charm.

The Musée Unterlinden ranks second only in France to the Louvre in the number of visitors. Its greatest treasure is Grünewald's magnificent 'Issenheim' reredos. Curator of the museum until his death in 1951 was Jean-Jacques Waltz, better known as Hansi, the writer and caricaturist who kept alive the free spirit of France throughout two long occupations. His *Mon Village*, published in 1914, earned him a year in prison for making fun of the occupying power.

The Colmar-born sculptor Bartholdi, on his way to Paris in 1870, drew inspiration from the Unterlinden. He is famous for the statue which stands at the entrance to New York harbour. He also immortalised Schwendi, who brought back the Tokay grape to Alsace. Bartholdi was born in Rue des Marchands in 1834 and his house now contains a small museum.

Strasbourg's 'Ponts Couverts' (covered bridges), the Kammerzell, Notre-Dame cathedral and Petite France, are well matched – Colmariens say surpassed – by Colmar's Petite Venise along the Lauch, the Pfisterhaus and the Ancienne Douane, the church of St-Martin and the refurbished Quartier des Tanneurs. The church is notable for its 14th-century Crucifixion and the carvings on the Portal St-Nicholas.

Around Colmar not only is there the Route du Vin with its picturesque villages to discover, but towards Marckolsheim and north towards Sélestat is the 'Ried', last remnant of the marshlands of the Rhine plain. In exploring, however, do not miss the delights of Colmar itself, which is particularly worth visiting at the time of the Festival in June or the wine fair in August.

THE LOIRE

ALTHOUGH IT TAKES ITS NAME from the greatest river of France, the Loire is far more than just a river. It is a richly varied region stretching from the Atlantic coast to the country's very heart, and incorporating soft, green river valleys, rolling hills covered with fruit and vine, vast open plains planted with cereals and huge tracts of forest, woodland and heath.

The Loire is a landscape of small towns and villages, churches, abbeys and châteaux marked by an instinctive feeling for architectural style and enriched with a wealth of ornament and detail that can be enjoyed in both grand buildings and ordinary houses. In all this stylistic diversity and flair an overriding sense of unity is achieved by the use of glowing white tufa stone and grey slate, both materials native to the region. The cities, Angers, Tours, Orléans, are also full of architecture and history.

Any exploration of the River Loire and its main tributaries, the Indre, the Cher, the Loir, the Vienne and the Sarthe, will bring the visitor face to face with history, in the form of early Christianity, the Plantagenet and Valois kings, the wars of the Middle Ages and the 17th century, and the impact of the Renaissance, all of which have left their mark on the landscape. Notable above all are the châteaux, whose transition from medieval fortress to ornamental mansion echoes the change from feudal strife to a golden age of civilisation. Bound up with the architecture is the literary tradition of the Loire, for here more than anywhere else in France are the castles of legend and fairy story brought to life in the concept of courtly love as expressed in the Romance of the Rose. This literary style was continued by Ronsard and Rabelais, both men of the Loire, while later writers maintained the tradition, among them Balzac, Péguy and Alain-Fournier.

Well watered and blessed with plenty of sun, the varied landscape of the Loire has always been fertile. The region is famous for wine and fruit, cereals and mushrooms, vegetables and cheeses – so much so that it has long been known as the Garden of France. It is also renowned for its gastronomic temptations, such as carp and pike served with creamy sauces, chicken in wine sauces and locally produced pork sometimes cooked in white wine with prunes. The forests of the Sologne, south of the Loire, are famous for game, and continue the centuries-old tradition of hunting established in the region by royal and aristocratic families.

Modern sculptures adorn the grounds of the Château de Chenonceau

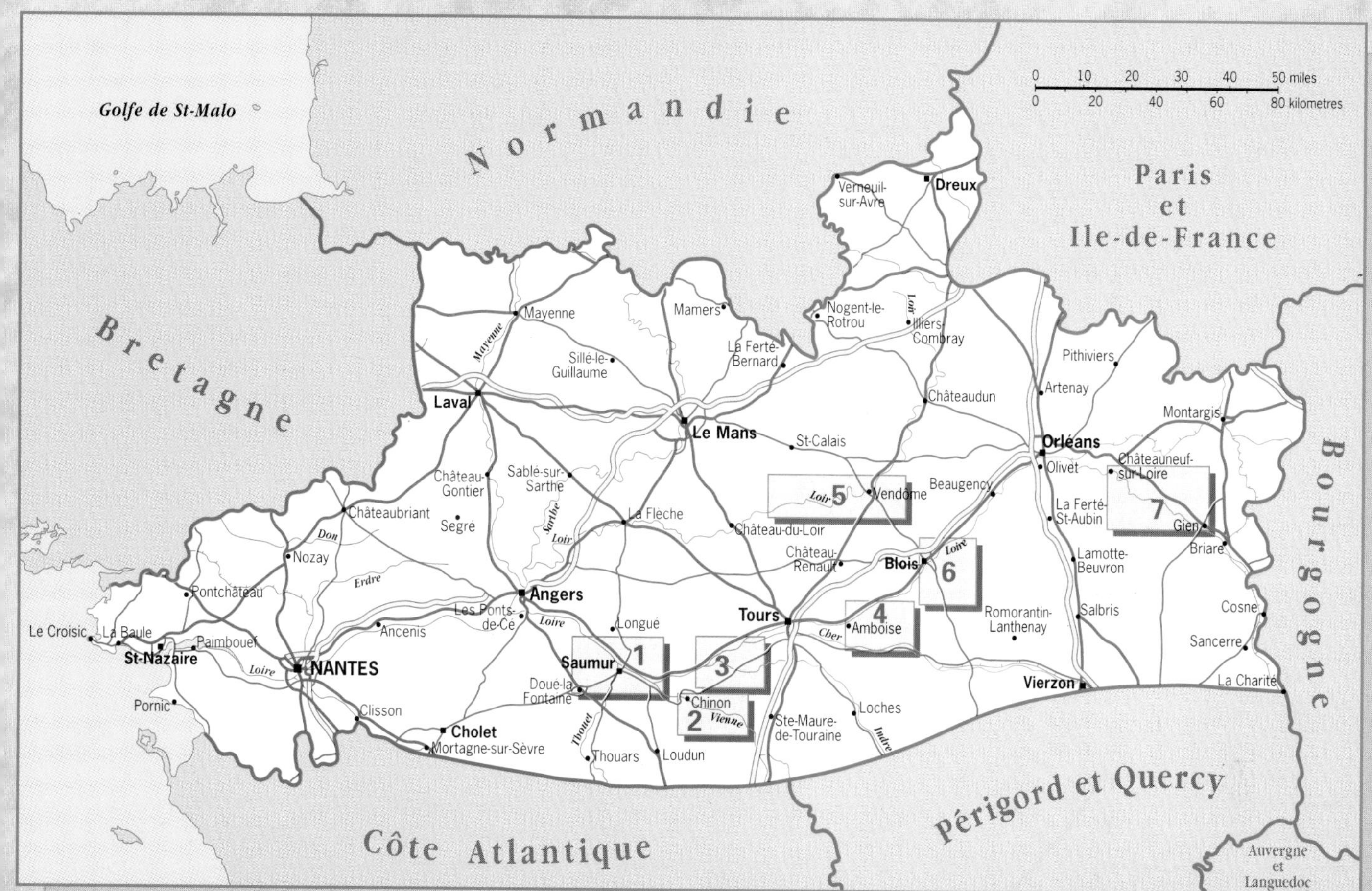

Golfe de St-Malo
Normandie
Bretagne
Paris et Ile-de-France
Bourgogne
Côte Atlantique
Périgord et Quercy
Auvergne et Languedoc
0 10 20 30 40 50 miles
0 20 40 60 80 kilometres
Verneuil-sur-Avre
Dreux
Mayenne
Mamers
Nogent-le-Rotrou
Illiers-Combray
Sillé-le-Guillaume
La Ferté-Bernard
Pithiviers
Artenay
Laval
Le Mans
Châteaudun
Montargis
St-Calais
Orléans
Olivet
Châteauneuf-sur-Loire
Château-Gontier
Sablé-sur-Sarthe
Segré
Vendôme
Beaugency
Châteaubriant
La Flèche
La Ferté-St-Aubin
Gien
Briare
Nozay
Château-du-Loir
Château-Renault
Blois
Lamotte-Beuvron
Pontchâteau
Angers
Les Ponts-de-Cé
Longué
Tours
Amboise
Romorantin-Lanthenay
Salbris
Cosne
Le Croisic
La Baule
St-Nazaire
Paimboeuf
Ancenis
NANTES
Saumur
Doue-la-Fontaine
Chinon
Sancerre
Vierzon
La Charité
Pornic
Clisson
Cholet
Mortagne-sur-Sèvre
Thouars
Loudun
Ste-Maure-de-Touraine
Loches
Loire
Loir
Mayenne
Sarthe
Don
Erdre
Cher
Vienne
Thouet
Indre

The Château de Chambord (below) is said to have inspired Versailles sablé, a Loire shortbread (right)

The town of Château-Gontier, founded in the 11th century, has an attractive position on the banks of the Mayenne, north of the Loire

As well as Chinon's regular street market (right) several fairs take place in the town. These include a medieval fair in August recreating the cookery, crafts, costumes and dancing and music of the Middle Ages

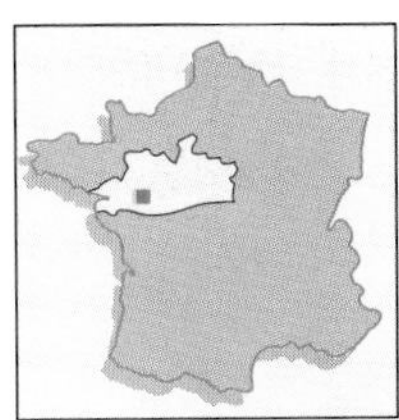

ANJOU – LAND OF WINE AND ROSES

THE BROAD LOIRE flows lazily through the heart of Anjou, dividing the low-lying landscape of the northern shore from the wooded hills of the south. Anjou's fame today is based on wine, roses and mushrooms, but always present is a strong sense of history, conveyed by the Romanesque churches, the abbeys and the châteaux – the legacy of the dukes of Anjou and the Plantagenets.

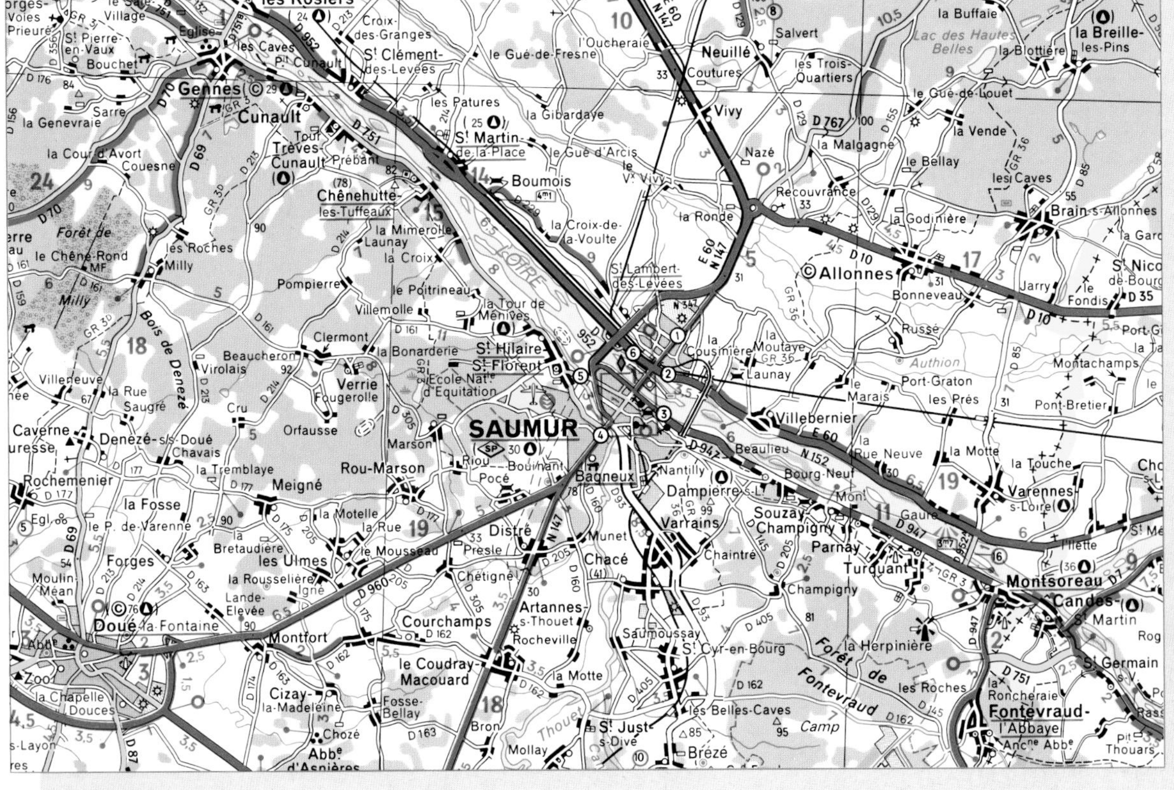

It is worth climbing the path from Candes-St Martin for the panorama of the Loire valley

Candes-St Martin

This pleasantly old-fashioned and flowery village, climbing gently up from the river's edge, is remarkable for its church, Gothic rather than Romanesque, and built in the 12th and 13th centuries on the site of the monastic cell in which St Martin died in 397. A powerful, soaring structure, rich in carved decoration, it venerates St Martin, the first Bishop of Tours. Behind the church a well-signposted but rather steep walk winds up past old cottages and former stone quarries to a field high above the village. From here there is a wide panorama of the confluence of the Loire and the Vienne, a classic landscape of the Loire valley. Those requiring refreshment after the walk can visit the many establishments along the riverside road between Candes and Saumur that offer *dégustation*, tasting, of the local white wines.

Château de Montsoreau

Montsoreau's château, a dramatic fortress towering above the Loire and the smart little village, was built in the middle of the 15th century. The grand but severe rooms were little used by the family that built it and its recent restoration followed many decades of decay.

Cunault

Most visitors to the Loire become familiar with the sight of Cunault's great abbey, rising above the stone walls and flowers of its tiny village. Yet far more memorable is the first view from the entrance along 70m of towering nave. Built over two centuries, and ranging in style from pure Romanesque to Angevin Gothic, the abbey is noted for its extraordinary carved capitals.

Comité Départemental du Tourisme d'Anjou
Place Kennedy - BP 2147
49021 Angers Cedex
Tel: 41 88 23 85

Touring:
use Michelin sheet map 232, Pays de Loire

The château at Saumur occupies a commanding position between the Loire and the Thouet

Mushrooms

A legacy of the Loire region's white tufa stone mining industry was a mass of caves driven deep into the soft stone cliffs, cool, dark chambers that proved excellent for storing wine.

Even more significant for the economy of the region was the realisation that the tufa caves would be ideal for the cultivation of mushrooms, and many now support a major industry that has contributed greatly to the local cuisine. In a typical cave at St Hilaire-St Florent, north-west of Saumur,there is a museum that explains all about mushroom cultivation.

Fontevraud-l'Abbaye

Set high in the wooded hills that flank the Loire's southern shore and surrounded by vineyards, this attractive village has inevitably become one of the region's most visited shrines. The reason is the great abbey, established by Robert d'Arbrissel early in the 11th century. It was a huge and remarkable establishment, incorporating on the same site a monastery, a nunnery, a home for fallen but repentant women and a lepers' hospital, and throughout its long life, until its final dissolution in 1789, the whole complex was always under the care of an abbess. Despite later use as a prison, the abbey retains an atmosphere of peace and harmony, underlined by the fine Romanesque architecture.

The abbey at Fontevraud was richly endowed by the royal Plantagenet family

Gennes

A small town often overlooked on the south bank of the Loire, Gennes is linked to its better-known neighbour on the north bank, Les Rosiers, by a long suspension bridge whose delicate grace enhances this stretch of river. The predictable appeal of Les Rosiers is based on its famous restaurants, tree-lined streets and chunky Renaissance church tower that dominates the flat landscape. Gennes is very different, with much of the village hidden below the steep, wooded hills of the southern shore.

It is essential to take the path that winds up through the woods to St-Eusèbe, both for the views over the soft greens of the river valley and for the moving memorial to the cadets from the Saumur Cavalry School who died defending the bridge against the German invaders in June 1940. There are two ancient churches: that of St-Eusèbe, parts of which date back to the 8th century, is a ruin, with the tower and spire being the most complete part. Not to be missed is the fine collection of Romanesque corbels, some surprisingly rude.

Saumur

Approached from the west along the Loire's northern bank, Saumur has a magical quality, the pinnacled skyline of its château looking like something from a 15th-century Book of Hours. Contained within the confluence of the Loire and the Thouet, and best entered by the old bridge that leads straight to its heart, Saumur is a small and compact town, easily explored on foot from the shaded riverside car park.

The château, built largely between the 14th and the 16th centuries by the dukes of Anjou, has in more recent times served as both barracks and prison. Today it houses two museums, one devoted to the decorative arts and the other to the horse. The latter is a fine collection of pictures, equipment and records of notable animals, including skeletons, telling the story of horsemanship through the ages.

Saumur is further closely connected with the horse through its famous Cavalry School, and the annual military tattoo, with displays by the pre-eminent Cadre Noir, is a high point of the summer. The town also has a museum of armoured fighting vehicles.

Roses

Flowers, both wild and cultivated, add greatly to the pleasures of the Loire. At different seasons the yellow iris, the soft-pink valerian and multicoloured geraniums enrich the landscape and the villages. However, memorable above all else are the roses, filling the hedgerows and gardens and climbing freely over cottages and village terraces.

Rose growing is carried on throughout the region, but one town is particularly well known as a centre for their cultivation. In Doué-la-Fontaine there is a famous rose show, held in July in one of the old stone quarries that surround the town. Market gardens and garden centres that specialise in roses are all over the town, and there is a rose-water distillery. Just outside Doué is the public Jardin des Roses, a changing display whose colours and scents provide an enduring memory.

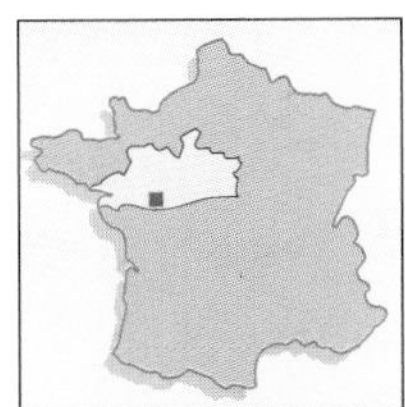

THE VALLEY OF THE VIENNE

THE VIENNE IS ONE OF the most attractive of the Loire tributaries, and the area has been settled since before Roman times. It was from the massive military fortress at Chinon that Joan of Arc set forth on her mission to rescue France from English domination. Rabelais was born and brought up in the woodlands south of that city, while further south Cardinal Richelieu created a grand palace and a new town that still carries his name.

Chinon's impressive château was a royal palace for a relatively short period, for the Court ceased to use it after the 15th century. The perspective of history reveals that Chinon was of far greater importance as a medieval military bastion, and it is an outstanding example of such architecture

Champigny-sur-Veude

The Veude, a quiet but engaging tree-lined river, winds its way from the Vienne to Champigny, passing through the centre of the village, whose restful, old-world atmosphere is put completely in the shade by the decorative magnificence of the Sainte-Chapelle. Early in the 16th century a splendid château was built here, but it was demolished a century later on the orders of Cardinal Richelieu, who wanted no rival for his own new château at Richelieu to the south. Little was spared, except for a few outbuildings and the chapel, and so today a small provincial village is graced with one of the most glorious Renaissance buildings in the whole of France.

Château de Rivau

Little known and rarely visited, Rivau is undeservedly overshadowed by the more familiar châteaux of the Loire. Part fortress and part mansion, it dates from the 15th century and still has its moat and drawbridge, as well as other original late-medieval features. With its stern grey stone walls softened by the surrounding parkland and woods, Rivau has a quality and an integrity often lacking in better-known but over-restored châteaux. On permanent view inside is a display of paintings by Pierre-Laurent Brenot.

Chinon

It is essential to approach Chinon from the south, to enjoy to the full the sight of the mighty fortress spread along its sheer cliff high above the town and the medieval bridge whose thirteen arches span the Vienne. Lacking any domestic refinement or grace, the château is a powerful memorial to the centuries of bitter strife that characterised the Middle Ages. It is really a fort and two châteaux, linked by a bridge. The smaller Fort St-Georges, now a ruin, was built by the Plantagenet King Henry II, while the more substantial Châteaux du Coudray and du Milieu were added by King

JOAN OF ARC

With the start of the English siege of Orléans in the autumn of 1428, the Loire had become the main battlefield in the long-running Anglo-French conflict. On 9 March 1429 Joan presented herself to the Dauphin in the Grande Salle of the Château du Milieu, successfully picking out his unobtrusive figure from the 300 people assembled in the room. She explained her dual mission, to raise the siege of Orléans and then to escort the Dauphin to Reims to be crowned king. Initially she was regarded with suspicion and was briefly held a virtual prisoner in Chinon and subjected to rigorous questioning at Poitiers. But eventually she was provided with armed men by the Dauphin, who was

desperate to raise the siege. In May Orléans was relieved, and in June Joan's army twice defeated the English, at Jargeau and Patay. On 17 July she led the Dauphin from Chinon on the way to his coronation at

Comité Départemental du Tourisme d'Indre-et-Loire
9, Rue Buffon - BP 3217
37032 Tours Cedex
Tel: 47 31 47 12

Touring:
use Michelin sheet map 232, Pays de Loire

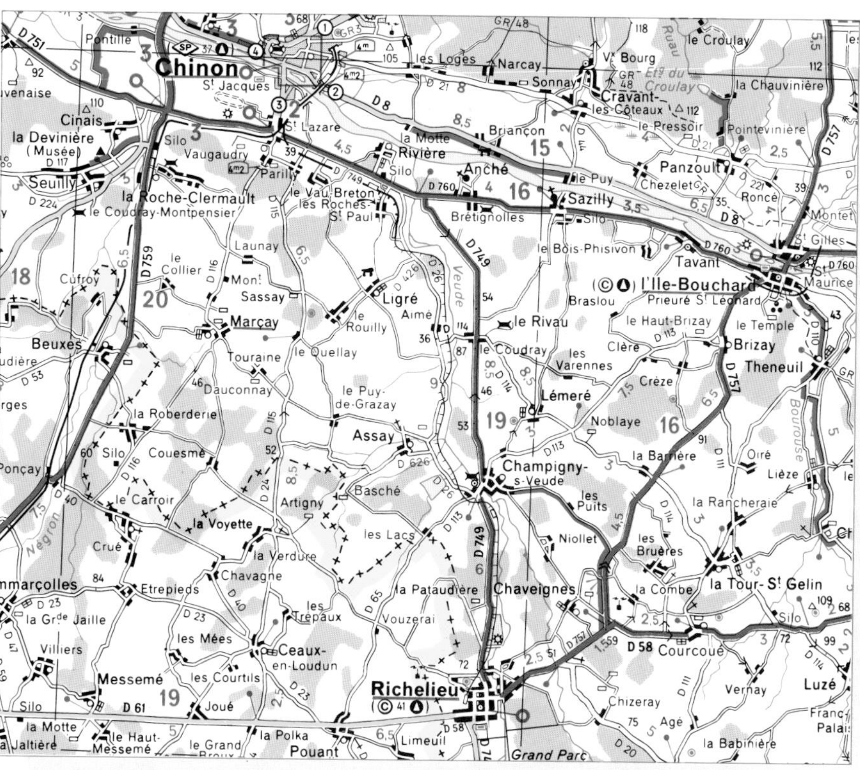

Philippe-Auguste. The Château du Coudray contains the royal apartments.

Below the château, huddled between the river and the cliff, is the town, a network of narrow streets lined with timber-framed houses often leaning at alarming angles. Hidden among the houses are little alleys and fine courtyards. Busy in summer, out of season Chinon is a delight. It offers a local museum in a fine 15th-century town house, a chapel cut from the solid rock of the cliff, a house with Rabelais associations, a barrel-making museum and, at various times of year, an interesting variety of fairs and markets. Among these is the annual wine festival, held in March, which features the famous local red wines that are always available in the town's many restaurants and cafés.

Flowers, grain, grapes and other fruit from the surrounding countryside are sold at Chinon's long-established market

L'Ile Bouchard

Formerly a trading port on the Vienne, L'Ile Bouchard was originally built on an island in the river, clustered around a 9th-century fortress. Today little remains of this historic past and the town has spread away from the island on to both banks. Pleasantly provincial, it is at its best by the river. The real treasure is to be found to the south, approached along suburban streets around the railway station. Here, on its own and apparently in a farmyard, is the ruined chancel of the former Prieuré de St-Léonard. A picturesque fragment, majestic in the open air, it is made memorable by its setting and by the ambitiously carved capitals on its broken columns, which feature New Testament scenes, foliage and sea monsters. Much can be seen simply by peering through the gate, but those requiring a closer look should go in the afternoon, when it is open to visitors.

Richelieu

Created from scratch in the 17th century at the instigation of Cardinal Richelieu, this is the perfect estate town. Built on a strict rectangular grid and surrounded by a moat and an enclosing wall pierced by elegant gateways, Richelieu is a delight in formal grey stone. Classical terraces cross the town, grand houses in the centre for the courtiers, smaller ones on the edge for the artisans.

Richelieu's slightly faded elegance is very restful and its open squares seem to cope easily with the needs of modern traffic. Just beyond the southern gateway there is a statue of the cardinal, surveying the entrance to the great park that housed his château. This mighty building, a rival to Versailles, and the *raison d'être* for the new town, was demolished long ago and only the park and a few outbuildings remain today as a memorial to Cardinal Richelieu's wordly ambitions.

Richelieu is a fine testimony to 17th-century urban planning, for an elegant uniformity is evident throughout the town

Sight-Seeing by Rail

An enjoyable way to visit the pretty valley of the Veude is to take the steam train from Chinon to Richelieu. The line wanders along the river valley, passing close to the Château de Rivau and through Champigny-sur-Veude on the way to its terminus just outside Richelieu's enclosing wall. Old carriages and an ancient SNCF locomotive contribute to making the journey memorable, while the gentle speed ensures ample time for enjoyment of the view. The service operates on Saturdays and Sundays from May to September.

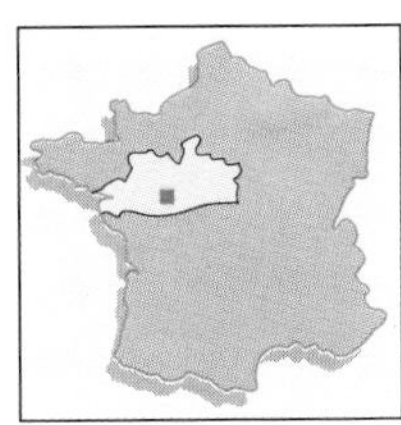

THE LOIRE, THE INDRE AND THE CHER

THIS WOODED REGION is watered by three great rivers, the Loire and its tributaries, the Indre and the Cher. It is rich in mysterious relics of the Roman period, towering medieval fortresses and decorative Renaissance châteaux that mark the transition from local conflicts to an era of national peace. It is also a region of massive market gardens and ornamental château gardens whose formality reflects man's control over nature.

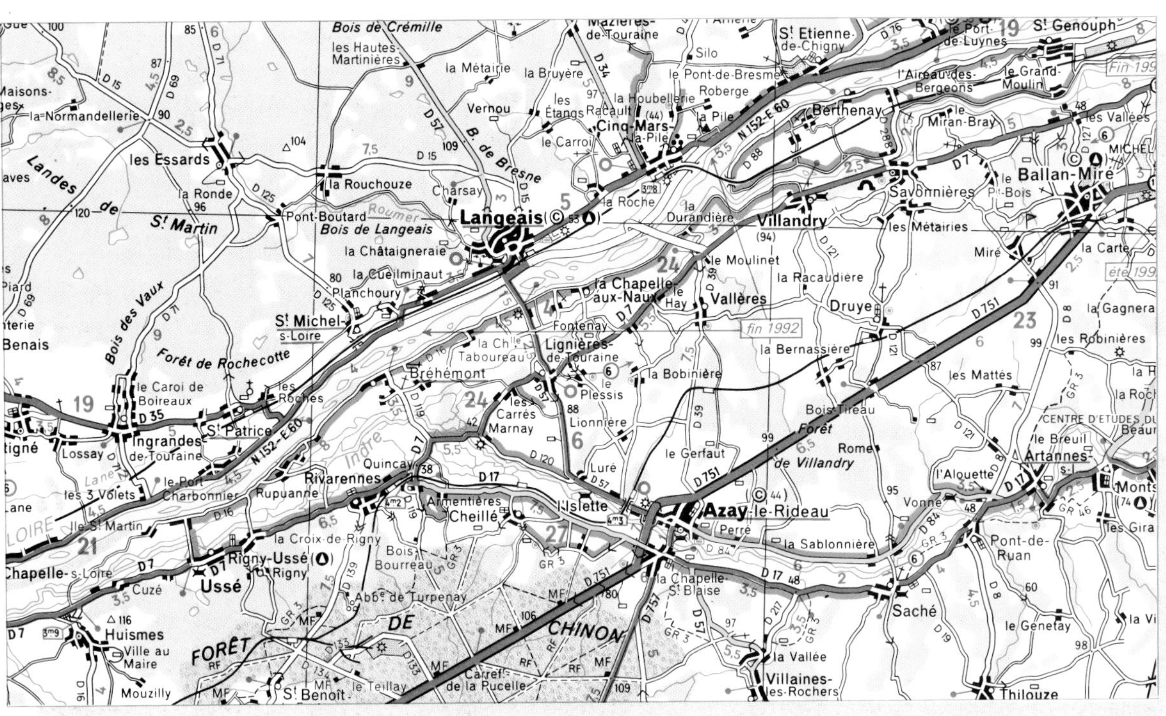

Comité Départemental du Tourisme d'Indre-et-Loire
9, Rue Buffon - BP 3217
37032 Tours Cedex
Tel: 47 31 47 12

Touring:
use Michelin sheet map 232, Pays de Loire

Azay-le-Rideau

The decorative elegance of the château of Azay-le-Rideau, rising from the waters of the Indre and half hidden by trees, must be one of the Loire's most popular sights. The appeal of this lovely building, an early 16th century gem, conceived entirely as a Renaissance mansion rather than a fortress, is understandable. Its delicacy is a vital foil to the grandeur, even pomposity, of so many Loire châteaux. The exterior and the setting are all that matter, but both are difficult to appreciate from the road. A visit is therefore essential, despite Azay's obvious popularity. Also of interest in Azay is the 11th-century St-Symphorien, a church with an unusual double gabled façade.

The village of Azay, busy, smart and full of tourist shops and expensive restaurants, has nonetheless retained an appeal and the mills and buildings by the river are worth a look. Those wanting to escape the crowds can enjoy the quieter roads that flank the Indre both west and east of the town.

Château d'Ussé

The only way to approach the château at Ussé is from the north, via the little road that runs along the Loire's south bank. Seen from a distance, the château's wonderful skyline of towers, spires and fortifications, set against the backdrop of wooded hills, seems to bring to life some fairy tale, and indeed Perrault did use Ussé as his model for the story of the Sleeping Beauty. Originally a medieval fortress, Ussé was steadily expanded from the 15th century to the 18th, yet its glowing white façade maintains a strong sense of unity.

The château is still privately owned and so there is plenty to see inside, but the best features are those dating from the Renaissance, notably the 16th-century chapel with its, later, Aubusson tapestries telling the life of Joan of Arc.

BASKET MAKING

Set in a valley to the south of Azay is the pretty village of Villaines-les-Rochers, whose houses line the banks of a little stream. Since 1849 this village has been a centre for basket making and wickerwork, and many of the inhabitants are still directly involved in the business. The cultivation and preparation of the osiers – willow stalks cut when they are between 0.8 and 2.6m high – and the manufacturing of the finished articles is a year-round activity demanding a range of traditional manual skills. Families work together either in their own homes and workshops or in the large cooperative in the centre of the village, where a vast selection of items, both traditional and modern, can be admired and

purchased. Various items of basketwork can also be bought directly from the small family workshops. The cooperative shows a video explaining the preparation of the osiers and the craft skills of the basket maker.

A blend of French and Italian styles, the formal gardens at Villandry (left) were designed to both reflect and inspire courtly manners

The imposing main entrance to the château at Langeais (below).

GARDENS

With its sea of fruit and vines and its flower-decked villages, the Loire is aptly known as the Garden of France. It is also an ideal region for studying the history of gardening and the changing ideas about the role of the garden. To be seen along the rivers are medieval monastic gardens, in which the growing of food and the cultivation of medicinal plants were at one time all-important.

The builders of medieval fortresses were not concerned with gardening but as conflict gave way to stability the châteaux turned first into hunting lodges whose surrounding forests were a natural garden and playground, and then into decorative and elegant mansions whose formal gardens were designed to reflect man's conquest of nature and symbolise the imposition of order upon chaos.

Château de Villandry

Built largely in the 16th century, Villandry contains the great keep of the original medieval fortress. Extensively restored in the 19th century, the château proudly overlooks the confluence of the Loire and the Cher. As little is to be seen inside, the setting is important, but Villandry's main glory is its garden, completely reconstructed by its 19th-century owner, Dr Carvallo. What is seen today is the most splendid and the most extensive example of a Renaissance formal garden in France. There are three great terraces, set above the Cher: a grand water garden, an ornamental garden and a vegetable garden, all in formal Renaissance patterns outlined by box arabesques, paths and canals. Villandry is a masterpiece of order.

Cinq-Mars-la-Pile

This small riverside village, dominated by the main road, takes the latter part of its name from a tall tower that stands just outside it. This massive structure – square, 30m high and topped by four pinnacles – overlooks the remains of a medieval fortress from its promontory above the confluence of the Loire and the Cher. Built with a rubble and cement core dressed with decorative brickwork, the monument has an uncertain origin. Some claim that it is Roman, some date it to the Dark Ages and some consider it medieval. Why it was built, and what it represents or commemorates, remains a mystery.

Langeais

Despite the heavy traffic, the best way into Langeais is still from the Loire, for the bridge leads straight to the town's old centre and the rather forbidding château. Visitors should not be put off by the château's appearance, for behind the grim façade is a decorative and well-furnished Renaissance mansion built, unusually for this region, uninterruptedly between 1465 and 1469. All that remains of its forerunner, a 10th-century fortress, is one battered tower, everything else having been demolished in 1427 on the orders of Henry VI.

On the outskirts of Langeais there are two museums, one devoted to old tools and the traditional life of the working man, a type of display not unusual in the region. The other museum, which is rather more unexpected, holds the largest collection of Cadillac cars outside the USA.

Saché

A quiet village set above the Indre, Saché has two claims to fame. First is the château, really a 16th-century manor house, beautifully sited by the river. It was the home for some years of the novelist Balzac, who moved there in 1838. A number of his books, including *Le Père Goriot* and *Le Lys dans la Vallée*, were written in the rooms that are now preserved as a Balzac museum, some of which are as he left them.

Saché's second, and rather more recent, famous resident was the American sculptor Alexander Calder.

VALLÉE DE L'INDRE

From Azay eastwards the Indre is a particularly attractive river, easily explored on quiet roads. The best of these runs through the trees of the north bank and is linked by pleasant old bridges to Saché and Pont-de-Ruan, the latter village notable for its lovely old water-mills. Further to the east, and also connected to the north bank by a bridge, is the hill village of Monts, with its traditional atmosphere and old shops, including the dynamic art deco tiled façade of the *boucherie*. Popular with fishermen, the Indre's quiet qualities can also be enjoyed by walkers and picnickers.

THE CHÂTEAUX OF THE LOIRE

IN THE LOIRE REGION AS A WHOLE there are probably 150 châteaux of some historical importance, and many more of lesser interest. They range in date from the 11th century to the 19th and reflect many of the architectural styles particularly associated with France. The habit of visiting châteaux was established in the 19th century, when the railways brought tourism to the Loire and its network of tributaries, and in more recent times the most famous examples – Angers, Saumur, Chinon, Azay-le-Rideau, Villandry, Amboise, Chenonceau, Chaumont, Blois, Chambord and Cheverny – have become household names. Every year many thousands of visitors come to see them, hoping perhaps to capture some hint of the spirit of creativity that brought them into being.

Many of the châteaux do stand beside the Loire, but others are on lesser rivers, the Cher, the Indre, the Vienne, the Loir and the Sarthe, or in woods or farmland well away from any river. Some are owned by the state, some by companies, some by private families, and their condition ranges from immaculate magnificence to a pile of broken stones. Yet all have played their part in the development of a region that has always been close to the heart of French history. There can be no river in the world with more historic associations than the Loire.

A WITNESS TO HISTORY

The history of the châteaux of the Loire is bound up closely with the history of France itself, for the great river, in its 1020-km sweep from the south to the Atlantic coast, has always been a frontier, a battleground and a vital line of communication. The invading Roman army followed the Loire in its conquest of Gaul, meeting stiff resistance from the local tribes. Christianity spread into France along the same route, and then came the Huns and the Saracens, invading forces who were stopped at the Loire. The next aggressors were the Normans, who used the river to transport their troops for attacks on towns such as Nantes and Tours. The legacy of the Norman invasion was chaos as feudal strife broke the region into small warring states.

By the 11th century Orléans, Touraine, Anjou and Maine were virtually separate kingdoms, and it was their rulers, semi-legendary figures such as Foulques Nerra, who built the first Loire châteaux, fortresses and strongholds to defend their frontiers. With the emergence of the Plantagenets, Anjou became dominant, establishing by the middle of the 12th century an empire that stretched from the Pyrenees to the north of England. Dating from this period are the earliest of the chateâux that can still be enjoyed today, great fortresses such as Angers. The Plantagenets' great enemy were the French Capetian kings, whose base was at Orléans, and the rivalry between the two royal houses led directly to several centuries of strife between England and France. During this time the fortresses of the Loire region were constantly being rebuilt, attacked and rebuilt again as the armies battled for the key towns and strongholds, and defended crossing points.

When the Dauphin set up his court, first at Bourges and then at Chinon, the Loire became the front line and with the intervention of Joan of Arc, whose battles all took place around the Loire, the balance swung to the French. By the middle of the 15th century English rule in France was at an end, and for the first time in centuries peace came to the region.

The 17 towers of Angers' 13th-century fortress are built of red schist and white stone

Azay-le-Rideau (far left) was erected between 1518 and 1527 by a wealthy financier. At this time châteaux were being built as homes rather than fortresses
The château at Blois (left) comprises elements ranging from medieval to 17th-century. Among the most striking is the staircase built by François I
It was Diane de Poitiers who extended Chenonceaux (below) across the River Cher in a series of arches
The massive château at Chambord (bottom), begun by François I but unfinished at his death in 1559, is regarded by some as the finest Renaissance building in France

The Golden Age of the Loire

With the peace came the relative stability of the Valois kings, who turned the Loire from a battlefield into the centre of Court life. Towering fortresses, their military life at an end, began to be turned into domestic palaces, and so there emerged the most characteristic of all Loire château types, the fortress containing within its heart a handsome mansion. Early in the 16th century François I came to the throne and this cultured king launched the golden age of the Loire. He established a sophisticated and artistic court, with an enthusiasm for Italy that brought the Renaissance to France.

The new generation of royal palaces – Amboise, Blois, Chambord – launched a new style of domestic architecture in France, and the royal creations were soon being echoed all over the Loire region as aristocrats, courtiers and financiers vied with each other in stately magnificence. For the first time ladies played a part, with figures such as Diane de Poitiers and Catherine de Medici adding style and elegance to masculine architecture. In the case of these two powerful rivals for the attentions of Henri II, it was the château at Chenonceaux that benefited.

Changing Fortunes

Peace was shattered by the violent religious wars of the end of the 16th century. These had a direct impact on the region, but château building continued nonetheless through the 17th century, inspired by leading figures such as Cardinal Richelieu. By the 18th century the royal influence had moved away from the Loire, but the château tradition was maintained by the aristocracy and newly wealthy industrialists and bankers. The new rococo and neoclassical styles came to the Loire, epitomised by Chanteloup, Ménars and Montgeoffroy, but the turmoil of the Revolution in 1789 brought an end to the Loire's powerful influence and prosperity.

An Enduring Legacy

In the 19th century industry and modern transport took their place beside the traditional agriculture of the region, and the new wealth encouraged the building of new châteaux and the restoration of many earlier ones. All this came to an end with the outbreak of the Franco-Prussian War in 1870. However, the important contribution of the 19th century remained the appreciation of the architectural qualities of those châteaux built between the 12th and the 17th centuries, a legacy enjoyed by inhabitants of, and visitors to, the Loire today.

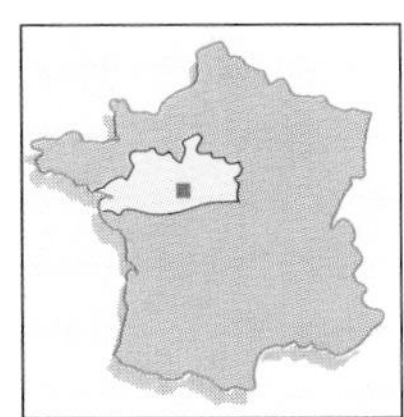

CHÂTEAUX OF THE LOIRE AND CHER

IN THIS REGION OF FOREST AND PARKLAND, bounded in the north by the wide course of the Loire and in the south by the gentler Cher, the Renaissance brought about the replacement of the medieval fortress with something far lighter and more elegant. Châteaux such as the daring Chenonceau came to overshadow the more traditional style of Amboise and Chaumont.

Amboise

Amboise is an attractive place, with narrow streets lined with a good range of decorative architecture, a postal museum, and Leonardo da Vinci's house, with its displays of models made up from his drawings. The Église St-Denis has a delicate 12th-century nave, and hidden among the medieval and Renaissance houses are many surprises. The town is probably best known for its *son et lumière* displays, the focal point of which is the château. This massive structure was built as a royal palace at the end of the 15th century, but declined after 1560.

Bléré

This small town, whose quiet streets and pleasant shops can be a relief after the turmoil of Amboise, grew up around a long-established crossing point on the Cher. Its former importance is reflected by several Renaissance buildings, the best of which is the Hôtel du Gouverneur.

Château de Chaumont-sur-Loire

The little town of Chaumont, essentially one street running parallel to the river, is wholly dominated by the château and indeed is little more than an estate village. The château, a grand but rather severe fortress built between 1465 and 1510, stands high on its hill above the river.

Château de Chenonceau

Visually the most exciting and, by its associations, the most romantic of the Loire châteaux, Chenonceau is in every way a remarkable building. Early in the 16th century Thomas Bohier, a Court financier, acquired the site of a medieval fortress beside the Cher, and began the construction of a formal but highly decorative Renaissance mansion. In 1526 the château passed to François I to pay off some of Bohier's debts and became a royal palace. Some 20 years later Henri II gave Chenonceau to his mistress, Diane de Poitiers, and it

ROYAL RIVALS

Considerably older than Henri II, Diane de Poitiers was far more than a mistress. Business manager, confidante and continual source of inspiration, Diane seems always to have outshone the queen, Catherine de Medici. The gift of Chenonceau to Diane, and her gardens and daring extension across the Cher, proved the final straw. When Henri died in 1559 Catherine took her revenge by forcing Diane to surrender Chenonceau for the gaunt walls of Chaumont. At Chenonceau Catherine flourished, expanding the building and linking the château's name with memorable masques and fêtes in the enlarged park. It was Catherine who fulfilled the promise of Chenonceau laid down by Diane, who spent the last seven years of her life in seclusion.

Amboise (above) is a typical Loire town and attracts many tourists in summer. They come not only to see the château but also to visit the old quarter and to attend various festivals, including one in September that celebrates the melon

Entry to the superb château at Chenonceau (right) is gained by passing through Bohier's original château

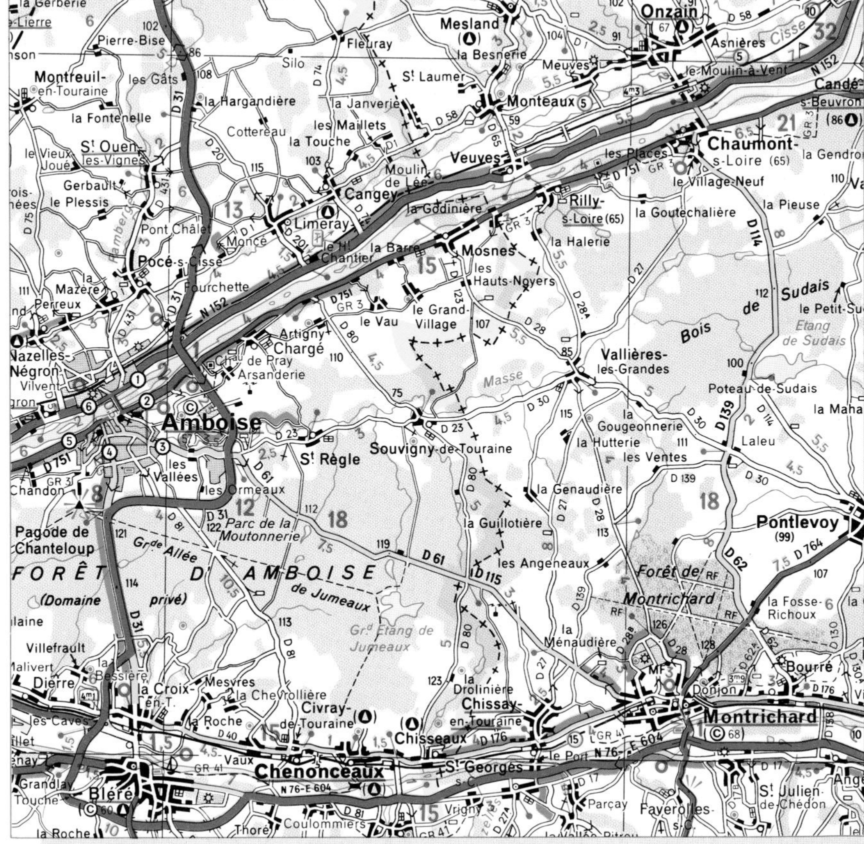

WINE

Among the many distinctive wines of the Loire region are those of Touraine, dry whites and reds, and the notable rosés associated particularly with the Mesland area north of Amboise. Taking their names from the region as a whole, from towns and villages or local châteaux, the Loire wines come in all qualities, from *Appellation contrôlée* to ordinary table wines. A number of grape varieties are used, including Gamay, Cabernet, Sauvignon and Chenin, and the changing soil conditions have resulted in a wide choice of wines.

Notable are the muscadets of the western Loire, the light rosés and whites of Anjou, the heavier sweet wines of the Coteaux du Layon, the light reds of the Angers region, the richer reds of Bourgueil and Chinon, the flinty-tasting white from Sancerre and, above all, the sparkling

varieties from Saumur, Vouvray and Montlouis. Many of these wines are made and stored in the old tufa-stone caves and there are plenty of opportunities for *dégustation*, roadside tasting.

it was she who extended it on a series of arches across the Cher. After Henri's death his widow Catherine took over the château and added two more storeys to the bridge.

The interior is full of fine architectural detail but there is little tangible evidence of the two rivals for Henri's affections.

Montrichard

The best way to see Montrichard is from the south, entering this attractive yet surprisingly little-known town via the 17th-century bridge across the Cher. This gives ample opportunity for the enjoyment of the splendid river front, with the ruined medieval fortress standing high above the town. There are pleasant old streets, lined with medieval, Renaissance and later buildings, lively shops and restaurants that have been spared the worst excesses of tourism and, in the centre, a little parish church.

Pagode de Chanteloup

Set on high ground at the edge of the Forêt d'Amboise, this entertaining fantasy is all that remains of an extensive château and park developed in the 18th century by the Duc de Choiseul. The château was actually much earlier and was bought by Choiseul when he was one of Louis XV's ministers. After falling foul of Madame du Barry, Choiseul was exiled from Court and spent four years confined to the Chanteloup estate. At the end of his exile, in 1762, he celebrated the loyalty of those friends who had made it bearable by commissioning the pagoda. Inspired by Sir William Chambers's structure in Kew Gardens, it was designed by the architect Le Camus, who turned it into something larger and more exotic.

From the top of the pagoda the magnificent view of the sweep of the Loire from Tours to Blois makes the climb up the twisting staircase well worth the effort.

Some fragments of the vanished château's décor are in the museum in Tours, but these can only hint at the lifestyle enjoyed by Choiseul during his exile, when Chanteloup became a rival to Versailles. Standing in the park today, it is hard to imagine the glittering society that inspired, among other things, Beaumarchais' play *Le Mariage de Figaro*.

Pontlevoy

The main feature of this quiet town is the huge abbey. Founded in the 11th century, it was greatly expanded in later centuries, and much of what can be seen today dates from the 17th century, a mass of simple classicism in white stone.

Comité Départemental du Tourisme d'Indre-et-Loire
9, Rue Buffon - BP 3217
37032 Tours Cedex
Tel: 47 31 47 12

Touring:
use Michelin sheet map 238, Centre/ Berry-Nivernais

The impressive abbey at Pontlevoy is the town's principal attraction. Originally founded in the 11th century, it combines fine 18th-century buildings with an earlier former abbey church

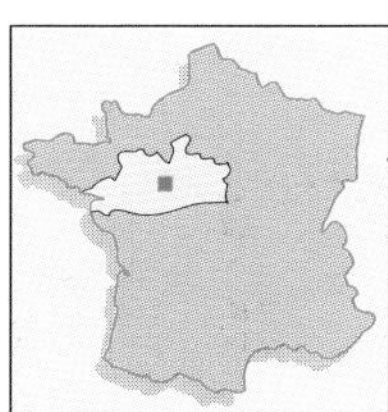

ALONG THE VALLEY OF THE LOIR

NOT TO BE CONFUSED WITH THE LOIRE, its grander neighbour, the Loir is a delightfully rural river. A tributary of the Sarthe, and thus of the Mayenne, it has its own medieval fortresses, Renaissance châteaux, Romanesque churches and interesting villages and towns, as well as a history reaching back to before the Roman occupation of France.

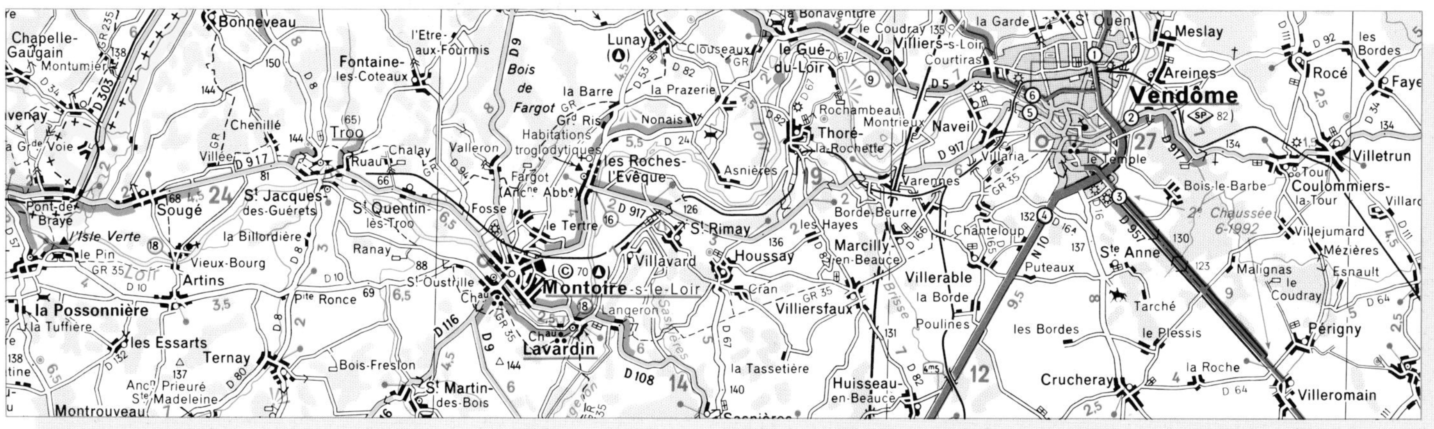

Comité Départemental du Tourisme du Loir-et-Cher
11, Place du Château
41000 Blois
Tel: 54 78 55 50

Touring:
use Michelin sheet map 238, Centre/ Berry-Nivernais

Lavardin

Set in a bend of the Loir, Lavardin is a remarkable little village, a cluster of old houses surrounding the hillside church, full of prettiness and picturesque detail and with only a hint of self-consciousness. Inside the church is a fine series of murals. However, Lavardin's most spectacular feature is its ruined 11th- and 12th-century castle.

Montoire-sur-le-Loir

In the Middle Ages the Loir formed a defensive barrier protected by a number of hilltop fortresses. Some have disappeared while others survive as picturesque ruins. Notable among the latter is Montoire, whose battered keep and fortifications stand high above the south bank of the river and are well worth exploring for the views along the wooded valley. Close by the river on the château side is the Chapelle-St-Gilles, with its deservedly famous series of 12th-century murals.

Montoire-sur-le-Loir's ruined château, with its 11th-century square keep

Poncé-sur-le-Loir

Almost out of place in the pastoral valley of the Loir is Poncé's fine château, a Renaissance building that owes more to the architecture of Chenonceaux and Azay-le-Rideau than any local tradition. Italianate and French design traditions come together, notably in the splendid coffered staircase that rises straight up for six flights. Poncé has the quality of a royal building, yet has no such associations. Nor is it known exactly when it was built, or by whom – mysteries that add to rather than diminish its lasting appeal.

To be seen in Poncé's church are good examples of the medieval wall paintings characteristic of this region. Painted in the late 12th century, the series includes a scene of a battle between Crusaders and Muslims.

Further examples of a similar date can be seen in the church at St Jacques-des-Guérets, which lies 10km to the east along the Loir.

CAVE DWELLINGS

A characteristic feature of the whole of the Loire region are the caves cut into steep riverside cliffs and hills during centuries of excavation of the soft, white tufa stone. Cool, dry, secure and often cut into huge caverns inside the hills, these caves have been adapted for domestic use since before Roman times. Many are used as stores, wine cellars or for the cultivation of mushrooms, but in a number of places there is an age-old tradition of troglodyte inhabitation. The valley of the Loir is well known for its troglodyte houses. The largest collection is cut into the hillside at Troo, but individual examples are to be seen in many other parts of the region. Some are quite clearly little more than inhabited caves, while others are on more than one storey and set behind a decorative architectural façade.

The village of Les Roches-l'Évêque lies in a wooded cleft between the Loir and sheer cliffs

Les Roches-l'Évêque

The setting of this little village is its main appeal. It is squeezed into the narrow strip of land that separates the Loir from the steep cliffs lining the river's north bank – squeezed so tightly that many of the houses are in the old tufa-stone caves. Some are actually not very old, for when demand outstripped supply the villagers simply carved out new cave homes, equipping them with all mod cons. Also partly in a cave is the church, decorated with 12th- and 13th-century frescos.

A variation to be found around Doué-la-Fontaine are the dwellings carved out underground rather than in caves in the riverside cliffs. At Rochemenier, for example, there is a subterranean village three times larger than the hamlet above ground, and dating back to the Middle Ages.

Troo

This is one of the most curious villages in the whole of the Loire, and it reveals its curiosities layer by layer. At first sight it is a pleasant traditional village with houses ranged in rows along the minor road that follows the Loir's north bank. But set high on the hill above is another Troo, a much older settlement with battered fortifications, an impressive gateway and a castle mount .

A walk down the hillside towards the river uncovers Troo's third, and most surprising, aspect. Here is the most extensive cave town in the Loire, if not in the whole of France. A network of paths reveals a whole nest of cave houses set into the steep hillside, many still in use.

Vendôme

The grandest town in this part of the Loire, Vendôme has been a settlement at least since the pre-Roman era and has subsequently had a colourful life. It was pillaged by the English, owned by the French royal family and the Bourbons, and attacked by the Germans in 1870 and 1940. It has associations with the 16th-century poet Ronsard and with Rochambeau, the leader of the French forces during the American War of Independence. High above Vendôme, and offering splendid views, is a huge and ruined medieval fortress, underlining the town's strategic importance in the Middle Ages. This is a delightful town to explore, its centre spread over several branches of the Loir ensuring a proliferation of little bridges and pretty waterfronts.

Near the central marketplace are two great towers: a 15th-century clock tower from the former parish church and a magnificent Romanesque campanile over 80m high, detached from its abbey church, La Trinité. The latter has fine sculpture on the Flamboyant Gothic west front.

Among Vendôme's several fine gateways is the Porte St-Georges

The scarce swallowtail butterfly, one of the many insects found in the Sologne

The Sologne

The Sologne, a region of wild forest and heath broken by streams and innumerable lakes, was formed when the Loire changed its course to swing in a great curve south-west towards the Atlantic. Bounded by Blois, Orléans, Gien and Vierzon, the Sologne is a huge area where centuries of isolation have developed a particular way of life. Notable are the single-storey terraces in the little towns and villages, all built in simple styles from local brick.

The thick forests are full of deer, wild boar and other game, and the lakes are rich in carp and other fish. The whole region is a secret paradise for wildlife and insects, much of it accessible only on foot or horse.

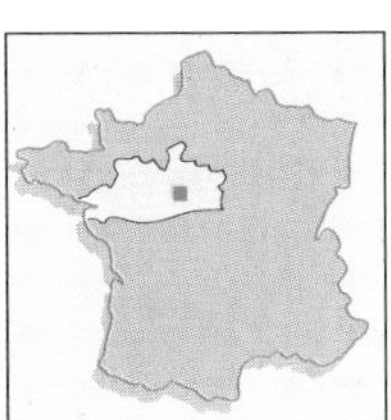

THE ROYAL HUNTING GROUNDS

EAST OF BLOIS AND SOUTH OF THE LOIRE the landscape is dominated by forest. The river itself, a royal highway linking Tours and Orléans, marks the boundary of the royal hunting grounds, a vast area of natural woodland whose abundant wildlife encouraged the construction of great châteaux such as Chambord and Cheverny.

Comité Départemental du Tourisme du Loir-et-Cher
11, Place du Château
41000 Blois
Tel: 54 78 55 50

Touring:
use Michelin sheet map 238, Centre/ Berry-Nivernais

The château at Blois has enjoyed a long connection with nobility and royalty. The earliest keep was erected in the 10th century by Thibault I. Later the quadrilateral château, which surrounds a spacious courtyard, was used by Louis XII, François I and Henri III

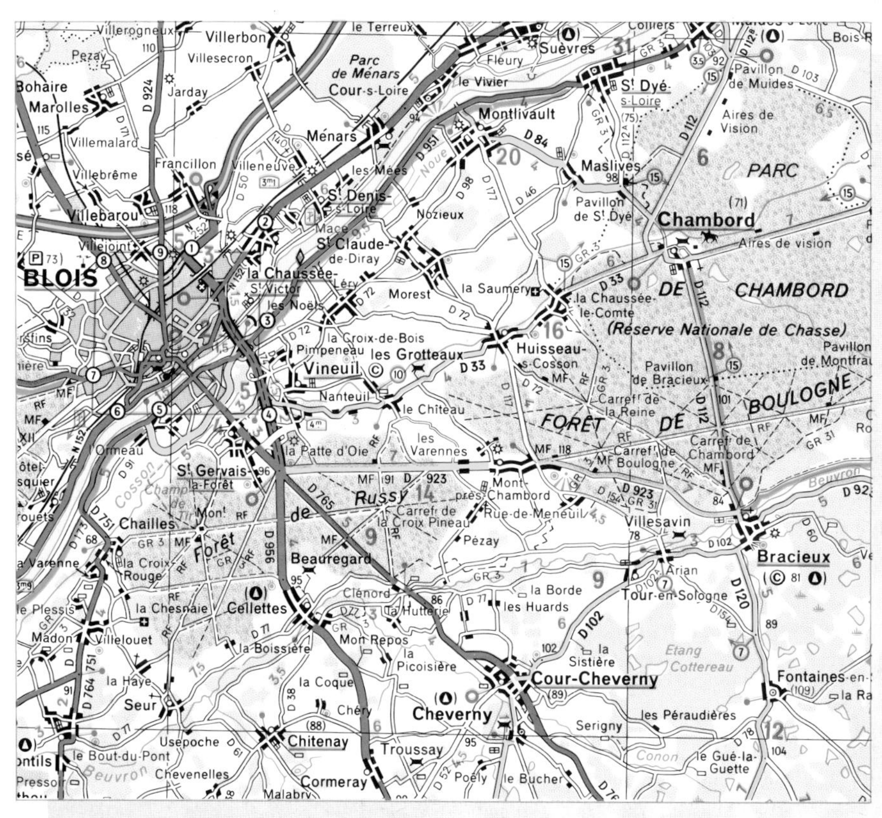

Blois

A thriving city and a major agricultural centre, Blois grew up around its massive château, which still stands at its heart. Built round a square, the château is an object-lesson in architectural style, for it shows the transition from medieval fortress to 17th-century classical mansion. The most exciting parts, however, are those built during the Renaissance, notably the famous octagon staircase and the mass of architectural detail. Throughout the 16th century the château at Blois was a royal palace and the centre of political and artistic life, and the impact of the château on the development of the town during that period can still be seen.

The capital of its region, Blois is of a size to be able to offer everything the visitor could need. The centre is relatively small, easy to explore on foot, and its history is easy to appreciate.

WATERWAYS OF THE LOIRE

The Loire, France's longest river by far, was for centuries a major navigation, a vital transport artery exploited by the Romans, then throughout the Middle Ages and during the 16th and 17th centuries, these two centuries being the period of major development of the region. The presence of the Loire as a navigation was a major stimulus for the spread of châteaux and civilisation along its banks. Navigation was never easy on a river that was fast-flowing and treacherous in winter and short of water in summer, but trade thrived until well into the 18th century. Barges that had carried their cargoes and passengers westwards with the current, aided by sails or oars, were either broken up at their destination, or painstakingly dragged back up the river by huge teams of men and horses.

Many of the Loire's tributaries were also navigable at this time and in the 17th and 18th centuries numerous improvements were made by dredging and by building locks to control the flow of water. A series of canals was also built from the 17th century to link the rivers of the region and to bypass the more hazardous sections. Inadequate roads made

the Loire navigation an economic necessity, and it was not until the coming of the railways in the 1840s that the battle to keep the river navigable was finally abandoned.

Today only very short stretches of the Loire carry anything bigger than a canoe or fishing punt. The centuries of river navigation are now a part of history, a story told in the museum at Châteauneuf-sur-Loire.

Château de Chambord

No one has ever been able to explain why François I, a king of great taste and style, decided in 1519 to create a massive palace in the heart of the Sologne forests. He was devoted to hunting, and the building he constructed certainly served as a hunting lodge. However, a lodge is no way to describe this extraordinary 440-room royal palace, perhaps the greatest legacy of the Renaissance in France.

The exterior is a remarkable blend of art and mathematics, and the same forces were brought together inside to create the double spiral staircase that rises through the full height of the building.

Château de Cheverny

Built by Henri Hurault, Comte de Cheverny, Cheverny is a noble château. This elegant and formally symmetrical mansion set in landscaped parkland illustrates the formality that came to characterise the country house in France in the 17th century. Henri Hurault's descendants still own Cheverny, and so the château presents the visitor with a rare chance to experience the atmosphere of a grand family house complete with its original 17th-century furniture and fittings. Cheverny is in a region that is famous for its hunting, and so its resident pack of hounds and hunting museum, which contains among other things 2000 deer antlers, add to the attraction of the château.

Château de Ménars

Set behind railings, the severely formal façade of Ménars is quite unlike that of any other Loire château. It was started in 1637 by a successful wine merchant, Guillaume Charron, who rose to become a viscount. His nephew, Jean-Jacques, enlarged the house and developed a park that ran down to the Loire, while using his political connections to become a marquis. In 1760 the château was sold to a lady of the Court, Antoinette Poisson, better known as Madame de Pompadour. She enjoyed Ménars for the last four years of her life, rebuilding the house with the help of Gabriel, the king's architect, and greatly improving the garden. Under her care Ménars became a grand neo-classical mansion, and the garden with its buildings, statues, urns and vistas a picturesque reflection of her artistic talents. The terraced slope between the château and the river still has its grottos and fountains. Now privately owned, the house, its contents and its gardens offer the chance to enjoy 18th-century classicism at its best. There is no village at Ménars, but the château and church form a good group.

It is worth a pause at Cour-sur-Loire to see the 16th-century stained glass, and then, escaping from the busy N152, to take a little road that runs right beside the Loire towards Suèvres and is overlooked by flowery gardens. Suèvres itself is a peaceful and pretty little town, with old houses decked with flowers, a stream running through its heart and a fine old mill.

Chambord is an ingeniously designed château: a perfect harmony of unbalanced forms that presents from all sides the illusion of symmetry. From a distance the eye is caught by the roof, with its mass of spires, towers, chimneys and domes. But as you get nearer your attention is drawn instead to the windows and the elaborate architectural detail, order replacing apparent chaos. The architect has never been conclusively identified, but some say that Leonardo da Vinci had a hand in Chambord's creation

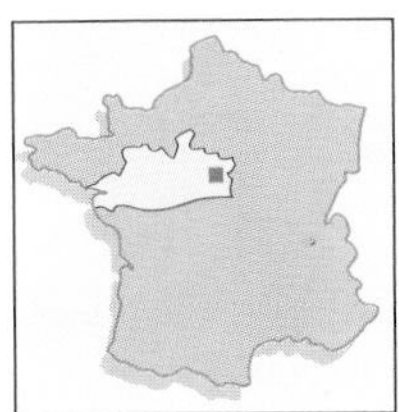

THE LAST CHÂTEAUX OF THE LOIRE

THE WIDE SWEEPS OF THE LOIRE separate the forests of Orléans from the empty heathland of the Sologne. The river itself is a band of civilisation and history flowing through this emptiness, its banks enriched with grand châteaux, with important associations with Joan of Arc and with sites vital to the development of Christianity.

Comité Départemental du Tourisme du Loiret
8, Rue d'Escares
45000 Orléans
Tel: 38 54 83 83

Touring:
use Michelin sheet map 238, Centre/ Berry-Nivernais

Château de Sully-sur-Loire

Badly damaged by bombing in World War II, the little town of Sully has never really recovered the style it must have enjoyed in the 17th century. The best approach is from the north, to enjoy the view of the château and the town while crossing the long bridge, preferably on foot. The château dominates the town completely, and there is really little else to Sully. It is a magnificent building, one of the most dramatic of all the Loire châteaux, wonderfully sited by the river and surrounded by a moat that reflects the glowing white stone to perfection. An excellent example of a Renaissance mansion inserted into an earlier medieval fortress, Sully is an harmonious mass of towers, fortifications and decorative detail.

The château enjoyed three distinct periods of history. The first was in the time of Charles VII and Joan of Arc, for it was from Sully that Joan set off in 1430 for her last battle, her capture by the English and ultimately her death. The second was in the 17th century when Henri IV's great minister the Duc de Sully rebuilt the château in its present form. The third was in the 18th century when the young Voltaire was exiled to Sully, bringing life and culture back to the old château. The interiors underline this varied history, but particularly impressive is the great hall, with its massive chestnut roof of 1363, one of the greatest of all medieval timber roofs. However, best of all is the view of Sully from the Loire, with its parapets, towers and pepper-pot roofs the quintessential medieval castle.

In medieval times there was a rudimentary fortress at Sully, guarding the Loire, and part of the original structure still faces the river. Maximilien Béthune (later Duc de Sully) made extensive additions in the early 17th century, so that the château is a fusion of medieval and Renaissance elements

Châteauneuf-sur-Loire

This smart market town grew up to serve its château, originally a medieval fortress that was destroyed in the 16th century. In 1646 the estate was acquired by Louis de la Vrillière, and a new château was built, a small Versailles with magnificent gardens beside the Loire. This in turn was almost completely destroyed during the Revolution. In the 1820s the gardens were landscaped in the English style and are still a delight to explore, particularly when the rhododendrons are in flower. The château's creator is commemorated in the 13th-century church by a statue, which was hidden during the Revolution.

Châteauneuf-sur-Loire is a pleasant town, with good shops and restaurants, and it is unusually blessed with two market halls, one wooden, dated 1854, and a later one in delicate cast iron. The château's former stables now house a museum of navigation on the Loire, bringing to life the boats, the boatmen and their families, the trade and the ports, of the once thriving river transport industry that died towards the middle of the 19th century (see page 84).

Louis XIV's Secretary of State, Louis de la Vrillière, built a small-scale replica of Versailles at Châteauneuf-sur-Loire. All that remains of it are the domed rotunda, the pavilions in the forecourt and the outbuildings

Pottery

France's association with the manufacture of decorative pottery dates back to the 16th century, when the industry was greatly encouraged by the spirit of the Renaissance. In many parts of France where suitable materials could be found pottery making became a major activity. The most common form was faience, an earthenware covered with a white tin glaze and then painted freehand with a wide range of designs based on oriental styles, Renaissance arabesques or natural forms. Production of faience continued well into the 19th century.

Also popular was creamware, based on English models, and factories to produce this ware were established in Orléans in the late 18th century. However, the Loire was never a major pottery-producing region and until the 19th century the emphasis was

on domestic wares and on bricks and tiles, particularly in the Sologne, where traditional factories still make a wide range of floor and roof tiling. In the 1820s faience and earthenware factories were established in Gien, and pottery making has remained the town's major industry and a tourist attraction.

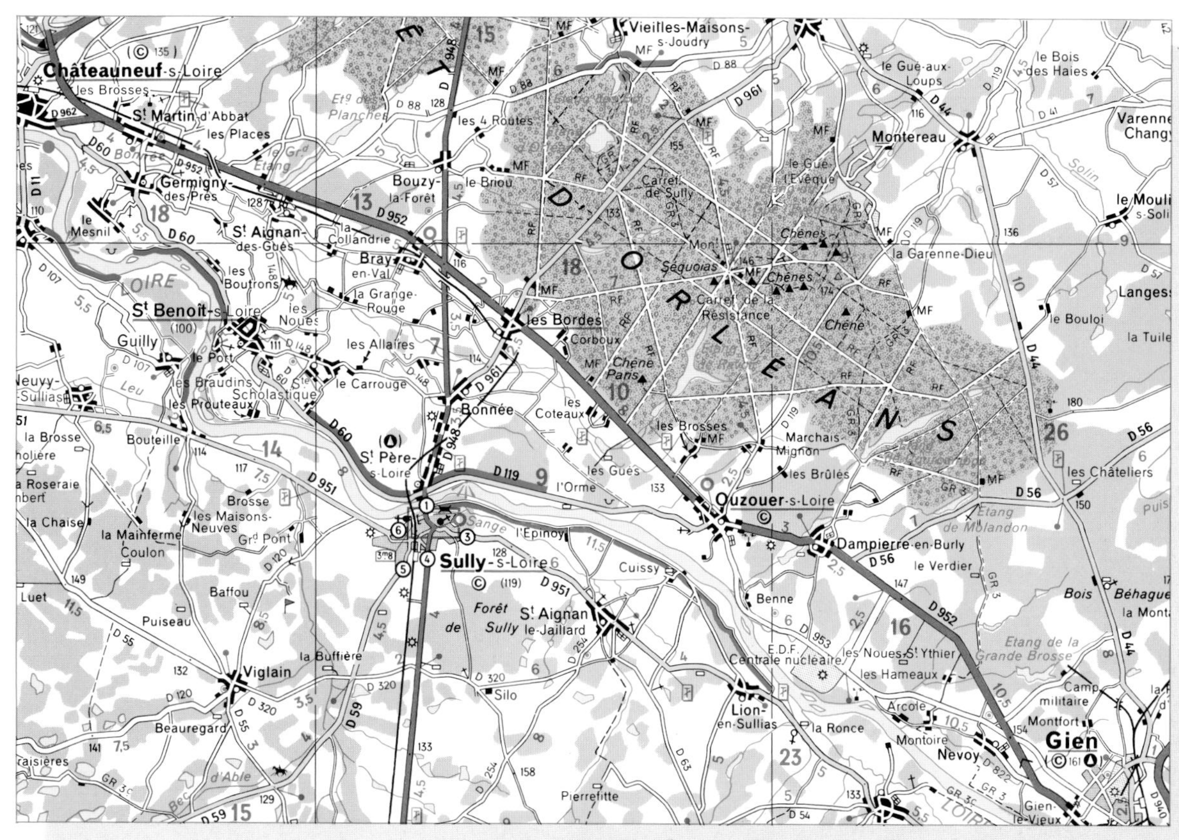

Gien

Seen from the south bank of the Loire, Gien is a fine sight. The town's church and château stand together on a hill, high above the clustered riverside houses and the multi-arched bridge. The château, all in diaper-patterned brickwork and dating from the 14th century, is the key to the town's development, and is additionally important in that it is geographically the last, or the first, of the châteaux of the Loire. It played its part in the dramatic career of Joan of Arc, for it was here that she first reached the Loire, on 1 March 1429, on her way to see the Dauphin. She was to stay here again four months later with the Dauphin on the way to his coronation at Reims.

Today the château houses a museum devoted to hunting, telling the history of a sport so significant in the Loire region. Much of the church is modern, for the building that Joan of Arc knew was largely destroyed by bombing in June 1940 – raids that also flattened Gien's river front. Much of the heart of the town has been carefully rebuilt in a sensitive manner.

Gien's heart, including its church and the area by the river, was badly damaged by bombs in World War II. However, much of the town's character has been regained through careful rebuilding with local materials

St Benoît-sur-Loire

In this little village is the abbey of Fleury, built between the 9th and the 11th-centuries. This is one of the foremost Romanesque buildings in France, notable for its early transept, choir and crypt and its multi-pillared porch.

A small road leads down to the old quays and cottages of St Benoît's long-disused port, which was a busy place in the 17th and 18th centuries, when Loire navigation was at its height.

PARIS AND THE ILE DE FRANCE

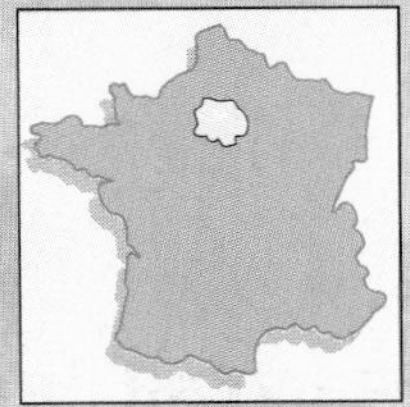

THE ILE DE FRANCE, WITH PARIS at its hub, remains the political, economic, artistic, cultural and tourist centre of France. First inhabited more than 5000 years ago by Bronze Age tribes who established a settlement on the banks of the Seine, the region has played a vital role in the country's development throughout the centuries. It was the ancient heartland from which the French kings gradually extended their control.

Today the capital city stretches across some 100 square kilometres of the Paris Basin, and has more than two million inhabitants, with another seven million spread throughout the surrounding metropolitan area. But despite the fact that it is among the world's most densely populated cities, it retains a balance between spaciousness and human scale. The last decade has witnessed many remarkable changes and alterations to the city's glorious and historic architectural treasures, and in that period these have been joined by some equally striking modern buildings.

Inevitably the demands of modern society and in particular those of motor transport have wrought many changes. Every day three million cars enter Paris via the Périphérique and its associated motorways, producing severe air pollution and causing massive congestion and parking problems. Although there is an excellent subsidised public transport system, many of these vehicles continue to come from the surrounding commuter towns and villages.

However, despite its remarkable population growth, the Ile de France has retained much of its original ancient forests, including those around Versailles and Fontainebleau, as well as the great royal palaces and châteaux of the 16th and 17th centuries. All of these lie within a few hours' drive of the centre of Paris, offering visitors an opportunity to view examples of a great variety of architectural styles. Development of the region continues, with the Ile de France providing the setting for the vast Euro Disney complex at Marne-la-Vallée, as well as a string of new towns spread around the capital.

The Eiffel Tower – long the most familiar symbol of Paris

A Métro sign lights Boulevard Haussmann (above)
Femme assise aux bras croisés *(below) is in the Musée Picasso*

The Basilique du Sacré Coeur looks down on Paris from its impressive position in hilly Montmartre, in the north of the city

The Moulin Rouge in Pigalle (above) is the home of the can-can. Founded in the last century, it remains the best known of the famous cabarets of Paris

Posters can only hint at the range and vitality of Paris's performing arts scene, which offers a choice of entertainment unsurpassed anywhere

I M Pei's glass-walled pyramid, 21.5m high, adorns the main courtyard of the Louvre (left)
The Centre Pompidou, opened in 1977, heralded a new, high-tech approach to museum design

MAJOR SIGHTS

Key to the major sights in Paris

Arc de Triomphe	D4
Avenue des Champs Élysées	D5
Basilique du Sacré Coeur	B8
Bois de Boulogne	E1
Bois de Vincennes	J13
Centre Georges Pompidou	E8
Cité des Sciences et de l'Industrie	A11
Conciergerie	F8
Les Halles	E8
Hôtel des Invalides	F6
Jardin des Plantes	G9
Jardin des Tuileries	G7
Jardin du Luxembourg	G7
Le Marais	F9
Musée Carnavalet	F9
Musée de Cluny	F8
Musée d'Orsay	E7
Musée du Louvre	E7
Madeleine	D6
Montmartre	B8
Montparnasse	G6
Notre-Dame	F8
Opéra	D7
Palais de Chaillot	E4
Palais de Justice	G7
Palais Royal	E7
Panthéon	G8
Place de la Concorde	E6
Place des Vosges	F9
Place Vendôme	E7
Pont Alexandre III	E6
Pont de l'Alma	E5
Pont Neuf	F8
Sainte-Chapelle	F8
Saint-Germain-des-Prés	F7
Tour Eiffel	F4

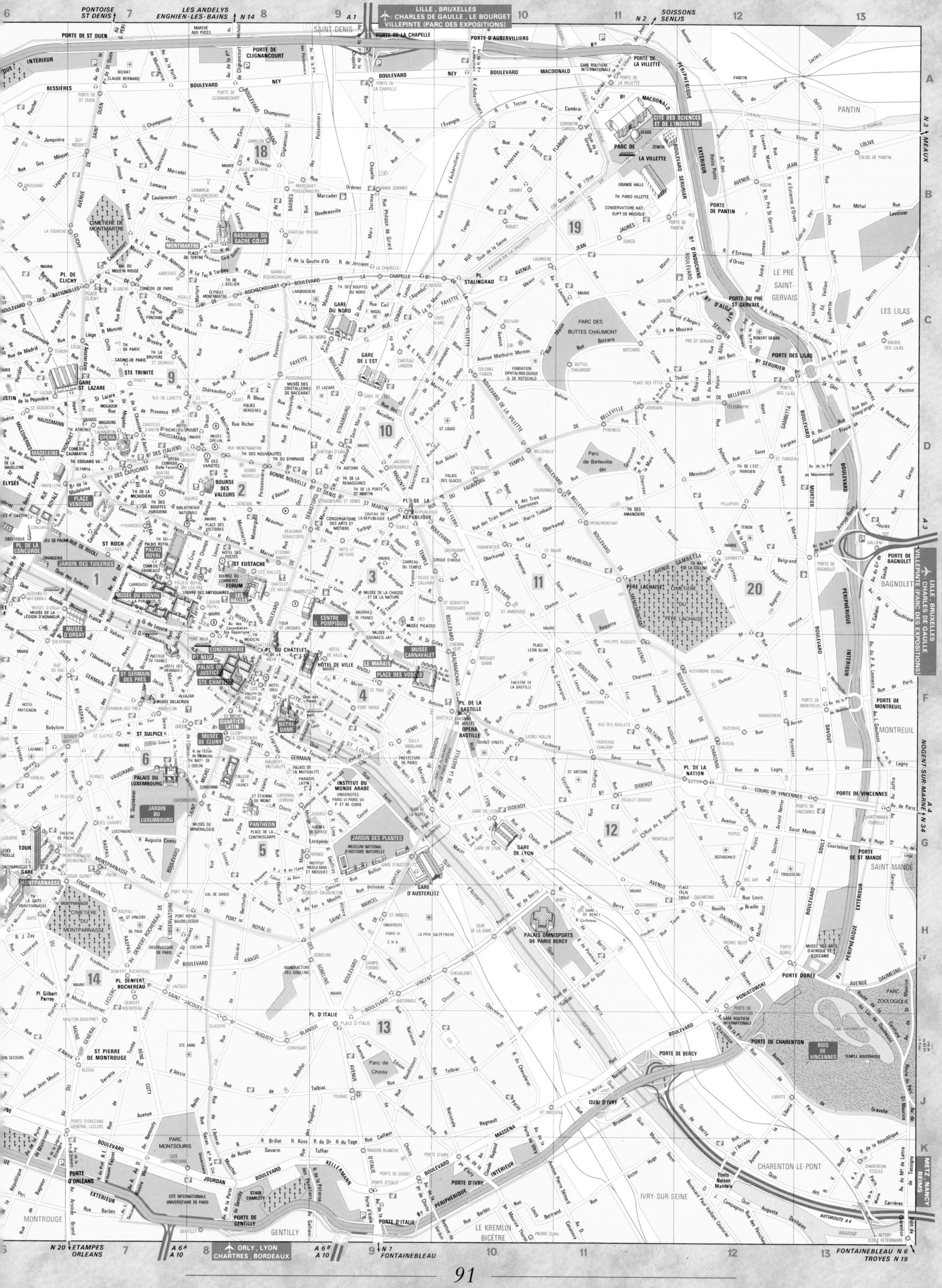

PONTOISE ST DENIS

LES ANDELYS ENGHIEN-LES-BAINS N 14

A 1 LILLE, BRUXELLES CHARLES DE GAULLE, LE BOURGET VILLEPINTE (PARC DES EXPOSITIONS)

N 2 SOISSONS SENLIS

N 3 MEAUX

A 3 LILLE, BRUXELLES CHARLES DE GAULLE VILLEPINTE (PARC DES EXPOSITIONS)

A 4 N 34 NOGENT-SUR-MARNE

METZ, NANCY REIMS

N 20 ETAMPES ORLEANS

A 6A A 10 ORLY, LYON CHARTRES, BORDEAUX A 6B A 10

N 7 FONTAINEBLEAU

FONTAINEBLEAU N 6 TROYES N 19

The magnificent Arc de Triomphe has a dual role: it commemorates the victories of Napoleon and pays tribute to the Unknown Soldier

ESSENTIAL SIGHTS

THE CITY OF PARIS, with a population of nearly 2.2 million, and the eight *départements* of the surrounding Ile de France, with over 10 million people, together provide France with a powerful engine – economic, political, administrative and cultural.

ARC DE TRIOMPHE

This, the world's largest triumphal arch, 50m high and 45m wide, was commissioned by Napoleon in 1806 to celebrate his military victories. Originally the monument was intended to be erected on the site of the Bastille and take the form of a similarly sized stone elephant squirting water from its trunk. It was also to incorporate an amphitheatre, banqueting hall and apartments. Fortunately the Emperor changed his mind.

The arch was designed by Chalgrin, and completed in 1836, only four years before Napoleon's body would be returned to Paris from St Helena to be transported on a chariot under the arch on its way to the Invalides. The main façades are adorned with colossal reliefs, of which the finest is *The Departure of the Volunteers*, which is better known as *The Marseillaise* by Rude.

In 1854 Haussmann redesigned the square surrounding the Arc, now Place Charles de Gaulle, adding a further seven avenues to the existing five.

On Armistice Day 1920 the body of the Unknown Soldier was laid in state beneath the arch to symbolise the dead of World War I, and the Eternal Flame, rekindled in a brief ceremony each evening, has burned there continuously since 1923.

EIFFEL TOWER

The prizewinning entry in a competition for a centrepiece to mark the Paris Exhibition held on the Champ de Mars in 1889, the 300-m tower designed by the engineer Gustave Eiffel was initially opposed on artistic grounds by influential figures such as Gounod, Zola, Huysmans and Maupassant. The losing entries included a giant guillotine and a mammoth lighthouse.

The tower was built in two years from 7000 tons of pig-iron and linked together by two and a half million rivets. Each of its 15,000 components is replaceable. But in spite of its overall size and weight, each of the four base pillars exerts a ground pressure no greater than that of a person sitting on a chair.

Originally intended to be a temporary structure, and to be pulled down after 20 years, the tower was saved from demolition by the invention of wireless telegraphy, for which purpose it was used during World War I. It was declared a national monument in 1964, and is still one of the tallest man-made structures in the world. The two lower stages accommodate restaurants and souvenir shops, while the platform of the third, on a clear day, offers panoramic views of the city and surrounding countryside as far away as Chartres, 72km distant.

The top of the tower is now crowned with TV antennae, which add a further 20m to its height. On a hot day the metal structure grows by another 15cm. At night a new lighting system illuminates the entire tower from within to create a dramatic golden tracery against the sky, underlining the fact the original objections to Eiffel's creation have faded with the years, and that it has come to be the best known and best loved landmark in Paris.

Long the most familiar symbol of Paris, the Eiffel Tower was originally intended to be a temporary structure when it was built in 1899

Napoleon's tomb lies in the baroque splendour of the Église du Dôme, the centrepiece of the Invalides, originally a home for wounded war veterans

PLACE DE LA CONCORDE

In spite of the crush of traffic, this is one of the world's most impressive squares, spanning 8.5 hectares. It was originally designed to provide the setting for an equestrian statue of Louis XV, unveiled in 1763. Seven years later, during a firework display to celebrate the marriage of the Dauphin and Marie-Antoinette, 133 people were crushed to death during a panic by the crowd – an ominous precursor of the revolutionary holocaust that lay ahead. A guillotine was set up here in 1793, close to the spot where Cortot's statue of Brest now stands, and more than 1100 people were executed in the renamed Place de la Révolution over the next two years, including Louis XVI, Marie-Antoinette, Charlotte Corday, the Girondins, Danton and Robespierre.

Place de la Concorde was given its present name at the end of the Reign of Terror, and the 23-m high Obelisk of Luxor, a gift from the Viceroy of Egypt to Charles X in 1829, was erected at its centre in 1836.

INVALIDES

This monumental group of buildings was commissioned by Louis XIV in 1674 to provide a home for wounded veterans, and 6000 invalid soldiers moved in on its completion two years later. Few soldiers now live here, but the military connection is retained in the form of the Musée de l'Armée, a magnificent collection of arms, armour, uniforms and banners from throughout the ages.

The impressive Église du Dôme is one of two adjoining churches in the complex. Its baroque interior houses the tomb of Napoleon, clad in red porphyry, in which his remains are contained in no fewer than six coffins, one inside the other. Others entombed here include the soldiers Turenne, Foch, Duroc, Jourdin, Grouchy, and Juin, the fortification-builder Vauban and Napoleon's son Joseph Bonaparte.

MONTMARTRE

Allegedly the site of St Denis' martyrdom in AD250 and rising 100m above the city, the Butte de Montmartre is crowned by the white towers and basilica of the Sacré Coeur (see page 95). Until the middle of the last century Montmartre was still a country village, bristling with windmills on the surface and undercut by gypsum mines. The district's picturesque charm and atmosphere, along with low rents, enticed artists, sculptors, writers and musicians to live and work here, and the heyday of bohemian Montmartre lasted until World War I.

Renoir, Dufy, Van Gogh, Matisse and Utrillo all worked here, and Picasso, Braque and Gris created Cubism in their studios at the Bateau-Lavoir. Toulouse-Lautrec immortalised the can-can dancers at the original Moulin Rouge, while the poet Apollinaire, novelist Boris Vian and illustrator André Gill were among the area's other noted residents.

Today the winding streets and peaceful, tree-lined squares retain much of their charm, but Place du Tertre, which is the hub of Montmartre, is now the preserve of tawdry souvenirs and street artists, and sadly Place Pigalle has descended from a racy vitality into outright sleaziness.

Place du Tertre (above) is in the heart of Montmartre, traditionally the artists' quarter and now a major tourist attraction

The Opéra (right), completed in 1875, remains a fitting monument to the opulence of the Second Empire

Style-conscious shoppers from all over the world descend on the stores in Paris (below right), long an international fashion centre

OPÉRA

This grandiose monument epitomises the extravagance of the Second Empire. Designed by Charles Garnier, on completion in 1875 it was the world's largest theatre. The façade is ornately decorated with columns, friezes, garlands, winged figures and busts of famous composers. The interior vestibule leads to a grand staircase of different shades of marble, with gold caryatids clasping elaborate candelabra. Although the whole building covers more than a hectare, the auditorium, resplendent in red plush and gilt, is surprisingly small, seating only 2158 people. The interior of the central dome was redecorated in 1964 by the Russian artist Chagall, producing an effect that many find inappropriate. The building contains a museum devoted to opera.

SHOPS IN PARIS

For most visitors to Paris shopping is one of the greatest delights. This is the city that gave the world the boutique, the small, specialised shop embodying the intimate nature of purchasing goods and services. Although recent years have seen the growth of large department stores and shopping centres, this legacy of the medieval trading system survives.

The world of *haute couture* and expensive fashion is still firmly based in and around the 8th *arrondissement*, while many of the antique and second-hand dealers can be found in the 6th. The bookshops of the Latin Quarter, the shoe shops of the Boulevard Saint Michel and the profusion of perfumiers around the Place de l'Opéra are other examples of this gregarious, yet competitive, approach to selling.

The redevelopment of Les Halles, Montparnasse and the district surrounding the Opéra Bastille has led to the establishment of new shopping centres filled with small boutiques, cafés and restaurants.

In Paris, simply window-shopping can be an experience in itself, since the French have elevated this form of display to a high art. And the bustling street markets in almost every *arrondissement* add their own special brand of open-air charm to buying and selling.

CHURCHES AND MUSEUMS

BASILIQUE DU SACRÉ COEUR

The white domes of the Sacré Coeur and its 80-m campanile, rising from the peak of Montmartre, are a familiar sight on the Parisian skyline. Initiated by the French government in 1873 as a reaction to the country's defeat in the Franco-Prussian War two years earlier, the basilica was built as a symbol of contrition and atonement for the 58,000 who lost their lives in the struggle.

Designed by Paul Abadie in a neo-Romanesque-Byzantine style, the church took more than 30 years to build, partly because of the difficulties of stabilising the foundations, which were unfortunately constructed on top of disused underground quarries. The material used was Château-Landon stone, which hardens and whitens with age, accounting for the brilliance of the exterior and the darker interior.

Although the Sacré Coeur was not consecrated until 1919, worshippers have maintained a constant day and night vigil of contrition before the altar since 1885, continuing even throughout the German occupation. The more secular visit for the panoramic views from the steps and the dome.

CATHÉDRALE NOTRE DAME

One of the great masterpieces of Gothic architecture, Notre Dame stands on the site of an earlier Gallo-Roman temple, dominating the skyline of central Paris with its beautiful, richly decorated façade and twin 69-m towers. Pope Alexander III laid the cathedral's foundation stone in 1163, but the building was not completed until 1330, and underwent further internal alterations during the 17th and 18th centuries.

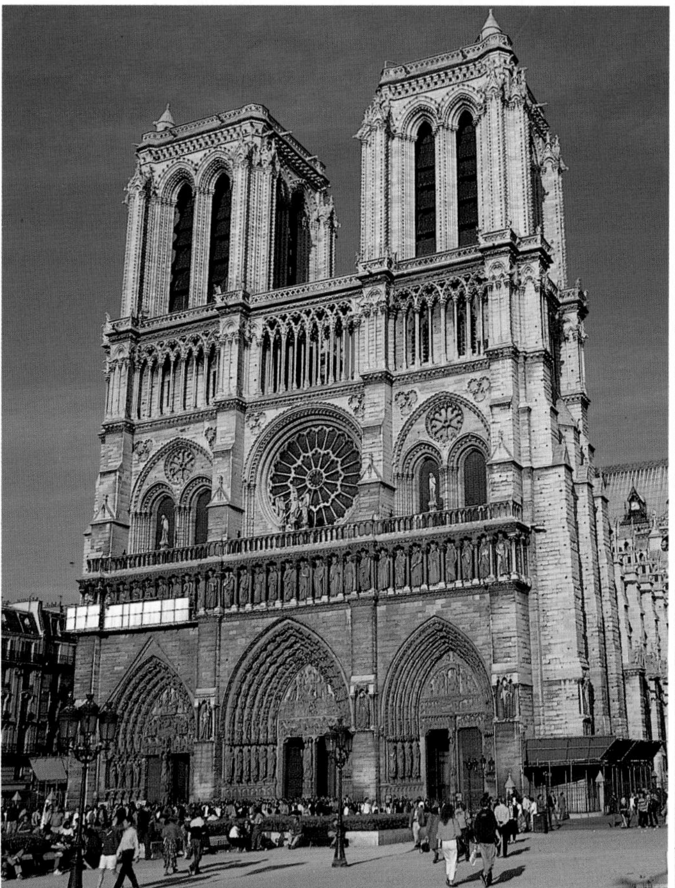

During the Revolution the statues around the portals were decapitated, orgies staged and the cathedral turned into a 'Temple of Reason'. By 1804, when Pope Pius VII was summoned from Rome to officiate at Napoleon's coronation, Notre Dame was a shambles but later in the century Viollet-le-Duc undertook its restoration. He replicated the carvings on the façade, including those of the 28 kings of Israel and Judaea and the panel representing the Last Judgement, as well adding the bestiary of gargoyles and demons that adorn the flying buttresses.

Inside the echoing building, capable of holding nearly 10,000 worshippers, the majestic walls rise in three tiers to a ribbed, vaulted ceiling 35m high. Illumination is provided by the three stained-glass rose windows, of which only the northern window retains the original 13th-century glass. The massive organ, with more than 7000 pipes, is France's largest, and is used for regular Sunday afternoon recitals.

The Sacré Coeur (above left) honours the soldiers who died in the Franco-Prussian War

Notre Dame is a supreme Gothic masterpiece (left) that was two centuries in the building

'Point Zéro' (below), in front of Notre Dame, is the point from which all road distances in France are measured

LOUVRE

This is Europe's largest royal palace, covering 18 hectares, the biggest single building in Paris and the largest museum in the Western world. The collections are divided into seven categories: Greek and Roman Antiquities, Oriental Antiquities, Egyptian Antiquities, Furniture, *Objets d'Art*, Painting and Drawing, and Sculpture.

Begun by François I, with 12 paintings looted from Italy, and added to by succeeding monarchs and Napoleon, the museum's greatest pride lies in its art collection. Leonardo da Vinci's *Mona Lisa* is a major attraction, along with other examples of his work, as are paintings by Titian, Raphael, Veronese and other Renaissance masters. Spanish masterpieces by Goya, Velázquez, Murillo and El Greco are also on show, as are paintings by pre-eminent artists of the French, Flemish, Dutch, German and English schools. Famous sculptures on display include examples of work by Michelangelo and Cellini as well as the *Venus de Milo* and the *Winged Victory of Samothrace*.

The Louvre's enormous wealth of material – more than 400,000 works of art – has meant that until recently only a small part could be on exhibition at one time. However, a massive programme of building and redevelopment has added to the museum's facilities to mark its bicentenary in 1993. The main courtyard is now graced by a 21.5-m glass-walled pyramid, designed by I.M. Pei, which serves as the central entrance to the museum and leads to new galleries. The Richelieu wing of the palace, formerly occupied by the Ministry of Finance, has recently been vacated and is now part of the museum, almost doubling the previous amount of exhibition space.

Like other great museums, the Louvre periodically rearranges its material. It also holds temporary exhibitions.

Most of the present Louvre (above) was built in 1546 as a palace for François I, who began the art collection that today makes the Louvre the world's largest museum, with over 400,000 works of art

The exposed services and vivid colours of the Centre Pompidou (above right and right) marked a decisive break with traditional museum design. The Centre combines the roles of arts centre, gallery and public library

MADELEINE

The foundation stone of this austere edifice, now dedicated to St Mary Magdalene (Marie Madeleine), was laid in 1764, but during the following 80 years the building was considered for use as a bank, banqueting hall, theatre, railway station and a temple to Napoleon's army, before finally being consecrated as a church. The façade of 52 soaring Corinthian columns is surmounted by Lemaire's relief of *The Last Judgement*, while the bronze doors carry bas-reliefs of the Ten Commandments by Triquetti. The interior, richly decorated with marble, is windowless and poorly illuminated but boasts a splendid organ once played by Saint-Saëns. It was on this that Chopin's *Funeral March* received here its début, at the composer's own memorial service in 1849.

CENTRE POMPIDOU

Inaugurated in 1977, Richard Rogers' and Renzo Piano's controversial five-storey jumble of high-tech plumbing and glass still attracts six million visitors a year. The revolutionary structure houses not only a language laboratory, cinema, music research centre, children's theatre and dance workshop, and the city's biggest public library with half a million books as well as slides and films, but also the Musée National d'Art Moderne, which is situated on the fourth floor. This, the largest art gallery of its kind in the world, features works by 20th-century artists as diverse as Picasso, Dali, Braque, Miró, Kandinsky, Matisse, Léger and Warhol in a comprehensive collection stretching from the Fauves up to the present day.

CIMETIÈRE DU PÈRE LACHAISE

Named after the Jesuit confessor of Louis XIV, whose house stood here, this is the largest and most select cemetery in Paris. The 47-hectare site was bought by the city in 1804 and the first interments were those of Molière and La Fontaine. The tomb of the country's most famous lovers, Abélard and Héloïse, was transferred here a few years later.

A detailed map showing the most famous graves is available from the custodian at the entrance. Among them are those of the writers Victor Hugo, Proust, Balzac, Beaumarchais, Sartre, Oscar Wilde and Gertrude Stein. Famous musicians buried here include Chopin, Bizet, Poulenc, Dukas and Cherubini and singers Adelina Patti, Maria Callas, Édith Piaf and American rock star Jim Morrison.

MUSÉE MARMOTTAN

This is a specially created basement gallery containing a marvellous collection of Impressionist paintings, pastels and drawings by Claude Monet, as well as works by Sisley, Renoir, Gauguin and Pissarro. Originally the collection of the 19th-century industrialist Jules Marmottan, and enlarged by his son Paul, it was bequeathed to the Institut de France in 1971. In the same building is the Wildenstein Collection of medieval miniatures.

MUSÉE RODIN

Auguste Rodin lived and worked in a ground-floor studio of this elegant Regency mansion during the last nine years of his life. It now houses a superb collection of his work and plaster casts arranged in chronological order, as well as some of his personal art collection.

Among the works on display are *The Kiss, St John the Baptist* and *The Burghers of Calais.*

MUSÉE D'ORSAY

This museum provides a chronological link between the Louvre collections and those at the Centre Pompidou. Constructed within the shell of the obsolete Gare d'Orsay, the Musée d'Orsay now provides 16,000 square metres of exhibition space on three floors.

More than 2000 paintings, 1500 sculptures, 13,000 photographs and other *objets d'art* span the years 1848 to 1914. Among these works is a remarkable collection of Impressionist masterpieces, many of which were transferred here from the Jeu de Paume. Paintings by Romantic artists such as Ingres and Delacroix, and by Degas, lead on to the Realists Daumier, Corot and Millet and the Barbizon landscape artists. The subsequent period is represented by outstanding works of Manet, Monet, Renoir, Sisley, Cézanne and Van Gogh. Also on display are paintings by post-Impressionists such as Seurat, Gauguin and Signac, and the Nabis.

Gently curving, tree-lined paths help to dispel any gloom aroused by Père Lachaise cemetery (above left). The celebrities buried here include Victor Hugo, Balzac, Oscar Wilde, Chopin and Maria Callas

The Musée d'Orsay (above), a converted railway station, is a showcase for 19th-century French art and culture

Over 200 of the painter's canvases can be seen in the Musée Picasso, including Mère et Enfant *(below) of 1907*

MUSÉE PICASSO

The 17th-century Hôtel Salé, built by the financier Aubert de Fontenay, whose fortune was based on the salt tax, now provides a home for the world's largest collection of Picasso's work. Although few of his masterpieces are here, the 203 paintings, 158 sculptures and more than 1500 drawings, along with his 30 sketchbooks, were acquired by the French government in lieu of inheritance taxes after Picasso's death in 1973.

The collection is exhibited in chronological order, with Picasso's early and late periods particularly well represented, enabling the viewer to gain an insight into the artist's development and thought processes. The exhibits also include his personal art collection, with works by Matisse, Braque, Cézanne, Renoir and Rousseau.

OUTDOOR PARIS

PARIS IS A CITY IN WHICH you can enjoy open-air pleasures for much of the year, and is best explored on foot. You can stroll the wide, tree-lined boulevards, savouring the atmosphere of the city, perhaps pausing to study some otherwise unnoticed detail on a building's façade. Or you may prefer to sit with a coffee at a pavement café and just watch the world pass by. The city's many parks and gardens offer a peaceful pause from the sounds of traffic, and some of the cobbled quais along the Seine soak up the river's tranquillity.

BATEAUX-MOUCHES

The 11-km stretch of the River Seine that passes through Paris is arguably the most beautiful length of urban waterfront in the world, and it has long provided painters with inspiration. The glass-topped *bateaux-mouches* that ply up and down the river are an ideal way to get a relaxed view of the city and its 33 graceful bridges. The Eiffel Tower, Louvre, Quai d'Orsay, Grand Palais, Institut de France, Conciergerie, and Notre Dame resplendent on the Ile de la Cité, are among the many monuments given a fresh perspective from a waterborne viewpoint. Many of the boats offer simple refreshments, while there are others that board, but at a considerable price.

BOIS DE BOULOGNE

The 900 hectares of woodland and open space of the Bois also encompass the 18th-century white villa and English-style garden of the Bagatelle, created by the Comte d'Artois in 70 days in a wager with Marie-Antoinette. The Pré Catelan is another self-contained oasis, with a magnificent copper beech whose branches have the widest span of any tree in Paris. It also contains the Shakespeare Garden, which displays the plants mentioned in the plays. The Jardin d'Acclimatation has an amusement park and zoo and, for the more energetic, boats can be hired on the Lac Inférieur. The Bois also has two racecourses: Longchamp for flat-racing and Auteuil for steeplechasing.

In the mid-17th century Louis XIV's gardener, Le Nôtre, imposed a formal design on the Jardin des Tuileries, creating the fine view along the central alley (above) and pools, one of which is now a boating pond (right)
Among the pleasures offered by the Jardin du Luxembourg are the Sunday concerts (below)

JARDIN DES TUILERIES

These 24 hectares of formal gardens, laid out by Louis XIV's gardener, Le Nôtre, are bounded by the Louvre, the Place de la Concorde and the Rue de Rivoli. But despite the nearby traffic they are an oasis of calm, studded with elegant statues of ancient gods and goddesses and allegorical figures, along with modern sculptures. On raised terraces at the western end stand the museum buildings of the Jeu de Paume and the Orangerie, while the new centre for fashion design, the Musée des Arts et de la Mode, will also occupy part of these grounds. It was through these that Louis XVI and his family made their escape from the mob in 1792.

JARDIN DU LUXEMBOURG

Situated in the heart of the Left Bank, these gardens were formally laid out in the Renaissance French style in 1612, but with Italian touches to please the owner of the adjoining palace, Marie de Médicis. Sadly neglected in the post-Revolutionary period, the gardens sank into disrepair, but a petition signed by 12,000 citizens succeeded in thwarting Baron Haussmann's intention to incorporate them into his new plan for Paris.

The Luxembourg is now one of the most popular open spaces in the city, a magnet for students from the nearby Sorbonne and for children, who sail their boats in the octagonal pond by the romantic Fontaine de Médicis. Tennis, *pétanque* and chess players have their own corners.

JARDIN DES PLANTES

Louis XIII initiated a medicinal herb plot here in 1626, but it now encompasses within its 28 hectares not only the botanical garden but also a zoo, a maze and the Muséum National d'Histoire Naturelle. The collections of wild and herbaceous plants are excellent, and in early summer the gardens make a magnificent display of colour.

The zoo was founded in the aftermath of the Revolution with the few surviving animals from Versailles – a hartebeest, a zebra, a rhinoceros and a sheepdog. During the siege of Paris in 1870-1, food shortages encouraged the city's inhabitants to try a more exotic cuisine based on the zoo's resident population. The zoo now contains large reptiles, birds and wild animals.

PLACE DES VOSGES

The oldest and possibly the most beautiful square in Paris was commissioned by Henri IV, and designed by Metezeau. Some of these 36 symmetrical red and gold brick houses linked by an arcade were originally intended to house a silk factory and its workers. But on the square's completion in 1612 all the buildings were quickly acquired by leading courtiers and senior ministers, including Cardinal Richelieu and the dramatists Molière and Corneille, and it became the capital's most fashionable address.

The central garden was originally a gravelled area used for games and spectacles, which the residents viewed from their balconies, but also for duels in which many aristocrats died. The wrought-iron railings and the fountains at the corners of the square were added in the early 19th century. The 186 lime trees, planted in 1976, are a replacement for earlier specimens but tend to obscure the impressive architecture.

The Jardin des Plantes (above) combines gardens and a zoo Place des Vosges (left) was once inhabited by figures influential in Parisian life

This café in Place des Vosges (below), benefits from an attractive setting in the heart of the restored Marais district

The Palais Royal, with its classical arcades (above), is a good place to visit antique shops or enjoy Daniel Buren's modern creation (below). His stark columns contrast dramatically with the Palais Royal itself

PLACE VENDÔME

Conceived by Louis XIV and designed by Hardouin-Mansart, this opulent octagonal square originally provided the backdrop for an equestrian statue of the Sun King. The graceful two-storey buildings, with their Corinthian pilasters and sculpted Bacchanalian masks, have recently had their limestone façades cleaned and now display all their 17th-century splendour.

The gilt statue of Louis was destroyed during the Revolution, and the heads of victims of the guillotine mounted on spikes briefly took its place. The central column commemorating Napoleon's victories in Germany was installed in 1810. It is faced by 378 spiralling sheets of bronze made from cannons captured at the Battle of Austerlitz, Napoleon's greatest victory.

PALAIS ROYAL

Built by Cardinal Richelieu in the 17th century as a private palace, the Palais Royal later passed into the hands of Philippe, Duc d'Orléans. He commissioned the architect Victor Louis to build matching terraces of apartments around the garden, with an arcade of 180 small shops and cafés. Completed in 1786, these became the setting for gaming and licentious behaviour of all kinds, and in July 1789, outside the Café de Foy, the lawyer and journalist Camille Desmoulins delivered the speech that sparked the Revolution. Today the elegant arcades are occupied by shops dealing in stamps, coins, military decorations and antiques.

The Palais Royal itself houses various government offices, while in the central courtyard there is a remarkable and controversial project by the sculptor Daniel Buren. It is based on 252 black-and-white columns, deep pools and airport lights embedded in the paving.

Night-time Paris

COME SUNSET, as befits any capital city, Paris doffs her elegant daytime garb and slips into apparel and a mood more suited to entertaining. The style and chic she presents to the world by night have long been one of the foundations of her worldwide appeal. Bedecked in the glittering jewellery of the floodlit buildings and monuments, and flashing street signs, she offers visitors and Parisians alike a dazzling choice of dining, dancing, music, theatre or cinema, cabaret or nightclub.

Cabaret and Clubs

Dinner and a glamorous floor show are one of the traditional ways for visitors to spend an evening in Paris, but it is far cheaper to skip the overpriced cafeteria-style food offered by many of the major establishments and buy a ticket just for the performance itself. Among the best-known cabarets, the Moulin Rouge has been providing its version of the can-can for more than a hundred years, while the Folies Bergère high-kicked its way into existence even earlier in 1860. The Lido still maintains its famous chorus line of 60 Bluebell Girls, amid spectacular lighting and special effects costing many millions of francs to stage. The Crazy Horse Saloon has its own extravagant theatrical production, offering a higher standard of humour and skimpier costumes.

For those who prefer to dance the night away, Paris contains a rich assortment of clubs and discos. However, a considerable number of these are open only to private members. The cocktail bar has also been enjoying a resurgence of popularity among Parisians in recent years.

Ever since the Belle Époque, Paris has retained an international reputation for the seedier side of its night-life. The area around Pigalle, with its plethora of sex shops, sleazy strip clubs and 'live' sex shows may lack sophistication and glamour, but manages by day and night to attract its fair share of adventurous, or just curious, visitors.

The Moulin Rouge (above), in Montmartre's Boulevard de Clichy, opened in 1889 and played host to cabaret stars such as Jane Avril, Yvette Guilbert and La Goulue

One of the best ways to see Paris by night is to take a trip along the Seine on a bateau-mouche

The extravagant shows staged by the Lido (left and top left), on the Champs Élysées, have made it one of Paris's best-known nightspots

Home of the can-can, the Folies Bergère (above), in Montmartre, first opened its doors in 1860

Eating outside (top right) is particularly popular on the Left Bank

Eating Out

Paris has more than 8000 restaurants and brasseries, catering for all tastes and purses, and it is beyond the scope of this book to recommend individual establishments. The French, quite rightly, take their food seriously, regarding gastronomy as one of the noble arts. Though this tradition has been undermined in recent years by the arrival of *le repas rapide*, the wide choice of eating establishments still reflects the importance Parisians attach to eating well. And while it is possible to spend a considerable sum dining at one of the noted three-star restaurants, the small *bistro du coin* and other eating places patronised by the local residents offer equally good value for money. Also, many of the cafés found in the side streets serve delicious snacks.

At night the busy street scenes of St Germain des Prés and the Boulevard Saint Michel on the Left Bank are especially popular with visitors, many of whom enjoy a late-night coffee at the Café de Flore or the Café des Deux Magots while watching the passing crowds.

Music

Paris may not be as well endowed with symphony orchestras as London or New York, but there is ample compensation in the feast of concerts and recitals held throughout the year in the city's churches and historic buildings. These are augmented during the summer months by the Festival de l'Ile de France, which presents excellent concerts in similiar settings across the whole region.

Grand opera has a new setting worthy of its title at the recently built Opéra Bastille, currently the largest auditorium of its kind in the world and capable of accommodating nearly a million concert-goers a year. The original Opéra still boasts a flamboyant setting for its own ballet and opera performances, while the Théâtre Musical de Paris caters for a wider audience at less extravagant prices.

Enthusiasts of rock music will find that most major concerts are held in one of four large venues: the Palais des Congrès, Palais Omnisports, Palais des Sports or the inflatable stadium Le Zénith in the Parc de La Villette. Smaller events take place at the Forum des Halles and the Rock'n'Roll Circus.

The French, and particularly the Parisians, have always been keen *aficionados* of jazz, and the capital has a good number of excellent clubs. Many of these can be found on the Left Bank, presenting not only fine local musicians but also a wide range of well known American and European performers.

Cinema and Theatre

The French tend to be more appreciative of film as an art form than either the British or Americans. Central Paris alone has several hundred cinemas, showing the latest international releases along with classics from the past, many of which are shown with their original English-language soundtracks. The major cinemas are to be found in the area around the Champs Élysées, along the Grand Boulevards between La Madeleine and Place de la République, and on the Left Bank.

There is no area equivalent to London's West End or New York's Broadway for live theatre but the 100 or so theatres spread across Paris offer a wide range of contemporary and period drama and music. The classic plays of Racine, Corneille and Molière still attract audiences to the Comédie Française, and typically Parisian café-theatre – a blend of satire, variety and slapstick – continues to flourish, particularly in Montmartre.

AROUND PARIS

CHARTRES

This masterpiece of medieval cathedral architecture dominates the surrounding plain of the Beauce, and its non-matching spires can be seen from 20km away. The sixth church to stand on the site, it was built over 25 years by a massive army of craftsmen and volunteers imbued with a great resurgence of religious faith, following the fire of 1194 that destroyed the cathedral's predecessor.

The speed of its construction accounts for the harmonious composition of the whole structure. This harmony is evident despite the fact that the architect was obliged to incorporate the remains of the original west front and work within the limits of the existing foundations. The central nave and choir consist of a series of stone canopies supported by tall piers and stabilised by flying buttresses that carry the weight of the vaulted roof, 37m high, out to a further set of piers, which also act as buttresses between the windows.

The 12th- and 13th-century stained-glass windows are the outstanding glories of the cathedral, with a galaxy of more than 2500 square metres of glass illuminating the interior of the building with its opalescent colours. The oldest example, and perhaps the most visually stunning, is *Notre Dame de la Belle Verrière* above the south choir. In order to grasp the delicacy of the detail and the craftsmanship involved, it is best to study the panels with binoculars.

Around the cathedral, and by the banks of the River Eure, are the streets of the old town where, outside the ramparts, the local industry of leather working was carried on. Many of the original buildings survive, along with riverside laundries, providing the foreground for some delightful views of the cathedral and giving an insight into the medieval world.

AUVERS-SUR-OISE

This small village north-west of Paris, stretching for 7km along the east bank of the River Oise, with wooded slopes rising behind, provided inspiration for the work of a small group of Impressionist painters who stayed here during the late 19th century. Although Pissarro, who lived for two years in nearby Pontoise, concentrated his attention on the surrounding countryside and its people, others, such as Charles-François Daubigny and Jules Dupré, were fascinated by the changing scenery of the river.

Dr Paul Gachet, an enthusiastic amateur painter, moved to the village in 1872 and subsequently shared his house and studio with Paul Cézanne, who painted more than 100 works while staying here. In May 1890 Vincent Van Gogh came to Auvers to place himself in Dr Gachet's care. He painted portraits of the doctor and the landlady at the Ravoux café, where he lodged, as well as three local scenes of the church, town hall and a field with crows. But in July that year, overwhelmed by his mental disorder, he shot himself while walking in the nearby countryside, and died in his room with his brother Theo at his bedside. His body lies in a simple grave in the local cemetery.

BARBIZON

Situated near Fontainebleau, south-east of Paris, this small and undistinguished village, with its long main street, became the centre for a group of mid-19th-century landscape painters. The members of the Barbizon School became identified with the village, having settled in cottages

The majestic cathedral of Chartres, seen here from the Porte Guillaume, is lent a striking appearance by its two spires in different styles

PAINTERS

The 19th century witnessed a cultural reawakening in France after the changes wrought in society by the Revolution. Nowhere was this more evident than in painting, and Paris and the Ile de France were in the vanguard of innovation and expression.

Under the *ancien régime* pictorial art had been bound to the service of the monarchs and the aristocracy, but now it sought to communicate with ordinary people and engage their interest by reflecting daily life. The Romantic painters, led by Géricault and Delacroix, were among the pioneers in this field. Their example was taken further by Camille Corot, who deserted his studio and painted the landscapes of the region and the work of the peasant farmers. His studies of tonal values and the contrasts of light and shade were followed by the work of the Auvers and Barbizon schools, and by Cézanne, Pissarro and Renoir. In their paintings naturalistic observation and atmospheric effects replaced the idealised classicism of previous centuries.

It was from this approach that Impressionism evolved, paying negligible attention to form and concentrating on the effects of light. The final break with the classical tradition came in 1863 at the famous Salon des Refusés, and the exhibition there of Édouard Manet's *Déjeuner sur l'herbe.*

The closing years of the 19th century and the Belle Époque witnessed the advent of modern art, with a prodigious development of different techniques and styles, including Pointillism, Symbolism, Fauvism, Cubism, Futurism, Dadaism and Surrealism. Paris, and particularly Montmartre and Montparnasse, became the internationally recognised art capital of the world – a position it was to retain until the outbreak of World War II.

Édouard Manet painted Déjeuner sur l'herbe *(below) in 1863. It was condemned as 'indecent' by Napoleon III and rejected by the Paris Salon. Today it enjoys the status of a masterpiece Van Gogh's memory is honoured in Auvers by a simple grave (below left) and by Ossip Zadkine's sculpture of him*

amid the surrounding woodlands of the Forêt de Fontainebleau. They were led by Théodore Rousseau, who came here in 1847 and remained until his death 20 years later, and Jean-François Millet. Both are now buried in the nearby Chailly cemetery. Their work, along with that of Diaz, Troyon, Charles Jacque and other members of the artists' community, is commemorated in the plaques affixed to almost every building in the village. An inn run by Père Ganne, where the painters gathered, now displays furniture decorated by them, as well as the work of contemporary artists. The barn used by Rousseau as a studio now houses a museum with a number of his works.

BASILIQUE ST-DENIS

This imposing Gothic cathedral housing the shrine of St Denis, the Apostle of France, as well as the tombs of royalty, rises from a grim industrial background. According to legend, the saint was executed by the Romans around AD 250 on the slopes of Montmartre but, having picked up his severed head and washed it in a nearby fountain, he walked north for several kilometres to this spot, where he finally fell and was buried by a peasant woman. The grave became a place of pilgrimage and the construction of the basilica was begun by the Abbé Suger in the 12th century. St-Denis represented a turning point in church architecture, and was a model for Chartres.

LE BOURGET

The Musée de l'Air et de l'Espace is installed in the former terminal building of this major airport north-east of Paris, where Lindbergh landed after the first successful transatlantic flight in 1927. The exhibits cover the history of manned flight from balloons and gliders to space capsules.

CHAMPS

This is one of the most distinguished houses in France, built in the first decade of the 18th century for the subsequently disgraced financier Beauvalais. Standing amid equally beautiful formal gardens 20km east of Paris, the château has a logical symmetry that is extremely pleasing to the eye.

Euro Disney is easily accessible from Paris and other parts of the Ile de France, thanks to a network of new roads. Many other Europeans are also keen fans

MAINTENON

The stone keep of this Renaissance château north of Chartres dates back to 1200, but the remainder of the tall-roofed brick structure was built 300 years later. It was purchased by Louis XIV for Madame de Maintenon, later to become his morganatic wife. She added a modest wing containing her own apartments between the gatehouse and the keep. The king also dispatched Le Nôtre to add his touch to the grounds, and he created a formal parterre and channelled the River Eure into a grand canal.

Nearby stand the remains of an aqueduct that was intended to form part of the scheme to convey water from the Eure 110km to Versailles. Between 1685 and 1688 some 30,000 soldiers and peasants were engaged in this mammoth undertaking, which was halted at the outbreak of war and never resumed.

VAUX-LE-VICOMTE

This superb 17th-century château was created by the architect Le Vau for Louis XIV's finance minister, Nicolas Fouquet. A costly extravagance that was to lead to Fouquet's downfall, its construction entailed the rasing of three villages and the employment of 18,000 workmen for five years. Standing on a raised terrace, and surrounded by a moat amid gardens landscaped by Le Nôtre, and with lavish interior decoration by Charles Le Brun, the imposing building makes an immediate and dramatic impact on the arriving visitor.

On the completion of Vaux-le-Vicomte in 1661, at a final cost of 18 million francs, Fouquet invited the whole of Louis' court to attend a dazzling celebration at the château, which lasted 14 hours and culminated in a grand firework display. But the king was furious that any subject should outshine him in this manner, and 19 days later Fouquet was arrested and sentenced to life-long incarceration in the fortress of Pignerol. The artists who had collaborated in the château's construction were all quickly commissioned by Louis to create Versailles.

EURO DISNEY

With the exception of the Channel Tunnel, Euro Disney, the first Disneyland in Europe and only the second outside the USA, is Europe's largest building project. It is scheduled to reach completion in 2017, when it will occupy more than 2000 hectares, one-fifth the size of Paris itself and only 32km from the capital. The first phase of the theme park was opened in 1992 and is linked to Paris by an express Métro line. There are also new roads from the nearby motorways.

Disney's Magic Kingdom, complete with Sleeping Beauty's castle, the re-creation of a fantasised Main Street USA and an assortment of themed rides and amusements, will all mirror their counterparts in Florida and California. The project will eventually include six luxury hotels, a Disney/MGM complex, a golf course, a man-made lake and a camp site.

Though the American cultural influence is paramount, the influences of Euro Disney's French hosts, along with those of the British and German patrons at whom its attractions are aimed, will be reflected in the completed project.

SENLIS

The whole of this ancient town, 45km north of Paris, is classified as an historic monument. Circled by the remnants of Roman walls 8m high and 4m thick, it has preserved its character of an old cathedral city with cobbled, winding streets that oblige the visitor to proceed on foot. The 12th-century Cathédrale Notre-Dame is contemporaneous with the Basilique St-Denis and was crowned in the mid-13th century with a slender 78-m spire.

During the Dark Ages the adjacent Château Royal was one of the main residences of the Merovingian and Carolingian monarchs. England's Henry V and Caroline of France were married here in 1420, but by the 18th century the building was in a state of decline and was finally demolished in the aftermath of the Revolution. However, the remains still give an impression of its former glory.

SÈVRES

The original factory producing the renowned soft-paste, gilded porcelain of Sèvres was situated at Vincennes, but moved to its present premises in 1756. Here, just to the west of Paris, it enjoyed the patronage of Louis XV and Louis XVI, and employed more than a dozen modellers and nearly a hundred painters. Advances in ceramic manufacturing techniques during the 18th century allowed the production of hard-paste ware, and the famous Sèvres blue porcelain has gained an international reputation. The factory houses a major museum of ceramics and porcelain from all over the world.

These two gilded Sèvres cups and saucers were made at the factory in Vincennes, and therefore before 1756

One of Versailles' many basins honours the Sun God, Apollo

ROYAL PALACES

VERSAILLES

Originally the site of a hunting lodge, and then a small stone and brick château built by Louis XIII, this grandiose structure, with its extensive park and adjoining town, stands as a permanent testament to his son's belief in the principles of absolute monarchy. The Sun King, who had a distaste for the French capital and its inhabitants, was spurred into commissioning the creation of Versailles by his finance minister's extravagant example in building Vaux-le-Vicomte, south-east of Paris. But Louis XIV's monumental undertaking was to cost the treasury 60 million *livres* and help to impoverish the nation.

The building was begun in 1661, under the direction of the architect Louis Le Vau. In 1678 the young Jules Hardouin-Mansart was engaged and, latterly, Robert de Cotte. The ornately decorated interior was largely the work of Charles Le Brun. The landscaping of the spacious gardens and park, which still cover 800 hectares and before the Revolution three times that area, was entrusted to André Le Nôtre. Work on the palace and its surroundings continued for 50 years, with 36,000 men and 6000 horses still labouring hard when Louis XIV moved his court and the seat of government here in 1682.

Versailles was to fulfil this crucial role for more than a century and at its peak more than 1000 members of France's nobility, accompanied by their servants, were in residence at the palace, preoccupied with the intricate etiquette and formalities that attendance on the Sun King demanded of them.

His successor, Louis XV, with his mistress, Madame de Pompadour, added further embellishments to the original grand design in the form of the rococo private royal apartments, opera house and their country retreat, the Petit Trianon. Later, Louis XVI and Marie-Antoinette disliked the atmosphere of the Court at Versailles, and took refuge from its formalities and routine in this rural mansion. Marie-Antoinette added a theatre to the building as well as creating a pretty hamlet, mirroring a counterpart at Chantilly.

Following the Revolution and the fall of the monarchy, most of the furnishings and contents of the palace complex were removed, and parts of the buildings and grounds were allowed to deteriorate. However, during the past century a comprehensive programme of restoration has given back to Versailles much of its original glory.

Fontainebleau

Less imposing than Versailles, and more subtle in its visual appeal, this beautiful Renaissance palace is largely the creation of François I. However, the mansion that preceded it had also been a royal residence since the 12th century and Louis XIII was born here. François, inspired by the architecture he had seen during his Italian campaigns, in 1528 replaced the medieval building with two main structures, decorated by pupils of Michelangelo and Guilio Romano.

Succeeding kings, and Napoleon, added other buildings, which are grouped around five courtyards. The palace, surrounded by formal gardens laid out by Le Nôtre and a thickly wooded park, is set in the heart of the Forêt de Fontainebleau.

The adjoining town, with its leafy avenues and graceful houses, exudes the charm and tranquillity that made Fontainebleau such a favourite residence of the French monarchs. The elegant frontage, with its sweeping horseshoe staircase, was the scene of Napoleon's emotional farewell to the members of his Imperial Guard after his abdication in 1814. The interior rooms on view to the public include the François I gallery with 14 Italianate frescos, the vast ballroom designed by Philibert Delorme, the royal apartments and the Napoleonic throne rooms and council chamber decorated with his emblem of the industrious bee.

Compiègne

The third of the royal palaces of France, Compiègne is very much a poor relation of Versailles and Fontainebleau. Of this group of buildings clustered around the nucleus of Charles V's medieval castle Louis XIV said 'I am accommodated as a king at Versailles, as a prince at Fontainebleau and as a peasant at Compiègne.' Nevertheless he chose to stay there 75 times during his reign.

The Galerie des Glaces, Hall of Mirrors, at Versailles

Louis XIV – The Sun King

The son of Louis XIII and Anne of Austria, Louis XIV succeeded to the French throne in 1643, at the age of five, but until 1661 was the subject of a regency under Cardinal Mazarin. On assuming power, he displayed an arrogant and unswerving belief in his own absolute authority to rule, and adapted the system of government he had inherited to suit his own personality and outlook. His motto – *Nec pluribus impar* (None his equal) – and his sun emblem exemplified this

philosophy.

The French people, weary of the internal civil disorder that had accompanied the Fronde uprising of 1648-53, accepted the tightening of his grip on the institutions of the state and his revocation in 1685 of the Edict of Nantes, which had earlier allowed a degree of religious dissent.

Under the Sun King's rule France reached a zenith of power and prestige. His patronage of the arts and industry resulted not only in the extravagant expansion of the Palace of Versailles and the purchase of the Gobelin tapestry factory, but also in the construction of many splendid new buildings in the capital, among them the Invalides, the Louvre colonnade and the Hôpital Salpêtrière.

It was to the lavish setting of Versailles and its spacious formal gardens that the king elected to transfer the Court in 1672. Here the traditionally querulous nobility were kept fully occupied in a continual round of pageantry and elaborate ceremonies, while being entertained by the music of Lully and Couperin and the comedies of Molière. But Louis' perennial preoccupation with *'La Gloire'* forced him to become involved in a series of military campaigns. While he had managed to extend France's eastern borders, these eventually proved a costly drain on the country's finances and bequeathed problems to his great-grandson, who became Louis XV on his death in 1715.

The painting (left) shows Louis XIV as the Sun in 1651.

The existing building dates from the time of Louis XV, and was designed as a summer palace by Ange-Jacques Gabriel but was unfinished at the time of the king's death. Louis XVI undertook the completion of the work, and it became his favourite residence. While the external appearance of the building has little to commend it, the rooms are light and airy, with the state apartments facing the park. The decoration and furnishings are a mix of the Louis XIV and Empire styles, since in 1810 Napoleon married the Archduchess Marie-Louise of Austria here. His nephew, the Emperor Napoleon III, with his wife, Eugénie, made it the setting for some of their most glittering weekend parties, conveying their guests, in fine weather, on excursions into the surrounding forest.

In a clearing near Rethondes, the Armistice of 1918 and the French surrender of 1940 were both signed in a railway carriage.

CHANTILLY

Chantilly comprises the 16th-century Petit Château and the 19th-century Grand Château, harmoniously linked.

The Château de Chantilly rises gracefully from the surrounding ponds, beyond which lie well-tended lawns

The former houses the library with its magnificent collection of manuscripts and breviaries gathered together by the Duc d'Aumale. The duke's family had inherited Chantilly from the powerful Condé family and in turn bequeathed Chantilly and its contents to the Institut de France at the end of the last century. The items on view include the treasured 15th-century illuminated manuscript *Les Très Riches Heures du Duc de Berry*, depicting the months of the year.

The adjacent Grand Château, completed in 1881, now displays the museum's most precious exhibits, including Raphael's *The Three Graces* and the Orléans Madonna, 40 delicate miniatures by Fouquet and the enormous pink diamond known as Le Grand Condé.

VINCENNES

Standing at the very gates of Paris, the group of buildings that make up this château occupy the site of a hunting lodge maintained by the French kings in the 12th century. Its main entrance, approached across an overgrown grassy moat, is dominated by the 51-m tower, one of nine that surround this rectangular site. The medieval keep now houses the museum of the château, which, until the transfer of the Court to Versailles, served as a royal residence. It was then occupied, in turn, by a porcelain factory, a cadet school and a small-arms factory. Napoleon converted it into an arsenal and in 1840 it was transformed into a fortress, before undergoing restoration at the behest of Napoleon III.

Fontainebleau's horseshoe-shaped staircase (below) and the François I picture gallery (right)

Vincennes' earlier historical associations also make it worthy of attention. Among those who died here were Jeanne de Navarre, Louis X, Charles IV, Charles IX, and Henry V of England, only a few weeks before he would have succeeded to the French throne.

Mata Hari was executed here in 1917, and during World War II the occupying German forces, who maintained a supply depot in the château, shot 26 Resistance members against the interior of the ramparts.

RAMBOUILLET

In some ways Rambouillet is the most unusual of the French royal residences, for it is by far surpassed in size by its accompanying offices and stables, and is triangular in shape as a result of alterations carried out by Napoleon. Originally the property of the d'Angennes family, it was initially acquired by Louis XIV in 1706 but passed into the hands of the Duc de Penthièvre, who remodelled the water gardens, before it was purchased by Louis XVI in 1783 for his hunting pursuits. To placate Marie-Antoinette, who disliked staying at the château, Louis arranged for the construction of the Laiterie de la Reine, the Queen's Dairy, in the grounds for her diversion. Nearby he also established what is now the Bergerie Nationale, the National Sheep Farm.

Rambouillet is currently used as the official summer residence of the President of France. Public access to the château is restricted when the President is not in residence there.

BURGUNDY

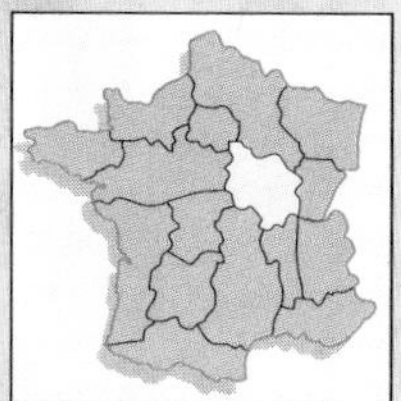

BURGUNDY IS ONE OF THE MOST underrated areas in France; thousands of travellers pass through but few take the trouble to explore it. This is a pity, for the region has much to offer. Not for nothing is it called the land of great art and good living. It offers varied scenery, picturesque towns and villages and a history as rich as that of any region in France.

It is also the home of some of the finest food and wines in the country.

For those who choose to leave the A6, Burgundy becomes a land of discovery, recalling an earlier age, as if the rush of the 20th century did not exist. Life seems to be lived at the pace of the snails that play such a part in Burgundian cuisine. The passing landscapes take a shape and form: the green becomes a range of high, tree-clad hills, an expanse of vineyards, a thick forest or meadows where white Charollais cattle graze peacefully.

What soon strikes the visitor to Burgundy is its size. It consists of Yonne, Côte-d'Or, Nièvre, and Saône-et-Loire, four *départements* that meet at Burgundy's heart, the Morvan. There is so much to see that here we can only pick out a few jewels from its many treasures and leave you to discover more. We uncover the character of the place, the mysterious mountains of the Morvan, the wine-producing slopes of the Côte-d'Or, gentle pastoral scenery and sparkling rivers and canals. We also look at the influences that helped shape Burgundy's character, such as the dukes and the monasteries of old, and we visit legacies of the latter: Dijon, Beaune, Vézelay, Fontenay and Avallon.

Sadly there is not space for places such as Mâcon, the lively wine town that was the birthplace of one of France's greatest writers, Alphonse de Lamartine; for Auxerre, capital of lower Burgundy and starting place of many boat trips along the canals, a town built in terraces on a hill overlooking the River Yonne; for ancient Autun with its numerous reminders of Roman occupation; or for Nevers, famous for its fine pottery, ducal palace and St Bernadette, who, like Sleeping Beauty, lies in a glass tomb at the Couvent St-Gildard.

Le Vigneron *can be seen in Beaune's Musée du Vin*

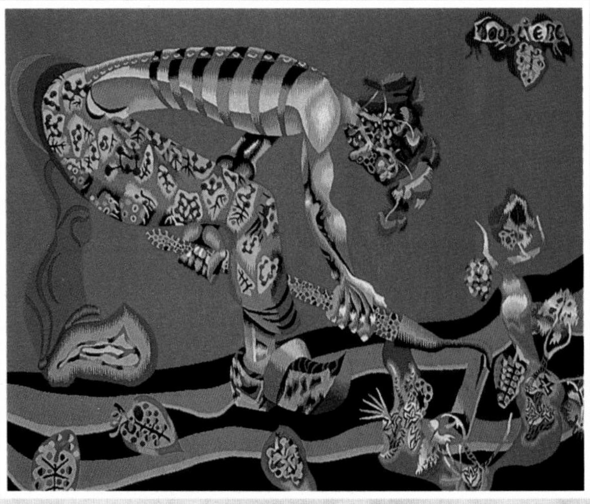

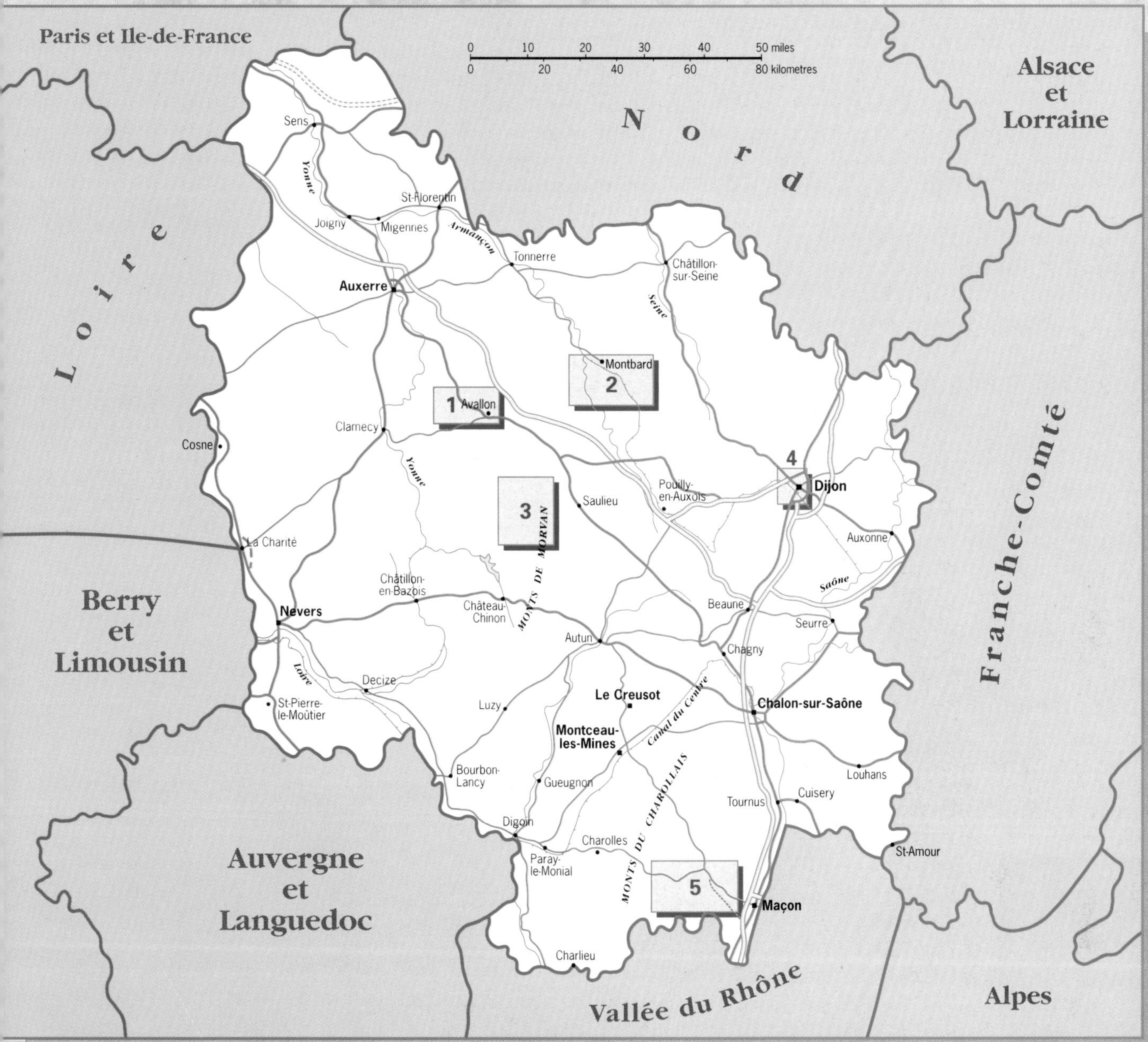
Paris et Ile-de-France
0 10 20 30 40 50 miles
0 20 40 60 80 kilometres
Alsace et Lorraine
Nord
Loire
Franche-Comté
Berry et Limousin
Auvergne et Languedoc
Vallée du Rhône
Alpes
Sens
Yonne
St-Florentin
Joigny
Migennes
Armançon
Tonnerre
Châtillon-sur-Seine
Seine
Auxerre
Montbard
2
1 Avallon
Clamecy
Cosne
Yonne
3
4
Dijon
Pouilly-en-Auxois
Saulieu
Auxonne
La Charité
Châtillon-en-Bazois
Château-Chinon
Monts du Morvan
Saône
Beaune
Nevers
Seurre
Autun
Chagny
Loire
Decize
Le Creusot
Canal du Centre
Chalon-sur-Saône
St-Pierre-le-Moûtier
Luzy
Montceau-les-Mines
Bourbon-Lancy
Gueugnon
Monts du Charollais
Louhans
Tournus
Cuisery
Digoin
Charolles
St-Amour
Paray-le-Monial
5
Maçon
Charlieu

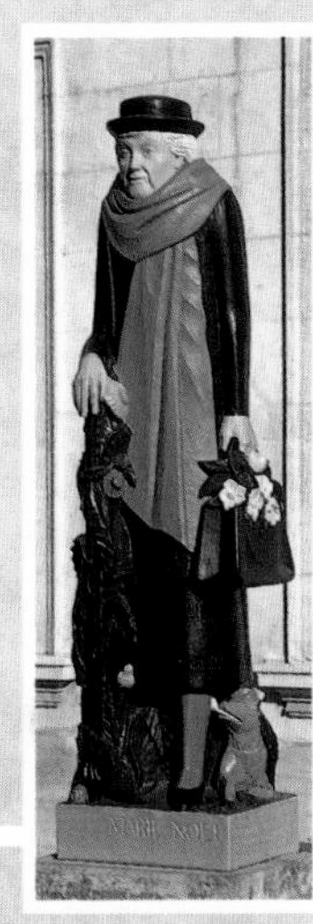

A bookshop sign (right) adds charm to pretty Noyers

BIBLIOTHEQUE

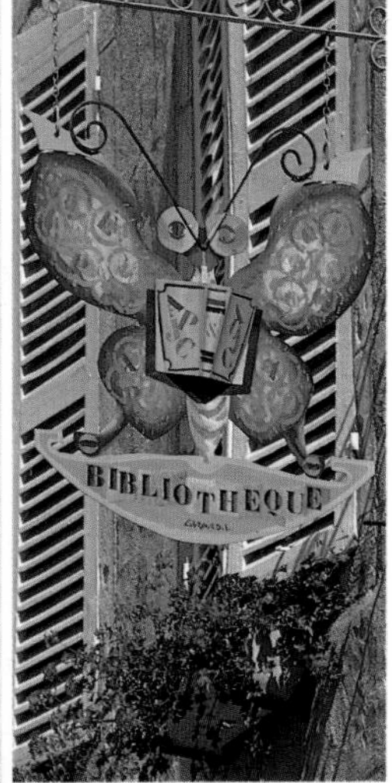

Sabot flowerpots (below) in St Amand-en-Puisaye, the centre of the local pottery industry

A statue in Auxerre by François Brochet commemorates the poetess Marie Noël (1883-1967), who was born in the city

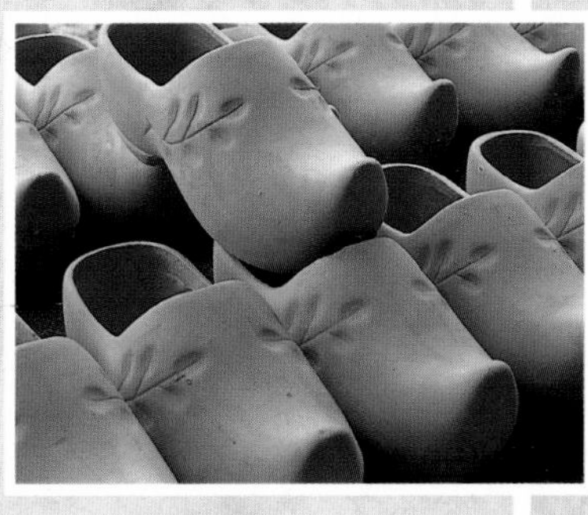

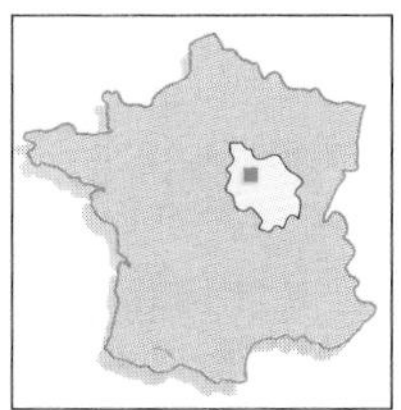

PILGRIMAGE TO VÉZELAY

FOR MORE THAN 900 YEARS pilgrims have flocked to the 'eternal hill' of Vézelay. They still come, but are now outnumbered by the tourists who want to see not just this remarkable sight but the surrounding landscape of rolling, wooded hills, fairy-tale valleys and delightful medieval towns.

Comité Départemental du Tourisme de l'Yonne
1/2, Quai de la République
89000 Auxerre
Tel: 86 52 26 27

Touring:
use Michelin sheet map 238, Centre/ Berry-Nivernais

CUISINE OF BURGUNDY

Burgundy has been described as a gastronomic paradise. Favourites such as *boeuf bourguignon*, a beef stew cooked in red wine, and *coq au vin*, chicken in red wine, are well known as main courses, but there are many other lesser known dishes that together make an attractive menu.

Jambon persillé, ham seasoned in parsley and a white-wine jelly, is a traditional starter, as are snails cooked in their shells. In winter, cabbage soup is a tasty warmer. Local cheeses are not well known outside Burgundy, but ones to look out for include Époisses, Cîteaux and St Florentin.

The façade of St-Lazare in Avallon displays a wealth of carved detail

Avallon

Occupying a picturesque position on a granite promontory overlooking the wooded Vallée du Cousin, Avallon is a charming town. The fact that the busy N6 passes through it is hardly noticed, for the town's main area of interest lies to the south of the road and is contained within the old fortifications, parts of which date back to the early 15th century.

The old town is divided in two by the main street, the Grande-Rue Aristide-Briand. This leads from Place Vauban, with its statue of the famous local military engineer, the Marquis de Vauban, to the Promenade de la Petite Porte, a terrace of lime trees high above the Cousin, from where visitors can walk around the ramparts. The Grande-Rue, cobbled and lined by several 16th- and 17th-century mansions, some embellished with turrets, passes under the famous clock tower, a main feature of the town since 1456, and in front of the mainly 11th-century Église St-Lazare. Opposite the church is an interesting museum containing Gallo-Roman remains from archaeological sites in the area.

Manoir du Chastenay

This manor house, dating from the mid-16th century, is almost hidden away in the pretty hamlet of Val-Sainte-Marie, just off the N6 in the Cure valley 3km north of St Moré. Behind high walls it displays a number of Renaissance features such as an hexagonal tower, mullioned windows and a richly sculpted portal and dormers. Among the treasures inside is a 14th-century polyptych portraying the story of Joseph.

Montréal

Like Avallon, Montréal shelters behind walls, perched on a hill. Narrow streets wind up from the lower gate and eventually pass through the upper gate, which also serves as a bell tower, to the 12th-century Église Notre-Dame.

Apart from the views from the terrace, the church is quite unremarkable from the

Vézelay is blessed with an attractive hillside setting overlooking vineyards

outside, but it is well worth a look inside for its oak stalls, elaborately carved in 1526 and depicting biblical scenes. Displaying some humour, the two brothers who carried out the work have also portrayed themselves enjoying some wine.

The chief glory of Montréal's church is its 26 carved oak stalls

St Père

Lying beneath the famous hill of Vézelay, the village of St Père has attractions of its own. Among them are the Église Notre-Dame with its graceful spire and delicately worked porch. Next to the church is the Musée Archéologique Régional, which includes exhibits unearthed at the excavations of the spring-fed Gallo-Roman baths at nearby Fontaines Salées.

Vallée du Cousin

Skirting Avallon's rocky promontory on the south side the River Cousin has created a beautiful verdant valley between the villages of Méluzien and Pontaubert. The narrow D427 follows the river's winding course past a succession of pretty sights including several old water-mills, two of them now converted to comfortable hotels.

Vézelay

A jewel of Burgundy, Vézelay sprawls up the side of a hill looking out over the hills and valleys of the Parc Naturel Régional du Morvan and surmounted by the Basilique Ste-Madeleine. One of the great pilgrimage churches of France and visible from some distance, Ste-Madeleine was one of the four departure points for the pilgrim trail to Santiago de Compostela in the Middle Ages and is still the scene of a pilgrimage every 22 July. It is best to leave the car at the entrance to the village and then follow the route of the pilgrims on foot up the steep and winding Grande-Rue.

Built in the 12th century, the basilica fell into ruin after the Revolution of 1789, but was restored some 50 years later by the controversial architect Viollet-le-Duc. Unusual use has been made of alternate light and dark stones in the arches of the nave, and with its remarkable purity of line and lightness the basilica is a wonderful monument to Romanesque art.

VIOLLET-LE-DUC

Eugène Viollet-le-Duc, the controversial 19th-century architect who carried out the restoration of the Basilique Ste-Madeleine in Vézelay, made quite a name for himself restoring medieval buildings. He worked on churches throughout Burgundy, notably at Auxerre, Beaune, Clamecy, Dijon, Semur-en-Auxois and St Père, as well as the Synodal Palace in Sens and the Gallo-Roman Porte St-André in Autun.

Vézelay was his greatest task, undertaken when he was less than 30 years old, but many people felt that his work there and elsewhere spoiled the original designs. Yet but for him many of Burgundy's treasures would have fallen into ruin.

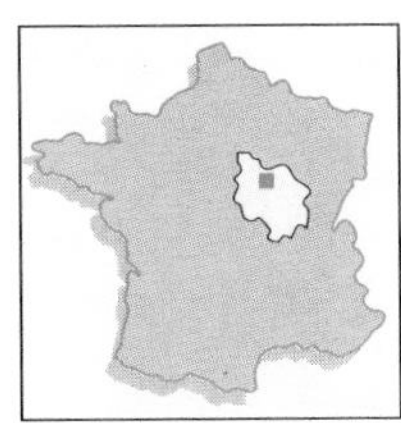

HISTORY IN THE AUXOIS

PICTURESQUE SMALL TOWNS AND VILLAGES set amid a variety of landscapes from wooded hills to fertile plateaux make this area a delight for leisurely touring. Here can be found a little of everything, from a fortified town that could almost be a film set, via a château and abbeys, to the site of Rome's final defeat of Gaul. The Auxois encapsulates the story of Burgundy.

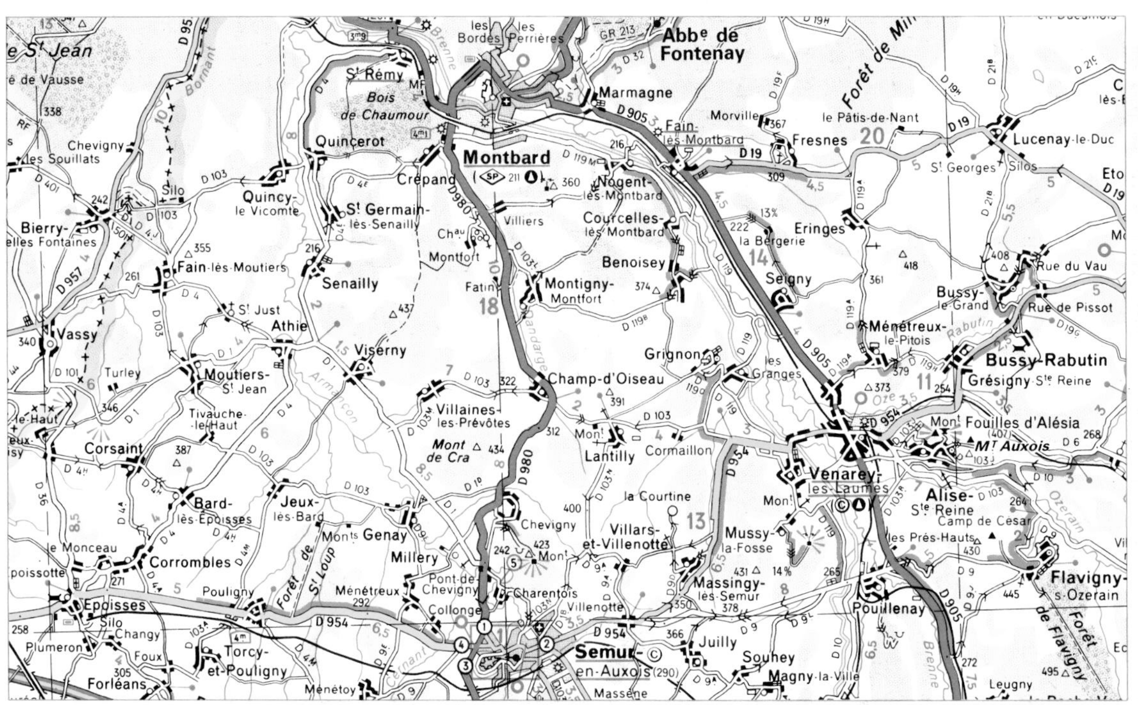

Comité Départemental du Tourisme de la Côte-d'Or
Hôtel du Département - BP 1601
21035 Dijon Cedex
Tel: 80 63 66 00

Touring:
use Michelin sheet map 243, Bourgogne/ Franche-Comté

Alise-Ste Reine

A pretty enough village nestling beneath Mont Auxois, Alise-Ste Reine is best known for its surroundings, for it was here that Julius Caesar finally defeated Gaul in 52BC. On the summit of the hill are the excavations of Alésia, the camp where the Gallic army held out against the Romans for six weeks before surrendering. Later the camp became a Roman town and many artefacts discovered at the site are now on display in the Musée Alésia in the village.

The second part of the village's name recalls a young Christian woman who was beheaded there by the Romans in the 3rd century. Every September pilgrims visit the village to commemorate the event.

Abbaye de Fontenay

The former Abbey of Fontenay, hidden away in a leafy valley not far from Montbard, is the oldest surviving Cistercian abbey in France. Founded in 1118, it was one of the most prosperous abbeys in France until the Wars of Religion (1562-98) brought about its decline. It was sold during the Revolution and until the early 20th century served as a paper mill for the Montgolfier family.

Now restored almost to its original state, the abbey gives a wonderful impression of what life was like for the 300 or so monks who lived there. A guided tour takes visitors to the church, cloisters, dormitory, bakery, the scriptorium and the huge forge.

Château de Bussy-Rabutin

This lovely moated 17th-century château, 4km north of Alise-Ste Reine, is largely the work of Roger de Rabutin, Comte de Bussy, who spent much of his life in exile there. Born in 1618, he was a soldier before turning to writing, which became more and more scurrilous in content until he was sent to the Bastille for ridiculing the *amours* of Louis XIV. While exiled at Bussy-Rabutin by royal order, he spent much time decorating the interior of the château.

BALLOONING

Although the Montgolfier family's connections with Burgundy are more ecclesiastical than avionic, the region nevertheless has strong links with their most famous invention, hot-air ballooning.

Ballooning is big in Burgundy and when conditions are right the skies can often be seen dotted with colourful shapes drifting lazily over the countryside.

Ever since the first flight by the Montgolfier brothers in 1783, ballooning has captured the imagination. Today numerous companies offer balloon flights over Burgundy, details of which can be obtained from local tourist offices. Flights are usually available all year round, though in summer launches take place early in the morning or late in the afternoon to avoid thermal currents.

Perhaps the most delightful view of Semur-en-Auxois, the main town of the Auxois region, is that from the Pont Joly (far left). Among the town's many solid medieval buildings is the tower of the former dungeons (left)

Flavigny's machicolated Porte du Bourg dates from the 15th century. The monks of the Benedictine abbey have a chapel and a refectory next to the gateway

Époisses

A quiet village 13km west of Semur-en-Auxois, Époisses was in the 6th century the seat of Burgundian power. The present château, grouped around a courtyard in lovely grounds on the edge of the village, dates mainly from the 14th to 18th centuries. The village is also known for its cheese, which is produced at a *fromagerie* in Place du Champ-de-Foire.

Flavigny-sur-Ozerain

Occupying a hilltop 16km east of Semur-en-Auxois, Flavigny is a fine example of a medieval fortified town. For a brief period 400 years ago it was even the capital of Burgundy. A mix of small houses and rather grander mansions, some with turrets, others with Renaissance façades, can be found within its walls. Many have undergone recent restoration.

Flavigny has also been, and still is, a religious centre. St Reine, martyred at Alise, was buried here in 864. The abbey, founded in the 8th century, is now a sweet factory, making the aniseed bon-bons for which Flavigny is known all over France.

Montbard

But for Georges-Louis Leclerc, Comte de Buffon, Montbard could well be seen as just a small industrial town. However, Buffon, who was born in the town in 1707, set about the work for which he is famed, the *Histoire Naturelle*, which ran to 36 volumes and took him 40 years to complete. At the same time he created the Parc Buffon, by demolishing most of the remains of Montbard's castle and landscaping the terraces with trees and flowers. He also set up an iron forge beside the River Brenne, just north of the town. No longer operational, it is open to visitors. Buffon died in Paris in 1788 and is buried in the Église St-Urse in Montbard beside the park he created.

Semur-en-Auxois

Almost encircled by a loop of the River Armançon, the fortified town of Semur is in one of the most attractive settings in Burgundy. With the four 14th-century round towers of its keep rising sheer from a rose-coloured granite spur, its position appears impregnable, though a huge crack inflicted on the Orle d'Or tower in 1589 shows that vigorous assaults occurred.

Overlooking the town is the 13th-century Église Notre-Dame, which has some interesting stained-glass windows and statues, including a 15th-century polychrome of the Entombment.

CANALS

An attractive feature of the Burgundy landscape is the network of canals that link the Seine, Saône and Loire. The main ones are the Canal de Bourgogne and the Canal du Nivernais, both completed towards the middle of the 19th century to make barge navigation possible from the Channel to the Mediterranean, but there are several minor ones too, some much older.

While commercial traffic has diminished considerably with the growth of the railways and roads, the canals are still used extensively. These days many holidaymakers hire comfortable and well-equipped cabin cruisers for leisurely cruises along the canals through the beautiful Burgundian countryside.

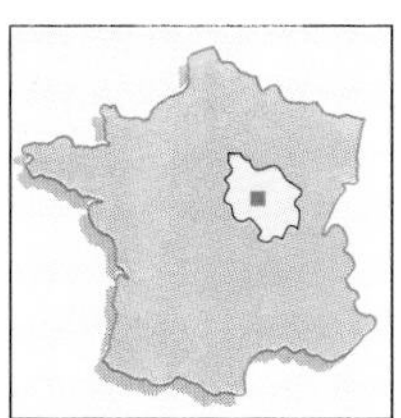

THE MORVAN NATURE PARK

ONE OF FRANCE'S LARGEST REGIONAL NATURE PARKS, the Morvan is a strange region of gentle wilderness, with lakes, hills and thick forests that conceal its scattered communities from the outside world. As such it served the local population well during the war and there are several reminders of the Resistance groups who operated here.

Comité Départemental du Tourisme de la Nièvre
3, Rue du sort
58000 Nevers
Tel: 86 36 39 80

Touring:
use Michelin sheet map 238, Centre/ Berry-Nivernais and Michelin sheet map 243, Bourgogne/ Franche-Comté

The candid Latin inscription above the door of the Abbaye de la Pierre-qui-Vire reads, 'I am the entrance'

Abbaye de la Pierre-qui-Vire

This abbey, hidden away among the woods and hills of the Morvan, was founded as recently as 1850 at the site of the Pierre-qui-Vire (Stone that Turns), a large granite dolmen that, according to legend, could be moved by one hand. The stone is still there in the woods, but is now surmounted by a statue of the Virgin. In accordance with the strict Benedictine laws of the abbey, most of it is not open to the public, though its Gothic-style church, which has recently undergone renovation, is. An exhibition room gives the visitor an idea of how the monks live. There are pleasant walks through the woods around the abbey.

Barrage Pannesière-Chaumard

This dam holds back the waters of the largest lake in the Morvan, the Lac de Pannesière, 7.5km long and 2.5km wide. Just below the dam a small hydroelectric power station operated by just two men produces 18 million kw per year. The lake, though less frequented than some of the other local waters, is in an attractive setting in wooded hills and is popular with anglers, especially fishing for pike and perch, and also lovers of sailing and canoeing. From the road along the top of the dam there are fine views across the lake.

Gouloux

This is a straggling village in an attractive area overlooking the valley formed by the Rivers Bridier, Caillot and Cure. A small family business makes clogs by hand from birch, beech or alder, for sale all over France, and a shop sells completed clogs to passers-by.

A short distance outside the village, close to where the D977 *bis* crosses the Cure, a footpath leads through woods to the Saut de Gouloux, a beautiful waterfall with a 10-m drop. There are also the ruins of an old water-mill.

A secluded area in the heart of Burgundy, the Morvan is dotted with dairy farms set among dense, hilly woodland

Ancient sarcophagi are strewn around the church of St-Georges in Quarré-les-Tombes, their significance still not fully understood

Quarré-les-Tombes

There is an air of mystery about Quarré-les-Tombes. Named after the large number of stone sarcophagi in the area, the village is thought to have been involved in their construction in the late 7th to early 8th centuries. Another, less likely, theory is that the town was the site of an ancient necropolis. Only about 100 sarcophagi remain and these are laid out around the Église St-Georges, which looks across the village's vast square. At the far end of the square is a memorial to members of the Resistance.

Lac des Settons

Dating from 1861, this reservoir was originally built to improve logging operations on the River Cure and to keep the Cure and Yonne navigable in times of drought. It is now a popular beauty spot and holiday centre and several communities have sprung up around the wooded shores. The biggest is Les Settons at the northern end, which consists mainly of hotels, restaurants, holiday homes and camp sites, but there are smaller centres at Les Branlasses and Chevigny. It is possible to drive right round the reservoir and there are several waymarked footpaths through the pine woods. Fishing is a prime attraction and other water activities are well catered for too.

The tranquillity of the Lac des Settons at sunset contrasts with the excitement generated by the regattas held here during the summer

Montsauche-les-Settons

Situated at an altitude of 650m, Montsauche is the highest village in the Morvan. During World War II its inhabitants provided aid and supplies for members of the Resistance living in the forest, until the Germans destroyed it in 1944. Rebuilt after the liberation, Montsauche is an ideal base for visiting the Morvan.

Roche de la Pérouse

Named after an 18th-century French explorer who, with his crew, was killed by Pacific islanders in 1788, this rocky promontory rises above the forest north of Dun-les-Places. It offers an extensive panorama south across the gorge of the River Cure.

St Brisson

A small, quiet, grey village, St Brisson is better known as the home of the Maison du Parc, the visitor centre for the Parc Régional du Morvan. Located at the Château de St Brisson beside the Étang Toureau, a haven for wildfowl just outside the village, the centre offers, as well as details about the park, a herb garden, an arboretum, a deer park, and a picnic area. The château is also home to the Musée de la Résistance en Morvan.

Resistance Groups

Because of its isolation and the difficult nature of the countryside, the Morvan became a stronghold of the Resistance during World War II. Between 1942 and 1944 some 15 groups operating from mountain refuges caused havoc among the occupying German forces, carrying out ambushes, capturing and destroying enemy equipment and aiding British agents parachuted in under cover of darkness.

The groups' success was such that towards the end of the war the increasingly frustrated Germans carried out reprisals in the region, including the destruction of villages. Numerous roadside memorials stand as witness to the high number of executions.

Religious Life

THE 9TH CENTURY WAS A TIME of great turmoil and instability in Europe. Barbarian hordes swept across the continent, bringing death and destruction, and as a result there was a resurgence of religious life. Benedictine law, the foundations of which had been laid by Benedict in Italy 300 years earlier, slowly spread northwards and by the late 9th century had reached France, establishing itself first of all in Burgundy.

The abbey at Charlieu (just outside Burgundy's present borders) was founded in 871 and seven years later came Vézelay, but it was Cluny, founded in 910, that became the real cradle of the Benedictine order in France. By the beginning of the 12th century Cluny was powerful and extremely prosperous, with 1450 foundations across Europe and more than 10,000 monks under its authority.

But some thought the Cluniac order, with its taste for rich decorations, had moved too far from the spirit of poverty and prayer that the Benedictine ideal upheld, and in 1098 a breakaway order, the Cistercian, was founded at Cîteaux. Under the guidance of St Bernard, who was extremely critical of Cluny's extravagance and was considered by many to be Christianity's true spiritual leader, the Cistercian order's influence spread far and wide.

Both the Cluniac and Cistercian orders flourished until the late Middle Ages, but the Wars of Religion (1562-98) caused great devastation and many abbeys and monasteries went into decline. For some the final ignominious end came with the Revolution in 1789.

In the Middle Ages abbeys were renowned seats of learning (above)

Daughters of Cluny

The priory, with its fine church, at La Charité-sur-Loire was built in the late 11th century and for a time this was the largest church in France after Cluny. Known as the 'eldest daughter of Cluny', and despite having suffered much damage over the centuries, it is a very good example of Romanesque architecture.

Started at about the time La Charité was completed, the Basilique du Sacré-Coeur at Paray-le-Monial is reflected beautifully in the still waters of the River Bourbince. A close

The secluded Cistercian abbey at Fontenay (below) was founded in 1118 by St Bernard

Great Cluny

Little remains of the great abbey at Cluny, but in spite of the senseless vandalism of the Revolution a visit today will give some idea of its extent. In its heyday it was the largest church, until St Peter's in Rome was built, in the whole of the Christian world.

Cluny was also a seat of great learning, a kind of university, and many Popes of the Middle Ages spent their early years there. Its influence, religious, intellectual and architectural, spread rapidly and new abbeys and churches were modelled on the original.

La Charité-sur-Loire's abbey church (above) is a fine example of the Romanesque style

The Clocher l'Eau Bénite (left) graces Cluny's magnificent abbey

copy of the abbey church at Cluny though on a smaller scale, this is the place to visit if it proves too difficult to imagine the original splendour of Cluny. The cult of the Sacred Heart was established here in the 17th century and Paray is now the most popular pilgrimage centre in France after Lourdes.

The pressures of Cluny took their toll on monks there and a few kilometres from the abbey, at Berzé-la-Ville, St Hugues, who was abbot of Cluny for many years, founded a small priory where they could rest.

Of the original buildings only the Chapelle des Moines still exists, the priory buildings themselves having been rebuilt in the 18th century.

THE CISTERCIANS

Like Cluny, the original abbey at Cîteaux is in ruins, but at the end of the 19th century the Cistercians returned to modern buildings. Today some 50 monks live there in simple self-sufficiency, their days of work and prayer starting at 3.30 a.m. and ending at 8 p.m. Once the owner of the vineyard at nearby Clos de Vougeot, Cîteaux today makes one concession to the good life: producing a fine cheese bearing the same name.

While the Cistercian influence was more widespread on a European scale, in Burgundy the Cluniac order was more successful. Even so, the finest abbey still standing in Burgundy belongs to the Cistercians: the Abbaye de Fontenay.

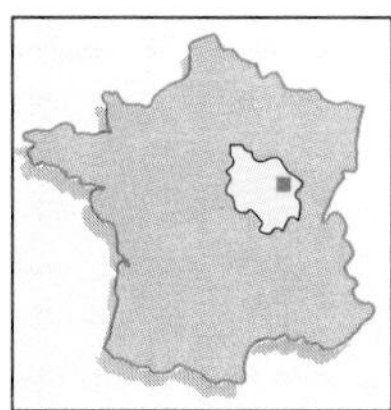

Along the Côte-d'Or

EXTENDING ALONG A RIDGE OF HILLS from Dijon to Chagny, the Côte-d'Or is one of the most famous wine-producing areas in France. From the N74, sign after sign leads through seemingly never-ending vineyards to tiny villages with huge reputations for their wine. But along the way there are many other places to explore, as well as treasures from earlier times to discover.

Comité Départemental du Tourisme de la Côte-d'Or
Hôtel du Département - BP 1601
21035 Dijon Cedex
Tel: 80 63 66 00

Touring:
use Michelin sheet map 916, Francia

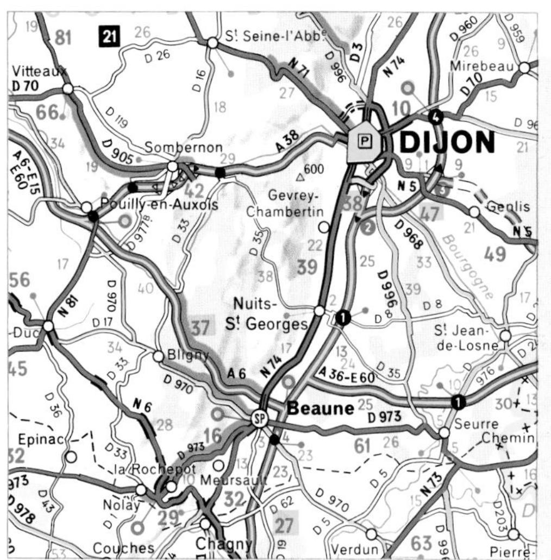

Winged angels guard the final resting place of Philip the Bold, Duke of Burgundy from 1364 to 1404, in Dijon's ducal palace

Beaune

City of wine and tourism, Beaune is a must for any visitor to Burgundy. Still enclosed with medieval walls, it contains a wealth of treasures, the most outstanding of which is the Hôtel-Dieu.

Founded in 1443 by Nicolas Rolin, chancellor to the Duke of Burgundy, the Hôtel-Dieu was built as a hospital for the poor, a function it fulfilled for more than 500 years. Visitors can see the paupers' ward, the chapel, the dispensary and the museum where a 15th-century masterpiece is exhibited, a triptych by Roger van der Weyden depicting the Last Judgement. But best of all, and symbolising Burgundy for many, is the Cour d'Honneur, the cobbled inner courtyard overlooked by a timber gallery and roofs of colourful varnished tiles.

Beaune, whose connections with wine go back 2000 years, is famous for its prestigious wine auctions held in November. Worth a visit is the Musée du Vin de Bourgogne in the former palace of the dukes of Burgundy, for it gives an insight into the history of wine production along the Côte-d'Or.

Wine pitcher on show in Beaune's fascinating Musée du Vin de Bourgogne

Clos de Vougeot

The enclosed vineyard of Clos de Vougeot, 5km north of Nuits-St-Georges, has a history going back to the 12th century, when it was founded by monks from the abbey of Cîteaux. More recent is the picturesque château, which dates from the Renaissance and appears to float like a great ship on a sea of vines. The château is now owned by the Confrérie des Chevaliers du Tastevin, a society pledged to uphold the quality of Burgundian wine. There are regular guided tours of the splendid cellars and chambers, and among the sights are four huge medieval winepresses made of oak. The vineyard itself, which each year produces around 200,000 bottles of one of the finest red wines in the world, is divided among about 80 owners.

Dijon

Burgundy's capital old and new, Dijon grew in importance once chosen by the early dukes as their seat. Today's lively city, famed for its gastronomy, centres on the former ducal palace, the Palais des Ducs et des États de Bourgogne, most of which was rebuilt in the 18th century and now houses the town hall and Musée des Beaux-Arts,

Dukes of Burgundy

Created a duchy in the Middle Ages, Burgundy acquired great wealth and possessions during the reign of the Valois dukes between 1363 and 1477.

When Philip the Bold became the first Valois duke, the duchy was smaller than today's province, but by marrying Margaret of Flanders he took over large tracts of land, including Flanders and Artois. He also made use of his access to Flemish painters, and Dijon, the dukes' capital, became a magnificent city of art.

Philip's son John the Fearless was not so successful. He often quarrelled with the king and was murdered in 1419 by supporters of the Crown. The Hundred Years War was raging at the time, and John's death led his successor Philip the Good to side with the English. It was

After five and a half centuries the Hôtel-Dieu in Beaune remains in excellent condition, a gem of Burgundian-Flemish architecture

he who sold the captured Joan of Arc to them.

With the Treaty of Arras in 1435, Philip made his peace with the king, as a result acquiring even more land. Burgundy now included much of Holland, Belgium, Luxemburg and northern France, and Philip lived like a king. In 1467 this massive inheritance fell to Charles the Bold, who immediately set out to achieve even more. Successful at first, he later suffered a string of defeats in battle and was killed at Nancy in 1477. With his death the Valois dynasty ended and Burgundy returned to the Crown.

one of the finest museums in France. It contains a wealth of paintings and sculptures and two dazzling tombs. The Musée Magnin specialises in lesser-known 16th-19th-century French artists.

In the pedestrian streets around the palace, notably the Rue des Forges, the Rue de la Chouette and the Place François Rude, are several fine medieval and Renaissance houses, while in the Place de la Libération is a crescent of elegant arcaded 17th-century houses. Among the churches worth seeing is Notre-Dame with its incredible rows of gargoyles and Jacquemart clock tower, St-Michel, a mixture of Gothic and Renaissance styles, and the cathedral, St-Bénigne, which was built in the Gothic style on the site of a Romanesque church. The crypt of the original church survives, full of pillars and superb sculptured capitals.

Nolay

Situated at the southern end of the Côte-d'Or, Nolay is a charming little town of narrow streets and half-timbered houses radiating from an attractive central ensemble around the Place Monge comprising the much rebuilt Église St-Martin with its attractive bell tower, the half-timbered Auberge du Centre and the 14th-century chestnut-framed market hall.

Nuits-St-Georges

The reputation of the wines of Nuits-St-Georges has been made over the last 1000 years and was given special impetus in 1680 when Louis XIV's doctor advised the king to drink only Nuits-St-Georges to cure an ailment. As a result the whole court wanted to drink it.

The town itself, on the busy N74, is attractive, with its pedestrianised main street, ivy-covered bell tower and St-Symphorien, one of the Côte-d'Or's most beautiful churches. Although it was built towards the end of the 13th century, this church is nevertheless a perfect example of the Romanesque style. The museum contains finds from the Gallo-Roman site of Les Bolards, south-east of the town.

La Rochepot

A small village not far from Nolay, La Rochepot is best known for its château, whose pepper-pot towers and glistening Burgundian tiled roof rise from a wooded hill on a rocky promontory above the village. In a state of ruin after the Revolution, it was restored earlier this century by Sadi Carnot, son of a former President of France. Tours of the interior – to gain entry at the drawbridge you must knock three times at the courtyard gate – take visitors to the dining room, guard-room, Captain's Room, kitchen and chapel.

Dijon Mustard

Dijon mustard goes back, like so much of Burgundy's history, to the 14th century, when Philip the Bold was given some by his wife Margaret as a gift from Flanders. Henceforth it became very fashionable and many tried their hand at making it.

However, the mustard's quality varied and in the 19th century the Dijon Academy laid down a standard. Even today the name Moutarde de Dijon is not protected by patent and producers in other parts of the world use it. The mustard's strong, spicy flavour comes from crushing the seeds of black or brown mustard and emulsifying them in verjuice, an immature wine obtained from unripe grapes.

The castle at La Rochepot was extensively restored in the present century

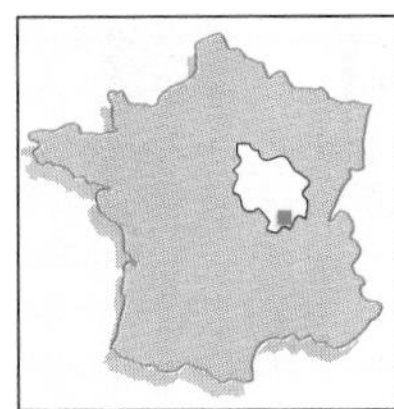

BETWEEN CHAROLLES AND MÂCON

THIS IS AN AREA OF GENTLE AND ATTRACTIVE SCENERY, with here and there a high point offering a panoramic view. Wine plays a significant role in the east, around the Mâconnais, although some outstanding natural features lend drama to the tranquil scene. But without a doubt it is the ancient religious centre of Cluny that takes centre stage.

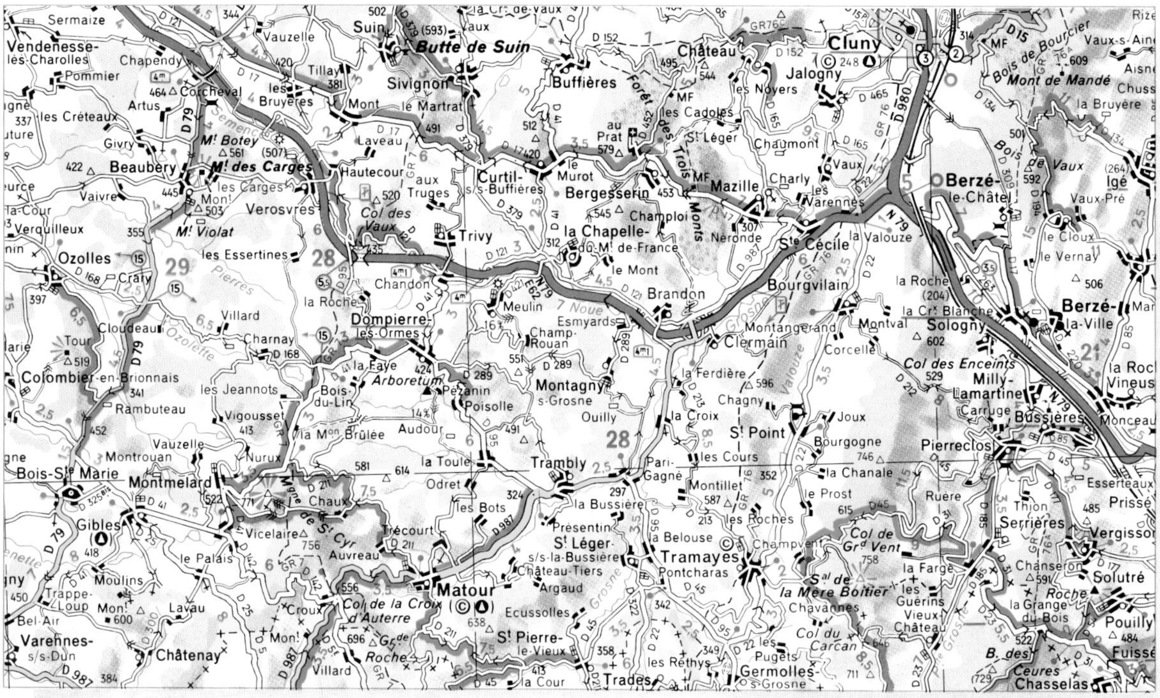

CHAROLLAIS CATTLE

Very much a part of the Burgundy countryside are the distinctive white or cream Charollais cattle, first bred at the Château de Chaumont south of Oyé in the mid-18th century.

Several other distinctive features, including a wide muzzle, short neck and great strength, mark the Charollais, but it is best known for the quality and tenderness of its exceptionally lean meat. The top breed in France for beef production, the Charollais numbers over three million head. They are exported to 68 countries worldwide, including well-known beef-rearing areas in South America and the USA.

Association Départementale de Tourisme
Maison de la Saône-et-Loire
389, Avenue de Lattre-de-Tassigny
71000 Mâcon
Tel: 85 39 47 47

Touring:
use Michelin sheet map 243, Bourgogne/Franche-Comté

Arborétum de Pezanin

Created in 1903 just outside the village of Dompierre-les-Ormes, this is one of the oldest arboretums in France. It suffered a severe set-back in 1982 when bad storms caused extensive damage, but the efforts of the Office National des Forêts, which owns it, have ensured a swift recovery. More than 400 species of trees and shrubs from all over the world, including some exotic varieties rarely seen in Europe, have been planted in a peaceful setting around a small lake. A short forest drive winds through the arboretum, but there are also waymarked footpaths allowing more leisurely strolls of up to an hour and a half.

Berzé-la-Ville

Once the site of a priory used as a country retreat by the monks of Cluny, Berzé-la-Ville is best known for its Romanesque Chapelle des Moines, which occupies a rocky spur above the village. Inside, its walls are covered with remarkably well preserved and colourful 12th-century frescos, including a Christ in Majesty, the martyrdoms of St Vincent and St Blaise and some favourite saints of Cluny. Nearby Berzé-le-Châtel, an imposing feudal castle on vine-covered slopes, formerly played a major role in the history of Cluny, guarding the abbey's southern approaches.

The mural paintings in the Chapelle des Moines at Berzé-la-Ville are a fine example of the art of the monks of Cluny

Lamartine

Born in Mâcon in 1790, Alphonse de Lamartine became a romantic poet of some repute, achieving instant success with the publication of his first volume, *Méditations poétiques*, in 1820. *Jocelyn*, published in 1836, was his most popular work. Several villages around Mâcon have associations with him, including Milly, Bussières, Pierreclos, Monceau and St Point, where the château became his home after his marriage. All are linked by a signposted tourist route. He died in 1869 and is buried in the grounds of the Château de St Point.

At the foot of the Roche de Solutré there is a museum of prehistory that gives a fascinating insight into how early man lived in this area

Butte de Suin

Midway between Cluny and Charolles and reaching a height of 593m, this is one of several rocky hills in the area. Surmounted by a statue of the Virgin and an orientation table, the hill, once the site of an impregnable fortress, offers panoramic views to other local high points. On a clear day it is possible to pick out the steeples of over 50 churches. The hill is now a popular launching point for hang-gliders.

Cluny

Despite the ravages of the Wars of Religion (1562-98) and the Revolution of 1789, modest Cluny, once the greatest religious centre in Christendom, continues to attract large numbers of visitors. Of the abbey buildings that still stand, the finest is the Clocher de l'Eau Bénite, but five of the original 15 guard towers also remain. One of these, the 11th-century Tour des Fromages, once used to store cheese, houses the tourist office and from the top provides panoramic views of the town and the abbey's surviving buildings. A model of the abbey and details of its history can be seen at the Musée Ochier in the town.

A climb to the top of the Tour des Fromages at Cluny is recommended, from where there is a good view of the other parts of the abbey and of the town

Montagne de St Cyr

This mountain, about 6km north-west of Matour along the D211 is, at 792m, the highest in the area. Signs lead by way of a wooded road to a picnic area from where a track leads to the top. There are two viewing areas: the orientation table and a large crucifix mounted on rocks.

Pouilly-Fuissé

Surrounded by gentle, vine-covered hills at the heart of the Mâconnais wine-producing area, Pouilly-Fuissé is in fact two villages that give their names to one of the best white wines in the world. A local saying goes, 'White is white, Pouilly-Fuissé is something else.' There are several *caves*, including the famous Château Fuissé, where tasting is possible.

Solutré

Another village known for its Pouilly-Fuissé vineyards, Solutré has more to it than wine, for its name has been given to the Solutrian Era, a period of the Stone Age around 18,000BC. This link with prehistory is connected with the spectacular Roche de Solutré, an enormous limestone outcrop just outside the village. At the rock's foot the dramatic discovery was made in 1866 of the fossilised remains of some 100,000 horses, which are thought to have been led to their deaths by early man.

Vergisson

Like Solutré, Vergisson occupies an attractive position beneath huge, golden cliffs, a fine limestone escarpment that is part of the same formation as its neighbour's famous rock. Surrounded by vineyards stretching up to the foot of the cliffs, Vergisson too produces Pouilly-Fuissé wine. This no doubt gives strength and courage to hunters of the fearsome P'teu de Vergisson, a mythical winged monster said to carry off farm animals in the area.

For many visitors to Solutré the local wine is the main attraction, for this is Pouilly-Fuissé country

FRANCHE-COMTÉ

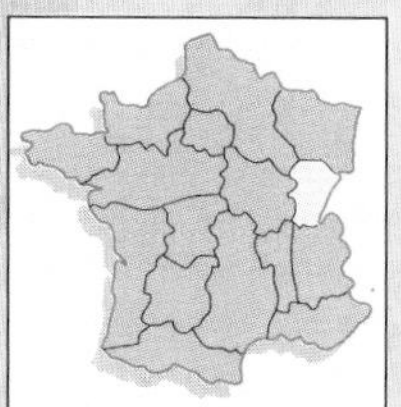

TO THE SOUTH OF ALSACE THE hills of the Sundgau lead into Franche-Comté and the Jura Mountains. From the top of sheer limestone cliffs you can look out over Switzerland and forests that still cover more than a third of this province, which comprises the four *départements* of Doubs, Jura, Haute-Saône and the Territoire-de-Belfort.

Multicoloured patterns of tiles, similar to those in Burgundy, cover the uniquely shaped church towers of Franche-Comté. This is a land of rivers and lakes, waterfalls and gorges, seducing the visitor into taking time just to watch the water ripple by. Many of the limestone cliffs hide grottos and caverns, carved out over millennia by subterranean rivers and rain. Many are open to the public but there are doubtless many others still to be discovered. Trout-filled rivers – the Doubs and the Loue are among the most picturesque – are confined for much of their length to steep-sided valleys, before finally seizing their chance to break through, over wide, shallow steps and spectacular cascades, to joint the Rhône and Saône. The Ain, now dammed to form the long Lac de Vouglans, itself boasts spectacular gorges to the south of Nantua.

The Jura is also a pastoral land, known for its Comté cheese and its red and white Montbéliard cows grazing peacefully in verdant meadows. The 'Route du Vin' runs from Beaufort, south of Lons-le-Saunier, to Arbois, near Salins-les-Bains. Salins, like Arc-et-Senans and Lons-le-Saunier, was once an important centre for the production of salt, a valuable commodity in the Middle Ages. The *gabelle* – a tax on salt not repealed in France until 1790 – provided as much as 40 per cent of the revenue of the rulers.

Franche-Comté can be enjoyed summer and winter. Light-green pastures and dark-green forests wear a glistening blanket of snow in winter. The blue of the sky is reflected in clear waters and there almost seem to be enough signposted paths to provide one for each summer rambler or winter cross-country skier. Throughout this unspoilt area, well known for its abbeys nestling in hidden valleys, a rich architectural heritage is proudly preserved.

Franche-Comté, like many areas of France, loves pétanque

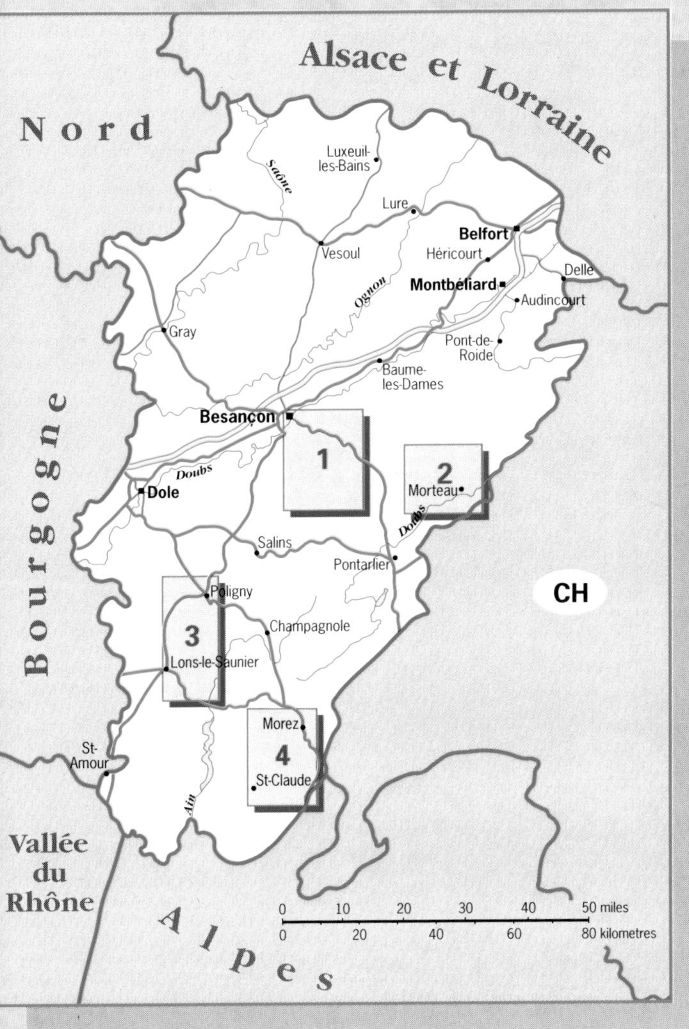

Morteau (left) was rebuilt after being largely destroyed by fire in 1865. Like St Dizier (below), it still possesses some attractive architectural details

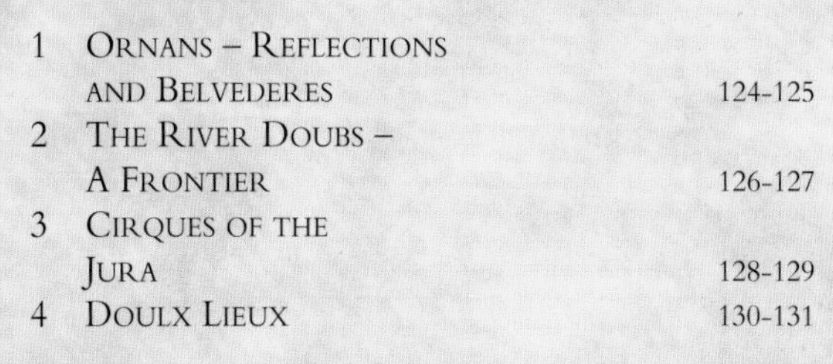

The source of the River Lison, east of Salins-les-Bains, is a typically pretty sight in this region of tumbling rivers

Colourful bread dolls are among the regional handicrafts to be seen in Franche-Comté

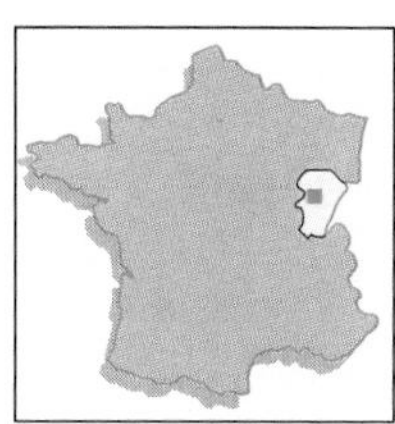

ORNANS – REFLECTIONS AND BELVEDERES

IF STAYING AT BESANÇON, see it first from the Citadelle and then from a bateau-mouche. On foot, see the old houses, the Porte Noire and the Cathédrale St-Jean. Around Ornans is a landscape of limestone cliffs, belvederes, caverns and waterfalls. The Loue has the loveliest river valley in France, unspoilt by the foundries, tanneries and distilleries of years past.

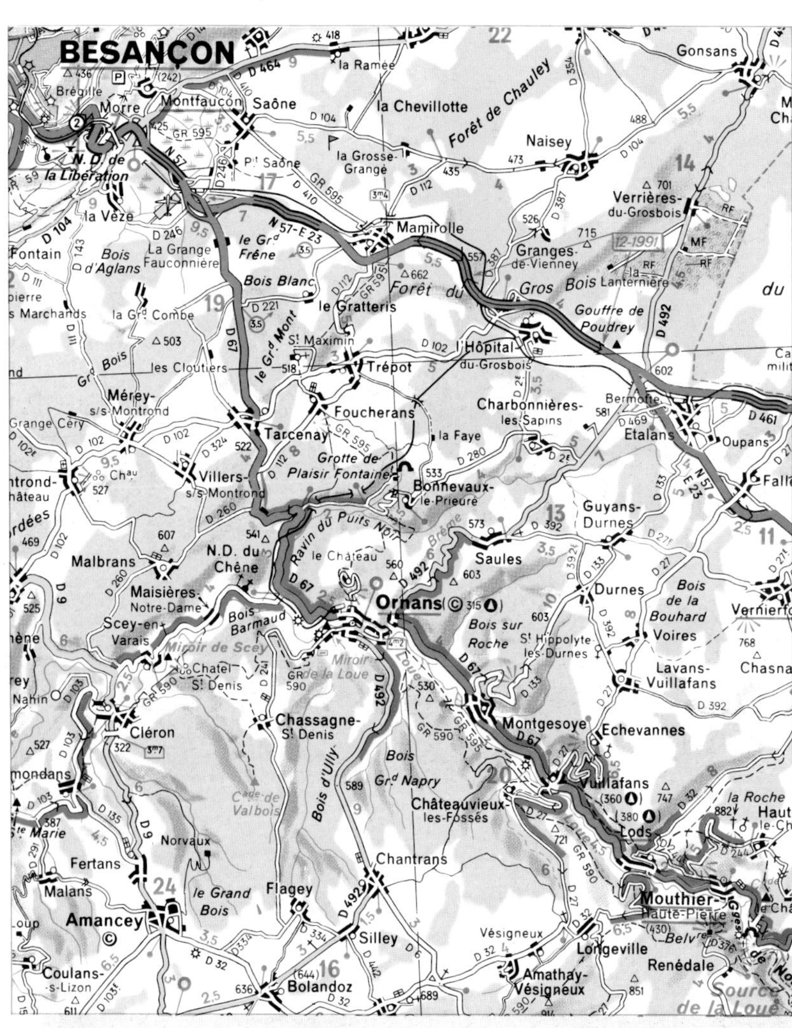

Château de Cléron

The château is open only in the afternoons, from mid-July to mid-August. On a calm day, from the bridge a wonderful series of reflections can be seen in the river – château walls and church tower – with the occasional leaping trout blurring the image.

As the D103 climbs up towards Amondans there is a view across the weir of the mainly 14th- and 16th-century château. Several of the villages hereabouts have large copper cauldrons – big enough to boil missionaries – once used to heat the milk to make Comté cheese. They are now used to hold floral decorations outside churches and are often seen by the pump or fountain in village squares.

On the same stretch of road are three belvederes. From that at Gouille Noire there is a view down into a thickly wooded cleft, in which you can hear the water rushing through the trees far below. The cows grazing along the banks, under limestone cliffs, are a typical sight in this peaceful pastoral region.

SOURCE OF THE LOUE

A stiff half-hour's walk from a small car park on the D67 out of Mouthier-Haute-Pierre brings you to the source. The narrow path runs halfway up a cliff and several hundred breathtaking metres above the bottom of the gorge. You can hear the river's noise rising from a sighing as of wind in the trees to a full-throated roar as you approach the dark cave from which it emerges, already 30m wide at birth.

Alternatively, you can take the D443 from Duhans as far as it goes, park the car and walk along the bottom of the valley to the source. This takes only half an hour, there and back.

Do not miss this chance to see a river plunging, full grown, from a dark cavern part of the way up a cliff. Afternoon light is best for photographs.

Agence de Développement Économique du Doubs
Hôtel du Département -
7, Avenue de la Gare d'Eau
25031 Besançon Cedex
Tel: 81 83 24 31

Touring:
use Michelin sheet map 243, Bourgogne/ Franche-Comté

The Château de Cléron is in a good state of preservation and benefits from a picturesque setting on the banks of the Loue

GUSTAVE COURBET

Born in Ornans in 1819, in the riverside house now turned into a museum of his life and works, Courbet was an independent and self-assured character. He was one of the Realist school, which took over as the Romantic and neoclassical schools declined. When asked to include angels in a painting for a church, he said, 'I have never seen one. Show me one and I will paint it'.

Courbet delighted in everyday scenes, two of which, *Enterrement à Ornans* and *L'Atelier du Peintre*, are in the Louvre. He loved to return each summer to Ornans, capturing the wild limestone landscapes and cliffs of the surrounding countryside. Many of these are in the Musée Courbet, as is the very 'realist' painting of the *Retour de la Conférence*. Happily inebriated clergy are returning home, among them the *curé* of Bonnevaux, easily recognisable on his little donkey. So recognisable was he that Courbet was never again invited to the presbytery wine cellars.

The house has been little modified since Courbet's family lived there, though it did serve as a brewery for a while.

Courbet's revolutionary leanings led him to take part in the destruction of the Colonne Vendôme in Paris in 1871. He was imprisoned but chose exile in Switzerland, where he died on New Year's Eve 1877.

Gouffre de Poudrey

Situated on the north side of the N57, to the north-east of Ornans, the entrance to this cavern, one of the ten largest in Europe, is marked by a statue reminiscent of Mickey Mouse – it is in fact a bat – in the car park, alongside souvenir shops and a café. Do not let this deter you, for the 60-m high ceiling and the sheer size – it could swallow up Notre Dame de Paris – together with the stalactites and stalagmites, the latter in both blue and white, and the dramatic lighting effects, are very impressive.

Lods

The River Loue, not far from its source, has escaped from the Gorges de Nouailles and tumbles over several small faults in its bed as it passes through the riverside village of Lods, which should not be confused with Nods, some 8km to the north-east. One single arch remains of an old medieval bridge across one of these 'weirs'. This, and the many old picturesque houses in the village, make it a pleasant spot in which to spend an idle hour.

Mouthier-Haute-Pierre

Only the name remains of the Benedictine abbey founded here in the valley meadows. The Roche de Hautepierre, 882m above, affords a view across the whole plateau, with the river below and the Vosges, and on clear days, the Alps, behind.

Ornans

Ornans, on the banks of the Loue, is home to the Musée National de la Pêche, the National Museum of Fishing. It was also the birthplace of the Realist painter Gustave Courbet. On a sheer bluff overlooking town and river is the site of the château, destroyed on the orders of Louis XIV when the region was wrested from the Spanish in 1674. Now occupied by a few houses and unmade paths and gardens, the spot affords a magnificent view on a sunny evening.

There is a tiny chapel to St George, founded in 1289 by Othon IV and rebuilt in 1500. At least one of the old castle wells gives water, for the owner uses it to water his garden and his chickens.

The medieval bridge and the series of little weirs that punctuate the Loue as it passes through the attractive village lend charm to Lods (pronounced 'Lô')

At the east end of the Église St-Laurent, in Ornans itself, is a strange table tomb, its inscription illegible now. The church was reconstructed in the 16th century.

Scey-en-Varais

In the little commune of Scey-en-Varais is the Miroir de Scey. A sweeping curve of the Loue reflects – in moods that vary according to the time of day and the skies overhead – a large rustic farmhouse on the far bank. It can also catch the jagged likeness of the Châtel St-Denis perched on the crag above.

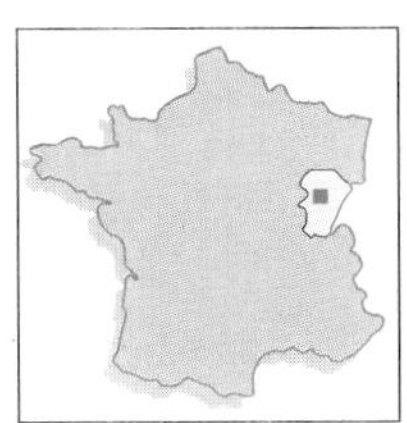

THE RIVER DOUBS – A FRONTIER

THE RIVER DOUBS is the undisputed star of this corner of France – and Switzerland – being assigned for part of its length the role of guardian of the frontier itself. The customs posts are not official but rather set up, tongue in cheek on 1 April, by the citizens of the Republic of Val du Saugeais, who have even elected their own President.

This stretch of the Doubs forms part of the border between France and Switzerland. The river's name derives from the Latin dubius, *which means doubtful, since for much of its length it takes a hesitant, sinuous course*

Cirque de Consolation and Roche du Prêtre

Follow the signposted route up to the Belvédère de la Roche du Prêtre. From the car park there is a pleasant walk until suddenly you are on the edge of a sheer drop down into the wooded valley. Far below is the seminary of Notre-Dame de Consolation. Three hundred and fifty metres of fresh air right at your feet is certainly exhilarating.

Défilé d'Entreroche

The D437 from Montbenoît towards Morteau certainly lives up to its name of the 'Defile between Rocks'. Once out of the narrowest part of the defile, at Pont de la Roche, the valley broadens considerably. The Doubs, with its wide bed and lush water-meadows, can absorb a large volume of winter flood water without problems; if it could not the road itself could very easily become impassable.

Grotte du Trésor and Notre-Dame de Remonot

These two caves in the base of the limestone cliff are close together and yet very different from each other. At the Grotte du Trésor, park alongside a broad, lazy sweep of the Doubs, cross the road, scramble down a culvert and up a dry watercourse, to the lip of a huge cavern with a rough, rocky floor that disappears into the gloom at the back.

Notre-Dame de Remonot is 2km along the road. A grotto once venerated by Druids, it was claimed for Christianity by hermits in the 8th century. The same underground stream that feeds the recesses of the Grotte du Trésor also flows here, and there is a small footbridge just behind the altar. However, mischievous water spirits from time to time flood the flagstone floor and float the chairs. For hundreds of years those afflicted with problems of sight have come here to bathe their eyes with the water running down the walls. Plaques on the damp walls give thanks for many a cure gratefully received.

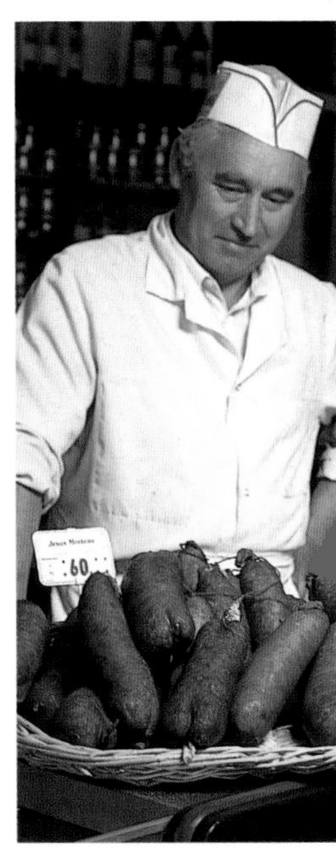

Smoked sausages are a speciality of Franche-Comté. The small ones known as 'Jésus' are used in a hotpot eaten in the Morteau area

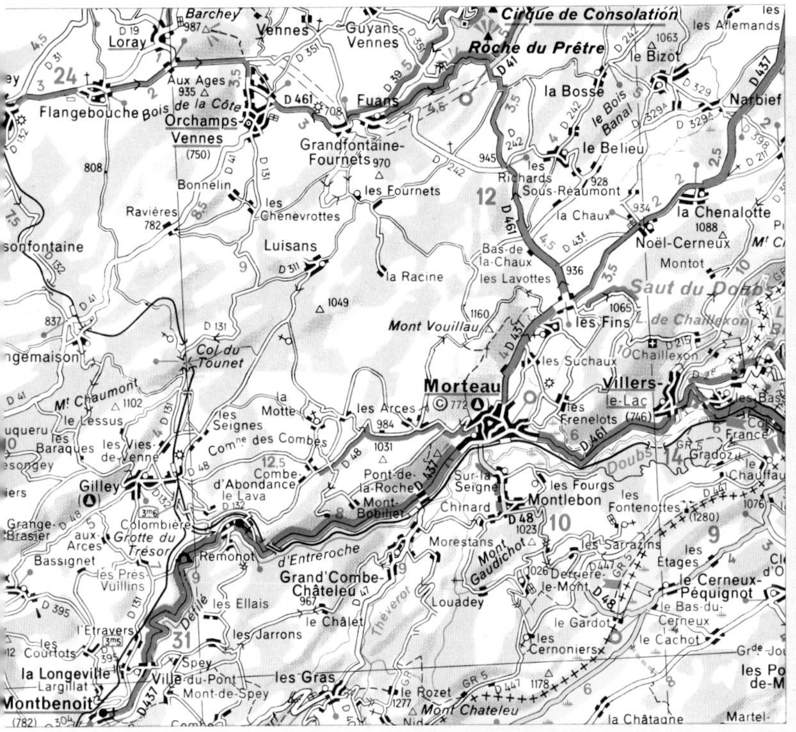

Morteau

The town grew up in the 13th century around a Benedictine priory and became, in the 19th, a centre for clock making. After the ravages of 17th-century wars and a disastrous fire in 1865, a few older buildings survive. The Hôtel Fauché, built in 1590, is now the town hall. The former Pertusier family home, dating from 1575, with its stone façade, mullioned windows, columns and colonnades, is one of the few such Renaissance buildings in the region. The gastronomic speciality of Morteau is its little smoked sausage, locally called Jésus.

VAL DU SAUGEAIS

At an altitude of over 800m, where the houses begin to look distinctly Alpine, is the Val du Saugeais, south of Montbenoît. Devastated and depopulated during wars three centuries ago, when France regained the Comté, this region was largely resettled from Haute-Savoie and elsewhere. The locals have their own dialect and customs, and have proclaimed their region the Republic of Saugeais, with their own elected President. They have even been known to set up unofficial customs posts on 1 April.

Agence de Développement Économique du Doubs
Hôtel du Département - 7, Avenue de la Gare d'Eau
25031 Besançon Cedex
Tel: 81 83 24 31

Touring:
use Michelin sheet map 243, Bourgogne/ Franche-Comté

Lac de Chaillexon

Formed by rockfalls, this lake, only exceptionally more than 200m wide, first winds its way between wooded slopes, its blue waters full of trout and other sport fish, before running between steeper cliffs. The short 3-km boat trip past the varied scenery feels like a much longer expedition.

Montbenoît

A clapper bridge crosses a bend of the Doubs in front of the abbey church of Montbenoît. Hidden at the end of its small valley, Montbenoît, 'capital' of the Val du Saugeais, is different, in patois and customs, from the other upland communities. In 1150 the local Sire de Joux offered land to monks from Valais. The abbey remained a feudal possession and many different architectural styles are represented. There are lovely carved choir-stalls, some depicting subjects unusually sensual for a church. The pillars of the tiny 15th-century cloister are carved with the monks' own interpretations in stone of local animals and flowers, in a pleasing style. As secular interest in the wealth of the abbey increased, so discipline and religious observance declined. Soon it was said to be 'gaining each year in gold what it lost in wisdom'.

The choir-stalls in Montbenoît's abbey church depict some surprisingly worldly scenes

Saut du Doubs

If you are not going to the Saut du Doubs by boat, take the not very clearly signposted left fork out of Morteau, at the Hôtel de France, for Saut du Doubs and Maiche. The road climbs steeply, giving a splendid view across the river, which has just become the Franco-Swiss border.

From the second car park there is a 500-m walk down to the cafés and souvenir stalls and a further 500m to the belvedere overlooking the fall itself. Boats come down river from Morteau and from Villers-le-Lac as well as from the Swiss shore. The border is marked by a garland of floating plastic buoys.

Villers-le-Lac

Boat trips along Lac de Chaillexon and to the Saut du Doubs start from here. The river has spread across the valley, before being confined again at Chaillexon. The exterior of the 17th-century Chapelle de St-Joseph-des-Bassots might not suggest that a stop is called for. However, the ceiling, formed of lozenges and hanging spindles, in blues, reds and gold, is unique. The reredos and choir-stalls also bear witness to the taste of the patron, Claude Binétruy, who built this sanctuary.

The Saut du Doubs plunges over a 27-m high ledge before being dammed

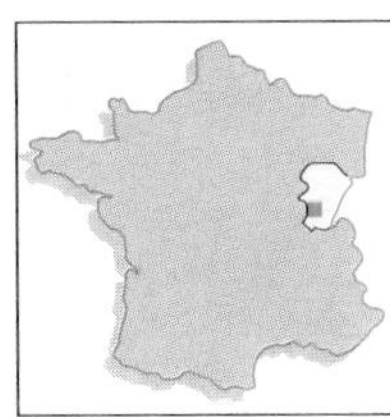

CIRQUES OF THE JURA

BAUME, REVIGNY, LADOYE – dead-end valleys known as *les bouts-du-monde* – are among the most spectacular cirques of the region. All around here you will come across, in village squares and outside churches, large copper cauldrons, once used in heating the milk for Comté cheese, now enjoying a new lease of life as containers for flowers.

Arbois

The wine capital of the Jura, Arbois is said to have produced one of the favourite wines of Henri IV. So, we are told, did Chalon, Jurançon and many other vineyards. Louis Pasteur, born at Dole, spent most of his youth and all his holidays in Arbois. The family home is now a museum explaining his research into rabies and serums, his contributions to the silk industry and, above all, his seminal work in the field of fermentation and wine production.

Cirque de Baume

The best vantage point from which to see the many small valleys that make up the Cirque de Baume is the Belvédère des Roches de Baume. A gorge over 1500m long, 300m wide and up to 200m deep suddenly opens at your feet. At the bottom of the gorge is the abbey and village of Baume-les-Messieurs.

At the bottom of the Cirque de Baume lies Baume-les-Messieurs, a village perhaps best known for its ancient abbey

Cirque de Ladoye

Seen from the top of its sheer 200-m cliffs, or from the bottom, this 600-m wide *bout-du-monde* is equally striking. A mountain road winds down the side of the cirque and the northern source of the River Seille rises, in a fountain called locally a *doye*, at the bottom of the cliffs.

Creux de Revigny

The River Vallière bursts forth from the foot of the escarpment. It is difficult to appreciate the sight without climbing part of the way up the overgrown scree slope. In the cliff face itself are a series of interconnecting grottoes and caves, carved by underground rivers long since disappeared. These served as refuge for the inhabitants of the village, terrorised for many years during the Thirty Years War by the Swedes.

WINES

The Côtes du Jura produce only 1 per cent of the wines of France, but their distinctive bouquet has a growing following. Local wine-growers do not make a wine to suit supermarket customers: 'Let the customer come and try our wines and he will soon come to appreciate them. If not, let him go back to the supermarket!'

At Château-Chalon is produced a deep-yellow wine, with a distinctive nose and flavour. It matures for a minimum of six years in part-filled barrels, under a yeast skin that excludes air. But 38 per cent of the wine evaporates – *la part des anges*, the angels' share – a much higher proportion than in cognac. Château-Chalon is the only wine sold in a 62-cl bottle rather than the EC 75-cl standard. Several grape varieties are grown hereabouts. Château-Chalon is made from Savagnin grapes, little grown elsewhere. Pinot Noir was introduced from Burgundy, having a more reliable record of production than the grapes that give such distinctive character to the local vintages. These grapes are Trousseau, which is used for Montigny, and Poulsard, from which Pupillin is made.

Salt Springs

Salarium meant wages – with which to buy salt – such was the importance to the Romans and others of salt. Production

of salt by evaporation of brine has been a valuable trade in this part of France as well as in the area around Marsal in Lorraine, for thousands of years. Salins-les-Bains, built along a river valley, is still guarded by two forts, Belin and St-André. It is the only place in the region where you can still see and understand the work of extraction and evaporation.

As wood was replaced for firing boilers by more expensive coal and as the warmth of the Mediterranean sunshine began to be used to do the job of evaporation almost free, Salins went into decline. The museum, in the 18th-century workings, gives a clear idea of the whole process. At Arc-et-Senans (above) the brine was pumped from Salins, along tree-trunk pipes, much being lost on the way. The project, which began in 1779, seldom produced even half of its Utopian target. It closed in 1895 but has been restored and since 1983 has been listed by UNESCO.

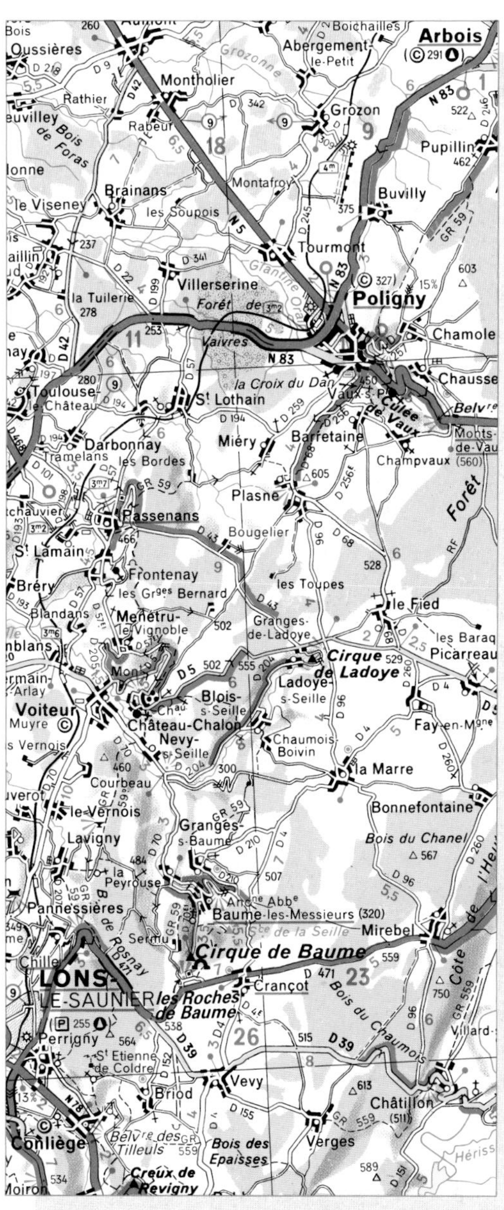

Lons-le-Saunier

Lons-le-Saunier is a pleasant centre from which to explore the 'Reculées', as the many spectacular gorges and chasms in the region are called. Salt springs exploited by both Gauls and Romans ceased production in the Middle Ages. Waters with some of the highest concentrations of chlorine and iodine in France are used today to treat lymph and rheumatic troubles.

Only the Tour de l'Horloge, the clock tower, remains of medieval walls that seem in no way to have deterred either the English in the Hundred Years War or the Swedes in the Thirty Years War. Lons-le-Saunier, like so many towns of the region, was sacked several times. Rouget de Lisle was born here. An engineer officer garrisoned at Strasbourg in 1792, he composed the *Marseillaise*. The theatre clock, in the Place de la Liberté, chimes a couple of bars of the national anthem each hour.

The Tour de l'Horloge in Lons-le-Saunier's Place de la Liberté once formed part of the town's medieval walls

Poligny

As with wines, there is an *Appellation Contrôlée* for Comté cheese. Poligny is the acknowledged capital of this industry. Only cows fed on fresh grass may supply the milk. The milk's quality varies according to the altitude of the farms.

Since no silage is used, there is little production in winter. As with Munster, some cheese is made straight away from the morning milking and another batch in the evening. Other Comté is made from a mixture of the two. The cream having risen and been skimmed off, this Comté has a lower fat content.

For a view over the whole town, climb up to the 'Trou de la Lune' near the Château de Grimont, once home to the counts of Burgundy, who ruled here. Among the roofs of the town seen from here are those of the Hôtel-Dieu, which has a fine collection of Poligny pottery, apothecary jars for the pharmacy, and of the Clarisses convent.

Pupillin and Fer à Cheval

Just south of Arbois, the Poulsard grapes planted around the village produce a light red wine, unusual and very fruity. After a *dégustation* the nearby Fer à Cheval is another of the cirques well worth seeing.

Comité Départemental du Tourisme du Jura
8, Avenue du 44e R.I. - BP 652
39021 Lons-le-Saunier Cedex
Tel: 84 24 57 70

Touring:
use Michelin sheet map 243, Bourgogne/ Franche-Comté

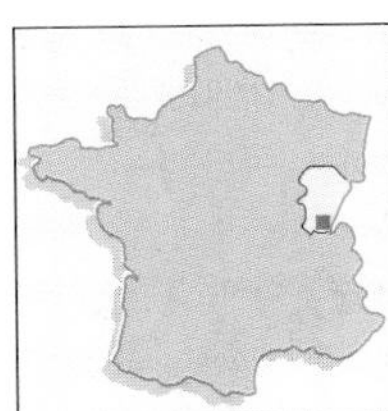

DOULX LIEUX

'DOULX LIEUX', 'GENTLE PLACES'. Thus did Cardinal Granvelle, a native of Ornans himself, counsellor to Philip II of Spain, describe his Jura to a friend at court. The Parc Naturel Régional du Haut-Jura, between the Swiss frontier and the road from St Claude to the Cascades du Hérisson, is a wilder, though equally inspiring landscape: convoluted limestone crags, carved by tumbling rivers into sheer gorges, fertile alpine meadows and crystal-clear streams, full of trout.

Col de la Faucille

Climbing up from the valley of the Valserine on a clear day, you may be lucky enough to see Mont Blanc nearly 100km away. It is a memorable sight, although more memorable still is the view from the top of Petit Mont Rond (1534m). The view down over Lac Léman, with Geneva to your right, is stupendous.

The layers of rock of the Chapeau du Gendarme, near St Claude, have bent upwards without breaking

Gorges du Flumen

Outside St Claude the D436 runs through the Gorges du Flumen, where the river drops spectacularly, one fall after another. From the Saut du Chien there is a view back to one of the best of these. Nearby is the Chapeau du Gendarme: a huge slab of sedimentary rock that was thrust up in the Tertiary era and has been gently bent without cracking or shattering.

Forêt du Massacre

This is another reminder of the region's turbulent past, the name recalling the massacre, by Savoyard troops besieging Geneva, of a force sent to the aid of the city by François I in 1535. The forest is criss-crossed with tracks and the views, especially from Crêt Pela (1495m), are splendid.

Les Rousses

Situated at an altitude of 1100m, the village of Les Rousses is a prime winter-sports centre. For summer visitors it has its lake and, just to the north, the Crêt des Sauges, and the Forêt du Risoux, which stretches into Switzerland. For some reason the timber cut here has special qualities of resonance and is much sought after by makers of musical instruments, such as those of Mirecourt.

HÉRISSON FALLS

These are among the finest falls in the region, the river dropping nearly 300m in about 3km. Within sight of the top car park at the end of the road from Bonlieu is the Saut de la Forge, a wide 12-m drop into a small shallow basin, where optimistic fishermen gather. The river tumbles on, over numerous small limestone lintels and steps, to Grand Saut, 500m downstream. Here the drop, confined in a V-shaped cleft, is a spectacular 60m. The path can become very slippery and muddy, so wear shoes with rugged soles, for smooth-soled footwear could be dangerous.

Further downstream is the Cascade de L'Éventail. Both the Grand Saut and the Éventail, where the river cascades 65m over a series of rounded steps, looking not unlike a bridal veil, are best seen from below. To this end, take the D326 out of Val-Dessous and park, amid the myriad coaches, cafés and souvenir shops, from where it is a five-minute walk to the bottom of the Éventail.

A series of waterfalls set in beautiful woodland, the Cascades du Hérisson are accessible on foot

PIPE MAKING

The making of pipes at St Claude grew from the religious objects – rosaries and crucifixes – produced by local wood carvers for sale to pilgrims. A French ambassador to Portugal introduced both tobacco and the pipe to France in 1560. Early pipes with silver bowls were beyond the means of most would-be smokers. Pipes of porcelain and meerschaum from Germany were also expensive but, above all, fragile.

Experiments with boxwood, pear, maple and walnut had little success. The wood burned as fast as the tobacco and the taste was horrible. Trials with horn were even more unpleasant. In 1854 the idea of using briar root was introduced from Corsica, where the root grew in abundance. By 1914 there were 1300 workers making five million pipes a year, most

for export. Mass production since 1945 has removed St Claude from its place as the maker of 90 per cent of the world's briar pipes.

A large collection of pipes can be seen at the Maison du Confrérie des Maîtres Pipiers (open 1 June-15 November), near the cathedral.

Morez

The River Bienne drops by more than 300m between Les Rousses and Morez. The town stretches for nearly 3km along the valley, its single street dominated by high escarpment walls and impressive railway viaducts.

The Bienne was a useful power source and around 1796 Morez became to spectacles what St Claude is to pipe making and it was here that the pince-nez was invented. There is a secondary industry, that of clock making, and a third, winter sports, as well as cheese making.

St Claude

This town is the natural centre from which to explore the region and possesses two tourist attractions itself: the Cathédrale St-Pierre and a pipe-making industry dating back 150 years. Near the cathedral is an exhibition of another established St Claude industry, the cutting and polishing of diamonds and gemstones.

St Claude clings to the precipitous banks of the ravine carved out by the Bienne and the Tacon, and the best overall view is from the Grotte Ste-Anne.

The site where the cathedral now stands was chosen as a retreat by two monks, the brothers Romain and Lupicin, in the mid-5th century. Monastic wealth soon attracted the worldly nobility, and monastic discipline relaxed scandalously over the years.

The glory of the 14th- and 15th-century cathedral, dedicated to St Peter, are the choir-stalls, finished in 1465 after 15 years' work, by the Geneva sculptor Jehan de Vitry. Carvers of the period seem to have had a similar puckish sense of humour and caricature: see, for example, the choir-stalls of the Collégiale St-Thiébaut at Thann, in Alsace. Unfortunately some 200 carvings, all those on the south side, were destroyed in a smouldering fire on the night of 26 September 1983. Since then, however, careful restoration has taken place.

Comité Départemental du Tourisme du Jura
8, Avenue du 44e R.I. - BP 652
39021 Lons-le-Saunier Cedex
Tel: 84 24 57 70

Touring:
use Michelin sheet map 243, Bourgogne/Franche-Comté

The main part of the Cathédrale St-Pierre in St Claude was built in the Gothic style in the 14th and 15th centuries, but in the 18th century the classical façade was added

THE ATLANTIC COAST

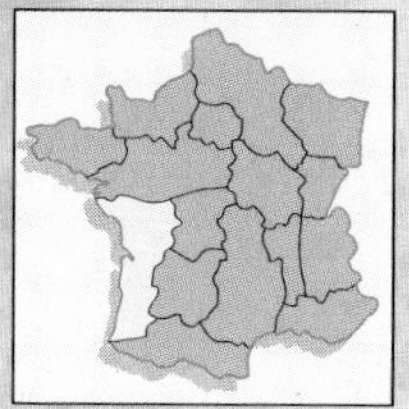

THE MEDITERRANEAN MAY BE warmer than the Atlantic, but in many other respects the Atlantic Coast and its hinterland have as much to offer as the more popular, and more crowded, Côte d'Azur.

You can certainly eat well here, seafood and goat's cheeses being just two of the regional specialities. As for wine, very few people would deny that the best wine in the world comes from Bordeaux. This is also France's famous cognac region, and although it is not covered here, you will almost certainly drive through it.

If you are interested in history and ancient monuments you will love this region. Here were fought many bitter battles during the Hundred Years War. There is an abundance of churches, châteaux and museums to explore, particularly around Poitiers.

But you do not have to be a history buff to enjoy the atmosphere of the many medieval villages. If you like night-life and shopping in smart shops, there are the stylish resorts of Arcachon and La Rochelle. Here, and in many other seaside towns, you can pamper yourself by having thalassotherapy – smooth and invigorating seawater treatment, very popular with the smart set these days. For sport, take your pick from walking, cycling, windsurfing, sailing, diving, canoeing, horse-riding, golf, swimming or simply paddling in the ocean.

For many city dwellers one of the most appealing aspects of the Atlantic Coast is quite simply that there is so much of it. It is very easy to find peace and quiet here, and even in the height of summer there are deserted beaches. But you need not be from the city to appreciate the pure air for which the whole region is known. Elsewhere the world's rain forests are being denuded, but the soil of the Landes area – a former swamp below Arcachon – has been fixed in place by the planting of thousands of pines, whose heady scent fills the air and clears the lungs.

The Atlantic Coast is also a haven for the environmentalist and nature lover. Offshore islands are on the migratory routes of many birds. On the islands themselves you can see the old salt plains as well as oyster beds and mussel farms. Inland, the mysterious reclaimed landscape of the Marais Poitevin, the 'Green Venice', exerts a powerful charm of its own. Its waterways are best explored by boat.

In some ways time seems to have stood still in this region, where the fields are still cultivated with the same crops and vines as they have been for centuries. But you can be abruptly brought back into the 20th century when you see the signs for nuclear power stations; or even thrust into the 21st by the Parc du Futuroscope, near Poitiers. The northern part of the region's coastline is known locally as the Côte de Beauté, and the southern, below Arcachon, as the Côte d'Argent. The whole Atlantic Coast could, equally aptly, be called the 'underrated coast'. But those who know it have always appreciated its charms.

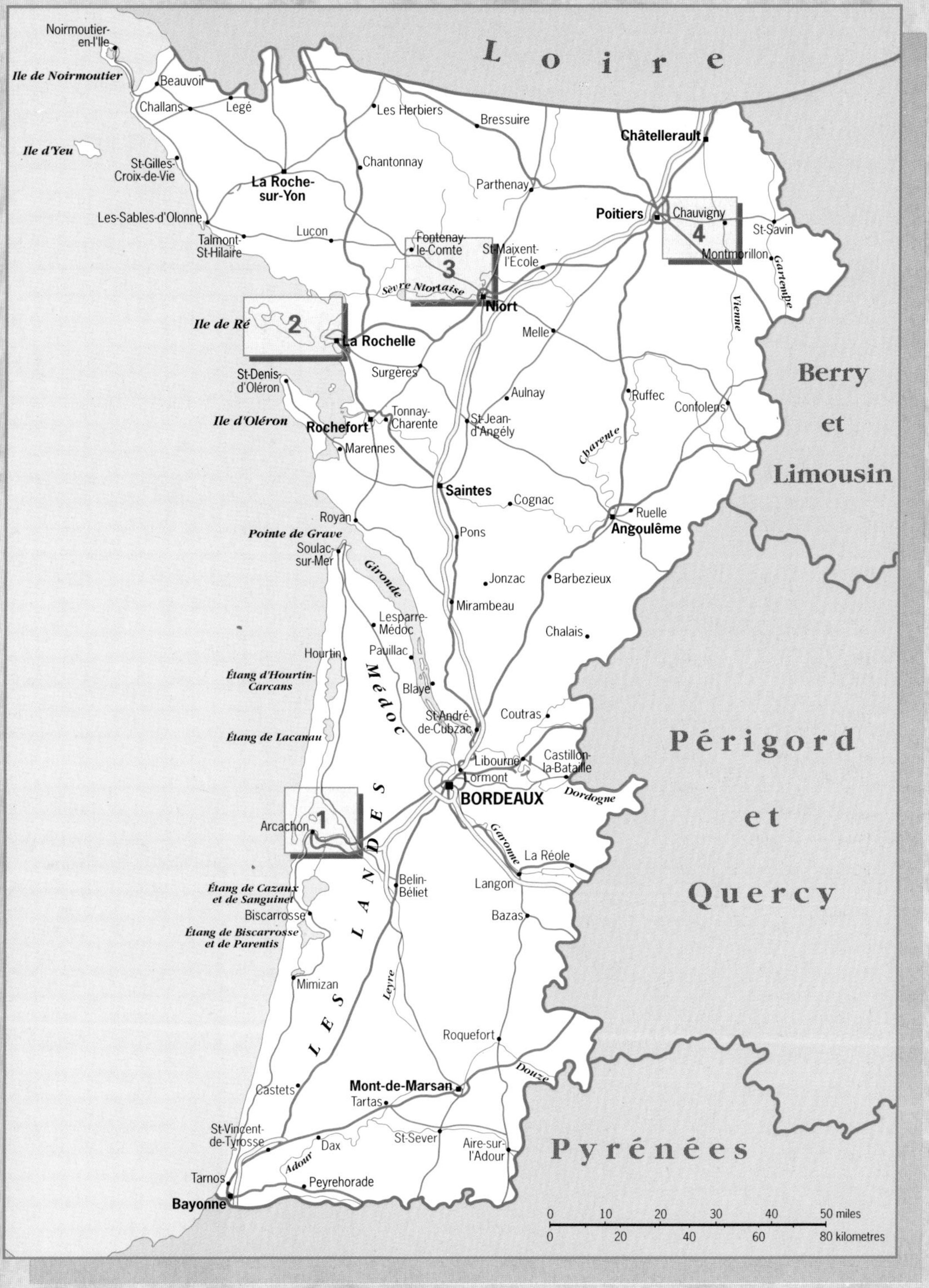

Loire
Noirmoutier-en-l'Ile
Ile de Noirmoutier
Beauvoir
Challans
Legé
Les Herbiers
Bressuire
Châtellerault
Ile d'Yeu
St-Gilles-Croix-de-Vie
La Roche-sur-Yon
Chantonnay
Parthenay
Poitiers
Chauvigny
St-Savin
Les-Sables-d'Olonne
Talmont-St-Hilaire
Luçon
Fontenay-le-Comte
St-Maixent-l'Ecole
Montmorillon
Gartempe
Vienne
Sèvre Niortaise
Niort
Ile de Ré
La Rochelle
Melle
St-Denis-d'Oléron
Surgères
Berry et Limousin
Aulnay
Ruffec
Confolens
Ile d'Oléron
Rochefort
Tonnay-Charente
St-Jean-d'Angély
Marennes
Charente
Saintes
Cognac
Royan
Ruelle
Angoulême
Pointe de Grave
Soulac-sur-Mer
Pons
Gironde
Jonzac
Barbezieux
Mirambeau
Lesparre-Médoc
Chalais
Hourtin
Pauillac
Étang d'Hourtin-Carcans
Médoc
Blaye
St-André-de-Cubzac
Coutras
Étang de Lacanau
Périgord et Quercy
Libourne
Castillon-la-Bataille
Lormont
BORDEAUX
Dordogne
Arcachon
Garonne
La Réole
Étang de Cazaux et de Sanguinet
Belin-Béliet
Langon
Biscarrosse
Bazas
Étang de Biscarrosse et de Parentis
LES LANDES
Mimizan
Leyre
Roquefort
Douze
Castets
Mont-de-Marsan
Tartas
St-Vincent-de-Tyrosse
Dax
St-Sever
Aire-sur-l'Adour
Pyrénées
Adour
Tarnos
Peyrehorade
Bayonne
0 10 20 30 40 50 miles
0 20 40 60 80 kilometres

The Écomusée de Marquèse shows Landes life, including the shepherds' use of stilts (below)
The Dune du Pilat is the highest sand dune in Europe (below)
A fireman is wed in Civray (bottom)

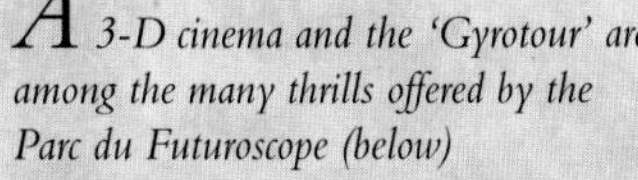

A 3-D cinema and the 'Gyrotour' are among the many thrills offered by the Parc du Futuroscope (below)

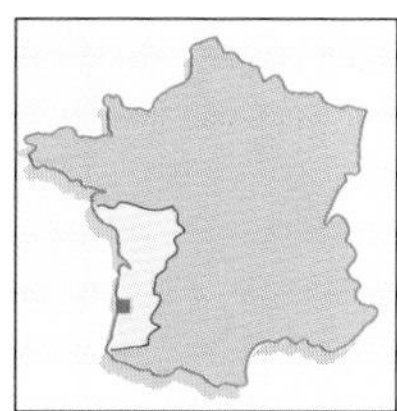

THE ARCACHON BASIN

THE SHELTERED basin of Arcachon, fringed with pine forests that anchor the sand dunes, is where the rolling Médoc meets the sea. Here the traditional industries of oyster and mussel farming still flourish. The basin is dotted with small resorts, varying from the simple to the stylish, but Arcachon is usually described as its pearl. To the south of the town, the local capital, lies the impressive Dune du Pilat, Europe's tallest sand dune.

The air in Arcachon is scented with a mixture of sea and pine, and sometimes on a breezy day there is a heady smell of eucalyptus. From the beach you can see Cap Ferret across the bay

Andernos-les-Bains

Here there is a picturesque harbour where you can watch the oyster boats being loaded. The Église St-Éloi was built on the site of a much older Gallo-Roman church and you can still see the 4th-century remains of the old basilica. Pines, oyster farming and tourism made this prehistoric village prosperous. The actress Sarah Bernhardt settled here during World War I.

Arcachon

This is one of France's most stylish seaside resorts and is very popular with the rich of Bordeaux, many of whom own weekend homes here. Originally a sleepy fishing village, it started to expand in 1857 with the arrival of the railway.

The town was formerly divided into four quarters named after the seasons of the year, and still has distinct summer and winter areas. The Ville d'Été is closest to the beach, and used to have a spectacular Moorish casino, but this was destroyed by fire in 1977. The surrounding park and gardens are still there and from the lift there are fine views of the town and bay. The Ville d'Hiver is more residential. Parking can be a problem in the town, and the best way to explore it is on foot.

Arès

This small oyster-farming and resort town was not given separate borough status from Andernos-les-Bains until 1851. A lady named Sophie Wallerstein was the resort's main benefactress and her large home in the middle of the park is now a retirement home for teachers.

Near the jetty is an old tower, all that remains of a former mill. It had started as a windmill, but when taxes were increased the sails were removed and the battlements added to make it look like a watch-tower. David Allegre, the inventor of the steam trawler, lived here. And it is perhaps surprising to discover, in such a sleepy town as Arès, that the world's first UFO-tracking station was launched on the beach here on 15 August 1976.

Cap Ferret

This is the long sand jetty that protects the Arcachon basin from the ocean. From its lighthouse there is a wonderful view of the whole basin and of the Atlantic. Until 1928, when the road was built, you could reach Cap Ferret only by boat, and this is probably still the best way. Another enjoyable excursion is to ride to the beach on the miniature steam train.

Comité Départemental du Tourisme de la Gironde
24, Rue Esprit-des-Lois
33000 Bordeaux
Tel: 56 52 61 40

Touring:
use Michelin sheet map 234, Aquitaine

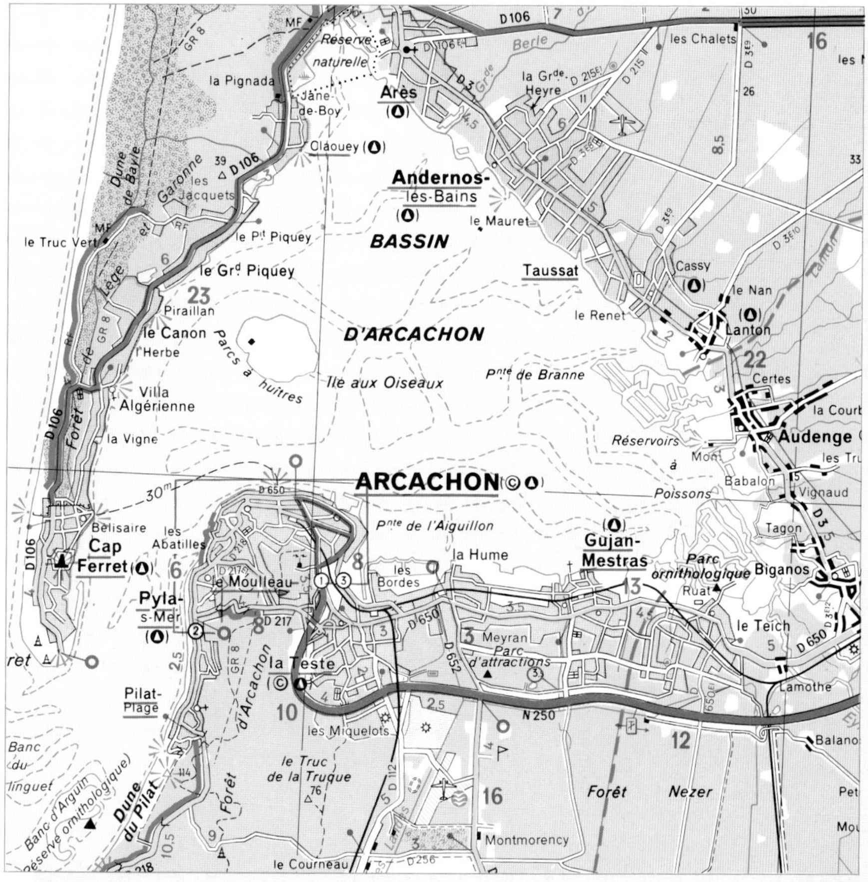

Landes Life

Until the 19th century the Landes was a huge swamp, edged by dunes. Today the area is planted with thousands of kilometres of trees. At the Écomusée de Marquèze (below), 15km east of Labouheyre on the N10 from Bordeaux to Bayonne, the traditional Landais way of life can be seen.

Shepherds used to wander the land on stilts and many of their dwellings were built on legs. Sheep and bees were the main basis of the economy, and today nearly every small farm still sells honey and every market sheepskin jackets.

The lighthouse on Cap Ferret (left) gives an excellent view of the Arcachon basin At over 100m high, the impressive Dune du Pilat (above) is the tallest sand dune in Europe

Dune du Pilat

Sometimes called 'Sahara by the sea', the Dune du Pilat is a must for anyone visiting the area. This natural sand dune, over 100m high and over 3km long, has continued to change and move since its formation. You can climb to the top up 190 steep wooden steps: the view of the sea, the channel between Arcachon and Cap Ferret, the thick forest of the Landes and the rolling dunes themselves are well worth the climb. And children love the (perfectly safe) slide down the dune.

Gujan-Mestras

This town is known as the oyster capital of the Arcachon basin. From its seven harbours you can find out everything you ever wanted to know about oysters, though tasting them is probably the best test. The town has a fine old church, and the Marinoscope – a museum of model ships. For children, there is the Aquacity leisure centre and the Cocinelle zoo.

Just outside Gujan is La Hume, which in summer plays host to a 'medieval village' of craft workers. Although a good hunting ground for souvenirs, it is very busy in the tourist season.

L'Herbe

This tiny oyster-farming village attractively sited between the sand dunes and the sea, with its narrow streets and its pine trees, is one of the most picturesque places in the Arcachon basin. In the last century its most famous residents were the Lesca family, who made a fortune in Algeria and built an Algerian-style villa and chapel here. Today only the chapel remains.

To reach the Écomusée you take a small steam train from Sabres to the clearing, with its re-creation of a typical Landais homestead. You can watch stilts being made and bread cooked traditionally over a fire. There is also a recreation area and restaurant. In addition, 20km north of Marquèze, you can visit a restored typical 19th-century Landais farmhouse and an old pine-resin processing plant.

BORDEAUX AND WINE

THE CITY OF BORDEAUX and its most famous product, wine, owe their origins to the Romans. Like Celtic tribes 300 years earlier, the Romans were attracted to the great crescent of the River Garonne. And today the port is still at the centre of Bordeaux's fame and fortune. The waterfront remains an impressive feature, dotted with imposing, if fading, houses built in the 17th and 18th centuries by wealthy wine merchants.

Bordeaux is synonymous with wine. What started as a result of the Romans' irritation that their precious cargoes of Italian wine were always late has culminated in the city's pre-eminence in the production of fine wines.

The land drained by the Rivers Dordogne, Garonne and Gironde is host to 112,000 hectares of vineyards that make the Bordeaux region the world's largest producer of fine wines. Each year the area's 3000 châteaux and 20,000 vineyard owners sell 3-5 million hectolitres of wine – a total of almost 500 million bottles.

18TH-CENTURY BORDEAUX

Behind the Quai Louis XVIII, on a curve in the river, is the Esplanade des Quinconces. This, reputedly the largest square in Europe, houses the botanical gardens and monuments and was established in the early 19th century. The statues of two of Bordeaux's most famous sons, Montesquieu and Montaigne, are at the river side of the square. This is the best place from which to begin a tour of old Bordeaux.

The Grand Théâtre is spectacular, with the style of an ancient temple but built in 1780. It is sumptuously decorated, and has an Italian-style auditorium with seating for 1000. Its fine domed staircase inspired the Paris Opera over 100 years later.

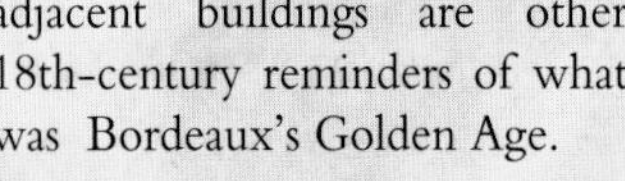

One place not to miss is the Musée des Beaux-Arts, a very special collection of paintings, including works by Titian, Van Dyck and Goya, housed in part of what once was the 18th-century Archbishop's Palace.

The Place du Parlement and adjacent buildings are other 18th-century reminders of what was Bordeaux's Golden Age.

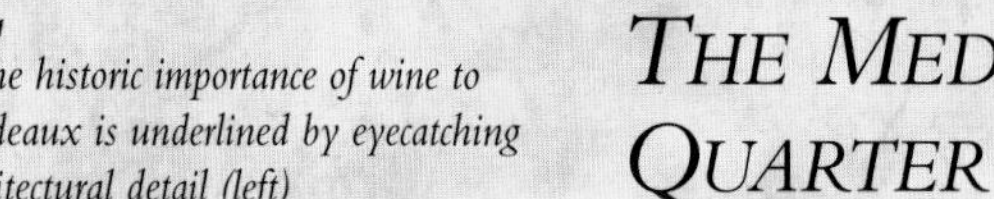

The historic importance of wine to Bordeaux is underlined by eyecatching architectural detail (left)

A fine memorial to the Girondins graces Bordeaux's magnificent Esplanade des Quinconces

THE MEDIEVAL QUARTER

Medieval and Gothic Bordeaux, just behind the dazzling range of buildings to be found in the Place du Parlement, is easy to miss. The Porte Cailhau is a fine example of Gothic military architecture built in 1500. The Grosse Cloche is a 13th-century gate, restored 200 years later, whose two round towers, 37m high, hold the bell that was formerly rung to announce important local events, such as the start of the grape harvest.

Situated in a position overlooking the Landes road, only one of the original five towers remains as a reminder of the Château Trompette, which once guarded the approach to the port of Bordeaux.

The oldest of the churches dotted around the old town is the Basilique St-Michel, close to the river in the old seamen's area. It was begun in 1376 and is famous for what is, at 114m, the tallest spire in France. The bell tower can be seen from all over Bordeaux and the top of its 228 steps provides the best view of the whole city.

THE VINEYARDS

In some ways the vineyards for which Bordeaux is famous are not of great interest to the sightseer. Most are in flat, dull countryside with few of the pleasant villages or even eating places that elsewhere make touring French wine regions such an enjoyable experience. There are relatively few places where dégustation, wine sampling, is readily available. By contrast, St Émilion is a beautiful old wine town within well-preserved city walls on a hill. It features a monolithic church carved out of the hillside, a medieval fortress and fine yellow-stone houses.

A tour of the Bordeaux vineyards begins right in Bordeaux itself, with the Graves-producing Château Haut-Brion. 'Graves' refers to the gravelly soil that sometimes produces white and red wines from the same vine. Start a visit to the region with the best known château, although this is not connected with a vineyard at all. La Brède, built in the 15th century, was the birthplace of Baron de Montesquieu. About 15km from Bordeaux, this fine old château is surrounded by a beautiful functioning moat.

Some 3000 châteaux produce wine in the Bordeaux area (above)

Bordeaux's old quarter (left) recalls the long history of this great city on the River Garonne

WINE CHÂTEAUX

The winding lanes leading to Sauternes are explained by the fact that the vineyards there produce some of the most expensive wines and therefore no land will be sacrificed for the sake of straight roads.

The most famous producer of the rich, sweet wines of the Sauternes district is Château d'Yquem. The medieval château is admirable but is not open to the public. But it is close to Château Filhot, which offers tastings. Just across the Garonne, Ste-Croix-du-Mont presents a beautiful vision of church and château perched on a cliff top.

Four great towers mark a medieval fortress built by Pope Clément V and the home of Roquetaillade. Another such château is Villandraut, the scenic background to the Uzeste music festival held during late August.

The most celebrated of all Bordeaux wine regions is Médoc. The definitive wine of the region, Médoc is produced by a thin strip of vineyards north-west from Bordeaux along the west bank of the Gironde estuary. Most of the 180 Médoc châteaux are open to the public, although it is necessary to book for the most celebrated of all, Mouton-Rothschild. A visit to the highly ornate mansion and the home of some of the world's rarest wines is a delight not to be missed. The wine museum there contains priceless exhibits and wine labels featuring the work of artists such as Dali.

The grapes of Bordeaux (above) produce classic wines such as those of Moulis-en-Médoc (right)

In Pauillac there are many well-known vineyards including Château-Latour and Château Lafite, which has guided tours. In St-Estèphe the architecture of Cos d'Estournel is reminiscent of the Orient and recalls the days when estate owners returned from the East Indies with ornaments. The Margaux château, designed by a pupil of the architect responsible for Bordeaux's Grand Théâtre, is similarly well worth a visit. The architectural style is based on Greek temples.

Only in the Bordeaux region does the word 'château' refer to the house, farm buildings and vineyard – the whole wine-producing estate. Many of these buildings are pleasing examples of local architecture.

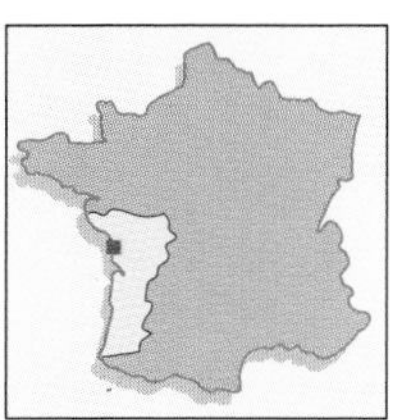

LA ROCHELLE AND THE ILE DE RÉ

LINKED by a modern road bridge, La Rochelle and the Ile de Ré are together the most attractive resorts on France's northern Atlantic Coast. Historically the Ile de Ré served variously as a protector to the harbour of La Rochelle and as a transit point for convicts awaiting deportation. Once an important maritime centre – the navy is still based nearby – the area is now more popular with well-heeled sailors of leisure.

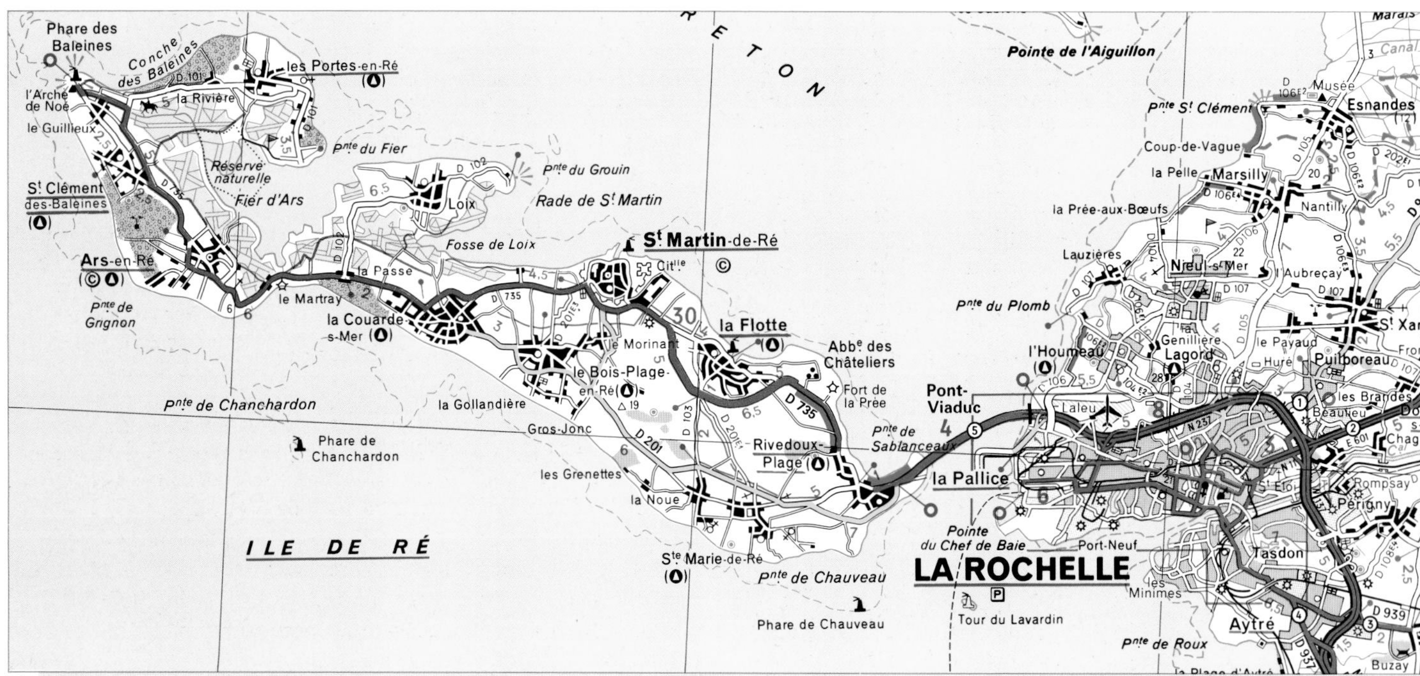

Comité Départemental du Tourisme de Charente-Maritime
11 *bis*, Rue des Augustins - BP 1152
17008 La Rochelle Cedex
Tel: 46 41 43 33

Touring:
use Michelin sheet map 233, Poitou Charentes

Abbaye des Châteliers

Driving along the main road from Rivedoux, the most striking sights you are likely to come across on the island are the ruins of the Abbaye de Notre-Dame de Ré, more commonly known as the Abbaye des Châteliers. Originally founded in the 12th century, it was burned down and rebuilt again many times until it finally fell into ruin in the early 17th century. There have been several excavations and the Musée d'Orbigny at La Rochelle contains a 13th-century tombstone from the abbey.

Ars-en-Ré

The economy of the Ile de Ré was founded on salt and wine. Many of the original salt-marshes have now been converted to oyster beds but you can still see others stretching for kilometres, in places such as Le Fier d'Ars. Ars-en-Ré, which today is a popular yachting centre, has very narrow streets, and you may notice that some of the corners have been cut off. This was so that people could turn round in the days when the horse and carriage provided the main form of transport.

Those interested in history should visit the 11th-century Église St-Étienne. Its black and white bell tower is a landmark for the island of Ars, and was in centuries past also used by navigators of passing ships. The church contains a 17th-century pulpit, an 18th-century lectern of painted and gilded wood and some interesting statues. Sunbathers may prefer to head for the lovely beach south of the town.

A striking modern road bridge joins the Ile de Ré to La Rochelle

Ile de Ré

Known locally as the 'white island bathed in light', the Ile de Ré is said by some to owe its name to the *ratis*, the fern with which it was covered in prehistoric times. Others say it was named after the Egyptian sun god Ra.

The harbour of La Rochelle is guarded by twin towers. For a contrast with the city's many historic buildings, you can enjoy a stroll in the beautiful wooded Parc Charruyer just behind the old city wall

Whatever the truth, this 30km-long island does have its own microclimate. It is, in fact, two islands – Loix and Ars – joined together by a narrow strip. It has had a turbulent history, mainly involving rivalry with Britain. However, today it is best known for the quality of its oysters, sandy beaches, pretty villages, wild birds and whitewashed cottages with green shutters. This is not to forget the taste of the local white wine, which some claim has the tang of seaweed. It is just right to accompany trout, oysters or any of the other seafood dishes for which the area is well known.

La Pallice

The commercial port on the western side of La Rochelle could scarcely be called attractive. But it has its points of interest, despite being heavily bombed in the war after the Germans built some huge concrete sheds as submarine bases. Being too difficult to demolish, some still remain in use. The navy has a base here. Close to La Pallice is the bridge linking the Ile de Ré with the mainland. The 2.9-km bridge was opened in 1988, 14 years after work began.

Pointe des Baleines

If you travel to the north-west tip of the Ile de Ré, you cannot miss the lighthouse on the Pointe des Baleines. It is one of the most powerful on the Atlantic coast, with its 47-km range. From its top you can see the whole island and get a good view of the Vendée coast. Children – and adults with a sense of fun – will enjoy a visit to the nearby 'Noah's Ark'.

La Rochelle

Sometimes called the French Geneva, this city claims, with some justification, to be France's most handsome port. Its origins were modest enough. In 1000 it was a simple Atlantic fishing village surrounded by marshlands. Eleanor of Aquitaine granted La Rochelle its charter in 1199, and ushered in a period of prosperity. Its still-bustling harbour, guarded by two towers that were part of its 14th-century fortifications, was once the site of a bitter siege. In 1627-8 Cardinal Richelieu blockaded the port because of the town's Protestant resistance to national unity. The population of 28,000 was reduced by famine to 5000. In more recent times it was the principal port for trade between France and Canada. But when Canada was liberated from France, in 1763, this trade all but died.

One interesting legacy of the association with Canada is the Musée du Nouveau Monde in Rue Fleuriau, which contains fascinating photographs of American Indians and old maps of America. The whole town is steeped in history, but you do not have to be a history enthusiast to enjoy atmosphere, the cobbled streets, beautiful parks, stylish shops and fabulous seafood restaurants. However, make a point of visiting the Gothic-style town hall, with its courtyard and Henry II staircase.

The towers that guard the entrance to the harbour are the Tour St-Nicolas (the patron saint of navigators) and the Tour de la Chaîne, the latter named after the heavy chain that was drawn between the two towers each night to seal off the harbour. Nearby, the Tour de la Lanterne formerly housed a large lantern that warned ships. From the balcony of this tower at low tide, you can see the foundations of the dykes built during Cardinal Richelieu's siege.

Convicts

In the 17th century the Citadelle de St-Martin, on the northern coast of the Ile de Ré, served to protect the island from foreign invaders. Later it found another use – as a prison, particularly as a transit point for deportees. The island was at one time known as the 'land of exile'.

The most famous deportees were the communards – 400 souls who were condemned by the Third Republic for insurrection. In 1872 they were sent to St-Martin before being shipped to New Caledonia. Many political or other prisoners who had been sentenced to hard labour or deportation found themselves spending a few months in St-Martin first. The prison was in use until 1947.

A statue in La Rochelle honours Eugène Fromentin, the 19th-century writer, who was born in the city

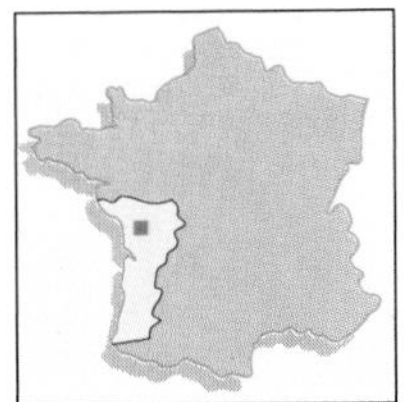

THE MARAIS POITEVIN

BETWEEN NIORT AND THE ATLANTIC lies the strange, misty landscape of the Marais Poitevin, reclaimed from the sea in the 11th century. It comprises two distinct areas, the dry marshes and the wet marshes, together now designated a Regional Nature Park. The wet marshes, known locally as the 'Green Venice', are the more beautiful and are best explored by boat. A further attraction is the surprising sight of churches and old abbeys – the legacy of the monks who originally drained the land.

Comité Départemental du Tourisme en Deux-Sèvres
74, Rue Alsace-Lorraine - BP 49
79002 Niort Cedex
Tel: 49 24 76 79

Touring:
use Michelin sheet map 233, Poitou Charentes

The Marais Poitevin is a secluded area divided up by an extensive network of canals. It is said that to this day not all of the 15,000 hectares of wet marshes have been fully explored

The remains of the 11th-century abbey of St-Pierre, near Maillezais. Boat trips can be taken from the quay at the abbey

Abbaye de St-Pierre

Situated right in the middle of the Marais Poitevin is the town of Maillezais, best known for the ruins of the Abbaye de St-Pierre, just outside the town. The abbey was originally built on an island in the 11th century and added to during the 14th and 16th centuries. In summer it is used for a dramatic *son et lumière*.

Château de Coudray-Salbart

About 6km north of Niort, on a rocky cliff overlooking the valley of the Sèvre Niortaise, are the ruins of the château, built by the lords of Parthenay in the 13th century. It is in the form of an irregular quadrilateral with six towers. One of these, the Tour Double, has walls over 6m thick.

Coulon

In the heart of the Marais Poitevin's wet marshes is the village of Coulon, with its low houses typical of the region. Each house has a small canal, and many farmers still rely on flat-bottomed punts for transport. Coulon is the best place to hire a punt to explore the whole area.

The area is now classified as a regional nature park. You can spot eels, pike, herons, snipes, duck, orioles, kingfishers and many other forms of wildlife. Worldwide interest in ecology is making this once relatively isolated area much more popular with tourists. Nevertheless it remains largely unspoiled, and has a slightly mysterious quality, owing to the fact that it is neither entirely land nor sea.

At Coulon, as elsewhere in the Marais Poitevin, punts provide a relaxing means of transport. The light filters gently through the poplar, ash and willow that line the tranquil canals

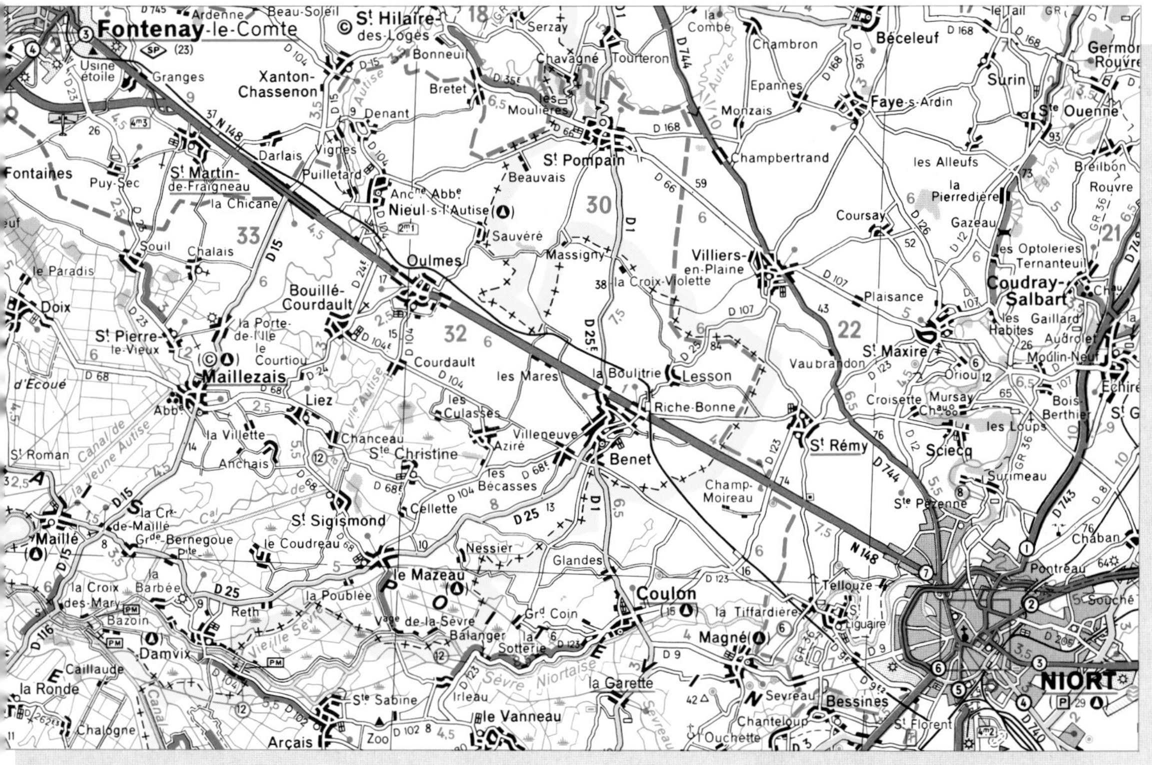

Marais Poitevin Food

The Marais Poitevin has a whole host of regional specialities when it comes to food and drink. Many include salt and cognac, which is produced nearby. Eels cooked in red wine sauce and snails in wine are very popular. Saddle of young goat with green garlic, mutton leg and local ham rubbed with salt and cognac are also local favourites. Meals are often served with *mojettes*, kidney beans, cooked in local butter, which is made from pasteurised cream. Goat's cheeses served with raspberry sauce make a rich ending to the meal. The whole region is proud of its goat's cheeses, which come in many different shapes.

Fontenay-le-Comte

Once the capital of lower Poitou, this town was given its motto by François I. It is engraved on the Renaissance Quatre-Tias fountain: 'Fountain and source of great minds'. During the Renaissance many writers and poets, including Rabelais, lived here. Today the old town still has many 16th- and 17th-century manor houses. Even the tourist office is sited in an old toll-house, and pretty walks abound.

Marais Poitevin

This is the low area between the Vendée plains in the north and the Niort plain to the east, with its apex in Coulon. Originally the land was covered by the sea, but as the sea retreated the land was reclaimed. Today there are 40,000 hectares of dry marshes, now mainly used as farmland – much of it given over to the beans that feature in so many local dishes – and 15,000 hectares of wet marshes.

Nieul-sur-l'Autise

This village is worth visiting for its Romanesque church, established in the 11th century. It has the only complete Romanesque cloister remaining in the entire Poitou region, and there are some good capitals on the main doorway.

Niort

A busy town situated on the Sèvre Niortaise, Niort once boasted a Plantagenet castle rumoured to be built by Henry II and Richard Lionheart. All that remains is the keep (Le Donjon), but it has a museum of Poitevin costumes where you can see jewellery, head-dresses, costumes and old tools.

Niort was once a thriving port and traded extensively with Canada. It also used to cultivate angelica and the local drink, *angélique de Niort*, dates from this time. Other local dishes include *matelotte des anguilles* (eels fried then baked in a wine sauce) and *mojettes à la maraîchaine* (kidney beans).

The town has several museums, including the Musée des Beaux-Arts, with several Dutch old masters in the gallery, and old houses. However, like so many of the towns in the Marais Poitevin, its chief attraction is its water, in this case the Sèvre Niortaise. There are also some very pretty walks near the town.

St Pompain

This is the site of one of the many Romanesque churches in the area. Monks were among the first settlers in the marshlands. The very first canal was called the Canal des Cinq Abbayes. These five abbeys were built on the first 'islands' left by the departing sea.

Oysters & Mussels

A luxury in most parts of the world, oysters are everyday fare on the Atlantic Coast. But they need a lot of care and attention and can take four years to mature. In the autumn lime-washed clutches are placed in oyster parks. After 10 months they are transferred to oyster beds, then to *claires*, running-water beds where they fatten. Oyster farmers must continually clean out the algae and weeds that inhibit the growth of the oysters. Their green exterior colour comes from a seaweed, the *navicule bleue*.

Mussels are grown on *bouchots*, wooden posts planted in the open sea to which the broods stick and grow. The most

traditional way to eat mussels is to place them upright on a wooden board, cover them with pine needles and then set them alight.

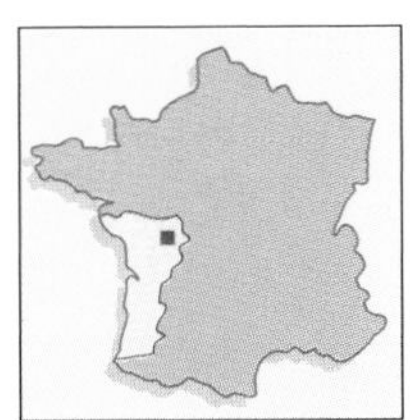

POITIERS AND CHURCH ARCHITECTURE

THE ROLLING PLAINS around Poitiers, with their crops of wheat and maize, have been marched across by many invaders over the centuries. Moors, Arabs, Visigoths and the English have sought control of the area and have left a rich legacy for today's tourist, particularly of religious architecture. Poitiers itself used to be on the pilgrims' route to Santiago de Compostela and lay at the heart of Eleanor of Aquitaine's domain.

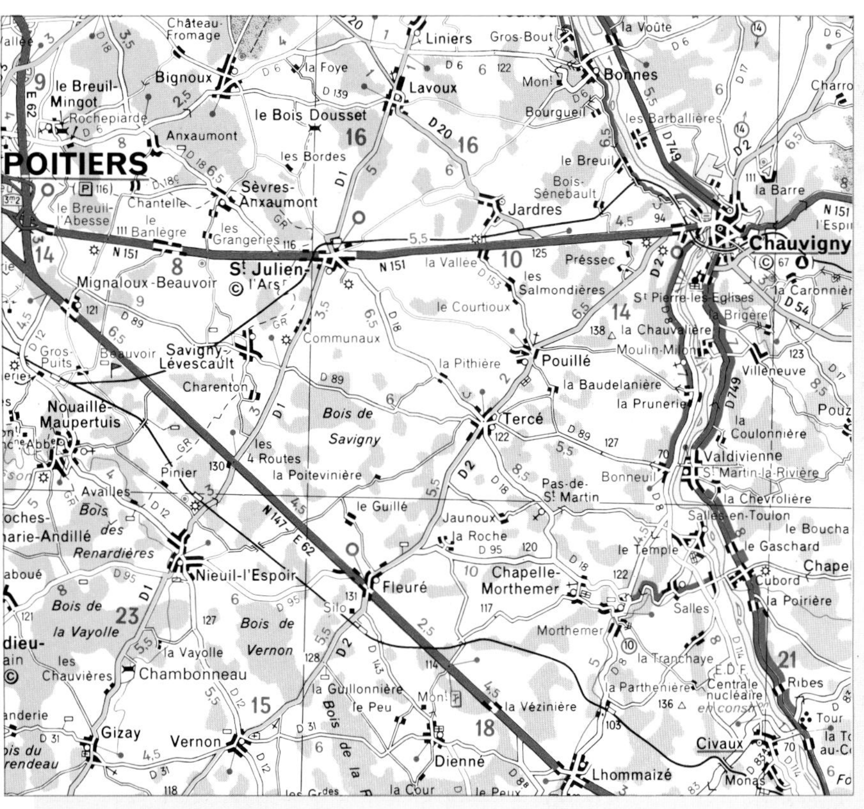

Chauvigny

This town boasts the ruins of five medieval castles set alongside the 11th-century Église St-Pierre, grouped together on a hill overlooking the town. The sculpted capitals of the church are justifiably famous, depicting scenes that are the stuff of nightmares – for example, a Siamese twin being gnawed by monsters! Lower down the town is the 11th- or 12th-century Romanesque Église Notre-Dame. On the river at the far south end of the town, St-Pierre-les-Églises has some 9th-century frescos.

Civaux

Civaux, a tiny hamlet on the west bank of the Vienne, has a 12th-century church in the middle of a Merovingian cemetery. Here was once a city of the dead with 20,000 tombs. Today there are still 2000 4th- and 5th-century sarcophagi containing those who fought to hold this land.

CHURCH MURALS

Some 20km to the east of Chauvigny is the small town of St Savin. Its abbey church, probably built in the 11th century on the site of a church founded earlier by Charlemagne, contains what is believed to be the finest example of Romanesque murals in France, if not in Europe. The wall paintings, which have been designated a UNESCO Heritage centre, include scenes from Genesis and Exodus, including Noah's Ark and workmen building the Tower of Babel. In the summer there are daily guided tours. While in St Savin, you should also visit the international centre for mural art and the medieval bridge over the River Gartempe, from where you get a beautiful view of the abbey church and its Gothic spire.

Office Départemental du Tourisme de la Vienne
15, Rue Carnot - BP 287
86007 Poitiers Cedex
Tel: 49 41 58 22

Touring:
use Michelin sheet map 233, Poitou Charentes

Chapelle-Morthemer

To get an idea of the immense power wielded by the barons of Poitou in the Middle Ages you have only to visit the château and church of Morthemer. Built on a massive scale, they tower somewhat menacingly over the little village and the valley of the Dive. The buildings date back to the 14th century, though architecture buffs will notice that the church has a strange mixture of Gothic and Romanesque styles. There are frescos of Christ and the Virgin, from when the church was first built. Another of the church's claims to fame is the 16th-century tomb of Renée Sangler.

The most striking aspect of the château is its rectangular turreted keep. Among the many who no doubt came to a sorry end in this gloomy prison was one John Chandos, a lieutenant of England's Black Prince who was wounded in the battle of Lussac.

St-Pierre-les-Églises at Chauvigny boasts fine relief carvings

There is a heavy concentration of ancient and beautiful churches in and around Poitiers. In the heart of the city is the 12th-century Notre-Dame-la-Grande

Nouaillé-Maupertuis

Every June there is a medieval festival in the town to commemorate the battle between England's victorious Black Prince and John the Good (Jean II), during the Hundred Years War. Even if you miss the festival, the town is still worth a visit. There is a Romanesque church with a 12th-century belfry, and a Benedictine abbey surrounded by walls, a moat with fortifications and a medieval garden.

The 4th-century Baptistère St-Jean is France's oldest Christian church

Poitiers

Set on a hill overlooking the Rivers Clain and Boivre, Poitiers used to be the capital of the Poitou region. From a distance it does not look inspiring. However, once you are inside the old city – and plenty of it remains – Poitiers reveals its true charms.

Historians rate it as one of France's most important cities, particularly for Romanesque art. In the Middle Ages it was a very important commercial and religious centre, at one time boasting 67 churches.

One of the most famous sites in Poitiers is the Église Notre-Dame-la-Grande, a 12th-century church originally built in the reign of Eleanor of Aquitaine. The sculptures on the outside, particularly the western front, are a masterpiece of Romanesque art. Today the church is surrounded by an open-air market where you can buy some of the goat's cheeses for which the area is famed. A short walk away is the Cathédrale St-Pierre, Poitiers' largest church. This has some spectacular 12th-century stained-glass windows and its wooden choir-stalls are believed to be the oldest in France.

Other Romanesque churches worth visiting include St-Hilaire, Ste-Radegonde and St-Porchaire. The oldest building in Poitiers is the 4th-century Baptistère St-Jean, the earliest Christian church in France. Try to see also: the French, Flemish and Italian paintings in the Musée Ste-Croix (the museum also has a section devoted to the history of Poitou – a useful prelude to a tour of the historical sites); the palace of the counts of Poitou; and the half-timbered houses of Rue de la Chaîne.

North of the old town is the Église de Montierneuf. In the 11th century it was the site of a Benedictine monastery, which was rebuilt in the 17th century.

The more modern – that is, 19th-century – building of the Palais de Justice encloses a medieval tower and parts of a ducal palace where Joan of Arc was cross-examined by doctors and bishops. It was here that Richard Lionheart became Duke of Anjou in 1170.

Futuroscope

In Jaunay-Clan, 7km north of Poitiers, is Futuroscope (below), Europe's first park devoted to technology: France's answer to the USA's Epcot Center. Its numerous attractions include: a Kinemax cinema with a 600sq-m screen; a 3-D cinema; a 'dynamic' cinema where spectators' seats react to the picture – for example, they shake when an earthquake is shown; a Gyrotour from which those with strong nerves can see the park from a rotating tower at a height of 45m; and an 'enchanted lake' with fountains. There is also a Lego exhibition spread over 2 hectares. Behind the scenes, not open to the public, Futuroscope has a serious side and includes a research centre, university and telecommunications centre.

BERRY AND LIMOUSIN

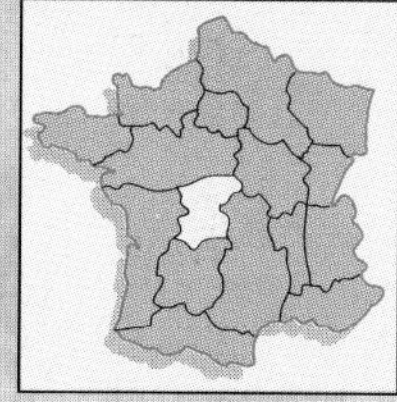

A FORGOTTEN REGION IGNORED by tourists in favour of the more spectacular, Berry and Limousin have few great monuments and little dramatic scenery. Nor is the area renowned for its food or wine. Yet the few that know better call it paradise. It has bred some of the greatest cultural achievements in France – Limoges enamel and porcelain and the Aubusson tapestries, to name but three – and inspired deep devotion in writers and artists, natives and visitors alike.

'I prefer to have a nettle in my Berry than a magnificent oak tree in any other place,' declared George Sand, the region's most famous daughter. The sentiment might sound extravagant, but it has long been shared by countless others.

Berry and Limousin lie at the heart of France. They also have a good claim to being its historic centre. As far back as the 6th century BC, Bourges, then known as Avaric, was a thriving Celtic city. At the collapse of the Roman Empire this was the first area settled by the Franks, who gave France its name. During the lengthy struggles leading up to and forming part of the Hundred Years War, it was within the island of land that was never ruled by England. In 1429 the Duc de Berry became Charles VII of France, the monarch who finally found the resources and the strength to drive the English out of France.

Since then the region's historic importance has faded. Limoges is the only city of any real size, and the only major industrial centre. Visitors today find themselves in a gentle, agricultural backwater dotted by small market towns and tiny villages, modest châteaux and minute Romanesque churches. In the north the great plain of Berry-Champagne is an area of open skies and prairie-like fields of wheat, framed with scarlet when the poppies are in flower. Further south the landscape gently gives way to rolling pasture patchworked by hedges and oak woodland. Creamy Charentais cows and russet Berry goats graze quietly while eagles and hawks swoop high above the fields. Wild boar and deer still roam the forest reserves.

Four main rivers – the Cher, the Indre, the Creuse and the Vienne – meander languidly across the limestone plateau, feeding the crops and drawing the tourists. Many of these come also for the water sports on the two main lakes, Chambon and Vassivière. But by contrast with the more famous neighbouring areas, here there are no great armies of tourists, no batteries of souvenir stalls, no vast complexes of holiday homes. Yet the area has plenty to offer sightseers and those who prefer to take it easy.

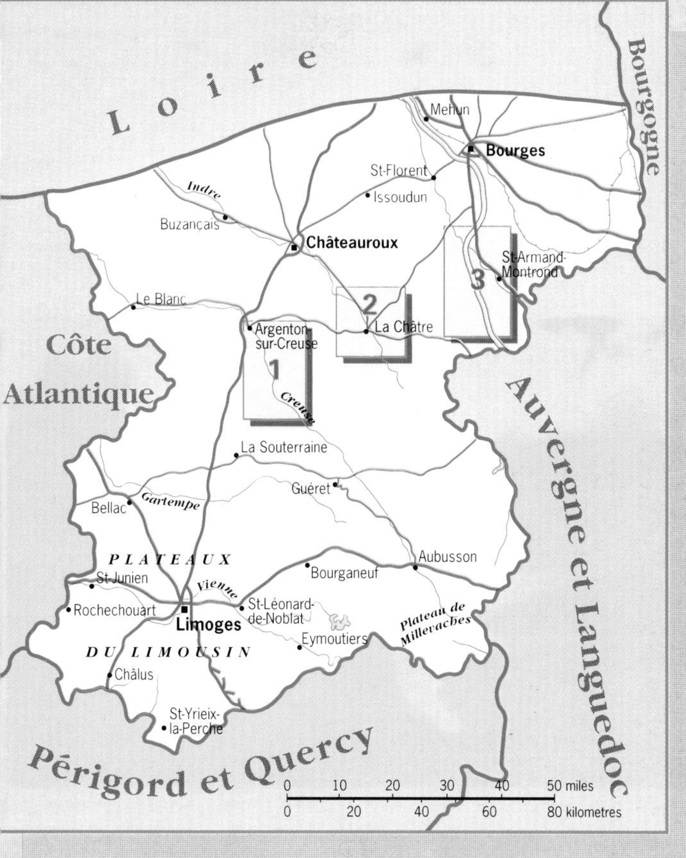

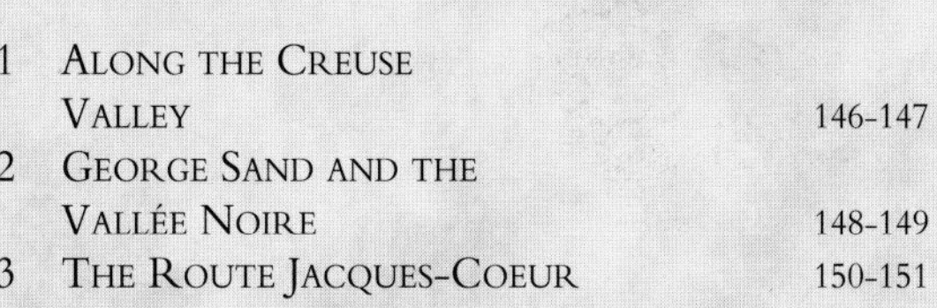

Berry is famed for the cheese produced by its russet goats (left)
George Sand and Chopin stayed in the Château de Culan (left below)
Sunflowers (left bottom)

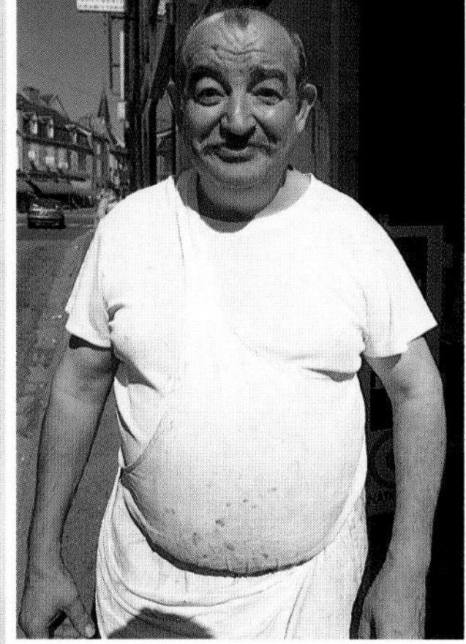

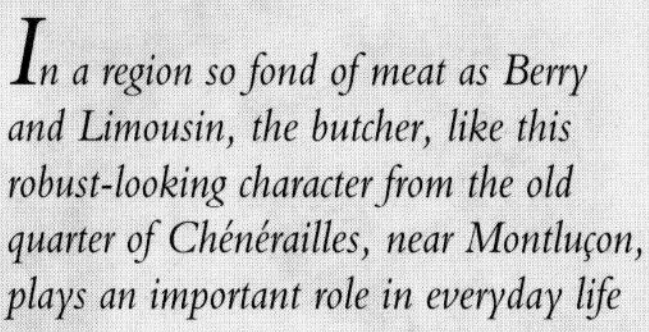

In a region so fond of meat as Berry and Limousin, the butcher, like this robust-looking character from the old quarter of Chénérailles, near Montluçon, plays an important role in everyday life

Wine-growers in Berry (top) produce a number of good red, white and rosé wines (above)

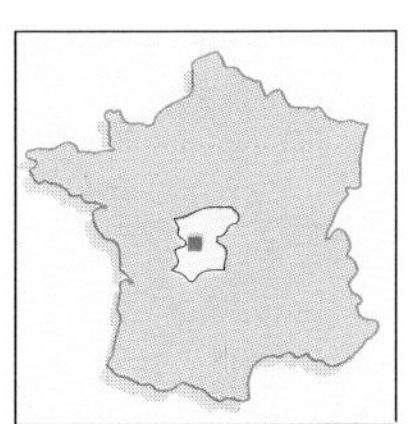

ALONG THE CREUSE VALLEY

UNLIKE THE GENTLE COUNTRYSIDE NEARBY, this stretch of the Creuse (literally 'hollow') cuts deep into the granite hills to create a long series of spectacular gorges beloved of many artists, including Rousseau and Monet. There are several historic sights of great interest, but this area is renowned above all for its scenery and as a centre for water sports.

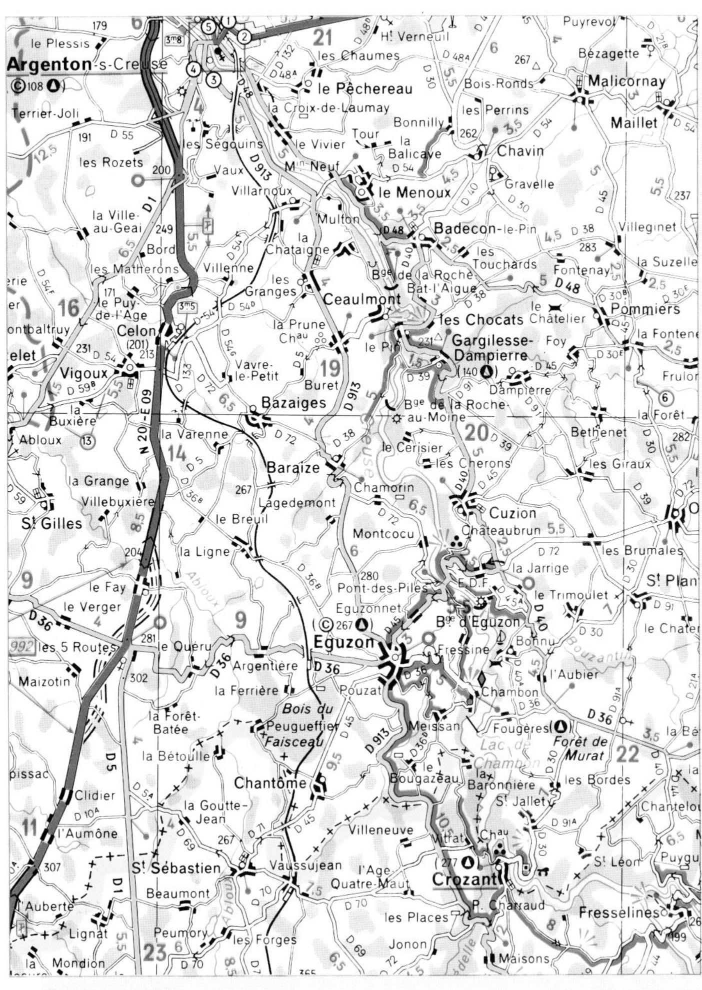

The ruins of the château at Crozant. Overgrown footpaths lead between the ivy-clad remnants of towers that still cling precariously to the wooded cliffs. There are magnificent views from the fortress

Château de Crozant

The fortress at Crozant was once one of the largest and most important in France. Built between the 13th and 15th centuries, it had walls over half a kilometre long, ten towers and a garrison of several thousand. It played a key role in the defence of Limousin and Aquitaine during the Hundred Years War (1337-1453) and the Wars of Religion (1562-98). However, severe damage, sustained both in battle and during an earthquake, meant that it was already in ruins by the 17th century. Nevertheless it remains one of the most spectacular sights in the region, since it is set high on a promontory overlooking the gorges of the Creuse and the Sedelle.

Comité Départemental du Tourisme de l'Indre
36, Rue Bourdillon
36000 Châteauroux
Tel: 54 22 91 20

Touring:
use Michelin sheet map 238, Centre/ Berry-Nivernais

Argenton-sur-Creuse

This bustling market town grew up at the foot of a vast fortress built in 761 by Pepin the Short, King of the Franks. Today only a few sections of the château walls and its chapel remain. The chapel was built in the 15th century on the site of the 2nd-century sanctuary of St Ursin, the first Bishop of Berry. In 1899 it was topped by a vast, gilded statue of La Bonne Dame d'Argenton. More than 6m high and weighing six tonnes, this has become the main local landmark. There is a panoramic view of the town from the terrace by the chapel, and from the Vieux Pont there are views of old riverside houses and mills.

Fresselines

The little cliff-top village of Fresselines has an august artistic pedigree: Monet, Rousseau and Rodin all worked here. It was also for a long time the home of the 19th-century poet and musician Maurice Rollinat, to whom there are two memorials: a *bas-relief* by Rodin in the back wall of the church, and a bust by Paul Surtel.

From the bridge over the Petite Creuse on the road to Nouzerolles, there are good views of both Fresselines and the Château de Puyguillon.

GOAT'S CHEESE

The one great claim of this area to gastronomic fame is its goat's cheese. There are six varieties, both hard and soft, all made from whole milk, with a creamy texture. None is strong. The best known is the *crottin*, which is the shape of a flat-topped cone. Its name comes from the small, clay oil lamp of the same shape that was at one time used in the area. The best cheese is said to come from the milk of the smooth-haired Berry goat.

Well-preserved 13th- and 15th-century frescos decorate the walls of the crypt of Notre-Dame-de-Gargilesse. The novelist George Sand gave a description of Gargilesse as it was in the last century in her Promenade autour d'un village

Gargilesse-Dampierre

One of the prettiest villages in Berry, Gargilesse-Dampierre is tucked away in a steep river valley. Probably the best view of the village, as well as of the confluence of the Rivers Gargilesse and Creuse and the iron Pont Noir is from just across the bridge over the Creuse.

It is a place of narrow streets and stone-built, geranium-clad cottages, liberally sprinkled with artists' studios. At the end of one alley is 'Algira', the small cottage bought for George Sand as a writing retreat by her lover, Alexandre Manceau. Today the cottage is a museum, with mementoes and work by both George Sand and her son, Maurice Sand.

The 18th-century château is closed to the public. In its grounds is the Romanesque Notre-Dame-de-Gargilesse, which has magnificent frescos and carvings. There are 129 capitals, all different. The themes include the Old Men of the Apocalypse, Old and New Testament stories and decorative designs. All are finely carved and in a remarkably good state of preservation. The frescos in the crypt date from the 13th and 15th centuries. Those in the apse and the two side chapels are still glorious. Centred round a huge portrait of Christ at the Apocalypse are scenes from the life of Christ and the Old Testament, and the patron saints of the various donors.

Lac de Chambon

This lake was created by the Barrage d'Éguzon, which, when it came into operation in 1926, was one of the first major dams to be built in Europe. Built primarily as a hydroelectric project, the dam is 59m high and 300m wide. There is an excellent view from beside the power station above the dam wall.

The narrow, 16-km long lake has become a major water-sports centre with its activities centred on Éguzon. This was once a fortified medieval village, although only the château's gateway remains as a sign of its illustrious past. Near here are a beach and a nautical club where you can swim or hire boats. The small roads round the lake do not follow the shoreline, but there are frequent access points.

Le Pin

About 2km north of Gargilesse-Dampierre, near the tiny hamlet of Les Chocats, there is a superb view over the Creuse gorges. Nicknamed Le Boucle, this stretch of the river loops tightly around the promontory of Le Pin in a last flamboyant gesture before leaving the granite hills for the gentle, flatter plain of Berry-Champagne. High on the opposite cliff you can see the Romanesque church of Ceaulmont.

Crafts

Fine enamels have been produced in Limoges since the 12th century. Early work was all *champlevé* ware, with the enamel being layered into hollows on an

engraved copper base. Since the 14th century, however, Limoges has also produced painted enamels. Porcelain production in the region was first made possible by the discovery of local kaolin deposits in 1768, allowing for the first time in France the production of delicate hard-paste porcelains based on a mixture of kaolin and sand. The first porcelain factory in Limoges was founded in 1771. Today Limoges produces more than half of France's china.

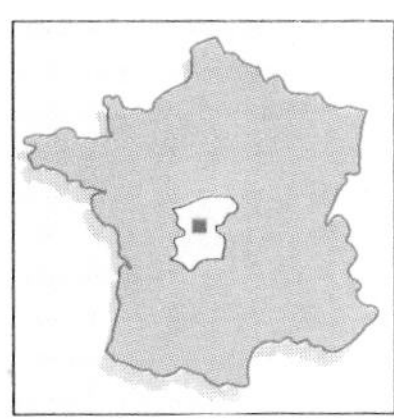

GEORGE SAND AND THE VALLÉE NOIRE

BUT FOR GEORGE SAND, few would have heard of the Vallée Noire. She set a series of pastoral romances here, creating an image of rural bliss. The farmers might no longer wear smocks, but this stretch of the Indre still exudes a sense of calm well-being that makes it easy to understand the writer's deep devotion to her lifelong home.

Château de Nohant

George Sand lived and worked in this rather run-down 18th-century château for most of her life. Here she gathered around her an artistic and literary circle of extraordinary talent, including Chopin, Liszt, Balzac, Flaubert, Dumas and Delacroix.

Now a museum, the château feels as if time has stood still since Sand's death. Faded place cards stand on the dining table, her pens wait to be picked up again and the curtain is ready to rise in the tiny theatre where she tried out her plays in front of a local audience before taking them to Paris. George Sand died at Nohant in 1876 and is buried in the family plot in the grounds of the château.

There is a charming but sadly neglected Romanesque church on the green outside the château gates.

Château de Sarzay

Built in the mid-14th century by Matthieu de Barbançois, the Château de Sarzay was in its prime a vast, moated edifice covering five hectares, with 38 towers and two drawbridges. All that remains today is the keep, a rectangular building with four circular corner towers, the fortified chapel and fragments of the outer wall. Even so, the château is remarkably impressive, its sombre elegance visible for several kilometres on every approach.

The current owners live in the farmhouse next door, the approach to which is through an attractive working farmyard. Inside, a thick layer of dust over the simple furnishings, together with the signs warning of ongoing restoration, give it an intensely atmospheric air, part building site, part fairytale castle. There are magnificent views over the surrounding countryside from the turrets.

LA BONNE DAME DE NOHANT

George Sand (1804-76) was born Aurore Dupin. Her father had royal blood, her mother was the daughter of a bird seller. Married briefly and unhappily to Baron Dudevant, she went on to live with various other lovers, both in Paris and at her family home of Nohant. She took her pen-name from Jules Sandeau, the lover with whom she collaborated in writing her first novel.

Today George Sand is commonly remembered both as Chopin's mistress and as a great eccentric (she occasionally wore trousers and a top hat and

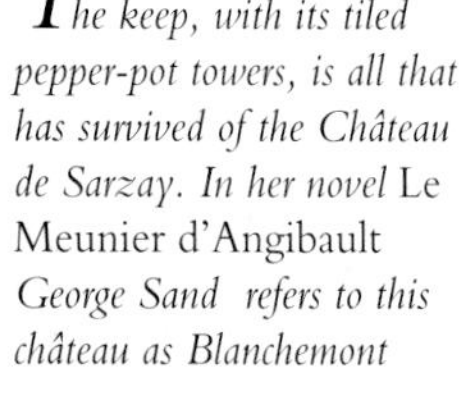

The keep, with its tiled pepper-pot towers, is all that has survived of the Château de Sarzay. In her novel Le Meunier d'Angibault *George Sand refers to this château as Blanchemont*

La Châtre

Although it has a population of only just over 5000, this little market town is the main centre on this stretch of the Indre. It is a charming place, built round a central market square, with a fine collection of half-timbered, 15th-century buildings as well as a number of 17th- and 18th-century stone houses. The arched Pont aux Laies across the Indre gives a good view back to the decorated roof lines and wooden balconies of the tanneries district.

The keep, which is all that still remains of the 15th-century Château de Chauvigny, now houses an eccentric but interesting museum with a collection of 3000 stuffed birds and a floor devoted to George Sand, with photos, original manuscripts, letters and first editions. The second floor is given over to the work of local artists and local crafts.

La Châtre is an important market town in the heart of the Vallée Noire

smoked cigars). During her life, however, her reputation as a writer was immense, and she enjoyed simultaneous critical and popular acclaim.

Sand was extremely prolific, writing 28 plays, and over 100 other works, including 80 novels. Some 20,000 of her letters have also been published. Many of her peers, from Dostoevsky to George Eliot, openly acknowledged her influence on their work. She was a committed socialist and remained politically active for most of her life. Although George Sand did not regard herself as a feminist, she was an early and influential exponent of women's rights.

In Berry George Sands (below) still enjoys the stature of a saint; she is 'La Bonne Dame de Nohant'.

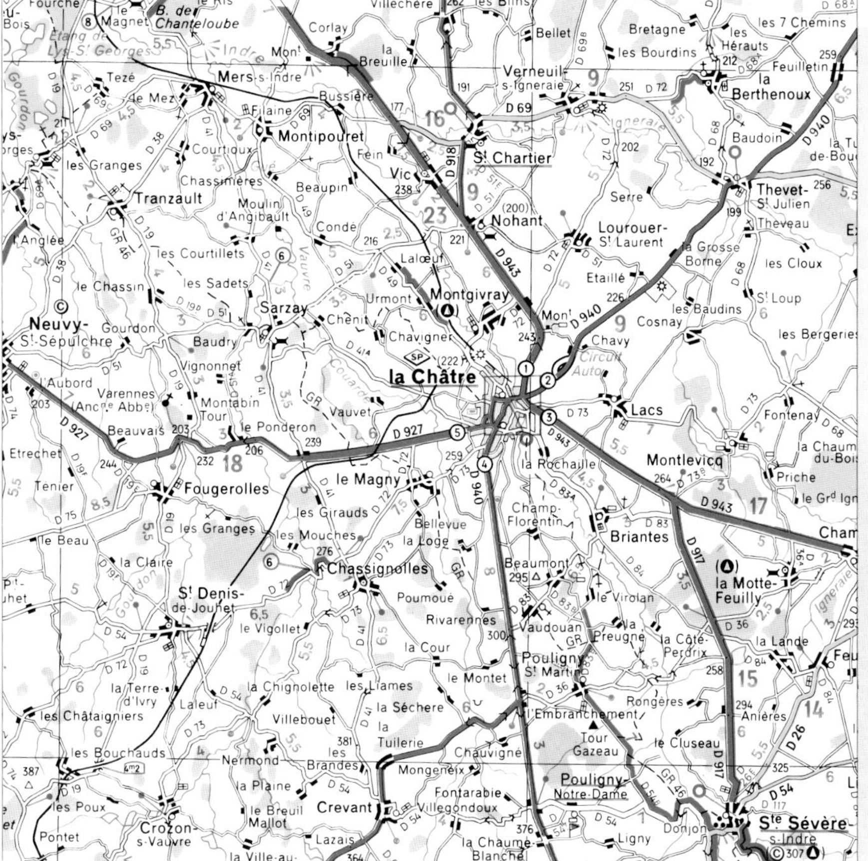

Neuvy-St-Sépulchre

Neuvy-St-Sépulchre lies about 20km to the west of La Châtre and there is a story attached to its name. When Eude de Déols came home from pilgrimage in the Holy Land in 1042, he was so taken with Jerusalem that he decided to build a copy of the Holy Sepulchre. The result is this extraordinary little basilica. The 22-m two-storey rotunda has a central ring of 11 heavy columns with fine sculptured capitals, and seven apsidal chapels around the outer wall. Above, a somewhat lighter ambulatory surrounds a central dome. An exhibition of sacred art is held here every summer. A central altar is placed directly under the dome. The iron strapwork door at the entrance dates from the 12th century.

The basilica was built on to an existing rectangular church with several small side chapels. This was to be demolished until word came from Jerusalem that the Holy Sepulchre had been extended, when it was decided to leave it in place. It was vaulted over in the 13th century and has been restored many times since. The resulting church is fascinating, if somewhat awkward, its two halves being forced by design to function separately. A few old buildings surrounding it are all that now remain of the canons' cloisters that were once attached to the church.

St Chartier

Chiefly famous as the setting of George Sand's novel *Les Maîtres Sonneurs*, this is a small attractive village with a pretty but undistinguished church that was heavily restored in the 19th century, and a 14th-century château, not open to the public. Each summer, however, it hosts a major international folk festival that keeps alive local musical and dance traditions. There are concerts and demonstrations by makers of bagpipes, lutes and hurdy-gurdies, all of which were traditionally made in the area.

Ste Sévère-sur-Indre

Perched on a cliff top overlooking the Indre, this pretty village has had an eventful history. Founded in 630 around an abbey long since vanished, it was later ruled by bandits, was sacked twice, and during the Revolution became a commune. In the central square are a 15th-century fortified gateway, a 16th-century stone cross and an open-sided 17th-century market hall, as well as other old buildings.

Comité Départemental du Tourisme de l'Indre
36, Rue Bourdillon
36000 Châteauroux
Tel: 54 22 91 20

Touring:
use Michelin sheet map 238, Centre/ Berry-Nivernais

In Berry and Limousin most people still live close to the soil (above)

The ancient beamed market hall in Ste Sévère-sur-Indre (top)

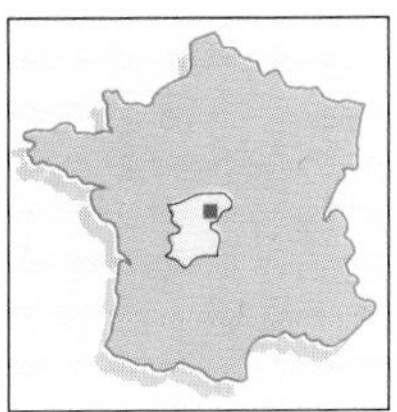

THE ROUTE JACQUES-COEUR

Comité Départemental du Tourisme du Cher
5, Rue de Séricourt
18000 Bourges (à partir 1/11/90)
Tel: 48 67 00 18

Touring:
use Michelin sheet map 238, Centre/Berry-Nivernais

THE BERRICHONS HAVE GIVEN the name of Jacques Coeur, the most famous son of the great medieval city of Bourges, to a route that carves its way through the heart of France. Few of the châteaux and churches along the way have any historical connection with Jacques Coeur, but together they paint a fascinating picture of French history, from the fearsome fortresses of the 11th century to the studied frivolity of the 18th.

The cloisters of the abbey at Noirlac. At its height Noirlac's 150 monks and 150 lay brothers spent eight hours a day in church, starting at 2 am

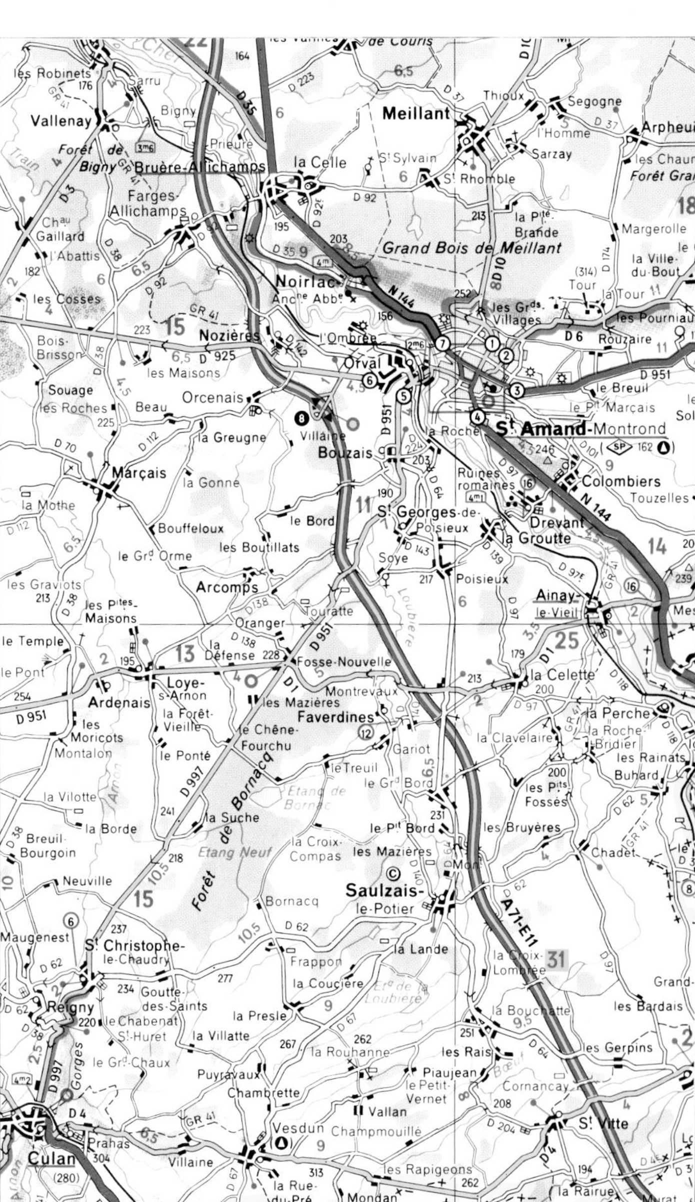

Abbaye de Noirlac

Founded in 1150 by Abbot Robert de Clairvaux, a cousin of St Bernard, the abbey at Noirlac, set in a peaceful river valley, is the only French Cistercian monastery to have survived almost intact. The vast, austere abbey church has no capitals, sculptures or paintings, and its windows are of grisaille glass, yet its simple arches have immense grace and its honey-coloured stone lends warmth and charm. Only three sides of the more elaborate 13th- and 14th-century cloister, with its ogival arches and traced windows, have survived.

Jacques Coeur

Despite humble origins in Bourges, Jacques Coeur made a fortune and became Master of the Mint to Charles VII, and thus one of the most powerful men in France. In 1451 jealous rivals falsely accused him of murdering the king's mistress, and the king seized his fortune and exiled him. But in 1457, a year after Jacques' death, Charles finally acknowledged his innocence.

Bruère-Allichamps

Since 1865 this little village on the banks of the Cher has been officially recognised as the geographical centre of France. It has a monument to prove it. Yet France has three hearts, say the diplomatic Berrichons, for two other nearby villages, Saulzais-le-Potier and Vesdun, hotly contest the honour – and they too have the monuments to prove it.

Château d'Ainay-le-Vieil

This small, octagonal, moated fortress, is by some nicknamed 'little Carcassonne'. Originally built in the 13th century, its nine towers and rampart walls have all survived intact. It was owned briefly by Jacques Coeur, then sold in 1467 to the Bigny family, who still own it today. In the late-

Restored in recent years, the Château de Culan (above) has a number of attractions, including exhibitions of medieval weapons of war and tapestries from several centuries

The extravagant external ornament of Meillant (above right) is matched by the attention to detail inside the château. In addition, the chapel in the courtyard has a beautiful 16th-century Rhenish altarpiece

15th century they built an Italianate Renaissance château into the wall. This has a small, highly decorated octagonal tower at the entrance and magnificent painted coffered ceilings in the main public rooms.

In the grounds a beautiful rose garden includes a number of old species, some of them dating back to the 15th century, as well as some scented and newer varieties.

A tiny but charming village is tucked under the château's walls.

Château de Culan

The setting of the Château de Culan is one of the most dramatic in this area: perched heavily on a cliff top over the gorge of the River Arnon, dominating both the town and its approaches. The château was begun in the 11th century, but only one side of the original massive, rectangular fortress still exists. This remnant is forbidding enough, with the circular towers at its corners in perfect condition, complete with roof and machicolations. The inner face and lower levels of the château have been altered at various times, the last major rebuilding occurring in the 17th century, to create an elegant and comfortable stately home.

The tour follows the centuries, with displays of 13th- and 14th-century soldiers and armoury, 17th- and 18th-century salons with fine Flemish and Aubusson tapestries, and a look at the bedroom used by George Sand and Chopin on their many visits. There are magnificent views over the valley from the terrace, and of the château itself from the bridge on the Montluçon road.

Château de Meillant

The Romans first settled Meillant as a garrison town. The village today is an attractive if slightly delapidated place, with buildings that date back to the 17th century.

The present château, an architectural gem, has its origins in the early 14th century moated fortress built by Étienne de Sancerre. In the late 15th century the Amboise family destroyed much of the rampart wall, incorporating some of the medieval towers into the south face of their new château. The curved east façade is a riot of decoration, a perfect example of 'flowering' or High Gothic architecture that nevertheless foretells the more classical lines of the Renaissance. Particularly spectacular is the central Tour du Lion (so called because of the small lead lion on its roof), which was designed by Giocondo, a close colleague of Michelangelo. The chapel and well date from the 16th century.

Inside, the sumptuously decorated rooms have a festive air. Especially notable are the dining-room, with hand-painted, embossed wallpaper, carved, painted frieze, painted ceiling and stained-glass windows, and the medieval Great Hall with its wooden ceiling and vast, formidable bosses of knights in armour.

Bourges

The capital of Berry, Bourges is a medieval masterpiece, a warren of cobbled streets lined with beautiful buildings, from humble stone cottages to timber-framed shops and grand palaces. The huge Cathédrale St-Étienne, built between 1135 and 1324, is one of the finest in France, with a series of magnificent stained-glass medallion windows (1215-25) in the apse. The Palais Jacques-

Coeur, commissioned in 1443 but not completed until after his disgrace, is grander than many royal palaces of the period. Other attractions include the 16th-century Hôtel Cujas, containing the archaeological and folklore collections of the Musée du Berry.

AUVERGNE AND LANGUEDOC

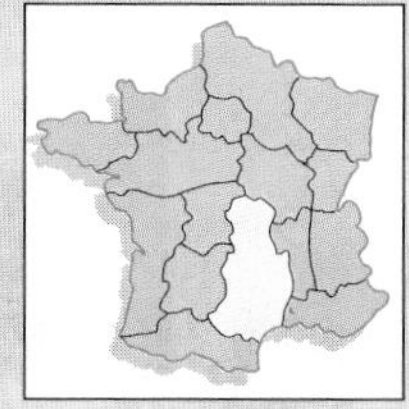

THOUGH WELL BELOW THE HIGH Alps and the Pyrenees in altitude, and lower than the peaks of Haute-Provence, the Auvergne and Languedoc region is thought of by many intending visitors as mountainous. This is because Auvergne in particular is synonymous with the Massif Central. Although they quickly change their minds, they are never disappointed, for what the region lacks in height and snowy peaks it more than makes up for in the sheer diversity of its scenery. Close to Clermont-Ferrand is the Parc Régional des Volcans d'Auvergne with its array of old volcanic cones.

Further south, the scenery of the Cévennes is so special that the area is designated a Parc National, one of only six in France, and is the only non-alpine such park on the mainland. Close by are the Causses, a huge area of raised limestone pavements that create a virtual rocky desert, the heart of which has been honeycombed by rainwater to produce some of the finest show caves in the world.

Between and around those high land blocks, the valley and plain scenery is equally good. Auvergne, which lies to the north of Languedoc, starts with Bourbonnais, a gently rolling, pastoral area surrounding the towns of Vichy and Montluçon. Vichy was, and is, a spa town. By contrast, Montluçon is a large industrial city.

Here we concentrate on that part of Auvergne below Clermont-Ferrand, exploring the unique scenery touched on above. Le Puy-en-Velay – perhaps the most spectacular town in France – is visited, though Clermont-Ferrand itself is not. Clermont is a sprawling industrial city, but it does have its points of interest, in particular the Basilique de Notre-Dame-du-Port, believed by many to be the finest example of Auvergne Romanesque architecture.

We also explore southern Auvergne, an emptier landscape where the visitor can the more easily appreciate the feel of the countryside. At inns in or between the villages and small towns the visitor can sample the enticing local foods. Auvergne is said to be the cheeseboard of France, such is the variety and quality of its cheeses. Then there is *potée auvergnate,* a stew of salt pork and vegetables; and Auvergne claims to have invented coq au vin.

To the south we enter Languedoc, an empty, secret land of lush valleys and low, wooded hills. This is beautiful country, so very different from Provence to the east, even if the menus of the two areas occasionally look very similar. To taste the difference, try cassoulet, a casserole of pork and haricot beans spiced with garlic and herbs, or *cousinat,* a stew of chestnuts (a local speciality), cream and fruit. Montpellier, the area's largest city, well planned and attractive, lies close to the Mediterranean.

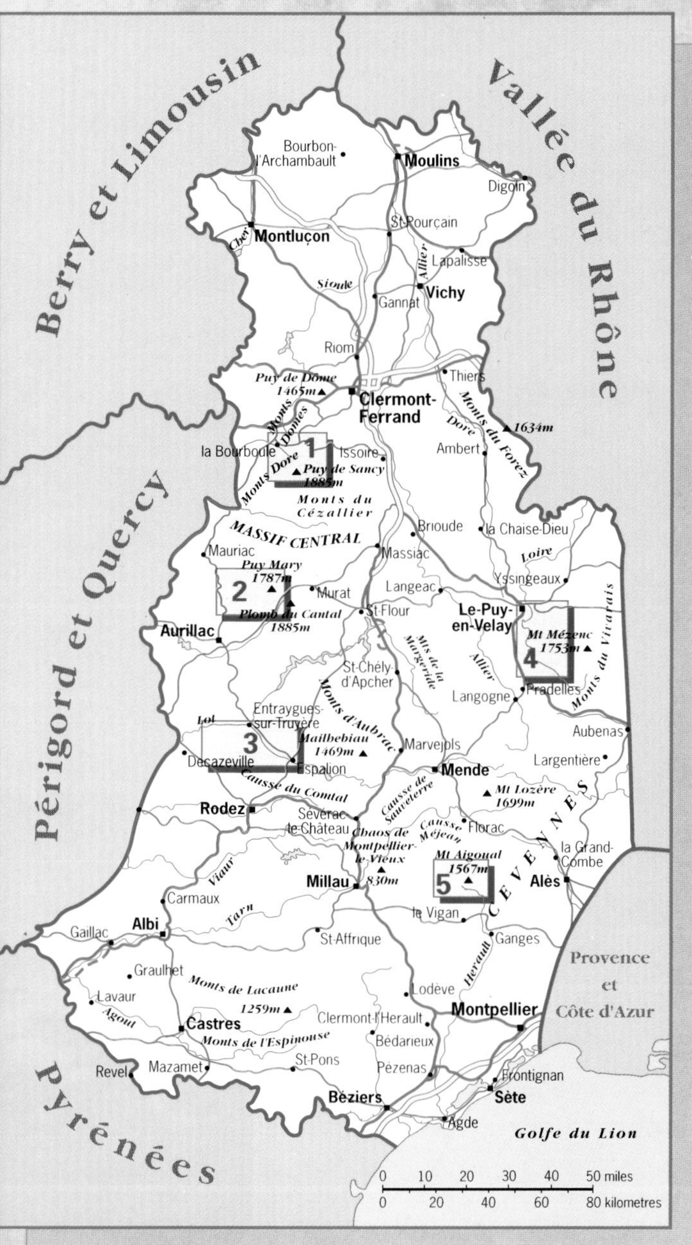

Of the more than 100 volcanoes of the Monts Dômes, the Puy de Dôme (above) is the oldest The Salers (below left) is a hardy breed of cow - nowadays very popular throughout France

The region's many markets offer fresh local produce and provide a good meeting place

Much of Auvergne and Languedoc is an agricultural region, whose inhabitants are fond of the outdoor life

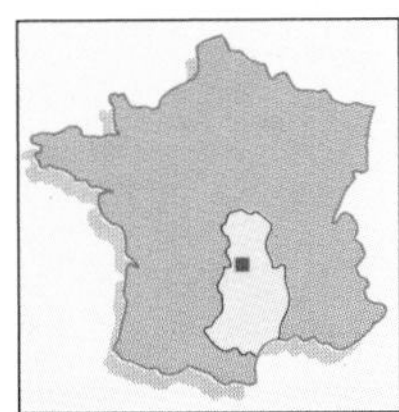

THE MONTS DORE

TO THE WEST of Clermont-Ferrand lies the Parc Régional des Volcans d'Auvergne, one of the most spectacular landscapes in France. The old volcanoes are laid out in a chain, with the Monts du Cantal to the south (see page 156-7) and the region's oldest and best known peak, the Puy de Dôme, lying to the north. Between these two are the Monts Dore, a superb piece of country, with impressive peaks hovering above equally fine villages.

Comité Départemental du Tourisme et du Thermalisme du Puy-de-Dôme
26, Rue Saint-Esprit
63038 Clermont-Ferrand Cedex
Tel: 73 42 21 21

Touring:
use Michelin sheet map 239, Auvergne Limousin

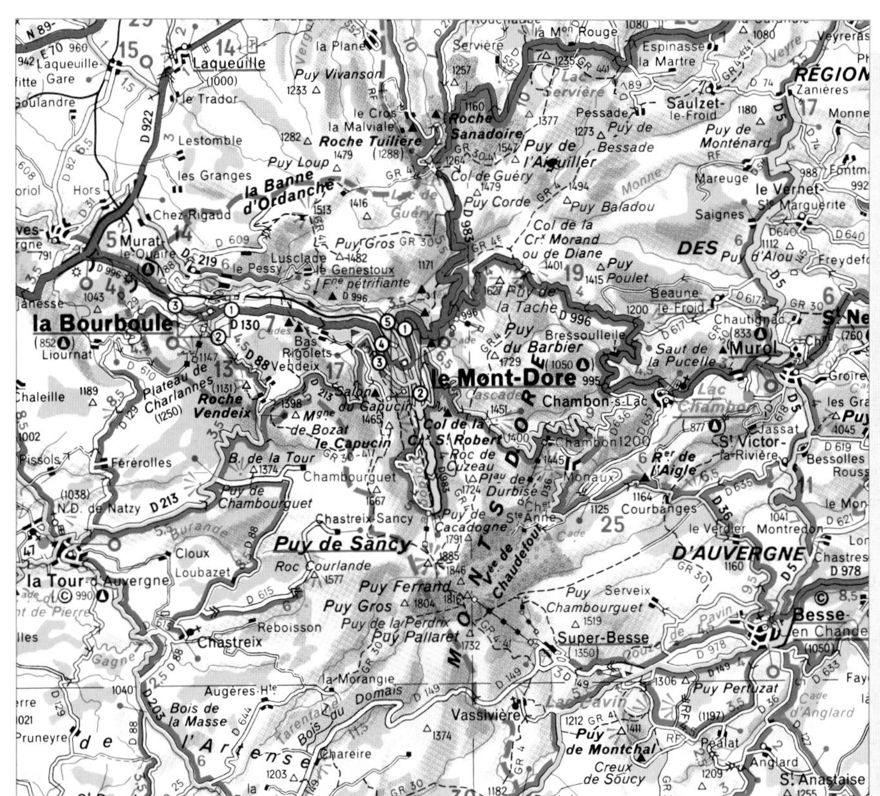

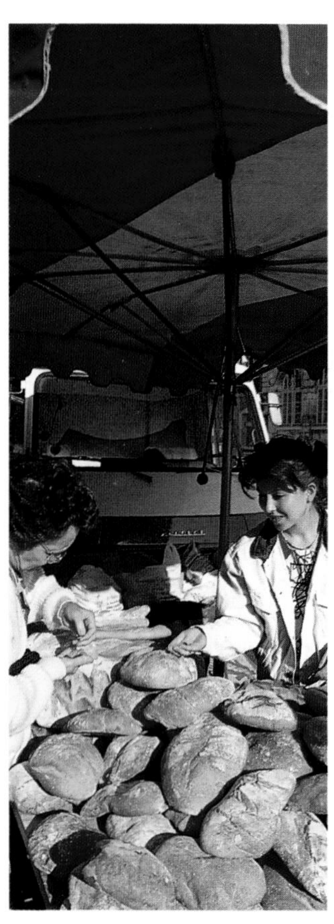
In an area of scattered rural communities the market town is an essential feature

Besse-en-Chandesse

The old and picturesque town of Besse-en-Chandesse was fortified in medieval times – though of the defences only the 16th-century Porte de Ville and the Tour de la Prison remain – and retains an air of venerable sophistication. Modernity is represented by the nearby centre for the study of plants and animals, an outpost of the university at Clermont-Ferrand, and the new winter-sports complex of Super-Besse. The best of the old town is seen in the Rue de la Boucherie, where the delightful houses are built of black lava. The Maison de la Reine Margot – at the far of the street as you approach from the church – is said to be named after Marguerite de Valois, the wife of Henry IV. The Église St-André is, in part, 12th-century and is famous for its 16th-century choir-stalls, and the ancient statue of Notre-Dame de Vassivière.

La Bourboule

Though it has been a recognised thermal centre since the 15th century, La Bourboule was really only developed as a spa town in the early 19th century, so that little of it is more than 150 years old. Nevertheless it is a delightful spot, with pleasant bridges over the youthful River Dordogne, and the airy Parc Fenêstre. The spa water has the highest arsenic content of any in Europe, though it is still recommended as a medicine rather than banned as a poison.

From the Parc Fenêstre, with its range of trees including the distinctly non-French sequoia, its fine river and lakeside strolls, a cableway serves the Plateau de Charlannes, where there is winter skiing and summer walking. It is possible to walk to the top of the Rocher des Fées, the 50-m granite mass that dominates La Bourboule. There is a fine view of the town from here.

La Bourboule, seen from the River Dordogne. The Rocher des Fées gives a contrasting panoramic view that many prefer

A six-hour walk from La Bourboule will take the serious walker to the top of the Puy de Sancy, at 1885m the highest peak in the Monts Dore range, from where there are spectacular vistas

Col de Guéry

Those travelling north from Le Mont-Dore pass the Lac de Guéry, a high (1244m) lake formed when a volcanic lava flow blocked the river valley. Further on is the Col de Guéry, a little higher at 1264m. From here there is a tremendous view of the valley to Rochefort-Montagne.

Le Mont-Dore

Although beautifully located, Le Mont-Dore is purely a spa town, with no reason for its existence other than hot water. Despite this singular reason for its existence it has a long history: there was a Roman settlement around the spring and perhaps even a Gallo-Celtic one before that. Those who are interested in the thermal station itself can take a guided tour.

Monts Dore and Puy de Sancy

The Monts Dore are the glaciated remains of a late Tertiary volcanic range, the volcanoes therefore being around three million years old, though the glaciers retreated only 10,000 years ago. The highest of the Monts Dore peaks, and also the highest peak of the Massif Central, is Puy de Sancy (1885m). The peak is the source of the River Dordogne, and its summit is easily reached by cableway. Leave Le Mont-Dore southward on the D983 to reach a large car park and restaurant. From the top of the cableway there is a short walk to the summit proper, from where, on a clear day, the Dauphiné Alps can be seen, as well as virtually all the major local mountain groups.

Murol

East of Le Mont-Dore is Murol, a delightful village set among trees with a castle that seems out of all proportion to the village's size and position. The castle is both picturesque and interesting: it dates from the 13th century with the final touches being added by the d'Estaings, one of Auvergne's noblest families. Among the family's 20th-century descendants is ex-President Valéry Giscard d'Estaing.

Super-Besse and Lac Pavin

Close to Besse-en-Chandesse is the new winter-sports resort of Super-Besse, at an altitude of 1350m. It has good facilities for both downhill and cross-country skiing and is also a convenient centre for the summer walker. A cableway links the resort with the summit of the Puy de Sancy, and a road links it with Lac Pavin. The lake, with its surrounding roads and trees, is claimed to be the most beautiful in Auvergne – a title for which the competition is stiff – and is on the route of the GR4 and GR30 long-distance footpaths. It is a popular spot with anglers, for it is well stocked with trout and *omble chevalier*, a species of char sometimes referred to as mountain trout.

Lac Pavin is almost exactly circular and very deep – nearly 100m – making it an almost perfect volcanic lake. Its name derives from the Latin *pavens*, frightening, because at one time it was said that if a stone were thrown into the lake violent local storms would result.

Black Virgins

It is believed that the first 'Black Virgin' was brought back from the Holy Land by Louis IX on his return from the Seventh Crusade. The original statue was lost in a fire at the time of the Revolution – the one now seen in the cathedral at Le Puy-en-Velay is a 19th-century copy – but its influence can be seen in churches all over Auvergne. Black Virgins were carved from walnut or cedar, which both age to almost jet-black. Originally the Byzantine icon style was used for the Virgin, but later

statues used the faces of local girls for a more pleasing effect.

The Black Virgin of Besse-en-Chandesse is one of the most famous of the statues. Each year on the first Sunday in July the statue is carried in procession 3km uphill to the Chapelle de Vassivière, and on the Sunday after St Matthew's Day it is carried back down to Besse's church.

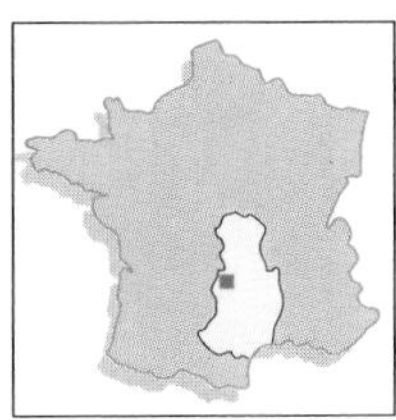

MONTS DU CANTAL

AT THE SOUTHERN END of the Parc Régional des Volcans d'Auvergne are the Monts du Cantal. It is now believed that the peaks of this range are the remnants of one massive volcano perhaps as much as 3000m high and over 70km across the base. Wind, rain, and Ice Age glaciers have eroded the huge peak down to the puys we see today.

The Monts du Cantal (top), of which the highest point is 1855m, are thought to be the product of the erosion of a single, much higher volcano
Salers (above), with its ornate, mainly 15th- and 16th-century houses, has a magical quality

Monts du Cantal

At 1855m the Plomb du Cantal is not as high as the Monts Dore's Puy de Sancy, but is still an impressive peak. It is also a good viewpoint, but by common consent the best panorama is provided by the summit of Puy Mary. This top (at 1787m) is reached in about 30 minutes from the Pas de Peyrol, at 1582m the highest pass in the Massif Central. From Puy Mary the volcanic ruins of the Cantal peaks are seen to perfection, as are the results of later glaciation. Laid out below are numerous valleys, enclosing the rivers that drain the high peaks.

St Cernin

This pretty village has a fine old church well known for the quality of its wood panelling. To the west of St Cernin, a drive along the D43 and then the D9 reaches the excellent Gorges de la Maronne. Beyond lies the Château de Bronzac, a picturesque ruin set on a ridge above the same river.

Salers

Make your way to the Grande-Place, the heart and centre of Salers, and look towards the church. This is a magical town: angled roofs set at all orientations, seemingly without order; turrets, chimneys and gables; an elegant bell enclosed in its wrought cage; old lamps and signs. It would be easy to see this small town, with its around 600 inhabitants, as having been built to a design in a children's fairy tale. Except, that is, for the dark, sombre nature of all the houses, which are built of the local lava.

Salers is set high, at 950m, which adds to the fairy-tale quality, and has almost no buildings from before the 15th century or after the 16th, which explains the architectural similarity among the apparent chaos. The earliest houses were built when the village was a refuge from bands of English soldiers and other ne'er-do-wells during the Hundred Years War. The later houses date from the time it was a successful local market town. The Hôtel de Ville, in Grande-Place, was built in the 15th century, as was the nearby Maison de Bargues, though this house – which is open to the public – is furnished in 17th-century style. Another fine building is the Maison des Templiers, just off Grande-Place, which

PARC NATIONAL DES VOLCANS D'AUVERGNE

About 60 million years ago, during the Tertiary era, the Massif Central was formed in the squeeze that created the Alps and Jura to the east, and the Pyrenees to the west. Faulting in the rocks of the Massif allowed magma from the earth's core to vent to the surface, creating volcanoes. This area's volcanic activity was neither continuous nor short and violent when it was in progress. In fact three distinct periods of activity are recognised. During the earliest, from 13 million to 3 million years ago, the volcanoes of the Monts du Cantal were active; from 6 million to 250,000 years ago those of the Monts Dore were erupting; while the youngest group, the volcanoes of the Monts Dômes, were probably still active when the earliest man arrived in Auvergne.

The Volcano Park is, at 348,000 hectares, the largest park in France set up to protect natural scenery. Within it, all the best features of volcanoes are present – typical volcanic craters, crater lakes, hot springs and pillars of volcanic rock. The latter are produced by the erosion of softer rock from around the hard-rock intrusions. The most famous examples are at Le Puy-en-Velay, which in fact lies outside the Park's boundaries.

The hot springs were known to the Romans, and indeed many of Auvergne's spa towns sit on Roman foundations. The spa water emerges at about 40°C, heated by sub-surface contact with rocks still hot from volcanic activity.

The most famous of the volcanic areas is the Monts Dômes, where there are over 100 old volcanic vents spread out in a 30-km ridge. The best known of these peaks is the Puy de Dôme. This has been an important pilgrimage site for thousands of years: it was a Gaulish holy site before the Romans built a temple to Mercury and in the 12th century a chapel was erected on the summit. Part of the explanation for this mystical hold on the locals could be the surprisingly warm temperatures recorded at the peak.

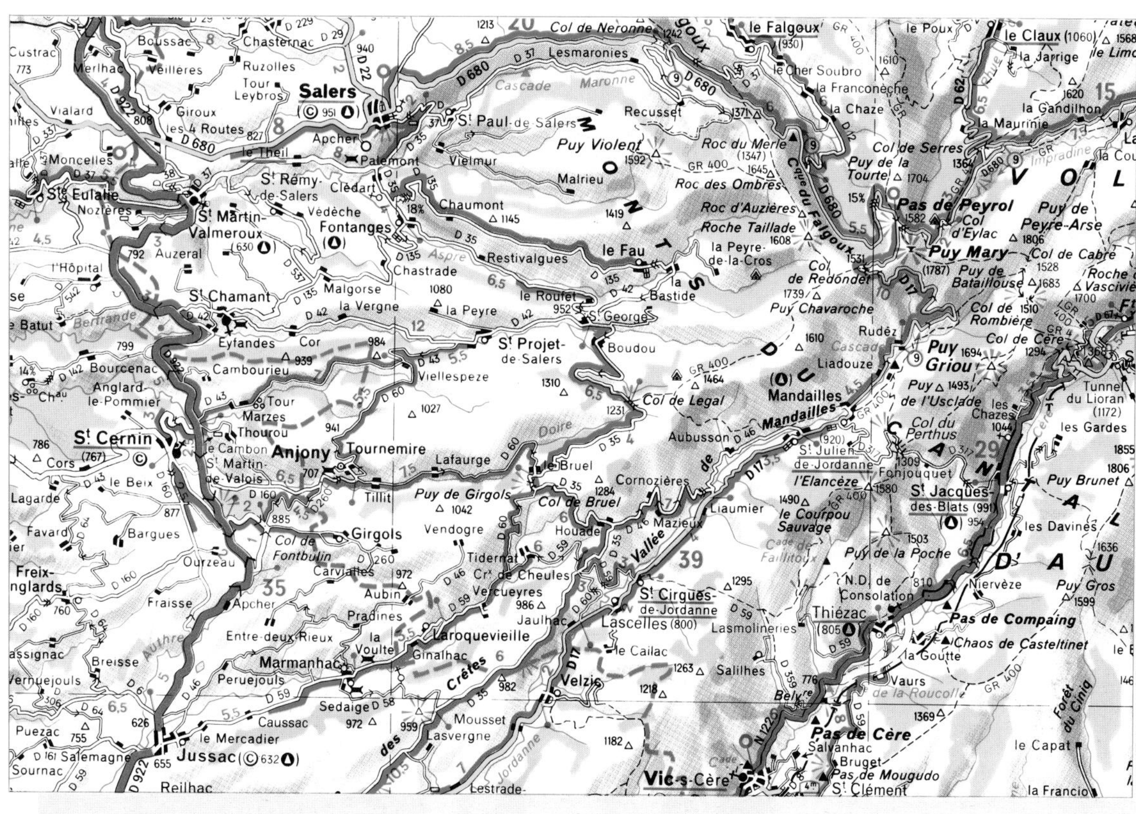

The town of Salers gave its name to a highly prized local breed of cattle

houses a folklore museum. Go past the museum to reach the Esplanade de Barrouze and a wonderful view of the valleys below Puy Violent (1592m).

Finally, the bust in Grande-Place is of Tyssandier d'Escous, the man responsible for obtaining countrywide recognition for the local breed of cattle, the Salers, which in France is now second only in popularity to the Charolais of Burgundy.

Vallée de la Cère

Many believe that the Cère valley is the finest in the Cantal, and with its lush greenness and the fine gorges of the Pas de Cère and Pas de Compainy it is certainly a strong candidate. At Thiézac, a village between the gorges, the valley opens a little, so that the village is delightfully situated. The chapel above the village, Notre-Dame de Consolation, was visited by Anne of Austria (see below), who prayed to a miraculous Virgin there for nine days. A lace altar-cloth she gave the chapel is now in the village church.

At the valley head is Le Lioran, where a tunnel driven through the mountain allows access to Murat even when snow blocks the high pass. The tunnel was hand-cut in 1839 and, at 1412m, was the longest in France at the time.

Vic-sur-Cère

This spa village is set in the lush lower region of the Cère valley. As a spa it was popular with the Romans, but achieved real fame as a result of a visit by Anne of Austria in 1837. Anne, wife of Louis XIII, was childless despite 22 years of marriage and was doing the rounds of spas and miraculous statues of the Virgin in the hope of providing the king with a legitimate heir. In 1838 she gave birth to the prince who would become Louis XIV, the Sun King, though there are several other places on her itinerary of the year before that could presumably claim equal credit for the 'miracle'. A fine 15th-century house in the village is named after the Princes of Monaco, Louis XIII having given an area around the town to them.

South of the village is the Col de Curebourse, the Pass of the Cutpurses, a favourite haunt of highwaymen. Further on is the Rocher des Pendus where they met their end by hanging after capture and sentence. The view from the rock is superb.

Comité Départemental du Tourisme du Cantal
Hôtel du Département - BP 8
15018 Aurillac Cedex
Tel: 71 46 20 20

Touring:
use Michelin sheet map 239, Auvergne Limousin

Churches of the Auvergne

FOR MANY AUVERGNE is the land of volcanoes and extravagantly sculpted limestone plateaux. For others the attraction is the local food and wine. But a significant number of visitors are drawn to the region by its superb early-medieval churches.

Dating from the 11th and 12th centuries, these are in Romanesque style, but in a version of it that is sufficiently distinctive to be termed Auvergne Romanesque.

The Earliest Auvergne Churches

It could be argued that the earliest churches in Auvergne – indeed, in Europe – were the megaliths of the New Stone Age and Bronze Age. For most people though, a church is symbolic of Christianity, and a search for Christian remains brings us forward by two or three millennia. In Clermont-Ferrand's cathedral there is a sarcophagus that is now believed to date from the 4th century. It lies in a crypt of the 9th or 10th century that formed part of the earliest cathedral on the site, consecrated in 946 by St Étienne. At that time Clermont-Ferrand was a part of the Carolingian Empire, and investigation of the cathedral – of which little more than the crypt now survives – suggests that it was built in a very early form of what was to become the Auvergne Romanesque style. Other churches surviving from the Carolingian period, most notably at Ris and Mozac, show similar characteristics.

Fine Auvergne Romanesque capitals adorn the church at Mozac (above), rebuilt in the 15th century

The Episcopal City of Le Puy-en-Velay

Le Puy-en-Velay, attractive as it is, is a city in which even the most enthusiastic visitor can grow weary of steps, so it is with trepidation that even more are suggested. They are, however, few and worthwhile. From the Place des Tables take the Rue des Tables so as to approach the Cathédrale Notre-Dame and its associated complex of religious buildings from the east, for the west front of the building is one of the most extraordinary in the whole of France. It is not Auvergne Romanesque, though there are elements of this style present, but then neither is it anything else in particular, being a mass of arches and coloured geometric patterns in which a Spanish (Moorish) influence can readily be seen. The façade is hardly beautiful, but it is certainly interesting. Inside, the overall effect is a little severe, but

St Gervais-d'Auvergne's mainly Gothic church (left) was fortified during the Hundred Years War

Ste Enimie, on a bend in the Tarn near Prades, has a 12th-century church (below)

the builders made elegant use of space, and there are fine details. The main altar is ornate, and topped by a copy of the most famous of the region's Black Virgins (see page 155). There are fine frescos, particularly that of the arts of Grammar, Rhetoric, Logic and Music in the Chapelle des Reliques. The treasury in the Sacristy includes the Bible of Théodulfe, a 600-page vellum Bible illuminated in gold and silver, which dates from the reign of Charlemagne, in the 8th century. In addition the building houses the largest painting of St Michael in France, over 5m high and dating from the end of the 11th century.

Next to the cathedral the visitor is offered a pleasant contrast to its sobriety in the Form of the restored cloister, with its red, black and white stonework. Finally, close by are the 11th-century Baptistère St-Jean and, beside it, the Maison du Prieur, formerly the prior's house but now occupied by a museum of local rural life and crafts.

Later Churches

In the 14th century the Gothic style of architecture, with its revolutionary use of ribbing for roof vaults, its soaring heights and wonderful lighting, evolved in northern France. The style reached its climax in the cathedral of Chartres, one of the wonders of Europe. To the south, Gothic architecture replaced the Auvergne Romanesque, but nothing to compare to Chartres was raised. The best example of Auvergne Gothic is the cathedral of Clermont-Ferrand, which has, in a small way, fused the earlier and later styles by retaining a slated roof. However, the severe look that results from the use of the dark local lava somewhat spoils the effect, and many visitors will prefer the lighter, limestone chancel of the Cathédrale Notre-Dame in Moulins.

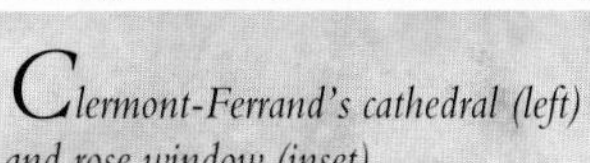

Clermont-Ferrand's cathedral (left) and rose window (inset)

Elsewhere, the churches of St Gervais-d'Auvergne and Royat are notable for the fortifications added to the original Romanesque buildings during the Hundred Years War (1337-1453). In the latter church especially, the Gothic battlements give the exposed side a formidable appearance.

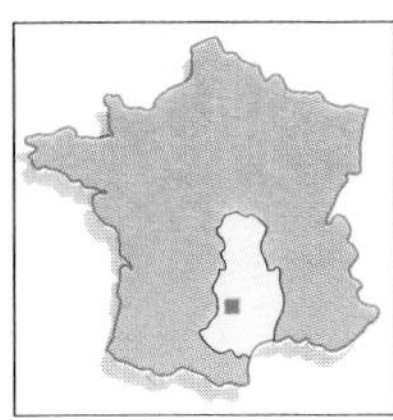

CONQUES AND THE VALLÉE DU LOT

THE FLAT PLAIN OF MIDI-PYRÉNÉES lies between Auvergne and the Pyrenees themselves. Across it drains the River Lot, which rises in the Massif Central and links with the Garonne before heading off to Bordeaux. In its early stages the Lot flows through a beautiful gorge in charming countryside.

The ancient village of Conques was a major religious centre in the Middle Ages and is still on one of the principal pilgrimage routes through France to Santiago de Compostela in northern Spain

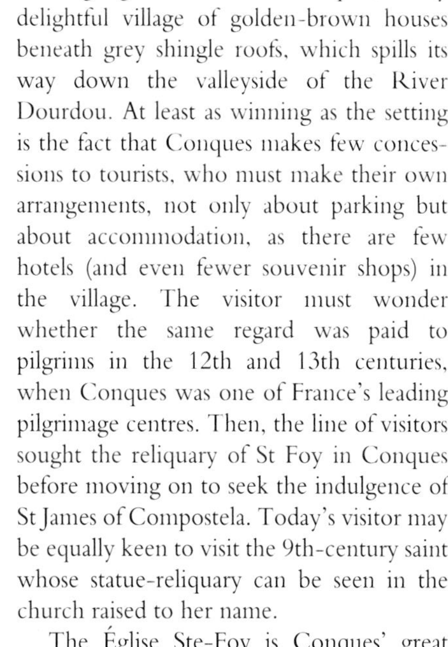

Conques

The highlight of the area is Conques, a truly delightful village of golden-brown houses beneath grey shingle roofs, which spills its way down the valleyside of the River Dourdou. At least as winning as the setting is the fact that Conques makes few concessions to tourists, who must make their own arrangements, not only about parking but about accommodation, as there are few hotels (and even fewer souvenir shops) in the village. The visitor must wonder whether the same regard was paid to pilgrims in the 12th and 13th centuries, when Conques was one of France's leading pilgrimage centres. Then, the line of visitors sought the reliquary of St Foy in Conques before moving on to seek the indulgence of St James of Compostela. Today's visitor may be equally keen to visit the 9th-century saint whose statue-reliquary can be seen in the church raised to her name.

The Église Ste-Foy is Conques' great treasure. It is built in 11th-12th-century Romanesque with a tympanum that brings experts from all over Europe. The work is above the west door and is a 12th-century representation of the Last Judgement. St Foy is depicted on the left side (as viewed).

Within the church, the treasury holds the finest work, the church itself being either dignified or austere, depending on your taste. The complete treasury represents one of the finest collections of early-medieval religious art in France, but the main attraction is the 10th-century statue of St Foy, carved in wood, covered in gold and set with precious stones. The saint is seated, with a small vessel in each hand.

Finally, for the best view of the village, take the D901 Rodez road and go left over the Dourdou after 500m to reach the Site du Bancarel.

Entraygues-sur-Truyère

Although named after the Truyère, the village actually sits at the confluence of that river and the Lot. The Truyère is usually a limpid river at Entraygues, the clamour of its excellent gorge – best reached from the village – being far behind. As it enters Entraygues it is crossed by a beautiful bridge, built at the end of the 13th century and comprising heavy buttresses separated by pointed Norman arches. In the village there is a fine collection of old houses, especially in the pedestrian-only Rue Basse, which represents the old quarter. Beyond, an old castle stands at the point where the Truyère meets the Lot.

East of the village the summit of the Puy de Montabès, reached by a straightforward

RURAL BUILDINGS

In Languedoc, to the south of the region, there is clay in the valleys and the houses are of brick, the roofs of clay tiles. This is a wine-growing area, the ground floors of the houses being wine 'cellars', the farmer and his family living on the first floor. The houses have small doors and windows so that the interior – and, most critically, the wine – is kept cool.

Further north the domestic architecture changes. In the Causses the walls and roofs are of limestone, as would be expected. What is not expected is that the roof trusses are also of limestone, for this countryside had few trees, and those stunted, making timber trusses a luxury. Since stone was in good supply the farmers had separate buildings for their animals, though the family still lived on the first floor, the lower floor being a tool shed. By contrast, in the Cévennes animals occupied the ground floor of the slate and schist (*lauze*) houses. Perhaps the difficulty of working the stone meant fewer buildings, perhaps it was the fact that 'spare' slate was used to face the windward side of the

Just outside Entraygues-sur-Truyère the river is spanned by a superb late-13th-century bridge

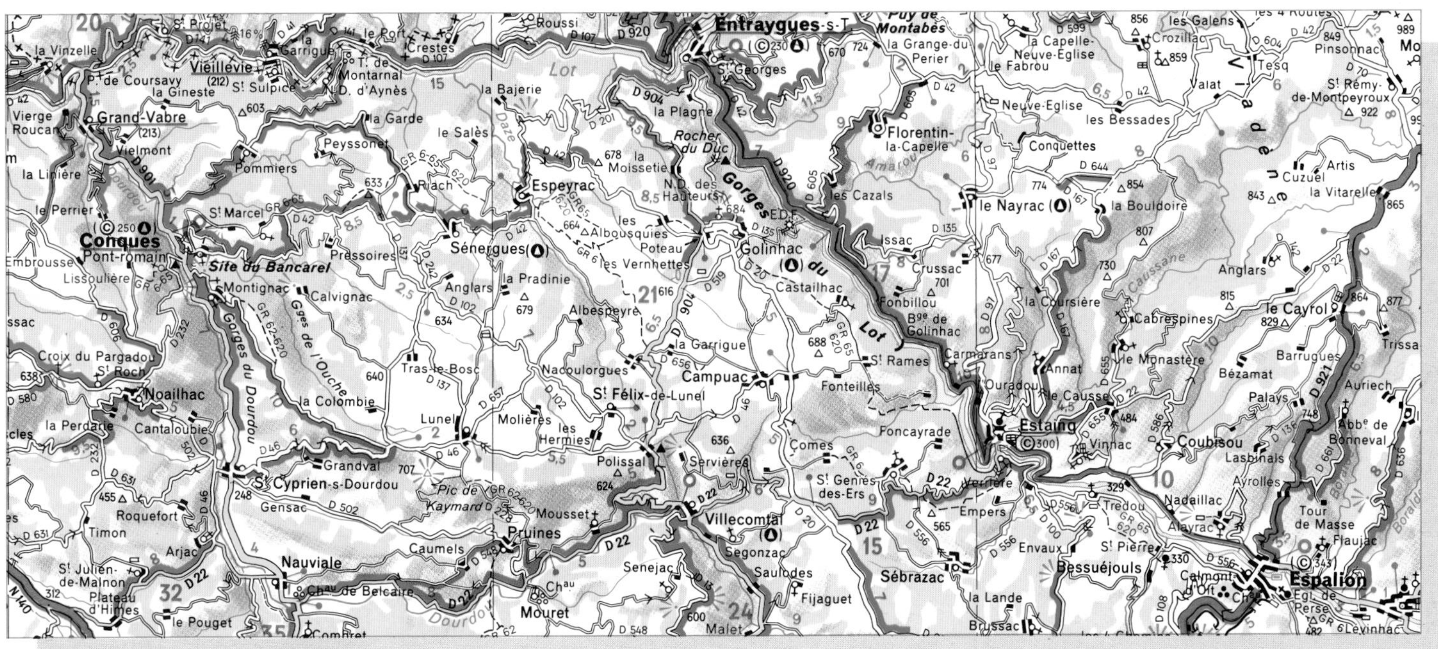

houses, as an extra protection against the wind and rain. North again the building material was volcanic rock, the houses being built smaller so as to offer a low profile to the wind and so that less stone was needed. Typical of this area is the *buron*, a cowman's shed that could be thatched or stone-roofed, and the *bergière*, a similar building for sheep.

10-minute walk from a car park, offers a superb panorama. With the help of a panoramic table and a little clear weather, the visitor can pick out the Monts du Cantal and the plateau of Aubrac, and even the cathedral of Rodez.

Espalion

Set on the Lot, and with a bridge as old as that at Entraygues – though not as picturesque, even if it is somewhat better set off by the village houses – Espalion is another delightful village. From the view-point near the car park on the southern side of the Lot, the old palace, the houses rising straight out of the river and the bridge make a beautiful picture. The palace is a 16th-century mansion in fortified Renaissance style. In the village centre old houses group around a good church dedicated to St Hilarion, a confessor of Charlemagne who retired to Espalion after a life of hectic service, only to be beheaded by Saracen invaders. Built in pink sandstone, the 11th-century church is a fine example of the Romanesque.

Surprisingly, in view of its size, the village has two museums. The Musée Joseph Vaylet, housed in an old church, has a collection of local arts and crafts, including furniture, while the Musée du Rouergue has costumes and religious vestments.

Estaing

At the entrance to the Gorges du Lot stands Estaing, a small village nestling below an old château and with a fine old bridge over the river. The name of the village recalls its association with the early history of the d'Estaing family. The statue of another member of the family, François d'Estaing, a bishop of Rodez, stands close to the Lot bridge. The d'Estaings lived at the château, but the family lost the building at the time of the Revolution when it was discovered that Charles-Hector d'Estaing, though a Republican sympathiser, had exchanged letters with Marie-Antoinette in the hope of securing the successful escape of the king and his family. Charles-Hector was arrested and, not surprisingly, executed. The château, built in the 15th and 16th centuries, is a fortress-like building now occupied by a religious community who will give a guided tour to visitors.

Gorges du Lot

Between the villages of Estaing and Entraygues the Lot, which until here has flowed in a wide valley, is cramped into a very picturesque gorge. The high, steep sides are topped by a ragged, rocky crest, the whole offering a very wild, if wooded, view. The Barrage de Golinhac, the 36-m high dam that is passed along the way, feeds water to a hydroelectric station.

Comité Départemental du Tourisme de l'Aveyron
33, Avenue Victor-Hugo
12000 Rodez
Tel: 65 68 11 43

Touring:
use Michelin sheet map 235, Midi-Pyrénées

A villager from Estaing

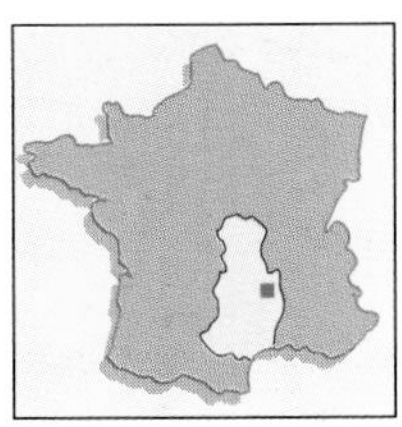

HAUTE-LOIRE

THE LOIRE, the most beautiful river in France, springs from the flank of the Gerbier de Jonc, a peak of the high Ardèche. Within a few tens of kilometres it has rounded Le Monastier and reached Le Puy-en-Velay, a most remarkable town where the region's volcanic chimneys have been put to extraordinary use.

Lac d'Issarlès

The lake is set in a volcanic crater and is about 140m deep. It is breathtakingly beautiful, the water an incredible clear blue. In the early 1950s this clarity was threatened by a hydroelectric scheme that took water from the bottom of the lake, replacing it by diverting streams. Following a national outcry it was agreed that all the inflowing water would be filtered to maintain water purity. As a result Lac d'Issarlès is nowadays as it was before.

Le Monastier-sur-Gazeille

The 19th-century Scottish writer Robert Louis Stevenson was not enamoured of Le Monastier-sur-Gazeille, where he found the people given to drunkenness and incivility. He must have been pleased when he and Modestine, his donkey, left the place to begin their literary travels through the Cévennes.

Today's visitor will be left bemused, for Le Monastier is a friendly place, a delight to visit. The chief attraction is the 11th-century abbey, restored after being damaged in the Hundred Years War.

The abbey treasure, which is only exhibited in high season, includes a very early wooden reliquary covered with silver and precious stones.

An ox cart still in use in recent times in Le Monastier-sur-Gazeille

Comité Départemental du Tourisme de Haute-Loire
12, Boulevard Philippe Jourde - B 185
43000 Le Puy-en-Velay Cedex
Tel: 71 09 66 66

Touring:
use Michelin sheet map 239, Auvergne Limousin

Arlempdes

Set almost as dramatically as Le Puy-en-Velay, Arlempdes has a gate bearing the date 1066, a remnant of the original fortifications. The castle, set on a volcanic spire, is later – with bits from the 12th to 15th centuries – and from it the view of the busy infant Loire is exquisite. The Romanesque church is a modest affair but the pillars of the portal and the sculpted capitals beneath an alveolate arch are worth seeing. Close to the village the Loire enters a fine gorge that can be explored if the water level is low.

The church in nearby St-Paul-de-Tartas is made of volcanic rock.

Le Puy-en-Velay

Certainly the most dramatic site in the Massif Central, and among the most extraordinary in France, is the town of Le Puy. So striking is it that all the roads into the town have numerous lay-bys so that the visitor can stop and wonder without endangering other road users. The town is built on an upside-down saucer of land, a volcanic dome, on which are set several

The approach to Le Puy-en-Velay is unmistakable. The Chapelle St-Michel d'Aiguilhe stands atop a dramatic spire, while above the old town the massive statue known as Notre-Dame de France perches on another volcanic rock

stacks of basalt, the remnants of the volcanic plumes. These stacks have been utilised by the town-builders in ways as dramatic as the features themselves. One stack is topped by the Chapelle St-Michel d'Aiguilhe (*aiguilhe/aiguille*, needle – a very apt name), a chapel that seems to grow out of the rock itself, and indeed it really does. To discover the truth of this, climb the 268 steps to the chapel. Construction started in the 10th century, though most of the work is a century older. The architecture took on the contours of the stack, with the basalt forming most of the flooring, the rock having been worn down by the feet of ages to a level smoothness. From the chapel the view to the town is excellent, the old cathedral dominating the scene.

Closer to the cathedral is the Rocher Corneille, on which sits Notre-Dame de France, a 16-m high, 110-ton statue made from 213 cannons captured at the siege of Sebastopol during the Crimean War. The statue is painted a garish red to prevent rust. The view from the top of the statue is good. In fact is is rather better than the view of the statue itself.

Lacemaking at Le Puy is mentioned as early as the first years of the 15th century, and in the 18th and 19th centuries it was a huge local industry. Machine-made lace and changing fashion all but killed the local trade, but of late there has been a revival, with both machine and hand laces now made in Le Puy. Hand lacemaking can be seen at the Centre d'Initiation de la Dentelle, while the Musée Crozatier is a museum to the history of the trade, as well as having other small collections.

There is much besides to admire in Le Puy. To capture the best of the atmosphere make your way to Rue Pannessac, and the roads that back on to it. Here there are Renaissance houses, outside which, in early September, there will be townsfolk in Renaissance dress as Le Puy celebrates the festival of Roi de l'Oiseau. The King of the Bird is a title given to the winner of an ancient archery contest in the town. Archers in medieval dress walk the streets at the time of the festival, mingling with other medieval folk and medieval bands.

Those who enjoy serious walking may like to try the Tour du Velay, a high-level route that encircles Le Puy.

The old quarter of Le Puy is clustered around the Cathédrale Notre-Dame, built in the 11th and 12th centuries, most of it directly on to rock

St Julien-Chapteuil and St Pierre-Eynac

St Julien is beautifully sited in a lush bowl amid volcanic stacks, and has a fine collection of houses built of the picturesque local stone. The village has a museum to Jules Romains, the 20th-century poet, novelist and dramatist. A little to the east stands the ruined castle of Chapteuil.

The nearby village of St Pierre-Eynac has a tiny church with a distinctive bell tower. From the village the D26 north to Aupinhac goes around the flank of Mont Plaux. From its high point there is a superb view down to Le Puy.

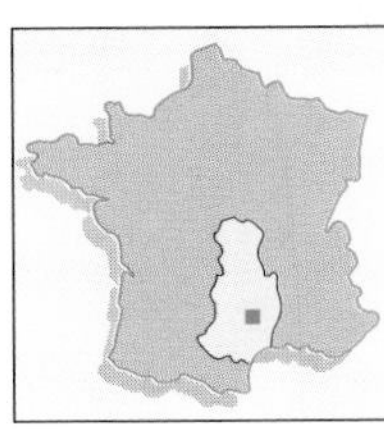

THE CÉVENNES

OF THE SIX FRENCH Parcs Nationaux, four are high mountain parks and one a marine reserve. The sixth is the Cévennes, covering a series of modest – by Alpine standards – peaks, deep gorges cut through green hills and the limestone plateaux known as the Causses. The area is distinctive and quite beautiful, its villages quiet and secret, its wildlife a naturalist's paradise.

Abîme du Bramabiau

Travelling from Meyrueis to the Col de la Séreyrède, the visitor passes the Abîme du Bramabiau. This is a chasm, the second part of the name meaning bellowing ox and referring to the noise the foaming stream makes as it emerges. This stream, the Bonheur, has cut down into the limestone plateau and then, instead of creating a deep gorge, has cut an underground channel about 700m long before returning to the surface. To date, over 10km of passages have been explored in the chasm.

In parts of the Gorges de la Dourbie rocks tower some 300m above the river

Col de la Séreyrède and L'Espérou

The Col de la Séreyrède can be reached from the summit of Mont Aigoual by road or by a fine 5-km walk along GR7. The Col is a surprisingly good viewpoint, despite being 250m lower than the summit, and can be used as a starting point for a trip to the waterfall on the River Hérault.

Nearby L'Espérou – also on GR7 – is set against the flank of the Col, which shelters it from northerly winds. Since it also faces south, towards the Mediterranean, the little village has an enviable climate, warm in summer with masses of flowers, shrubs and trees, yet high enough to be a small winter-sports centre.

Gorges du Trévezel and Gorges de la Dourbie

The northern flank of the Aigoual massif is drained into the Dourbie valley by the Trévezel stream, which passes through the delightful, wild and narrow Gorges du Trévezel. The narrowest part of the gorge, no more than 35m wide, is known in local dialect as the Pas de l'Ase.

In its lower reaches the Dourbie flows through a pleasant valley, but its youthful vigour is entrapped by a delightful gorge, not as tight as the Pas de l'Ase, but with the attraction of a string of fine gorge villages.

Meyrueis

Set at the junction of not two but three rivers, Meyrueis is a pleasant little town that is a good centre for local explorations. One of the town's hotels, an old Benedictine monastery, boasts General de Gaulle as a former guest. Its old round tower, part of the original town fortifications, is topped by a clock tower, which is itself finished by a caged bell.

PARC NATIONAL DES CÉVENNES

Of the five Parcs Nationaux that are land-based (the sixth is part island and part marine), the Cévennes is the only one that does not lie in high mountain terrain, this section of the Massif Central being, in the main, a medium-height (around 1000m) plateau. The Park was created in 1970 and covers a triangular section of limestone plateau around which are grouped several mountain chains. The Lozère range, grouped around Mont Lozère itself, the Park's highest peak at 1699m, are volcanic plugs, characterised by poor soil and a harsh climate, with peat bogs and a strange flora. The Bougès are lower and granitic, with a thin soil, except in the valleys, which are deeply wooded. The final group, Aigoual/Lingas –

Comité Départemental du Tourisme de Lozère
14, Boulevard Henri-Bourillon - BP 4
48002 Mende Cedex
Tel: 66 65 34 55

Comité Départemental du Tourisme du Gard
3, Place des Arènes - BP 122
30011 Nîmes Cedex
Tel: 66 21 02 51

Touring:
use Michelin sheet map 240, Languedoc Roussillon

including Mont Aigoual, perhaps the Park's finest peak – are limestone peaks rising to 1500m with a typical limestone flora, inset by granite masses that add a variation to the scenery. Set between these ranges are good valleys, the best of which are the Gardons valleys, cut in schist and the most agricultural area of the Park. The agriculture supports few now, though life has always been hard in the Cévennes, where summers are very hot and winters very cold. Today under 1000 people inhabit the high central section of the Park. A few of them are engaged in bee-keeping (left).

The Park's wild flowers include beautiful tracts of wild daffodils in spring and over 40 varieties of orchid. Its birds include the Egyptian vulture (if you are really lucky), golden eagles and eagle owls, hen and Montagu's harriers, little bustards, stone curlew and choughs. And for the animal lover there are wild boar, genet cats and several species of deer.

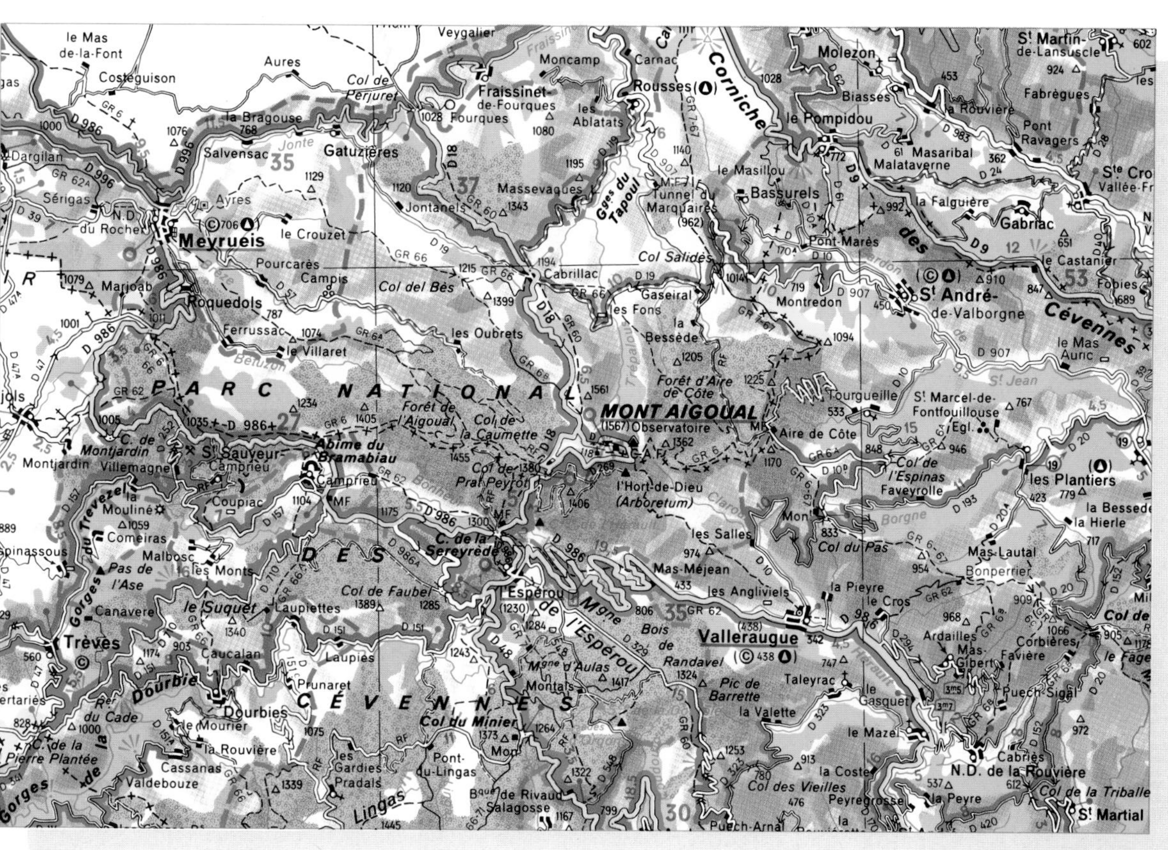

Mont Aigoual

The Massif de l'Aigoual, of which Mont Aigoual is, at 1567m, the highest point, is of critical importance to the water flow of the country on all sides. It stands between the Atlantic and the Mediterranean and collects clouds from each, the rain from which averages over 2m annually. This is not a great deal in comparison with some of the wetter areas of Europe, but for the peak's position, close to the arid south of France, it is a very great amount and has earned it its name, from the local dialect word for water, *aiqualis*. It must also be said that it does not rain often on Mont Aigoual, but when it does it comes down in torrents.

The summit is easily reached – by road, with no walking involved – and there the visitor finds a meteorological station built in 1887 for the Water and Forests Department. This organisation planted trees on the peak, turning a bare mountain into one that became covered in beech and pine in only 100 years. From the summit the view towards the Mediterranean is superb, as is that towards the closer Causses country. On clear days Mont Blanc is visible to the north-east, beyond Mont Ventoux in Provence, while to the west the Pyrenees can be seen.

St André-de-Valborgne

With its narrow streets hemmed in by old houses of great character, this delightful village owes its prosperity to the local silk industry. Those wanting to know more about this fascinating subject should visit the Écomusée de la Soie at St Hippolyte-du-Fort, which lies about 20km to the south-east of St André. The eggs of the moth, whose caterpillars are the silk 'worms', were incubated in pouches hung between local women's breasts.

Valleraugue

This pleasant market town is also a centre for apple growing as almost any visitor will realise on seeing the orchards on both sides of the D986 into Valleraugue. The town offers gentle strolls with no particular highlight, and those looking for a more energetic outing and a genuine goal should visit the 12th-century church. From there a long walk – known, optimistically, as the Path of 4000 Steps – leads to the top of Mont Aigoual.

In the predominantly rural Cévennes there is plenty of local produce on sale in the market towns dotted throughout the area

LIMESTONE SCENERY

IN ADDITION TO THE VOLCANOES of Auvergne the region possesses one other unusual feature, the Causses. This area, bordered by the Cévennes to the east, the eastern edge of Aquitaine to the west, the valley of the River Lot to the north and the Hérault plain of Bas Languedoc to the south, is a limestone plateau of around 1000m in height and presenting a chiselled landscape to the visitor. Its climate is harsh, with hot, dry summers followed by cold winters during which the area is scoured by high winds. The limestone is carboniferous, permeable to water, so that vegetation has little soil and even less water.

The Causses is divided into four blocks by steep valleys that carry rivers out of the area. These rivers spring from neighbouring hill ranges and traverse the area along beds of the impervious marl strata that lies below the limestone. The Causse de Sauveterre lies between the Lot and the Gorges du Tarn; it is the least arid and is mostly arable. The Causse Méjean is next. Lying between the Gorges du Tarn and the Jonte, it is the highest Causse, a harsh area. The Causse Noir lies between the Jonte and the Dourbie. It is the smallest Causse, named after an ancient, dark, pine forest that once grew on it. Finally, south of the Dourbie, is the Causse de Larzac, the largest of all, mainly a high, dry plateau covering over 1000 square kilometres.

The harsh Causse Méjean is the highest-lying of the Causses

CAVES

The limestone of the Causses is a basic calcium-carbonate rock. Rain, a mild acid as a result of dissolved carbon dioxide, attacks the rock when it falls on it. In some cases rainwater percolates down vertical fault lines, eventually reaching horizontal or inclined rock beds along which it can flow. The flowing water carves out tunnels and chambers in the rock, and occasionally eats its way through to a lower level so that a tunnel or series of tunnels are left literally high and dry.

These dry tunnels and occasionally the wet ones are the caves explored by speleologists. Ultimately the underground river reaches a layer of impervious rock – under the Causses it is a bed of marl – runs along it and reaches the surface again at a point where the limestone cap has been eroded, or at a geological fault. The point of re-emergence is known as a resurgence.

Sometimes the surface rainwater erodes the rock into a shallow

MARTEL, SPELEOLOGIST EXTRAORDINARY

Though Stone Age man inhabited caves perhaps as long as 50,000 years ago, and lived in them for many thousands of years, by medieval times the holes and caves of the Causses had become places of dread for the locals. At best they were the homes of demons, at worst gateways to Hell. Not surprisingly no one even contemplated entering them for fun. Though attitudes towards caves changed in later centuries it is believed that it was not until the 18th century that the first tentative visits were made. Even these did not amount to much in the way of investigation, and it was not until the late 19th century that any systematic exploration took place. The man at the forefront of this exploration was Édouard-Alfred Martel. He was born in 1859, was interested in geology and geography from a very early age and by the early 1880s was exploring the caves of the Causses, often in the company of Louis Armand, a locksmith from Rozer.

Most of the great caves of the area were first explored by Martel: Demoiselles from 1884, Dargilan and Bramabiau from 1888 and Armand from 1897. Indeed, only Clamouse of the great local caves was not first explored by Martel. In addition to his work here, Martel also explored caves in Spain, Austria and Britain, and virtually founded the science of speleology with his writings on underground geography. Back in the Causses he also helped the locals by studying regional water flow and so aiding the creation of a more hygienic water supply.

The Grotte des Demoiselles lies south-east of Ganges

ROCHERS RUINIFORMES

Interspersed within the calcium-based limestone matrix of the Causses are nodules of a magnesium-based rock known as dolomite. This rock is more famous as the basis of the sharp towers it has produced in the region of northern Italy that bears its name, but since it was named after Dolomieu, a French geologist, it is not out of place here. Dolomite is a harder rock than limestone, more resistant to water and the wind. Where it outcrops it therefore tends to be left behind as the softer, calcium-based limestone dissolves or erodes. Where this happens the lumps of dolomite that remain form *rochers ruiniformes*. The name means 'town-ruin rocks', because, from a distance, they look like the remains of an old town. The very best example is Montpellier-le-Vieux in the Causse Noir.

The site can be explored on foot: drive to the car park from the Auberge de Maubert on the D110 and start from there. The path around the site from there is about 1.5km long and very worthwhile. At the first path junction go left – to reach the viewpoint of Rampart. Beyond is the Porte de Mycènes, named by Martel after the Lion Gate at Mycaenae, one of the site's best features, a 12-m natural arch. Further on again – beyond a rock evocatively named the Nez de Cyrano – is a cave, the Grotte de Baume Obscure (*baume* being a local word for cave), in which Martel found the remains of cave bears. On again is a superb viewpoint and a 53-m deep *aven*.

The 'rochers ruiniformes' of Montpellier-le-Vieux (left and right) cover 100 hectares. Édouard-Alfred Martel drew the first plan of the site in 1885

depression known in the region as a *cloup*. As the depression erodes down it becomes a *sotch*, more of a pit than a hollow. Further erosion creates an *aven* or *igue*. *Avens* are steep-sided chimneys and are at their most spectacular where they link with underground chambers. In such chambers water from the *aven*, or just from percolation, creates stalagmites as calcium carbonate is re-deposited, having been taken into solution as the water dissolved the rock. It is these formations that make a visit to the caves of the area so worthwhile. The Grotte des Demoiselles has a chamber 120m long and over 50m high. The Grotte de Dargilan, with its 100-m wide and 40-m high waterfall, and its Salle Rose, is also spectacular.

AVEN ARMAND

This superb cave started, as is usual, with the percolation of water through the Méjean limestone pavement, the water forming vertical chimney-like holes that all joined together in a huge, water-eroded chamber. Ultimately the detached blocks formed at the base of the percolation chimneys collapsed into the chamber, blocking the outflow from it. Much later the blockage also collapsed so that water could again flow freely. Then, on top of the blocks on the chamber floor, and from the chamber roof, respectively, stalagmites and stalactites began to form.

The local shepherds knew of the *aven* and Martel, hearing of it from them, brought a ton of equipment and his trusted partner Louis Armand for an exploration. It was Armand who first descended into the cave, bringing out news of the wonders below. Today's visitors enter by way of a 200-m tunnel bored directly into the main chamber. When they emerge into it they are confronted by a forest of stalagmites, some of the most beautiful so far found in any cave.

GORGES

These are formed either where the rock roofs above underground rivers have collapsed, or, more usually, where surface rivers have cut right through the limestone plateau to reach the impervious marl bed beneath. Occasionally the cutting has created ordinary valleys, wide and lushly vegetated, but more frequently the gorges are tight and high-sided, the scenery dominated by angular rocks. The gorges of the Jonte and the Dourbie are worth visiting, but best by far is the Gorges du Tarn. This beautiful gorge is 50km long and can be followed by car – the easiest way – by boat – the most exciting way – or by foot. The last way is hard work but undeniably worth the effort.

Whether seen from road, cliff top or river, the Gorges du Tarn (above, right and below) are among the most dramatic sights in France

The Tarn has no tributary streams in the Gorges, other than one or two that are a few tens of metres long, but is fed by water from over 40 resurgences – much of the water inflowing as waterfalls. This gives some impression of the degree to which the Causses are penetrated by rainwater. Never more than 500m wide and occasionally narrowing to just 30m, the sides of the Gorges are always steep, sometimes vertical and occasionally overhanging.

Consequently the drive along the Gorges is thrilling. If you are driving, start at Molines, passing the 16th-century Charbonnières castle near Montbrun, before reaching the enchanting village of Ste Énimie. Beyond are two cirques (see below), the Cirque de St Chély and the Cirque de Pougnadoires, before the Point Sublime is reached. From the Point, close to which is a memorial to Martel, there is the very best view of the Gorges. The section in prospect includes Les Détroits and the Pas du Souci, but both of these features are best viewed from the boat that can be boarded at La Malène. Les Détroits are 400-m sheer cliffs, while in the Pas du Souci the Tarn flows over and under huge blocks created by the collapse of part of the wall of the Gorges.

Roquefort

Many thousands of years before the village of Roquefort existed, the edge of the Cambalou plateau collapsed into the Soulzon valley, creating a jumble of huge rocks on the impervious marl of the valley's floor. In the caves created by the stabilised blocks a specific form of penicillin, *Penicillun glaucum roquefortii*, formed. Neolithic man inhabited the caves, but it is doubtful whether he noted the effect of the bacteria on cheese – though it was known by the time of the Romans. Nowadays this pungent cheese is big business, and only those visitors to Roquefort who have lost their sense of smell can be unaware of its existence.

Roquefort's blue-marble appearance is unmistakable

The basic ingredient of the cheese is sheep's milk, the efforts of half a million sheep in the Causses now being supplemented by imports. The milk, obtained by milking machines, just as from cows, is not pasteurised or in any other way altered before 'standard' cheeses are made from it. After the round cheeses have been formed – by about 10 cheesemakers, a number that is surprisingly large in modern industrial terms, but rather small for such a cottage industry – they are taken to the caves formed by the ancient rockfall and stored on oak tables for three months. In the cool (about 10°C), humid air the penicillin grows in the cheese, producing the famous blue-marble appearance. Today about 17,000 tons of the cheese are produced annually.

Cirques

Occasionally the rivers that cut down through the limestone form a meander and then, by cutting away a cliff in the bed, cut a straighter path, leaving the old bend behind. In a river plain, and on more impermeable soil, the old bend usually remains filled and is termed an oxbow lake. In the Causses the bend empties of water and becomes a dry gorge called a cirque. The best example is the Cirque de Navacelles, close to the Gorges de la Vis on the Causse du Larzac. The tiny village of Navacelles has a splendid bridge over the River Vis and is a good starting-point for a trip to the local viewpoints. To the south is La Baume-Auriol, while to the north is the honestly named Belvédère Nord, and from either the bleached, plant-less sides of the cirques are well seen. For those wanting a clearer look, GR7, one of France's system of long-distance footpaths, visits the Cirque.

The region's best-known cirque is that of Navacelles (left)
Mourèze (above) is near a fine cirque

Another fine cirque is to be found close to Mourèze at the southern end of the Causse du Larzac. Rocks at the Cirque de Mourèze have weathered into fantastic shapes.

THE RHÔNE VALLEY

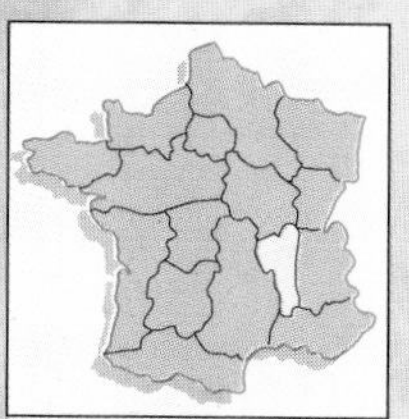

FRANCE'S MAIN NORTH-SOUTH highway, the Rhône Valley is used by travellers by road, rail, river and canal, and consequently there is a sense of frenetic rush throughout its length. A great deal of industry is concentrated in the river valley itself and with it all the ugliness that industry attracts. But concentrating too much on these aspects is unfair to the Rhône Valley, for they are arguably the price of modern living, and besides there is much more about the region that is positive.

In the valley itself the countryside is largely spoiled and uninteresting in its flatness. Yet not very far from either side of the river, hills rise, steep and high, in places opening up huge vistas of the valley, which from a distance gains a beauty not always evident at close quarters. These hills also allow visitors wishing to escape the rush and industry of the valley floor to enter a world of peace and beauty.

To the north-east of Lyon, that tranquillity comes in the strange world of Les Dombes, a flat region dotted with hundreds of lakes and home to many species of bird. West from there, on the right bank of the Saône and between the vineyards of Burgundy and the Côtes du Rhône, lies the Beaujolais region, where attractive little villages quietly prepare their young red wines for the mad November rush. Much farther south, to the south-west of Montélimar, there are the Gorges de l'Ardèche, without a doubt some of the most dramatic scenery in the whole region, where many people leave their cars for a while to make the journey by canoe.

Whether taken at a rush or at a more leisurely pace, the Rhône Valley has a lot to offer. In fact, for any traveller in a hurry just one stop could be enough to cause the rush to be abandoned for a while.

Water sports are popular in this region of rivers

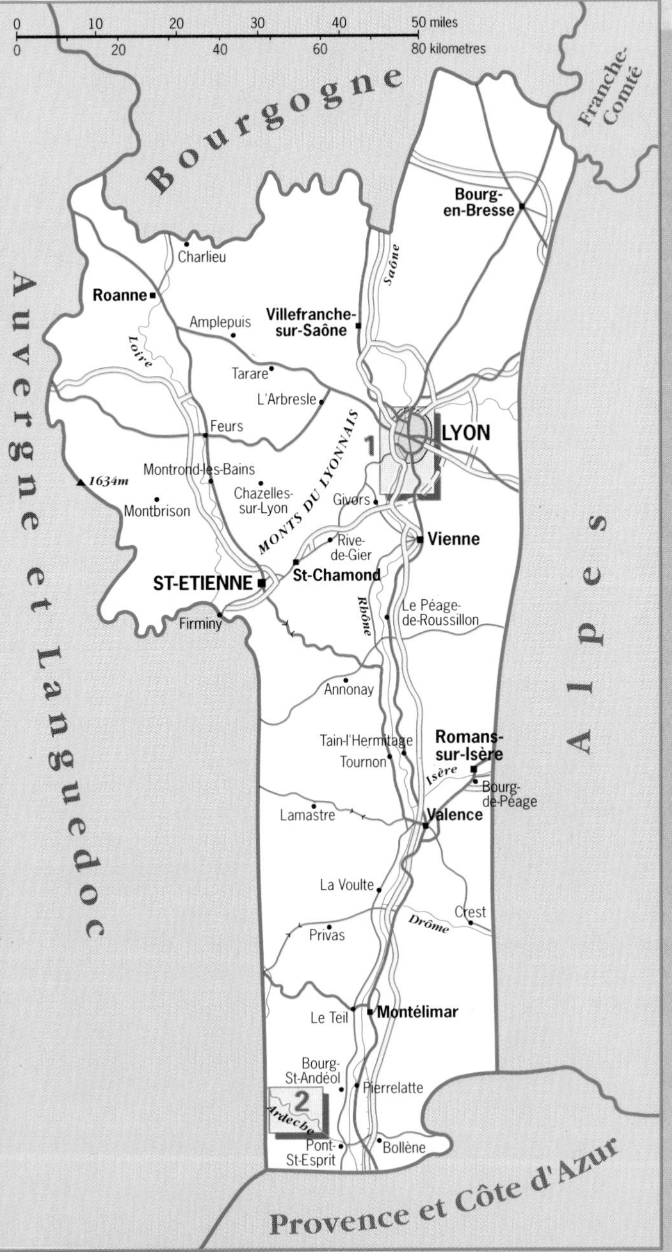

The Chartreuse de Valbonne (left) lies in attractive wooded country south of the Gorges de l'Ardèche, spectacular cliffs towering over the river

At Juliénas a colourful mural can be seen in old wine cellars. It depicts the frolics associated with Bacchus, the Greek and Roman god of wine

A game of boules (right)

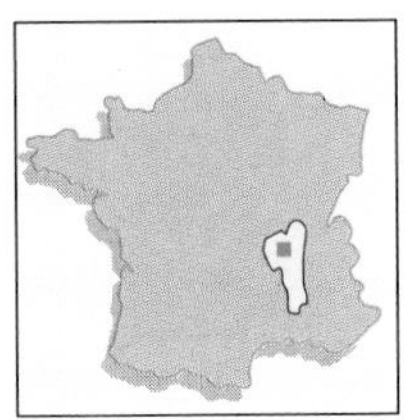

ALONG THE RHÔNE

THE RHÔNE TRACES a major communications corridor between northern and southern France, sharing its valley with two trunk roads, the RN7 and RN86, an *autoroute*, the A7, and two railway lines. Despite these, and a subsequent growth in industry that demands three nuclear power stations between Lyon and Pont-St Esprit, there is much along the Rhône Valley to draw the traveller's attention.

Comité Départemental du Tourisme du Rhône
15, Rue de Sévigné
69003 Lyon
Adresse postale : 146, Rue Pierre-Corneille
69426 Lyon Cedex 03
Tel: 72 61 78 90

Comité Départemental du Tourisme de la Drôme
1, Avenue de Romans
26000 Valence
Tel: 75 43 27 12

Touring:
use Michelin sheet map 916, Francia

Corniche du Rhône

A high-level route between Tournon-sur-Rhône and Valence, passing on its way the lofty ruins of the Château de Crussol, the Corniche du Rhône runs to the west of the river via St Romain-de-Lerps. From various points along its route there are marvellous views of the valley, but the best is at St Romain itself. All-round panoramas from the viewing table at the tiny Chapelle du Pic are immense, encompassing no fewer than 13 *départements*.

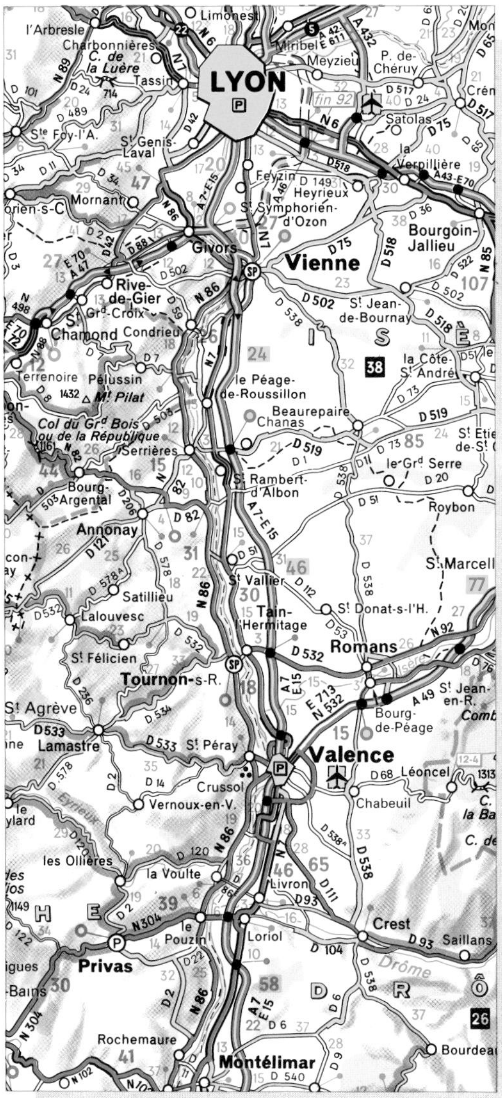

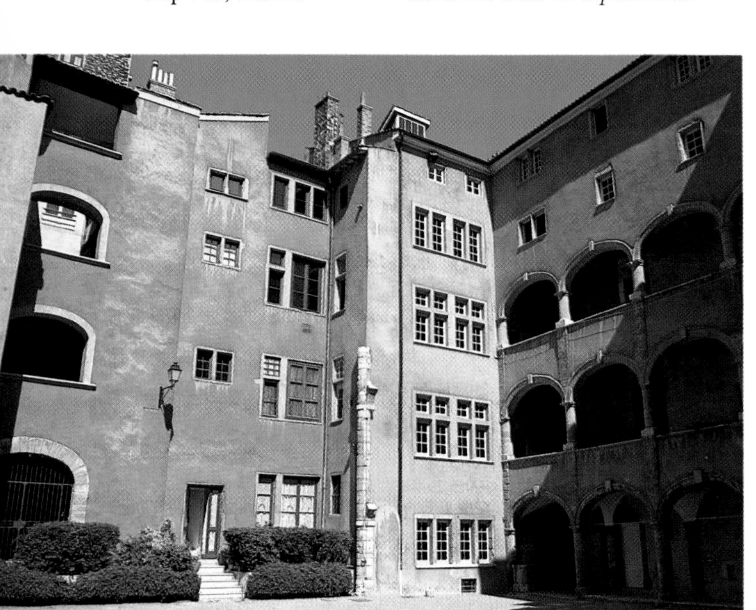

The centre of Lyon retains a wealth of Renaissance building. Its narrow streets, most of them pedestrianised, are lined with many fine mansions of the period

Lyon

Situated at the confluence of the Rhône and Saône, France's third-largest city is worth a visit of several days. Built on silk, banking and insurance, Lyon is a prosperous city with hundreds of restaurants and 24 museums (from fine arts to puppets).

The heart of the city is the Place Bellecour, one of the largest squares in Europe, from where it is just a short distance across the Saône to Vieux Lyon. This area, around the Cathédrale St-Jean, is the largest Renaissance centre in France.

Overlooking the old quarter of Lyon is the Fourvière district, where the city was founded by the Romans. Visitors can take a funicular railway to the top of the hill to see the gaudy Basilique Notre-Dame, Roman amphitheatre and Musée de la Civilisation Gallo-Romaine. Views from the basilica's terrace are extensive, stretching from the Parc de la Tête d'Or in the north to the riverside petrochemical works in the south, and show a red-roofed city virtually devoid of high-rise buildings. The exception is the soaring Crédit Lyonnais tower.

THE SILK TRADE

Lyon owes much of its wealth today to the silk industry established in 1536. Progress was slow at first and in the latter half of the century was interrupted by the Wars of Religion. With peace restored, the famous horticulturist, Olivier de Serres, suggested to Henri IV that to help revive the economy, silkworms and their staple diet, mulberry trees, should be introduced to the Rhône Valley. Several farms were established and by the mid-17th century locally produced raw material was supplying 10,000 looms in Lyon.

The Revolution caused further setbacks and Napoleon came to the industry's rescue. New looms were introduced, enabling one *canut*, as the weavers were called, to do the work of five, and new premises were built in the Croix-Rousse district to accommodate them. But workers' pay and conditions were far from good and the mid-19th century saw bloody revolts. With the advent

Tournon-sur-Rhône is a compact little town facing Tain-l'Hermitage across a broad stretch of the river

Montélimar

A quiet but colourful town just east of the Rhône, Montélimar is best known for nougat. This is made with almonds, which were first introduced from Asia by the horticulturist Olivier de Serres in the early 17th century. Other ingredients, such as honey and eggs, were available locally and for the next 300 years nougat thrived as a cottage industry. Only since early this century has production been factory-based.

The town centre, around the 15th-century church of Ste-Croix, is pedestrianised and has several old mansions, while at the eastern edge is the feudal castle of Mont-Adhémar, which gave the town its name.

Tournon-sur-Rhône

The Rhône is wide at Tournon, slowly flowing between the town and the vine-covered slopes of Tain-l'Hermitage opposite. It was between these twin towns that the first suspension bridge across the river was built in 1824 by the engineer Marc Seguin, who was also responsible for the first steamboat service on the river and for the first French railway, between Lyon and St-Étienne. A steam railway still runs from Tournon, following the scenic Gorges du Doux to Lamastre.

Tournon, with its attractive riverside terrace shaded by huge plane trees, has several other interesting sights. Overlooking the river is its 15th-century château, which houses the museum, the latter showing the use of the Rhône for trade. In the Grande Rue are several imposing town houses and the 14th-century church of St-Julien with its unusual timber ceiling.

Valence

Squeezing the RN7 and A7 to the banks of the Rhône, Valence rises on the slopes to the east and for travellers from the north offers the first taste of the Midi. Enclosed within broad boulevards, the town centre hides tree-shaded squares where numerous restaurants vie for business. Among several Renaissance houses is the Maison des Têtes in the Grande Rue, which has 45 heads carved on its façade, in the entrance passage and in the interior courtyard. On terraces overlooking the Rhône are the Cathédrale St-Apollinaire, rebuilt in the 17th century, and the lovely Parc Jouvet.

Vienne

A town of churches and Roman remains, Vienne is not a place to hurry past. The Cathédrale St-Maurice is one of the most important Romanesque and Gothic churches in the Rhône Valley, but much older is the former church of St-Pierre, now an archaeological museum, parts of which date from the 5th and 6th centuries. The Romanesque St-André-le-Bas has a charming little cloister.

For a town of its size, Vienne has a remarkable number of Roman remains. The largest is the amphitheatre below Mont Pipet, which is still used. Other remains include the Temple d'Auguste et de Livie, an archaeological garden, the settlement of St-Romain-en-Gal on the opposite bank of the Rhône, and a strange structure called the Pyramide, formerly an arena.

of mechanisation early this century, the Croix-Rousse workshops fell into decline and today most of the city's silk production has dispersed to high-tech factories elsewhere in the region.

Lyon's Musée Historique des Tissus, to the south of the Place Bellecour, has a particularly fine collection of silk, and at the Maison des Canuts in the Croix-Rousse a small number of artisans produce silk by traditional methods.

One of the last silkworm farms still operating can be visited at Les Mazes, near Vallon-Pont-d'Arc in the Ardèche.

Vivarais Railway

Running between Tournon-sur-Rhône and Lamastre, the Chemin de Fer du Vivarais is the only passenger service operating in the Ardèche *département*. Built in 1891, the line winds through the Gorges du Doux, the steam locomotives and wooden carriages taking two hours to complete the 33-km journey.

The train first passes orchards and vineyards before reaching the wilder mountain scenery of heather and fir. Just before reaching Lamastre the line crosses the 45th parallel, which is where the Midi, or southern France, begins.

Trains run daily in July and August and on a restricted basis from the beginning of April to the end of June and from the beginning of September to early November.

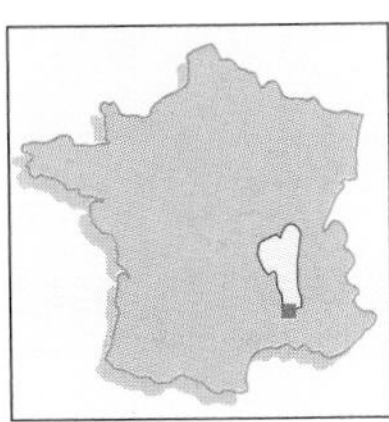

THE ARDÈCHE GORGES

THE ARDÈCHE REGION, with its many outstanding natural sights both above and below ground, makes an attractive contrast to the rush and industry of the nearby Rhône Valley. A sparsely populated limestone plateau covered in forest, it has been shaped by the action of water, and the visitor is presented with one of the most beautiful gorges in France as well as a number of spectacular caves.

Coloured stalactites and stalagmites can be seen in the Aven d'Orgnac

Aven de Narzal

Reached by a staircase through its roof, this chasm is not as big as that of Orgnac, but it is just as beautiful. Strategically placed lights pick out the shapes and colours and cause minute crystals in the rock to sparkle. On the surface there is a museum of caving.

Aven d'Orgnac

This is the largest of the caves in the Ardèche open to the public, but despite its size it is only a fraction of a system that has still to be fully explored. Strictly speaking a pothole because it has a vertical entrance, it was known for many years but only entered for the first time in 1935 when the speleologist Robert de Joly made a descent. Consisting of several chambers, one of them 250m long, it has magnificent stalactites and stalagmites in all sorts of weird and wonderful shapes and colours, some reaching 25m in length. The growth rate is about a centimetre per century.

Gorges de l'Ardèche

For around 30km between Vallon-Pont-d'Arc and St Martin-d'Ardèche, the Ardèche flows through some of the most spectacular scenery in southern France, part of it a nature reserve. Precipitous limestone cliffs, some 300m high, tower over the river, which from autumn to early spring rages with white water. A road follows the northern rim but the best way to see the Gorges is from the river itself and every spring, especially during May and June, when conditions are at their best, thousands make the journey by canoe, most completing it within a day.

For those who prefer a more leisurely pace there are a couple of riverside camp sites. One of the most fascinating sights on the way is the Pont d'Arc, a huge natural arch over the river.

THE *MAS*

The *mas* is the typical farmhouse of the region. Quite low despite its two storeys, it has stone walls beneath a gently sloping roof of curved terracotta tiles. The windows are small to keep it cool in summer but large enough to allow in light.

The focal point of the house is the kitchen, which traditionally comprises a hearth, sink and oven plus simple furnishings. The bedrooms and sometimes a sitting-room, all with terracotta-tiled floors, are upstairs.

The outbuildings, grouped round a courtyard, consist of a cellar, storeroom, bread oven and sometimes a cocoonery from the days of silk production.

Spanning the Ardèche some 4km below Vallon-Pont-d'Arc, the Pont d'Arc is in summer a popular place to relax and sunbathe

The Belvédère de la Madeleine is one of the finest viewpoints on the high cliffs of the dramatic Gorges de l'Ardèche

Haute Corniche

Opened as recently as the late 1960s, the D290 road along the Gorges de l'Ardèche follows as closely as it can the curves of the river, often along the cliff tops. There are frequent stopping places, but the most spectacular section of the journey is the Haute Corniche, from where at almost every bend in the road there are outstanding views of the river below. Particularly dramatic are the views that can be enjoyed from the Belvédère de la Madeleine and the Belvédère de la Cathédrale.

Grotte de la Madeleine

This cave, which overlooks the Gorges de l'Ardèche and was discovered in 1887, has been open to the public only since 1969, shortly after the scenic road was built. In its chambers are beautiful and richly decorated rock formations, some flowing almost like water or shaped like hanging curtains, others having the appearance of flowers and coral. In addition, the remains of Ice Age animals such as reindeer, stags and bears have been found in the cave.

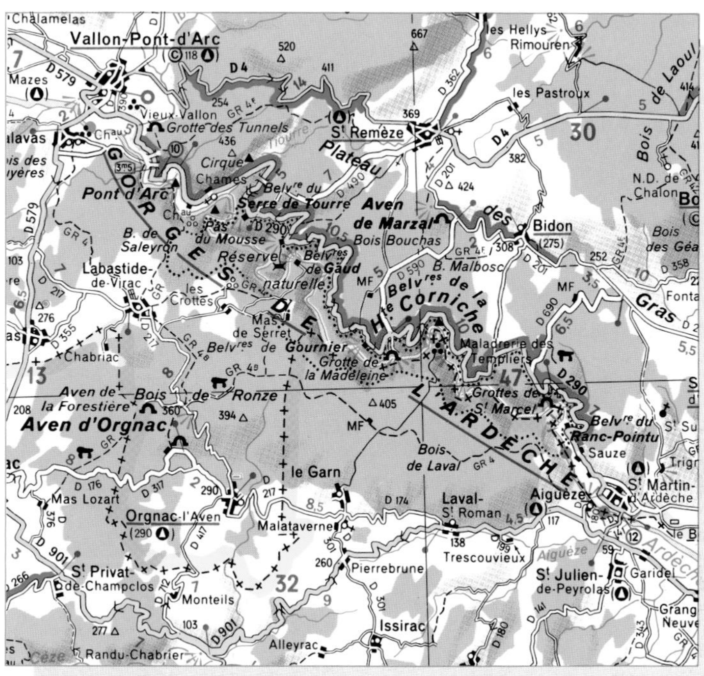

Grottes de St Marcel

These caves are not far from St Martin-d'Ardèche at the southern end of the Gorges. Discovered in 1835, they have only recently been opened to the public. Previously access was restricted to scientists, who have explored a network of more than 20km. Some of the chambers are enormous and have outstanding natural vaulting and concretions – small, round masses of rock particles embedded in the limestone.

Vallon-Pont-d'Arc

This town is the main tourist centre for the Gorges de l'Ardèche, with many hotels, camp sites, restaurants, bars, souvenir shops and canoe rental centres. For most visitors Vallon-Pont-d'Arc is the starting-point for the journey through the Gorges, either by canoe or by car.

Wandering around the town, though, away from the hubbub, the visitor will find attractive old squares and alleyways reminiscent of some of the medieval villages in the area. The town hall, a Louis XIII-style mansion, has on show a fine collection of Aubusson tapestries.

Comité Départemental du Tourisme de L'Ardeche
8, Cours du Palais
- BP 221
07002 Privas
Tel: 75 64 04 66

Touring:
use Michelin sheet map 240, Languedoc Roussillon

THE ALPS

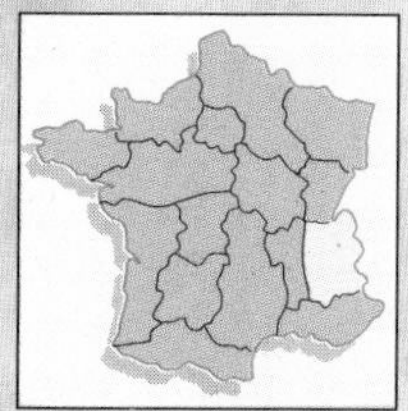

BORDERING SWITZERLAND AND Italy, the French Alps offer a diversity and grandeur unmatched in Europe. They include not only the single highest mountain, Mont Blanc, but also hundreds of other peaks that attract climbers and tourists alike. In the north of the region is Chamonix, the world centre for Alpinism, where dozens of needle-like peaks thrust skywards, demanding attention and holding a fascination for all who gaze up at them. Beyond, the creamy-white summit of Mont Blanc lures thousands of climbers each year.

To the south, huge valleys linked by high passes delineate different Alpine regions. The Parc National de la Vanoise, a magnificent area for wildlife, is far less commercialised than the northern Alps, as is the Parc National des Écrins, south-east of Grenoble. This latter area is one of the largest mountain bulks in the Alps and although it is popular with Alpinists, it remains free from the heavy tourist-related developments of many other areas.

Towards the Italian frontier is the Queyras, famous for its wild flowers, high villages and stunning scenery, while to the south again is the Vercors. Gorges of unfathomable depth, tremendous limestone cliffs leading on to huge plateaux and dense woodland characterise this landscape of outstanding quality.

To the south-west of Chamonix, Lac d'Annecy and Lac du Bourget and their surroundings demonstrate yet another stark contrast. The larger towns are important cultural and historical centres, while the lakes themselves are the perfect complement to the nearby peaks.

Wherever there are mountains there will be climbing and walking, and the Alps have a superb selection of both, from the gentlest stroll to the most demanding north face. In addition there are many other activities, such as paragliding, canoeing, mountain biking, skiing and sailing, making the Alps one of the world's great outdoor playgrounds.

Below the majestic peaks are dozens of small and friendly villages, ranging from the austere, granite-clad settlements of the high eastern Alps to the mellow, bleached limestone houses of the Vercors. Each area has its own distinctive quality, and in many cases its own food and wines. The traditional dishes of Haute-Savoie are the fondue and the *raclette*, both of which can take several forms. You may have sampled these delights elsewhere, but they are even better in the right environment, ideally after an energetic day on the mountain, when your appetite is likely to match the generous portions. Locally produced wines are also a good bet.

Some places have had to be left out, for lack of space. Grenoble is one of these. A modern city often referred to as the capital of the French Alps, Grenoble is strategically placed, economically important and a good cultural centre.

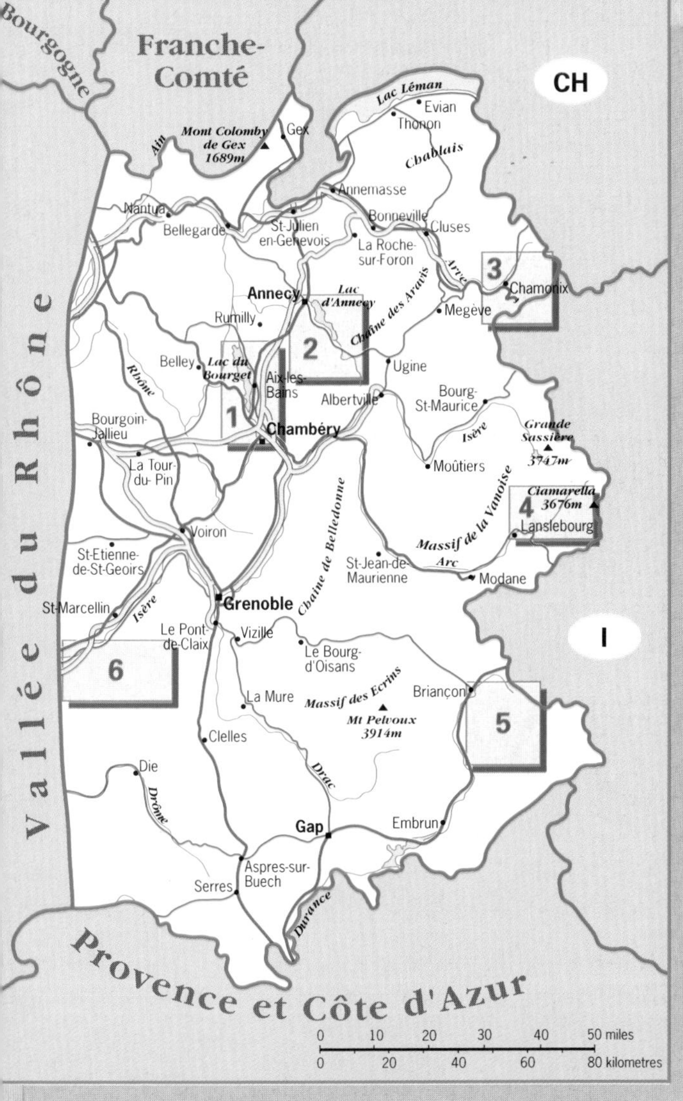

The old quarter of Annecy (left) is largely built around the River Thiou

Rural Savoy is proud of its crisply starched traditional costume (below)

Behind the village of St Michel-les-Portes (above) Mont Aiguille (2086m) can be seen to the left and the Grand Veymont (2341m) to the right

The town choir of Beaufort (right), a strong community, rehearses for a festival

The Beaufortin is a gentle Alpine area with no massive peaks or glaciers

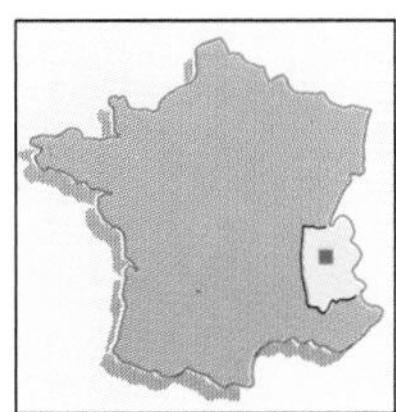

Lac du Bourget

THIS REGION OFFERS historical and cultural interest of a quality to match its superb natural scenery. Dark forests that frame the limestone peaks sweep down to waterside meadows, while Lac du Bourget itself constantly changes in hue and mood with the subtle shifts in light. The main towns of Chambéry and Aix-les-Bains offer first-class facilities, and there are many delightful villages in the surrounding countryside.

At the north end of Aix-les-Bains is the Grand Port. Busy with pleasure boats, the port is lined by attractive, tree-shaded promenades

Aix-les-Bains

The hot springs that have made Aix-les-Bains famous were taken advantage of by a Celtic race, the Allobroges, as long ago as 400 BC. But it was the development of the thermal baths in the mid-18th century and the rapid expansion of the town in the late 19th century that created the present-day Aix-les-Bains, an affluent and well looked after town that attracts visitors from all over the world.

Aix is set on the gentle hillsides above the lake, and has many attractions. The Musée Faure, for example, has a good collection of Impressionist paintings and sculptures, and the tourist information centre (in the square that is in front of the thermal baths) has a selection of Roman relics ranging from coins to headstones. Most importantly, you should visit the baths, where the waters are used, in one form or another, to treat an extremely wide variety of ailments.

The Grand Port, with its fine old willows, is a good place for a gentle stroll.

Le Bourget-du-Lac

This small town, previously a busy port with boats using the Canal de Savières to reach the Rhône until 1859, is now a thriving centre at the southern end of the lake. There are lakeside strolls, all kinds of water sports and a beach, though the church, priory and gardens alone make a visit worthwhile. The priory is just to the right of the church and is entered by a series of courtyards, including an inner one some-

Lac d'Aigue-belette

Easily reached from the Chambéry to Lyon motorway, the lake is situated at the junction of the Col de l'Épine and the rolling, partly wooded rural area to the west. Its two islands support a delicately balanced ecology and it has the richest flora and fauna of the Savoyard lakes, despite being the smallest. Summer bathers will find a typical surface temperature of 28°C very agreeable.

Association Départementale du Tourisme de la Savoie
24, Boulevard de la Colonne
73000 Chambéry
Tel: 79 85 12 45

Touring:
use Michelin sheet map 244, Rhône-Alpes

A Royal Abbey

The Abbaye Royale de Hautecombe is magnificent both in structure and in setting. Situated at the foot of the forested slopes bounding the limestone plateau, and overlooking the shores of Lac du Bourget, it is a very popular attraction. Although besieged by coach parties for much of the main holiday season, the abbey is well worth a visit.

A superb old barn houses a display depicting the daily life of the monks, and the site can be viewed from boats that sail regularly from the adjacent jetties. Regular guided tours take visitors round the chapels and the church, where works including a *pietà* by Cacciatori are on show.

times used for concerts. To the rear are some superb formal gardens, now fully restored.

Chambéry

Situated in a fine and sheltered setting to the south of Lac du Bourget, Chambéry is the meeting point of several roads. Stylish, elegant and wealthy, its affluence owes much to its historical importance as the capital of Savoy, then an independent nation stretching from Berne to Nice and from Lyon to Turin. Although the outskirts are given over to commerce, the centre, and in particular the famous Vieille Ville, is full of character and curiosities. Sombre, arch-covered alleys and tiny courtyards lead to long avenues lined with chic shops and less expensive bars and cafés. There are too many attractions to list, but the Fontaine des Éléphants is a must, as are the castle of the dukes of Savoy, the Cathédrale St-François-de-Sales, the statue of the writer and philosopher Jean-Jacques Rousseau and several excellent museums. There are many cultural and commercial events, including September's Jazz Festival, April's Great Spring Flea Market and the October Motor Show, as well as dozens of street performances of music, theatre and dance.

Chapelle Notre-Dame de l'Étoile

This is to be found just off the D914, across the lake from Aix-les-Bains. Well signposted from the road, and just five minutes' walk from the parking area, the 14th-century building was last restored in 1888. Interesting in itself, it also offers views of the limestone summits and the Dent du Chat to the rear, Aix-les-Bains opposite, Le Grand Colombier to the north and the Massif d'Allevard to the south.

Lac du Bourget

This, the largest Savoyard lake, can easily be driven round in a day, though two days would give you time to enjoy its main attractions at a more leisurely pace. Although its immediate surroundings are steep, forest-clad hillsides topped with starch-white limestone pinnacles, the lake still feels spacious and exhilarating. The water itself is renowned for its ever-changing hues and shades, at times possessing great clarity, at others a milky opalescence. A boat trip from Aix-les-Bains or Le Bourget-du-Lac is the very best way to view the lake and its surroundings.

Mont du Chat

Yenne and Le Bourget-du-Lac are separated by a range of limestone hills, tree-covered except for large and well defined molar-like pinnacles. The serpentine road that links the two towns reaches its highest point at a radio and television mast at 1504m, from which some walking is necessary to reach the best viewpoints. These are the Molard Noir – from where the Aiguilles de Chamonix and the Massif de la Vanoise can be seen – and Mont du Chat itself. The former is about half an hour's walk from the col, the latter a little less.

A splendid position overlooking Lac du Bourget is but one of the charms of the Abbaye Royale de Hautecombe. The church is adorned with fine frescos and a pietà *in marble by Benoît Cacciatori can be seen*

The Fontaine des Éléphants is one of the essential sights of Chambéry, a city of great historical, cultural and commercial vitality

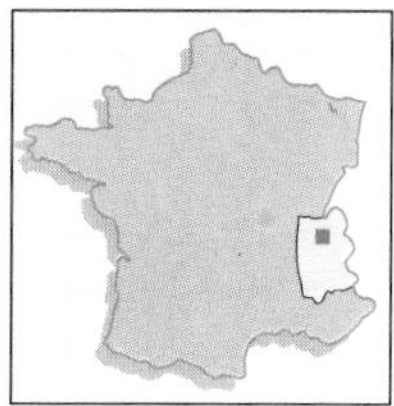

LAC D'ANNECY

ANNECY, the lake bearing its name and the surrounding peaks and forests all possess a character very different from that of the higher region to the east. The land is gentler, the accent is on sailing as much as climbing and the climate is less harsh. Annecy itself is a marvellous centre, charming and with an air of well-being. The region provides cultural and outdoor interests to suit all tastes.

Association Touristique Départementale Haute-Savoie/Mont-Blanc
56, Rue Sommeiller - BP 348
74012 Annecy Cedex
Tel: 50 51 32 31

Touring:
use Michelin sheet map 244, Rhône-Alpes

Annecy is an ancient town, its name deriving from the Roman Villa Aniciaca. A large part of the town's old quarter grew up around the River Thiou. Important past residents of Annecy include St François de Sales and the 18th-century writer and philosopher Jean-Jacques Rousseau

Annecy

This fine town commands a magnificent position at the northern end of the lake. On the lake front are the Jardin d'Europe, the boat-lined Canal du Vasse, with its photogenic Pont des Amours, and the wide, open spaces of the Parc du Paquier. From here can be clearly seen the saw-tooth ridge of the Tête du Parmelan and the jagged pinnacles of La Tournette. With the royal, tree-lined Avenue d'Albigny behind it, the park is a deservedly popular place. Opposite the inland end of the canal is the Centre Bonlieu, which houses an information centre, library and theatre.

The old quarter is worth a special visit. On its lakeside edge are the Église St-Maurice and the Église St-François. The former has a mural dating from 1458 and representing the mortal remains of Noble Philibert de Monthouz that was rediscovered during the restoration of the church in 1953. Much of the old town is built around the River Thiou, which is bridged several times in this short length. The sinuous streets are lined with houses painted grey, ochre, fern and salmon, and window-boxes brighten the bleached paintwork. Some streets have squat, pillared archways and small, cave-like arcades with dozens of inviting shops and bars. An exceptionally fine and busy food market can also be found here, where superb cheeses are brought in and sold by farmers from the nearby hills. The Palais de l'Isle, which divides the river like the bows of a boat, is one of the most famous attractions in the old town. Formerly the Governor's house, a court, prison and mint, it now contains a small but interesting museum of local history.

Cimetière des Glières

Between Annecy and Thônes, and overlooked by the Tête Ronde, the Tête de Turpin and the Plateau des Glières, there are a cemetery and a museum dedicated to the Resistance. The message on the cemetery's monument reads simply 'Live free or die'. The place is a forceful reminder of the dark days of World War II.

Crêt de Châtillon

A gruelling drive up through the forests and then out into the Alpes, the high pasture land that gave these mountains their name, leads to the area just below the summit of the Crêt de Châtillon. Ten minutes' walk up to the cross on the summit itself is rewarded with a stunning 360-degree panorama. The orientation panel will help you to pick out Mont Blanc and the Aiguilles de Chamonix, the Dents de Lanfon, La Tournette and the Dents des Portes, among many other peaks.

This is a popular paragliding, walking and Nordic-skiing centre.

COMBE D'IRE

At the southern end of Lac d'Annecy lies the long valley of the Combe d'Ire. Even at the turn of the century this was one of the wildest and least known valleys in the French Alps. Although it is possible to drive some

way up the valley, through dense woodland and alongside a swift stream, there is no vehicular access into its upper part, which is a strictly controlled nature reserve. Chamois, ibexes, marmots and many other forms of Alpine wildlife inhabit this area, which has well-marked footpaths.

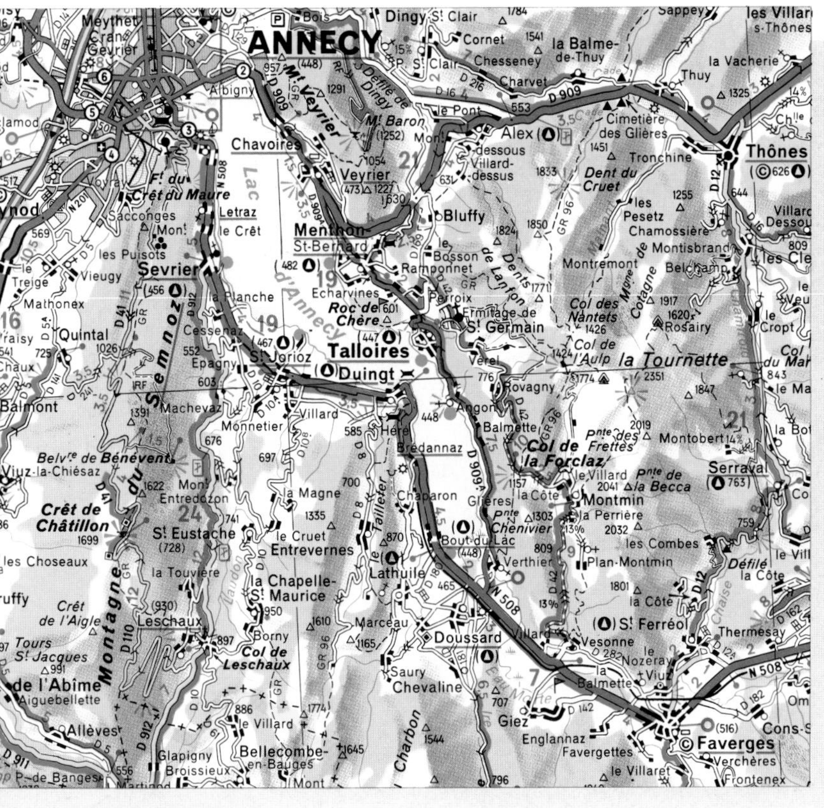

Pleasure boats make regular trips around Lac d'Annecy from the mouth of the River Thiou in Annecy

Duingt

Despite its main-road location, Duingt is a delightful lakeside village. The ancient wooden houses, with their exterior stairways and trellises overflowing with honeysuckle and wistaria, are fine examples of Savoyard domestic architecture.

On the lakeside is the Château de Duingt, also known as the Châteauvieux, property of the de Sales family and best viewed from the small square named after St François de Sales.

Ermitage de St-Germain

This impressive spot is where St François de Sales came to see out his days in 1621. The tiny church has many paintings and sculptures, and the Belvédère de la Vierge presents a wide and truly superb panorama over Lac d'Annecy, to Duingt and to the Crêt de Châtillon.

Lac d'Annecy, widely regarded as the jewel of the Savoy Alps, is used for water sports of all kinds, of which sailing is the most popular

Lac d'Annecy

The lake is now well protected, and is reputed to be the purest in Europe. There are plenty of opportunities for water sports and fishing, and many beaches have lifeguards. With a water temperature as high as 23°C in midsummer, swimming is possible from June to the end of September.

Talloires

This is a well looked after and popular village that exudes affluence and a high quality of life. There are plenty of outdoor activities on offer, including paragliding, sailing, diving and water-skiing.

In 1031 a Benedictine priory was established at Talloires, serving as the residence of the head monk and a centre of daily monastic activities until the Revolution. Now it is a centre for international conferences and academic studies.

Thônes

The approach to Thônes is industrial and unattractive, but the town centre is open and pleasant, sheltered by the surrounding tree-clad hillsides. The regular cheese market is a gastronomic delight and the church, with its typically baroque interior, and the nearby museum of local history and arts and crafts, should be on every visitor's itinerary.

Viuz

Just north of the industrial centre of Faverges is Viuz, which has a small archaeological museum next to its 12th-century church. It also gives views of the creamy-white summit of Mont Blanc, which peeps over the nearer Mont Charvin.

Chateau de St-Bernard

The château occupies a truly commanding position. The site probably dates back to pre-Celtic times, though the château is the result of work carried out between the 12th century and World War II.

The Menthon family has occupied the château for a virtually unbroken period of over 700 years and has played prominent roles both locally and nationally. St Bernard de Menthon, the patron saint of mountaineers and mountain dwellers, is reputed to have been born there in 923. There are regular trips around the château, which has a beautiful chapel and a fine library.

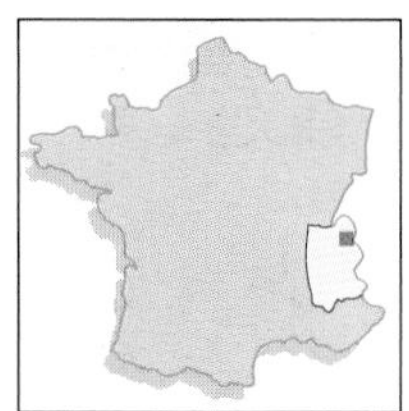

Chamonix and Mont Blanc

CHAMONIX and its nearby mountains, the most famous of which is Mont Blanc, dominate a wide area that is without equal for climbing and skiing. Indeed Chamonix has long been known as a centre where the standards of Alpine sports are pushed ever higher. Many of the area's facilities are used by the adventurous and sedate alike, climber and tourist sharing a love for this special place.

Association Touristique Départementale Haute-Savoie/Mont-Blanc
56, Rue Sommeiller - BP 348
74012 Annecy Cedex
Tel: 50 51 32 31

Touring:
use Michelin sheet map 244, Rhône-Alpes

Paragliding

On any fine day in the Chamonix valley you are likely to see dozens of brightly coloured paragliders drifting down to the valley floor, from take-off sites served by the many chair-lifts. Pilots seek out the uplift provided by thermals,

which can keep them aloft for several hours, enabling them to fly considerable distances across country. Landing into the wind, pilots apply both brakes at once to slow the canopy, and with luck touch down gently. Dual flights and lessons are available locally, but be warned – the sport can soon become highly addictive.

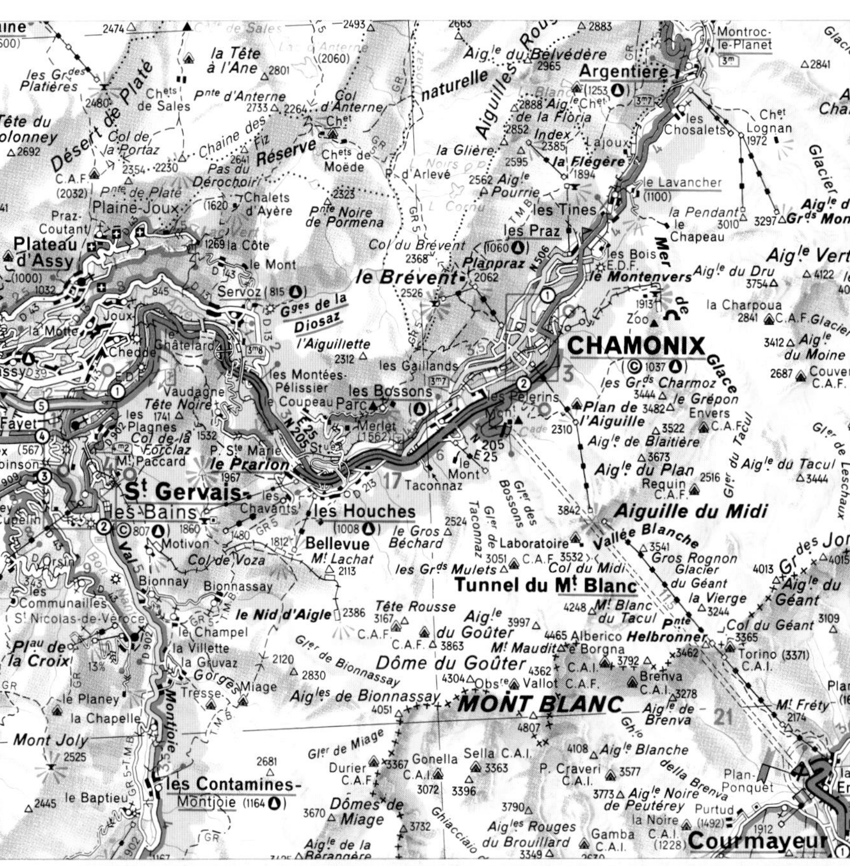

Aiguille du Midi

One of the most spectacular cablecar rides in the world takes you up in two stages via the Plan de l'Aiguille to the summit of the Midi, the most southerly of the famous Aiguilles de Chamonix. The views from here are stunning. The Chamonix valley lies over 2500m below and behind the town Le Brévent and the Aiguilles Rouges look gentle in comparison with the savage views closer by. Apart from the granite spires of the Aiguilles, you can see the Grandes Jorasses, Mont Blanc du Tacul and distant peaks too numerous to mention. The cable-car goes all the way to Helbronner, on the Italian border, after crossing the Vallée Blanche. There is much opposition to this part of the route, as it intrudes into the very heart of the Aiguilles, and its future is in some doubt.

Argentière

A major settlement of the Chamonix valley, Argentière has retained an old quarter of some character, despite the obvious pressure of more recent development in the town. It is the base for ascents by the Grands-Montets cableway, which serves a very important skiing area.

Le Brévent

A cableway on the west side of the Chamonix valley gives access first to Planpraz, then to the summit of Le Brévent. There are some fine walks and excellent views from the first stage, and a walk back down to the valley is a popular option. From the summit, the views to Mont Blanc and the Aiguille du Midi are superb.

At 1252m, Argentière is the highest of the winter-sports centres in the Chamonix valley. Close by are the Glacier d'Argentière and the Réserve Naturelle des Aiguilles Rouges, which has a good variety of wildlife

The imposing Aiguilles de Chamonix look down on the town. Chamonix also lies close to Mont Blanc

Mountain Guides

The Compagnie des Guides de Chamonix is the oldest and best known of all the Alpine guiding agencies. With 150 members available to guide clients on walks and climbs of all standards, it is well equipped to deal with the demand for activities around Chamonix, the world's leading Alpine centre.

Popular excursions include the ascent of Mont Blanc by the Dôme du Goûter or Grands Mulets routes, glacier walking and rock climbing of all standards, from the low-level peaks of the Petit Charmoz to the formidable North Face of the Grandes Jorasses. A bronze statue in Chamonix (above) depicts the naturalist Saussure and the famous guide Balmat together contemplating the wonders of Mont Blanc.

Chamonix

The bustling tourist centre of Chamonix is often described as the world's top Alpine resort, where climbers and visitors of every nationality rub shoulders beneath some of Europe's most formidable peaks. The town is well equipped with all manner of accommodation, a wide range of sporting facilities and entertainment to suit virtually all tastes.

There are many fine examples of Victorian architecture and Alpine chalets, though the mix of these and some of the newer developments is not always pleasing. Chamonix exists above all because of its location at the foot of the highest summit in the Alps, and inevitably mountain views dominate the town. The Musée Alpin relates the history of the Chamonix valley and of mountaineering in the Alps, and holds a mineralogical collection.

Index

A cableway begins at Praz, a little way to the north of Chamonix, and is in two stages, finishing at the Index station. (The mountain known as the Index is just above here.) The terminus is a marvellous place to watch paragliders take off and it offers spectacular views of the main peaks, in particular the Grand Dru and the Petit Dru, the Grandes Jorasses and the Aiguilles de Chamonix. The descent from the Index to La Flégère is an easy and popular walk.

Mer de Glace

A small train from Chamonix ascends the steep, forested hillsides and arrives at Montenvers, right on the edge of the Mer de Glace, probably the most famous glacier in the Alps. Although this is a very busy place in the high season, the views are exceptional, and particularly prominent are the Grand Dru and the Petit Dru, Le Moine, La Verte and the famous North Faces of the Grandes Jorasses.

St Gervais-les-Bains

An extremely popular and busy town, famous for its thermal waters, St Gervais-les-Bains is well connected by train and cablecar to other parts of the region and is often used as a lower-level alternative base to Chamonix. A popular excursion is to take the small train to the Nid d'Aigle, the Eagle's Nest. At an altitude of 2386m, this is an excellent viewpoint.

The Mer de Glace is a huge swathe of ice, cracked, distorted and seamed with crevasses, which flows down unceasingly from the high peaks towering above

ALPINE MOUNTAINEERING

IT IS DIFFICULT TO KNOW who first started to climb mountains for pleasure. Perhaps it was one of the early Swiss naturalists, or a shepherd inspired by the promise of some marvellous view. Probably the first major ascent was that of Mont Aiguille in 1492, made on the orders of Charles VIII of France, and employing ladders in a way that would be more at home on a building site than a mountain. Antoine de Ville and his companions returned with tales of strange and terrible beasts that inhabited the summit plateau, a common fear in those days, and one that was to play its part in inhibiting mountaineering for several centuries. Mountain folklore was still full of evil in the 17th and 18th centuries. Murderous witches and warlocks were supposed to hurl their terrified victims down hideous precipices, and dragons were allegedly to be found throughout the Alps. Bearing in mind the strength of these fears, and considering the difficulty of normal travel in those times, let alone the hazards of avalanche, glacier crossing and sheer verticality, it is no wonder that the mountains were left well alone.

GREAT ADVENTURES

Ever more adventurous feats were attempted during the 18th century, as chamois hunters and crystal collectors made regular forays into the higher Alpine regions. In 1785 Dr Michel-Gabriel Paccard and Jacques Balmat, a crystal hunter from Chamonix, reached the summit of Mont Blanc, the highest peak in the Alps, so beginning an era of great adventure.

The pair returned to Chamonix after three days on the mountain, Paccard snow-blind and both men exhausted. There

Mont Blanc (above), at 4807m, is the highest peak in Europe

The Aiguilles de Chamonix (right) look down on the town that lies at the heart of Alpine mountaineering

followed an extraordinary series of controversies and in-fighting, fired by the jealousy and inadequacies of another would-be conqueror of the heights, who suggested in an unjust written attack that Balmat was the hero, having dragged Paccard to the summit. In fact the reverse had been the case. Though Mont Blanc's first ascent will always be tainted by this bickering, it was nonetheless a magnificent and brave feat by two exceptional men. In 1809 the first woman, Marie Paradis, a Chamonix maid servant, reached the summit.

Bernard Voegeli was the first to climb the Pic du Toedi, in 1837

PERSONAL ACHIEVEMENT

As the 19th century progressed, people started to climb mountains regularly for reasons other than scientific curiosity or to fulfil a personal ambition.

There was an element of joy, of wanting to climb for climbing's sake, to experience the savage grandeur of the mountains at first hand.

The major peaks were gradually conquered in the so-called Golden Age of mountaineering, when climbers could find almost at will an untrodden peak to climb, and when mountaineers of many nationalities joined forces at the Alpine centres.

But later, with all the major summits climbed, a new generation of climbers had to find alternative ways to demonstrate their talents and satisfy their desire for discovery and exploration. They did this by seeking new and more difficult routes up mountains that had already been ascended many times. The quest for ever greater difficulty was on, and this has been the predominant theme of Alpinism over the last half century. Gradually the valley crags are now being found on the very highest faces.

A climber tackles a difficult rock face near Chamonix

MODERN MOUNTAINEERING

The French have played a great part in the development of mountaineering. Great Alpinists such as Patrick Vallençant, Jean-Marc Boivin, Christophe Profit, Thierry Reneault and Nicolas Jaeger, some of whom are now tragically dead, have placed France at the forefront of modern Alpinism, often bringing commercialism into the sport along with very high standards.

In recent years changes in equipment and attitudes have given rise to some remarkable feats. Faces that would once have been considered difficult climbs have been descended on skis, and most of the high peaks have now been descended by paraglider. But there will always be 'the last great problem', and we can be certain that the techniques of Alpine-style climbing will be transferred to the other great ranges of the world, where challenges still beckon.

Safety in the mountains demands the best modern equipment

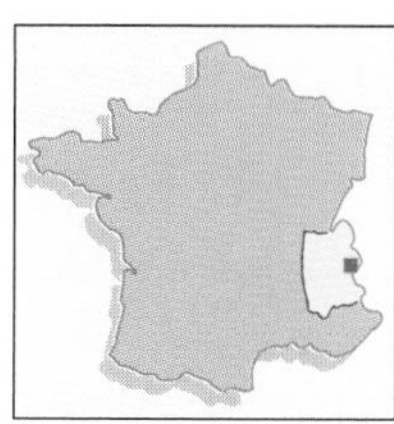

The Vanoise

THIS REMOTE and spectacular area is crossed by one route only, the Col de l'Iseran, which divides the Maurienne and Arc valleys from the Tarentaise mountains to the north. The scenery is characterised by a bleak grandeur that is reflected in the squat stone houses, built to withstand the harsh climate. For high-level mountain walking the region ranks with the best, and is less touched by man's influence than many other Alpine areas.

Bessans

This village is situated on a small, high plain surrounded by steep-sided peaks, and it seems that whichever direction you look in there is a glacier, high snowfield or milky waterfall tumbling down from unseen heights. Lying in the heart of the Maurienne mountain region, Bessans retains much of its traditional character, despite being an increasingly popular winter-sports centre, and has some fine old buildings.

Above the village stands the church and the Chapelle St-Antoine. The church has some statues from the 17th century, but it is the chapel that is particularly impressive. It houses some fine examples of the ornate works that are found throughout the Arc valley, as well as murals, wood carvings and frescos dating from the 15th century.

Bonneval-sur-Arc

Situated at the very foot of the Col de l'Iseran, Bonneval is one of the classic villages of the French Alps. There are no telephone lines, television aerials or electricity cables to be seen, and only local vehicles are allowed into the village. The houses huddle together as if sheltering one another from the harsh climate, and the rough, rust-coloured stone roofs are almost works of art. Wooden balconies and ancient doors complete this rustic scene, and when it is quiet you could be in another century.

In the village centre is the Grande Maison, a huge old chalet that now houses the butcher's and baker's shops and an information centre. On the outskirts of the village is a cheesemaker who sells local cheeses such as Emmental and Beaufort.

Parc National de la Vanoise

Covering 7 per cent of its land surface, France's Parcs Nationaux are a relatively recent contribution to conservation. The Parc National de la Vanoise is the oldest, founded in 1963. Sandwiched between the high valleys of the Maurienne and the Tarentaise mountains, the Vanoise has a high point of 3855m and a low point of 1280m. A wide variety of rock types has led to a great diversity of flora and fauna, the Alpine and sub-alpine zones being especially interesting. These hold chamois, ibexes, golden eagles and a splendid selection of Alpine plants.

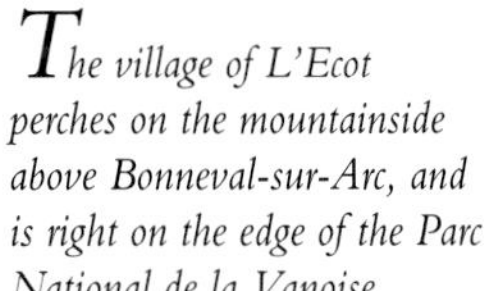

The village of L'Ecot perches on the mountainside above Bonneval-sur-Arc, and is right on the edge of the Parc National de la Vanoise

Association Départementale du Tourisme de la Savoie
24, Boulevard de la Colonne
73000 Chambéry
Tel: 79 85 12 45

Touring:
use Michelin sheet map 244, Rhône-Alpes

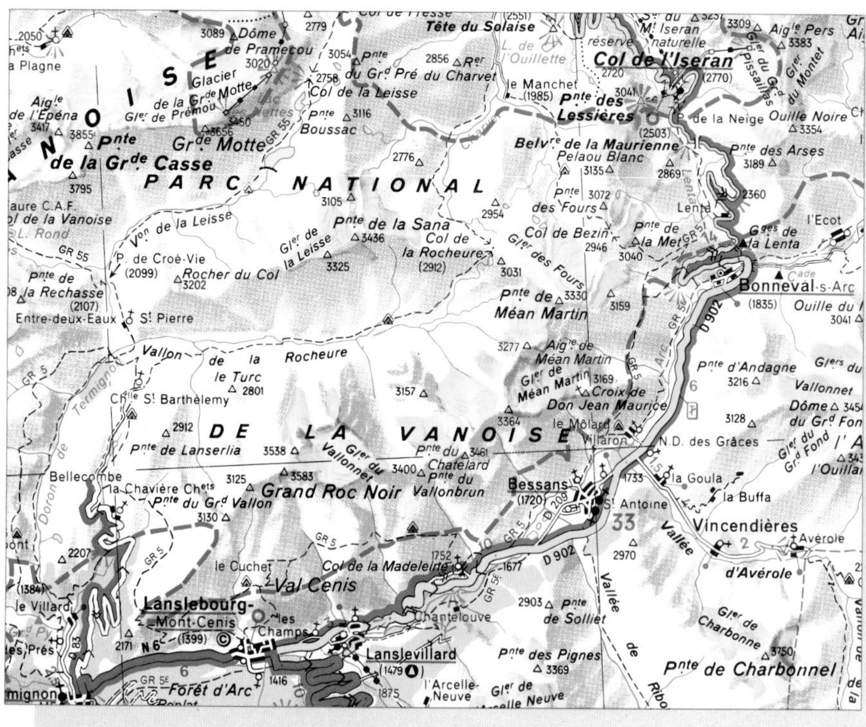

Col de l'Iseran

The highest major European pass, the Col de l'Iseran is a desolate and austere place. From Bonneval the road twists tortuously up very steep hillsides (with good views of the village), rising almost 1000m from the valley to the Col itself. There are several excellent viewpoints, for example the Belvédère de la Maurienne, located immediately past the Pont de la Neige tunnel. This provides a particularly good view of the Albaron, the snowy pyramid of the Pointe de Charbonnel, the Pointe de Ronce and the dramatic ridge of the Massif du Mulinet.

There is always plenty of snow near the Col, and there is a summer ski area, the Glacier du Grand Pissaillas, which is well signposted. Snow can fall at any time of the year here, and the road is almost certain to be blocked from November to June. At the Col itself there is a shop, built to withstand the extremes of climate, and a small church built in 1939, just three years after the route was opened.

The finest viewpoint of all is the Pointe des Lessières, the peak to the immediate west of the summit. However, this is a route for experienced and properly equipped walkers only, and the inexperienced should limit their walks to the environs of the Col.

The stern beauty of the Col de l'Iseran, with its fine viewpoints, attracts many walkers. Bonneval-sur-Arc, situated at the foot of the Col, is the closest village to the Col's summer skiing area, and is a good base for both summer and winter activities

Vallée d'Avérole

This is a remarkable high valley of the Haute Maurienne that contains tiny, unspoilt villages such as La Goula, Vincendières and Avérole. It is overlooked and dominated by the Pointe de Charbonnel, with its attendant glaciers and ice cliffs that teeter on the edge of the vast rock walls below. It is a wild and savage landscape, where large, dirty snow patches, often the residue of winter avalanches, lie next to the road until well into the summer.

Chalets of the Maurienne

The high valleys of the Maurienne contain villages that have survived and developed despite the harsh environment. The hardy and adaptable inhabitants have had to construct homes able to withstand the extremes of climate.

The traditional permanent chalets at lower levels are normally constructed of stone, with some wood, and have barns to the rear for hay, tools and implements. At higher levels the chalets are constructed solely of stone, their front sections designed to house both animals and people, while at the rear hay is stored for the winter. The roofs are often striking, with their huge granite tiles.

Vincendières, nestling beneath the massive mountainsides that form the Vallée d'Avérole, is a typical stone-built village of the Haute Maurienne

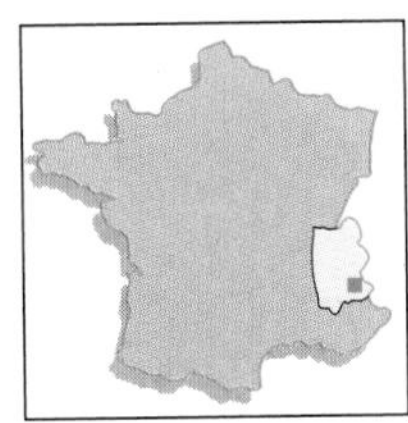

THE QUEYRAS

THE PARC RÉGIONAL DU QUEYRAS is a mountain paradise, closed off from Italy by a wall of 3000-m peaks and presenting a fine combination of flowery meadows and high pastures, villages that cling doggedly to steep hillsides and a reasonable climate. Further north the awesome Col d'Izoard leds to Briançon, a strategic stronghold since Roman times and now a busy Alpine centre.

Comité Départemental du Tourisme des Hautes-Alpes
5 *ter*, Rue Capitaine-de-Bresson - BP - 46
05002 Gap Cedex
Tel: 92 53 62 00

Touring:
use Michelin sheet map 244, Rhône-Alpes

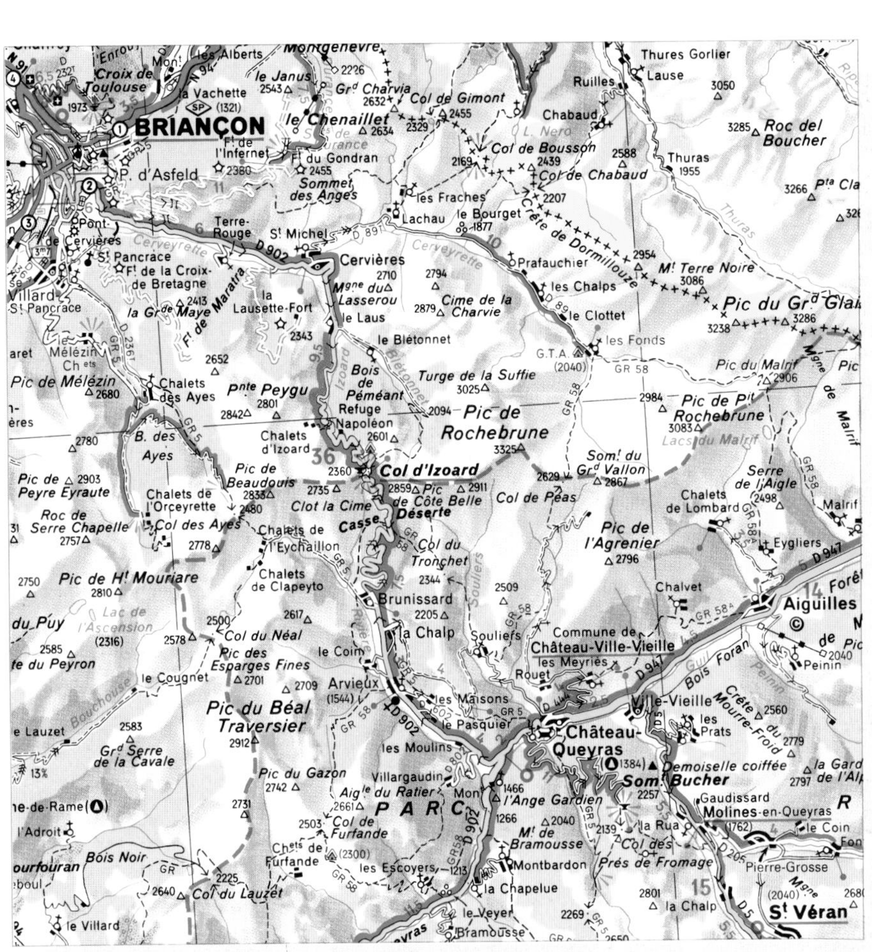

From the perimeter of the fort of Château-Queyras, perched on an outcrop of rock, there are fine views to the east. The village nestles just below, in times past grateful for the fort's protection

Briançon

The highest city in Europe, and the most important in this part of the Alps, thriving Briançon developed as a result of its strategically valuable position. There have been military fortifications here since Celtic and Roman times and the Fort des Salettes still stands impressively above the Ville Haute.

This part of the city is particularly worth a visit. After parking at Champ de Mars or Porte d'Embrun, you can gain access on foot through stout, studded wooden doors. The newer, low town has excellent year-round sporting facilities.

Shops and bars are plentiful in Briançon and though it is a busy place, the mellow colours of the rock, the steepness and the pleasing architectural styles lend it a relaxing air. In the north-west corner is the Collégiale Notre-Dame, built between 1703 and 1726. Inside is a 16th-century tapestry of St George and the Dragon and many other superb paintings and tapestries. Behind the church is an orientation panel. There are many other things to see, including the Place d'Armes with its sundials, the town hall and the Pont d'Asfeld.

Château-Queyras

The huge fort of Château-Queyras, which remained in military use until 1967, completely dominates this upper part of the valley. There have been important fortifications on this natural rock barrier since the 14th century, but most of the present structure was built in the 18th and 19th centuries.

PARC DU QUEYRAS

France's Parcs Régionaux differ from its Parcs Nationaux in that alongside the promotion of nature conservation and the protection of sites of, for example, archaeological, historical and geological interest (below), they also encourage outdoor sports. These include walking, ski touring, paragliding and canoeing, and the establishment of a long-distance footpath, the Tour du Queyras, is a good example of this initiative. As a result, economic considerations do not predominate over landscape and wildlife conservation.

The Parc Régional du Queyras, which is famous for its wildlife, was created in 1977, and provides an excellent illustration of how careful development can coexist with a policy of conservation of the environment.

In the Parc Régional du Queyras, a mountainous and wooded area on the border with Italy, efficient environmental management goes hand in hand with prudent development of leisure activities

Casse Déserte

From Château-Queyras, the road north to Briançon runs over the Col d'Izoard, a high-level pass often blocked by snow from October to June. However, it becomes accessible in summer, when one of its most awesome sights is the Casse Déserte, a huge mountainside of grey scree slopes, out of which sprout dozens of dramatic rocky pinnacles, some in groups, some in isolation. This lunar landscape has been created by natural forces, as wind, rain and extremes of temperature have eroded the softer rock, wearing it down into scree and leaving extrusions of harder rock in the form of these contorted and grotesquely shaped pinnacles.

The true extent of this massive desert of bare scree is difficult to grasp. There are no trees to give it scale, and not even the hardiest plant clings to the ever-moving slopes. The area's beauty lies in its uncompromising barrenness and no one can fail to be overawed by it.

Col d'Izoard

One of the highest Alpine passes, at 2,360m, this Col is well known as the summit of one of the toughest routes taken by the Tour de France. The approach from either direction is long and arduous, as forest gradually gives way to open mountainside, scree and snow, the road taking an unrelenting series of hairpins. The names of famous riders are painted on the road, and at the summit there is a cycling information centre.

Behind here a short walk leads up to a viewpoint and an orientation panel that points out the magnificent views south to the summits of the Queyras and north to those of the Briançonnais.

Lower down on the south side of the Col is a plaque commemorating Tour de France stars Fausto Coppi and Louison Bobet.

Montbardon

As you drive north through the Combe du Queyras towards Château-Queyras it seems impossible that there should be habitation on the vertical valley sides. Yet there is, and one of the loveliest small villages in the area, Montbardon, lies at the end of a narrow and tortuous road. It is set amid high pastures dotted with fir and pine and carpeted with wild flowers.

St Véran

The highest village in Europe, at over 2000m, St Véran is also one of the most visited. That it is heavily commercialised is without question, but it has not been destroyed, as have villages in many other areas. All visitors' vehicles have to be left below the village, necessitating a short, uphill walk. Many of the buildings date from the 17th and 18th centuries, with wood featuring strongly in the construction, along with some typical Haute-Savoie stone-tiled roofs. The massively overhanging eaves, wide balconies and contorted, ancient beams, together with the narrow streets and lack of the outward signs of modern life, lend a genuinely old-fashioned air to the place.

Sommet Bucher

The road to this supreme viewpoint is signposted from near the Lou Tou sports shop, which is down in the low town of Château-Queyras, below the fort. The 11-km drive through the forests is rough in places, but presents no real difficulties, and leads eventually to the summit plateau, an open area of high pastures. A short walk from the car park takes you to the viewpoint, with its beautifully crafted orientation panel.

St Véran's church, which has a wall-mounted sundial, watches over the upper part of this enchanting village

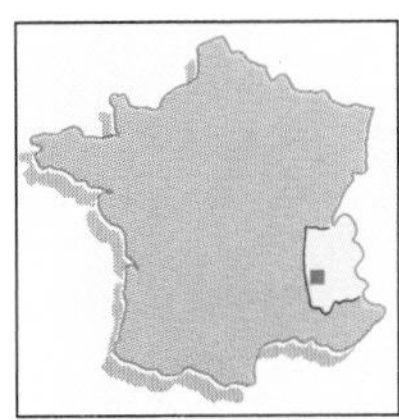

The Vercors

THE VISITOR to the Vercors will be captivated by a stunning combination of gorges and waterfalls, dark forests, precipitous limestone escarpments and delightful villages that are linked by some of the most exciting roads in Europe. Both relaxing and invigorating, this is an area to enjoy at a leisurely pace.

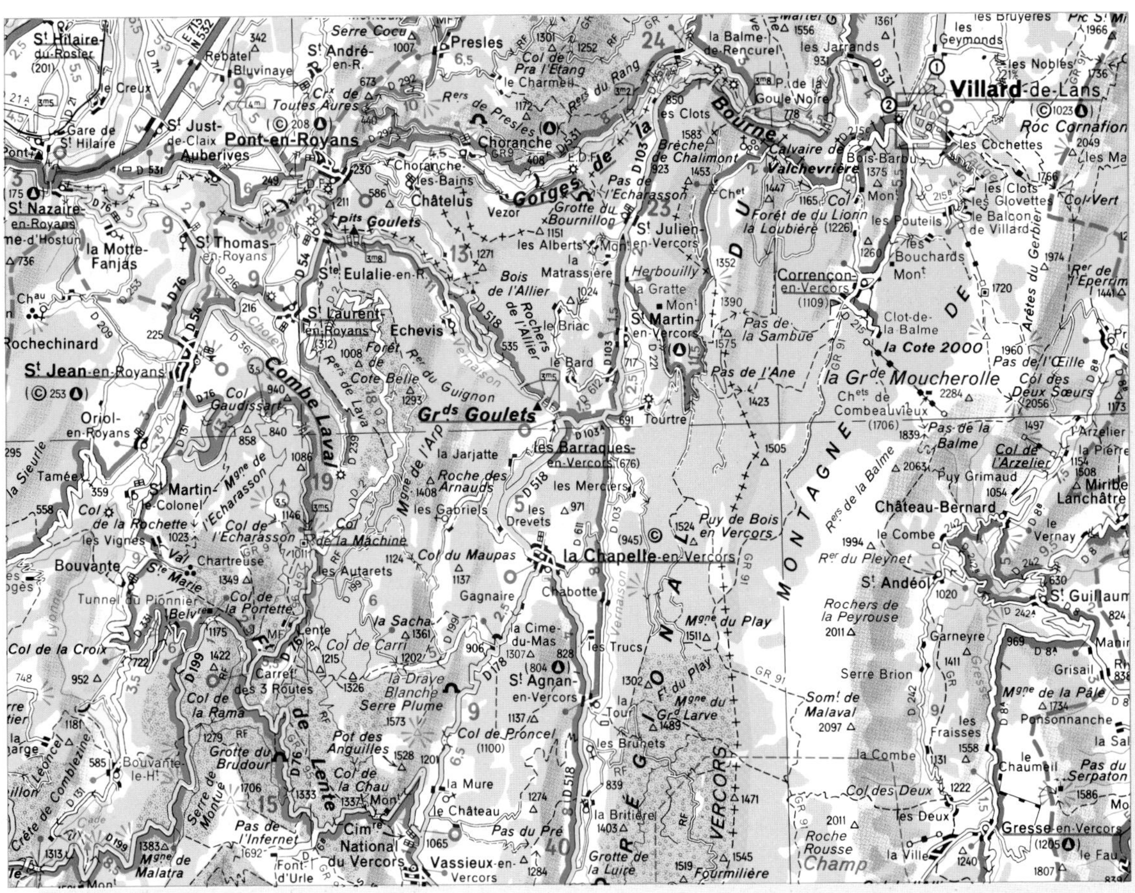

Mont Aiguille

Standing in proud isolation at the south-east corner of the main Vercors massif is Mont Aiguille, a huge and seemingly impregnable limestone tower reaching 2086m. It is best viewed from the road travelling south from Gresse-en-Vercors, when its impressive north-east prow dominates the panorama.

The mountain is particularly interesting as it was the first Alpine peak to be ascended, though the mass of ropes, ladders and accessories employed would be found amusing by modern Alpinists.

Comité Départemental du Tourisme de l'Isère
14, Rue de la République - BP 227
38019 Grenoble Cedex
Tel: 76 54 34 36

Touring:
use Michelin sheet map 244, Rhône-Alpes

Combe Laval

There is no more supremely crafted road, no route with finer views or more startling vistas than the Combe Laval. From the Col de la Machine the route forks left, suddenly opening up a stunning view across to massive escarpments and to the valley far below. There is a small parking area here, from where the line of the road can be fully appreciated, and just in front a rock pinnacle appears to defy gravity, existing where it ought not to.

The road is masterfully engineered, tunnelling through some parts of the vertical hillside, and then abruptly forsaking its womb-like safety as it hugs the cliff edge, suspended seemingly impossibly over awesome drops. Extremely careful driving is called for here. As you descend, each section of the road seems more impressive than the last.

Forêt de Lente

This huge expanse of woodland lies on a high plateau north-west of Vassieux-en-Vercors. It is an excellent area for walking and cross-country skiing. Just out of the forest is Font d'Urle, a very different landscape consisting of vast open meadows on a limestone plateau. It is particularly good for flowers, walking and ski touring.

Gorges de la Bourne

The road between Pont-en-Royans and Villard-de-Lans follows a superb gorge system, lined by massive limestone crags coloured white, ochre, gold and black. Three kilometres out of the village of Choranche-les-Bains, with its neat houses and welcoming bars, is the magnificent cave

they are cool and wet. Water drips from the limestone overhangs and ferns sprout luxuriantly from rocky gullies.

The road snakes through dark tunnels, beneath huge, leaning rock buttresses, and a long valley drops away in the distance. This is an entertaining drive, but expect a bit of crowding and manoeuvring at busy times on this popular road.

Constructed between 1844 and 1851 by the father-and-son team of Adrian and Ernest Joubert, the road that twists its way through the Grands Goulets leads eventually to attractive Pont-en-Royans via the Petits Goulets

The village of Pont-en-Royans (top) has a dramatic riverside setting below the Gorges de la Bourne (above)

system of Choranche.

Further along towards Villard-de-Lans, the road and the overhanging limestone crags suddenly meet, the way continuing thanks to a series of tunnels and excavated overhangs. The route then suddenly veers at right angles to the main gorge, and the motorist is shielded from the precipitous drop by no more than a low wall. The view is first-class, but only for passengers! The fun continues as the gorge narrows once again and a further few kilometres of intimidating and impressive road must be negotiated before the angles suddenly soften and the ascent of the gorge is over.

Grands Goulets

Access to the Grands Goulets is from Les Barraques-en-Vercors, and it is best to park and walk down the first sections, to savour the atmosphere to the full. On a hot, dusty summer day, the stark contrast as you walk into the first area of tunnels is welcome, for

Pont-en-Royans

This charming village at the foot of the Gorges de la Bourne is an ideal base for touring the western Vercors. Most of its sun-bleached houses are huddled at the bottom of steep cliffs, while some of them – the famous Maisons Suspendues – cling precariously to the rock faces.

The narrow streets ooze charm and character and there is an attractive walk along the banks of the Bourne. An excellent viewpoint, the Panorama des Trois Châteaux, can be reached on foot from the Place de la Porte de France.

Villard-de-Lans

A friendly, busy town, Villard-de-Lans is a well known ski centre that enjoys a good sunshine record, has excellent facilities for children and is a convenient base for walking. Higher than most other towns in this region, it is more traditionally Alpine in character and appearance, yet has excellent amenities. The town sprawls rather than huddles and has a more open aspect of meadows and woodland, with a high mountain backdrop.

The Resistance

The Vercors region produced one of the most famous symbols of the Resistance – the Maquis. These tough and fiercely nationalistic people provided motivation and inspiration to the Resistance throughout France and caused the Germans many problems. Several towns were totally destroyed when in 1944 the Germans sent in huge numbers of troops to crush the Maquis, who fought nobly and with great valour. At Vassieux-en-Vercors the Musée de la Résistance provides a sobering reminder of those hard times, while throughout the Vercors monuments and displays likewise ensure that these brave people are not forgotten.

PÉRIGORD AND QUERCY

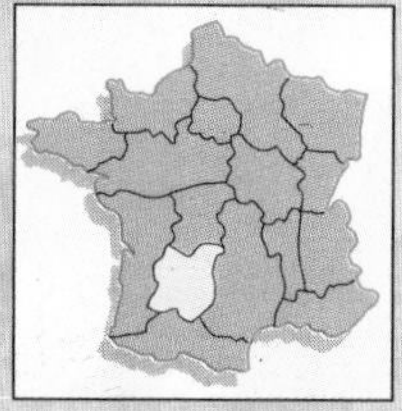

THERE IS A MAGICAL, ALMOST magnetic, quality about Périgord and Quercy, the areas around the Rivers Dordogne and Lot. The dramatic limestone cliffs, the rivers running down from the Massif Central to their eventual destination in the sea, the waterfalls and the distant views that drew early man to settle here, all exert a similar pull on everyone who visits the region.

This is an area that is rich in many ways: scenery, agriculture, food, caves and other prehistoric sites, châteaux, medieval villages and attractive towns. Lack of space forces us to make a selection of places of interest. But doubtless you will discover many of your own, for if you like to just drive where your fancy takes you, this is the ideal region. Wherever you choose to stop you can be sure there will be something to catch your eye, whether it is a pretty waterside village, a majestic castle perched on a hill, a cave or simply a lively local market or restaurant.

When you first see villages such as St Cirq-Lapopie, set high on a hill, with all its turrets and towers overlooking the winding Lot – which, when full, runs almost blood-red with sandstone – you begin to believe in fairy stories.

Périgord has recently been conveniently colour-coded by the local tourist office. Historically, there was Périgord Blanc, named after the white rocks that dominate the central region, and Périgord Noir, from the dark leaves of the oaks that covered the south-east of the area. Here, too, you can enjoy those darkest of delights – truffles. To these areas have now been added Périgord Vert (around Nontron) and Périgord Pourpre (near Bergerac and the purple grapes of the wine region).

The Vézère valley, the area between Lascaux and Souillac, including Sarlat-la-Canéda, is the striking heart of Périgord Noir. It is rich beyond belief in cave paintings and historical sites. However, further south, the Quercy region around the Lot is less crowded and also has cave paintings, fine river views and wonderful wine, so deep red it is almost black.

Both the Dordogne and Lot valleys are studded with castles, built mostly for defence and in many cases bearing the battle scars of the Hundred Years War and the Wars of Religion.

Bastide towns, medieval garrisons, today sleepy in the sun and with attractive markets piled high with walnuts, fruits, duck and goose products and wholesome vegetables of every description, are another enjoyable and typical feature of the landscape. It is chilling to learn how bitterly they were fought over.

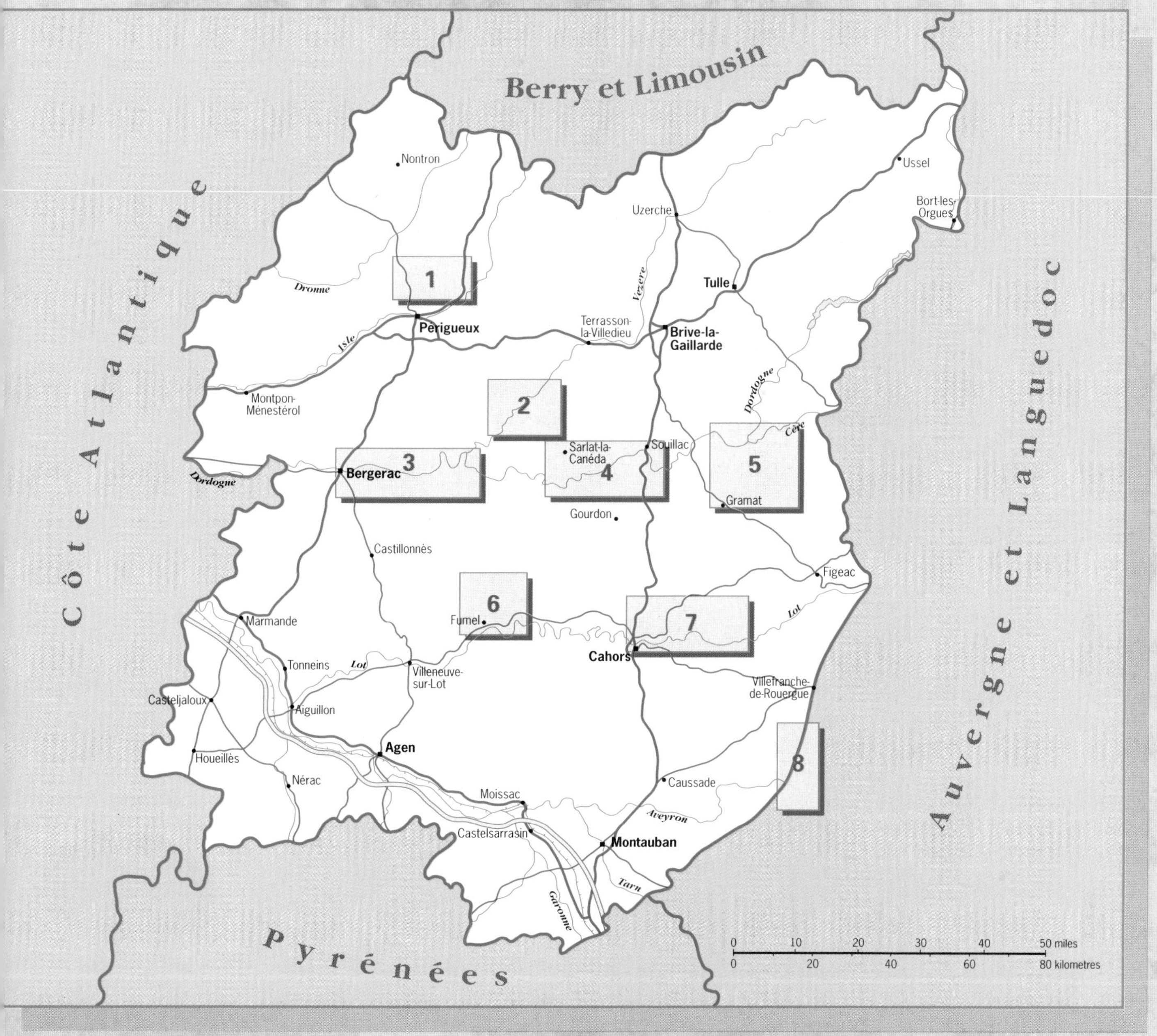

Berry et Limousin
Côte Atlantique
Auvergne et Languedoc
Pyrénées
Nontron
Ussel
Uzerche
Bort-les-Orgues
Tulle
Dronne
Vézère
1
Périgueux
Isle
Terrasson-la-Villedieu
Brive-la-Gaillarde
Montpon-Ménestérol
2
Dordogne
Cère
Sarlat-la-Canéda
Souillac
Bergerac
3
4
5
Gramat
Gourdon
Castillonnès
Figeac
6
Fumel
7
Lot
Marmande
Cahors
Tonneins
Villeneuve-sur-Lot
Villefranche-de-Rouergue
Casteljaloux
Aiguillon
Agen
8
Houeillès
Nérac
Caussade
Moissac
Aveyron
Castelsarrasin
Montauban
Tarn
Garonne
0 10 20 30 40 50 miles
0 20 40 60 80 kilometres

Beynac (right) stands on one of the most attractive stretches of the characterful River Dordogne

Périgord's geese (below) provide renowned pâté de foie gras

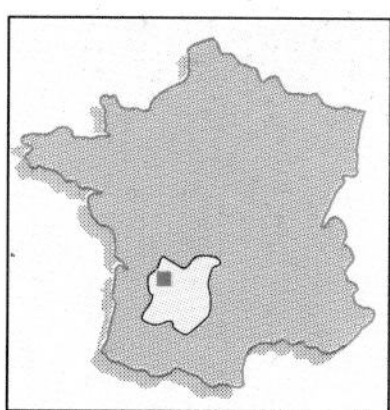

Around Brantôme

BRANTÔME IS one of the best gateways to Périgord. Its mellow buildings, its abbey and its island location on the River Dronne are a pleasant foretaste of what is to come in a tour of the region. However, its attractions are so well publicised that you may find it crowded in high summer. The area contains a number of interesting châteaux and a few prehistoric cave paintings, but its greatest asset is undoubtedly the charm of its riverside towns.

Office Départemental du Tourisme de la Dordogne
16, Rue Wilson
24000 Périgueux
Tel: 53 53 44 35

Touring:
use Michelin sheet map 233, Poitou Charentes

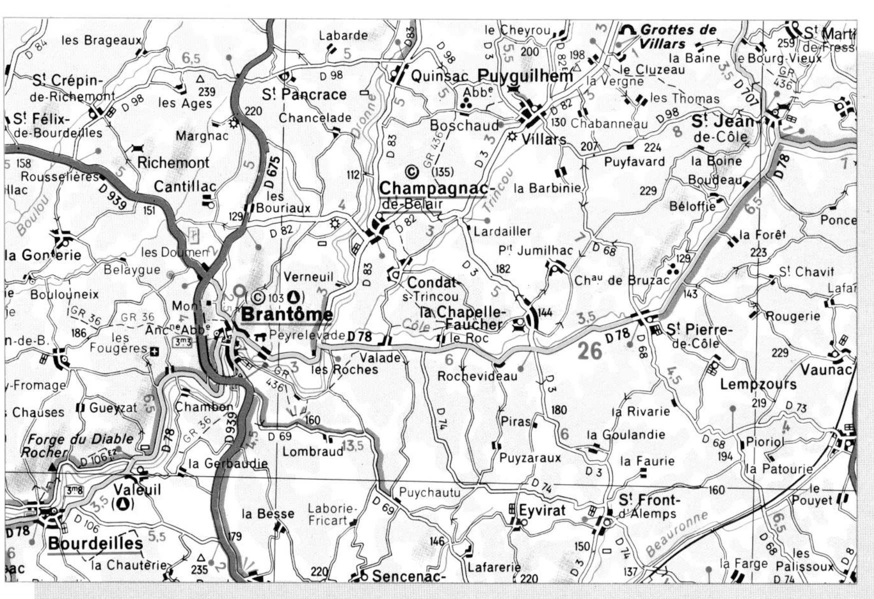

Walnuts

Périgord and Quercy are France's second largest producer of walnuts. Here the main areas of cultivation are north of the Dordogne, south of the Corrèze and many parts of the Lot. During October and November many towns hold walnut markets.

Walnut oil is the chief ingredient of the local salad dressing and is also widely used for cooking. In the Lot Marbot and Grandjean walnuts are often sold broken for making bread, cakes or oil. Many restaurants serve walnut bread with cheese. Walnut mousse (above) is also popular.

The chestnut is the other much prized local nut. Even the smallest village shop sells canned *marrons glacés* as souvenirs.

Monumental rock carvings were executed in the caves behind the abbey at Brantôme in the second half of the 15th century. They depict the Crucifixion and the Last Judgement

Bourdeilles

This was the birthplace of the 16th-century chronicler Pierre de Bourdeilles, who used the pen-name Brantôme. Occupying an imposing position on the rocks above the Dronne are a 13th-century castle and a Renaissance château, with the village clustered below by the river. Among the castle's claims to fame is a bed that was supposedly slept in by Emperor Charles V. From the castle there is a beautiful view of the restored 17th-century water-mill, built in the shape of a ship and surrounded by the green waters of the river.

Brantôme

A beautiful medieval and Renaissance town, Brantôme is known as the Venice of Périgord, as it is a little island held between the arms of the Dronne. It is a wonderful place to stroll, with its old balconied houses with their flowers and trellises and its five bridges. The town is dominated by the abbey, parts of which date back to the 8th century. The abbey has a bell tower built on an imposing rock in the 11th century, while the riverside gardens, originally created by the monks, are one of Brantôme's most attractive features. The monks used the caves behind the abbey to store wines and executed some carvings in them, one of which depicts the Last Judgement. This cave is now used as a theatre, and provides a dramatic backdrop to performances during the summer, when Brantôme plays host to the International Festival of Classical Ballet.

Brantôme has not achieved its immense

Brantôme, with its attractive mixture of medieval and Renaissance architecture, provides an excellent introduction to Périgord

Fishing

For the fisherman, a holiday in the Dordogne and Lot region provides plenty of opportunities for sport. It is best to ask for information at the local tourist office first, as you will probably need a temporary licence to fish. Many of these offices have free maps showing where you can fish.

Trout, roach, perch, bream and carp are the local fish. But there are closed seasons for certain fish and the tourist office can advise on the regulations. The best fishing is said to be wherever the river widens. Further information can be obtained by writing to the Fédération Départementale de Pêche, 182 Quai Cavaignac, 46000 Cahors, or telephoning 65 35 50 22.

popularity simply on the strength of its archaeological and historical sites; an equal attraction are its many fine restaurants, featuring the best of the region's cuisine.

Champagnac-de-Belair

This small town is worth visiting for its Monday markets, and if you are there on the last Sunday in August you will see the sheep fair. It has the 16th-century Château de la Borie and a fine old church. But the town's greatest appeal lies in its location overlooking the Dronne.

La Chapelle-Faucher

The village boasts a wonderful château set above the River Côle. Although part of the château was destroyed by fire, it is still apparently inhabited. Nearby is the little village of Jumilhac, whose springs supply the area with water, where the ruins of the priory of Puymartin and the Château de Bolaurent can be seen.

St Jean-de-Côle

Situated on the Côle, a tributary of the Dronne, the village has often been used as a location for historical films. Its narrow streets contain half-timbered medieval houses typical of the region and there is a humpback bridge over the river. The church, which has its origins in the 11th century, has several unusual features, including a curiously shaped bell tower with windows. The remains of the 12th-century Château de Marthonie dominate the village square. Open to visitors in July and August, they house a permanent exhibition of old publicity posters and the handmade paper for which the region was at one time famous.

St Jean-de-Côle has provided the location for many films which have a medieval setting

Villars

This traditional village, with its old covered market and distinctive fountain set in a circular basin, has three interesting sites. The Château de Puyguilhem was built in the early 16th century by Mondot de la Marthonie, the first president of the Paris and Bordeaux parliaments. It is very much in the style of the châteaux of the Loire, on which he modelled it. The renovated château is open for tours.

Nearby are the Grottes de Villars, caves featuring prehistoric wall paintings and stalactites and stalagmites. The most famous painting depicts a blue horse. Unusually, the paintings also show human figures. Also situated near Villars is the 12th-century Abbaye de Boschaud, abandoned at the Revolution. It has undergone restoration but is still partly in ruins. It was one of just four Cistercian abbeys in Périgord.

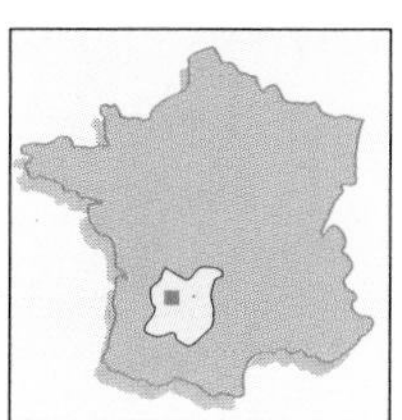

THE VÉZÈRE VALLEY

ALTHOUGH THE VÉZÈRE VALLEY is best known for its many important archaeological sites, what drew primitive man to the area – its rivers, its lush vegetation and its dramatic cliffs – make it attractive to the modern tourist. It is impossible to visit a region that saw the dawning of early man without finding your curiosity awakened.

Les Eyzies-de-Tayac lies at the heart of a region renowned for its wealth of connections with prehistory. Near here, in 1868, the remains of Cro-Magnon Man were found

Les Eyzies-de-Tayac

This town, sited dramatically below the limestone cliff where the Vézère meets the Beune, is at the heart of a region where early man is known to have lived, and is therefore known as France's centre of prehistory. The many caves in the cliff reveal some of the secrets of early man, and throughout the area there is a concentration of such caves and prehistoric sites. Situated to the east of Les Eyzies, in a 13th-century fortress on a rock halfway up the cliff overlooking the town, is the Musée National de Préhistoire, which displays, among other items, major local archaeological finds.

Just off the D47 to the north-west of the town you can visit the Gorges d'Enfer, where tigers, deer, horses, boars and many of the animals painted in the caves roam in semi-captivity.

Grotte de Carpe-Diem

The cave, off the D47 a few kilometres north-west of Les Eyzies, winds through the rock for 180m and has some fine examples of stalactites and stalagmites. Its mysterious chambers have been named after what these formations suggest – for example, Salle de l'Aigle and the Salle de la Vierge.

Grotte du Grand Roc

Close to Laugerie Haute and Laugerie Basse, where primitive man lived for 20,000 years and hundreds of prehistoric items have been found, is the natural cave known as the Grotte du Grand Roc. From the stairs leading up to the cave and the platform at its mouth there are excellent views of the Vézère valley and the valley of Tayac and Les Eyzies. Inside there is an impressive display of stalagmites and unusual crystalline formations, which seem to defy gravity.

EARLY MAN

the Vézère valley is of prime archaeological importance because it was here that Cro-Magnon Man was discovered. This early form of *Homosapiens* appeared in Europe about 30-40,000 year ago, after Neanderthal Man, who lived 150,000 to 40,000 years ago. The latter had a short, stocky body, a wide pelvis and an enormous nose, all probably the result of adaptation to the demands of the Ice Age.

Cro-Magnon Man was taller, with a smaller face and a higher brow. He is also distinguished from his Neanderthal predecessors by using tools differently, by the evidence of art and decoration discovered in his dwellings and by his wearing of 'jewellery' such as beads and pendants.

In the caves at Lascaux II are facsimiles of the paintings in the original caves. Particularly striking is the Salle des Taureaux, the Bulls' Hall, from which a detail is shown here

Montignac

This is the only place where you can buy tickets for the cave system of Lascaux II. Montignac, on the banks of the Vézère, was once a fortress town belonging to the counts

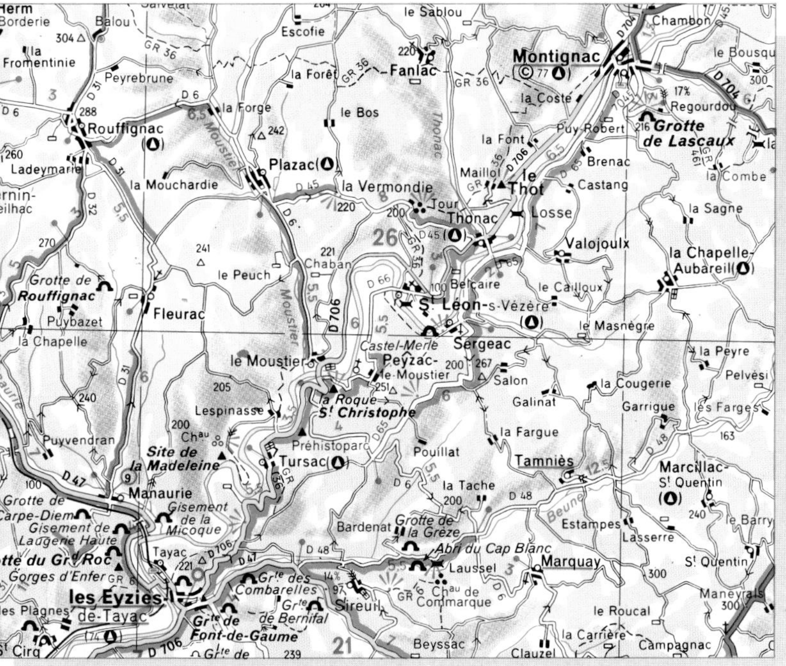

of Périgord and the original tower remains. Thanks to the discovery of Lascaux, it is no longer a sleepy village but an extremely busy tourist centre. Nearby is Regordou, where in 1954 were found the 70,000-year-old skeleton of Regourdu Man and a burial ground containing the bodies of bears.

Office Départemental du Tourisme de la Dordogne
16, Rue Wilson
24000 Périgueux
Tel: 53 53 44 35

Touring:
use Michelin sheet map 235, Midi-Pyrénées

Peyzac-le-Moustier

Where the stream of Le Moustier joins the Vézère, there was in prehistoric times an *abri*, a shelter. Apparently, our ancestors preferred to live in shelters formed by overhanging rocks on the cliff face. The cliffs of the Vézère valley are riddled with such shelters, providing archaeologists with rich pickings. At Peyzac in 1908, German explorers discovered a Neanderthal man. They shipped his remains to a museum in Berlin, where they were unfortunately bombed during World War II.

At the Abri du Cap Blanc, a similar shelter east of Les Eyzies, a skeleton of a woman was found. She ended up in an American museum, but you can see a replica of her and some sculpture over 10,000 years old.

Préhistoparc

You can get a good idea of how our early ancestors lived without setting foot in a cave, by visiting this park at Tursac. It has been laid out with models that reconstruct the life of early man by showing, for example, the cutting up of reindeer, cave painting, fishing and hunting. Early animals are also well represented. The setting of the park, in woodland between cliffs, where we know prehistoric man actually dwelt, adds a certain magic to what might otherwise be just another theme park.

Also at Tursac is the archaeologically important site of La Madeleine, a narrow, rocky limestone promontory that has been inhabited from prehistoric times. By the river in a rock shelter the remains of early man have been discovered. Further up the cliff are troglodyte dwellings, inhabited from the Middle Ages until the beginning of the 20th century. Above are the remains of a ruined castle.

La Roque St Christophe

Believed to have been inhabited from prehistoric times to the 16th century, this sheer cliff 80m high and 1000m long is a honeycomb of hundreds of caves and shelteres, stacked in five tiers, like a prehistoric block of flats. From the terrace there is a commanding view over the Vézère valley – once the steep steps up to it have been climbed. This is one of the oldest and most important cliff fortresses in the world, and those who have sought its shelter over the centuries include Neanderthal Man, Vikings and Huguenots.

St Léon-sur-Vézère

This pretty village lying in a loop near the river valley has no caves. But it does boast a fine 12th-century Romanesque church, made of honey-coloured stone, that was formerly a Benedictine priory, and two châteaux which are not, unfortunately, open to the public. Close by is the imposing 16th-century Château de Belcayre.

MARKETS

Almost every town in France has a market. This is usually held in the main square and takes place on Saturdays and also one weekday, often

Wednesday. Here is a chance to see – and sample – the local produce: vegetables, fruits, flowers, honey, cheese, bread and, of course, the ducks and geese for which the area is renowned. One of the liveliest markets in the Dordogne is the Tuesday market in le Bugue, about 30km west of Sarlat-la-Canéda, not far from where the Vézère flows into the Dordogne. Held in the Place Mairie, the market spills over into neighbouring streets.

If you want to see livestock sold, there is a sheep fair in Cénac in August; and Bergerac has livestock sales on the first and third Tuesdays of the month and Beynac on a fixed date, the 28th.

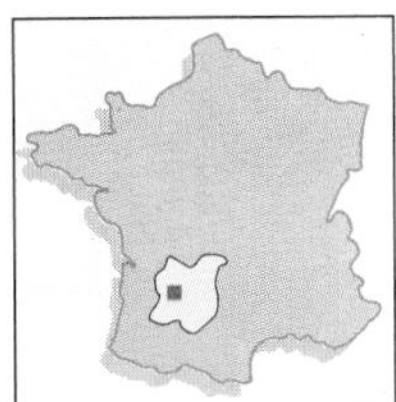

THE WESTERN DORDOGNE

THE WIDE RIVER VALLEY of the western Dordogne, flat and quite different from the country surrounding the river itself, has consequently created different kinds of communities. This area embraces Bergerac, once a rival to Bordeaux for wine and still France's tobacco-making centre, and the unspoiled town of Trémolat, with its spectacular snake-bend location.

Office Départemental du Tourisme de la Dordogne
16, Rue Wilson
24000 Périgueux
Tel: 53 53 44 35

Touring:
use Michelin sheet map 235, Midi-Pyrénées

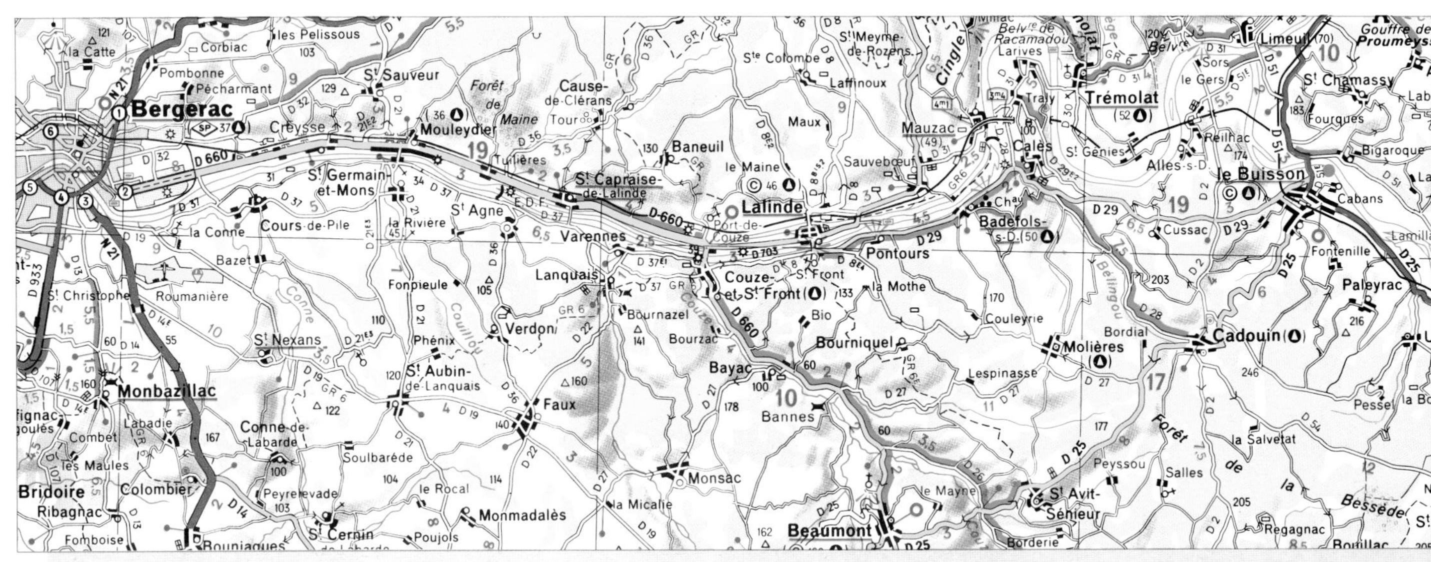

Beaumont

This small 13th-century village was one of the first English-built fortified towns. Known as *bastides* and built by both the French and the English, these were centred on a square surrounded by covered arcades. Most had fortified churches and a town wall with towers and gateways. Beaumont was constructed in the shape of an 'H', in honour of Henry III.

The massive and unmistakably militaristic church still has its four defensive towers with a parapet walk. Although the market square has suffered many changes, it still has two sides of elegant vaulted arcading.

The old quarter of Bergerac contains elegant squares and a number of well-preserved medieval houses

Bergerac

Bergerac is an historic town that at one time contended with Bordeaux for wine-making supremacy and has been for 400 years the capital of France's tobacco industry. Its illustrious past and the wide and attractive reach of the River Dordogne that it spans, together make Bergerac a thriving yet stylish place. The fine main bridge makes the town still the most important crossing point of the river. When you stand at the southern end of the bridge, the reasons for Bergerac's importance are clear. It is a perfect south-facing site for a settlement, 'easy' terrain for farming, partly protected from west winds by the low hills, and the first easily navigable stretch of river south-west of the Dordogne's source. Much of the town's medieval quarter, which lies along the north bank, is pedestrianised.

Bergerac's Musée du Tabac, housed in the fine early-17th-century Maison Peyrarède, traces the history of tobacco. It displays tobacco-containers of all kinds, pipes, cigarette holders and paintings on the theme of smoking

The 16th-century Château de Monbazillac, which produces the most renowned of the wines of Bergerac, commands a fine view over the Dordogne valley to the north

CYRANO

Cyrano de Bergerac has found renewed fame in recent years as a result of the popular film. A brilliant swordsman, he was supposed to have had a big nose that made him so ugly that he was forced into duels to defend his honour. In Rostand's play, written in 1897, Cyrano wrote love letters, on behalf of a friend, to the love of his life.

There is a street named after Cyrano in Bergerac and his large nose has frequently been used in

posters advertising wine. Some 10,000 hectares of vines stretch along the Dordogne. Among these, that of Bergerac is famous for its dark red *robe*, or skin, the reason why the area is called Périgord Pourpre.

There are two fascinating museums that every visitor should see: the Musée du Tabac and the Musée du Vin, the latter also telling the story of river boating and cooperage. The most famous wine-making château to visit is that of Monbazillac (see below), whose museum also chronicles the region's war-torn religious history.

Bergerac is surrounded by vineyards, tobacco plantations and cereals, part of the riches bestowed on it by the calm river and the wide, fertile valley that it straddles.

Cadouin

Away from the river in a valley alongside the Forêt de la Bessède, Cadouin is best known for the remains of its early-12th-century Cistercian abbey, with a splendid 15th-century Gothic-style cloister featuring beautiful, intricate carving. For 800 years the abbey profited from its display of a holy shroud. This was exposed as a fake, albeit an extremely precious one, in 1934.

Château de Monbazillac

Monbazillac is an imposing 16th-century hilltop château lying south of the Dordogne, in the most famous of all the Bergerac vineyards. Unlike the majority of local wines, which are red and full-bodied, Monbazillac is white and sweet. The majestic château itself is open to the public, as is a wine museum in the cellars.

The château is well preserved and furnished with fine 17th-century pieces, including an ornate bedchamber. From the north terrace there is an excellent view of the whole vineyard, and of Bergerac, in the valley of the Dordogne.

Lalinde

This town, with its fine views of the river, retains few memories of its life as an English-built, 13th-century *bastide*. The only traces of the fortified town are the chequered pattern of its streets, the remnants of ramparts and the western gate. Most of the medieval fortifications were finally destroyed by German shells during World War II.

Lalinde is located between the river and a canal, and retains many houses from the 15th and 16th centuries. A pleasant 13th-century building, now a hotel, was a formidable fortress with pointed turrets.

Trémolat

The course of the Dordogne offers plenty of surprises, none more spectacular than the snake bend at Trémolat.

It is the river that brings most tourists to Trémolat. The west bank of the mighty bend is perhaps the world's prettiest water-sports centre, where the cliffs and the rural splendour compete with regattas for the attention of spellbound visitors.

The 12th-century fortified church in the main square is an almost windowless decaying fortress, built on the foundations of one dating from the time of Charlemagne. The inside and outside are fairly Spartan – of necessity for a building made to house the entire population of the village – with internal and external firing points for defence against invaders.

Trémolat is so typically French that Chabrol chose it as the setting for his chilling murder mystery Le Boucher. *But there is nothing sinister about this handsome village*

PÉRIGORD NOIR

THIS AREA OF PÉRIGORD is perhaps the most attractive, with its massive cliffs topped by golden châteaux, fascinating history, fine food and the beautiful old regional capital, Sarlat-la-Canéda. Yet the most impressive sights are not the towns, however appealing. It is the landscape of cliffs, rivers and trees that lingers in the memory.

The Château de Castelnaud looks across a bend in the Dordogne at its former adversary, the Château de Beynac

Beynac-et-Cazenac

From the terrace of the medieval château here, there is a fabulous view along the winding Dordogne as far as Domme, and of the châteaux of Marqueyssac, Castelnaud and Fayrac. The château is perched on top of a rocky cliff. The easy way to reach it is by road, but walking up gives you a better idea of how difficult it was to storm.

A cluster of houses, in the same golden stone, huddle beneath the château: the little village of Beynac-et-Cazenac, where you can visit a small museum of folklore. From the old quays you can take a boat trip along the river, or hire a canoe or kayak. During the Hundred Years War the English occupied Beynac and the French held Castelnaud across the river, the Dordogne forming the boundary between the two.

Carsac-Aillac

This peaceful village on the green river banks has a beautiful Romanesque church in golden stone, with a huge bell tower and dramatic modern stained-glass windows. It stands beside the ruins of a château, and farther along the river, at Aillac, there is a very similar church, in a similar setting.

Château de Castelnaud

Beynac's great rival during the Hundred Years War, the château is said to have been destroyed and rebuilt 10 times during its turbulent history. The latest renovation began in the late 1960s and is nearly complete. The château now houses a museum of medieval siege warfare. As with the château at Beynac, one of the best reasons to visit it are the panoramic views over the Dordogne across the terrace.

Close by is Les Millandes, the château where the entertainer Josephine Baker set up a home for orphans from all around the world. Unfortunately she had to sell it in 1964. In a farmyard she owned there is now an agricultural museum.

Cingle de Montfort

The great loop in the Dordogne is best viewed from a car park on the D703 built for this purpose. On top of the cliff is the Château de Montfort. Simon de Montfort

TRUFFLES

Probably the most expensive vegetable in the world, truffles are an edible fungus that grows underground close to the roots of certain trees, especially oaks. Truffles like a dry limestone soil, which is why they thrive in Périgord. They are harvested between December and February, when gourmets and chefs from around the world descend on Périgord for the truffle hunt.

Traditionally, pigs or specially trained dogs sniff out the truffles when they are in peak condition. Sows were originally used because the smell of a ripe truffle apparently resembles that of a male pig. Neither sows nor dogs have the temerity, it seems, to eat these 'black diamonds'.

There are some 30 types of truffle, but the type from Périgord is the most famous. Truffles feature in many regional dishes, but nowadays only tiny shavings are used, for as with garlic, a little is said to go a long way. A full-grown truffle weighs about 100g. Their aromatic, earthy flavour goes well with eggs, fish and chicken.

Near Sorges, on the N21 north of Périgueux, is the Maison de la Truffe, a truffle museum.

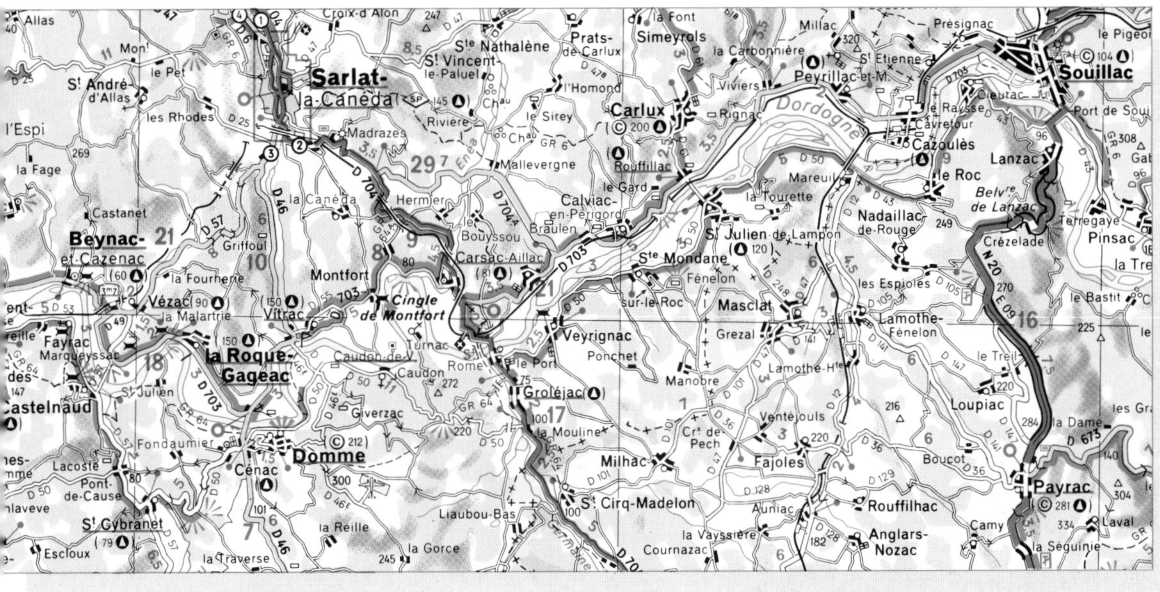

Office Départemental du Tourisme de la Dordogne
16, Rue Wilson
24000 Périgueux
Tel: 53 53 44 35

Touring:
use Michelin sheet map 235, Midi-Pyrénées

Foie gras

Geese (below) and ducks are a common sight in Périgord and Quercy, and they feature on practically every menu in one way or another. Foie gras has been popular, particularly in this region, since the 15th century. Often made into a pâté, it is produced by force-feeding geese or ducks until their livers swell to a weight of 1500g.

Another local speciality is *confit* of duck and goose, in which the wings or legs are preserved in their own fat. The *confit* was the traditional way of preserving geese before refrigeration was invented.

rased it in 1214, it was rebuilt by the Turenne family and then it was captured and destroyed twice more; hence the mixture of styles. Unfortunately it is not open to the public, but as it dominates the little hamlet below you can get some good views of it. Nearby is the Château de Fénelon, the home of the the 17th-century writer and archbishop of that name.

Domme

This is one of France's most spectacular *bastide* towns, built in 1280 for Philip the Bold. The northern end of the town has such a steep drop down the cliffs that it never needed to be fortified. Domme does not possess the strict rectangular formation of other *bastides*. Instead, its design took advantage of the lie of the land.

The history of Domme is recounted in the Musée Paul-Reclus. From the traditional covered market in the town centre, you can visit the 400m of caves, where the villagers took refuge during the Hundred Years War. In one of the three gates in Domme's massive walls, the Porte des Tours, are two towers, one of which contains the names of the Knights Templars who were held prisoner there during the 14th century.

La Roque-Gageac

La Roque-Gageac is frequently described as one of France's most beautiful villages, so in the summer months it is quite busy. Exploration of its narrow streets is best done on foot. There is a 16th-century manor house with a pepper-pot roof, the Manoir de Tarde. At the other end of the village is the 20th-century Château de la Malartrie, inspired by the style of the 15th century. Near the riverside car park you can take a trip in a *gabarre*, a flat-bottomed boat.

Sarlat-la-Canéda

This medieval town, with its honey-coloured buildings with twisted towers, turrets and gables, alleys and courtyards, is best explored on foot. Parking can be a real problem, especially in the summer. Sarlat originated in the 8th century, when a Benedictine abbey was founded there. The monks built their abbey 10km from the river, to protect themselves from river-borne looters. Although the medieval centre has spread somewhat beyond its original boundaries, it is remarkably unspoiled and provides a magical contrast with the suburbs. There is a lot to see in the old quarter, including the Lanterne des Morts, a strange tower with a conical roof, and the Cathédrale St-Sacerdos. But Sarlat's charm does not lie so much in its many individual monuments as in the total feel of the place.

La Roque-Gageac's Manoir de Tarde, built of the local golden stone and with a pepper-pot tower, stands beneath cliffs that tower over the village and the Dordogne. High up on the cliffs, there are the remains of long-abandoned cave dwellings

One of the best places to view Sarlat is the public gardens above the Palais de Justice, which were once the private gardens of the bishops of Sarlat. Originally laid out in the 17th century, they are still very beautiful. On Saturdays there is a market that spreads over many streets and all the riches of Périgord Noir, including truffles, chicken, geese and other livestock, can be bought here.

PREHISTORIC DORDOGNE

THE AREA ROUND LES EYZIES-DE-TAYAC is known as the cradle of prehistory. Here, some 30-40,000 years ago, Cro-Magnon man settled in caves where the Vézère meets the Beune. The limestone cliffs provided shelter and the reindeer that roamed the area provided meat. In the countless caves of the Dordogne many of the secrets of early man are uncovered. Of course, it is not only France that has cave paintings and prehistoric sites, but few areas of the world have such a concentration.

Tools, artefacts and bones found in the Dordogne have enabled archaeologists to trace the development of *Homo sapiens* long before history was recorded. The remains of Cro-Magnon Man were first discovered in 1868, during the building of the railway from Périgueux to Agen.

An essential pilgrimage for those interested in early man is to the Musée National de Préhistoire in Les Eyzies. A huge stone giant, carved in 1930 to portray Cro-Magnon Man, confronts the arriving visitor. Inside you can monitor the slow progress of man from his hazy origins to the present day. You need not be a student of prehistory to enjoy the drama of the caves and the cave paintings, but a little knowledge will help you to appreciate the miracle more. The area around Les Eyzies has the biggest concentration of prehistoric sites, but all over the Dordogne and the Lot are other reminders of early man. One of the most spectacular is at Cabrerets.

LASCAUX

Hidden from the world for an estimated 20,000 years, the caves at Lascaux were discovered in 1940 by four schoolboys. They were, so the story goes, looking for their dog when they stumbled into a cavern decorated with animal paintings. They told the village schoolmaster, who reported the matter to the Abbé Breuil, a specialist in prehistory. The priest verified the origins of the paintings, which had been preserved by the formation of a layer of vitreous calcite.

Altogether, 200 paintings and 1500 engravings were discovered. They included bold images of horses, stags, oxen, bison, deer and bulls, painted in black, vivid purple, yellow and red. Drawings were superimposed, as if the artists had run out of space. Many of the animals are female and pregnant, a representation believed by some experts to reflect the wishes of early man for fertile hunting grounds.

The paintings at Lascaux illustrate just how close in spirit and intellect early man was to us. However, why he daubed these images and signs in dark, hidden caves has never been fully explained. One theory is that the caves were sacred places where magic rites were performed by the hunters to bewitch their prey. Certainly prehistoric man had to overcome his natural fear of the dark and burrow into places he did not inhabit to do the paintings. Historians know that these caves were uninhabited, as no tools or weapons were found there.

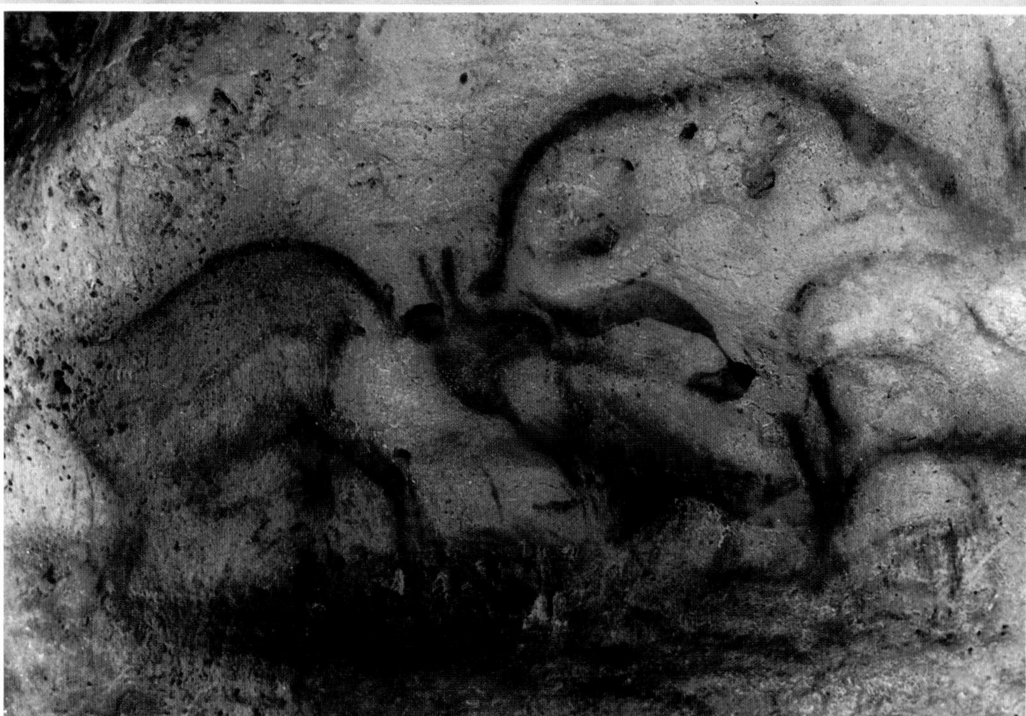

A bison and a reindeer are shown fighting in a cave painting in the Grotte de Font-de-Gaume

Anyone lucky enough to have seen the original caves at Lascaux must have been filled with a sense of awe – and perhaps of magic. But sadly, within 20 years of the caves opening, traffic fumes and the breath of the thousands of visitors who descended on Lascaux achieved what thousands of years of nature had not. The paintings began to deteriorate and the rock surface was crumbling, so the caves were closed to the public in 1963. However, an exact copy of the caves, including the spectacular Salle des Taureaux, has been created, using the original materials, in a woodland setting at Montignac known as Lascaux II.

ROUFFIGNAC

One of the most impressive caves in the area is Rouffignac, 18km from Les Eyzies. The cave stretches for 8km, but thankfully an electric railway takes you deep inside and the guide points out along the way some of the 250 mammoths and other animals drawn on or etched out of the rocks. Inside the cave the train stops in a hall whose low roof is decorated with horses, variously galloping, grazing and standing still.

The cave paintings at Lascaux II faithfully reproduce those at the original site, now closed to the public

The Colonnes d'Hercule, stalagmites measuring 8.9m in height, are found in the Grotte de Presque, near St Céré

THE GROTTE DE FONT-DE-GAUME AND GROTTE DES COMBARELLES

The Grotte de Font-de-Gaume, discovered in 1901, features some of the most impressive cave paintings in France. On either side of the 130-m long natural corridor are dramatic polychromatic paintings of horses, reindeer, bison, mammoths and other magic symbols similar to those found in Lascaux. Particularly striking is a frieze of black bison on white limestone. The nearby Grotte des Combarelles also has a fabulous gallery of 300 animal paintings, and some human figures. Access is limited, so it is advisable to arrive early.

Prehistoric human remains can be seen at Les Eyzies-de-Tayac

The caves at Les Eyzies-de-Tayac contain clay reliefs of bison

SCULPTURE

In addition to caves that have wall paintings, the area around Les Eyzies is rich in other prehistoric caves, some 10 of which contain sculptures. Those at the rock shelter of the Abri du Cap Blanc are believed to be the best. Other important sites worth visiting include Laugerie Haute and Laugerie Basse, where primitive man lived for 20,000 years.

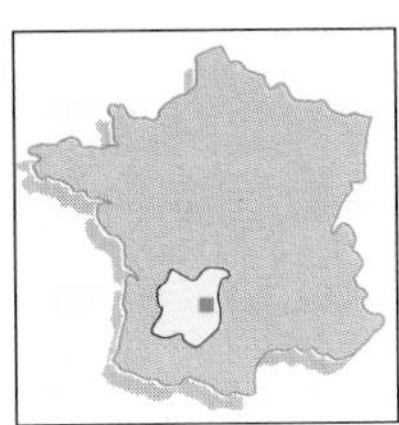

Upper Quercy

LIKE MUCH OF THE REGION, this is an area of great contrasts. The high limestone plateau that links the Dordogne to the Lot and Célé is nature unrestrained. A trip to the Gouffre de Padirac, for example, makes you realise how hostile the natural world can be. The charm of riverside villages such as Loubressac lies partly in their smallness, which is reassuring when compared with the awesome character of the landscape.

The lovely village of Autoire is typically Quercynois, with its mellow stone houses with brown-tiled roofs and its turreted grander dwellings

Autoire

This is a well-preserved picturesque village, officially one of France's prettiest, with its half-timbered houses, turreted mansions and fountain. From the terrace near the beautifully sculptured church you can see the Cirque d'Autoire, an amphitheatre of rocks. Also nearby is a ruined castle with a dramatic waterfall tumbling down the cliff face. The gorges of the River Autoire are also a striking sight.

Carennac

The village benefits from a beautiful setting on the banks of the Dordogne, facing the little island of Calypso. Houses with brown roof tiles, typical of Quercy, and villas with turrets are clustered round an old priory where Fénelon, the 17th-century writer, was the prior. The 12th-century church of St-Pierre has a handsome carved doorway.

Château de Castelnau-Bretenoux

At one time 1500 men and 100 horses were garrisoned in this huge medieval fortress on a spur overlooking the village of Prudhomat, close to the spot where the Cère joins the Dordogne. It was originally built in the 11th century and was restored at the beginning of this century by the opera singer Jean Moulierat, who left it to the nation. The château gives superb views over the Dordogne and is an unmistakable landmark. To the north-west you can see the remains of the Château de Turenne, once its bitter rival. Attractions inside the château include Aubusson and Beauvais tapestries and a lapidary museum.

Comité Départemental du Tourisme du Lot
Chambre de Commerce et d'Industrie
107, Quai Cavaignac - BP 71
46001 Cahors Cedex
Tel: 65 35 07 09

Touring:
use Michelin sheet map 239, Auvergne Limousin

St Céré is a thriving market town situated at an important crossroads in the valley of the River Bave. Looking down on the town are the imposing medieval towers of St-Laurent

Rocamadour

The spectacular village of Rocamadour is dramatically sited on a steep rock face in the gorge of the River Alzou. The best view is from the belvedere in the hamlet of L'Hospitalet above it, which still has the ruins of an 11th-century hospital for the care of pilgrims.

Rocamadour is dominated by its 14th-century castle, which is reached from the village by a steep flight of steps marked by the Stations of the Cross. For hundreds of years pilgrims have flocked here to pay homage to the Vierge Noire, carved out of walnut wood. Penitents used to climb the 216 stone steps in chains to receive absolution in the Chapelle Miraculeuse. The chapel also houses an ancient bell, said to toll itself before a miracle occurs. Seven churches are grouped together on the site, which was believed to have contained the grave of one of Christ's disciples, St Amadour.

Because of its beauty and history, Rocamadour is the second most visited historic site in France. Inevitably the village gets very congested and is highly commercialised, but it is still a marvellous place to visit.

Château de Montal

This medieval and Renaissance château on a wooded hillside above the Bave has a sad and romantic history. The widow Jeanne de Balsac d'Entraygues built it in 1534 for her eldest son, who was fighting in Italy at the time. She used master craftsmen and artists, and when it was completed she sat at a high window, watching for her son. He never returned, and she had the window boarded up and the words *'Plus d'espoir'* (Hope no more) carved beneath it. It was restored at the beginning of this century by one M. Fenaille, who gave it to the nation.

Gouffre de Padirac

This huge crater, 90m in width and depth, was originally caused by the collapse of a cave. Through it flows a subterranean river. Although in the summer it is very busy, it is still an awe-inspiring site. After descending by a lift you can take a boat trip through floodlit limestone caves, of which the enormous Grand Dôme, 100m high, is the most dramatic.

Gramat

The town is the capital of the Causse de Gramat, the massive limestone plateau that runs from the valley of the Dordogne near Souillac to the Lot and Célé near Cahors. The Causse has an average height of 350m and along its route are some unusual and dramatic landscapes. Gramat itself is a bustling town that serves as a market for many of the villages around, and its many markets sell all the local produce from sheep and nuts to truffles. It is also famous for its training centre for police dogs and handlers, where there are tours and special displays during the summer months. Just outside the town is the Parc de Vision de Gramat, a 40-hectare zoo. Among its attractions are animals in their natural environment and a botanical park featuring typical trees and shrubs of the Causse.

Loubressac

A charming fortified village built on a rocky spur overlooking the River Bave, Loubressac offers views across the river to the Château de Castelnau-Bretenoux. It is dominated by a 15th-century château of its own, unfortunately not open to the public.

St Céré

A picturesque old town situated 3km west of Montal, St Céré lies clustered in the valley of the Bave, overlooked by the medieval towers and curtain wall of the Tours de St-Laurent. It has many fine old houses and in the Galerie du Casino there is a large collection of Jean Lurçat's tapestries. Having trained in Aubusson, Lurçat lived in St Céré from 1945 until his death in 1966, when his widow bequeathed a representative selection of his works to the town.

St Céré is still a prosperous town, with a market that is particularly noted for the plums and strawberries it sells from local farms. It also has a fascinating car museum. Some 16km along the river is Latouille-Lentillac, with the little pilgrim chapel of Notre-Dame de Verdale.

Souillac

A busy town situated where the main road between Brive-la-Gaillarde and Cahors crosses the Dordogne, Souillac has been an important river trading post and crossroads for hundreds of years. Boats would travel from Souillac to Libourne laden with salt and wood for wine stakes and barrels. It is still an important market town for farms in the region, but now the river is used for swimming, fishing and canoeing.

There is little left of the original medieval town, apart from a beautiful church (above), all that remains of a Benedictine abbey. It is said to compare favourably with the cathedral at Cahors. Souillac also has a fascinating mechanical-model museum.

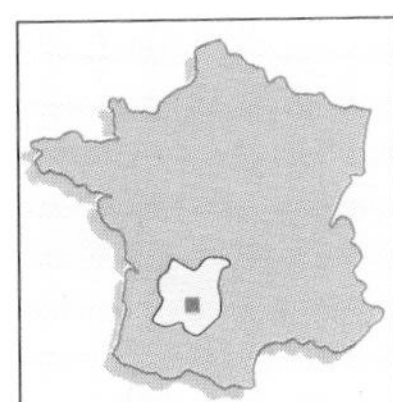

LAND OF *BASTIDES*

THIS LANDSCAPE is so studded with the fortified towns known as *bastides*, and with castles, that you cannot but wonder about its history, which often turns out to be bloodchilling. But there is a welcome contrast. Pretty riverside towns such as Puy-l'Évêque have great charm, and the best thing about the *bastides* today is their markets, which have long sold all the regional delicacies.

Originally raised in the 12th century, the Château de Biron (above) is a mixture of architectural styles. There are plans to site here a museum of the Hundred Years War

Monpazier (right), built by Edward I of England, is one of the finest bastides

Château de Biron

Romantically sited on a high rock 8km from Monpazier, the Château de Biron is a massive landmark and from its sentry walks there are wonderful views. It was originally built in the 12th century by the Gontaut family, who held it until the present century. It has been added to and altered so many times that it represents nearly every architectural style through the centuries.

The hamlet of Biron is within the outer walls of the château and a remnant of the class system is seen in the chapel, which has an upper storey for the family and one below for the villagers. But you will have to go to New York's Metropolitan Museum of Art if you want to view what some historians believe were the chapel's best treasures: a carved tomb depicting angels around the body of Christ and a *pietà*.

Château de Bonaguil

This was one of the last medieval castles to be built, during the 15th century. It was begun by Bérenger de Roquefeuil in 1447 and took 40 years to complete. It had 350m of wall, 13 towers and turrets, an inner moat and dozens of concealed passages. Ironically, this fortress built to withstand an attack by 10,000 men was never challenged. It came under siege only during the Revolution, and even so the bulk remains. As well as tours of the romantic ruins, musical evenings are held during the summer.

Monpazier

Founded in 1284 by Edward I of England, Duke of Aquitaine, Monpazier is a perfect example of a *bastide* town, eight blocks around a central square, and has miraculously survived largely unchanged. During the Hundred Years War it was captured by the French and English several times in turn and in the 17th century

BASTIDES

The countryside of south-west France is dotted with *bastides*: towns built in the Middle Ages for defensive purposes. Life in the French countryside at that time was far from safe. Kings and the nobility had to protect the peasants from robbers and marauding bands, to keep them living and farming locally. The fortress-like *bastides* were sometimes built when peasants switched allegiance to a new lord. Later, they were needed as protection during the wars with England.

Bastides are instantly recognisable by their pattern of three longer straight roads criss-crossed by smaller ones. The market-place is usually at the centre, and the town is walled. Churches in *bastides*, Gothic in style, also tend to be heavily fortified. Although Monpazier, for example, is built on the plan described above, most *bastides* are less regular in design, laid out in response to the lie of the land. Beaumont, Domme and Monpazier are three of France's finest surviving examples.

Puy-l'Évêque is a handsome, stone-built town on the banks of the Lot. Its fine castle keep was, in times gone by, the residence of the bishops of Cahors

Mushrooms are a speciality of the region, and are sold in many places, including the spacious covered market in Villefranche-du-Périgord

witnessed a bitter peasants' revolt.

The central square, with its medieval covered market-place, is impressive and on the third Thursday of each month there is a fair. Originally this square was the corn market. The town has many old houses, a *lavoir* where the village women used to wash clothes, an old tithe barn and a 14th-century church. In spring and autumn Monpazier is shaken out of its sleepiness by its renowned mushroom markets.

Montcabrier

This is a small *bastide* founded by Guy de Cabrier in 1297. Several very old houses overlook the central square. Inside the old church is a 14th-century statue of St Louis, patron saint of the parish, to which local pilgrimages were formerly made.

Puy-l'Évêque

A good place to stop for lunch, this picturesque town, with its golden-stone houses stretching down to the banks of the Lot, is dominated by the church and the castle keep. The best way to appreciate the beauty of Puy-l'Évêque is from across the river. In the town itself there is a stunning view of the Lot valley from the Esplanade de la Truffière, between the original keep and the town hall.

The town's shape is said to have been determined by the English, who occupied it many times and changed its defences. It is now on the official wine route between Cahors and Fumel. The fertile red soil of the area produces what most experts agree are the best wines of Cahors. These rich, red wines are usually matured for three years in oak casks.

St Martin-le-Redon

A few houses clustered round a church that most people simply drive through on their way to Bonaguil, the village at one time found fame as the source of St-Martial water, which was believed to be capable of curing skin ailments.

Villefranche-du-Périgord

In times past this Catholic *bastide,* which dominates the valley of the River Lémance, was a great rival to Monpazier, the towns taking it in turns to raid each other. Built over the years to defend the way to Quercy, it was several times captured and destroyed, then rebuilt. Although Villefranche-du-Périgord is not as well preserved as its former rival, its large covered market surrounded by arcades clearly identifies it as a *bastide.*

Office Départemental du Tourisme de la Dordogne
16, Rue Wilson
24000 Périgueux
Tel: 53 53 44 35

Comité Départemental du Tourisme du Lot
Chambre de Commerce et d'Industrie
107, Quai Cavaignac - BP 71
46001 Cahors Cedex
Tel: 65 35 07 09

Touring:
use Michelin sheet map 235, Midi-Pyrénées

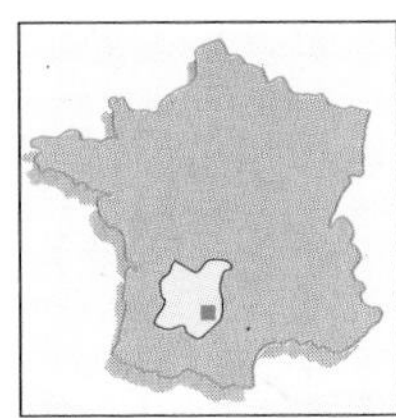

THE LOT AND CÉLÉ VALLEYS

THE PERENNIAL POPULARITY of the Dordogne leads many visitors to the region to overlook the valleys of the Lot and Célé. This implied comparison strikes the more adventurous traveller as unjust, for the Lot is flanked by spectacular limestone cliffs topped by villages and castles, while the Célé runs through dramatic narrow limestone gorges with old mills and little waterfalls. In short, the area's scenery is matched by its rich history and its prehistoric sites.

Comité Départemental du Tourisme du Lot
Chambre de Commerce et d'Industrie
107, Quai Cavaignac - BP 71
46001 Cahors Cedex
Tel: 65 35 07 09

Touring:
use Michelin sheet map 235, Midi-Pyrénées

Cabrerets nestles below towering cliffs where the Célé and the Sagne meet

Cabrerets

The road to the village of Cabrerets weaves between the river bank and a sheer wall-like cliff face in a spectacular manner. Allow yourself plenty of time to view the outside of the two châteaux that look down on this beautiful village at the intersection of the Célé and the Sagne. You will see the 14th-century Château de Gontaut-Biron, some of whose balustrades overhang the road some 25m below. Unfortunately, it is not open to the public. Opposite, clinging to the steep Rochecourbe cliffs, are the ruins of the Château du Diable.

Cahors

Roman in origin, Cahors stands in one of the many loops in this part of the Lot. The town is famous for the fine twin-domed Cathédrale St-Étienne and the magnificent Pont Valentré. This bridge, with its three 40-m towers and seven spans, is a 14th-century engineering masterpiece. One of the most photographed monuments in France, it is undoubtedly among the most beautiful bridges in the world.

There are some remnants of Roman baths, a theatre and the aqueduct that brought water to Cahors. You should also see the old paper mill overlooking this ancient town. A fine panoramic view of the town can be gained from a viewpoint on nearby Mont St Cyr. Indeed, most of the best views of what was one of medieval France's most important cities, are from the hills that almost surround it.

Calvignac

This beautiful old village, some 15km east of St Cirq-Lapopie, offers lovely river views. The huge Château de Cénevières stands atop a vertical rock face above the river. (There are guided tours during the summer.) The 13th-century Tour de Gourdon has secret dungeons and a fine Renaissance gallery. From the terrace there are breathtaking views of the Lot valley.

FESTIVALS

Throughout the summer there are numerous festivals in Périgord and Quercy. Nearly every town and village celebrates its own saint's day with a fair, which is typically rounded off with a firework display. There are also annual fairs, such as Cénac's wine festival (August), the harvest festival in Gourdon (August), Rocamadour's pilgrims' week (September), Cahors' blues festival (July/August), and Sarlat's theatre festival (July/August). Figeac and St Céré usually have concerts and music, dance and folklore festivals each year in July and August.

But the most famous festival in Périgord is the Félibrée, which is celebrated by a different town in the region each year. The town is decorated with masses of paper flowers and people flock to the area in traditional dress. The Queen of the Félibrée is ceremonially given the keys of the town and there is a spectacular procession to Mass.

From the cliff-top château at Calvignac there are extensive views over the Lot valley

Grotte du Pech-Merle

This prehistoric site beneath the steep cliffs just outside Cabrerets contains some of France's most interesting caves. Large interconnecting chambers may have been used as a temple sanctuary over 20,000 years ago, but they were only rediscovered in 1922. You can walk through the huge chambers and corridors for 2km or so, gazing at vivid drawings, paintings and etchings of bison, mammoth, horses and people. There are also prehistoric footprints on the floors, hand prints on the walls and the roots of a tree pushed down to find water. A frieze depicting animals, 10m long and 3m high, possibly dates back 25,000 years.

These large, accessible caves are altogether more beautiful than others of their age, and are decorated with spectacular stalactites and stalagmites. They are thought-provoking too – for example, when you confront the skeleton of an animal that has lain there for 20,000 years.

At the Grotte du Pech-Merle cave paintings can be seen from 25,000 years ago. The admission charge includes a film and entry to the Musée Amédée-Lemozi

St Cirq-Lapopie

Close to the Grotte du Pech Merle is one of the prettiest villages in France, perched on an escarpment high above the Lot. The steep, cobbled medieval lanes and timber-framed houses of a village built into the side of a rugged cliff are such an attraction that most people tire themselves out walking up the hills to get there, for car parking is difficult and the buses stop at the valley.

The village and its fine 15th-century church (and separate belfry tower) have been restored by what seems like a whole village of modern artists and craftsmen, who have turned the gabled houses into studios and galleries. From the church's rock terrace there are excellent views of the river and the surrounding countryside. But the best viewpoint is above the village, among the remnants of the château.

Sauliac-sur-Célé

The houses of this village cling to a steep cliff of coloured rock like birds' nests. Above are strengthened caves used as war refuges and accessible only by ropes and ladders. During the Hundred Years War, which left such a mark on this whole region, whole families of adults, children and farm animals were hoisted into these caves to escape from pillaging soldiers. Nearby is the Domaine de Cuzals, an open-air museum featuring farm buildings and agricultural machinery ancient and modern. In Sauliac there is also a museum of childhood and toys to keep children amused.

Vers

This sleepy, flower-adorned village of honey-coloured stone lies beneath the cliffs on a loop in the Lot. It has the remains of an ancient Roman aqueduct that once supplied the thermal baths of Cahors. Just before you enter the village there is a Romanesque church, rising above the fields and walnut trees. This was once an important pilgrimage point for the sailors for whom the Lot was an important, and dangerous, trading route.

Cahors Wine

The local wine is very distinctive in being almost black. Although the region has long been overshadowed by Bordeaux, wine has always been important hereabouts and there have been vineyards along the Lot since before Roman times. The vines were destroyed by phylloxera at the end of the 19th century but were replanted. The lower slopes of the Lot valley, west of Cahors, are the main growing area, since they are the hottest in the area.

A meal in Quercy often begins with a *tourin*, a hearty soup. The locals then pour Cahors wine on to the dregs in the bottom of the bowl and drink the resulting *chabrot* straight from the bowl. In addition to wine, the area produces a range of strong *eaux-de-vie,* made from walnuts or plums.

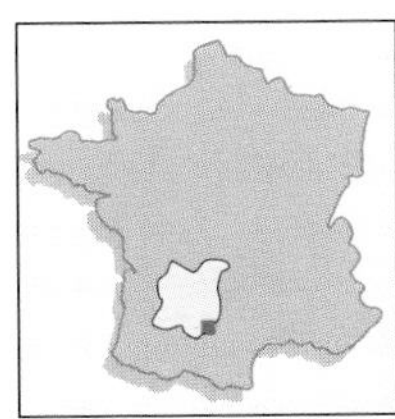

The Aveyron Valley

DRAMATIC SCENERY and sparse populations in scattered communities perched on hilltops or sheer cliffs characterise this wild countryside that illustrates so well how France was fought over. The area also possesses several attractive medieval towns where so much remains unchanged after centuries.

Among the many attractions of Cordes is the Maison du Grand Fauconnier, which has fine carved falcons on its façade and is today used as the town hall. The 14th-century market hall is still intact and has a splendid timber roof and a well said to be over 100m deep. The Maison Portal, with its fine paintings, and the Gothic church of St-Michel are also worth seeing

Bournazel

The look of this tiny village on a rocky outcrop north of Cordes is typical of the region. It features a 15th-century church with a restored tower and an unfinished château with two 16th-century wings.

Les Cabannes

The Gothic church has a painting of the Assumption dating from 1653 and an iron cross whose base is decorated with the fleur-de-lys. A broken tower is all that remains of a château. There is a 19th-century bust of Vice Admiral St Félix in the middle of the beautiful square. He distinguished himself in the American War of Independence. In a battle during the Napoleonic wars he was in command of the only ship that halted the English advance on the French line.

Cordes

This exceptionally pretty town, sometimes called 'Cordes-sur-ciel', is built on a hill with a marvellous view of the surrounding countryside, and seems to reach up to the sky. It was a *bastide* town (see page 206), founded early in the 13th century. But the name 'Cordes' probably derives from the leather and hemp industries through which the town became prosperous in the 13th and 14th centuries. Energetic visitors leave their cars at the bottom of the hill and walk, the better to imagine the scale of the defensive walls that surrounded the town. Many of the gates remain almost intact and, although tiring, the climb up the steep, narrow streets past old houses with exposed beams is very worthwhile.

Gorges de l'Aveyron

The River Aveyron forms the south-western boundary of the Massif Central. The main roads connecting Villefranche-de-Rouergue, Albi and Montauban form a triangle of wild, sparsely populated countryside through which the Aveyron runs south to the village of Laguépie and then west to join the Tarn north of Montauban.

The Gorges de l'Aveyron offer stunning steep cliffs, up to 500m above the river, widely contrasting landscapes, grottos, many kilometres of shaded lanes and brooks full of trout. This is an ideal area for those who love to canoe, cycle, ride, walk, climb, pot-hole or hang-glide.

The area between Laguépie and Villefranche-de-Rouergue has been an important mining area for many centuries. In Roman times metal from local mines was used to make coins and in the 16th century German miners discovered substantial deposits of silver. Although the mines later fell into disuse, it was the wealth they promised that brought the railway to the Gorges de l'Aveyron in the 19th century, during which time they were once again heavily worked. During World War II, it is believed, the Germans carried out exploratory mining for copper here.

Cordes, with its gateways and steep streets, is a town best explored on foot. Many of the old houses are now occupied by artists and craftsmen, who can be seen at work on canvas or loom, or with metal or stone

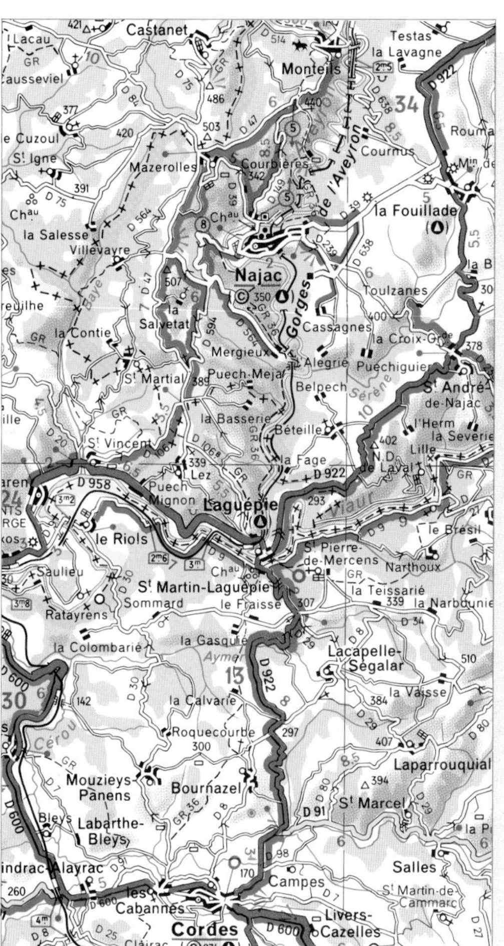

Comité Départemental du Tourisme du Tarn
Maison Départementale du Tourisme
Hôtel du Département
81014 Albi Cedex
Tel: 63 47 56 50

Comité Départemental du Tourisme de l'Aveyron
33, Avenue Victor-Hugo
12000 Rodez
Tel: 65 68 11 43

Touring:
use Michelin sheet map 235, Midi-Pyrénées

QUERCY

The old houses of Quercy are one of the region's greatest attractions. Traditionally built from local stone that seems to glow in the sunlight, they usually had space for animals on the ground floor and living-rooms on the first floor. The top floor was reserved for drying tobacco or preserving foodstuffs. Dovecots are a common sight, and are mostly balanced on square stone pillars. Pigeons were kept mainly for manure, very important for the land; hence the height of the dovecots.

Najac

This is a quiet little town, built, unusually, on twin hills. The houses lie along the ridge of the hills, to one side of which is a sheer drop to the Aveyron, in its beautiful gorge. Najac has always been dominated by the castle, now in ruins, which is located strategically on a cliff all but surrounded by the river. This is surely the most romantic setting in France for a medieval fortress. A castle was first built here in 1110 and rebuilt in 1253 by Alphonse de Poitiers, brother of St Louis. Its continuing visual impact on the place is striking: you keep glimpsing it from the hilltops and losing it from view as you dip into ravines. The houses below the castle were formerly soldiers' billets.

Despite its predominantly military history, Najac is a colourful, flower-decked tourist centre with adjacent holiday villages. But you will need energy and determination to climb its steep ancient streets.

Varen

Situated on the Aveyron about 10km west of Laguépie, and outlined by a string of poplar trees, is the lovely market town of Varen. Long ago it was highly defended,

and you still enter the medieval quarter through the fortified Porte El-Faoure. Here the winding streets have timber-framed houses and interesting flat roofs with round tiles. The tower and gatehouse of the fortified 14th-15th-century château lie beside a 12th-century Romanesque church that has a dungeon in the dean's house.

Viaur

The River Viaur, which meets the Aveyron at Laguépie, is a water-sports centre, though it has variations in its water level because of its dams. It is fished for trout but the Aveyron has a more varied catch and teems with roach, tench, gudgeon, carp and rainbow trout. About 40km east of Laguépie the river is spanned by the elegant structure of the Viaduc du Viaur, 460m long and 116m high.

Vindrac-Alayrac

Vindrac-Alayrac, north-west of Cordes, was originally built as a defence for that town, and its church has a watch-tower 17m high. The church's interior was restored in the 16th century and its attractions include a gilt wooden statue of the Virgin and St Joseph from that period. Underneath the building is a subterranean refuge. Adjacent to the church is a château that now belongs to the Anselme family but was once the home of the Tapie de Celyrans, relatives of the 19th-century artist Toulouse-Lautrec, who are buried in the cemetery.

Najac is overlooked by a 13th-century fortress and a church of similar date (top). The former occupies a highly defensible position on a cliff encircled by the Aveyron. The Gothic church is plain but distinctive. Most of the houses in the town are of stone (above) or timber-framed and lack cellars because they are built on granite

THE PYRENEES

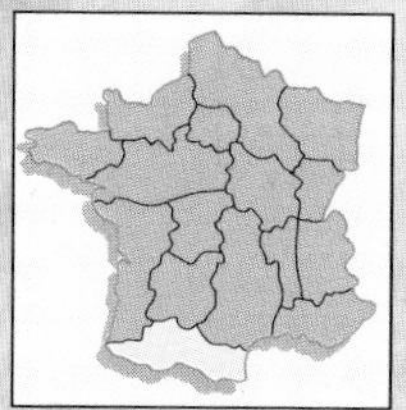

STRETCHING THE WIDTH OF south-western France, from the wind-scuffed surf of the Atlantic to the gentle drift of the Mediterranean, the Pyrenees form a magnificent backdrop of mountains, some 400km long. In the west they are green and rolling, and heavily wooded, with neat Basque villages nestling in their folds. In the east, where the climate of Catalonia influences both landscape and lifestyle, vines, orchards and an aromatic scrub clothe the hillsides.

Between these extremes the region is one of rich scenic and cultural variety, for its history reaches back 20,000 years and more; yet it is also at the forefront of modern technology. It is an undulating land watered by big rivers and numerous *gaves* (mountain streams), among them the Nive and Oloron, Adour and Aure, Ariège, Aude and Garonne. There are dramatic waterfalls, stark limestone gorges, snow-clad peaks and hundreds of tiny lakes sparkling among glacial cirques.

The Pays Basque, comprising Labourd, Basse-Navarre and Soule, is a land of *pelota* and sheep; each village has its fronton, where *pelota* is played, every hillside its grazing flock. Coastal Labourd has palm trees and sandy bays with great appeal, while inland the pastoral heights of Basse-Navarre are carpeted with bracken and gorse where snaking roads exploit enchanting vistas. Soule, however, is genuine mountain country, sliced by the gorges of Holçarté and Kakouetta on the edge of the High Pyrenees.

Hautes-Pyrénées is truly mountainous, with a number of 3000-m peaks and the cirques of Gavarnie, Estaubé and Troumouse forming a rim to the Parc National des Pyrénées and the adjacent Réserve Naturelle de Néouvielle. The world-famous pilgrimage town of Lourdes is the gateway to this big country.

Haute-Garonne reaches from the frontier above Bagnères-de-Luchon, beyond magnificent St Bertrand-de-Comminges in the foothills to the plain of Toulouse. Economic capital of the Languedoc and France's fourth town, Toulouse lies too far north to be included here.

The forested heights of Ariège spill down to St Lizier and Foix, whose architectural splendours mark another age. Yet the whole region is riddled with history, from the caves of Lombrives, Niaux and Mas d'Azil, to the cliff-top remains of the Cathar castles of Roquefixade and Montségur.

Far to the east, and with its bright Mediterranean influence, lies the country of Roussillon, whose undisputed overlord is the Canigou rising between the Vallespir and the Conflent. Bleached villages beam at the sun, beneath their undulating, orange-tiled roofs. Orchards and market gardens smother the lowlands, while an extravagant flora, highly fragrant and alive with insects, spreads palettes of colour across the hillsides before these subside among the waters of the Côte Vermeille.

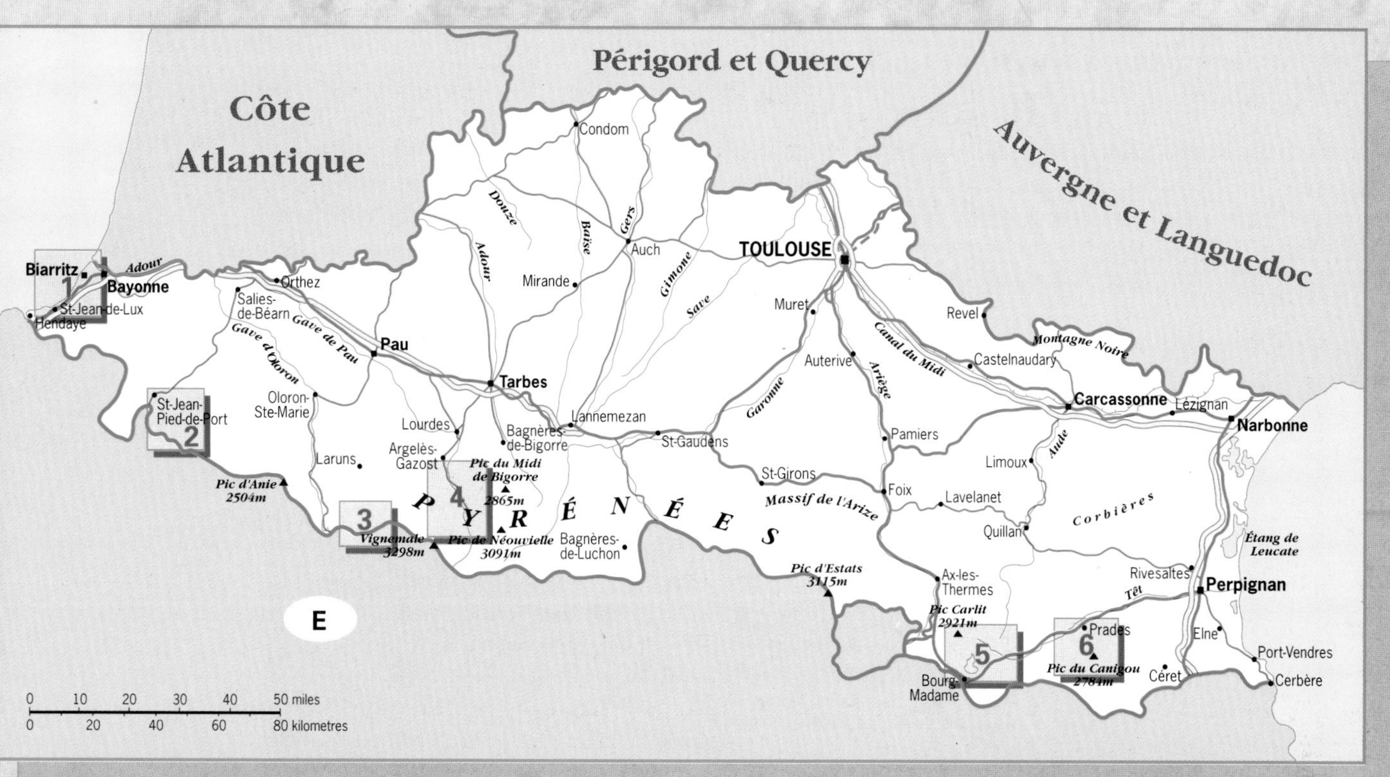

Features

Away from the coastal resorts such as St Jean-de-Luz (right), life in the Pyrenees is quiet for many people, including this couple (below)

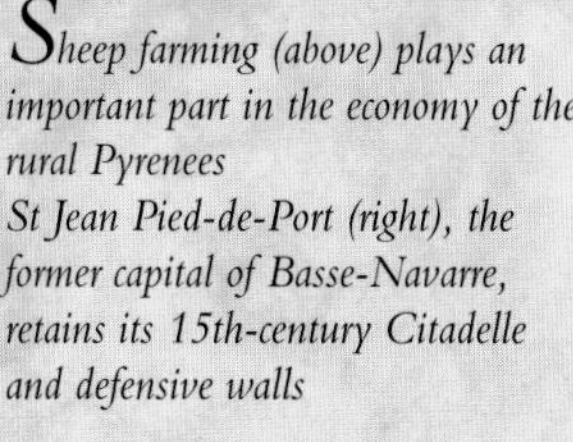

Sheep farming (above) plays an important part in the economy of the rural Pyrenees

St Jean Pied-de-Port (right), the former capital of Basse-Navarre, retains its 15th-century Citadelle and defensive walls

The dramatic Col d'Aubisque (above) lies on the 48-km long Route d'Aubisque, which goes from Laruns to Argelès-Gazost. The Col, which is usually blocked by snow between November and June, has in the past been one of the challenges of the Tour de France

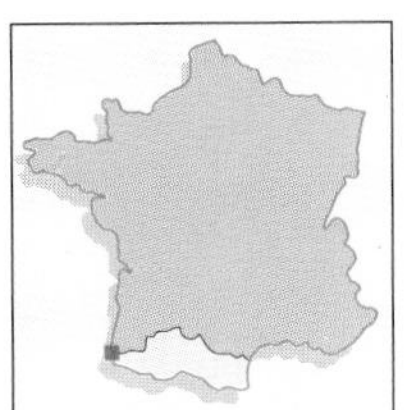

THE BASQUE COAST

A GENTLE, undulating roll of green hills breaks above the sandy bays and coves that line the Bay of Biscay. From Biarritz to St Jean-de-Luz these half-moon beaches receive the Atlantic surf, and the resorts that have grown up behind them offer a wide choice of accommodation and facilities. With a mild climate and glorious scenery, the Basque coast is at its best in the early autumn.

Mission de Développement Touristique des Pyrénées-Atlantiques
22 *ter*, Rue Jean-Jacques-de-Monaix
64000 Pau
Tel: 59 30 01 30

Touring:
use Michelin sheet map 234, Aquitaine

The excellent sandy beach at Biarritz (top) helps to make it the main holiday centre on this stretch of the Atlantic coast. At the southern end of the beach is the tiny port from which whalers once put to sea. At the northern end is the lighthouse (above)

Biarritz

An air of genteel respectability lingers on in Biarritz, long after the last of Europe's holiday-making monarchs has departed. But it is impossible to visit this 'queen of resorts and resort of kings' and not sense its past grandeur. The elegance of the Hôtel du Palais dominates the Grande Plage; enlarged and reconstructed, it was originally built for Napoleon III's Empress Eugénie, who brought the town its fame in the mid-19th century. The Grande Plage is a broad sweep of superb sand with bastion-like stacks standing offshore as it to interrupt the endless breakers that make modern Biarritz such a mecca for surfers.

Bidart

When travelling down the coast from Biarritz, Bidart is the first real introduction to Basque architecture and culture. A handsome village and one of the highest along this stretch of coastline, its open square is dominated by the church and a large, pink-walled *fronton*. Nearby hotels and restaurants, with their balconies, overhanging eaves and rust-coloured shutters, are all the very essence of the architecture of the Basque country.

Inside the 16th-century church triple galleries run round the nave, and from the wood-panelled ceiling there hangs a model sailing barque. An effigy of Joan of Arc stands next to the altar. At the end of a narrow side road leading from the square is the white-walled Chapelle Ste-Madeleine.

BASQUE MUSEUM

Contained in a 16th-century town house on the right bank of the Nive in Bayonne, the Musée Basque displays artefacts and costumes, reconstructions of dwellings, games and dances, together with historical documents. These combine to summarise the history and traditions of the Basque race in an entertaining yet intelligent way. Here you can learn all about *pelota,* the suppression of witchcraft throughout the region in the 16th and 17th centuries, and the seafaring exploits of its intrepid mariners.

RAVEL

On the quay named after him, the composer Maurice Ravel (1875-1937) was born in a Dutch-style house facing the harbour in Ciboure. Ravel was a highly respected innovator, both of piano technique and of orchestration, whose compositions include piano and orchestral music, ballet, opera, songs, concerti and chamber music.

Although the family moved to Paris when he was only three months old, Ravel often returned to the town of his birth, using it as a 'listening-post' for musical ideas. A number of Ravel's compositions clearly bear a local, or Spanish influence, especially *Bolero*, on which he worked in St Jean-de-Luz in 1928.

Chambre d'Amour

Anglet's beach, enclosed by rocky projections and backed by vegetated cliffs, is named after a legend that tells of the secret seashore rendezvous of a poor peasant girl in love with the son of a local nobleman. Unable to meet in public, the couple were engulfed in their passion by the onrushing tide and died in each other's arms. More prosaically, it was here in 1808 that Napoleon I heralded the idea of sea bathing. The water was first tested by members of the Imperial Guard, then Napoleon ventured forth, accompanied by the music of a military band, while the guard stood by in case of accident.

Ciboure

Linked by a bridge to St Jean-de-Luz, Ciboure escapes the crowds that congregate across the harbour. Smaller, less spread out than its better known neighbour, it hugs the western side of the port from which, in centuries past, its citizens set sail on voyages of piracy. In the courtyard of the 18th-century town hall there is a bust of Ravel, the town's most illustrious son, and next to it is the pelota court. Not far away is a 17th-century fountain adorned with Ciboure's coat of arms. Along Rue Pocalette there are some interesting 17th- and 18th-century houses, and these and the church interior are good examples of the architecture of the Basque country.

The fishing port of Ciboure, on the left bank of the Nivelle, faces the popular resort of St Jean-de-Luz across the river

Guéthary

An attractive hilltop village with a number of fine houses, Guéthary is bisected by the Paris-Madrid railway, which passes through a deep cutting. The beach consists of tilted rocks sloping to sand and sea, with a view back to Bidart.

St Jean-de-Luz

This is a busy resort with the most perfect of bathing beaches: a crescent-shaped bay whose extremities manage to deflect the rolling Atlantic waves and ensure a haven of calm water. The fishing port is likewise protected and is a colourful place at the mouth of the Nivelle. Adjacent to it is the oldest part of town, that which was rebuilt after the Spanish rased it in 1558. Place Louis XIV faces the harbour and contains the town hall, built in 1635, in which the Sun King stayed before his marriage to the Infanta, Marie-Thérèse, in 1660. St-Jean-Baptiste, the church in which the marriage ceremony was performed, is close by.

The town has some interesting buildings, including several excellent town houses.

St Jean-de-Luz is an elegant town with a number of well-preserved mansions in the Basque style, a fine beach and a busy fishing port

THE BASQUE COUNTRY

A GREEN AND WELL-WATERED COUNTRYSIDE adequately describes the *département* of Pyrénées-Atlantiques, a rural landscape abounding in sheep, running with streams and punctuated with delightful villages where art and architecture blend together beneath projecting eaves. But Eskual Herria, the Land of the Basques, is more a country of racial identity than of political boundaries, for the people themselves, unique and mysterious in origin, have dwelt among the western hills and sea coasts of the Pyrenees since long before the birth of France and Spain as we know them today, and with some justification claim to be Europe's oldest race.

Since they have lived in a state of virtual self-isolation for centuries, speaking a language, Euskara, that is unrelated to any other Indo-European tongue, it is perhaps not surprising that the Basques should have developed a number of distinct social, intellectual and architectural features. This uniqueness is most immediately apparent in the difficult, tongue-tying names such as Choldocogagna (one of the western hills), Oxocelhaya (a cave system near Hasparren), the Crête d'Uthurkokotcha in the Forêt d'Iraty, and the minor summit of Léchoukohéguia, to name but a few. Road signs often display two names for a town or village, one being the French spelling, the other giving its Basque identity. These names are almost always polysyllabic and often include x, y or z.

THE VILLAGE

While there are several small towns in the Basque country that have undeniable appeal – Cambo-les-Bains and St Jean-Pied-de-Port immediately spring to mind – it is among the neat land-locked villages that the essential Basque quality of bucolic harmony, the peace of the peasant, is best observed. Although each province has its own specific building style, perhaps the most attractive houses are to be found in Labourd in the west. Here the white loam walls contrast with exposed timbers, painted rust-brown, beneath large, shallow-pitched tiled roofs.

Individual houses stand out in the pastoral landscape, but gathered together in orderly groups they are some of the loveliest villages in all France. Aïnhoa is a classic example, with its wide main street lined with ageing but well-maintained buildings, often with the date of construction and the name of the builder or owner carved in the lintel over the front door. Biriatou, Sare and Ascain fall into a similar category of architectural beauty.

Typical Basque houses are to be found in many villages, including Aïnhoa (far left) The characteristic dress of the Basque region (left)

PELOTA

No introduction to the Basque country would be complete without mention of *pelota*, the game that appears to dominate life throughout the region, and whose top players become local heroes. Age-old in concept, *pelota* has undergone a number of changes and variations, but basically the game consists of hurling a ball, the *pelota*, against the high *fronton*, or wall, and playing it back again, either bare-handed or with a curved wicker scoop known as the *chistera* or with a wooden bat, the *pala*. (One of the greatest ever players was Chiquito, from Cambo-les-Bains, who, it is claimed, once won a match using a champagne bottle.) It is a very fast, vigorous sport, with the players dressed in brilliant white and the *chacharia*, the umpire, calling the score.

Most Basque villages have an outdoor pelota court, with the *fronton* occupying a prominent position in the main street – usually close to the church, whose wall was formerly adopted temporarily for the country priests often being renowned as enthusiastic devotees.

Pelota is the foremost sport of the Basque country

A Love of Dance

In many villages the square and pelota court are one and the same. The weekly market is held in them, and so too are the dances of which the Basques are particularly fond. Traditional Basque folk dances demand agility and sure-footed concentration, not least for the powerful and spectacular leaps (the famous *saut basque*) required in many of them. The torso and head are held erect, the face set and emotionless. Apart from the *fandango* and *arin-arin*, dances are by custom performed only by males and accompanied in rudimetary style by a stringed tambourine, a small drum and a three-holed flute, the *tchirulä*.

The *Zamalzain* is one of the oldest dances, a charade of Good against Evil in which two teams perform. One team is dressed in ornate and colourful costume, with the leader wearing a wicker frame representing a horse, the other in grotesque masks and tattered clothes. As a climax the lead dancer of each team carries out a series of intricate steps around a wine glass, leaping momentarily on to it and then off again. Should the dancer symbolising Good manage to finish the dance without spilling any wine, and Evil knocks the glass over – as intended – the dance will have been successfully completed according to tradition, and, to the superstitious, the future will bode well.

Galleried Churches

The church plays an important role in the life of the Basque village, although it may not always be seen as its most notable building. While the exterior varies in architectural style from province to province and is generally rather plain, internally there is a common layout with two, and sometimes three, carved wooden galleries overlooking a wide, wood-floored nave. Men sit in the galleries while women, children and the infirm only are allowed in the nave. In some coastal churches a model sailing ship hangs above the nave as a reminder of the close affinity the Basques have with the sea. Inland, in the province of Soule, many churches have impressive triple belfries, that at Gotein being a fine example.

In a number of churchyards, among them those at Biriatou, Ascain, Sare and Ste-Engrâce, old and unusual discoidal gravestones are seen, some of which have been engraved with the Basque cross, reminiscent of the swastika. Others are decorated with a wheel or solar rose motif.

The Basque country is mainly green and lush (below) and many white churches, simple in form, punctuate the landscape (inset)

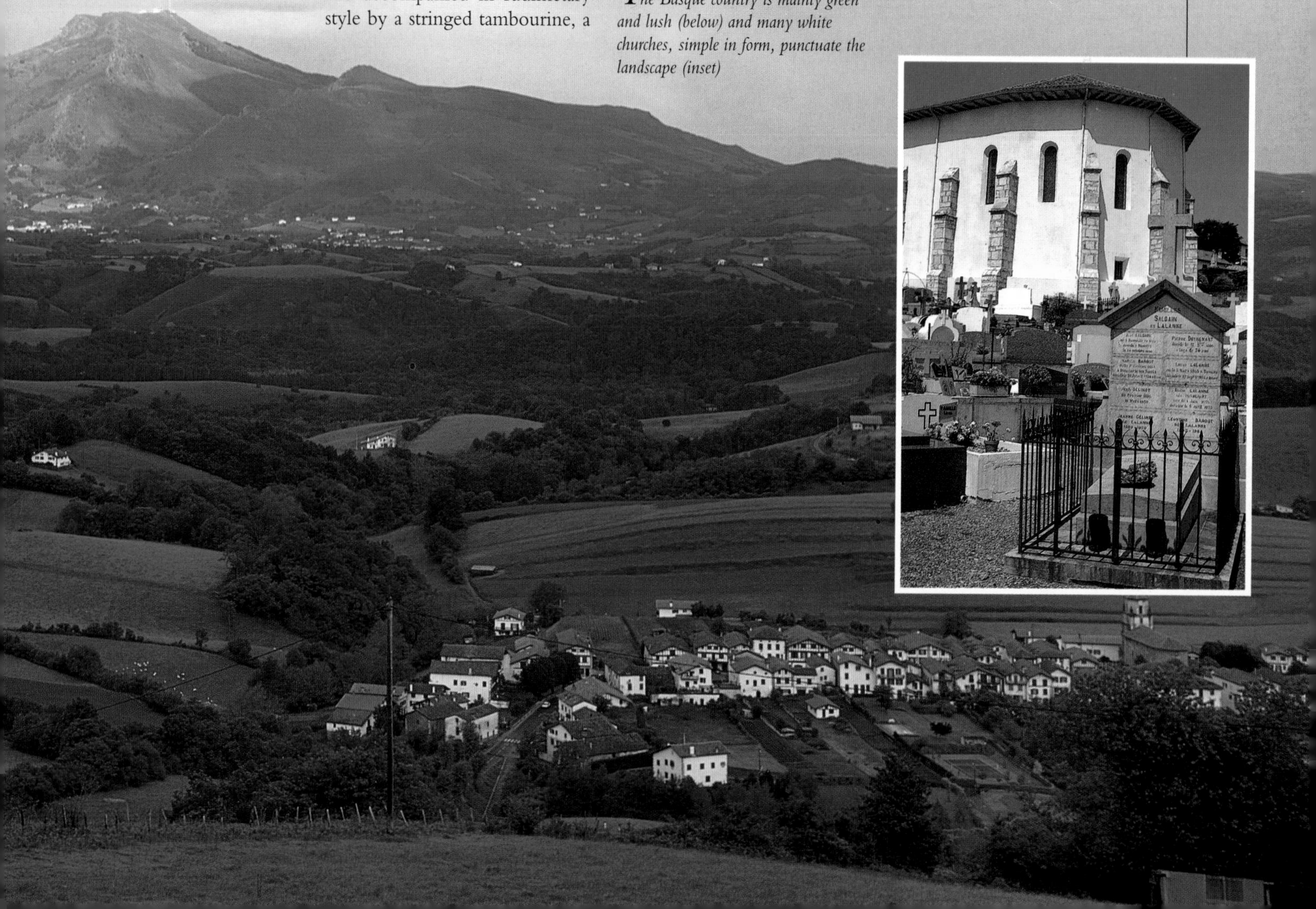

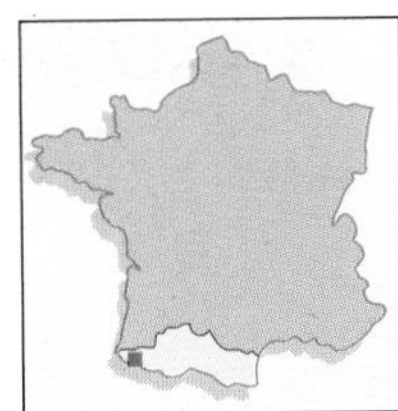

The Heart of the Basque Country

SHARED BETWEEN Basse-Navarre and Haute Soule, the heartland of the Basque country is a broad spread of beech woods and steep hillside pasture. It is sparsely populated, with winding, narrow roads and forest tracks that link shepherds' huts and secluded farmsteads. Few villages break the sense of isolation, and only St Jean-Pied-de-Port is large enough to be considered a town.

Limestone Clefts

South-east of Larrau the frontier hills are sliced by huge limestone clefts sculpted over countless millennia by the industry of innocent-looking streams: the Crevasses d'Holçarté and the gorges of Olhadibie, Kakouetta and Ehujarré. Holçarté and Olhadi are reached easily from Laugibar below Larrau. Kakouetta and Ehujarré are both accessible from the valley of Ste-Engrâce.

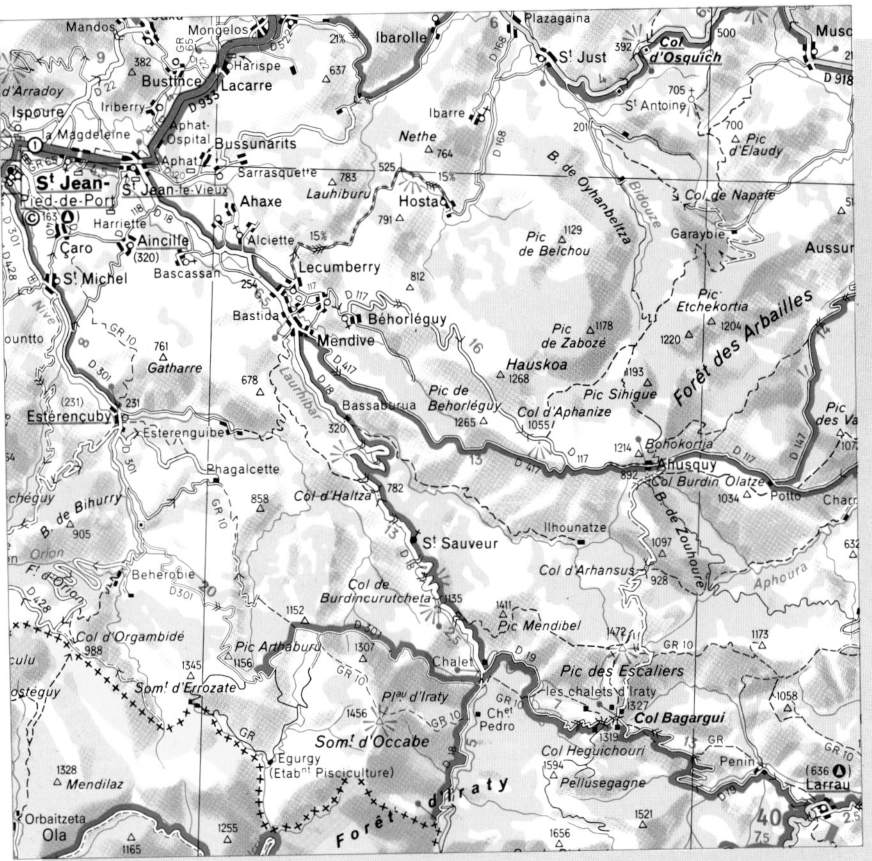

Chapelle St-Sauveur

Unseen from the road but set on a magnificent green crest high on the approach to Col de Burdincurutcheta, the chapel, site of an annual Corpus Christi pilgrimage, is barn-like in size and appearance and surrounded by 13 small crosses with one larger stone pedestal cross set aside from it. On the stone cross is carved a crude but effective Crucifixion. There is a well just below the chapel and a small farm nearby.

Col de Burdincurutcheta

The main western access to the Forêt d'Iraty is by way of Col de Burdincurutcheta (1135m), a high, natural gateway in the northern ridge of the Sommet d'Occabé. The road up to the pass from the valley of Laurhibar is long and twisting, but scenically engaging. Views from the pass itself are far-reaching, with Pic d'Orhy (2017m) peering above the shoulders of nearer mountains.

The Chapelle St-Sauveur, which stands at the entrance to the Col de Burdincurutcheta, is of unusual design, looking rather a barn from a distance

Mission de Développement Touristique des Pyrénées-Atlantiques
22 *ter*, Rue Jean-Jacques-de Monaix
64000 Pau
Tel: 59 30 01 30

Touring:
use Michelin sheet map 234, Aquitaine

Ahusquy

This is a beautiful, secluded, high pastureland on hillsides between the Forêt des Arbailles to the north and the Forêt d'Iraty to the south. Ahusquy enjoys a magnificent panorama that includes far-off frontier peaks and consists of a lonely hotel, small cottage and a nearby spring, the Fontaine d'Ahusquy. The waters from this spring are said to be beneficial to those suffering kidney or bladder disorders. Ahusquy stands at the junction of several narrow roads, variously linking St Jean-Pied-de-Port, Tardets-Sorholus and a number of hidden shepherds' dwellings. The road from St Jean, going through Col d'Egurcé and Col d'Otxolatzé, demands concentration from drivers, but makes a spectacular journey.

Col d'Osquich

On the boundary between Basse-Navarre and Soule, this undemanding low pass (392m) provides the easiest crossing of the hill country east of St Jean-Pied-de-Port and is therefore popular with motorists touring the Basque country. From both sides there are superb views to enjoy – the soft Basque valleys and snow-dusted tops of the frontier range – while from the summit the western Pyrenees spread out in a lavish display of green undulations. An hotel on the pass exploits these views.

Fortifications dating from the 15th century surround the medieval quarter of St Jean Pied-de-Port. The ramparts of the Citadelle, built during the following century, make an interesting walk and give fine views over the town

GR10 AND THE HRP

The mountains and hill country of the Pyrenees provide some of the most stimulating walking in all Europe, from short outings to multi-day epics full of challenge and reward. Two of the longest are the GR10 (Grande Randonnée) and the Haute Randonnée Pyrénéenne, commonly known as the HRP. Both cross the mountain range from the Atlantic to the Mediterranean, the first keeping mainly to the lower hills and valleys, the second following the frontier crest as far as possible. For much of the way across the Basque country the two routes share common footpaths and enjoy huge vistas. In recent years they have become immensely popular among Europe's outdoor fraternity.

Forêt d'Iraty

Predominantly beech and yew, this is one of the great forests of the Pyrenees. It sprawls over both sides of the international frontier and is managed by joint communities from the upper Nive valley and the Soule. In the past large quantities of timber from the forest were sent to the coast to be used in the manufacture of ships' oars, and in the 17th century fears of deforestation had reached Paris. As a result, Louis XIV's finance minister, Colbert, sent a forester to check on its condition. Today the abundant beeches are interspersed with open pastures. Many footpaths and tracks wind through the forest and alongside the road between Burdincurutcheta and Bagargui picnic areas have been set aside. At the summit of Col Bagargui there are tourist facilities.

St Jean-Pied-de-Port

Once the capital of Basse-Navarre, this small and pretty town on the River Nive makes a perfect base from which to explore the surrounding countryside and is very popular among trout anglers. As its name suggests, St Jean lies at the foot of a *port*, or pass – that of Roncesvalles, otherwise known as the Ibañeta, which was crossed in the Middle Ages by thousands of pilgrims from all over Europe *en route* to the tomb of St James the Apostle in Compostela. St Jean-Pied-de-Port was a regrouping centre and the last stopping-place before entering Spain, and as large groups of pilgrims descended on the town bells rang out as if to warn the housekeepers of the refuge in the Rue de la Citadelle to prepare for an influx of visitors.

It is still possible to follow the pilgrims' route through the town today, entering by the Porte St-Jacques and leaving by the Porte d'Espagne. Cobbled streets lead past the church of Notre-Dame-du-Pont and across the old bridge over the Nive, which makes a focal point for picturesque views along the river. The old town is contained within 15th-century fortifications, while the Citadelle, built on the orders of Richelieu in 1628, was redesigned by the military engineer and architect Vauban in 1685.

Sommet d'Occabé

This broad, bald mountain top is, at 1456m, the highest summit reached when travelling on foot from the Atlantic, and is crossed by the GR10. The summit is noted for its low, Iron Age circle of cromlechs, or standing stones, and may be gained by a little more than an hour's walk from Chalet Pedro, a restaurant near the Plateau d'Iraty, below Col de Burdincurutcheta.

The red sandstone church of Notre-Dame-du-Pont in St Jean Pied-de-Port has a fine position by a bridge over the Nive, but has been heavily altered over the centuries

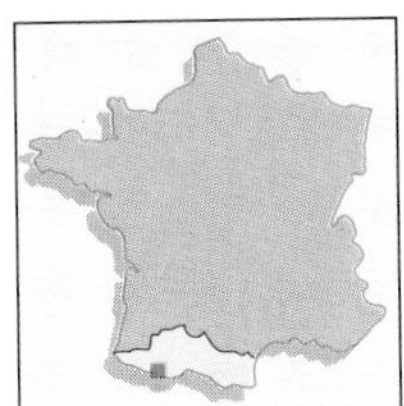

THE HIGH PYRENEES AND THEIR RESORTS

THE THERMAL RESORTS of Barèges, Cauterets and Luz-St Sauveur line the edge of the Parc National des Pyrénées, providing access to some of the most stimulating scenery of this great mountain range. Barèges has the Massif de Néouvielle on its doorstep, while above Cauterets cascades pour from a trio of beautiful valleys. Beyond Luz the great cirques of Troumouse, Estaubé and Gavarnie have undisputed attractions all their own.

The Grande Cascade, a 400-m ribbon of tumbling water, adds to the already superb spectacle of the Cirque de Gavarnie

Cauterets

Known to the Romans, a dozen sulphurated springs first brought Cauterets its fame, and through the centuries the number of illustrious visitors has included Gaston Fébus, who recovered his hearing there, Marguerite de Navarre, who wrote part of the *Heptaméron* while being treated for rheumatism, George Sand, Chateaubriand, Victor Hugo, Flaubert and Tennyson. Today the spa is enjoying something of a revival, while the fortunes of the town itself rely on the drawing power of the surrounding mountains, which attract visitors in both winter and summer. There is no shortage of excursions for motorist, pedestrian or athletic climber.

Barèges

A winter-sports resort and centre for mountain activities in summer, Barèges is also the highest Pyrenean thermal spa. In 1787 Ramond de Carbonnières based himself there for several weeks, during which he made a number of explorations in the heart of the range, effectively heralding the advent of mountaineering in the Pyrenees.

Cirque de Gavarnie

Without question the Cirque de Gavarnie is the best-known feature of the Pyrenees, drawing tens of thousands of visitors each summer. Rising almost sheer from the valley floor to a summit ridge topping 3000m, the limestone walls are divided by two main snow platforms. A long ribbon of waterfall, the Grande Cascade, showers from the upper crags of Marboré (3248m), while across from it to the west the great gash of the Brèche de Roland, said to have been made by the sword of Charlemagne's nephew, provides access for fit mountain walkers to the Ordesa canyon in Spain.

The village of Gavarnie is a whimsical place of hotels, restaurants and postcard and trinket stands. Its streets are crowded with ponies and donkeys, which are employed to convey visitors up the valley to the Hôtellerie du Cirque for a close view of the Grande Cascade and the mountain walls towering dramatically overhead.

HENRY RUSSELL

On the outskirts of Gavarnie the statue of a wisp-bearded figure lounges above the road, gazing at the Vignemale. Comte Henri Patrick Marie Russell-Killough (1834-1909) was the greatest mountaineering eccentric of all time. His exploits are known throughout the Pyrenees and his love affair with the Vignemale is legendary. He climbed it 33 times, made its first winter ascent and excavated a total of seven caves on its rocky flanks near the summit. Here he lived for weeks at a time, holding lavish dinner parties and celebrating Mass on the Glacier d'Ossoue.

The fit walker and the experienced climber will both find an enormous choice of challenges in the Pyrenees

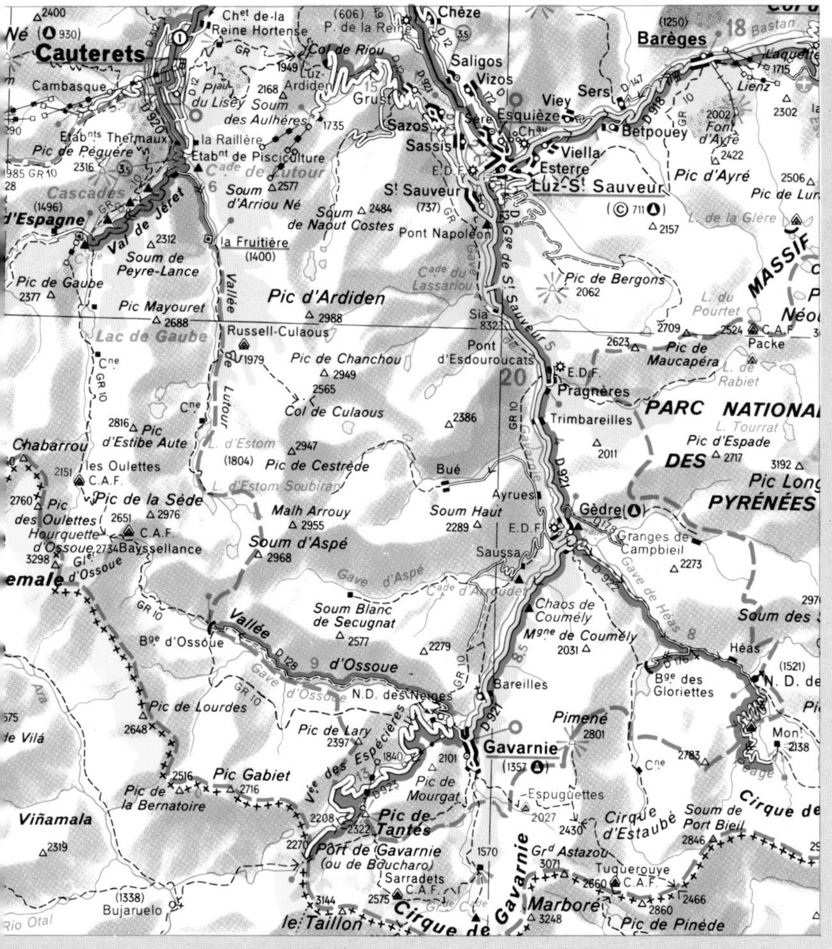

Luz-St Sauveur's church was built in the 12th century and fortified two hundred years later to keep out invaders from the other side of the Pyrenees

Cirque de Troumouse

Reached from Gèdre by way of the hamlet of Héas, the Cirque de Troumouse is larger than the Cirque d'Estaubé and the Cirque de Gavarnie to the west. It is a superb 10-km wall of mountains with rough pastures and a scattering of tiny lakes trapped beneath. A steeply climbing toll road, offering fine views, winds into the mouth of the cirque from Héas.

Luz-St Sauveur

Luz and St Sauveur are divided by the Gave de Pau, a mountain stream that has carved a deep defile between them. St Sauveur is a thermal spa, a single street of tall buildings. The lower part of the avenue is named after the Duchesse de Berry, wife of the second son of Charles X, the upper part after the Empress Eugénie, who spent two months there in 1859 with Napoleon III. To commemorate the imperial couple's sojourn, the single-span Pont Napoléon was built across the gorge above St Sauveur.

Luz itself is more interesting than the spa and occupies a basin at the junction of two valleys. Its 12th-century church was fortified by the Hospitallers of St John in the 14th century as a defence against marauders from Spain; it has an impressive Romanesque doorway, two square towers and a crenellated wall. The nearby Maison du Parc houses a number of displays detailing the natural history of the Parc National des Pyrénées. Above the town stand the ruins of the Château Ste-Marie, which once had an important role as the principal stronghold of the valley of Barèges.

Parc National des Pyrénées

Created in 1967, the Parc National des Pyrénées stretches from the Aspe valley in the west to the Massif de Néouvielle in the east and, butting against the Spanish frontier, covers an area of almost 500 square km. Within its boundaries rise many of the finest individual peaks of the range: Pic du Midi d'Ossau, Balaïtous, Vignemale, Marboré and the cirques of Gavarnie, Estaubé and Troumouse. While tourist developments are permitted on the periphery, the park itself is protected as a sanctuary where the natural life and beauty of the mountains are preserved

Pont d'Espagne

At the road-head of Val de Jéret above Cauterets, Pont d'Espagne gives access to two major valleys worth exploring on foot. The first of these is the Vallée du Marcadau, in whose upper reaches gentle pastures lead to a wonderland of mountain lakes and inviting peaks; the second is the Vallée de Gaube, with the popular Lac de Gaube a short walk from the road. The head of the valley leading to the lake is blocked by the savage north face of the Vignemale, at 3289m the highest peak on the border with Spain.

Comité Départemental du Tourisme des Hautes-Pyrénées
6, Rue Eugène-Tenot - BP 450
65005 Tarbes Cedex
Tel: 62 93 03 30

Touring:
use Michelin sheet map 234, Aquitaine

Lourdes

More than four million people a year visit Lourdes, the majority of them pilgrims bound for the grotto where Bernadette Soubirous had the first of her visions of the Virgin in 1858. Many are invalids hoping to join the list of

the faithful who have been cured during their visit. Lourdes is now the site of the world's greatest pilgrimage. Because the extravagant Basilique du Rosaire was unable to contain the crowds, another, underground and large enough to hold a congregation of 20,000, was consecrated in 1958.

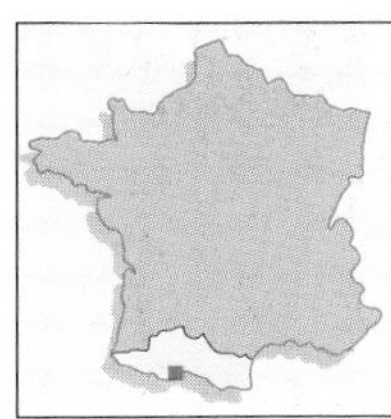

The Aure Valley

HANDSOME GREY VILLAGES, typical of Bigorre, line the fertile valley of the Neste d'Aure, which once formed part of the Pays de Quatre Vallées. Pastures carpet the valley floor, but patches of forest adorn the hillsides that wall it. On the western flank ski grounds nudge against the boundary of the Réserve Naturelle de Néouvielle, an area of lakes, gaunt peaks and wild corries, while to the south lie charming, secluded valleys.

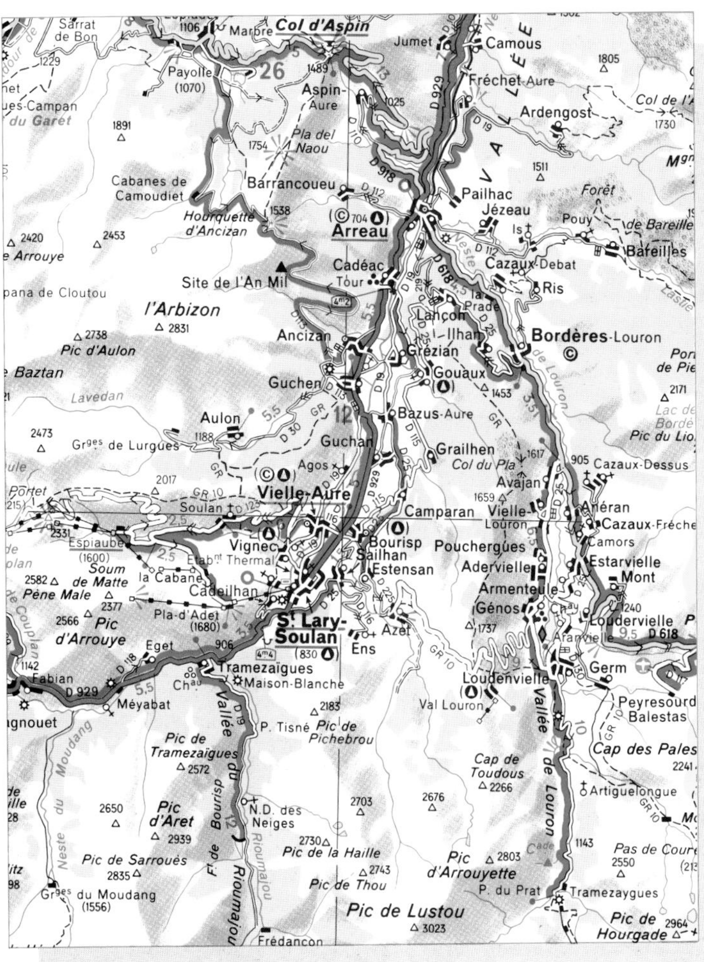

Comité Départemental du Tourisme des Hautes-Pyrénées
6, Rue Eugene-Tenot - BP 450
65005 Tarbes Cedex
Tel: 62 93 03 30

Touring: use Michelin sheet map 234, Aquitaine

Arreau

Formerly the capital of the Pays de Quatre Vallées, Arreau is a pleasant little market town, strategically placed between Col d'Aspin and Col de Peyresourde at the confluence of the Neste d'Aure and the Neste de Louron. In the days when cross-border trade with Spain was flourishing, Arreau was able to exploit its position and the town prospered, although there are few grand buildings to show for it. The covered market in the main street on the left bank of the Louron stands opposite the attractive 16th-century Maison du Lys, whose exposed timbers have been carved with numerous fleur-de-lys motifs. On the far side of the Louron the 13th-century Église St-Exupère has an octagonal tower, an imposing Romanesque doorway and in the porch a wooden corn bin that was formerly used to collect tithes. The Château des Nestes, near the post office, houses a museum of Pyrenean life.

Bourisp

Noted for the lurid 16th-century frescos in its church, this small, grey stone-built village rests on the east slope of the valley. The church dates from the 15th century but has a Norman tower, and the frescos depicting the Seven Deadly Sins show court ladies mounted on strange beasts with hideous demons behind them. On a raised square near the church there can be seen a simple but lovingly carved mother and child.

Cadéac

On a high, bushy knoll overlooking the village stand the ruins of a 12th-century feudal watch-tower. The village is small and has some of the coldest sulphur springs in the Pyrenees; these, however, give it the dignity of a spa. As it passes through, the main valley road narrows to ease beneath the archway porch of the small chapel of Notre-Dame-de-Pène-Taillade.

Col d'Aspin

The comparatively low altitude of Col d'Aspin (1489m) belies the extent of its summit panorama, which is dominated in the west by Pic du Midi de Bigorre. Half an hour's easy walk to the south enables you to enjoy an even more extensive view than that from the pass. It includes the jagged rim of the Massif de Néouvielle, a hint of the Cirque de Gavarnie and above that, Spain's Monte Perdido. The pass itself is a broad

Mountain Contrasts

The differences between one side of the Pyrenees and the other are striking, not just scenically but in vegetation, climate and culture too. 'Europe ends at the Pyrenees' is an old cliché, but while not geographically true, it is given a degree of credibility by those travelling south through the 3-km long Bielsa Tunnel, which links the upper reaches of the Vallée d'Aure and the Spanish valley of the Río Barrosa. Leaving behind green, well-watered France with clouds brushing the peaks, the motorist emerges five minutes later to a bare, scorched landscape of brown hills, dusty valleys and bleached sierras blending into the distance. The contrast is profound.

Striking frescos decorate the porch of the little 15th-century church at Bourisp. Painted in 1592, they warn of the Seven Deadly Sins

Néouvielle Nature Reserve

Skirting the edge of a series of lakes dammed for hydroelectric purposes, the Réserve Naturelle de Néouvielle is a region of tarns, forests of mountain pine and granite peaks topped by Pic de Néouvielle (3091m). Reached by way of a steeply climbing road heading north from Fabian, the Reserve was established in 1935, but has since been reduced in size by the activities of the hydroelectrical engineers. The lakes of Orédon, Aubert and Aumar are accessible by vehicle, but elsewhere only rough paths intrude. The scenery is raw and uncluttered, but brightened by low-growing shrubs and the dazzle of sunlight on water. Chamois and marmots have both been reintroduced and may be seen in the remote inner regions, which are a paradise for walkers.

saddle of pastureland between wooded crowns. The western approach from the Vallée de Campan is through forest, but the descent to Arreau winds among steep pastoral hillsides flush with wild flowers in early summer and lined with sprays of overhanging broom. Squeezed into a deep cleavage immediately below the pass is the tiny village of Aspin-Aure.

Granges du Moudang

This summer grazing hamlet, consisting of a number of shepherds' cottages and barns, occupies a pastoral basin at the junction of two streams in an amphitheatre at the head of the Moudang valley. Accessible only on foot, this pretty scene is reached in a little under two hours from the Pont de Moudang below Fabian.

St Lary-Soulan

Tourism – predominantly winter, but summer also – has turned this once-quiet mountain village into a bustling, growing resort whose original heart is being submerged by modern development. The village now sprawls across the meadows towards Vignec, and overlooking it, conspicuous and incongruous, stands Pla-d'Adet, the concrete blocks of apartments that serve the main ski area. In St Lary itself the Maison du Parc has a fine exhibition depicting the wildlife of the Parc National des Pyrénées, housed in an attractive rugged-stone building. The town is a good base for exploring the Néouvielle massif.

Vallée de Louron

With Pic Schrader and Pic d'Aygues-Tortes rising at its head, the Vallée de Louron is a fine, peaceful trench of greenery, flat-bottomed and with a small lake, Lac de Génos, lying midway along it. Vielle-Louron has a Romanesque church with 16th-century murals and the tomb of St Mercurial.

Vallée du Rioumajou

This beautiful, heavily wooded valley leads to open pastures at its head. Waterfalls tumble from the craggy heights and the meadows are dotted with ancient barns. At the end of the track-cum-road stands the renovated Hospice de Rioumajou, a once-romantic, barn-like building formerly used by both shepherds and mountaineers. The valley is a popular walking area, with several trails that cross high passes into Spain.

Vielle-Aure

Lying mostly on the left bank of the Neste d'Aure, the village is a neat cluster of grey slate roofs and solid-looking houses. Partially hidden galleried courtyards are glimpsed from narrow streets lined with houses of the 17th-19th centuries. There is a tiny chapel in one side street, in addition to the 12th-century parish church.

The fertile terrain around the village of Guchan is typical of this relatively gentle part of the Pyrenees

St Lary-Soulan retains an ancient heart, but, in common with a number of other small towns in the area, it is under pressure from the demands of the winter-sports industry

CATHAR CASTLES

MONTSÉGUR

The tall but narrow rectangular castle, perched like an eyrie on top of a steep 1207-m *pog* (rock), appears utterly impregnable. It was built in the early 13th century at the request of Esclarmonde de Foix as a refuge and place of worship on a site considered secure from attack. For 30 years it was the religious and political headquarters of the Cathar heresy.

Between 450 and 500 Cathars and troops were lodged within the walls of Montségur and on patches of steep ground outside when, in May 1243, the crusaders began their siege. At times there were as many as 10,000 mercenaries surrounding the castle, yet supplies still managed to get through and the siege continued all that year and through the following winter.

After nine months a breakthrough was made and terms of surrender offered. More than 200 Cathars refused to renounce their faith and were led down the hill to a grassy site known as the Camp des Crémats, where they were burned on a single pyre. Three of their number escaped, however, in order to carry the sect's treasure to safety. It has never been found.

CARCASSONNE

This most perfect of fairy-tale walled cities owes its foundation to the Romans of the 1st century AD. A magnificent hilltop town fortified with a double ring of walls and numerous towers, it was besieged by the Franks some 400 years before the crusade against the Cathars. Following the sacking of Béziers in 1209, Simon de Montfort turned his attention to Carcassonne, where the young Viscount Raymond-Roger Trencavel, together with his uncle, Count Raymond VI of Toulouse, organised the Albigensian resistance.

During the siege the town ran short of water. Trencavel was persuaded to leave the safety of Carcassonne to negotiate with the crusaders, but was immediately seized and put in chains. Carcassonne surrendered and Trencavel was imprisoned in a tower within his own fortifications, where he died six months later. The official account of his death says that dysentery was the cause, but he is thought to have been assassinated.

During the Middle Ages the area around the eastern Pyrenees was a stronghold of Catharism, also known as Albigensianism, one of the major heresies of the period. The Cathars, or 'Pure Ones', reacted against the materialism of the Catholic Church, and rejected the Sacraments and the doctrine of the Virgin Birth. They were pacifists, and their leaders, the *parfaits*, were recognised as being far more devout than the slack priests of orthodox Christianity. Opposed to papal decrees and institutions, they were drawn into the dangerous world of politics and feudal manipulation and a major confrontation with Church and State became inevitable.

In 1208 Pope Innocent III preached against the Cathars, and the following year a crusade from the north was organised against them. For although this area was not yet a part of France, the king was ambitious to extend his power and used the crusade as a means of gaining control over the south. Under Simon de Montfort and his mercenaries the crusade attacked Béziers, Carcassonne and many other Cathar strongholds, burning at the stake all heretics who refused to recant. The culmination of this bloody campaign was reached in 1244 when, after a lengthy siege, more than 200 Cathars surrendered at Montségur and were burned on a communal pyre.

The Château de Quéribus was the last stronghold of Cathar resistance

PUIVERT

This castle, overlooking the Pays de Sault, enjoyed the favours of a number of illustrious visitors during the Cathar years, including Esclarmonde de Foix, Eleanor of Aquitaine and the Trencavels. It was also closely associated with the troubadours, who, through their unrestrained movements, were able to provide an undercover information network linking centres of Catharism during the persecutions. Puivert fell in 1210 after three days of fierce battle.

PUYLAURENS

Standing high above the confluence of two valleys to the east of Axat, the Château de Puylaurens has some well-preserved remains, including sturdy towers and battlements and large sections of outer wall. The castle was enlarged and given ramparts in the 12th century, when it was the refuge of the local lords. Cathars sought shelter in Puylaurens during the early crusades against them and from it made regular sorties to attack Simon de Montfort's army.

QUÉRIBUS

Standing astride the one-time border between France and Aragon, and commanding a huge panorama, the Château de Quéribus was the last stronghold of Cathar resistance, lasting for 11 years after the fall of Montségur in 1244. Like Montségur it occupies a magnificent ridge-top position and gives every impression of impregnability. On his return from the Holy Land Louis IX (St Louis) was angered to find Cathars still occupying Quéribus and ordered it to be taken at all costs. Chabert de Barbéra, who was defending it, was persuaded by his friend Olivier de Termes to surrender to the king's representative with-

out a lengthy siege. It is thought that the Cathars escaped to Spain. The remains of the castle have been partially restored, and from it there are superb views to the Canigou.

Peyrepertuse

Charlemagne is said to have built a fortress here in about 707, but the first mention of the Château de Peyrepertuse dates from the 10th century. The remote and rocky site is dramatic, and the fortress itself is the largest in Aude, with walls that follow the extensive outline of the mountain crest on which it stands. During the campaign against the Cathars Peyrepertuse was occupied by Guillaume, lord of Montgaillard, until it was confiscated by Simon de Montfort. Unlike many other Cathar strongholds, it was not destroyed by the crusaders, but was extended and modified on behalf of the king. A garrison was maintained at the fortress until the time of the Revolution.

When captured from the Cathars, the Château de Peyrepertuse (left and inset) was extended by royal command

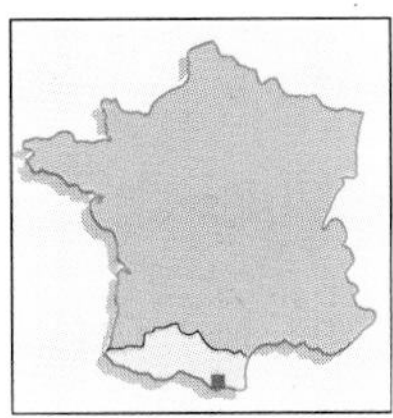

The Cerdagne

THE CERDAGNE is the only broad, flat-bottomed valley in the Pyrenees. Half French, half Spanish, this high plain is a sun-trap enjoying almost 3000 hours of sunshine a year. Formerly the basin of a glacial lake, this fertile region is protected from northerly winds by the Carlit mountains, and walled in to the south by the Puigmal range. Virtually lacking in humidity, the air is dry and bracing.

Comité Départemental du Tourisme des Pyrénées-Roussillon
Quai de Lattre-de-Tassigny - BP 540
66005 Perpignan Cedex
Tel: 68 34 29 94

Touring:
use Michelin sheet map 235, Midi-Pyrénées

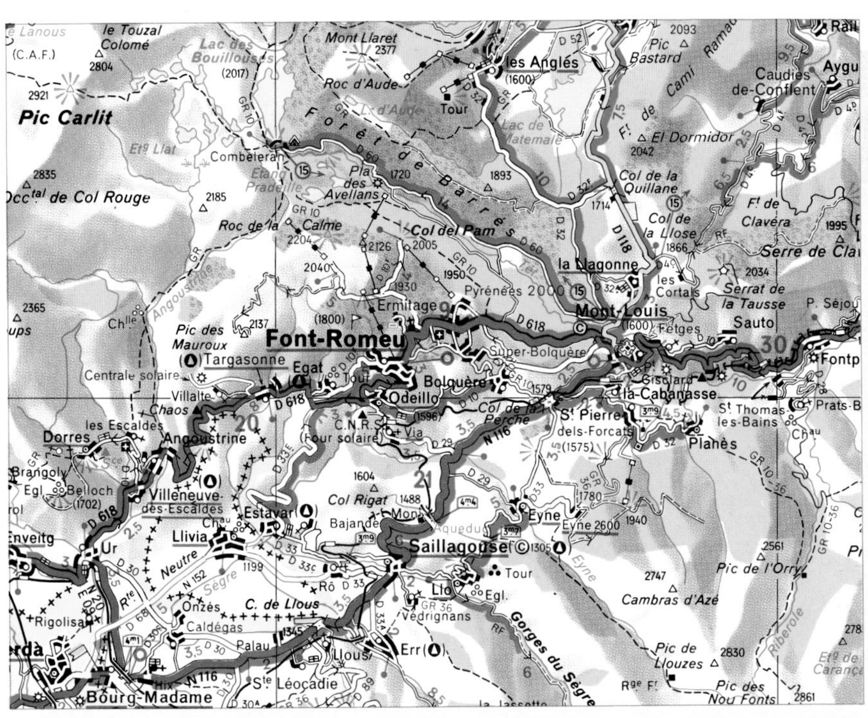

The Little Yellow Train

Between Villefranche-de-Conflent and Latour-de-Carol, the *Petit Train Jaune* links Perpignan with the main Paris-Toulouse-Barcelona railway. This once-essential local service run by the SNCF is now very much a tourist attraction, a romantic 'runaway train' decked out in yellow with red trim. Unlike standard state railway services, however, the *Petit Train Jaune* allows passengers who wish to board it at a minor station to wave it down. Similarly, those who need to disembark at a minor stop must sit in the front carriage and inform the driver as their destination approaches. Along the Cerdagne the railway picks its way easily from village to village, but the route through the steep Têt valley is spectacular, crossing suspension bridges and viaducts that span deep defiles.

Alpine plants adorn the quiet meadows of the Eyne valley, a beautiful, secluded part of the Cerdagne

Bourg-Madame

Formerly called La Guinguette, this small frontier village changed its name in honour of the Duchess of Angoulême, daughter of Louis XVI, after she and her husband passed through in 1815. Across the Sègre, which marks the frontier, stands Puigcerdà.

Col de la Perche

Of modest altitude (1581m), Col de la Perche, on the N116 west of Mont-Louis, nonetheless enjoys a magnificent panorama; to the east the deep valley of the Têt, with Mont-Louis commanding it, to the west the broad Cerdagne from the Carlit massif to Sierra del Cadi in Spain. Sweeping from the col to Cambras d'Azé, the countryside has a moorland-like aspect, but below are lush pastures and fields under cultivation. Nearby Signal de la Perche (1621m), or Perche Belvédère, on the side road (D33) that leads to Eyne and Llo, extends the view even farther and is worth the diversion.

Eyne

The village nestles against the hills, its soft, sand-coloured stone glowing in the sunlight. At first glance it appears not to belong to this century, a small, shy hill village linked with nearby Llo by a scenically delightful narrow road. In the church Notre-Dame-du-Remède is worshipped as a deliverer from ill health. Behind, the Eyne valley is noted for its wealth of plants while Col de Nuria at its head is one of the most important migration routes in the Pyrenees. In the autumn a magnificent variety of birds crosses the mountains there, heading south.

Font-Romeu

This 'Pilgrim's Fountain' has changed from its original role as a place of pilgrimage to one of the most popular and best equipped of Pyrenean ski resorts. Set high above the

Solar Mirrors

Just above Odeillo, near Font-Romeu, stands an astonishing piece of engineering work built by the Centre National de la Recherche Scientifique. It is the Four Solaire, a solar furnace in which almost 10,000 small mirrors, fixed to a concave surface and directed by movable reflectors, managed to concentrate the sun's rays into the centre of a huge dish where temperatures in excess of 3500°C were achieved. Work began with the solar mirrors in 1969, but ceased in 1986. The Four Solaire now helps France's space-science research programme.

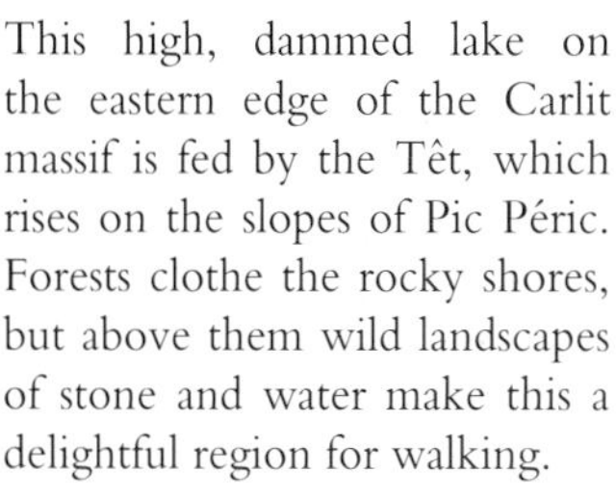

Cerdagne, with a superb outlook and a reputation as the sunniest place in France, it is very much a resort in the modern idiom but, despite the variety of its buildings, not even winter snow can hide its architectural shortcomings. The most prominent of its many hotels is the large and imposing Grand, built just before World War I broke out, and consequently it was several years before it was put to use. Athletes used Font-Romeu for altitude training in preparation for the Mexico Olympics of 1968.

Lac des Bouillouses

This high, dammed lake on the eastern edge of the Carlit massif is fed by the Têt, which rises on the slopes of Pic Péric. Forests clothe the rocky shores, but above them wild landscapes of stone and water make this a delightful region for walking.

Llivia

The former Roman capital of the region, known then as Julia Livia, is one of the anomalies of France: a Spanish enclave surrounded by French territory. Under the Treaty of the Pyrenees of 1659 it was agreed by delegates from both sides that 33 villages in the Cerdagne would be ceded to France, but a year later it was pointed out that Llivia was in fact a town and therefore should remain a Spanish possession. Agreement was eventually reached on the assurance that it would never be fortified, and that the connecting road be considered neutral territory. Llivia today has narrow alleyways, a 15th-century fortified church, the Torre de Bernat adjoining it, and the municipal museum opposite.

Llo

The village blends into the shape and texture of the hills among which it sits. It has one of the finest Romanesque churches in the district, and a ruined tower standing above it. The church's eyecatching doorway has two pairs of pillars that are accompanied by detailed carvings depicting grotesque faces and other subjects. Behind the village stretch the Gorges du Sègre, or Gorges du Llo.

Mont-Louis

Fortified by Vauban following the Treaty of the Pyrenees and named after Louis XIV, this small military town is a sturdy place contained within low, moat-ringed walls. No longer a resort, it has the air of a garrision, heavy and masculine, but trees have been planted to soften the approach and the views it commands over a wide territory include Cambras d'Azé and neighbouring mountains on the south side of the Cerdagne. The citadel at the top end of the town houses commandos who use the surrounding countryside for exercises. Near the austere citadel stands a memorial to Emmanuel Brousse, one-time Deputy for the *département*.

The Cerdagne is a high-lying plain blessed by abundant sunshine and sheltered by mountains to both north and south

The church at Llo has a fine open belfry with three bays, but the carved doorway attracts the most attention. Hideous faces, shells and patterns, all skilfully executed, decorate the arch and the jambs

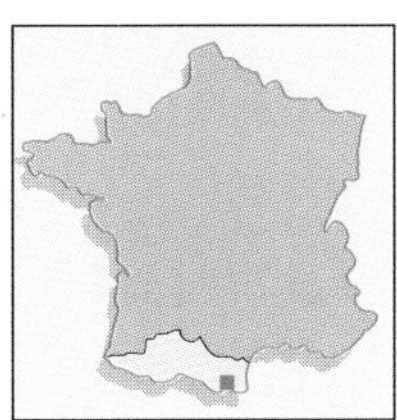

THE CONFLENT

DOMINATED BY Pic du Canigou, and full of abbeys and villages, the Conflent, or valley of the Têt, is very much a land of the Romanesque. Portals of sun-warmed stone look out to market gardens and orchards flush with blossom in spring. The upper valley is a steep defile draining below Prades to the plain of Roussillon, its weathered hamlets clinging to hillside terraces above the river.

Abbaye de St Martin

The romantic eyrie of this isolated red-tiled abbey is one of the wonders of the eastern Pyrenees. Perched on a rock rising from forests of sweet chestnut and beech in the lap of the Canigou, St Martin was founded as a monastery by Guifred, Comte de Cerdagne, at the beginning of the 11th century, but was partially destroyed by an earthquake in 1428. By the time of the Revolution it was in a state of abandoned decay, its cloister columns taken by villagers from Vernet and its treasures scattered.

In 1902 the Bishop of Perpignan set about the abbey's restoration, at first at his own expense, later with state help. He managed to recover some of the original columns and bells and recreated order out of disorder, and today the abbey is once more in use. The cloisters, with their mountain outlook, are delightful, the two-storey church admirable, with its contrasting architectural styles and its columns adorned by simple capitals. But it is the setting that creates the greatest impression.

Abbaye de St Michel-de-Cuxa

The abbey, situated at the foot of Pic du Canigou, was founded in the 9th century to replace a flooded Benedictine monastery on the Têt. It became the most important ecclesiastical building in Roussillon, reaching the height of its influence in the 11th century. After this, however, it entered a steady decline and finally closed in 1790. During the Revolution it was burnt and many of the most notable features sold by lots, the cloisters were dismantled and one of two towers collapsed in a storm. But in 1952, like the Abbaye de St Martin high above it, it was partially restored and a number of original items of stonework were retrieved.

MUSIC FESTIVAL

Few settings for a music festival could be more romantic than that of the restored abbey of St Michel-de-Cuxa (below) nestling among mountain-backed orchards south of Prades. The exiled Catalan cellist Pablo Casals (1876-1973) settled in Prades during the Spanish Civil War. He stayed on to compose and develop his own unique style of playing and became the inspiration behind the summer music festival at St Michel-de-Cuxa, which began in the 1950s. This has since become the most distinguished of all such festivals in this corner of France and annually attracts music lovers both by the quality of its programme and the idyllic setting.

The Abbaye de St Martin enjoys a spectacular outlook, particularly from the cloisters, as a result of its position on a steep spur of rock nearly 1100m high

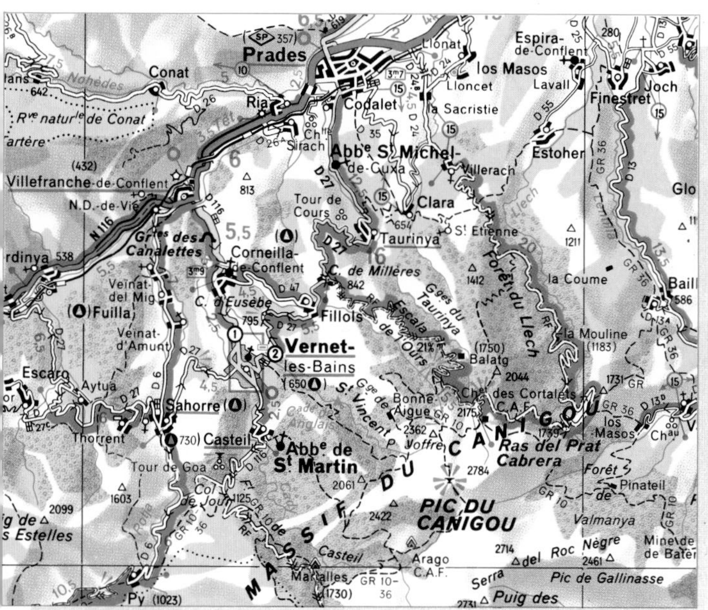

CANIGOU, KING OF ROUSSILLON

So completely does it dominate the eastern Pyrenees that Pic du Canigou (2784m) was long considered the highest mountain in the range. Although of no great altitude, even by European standards, it stands isolated and, rising in conical form, is seen from a great distance and treated almost with reverence throughout the district. At its foot there are olive groves, orchards and vineyards, and towards its summit alpine plants. In 1276 King Pedro III of Aragon set out from Perpignan to climb the mountain. This he did, but his account described a lake on the top in which he discovered a dragon 'which began to fly about and... darken the air with its breath'. Dragons or no dragons, the panorama from the summit is vast indeed and said to stretch from Barcelona to Montpellier.

Corneilla-de-Conflent

Leaning against the mountain slope, Corneilla was the seat of the Comtes de Cerdagne, who built themselves a castle there in the 11th century; but this disappeared long ago. The Romanesque church, however, graces the heart of the village, its richly decorated doorway being much admired, as is the ornamented apse. Inside, the choir is adorned with two Virgins. The most striking of these is a carving in wood, typical of the 12th-century Catalan School. The other, in marble and from the 14th century, depicts the Virgin with Child. In the nearby square a fountain is topped by the figure of a scantily clad shepherd boy draining his water bottle while his dog looks on in envy.

Grottes des Canalettes

Entry to these impressive limestone caves is gained from the Vernet road south of Villefranche-de-Conflent. They extend much farther than is accessible to the public, but walkways lead to a series of spectacular dripping chambers. These are adorned with stalactites, stalagmites, ceiling fins and huge overflowing candle-like pillars that are fascinating to study, their beautiful colours, shapes and textures picked out by electric lights. The caves were discovered in 1951, and the 160-m entrance passage is thought to have been hollowed out some 395 million years ago.

Prades

Capital of the Conflent, Prades is a notable centre from which to explore the many interesting and attractive villages, abbeys and landscapes on its doorstep. It has a certain charm while lacking any real architectural gems, although the Gothic church has a Romanesque tower of rich golden stone and there are many buildings where local pink marble has been used to good effect in neighbouring streets. Surrounding the town, set in the midst of a broad, open plain below the Têt's defile, are orchards and flower-filled market gardens.

Vernet-les-Bains

Comfortable-looking on the slopes of the Canigou, Vernet-les-Bains is a small thermal spa enriched by neat and colourful gardens. The old village, crowded below the 12th-century church and the much-restored castle, is picturesque with its narrow alleyways and flower-decked houses.

Villefranche-de-Conflent

The little town almost blocks the valley, leaving just enough room for the river one side and the road on the other. Dating from 1092 and once the capital of the Conflent, Villefranche consists of two parallel streets contained within lofty, fortified walls remodelled by Vauban following the Treaty of the Pyrenees. There are two handsome main gateways, Porte de France and Porte d'Espagne, providing access to the atmospheric streets of restored Catalan houses, a 12th-century church and a pair of towers. A walk along the ramparts enables the visitor to obtain views of the rooftops of the town, and illustrates how vulnerable it was to attack from above. Vauban added considerably to the château that overlooks Villefranche from the north, turning it into a citadel reached by 999 underground steps. In World War I it held German POWs.

Comité Départemental du Tourisme des Pyrénées-Roussillon
Quai de Lattre-de-Tassigny - BP 540
66005 Perpignan Cedex
Tel: 68 34 29 94

Touring:
use Michelin sheet map 235, Midi-Pyrénées

Corneilla-de-Conflent's church of Ste-Marie has a fine 14th-century marble Virgin with Child (top) Villefranche-de-Conflent (above) preserves much of its medieval character

PROVENCE AND THE CÔTE D'AZUR

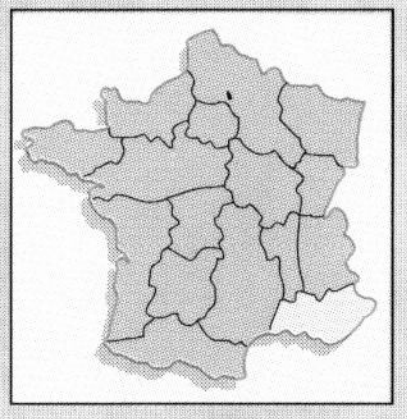

FOR MANY VISITORS THE SOUTH of France means the adjacent regions of Provence and the Côte d'Azur, even though these account for only about half of France's Mediterranean coast.

So many have praised the Provençal light that their adulation has become almost a commonplace. But this remarkable light is not all that makes Provence special, for it also has Roman and medieval antiquities, the Camargue and its world-famous herbs. Provence is a region of wide vistas that are dominated by low scrub of one of two forms. Where original forests have been thinned there is the *maquis*, a scrub formed of tree-heather, strawberry trees, juniper, myrtle, broom, cistus and turpentine trees. Larger tracts of open land exist where the underlying rock is so close to the surface that trees were unable to gain enough purchase, so that there was never a forest to thin. Here there is the *garrigue*, a mix of aromatic herbs, kermes oak, gorse and ling heather.

In contrast to Provence, which represents an older way of life, provincial southern France, the Côte d'Azur, is modern living epitomised. The coast, especially from Cannes to the Italian border, seems to be one long promenade running between a line of luxurious high-rise hotels on the landward side and a marina full of expensive boats on the seaward. But that is not a criticism; it is just a fact, and should not deter you, for the Côte d'Azur is a wonderful area, with sea the colour of its name and ancient ports as picturesque as you could hope for.

Inland from the coast the picturesque qualities are maintained, with pretty hill villages set on the flanks of the Haute-Provence peaks. Here are the lavender fields that provide the raw material for Grasse's perfume industry, and here too the stupendous Grand Canyon du Verdon, one of the natural wonders of France (and Europe). The hills of Haute-Provence lie within the borders of the Parc National du Mercantour, an area of high peaks that includes at its eastern end the valley of Merveilles and Mont Bégo, one of the world's finest sites for Bronze Age art. The area is also home to most of Europe's mountain animals.

Birds, rather than animals, are the main attraction of the Camargue, and include flamingos, one of Europe's most exotic avian residents. Close to the Camargue are Marseille and Toulon, neither of which can be described in detail here. Toulon is a naval port with fine museums on the history of the French Navy. Marseille is France's second city and a major port. Its history is fascinating, and the Musée des Docks Romains explores the first port, the Musée de la Marine its later development.

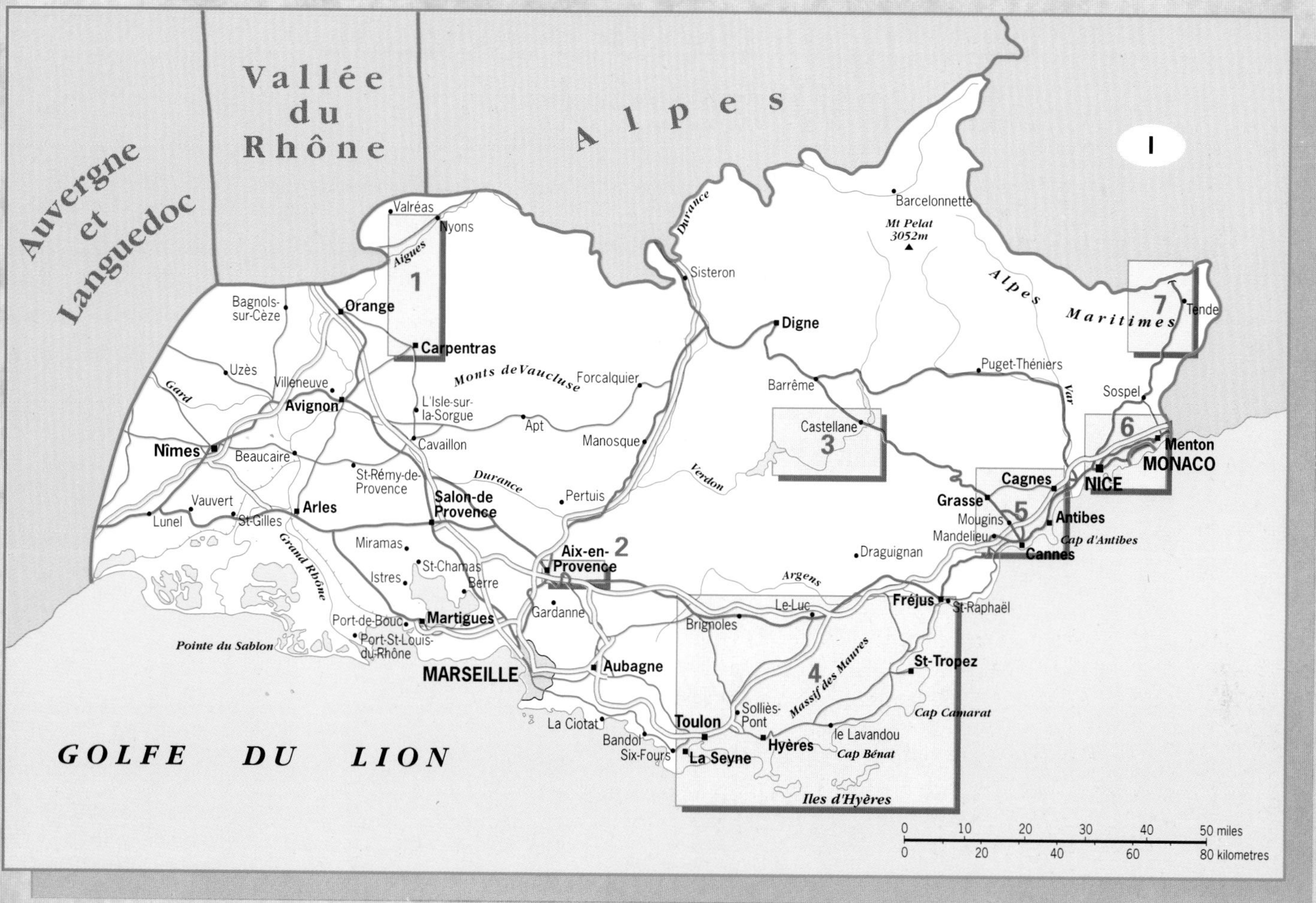

Vallée du Rhône
Auvergne et Languedoc
Alpes
I
Valréas
Nyons
Aigues
1
Bagnols-sur-Cèze
Orange
Carpentras
Uzès
Gard
Villeneuve
Avignon
L'Isle-sur-la-Sorgue
Monts de Vaucluse
Forcalquier
Apt
Cavaillon
Manosque
Nîmes
Beaucaire
St-Rémy-de-Provence
Durance
Pertuis
Vauvert
Lunel
St-Gilles
Arles
Salon-de Provence
Grand Rhône
Miramas
St-Chamas
Istres
Berre
Aix-en-Provence
2
Port-de-Bouc
Martigues
Gardanne
Port-St-Louis-du-Rhône
Pointe du Sablon
MARSEILLE
Aubagne
La Ciotat
Bandol
Six-Fours
La Seyne
Toulon
Solliès-Pont
Hyères
le Lavandou
Cap Bénat
Iles d'Hyères
Cap Camarat
St-Tropez
Massif des Maures
4
Brignoles
Le-Luc
Argens
Fréjus
St-Raphaël
Draguignan
Verdon
Castellane
3
Barrême
Digne
Sisteron
Durance
Barcelonnette
Mt Pelat 3052m
Alpes Maritimes
Puget-Théniers
Var
7
Tende
Sospel
6
Menton
MONACO
NICE
Cagnes
Grasse
Mougins
5
Antibes
Mandelieu
Cap d'Antibes
Cannes
GOLFE DU LION
0 10 20 30 40 50 miles
0 20 40 60 80 kilometres

FEATURES

The Roman theatre at Orange (left) has survived in splendid condition and is still used today
Sweet chestnut on the Massif des Maures (below)

Like many coastal towns on the Côte d'Azur, Menton (above) combines the role of fishing port with that of smart holiday resort

An ornate tiled cupola decorates Menton's 17th-century harbourside fortifications (right) Provence is renowned the world over for its herbs (centre right)

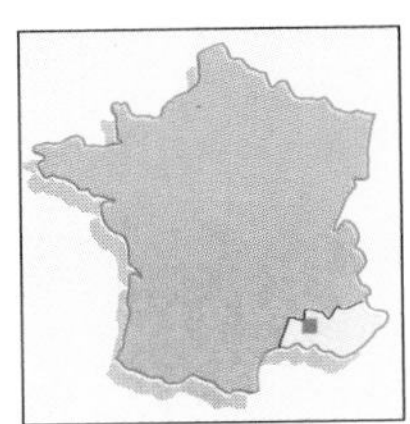

THE DENTELLES DE MONTMIRAIL AND MONT VENTOUX

AS THE RHÔNE flows down towards Provence it swings westward, avoiding the Roman town of Orange. To the east of Orange are the low, attractive hill ranges of the Dentelles de Montmirail and Mont Ventoux. On the flanks and around the bases of the hills are vineyards, while to the north Nyons is a centre for olive oil.

The limestone hills of the Dentelles de Montmirail (top) continue to attract walkers and climbers, as well as artists and nature lovers

The presence of the Romans in Provence is recalled by a carving near the cathedral in Carpentras (above)

Carpentras

Set at the edge of the pastoral land at the southern edge of the Dentelles de Montmirail and Mont Ventoux, Carpentras is both the market town for the local market gardens and a light-industrial town. Of chief interest here is the Cathédrale St-Siffrein, a 15th-century Gothic edifice entered through the Porte Juive (in the Flamboyant Gothic style). The door was thus named because it was through it that Jews converted to Christianity went for their baptism. Carpentras had a thriving Jewish community and until the Revolution there was a ghetto of about 1200 Jews. The synagogue is the oldest in France, dating from the 15th century. Visitors can view its ground-floor baths and kosher bakery, as well as the first-floor temple.

To the west of the cathedral, in Boulevard Albin-Durand, is a museum complex that includes the Inguimbertine library, an extensive collection of volumes assembled by an 18th-century town bishop, including some fine and rare books.

Dentelles de Montmirail

Geologically, the Dentelles are the last section of the Ventoux ridge. They would be rounded hills, covered in vineyards and topped with pine and oak woods, had not folding of the earth's crust pushed the limestone rock into a jagged line of points like the edge of lace, from which the range gets its name. The peaks are beloved of rock climbers and those seeking a hard day on difficult terrain. The best approach is from Suzette on the eastern side or Gigondas to the west.

Below the Dentelles lie a string of charming wine villages. Séguret nestles below a sheet of rock and would be worth a visit for the views alone. However, among its further attractions are the steep streets with their old houses, a 12th-century church, a 15th-century fountain and a ruined castle.

From Séguret a road skirts the base of Montmirail to reach Gigondas, whose Grenache is reckoned to be second only to Châteauneuf-du-Pape as a red wine of quality. From the village a road climbs up to the Col du Cayron, which lies in the heart of the Dentelles.

Mazan

Of particular interest in this village are a set of Roman sarcophagi that make up a wall of the cemetery, and the chapel of Notre-Dame de Pareloup, Our Lady Protectress against Wolves, half buried in the same cemetery. The chapel was built in the 12th century to protect the buried from being eaten by demons disguised as wolves.

MONT VENTOUX

In geological terms Mont Ventoux is the westernmost ridge of the Alps. Its high point (1909m) is laid bare of vegetation by the scouring of the wind, which seems to blow constantly. In Provençal the peak's name is *Ventour,* meaning Windy Mountain.

The mountainside is

clothed in pine, oak and beech woods, but these soon give way to broom, and finally to a few alpine flowers. On the summit there is a weather conservatory, a TV mast and a radar station. The view from the top is a 360-degree panorama, and an orientation panel helps to identify the Lubéron

Chambre Départementale de Tourisme
Place Campana - BP 147
84008 Avignon Cedex
Tel: 90 86 43 42

Comité Départemental du Tourisme de la Drôme
1, Avenue de Romans
26000 Valence
Tel: 75 43 27 12

Touring:
use Michelin sheet map 245, Provence/ Côte d'Azur

hills, the Alpilles and the Montagne Ste Victoire. In summer you can walk along the bare limestone ridge, following in the footsteps of the Italian poet Petrarch, whose ascent of the peak in 1336 is the first recorded conquest of it.

Because of its shape, Mont Ventoux has always attracted competitive cycling. It was used as a hill-trials course for over 70 years until 1973, and frequently features as a climb in the Tour de France. It was on the flank of Mont Ventoux that the English cyclist Tommy Simpson became the race's only fatality. You can cross Mont Ventoux by car by driving east from Malaucène on the D974. The return journey along the southern flank of the mountain allows a visit to Caromb, which has a fascinating museum of old agricultural tools, and to Le Barroux, where there is a restored Renaissance château.

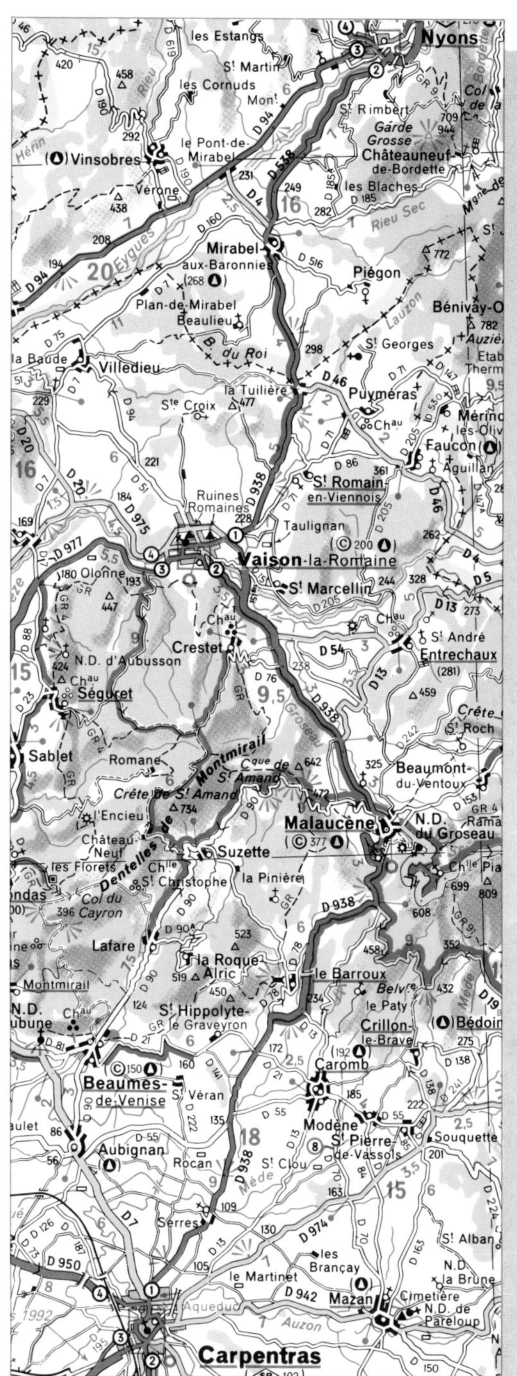

Nyons

The town of Nyons is in Drôme rather than Provence, yet its climate and appearance are Provençal and it makes a good introduction to the South. It is popular as a summer and winter retreat. In winter the surrounding shrub-dotted hills give protection from the *mistral*, while in summer a cooling breeze, the *pontias*, blows down the Eygues valley and keeps the occasionally searing heat at bay. The name of the river is sometimes written as Aigues, but both words simply mean water.

At the northern end of the town arcaded streets lead into the Quartier des Forts, built in medieval times. The 13th-century Tour Randonne encloses a tiny chapel. Take the beautiful, covered Rue des Grands Forts to reach an old gateway that is most of what remains of the town's fortifications. The old bridge over the river, with its single 40-m arch, dates from the 14th century.

Although Vaison-la-Romaine has Roman remains, the medieval town, including the 13th-century cathedral, is no less impressive

Vaison-la-Romaine

The suffix to this town's name is a clue to its Roman ancestry and to its Roman remains, which are discussed further in the feature on the Romans in Provence, on pages 238-9. But there is more to Vaison-la-Romaine than its Roman past. Notre-Dame-de-Nazareth is a superb 13th-century cathedral in the simple but elegant Provençal Romanesque style. Inside there is the sarcophagus of St Quenin, the 6th-century bishop of Vaison-la-Romaine. It is set before the bishop's throne in an apse of exceptional beauty.

On the other side of the River Ouvèze a steep road leads to the upper town, which is dominated by a ruined castle of the Counts of Toulouse. This part of the town is well worth seeing. There is a fountain at the centre of Place du Vieux-Marché, and narrow alleys lead off the square in apparently haphazard fashion. Many of the tall houses have ornate wrought-iron gates.

It is worth seeing one of the olive-oil mills that are open to visitors in Nyons. Here you will find the local speciality: black olives pickled in brine

AVIGNON AND ARLES

TO THE WEST of Marseille lies the Camargue, one of the most remarkable areas in Europe, a salt-marsh with an almost African bird life. On the northern edge of the Camargue, where the Rhône enters the salt-marshes, is Arles, the artistic centre of Provence and the town most closely associated with Van Gogh. North again, through an area sandwiched between the Rhône and the hills of the Alpilles and rich in history, is Avignon, the seat of medieval popes.

ARLES

The site that is now occupied by Arles was first settled by Celtic-Ligurian peoples, though it is to the Greeks that the name is owed. Aptly they called their settlement Arelate, the 'town in the marsh'. Later the town became the most important Roman settlement in southern France. In medieval times Arles was caught up in the strife between the Holy Roman Empire and France, and when it was finally absorbed into France it entered a decline. For centuries the Rhône ensured a certain level of commercial activity, but the coming of the railways put an end to even that trade.

By 1888 Arles was an historically interesting place, a little down on its luck perhaps, but still blessed with pure Provençal light. In February of that year Van Gogh took rooms in Place Lamartine in the town.

Van Gogh spent only 15 months at Arles and yet in that time produced almost 200 canvases, half of them of local landscapes, with around 50 portraits and 40 still lifes or interiors. This period in Arles was one of the most creative of his life, and yet there is almost nothing in the town to remind the visitor of his presence. *The Yellow House* where he roomed in Place Lamartine was destroyed by bombing in 1944 and the café of *Café Terrace at Night* is now a furniture shop. The Pont de Langlois, the famous drawbridge, still stands, but it is in a different spot, reconstructed after its demolition in 1926. Yet no one who has seen the works of Van Gogh can be unmoved by Arles. In the surrounding fields grew the artist's *Sunflowers*; the *Alyscamps* are still here, and much that must have inspired him remains: the church of St-Trophime, with its Gothic, rib-vaulted cloisters, standing at the edge of Place de la République; the cobbled, stepped backstreets, the river bank.

While he was staying at Arles Van Gogh sold not one painting. Indeed he had to barter several for food, and it is said that one masterpiece was found years later boarding up the broken window of an outhouse. It is ironic therefore that Arles does not have a museum of his work – for the simple reason that it cannot afford to buy the work needed to fill it. Instead it has the Espace Van-Gogh, a library of books on art and the artist, in the Hôtel-Dieu-du-St-Esprit.

Around Place de la République in Arles (above) can be seen, from left to right, the town hall, the church of St-Trophime and the library
Arles commemorates Van Gogh in simple style (left)

AVIGNON

In 1309 the French Pope Clement V moved the papal seat from Rome to Avignon. Even now there is a difference of opinion among academics about the reasons behind this move. Most believe that Clement retreated among his own countrymen when internal strife in Italy and the threat of invasion from the east made Rome an insecure papal capital. Others believe that the move was a virtual kidnap by Philippe IV, who was anxious to control the Papacy in order to stop mutterings about his expansionist policies and the horrifying cruelty of the Albigensian Crusade against the Cathars in southern France. Whatever the reason the town of Avignon, then just a crossing point on the Rhône, was thrust on to the turbulent centre stage of medieval politics.

Clement V remained in Avignon throughout his papacy, as did his successors until 1377. During the early years of the Avignon Popes, and particularly

in the case of Clement V, it does appear that they were virtual prisoners in their palace, though towards the end of their stay their position was clearly not that of captives. When the Great Schism of 1378 to 1417 occurred, and an 'antipape' was elected in opposition to the one in Rome, it was to Avignon that the former, favoured by France, Spain and northern Italy, retreated. By then the Papal State owned Avignon and the surrounding area, a situation that lasted until the late 18th century, when the Papal State was annexed by France.

The Avignon Popes of the 14th and early 15th centuries occupied a fortress-like palace (above)
Avignon's light still attracts artists (above right)
The Pont St-Bénézet in Avignon (right) has undergone much rebuilding over the centuries. The dancing of the nursery song took place beneath the bridge

In Avignon the Popes occupied the Palais des Papes, a huge and impressive, if somewhat austere, building of pale grey stone. More fortress than mansion, the palace mirrors the insecurities the occupiers must have felt, with its soaring walls, towers and battlements. It covers a hectare, with a myriad of rooms leading off from the central Great Courtyard. The rooms themselves are mostly bare of furniture – though this merely adds to the stern grandeur of the huge Great Hall – but a visit to the Robe Room with its fine tapestries is recommended. Beside the palace is the Petit Palais, which now houses a museum of medieval art.

Elsewhere in the town there are fine museums set in a street plan that successfully integrates narrow alleys and wide, airy boulevards. From the Palais des Papes a narrow, enclosed series of alleys spirals down to the Pont St-Bénézet. The bridge, made famous by the nursery song, was built in the later 12th century, but time and floods have reduced it to half its original length, so that it now stops forlornly in the middle of the Rhône. The visitor comes to see the bridge on which occurred the famous dancing sung about in the nursery song. But the song has not travelled the centuries well and should read not *'sur le pont'*, but *'sous le pont'*, for the dancing took place on a now long disappeared island surrounding a central pier of the bridge.

Camargue Wildlife

Just north of Arles the Rhône splits into the Grand Rhône and the Petit Rhône. These rivers, flowing almost at right angles to each other, below Arles form with the coastline a triangular delta that has been semi-flooded to form a flat salt-marsh interspersed with wider expanses of brackish lagoons known as *étangs*. Within this area, the Parc Nature Régional de Camargue, the bird life is unique in Europe: flamingos flock and nest – the only place in Europe where they do so – vultures soar overhead and egrets stand erect among the reeds.

There are avocets and stilts, storks and herons, bee-eaters, rollers and hoopoes. Turtles swim in the waters and beavers still survive, though they are very rare. Much more common are the small black Camargue bulls that live semi-wild among the reed margins. Each year they are herded by the *gardians*, gaucho-like cowboys who ride white horses, herds of which also roam freely among the marshes.

A little egret, one of the Camargue's inhabitants

The bulls fight in the Provençal bullfights held at Arles and Nîmes. These differ from the Spanish variety in that the bull lives to fight another day, but the action is no less exciting.

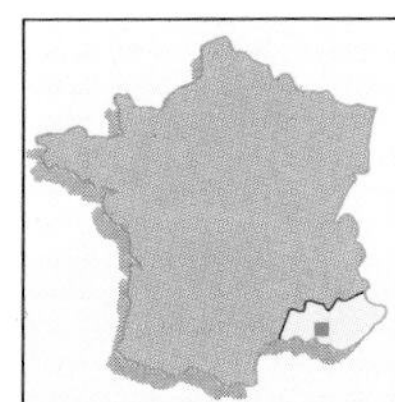

AROUND AIX-EN-PROVENCE

ONLY A FEW kilometres north of Marseille lies a town that could hardly be more different. While Marseille is big and impersonal, crowded and noisy, Aix-en-Provence is small and quiet, a sedate university town where there is always time for a coffee and some lazy exploration.

Comité Départemental du Tourisme des Bouches-du-Rhône
6, Rue du Jeune-Anacharsis 13001
Marseille
Tel: 91 54 92 66

Touring:
use Michelin sheet, map 245, Provence/Côte d'Azur

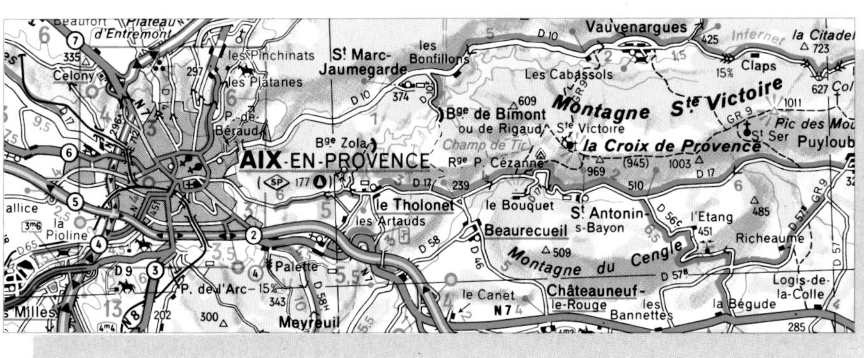

Aix-en-Provence

Although Aix was the seat of the dukes of Provence, it had an unremarkable history until the 15th century, when the dukedom passed to René (1409-80), who was also King of Sicily and Duke of Anjou. René was a committed 'green' at a time when such concerns were viewed with suspicion if thought about at all. In addition he was a patron of the arts, a linguist, a mathematician and a lawyer. He was also a rather incompetent ruler, but that seems to have been overlooked. René is credited with introducing the muscat grape to Provence, from Sicily, and with importing the first silkworms. A statue of him, holding a bunch of grapes, can be seen at the end of Cours Mirabeau, the finest boulevard in Aix. But the visitor will also notice frequent reference to René in shop, café and restaurant names, for Aix is now very fond of its eccentric ruler.

The ornate 16th-century Tour de l'Horloge, with its bell in a wrought-iron cage, stands next to the town hall in Aix-en-Provence

Cours Mirabeau is named after a citizen of the town at the time of the Revolution, an ugly man of ugly habits who, nonetheless, was a superb orator, and beloved of the common folk. The boulevard is wide and airy, each pavement planted with a double row of plane trees that offer welcome shade from the summer sun. In the centre of the boulevard is a moss-encrusted hot-water fountain, supplied by the same source that the Romans tapped in 122 BC. The water is a brew of mineral salts and is mildly radioactive; it reaches the surface at 36°C.

The north side of Cours Mirabeau is lined with cafés, restaurants, bookshops and shops selling *calissons* (see box on facing page), while the south side is more formal, with the occasional elegant mansion from the 17th century, its façade enriched with caryatids and wrought iron.

Vieil Aix, the city's oldest and most charming section, lies between Cours Mirabeau and the cathedral. Some of the streets here are pedestrian-only and are lined with smart fashion shops, antique dealers and shops selling Provençal handcrafts. To get the real flavour of the old town, follow Rue Roumer from Cours Mirabeau and turn right into Rue Espariat. Here the Hôtel Boyer d'Éguilles houses the Muséum d'Histoire Naturelle, which, among many other things, has a collection of dinosaur eggs unearthed on the Montagne Ste Victoire. Thousands of eggs were discovered, and to date no satisfactory explanation has been found as to why they failed to hatch.

A wealth of brightly coloured vegetables and fruits adorn street markets, like this one in Aix, all over Provence

Rue Espariat leads into Place d'Albertas, the most delightful of the little squares of old Aix, cobbled, and with elegant terraced houses around a central fountain. Close by is Place des Prêcheurs, where a food market is held on Tuesday, Thursday and Saturday mornings. North again are the Tour de l'Horloge (Clock Tower) and the Cathédrale St-Sauveur, two of Aix's landmarks. The first dates from the 16th

CÉZANNE

Paul Cézanne was born in Aix in 1839, at 28 Rue de l'Opéra. He was baptised in the chapel of Ste-Marie-Madeleine in the same year, and attended a primary school in Rue des Épinaux from 1844 until 1849. The family moved to 14 Rue Mathéron and Paul attended the Collège Bourbon – now the Lycée Mignet – in Rue Cardinale, where he was a pupil at the same time as Émile Zola. Cézanne's father, a well-to-do man, acquired an estate about 4km south-west of Aix called Jas de Bouffan; this is now home to the Vasarely Foundation, showing the work of the Hungaro-French geometric artist. In 1859 Cézanne went to Paris intending to study law. There, however, he decided to fulfil his dream of becoming a painter. He left Paris in 1881, disillusioned by

The Montagne Ste Victoire is probably the most familiar natural landmark in Provence. Cézanne, who was particularly fond of it, painted it many times (see picture below)

what he saw as the limitations of Impressionism, but also by the public reaction to his Impressionist friends, whose work he believed to be critical to the development of art. Back in Aix, he rented rooms in several locations, most importantly in the Château Noir, on the D17 to the west of the town, and at 23 Rue Boulegon, where he died in 1906. In 1902 he rented a studio at number 9 in the avenue that now bears his name. The studio is now the Atelier Paul Cézanne, a museum devoted to the artist's work.

Cézanne was a modest man, but clear about his own position in art. 'A painter like me,' he said, 'there's only one every other century.' His ideal was to create strictly

harmonious pictures, for he admired greatly the balance of the great classical artists. He imposed this balance on his landscapes, creating paintings that appear to be patchworks or mosaics, blocks of colour which complement each other in addition to portraying the subject.

century, but the lower statues of Night and Day are modern. The wooden statuettes of the four seasons are each visible for three months at a time. The cathedral has a 5th-century baptistery, and work from many different architectural periods is incorporated in this impressive 16th-century Gothic building.

South of Cours Mirabeau is another attractive old neighbourhood, the Quartier Mazarin, smaller and more restrained than Vieil Aix. Beyond the Musée Archéologique Paul-Arbaud, which houses sculptures and paintings by local artists, the Fontaine des Quatre Dauphins stands in the square of the same name. At the head of Rue Cardinale, which leads off the square, is the Musée Granet, which has important works by French, Italian, Flemish and Dutch artists as well as a separate gallery of paintings by Cézanne.

Montagne Ste Victoire

When the Romans moved into this part of Provence they discovered the hot springs that still feed the fountain in Cours Mirabeau, and founded Aquae Sextiae Saluviorum – the future Aix – around them in 122 BC. Twenty years later, Roman historians record, a band of Teutonic barbarians invaded the area and were confronted by a Roman army on the hillside to the east of the town. In the battle 100,000 barbarians are said to have been killed and the same number captured. The mountain above the battlefield was called Victory to commemorate the slaughter, and it still bears the name.

The mountain was beloved of Cézanne, and a visit to it can feel like a pilgrimage. Those willing to punish themselves in true medieval pilgrim fashion can climb up to the Croix-de-Provence, on the highest peak of the long ridge. Starting from Les Cabassols, on the D10, this route involves a 550-m climb and takes about two and a half hours. The reward is a close-up sight of the summit cross and a breathtaking view.

Vauvenargues

This pretty village is famous for its Renaissance château, which was inherited by Pablo Picasso in 1958 and is where he died in 1973. Picasso is buried in the château's extensive park, but neither park nor château is open to the public.

Provençal Sweets

So much has been written on Provençal cooking, particularly on *bouillabaisse* and *aïoli*, that other specialities of the region are sometimes overlooked. One of these is sweets, and at Aix one of the most famous is made. These are *calissons*, small, diamond-shaped biscuits that are made of iced almond paste.

You could also try crystallised fruit or jam from the small town of Apt; or the preserved melon from Avignon. Carpentras is famous for its *berlingots*, caramel sweets, while Sault, on Mont Ventoux, produces a nougat made from honey that is every bit as delicious as the more famous sweet from Montélimar. Montélimar nougat started as a local, home-made sweet, but is now a full-scale industry. The nougat is a blend of almonds and honey, but the detailed recipes of the different manufacturers are closely guarded secrets. Tarascon, between Avignon and Arles, specialises in chocolates called *tartarinades*.

Elsewhere, do not turn down the chance of sampling *beignets de fleurs d'acacia*, a pancake flavoured with acacia blossom, or a *torta bléa*, a cake made with raisins and crushed pine seed.

THE ROMANS IN PROVENCE

ALTHOUGH THE CELTO-LIGURIAN TRIBES occupied Gaul, as the Romans were to call France, the Greeks and Phoenicians held the Mediterranean. It was the Greeks who established the first settlement on the coast, called Massalia, on the site of what is now Marseille. With the rise of the Roman Empire and its embracing of Hellenistic culture, Massalia gave Rome support in the Punic Wars. Inland, however, the Celts sided with Carthage, showing Hannibal's army the way across Provence to the Alps in preparation for his attack on Rome in 218 BC. The Romans forgot neither Massalia's help nor the Celtic action.

Within a century Rome controlled much of southern Gaul and Massalia was established as a Roman port. The Romans built roads to service their garrisons and ports, the Via Aurelia being the main route linking the Italian Ligurian coast with the ports of Nice, Antibes and Marseille (Massalia). Later Julius Caesar built the harbour of Fréjus, also on the Aurelian Way. This route is now followed by the RN7. Other roads took soldiers and supplies inland, the Via Agrippa following the Rhône valley to link Arles with Orange. Each of these towns had been founded by the time of Caesar's rise to power, and Arles chose to support him in his battle with Pompey. Marseille took Pompey's side and, when he was defeated, fell into decline at the expense of its Camargue neighbour.

The period that followed was prosperous as never before, the great buildings at Orange, Nîmes, Arles and Pont du Gard dating from that time. The Pax Romana lasted three centuries, until the Visigoths invaded the area in the early 4th century. That early invasion was unsuccessful, but the power of Rome was waning and it was only a matter of time before Roman Provence fell. The Franks finally took control in AD 536.

The Pont du Gard (left) is a miracle of Roman engineering

The amphitheatre at Arles (right) could hold 25,000 spectators

PONT DU GARD

The Pont du Gard aqueduct is impressive in several ways: it is a statement in stone of the Romans' thoughts on the permanence of their empire; it is a remarkable technical achievement; and it is very beautiful. An aqueduct was constructed to take water from Uzès to Nîmes, 50km away, and to carry it across the Gardon valley the Pont du Gard was built, a triple-arcaded aqueduct nearly 300m long. Visitors may walk along the top, but be careful: where the water channel covers are intact you must walk on them. There are no guard-rails and there is a drop of 130m.

The entire aqueduct had an average fall of 1:300, and supplied 400 litres of water daily for every inhabitant of Nîmes – more than is supplied today.

VAISON-LA-ROMAINE

The Roman remains at Vaison-la-Romaine are divided into the Quartier Puymin and the Quartier Villasse. The latter quarter comprises the remains of houses, shops and a basilica and includes a colonnaded street, while the Quartier Puymin includes a theatre, several more houses and the site museum.

ARLES

The chief attraction at Arles is the huge stone amphitheatre, built in the 1st century AD. The oval building is 137m long, 107m across and has three tiers of seats below a towered and arcaded final wall. It seated up to 25,000 spectators, and the cages that held wild animals for gladiatorial bouts can still be seen below the walls. In the Middle Ages a small village grew within the protecting walls, though now the amphitheatre is much as it was in Roman times. It is still used for Provençal bullfights. The theatre of Arles was built in the 1st century BC, to hold about 7000 spectators, but it has not stood the ravages of time well. An earlier arena, of wood, may have existed at the same time.

The Palais Constantin is also known as the Thermes de la Trouille, for it is in fact a Roman baths, dating from the 4th century. Water is supplied by aqueduct from Eygalières, 25km away.

The Alyscamps is a necropolis with its origins in the 4th century. Van Gogh painted it during his stay at Arles.

The best archaeological exhibits from Roman Arles are to be found in the twin Musée d'Art Païen and Musée d'Art Chrétien, which tell the story of pagan and Christian art.

NÎMES

The amphitheatre at Nîmes, while not the biggest of those left by the Romans, is by common consent the best preserved. For the visitor it is awe-inspiring, not just for its size and architecture, but because its position – on its own in the centre of a square and completely open on its southern side – allows a real appreciation of its splendour. Like its counterpart at Arles, the amphitheatre is oval in shape, although it is a little smaller. It too, is still used for Provençal bullfights, and as many as 20,000 spectators are able to gather inside.

While the amphitheatre is the most impressive of Nîmes' Roman remains, the Maison Carrée is perhaps more unusual. The name means 'square house', which is both geometrically inappropriate and an understatement, for this very Greek-looking building is actually a temple, built in the 1st century BC. A museum within the temple has an exhibition of the best finds of Roman Nîmes.

In the Jardin de la Fontaine are the remains of another temple, the Nîmes baths and a watchtower dating from the 1st century AD. Also in the town is the collecting basin for water from the Pont du Gard aqueduct. The water fed into 10 canals for distribution, and these can still be seen. A similar system is still in existence at Pompeii.

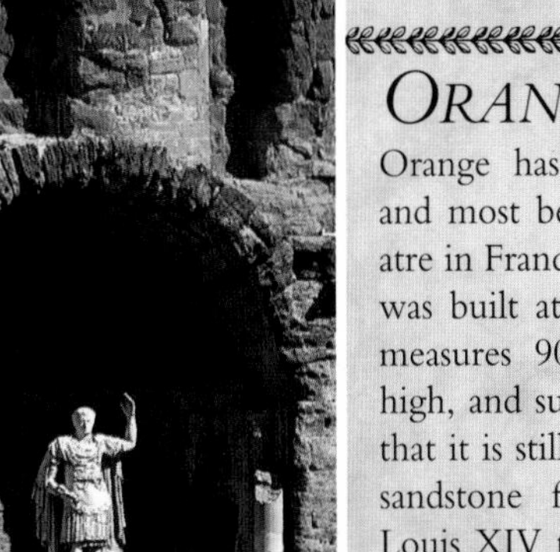

The Roman theatre at Orange

ORANGE

Orange has the best preserved and most beautiful Roman theatre in France still in existence. It was built at the time of Christ, measures 90m across and 36m high, and such is its preservation that it is still used. The huge red sandstone façade was said by Louis XIV to be 'the finest wall in my kingdom'.

The top tier of seating is the best place to view and appreciate the craftsmanship employed in the building of the theatre. The statue in the niche above the stage is of the Emperor Augustus and is 3.5m high; it has been carefully rebuilt, right down to the Imperial baton, from fragments found at the site. Beside the theatre are the ruins of the only known gymnasium in Roman Gaul.

St-Rémy-de-Provence's municipal arch and mausoleum

ST-RÉMY-DE-PROVENCE

About 1km south of St-Rémy-de-Provence are the excavations of Glanum, one of the most important Roman sites in France. Believed to date from around 30 BC, the site has only been partially excavated, but so far the remains of the forum and baths have been uncovered, as well as several houses and temples. The most significant remains are a municipal arch from the time of Augustus (63 BC-AD 14), with carved reliefs commemorating Julius Caesar's victories in Gaul, and a mausoleum to the memory of his two adopted sons.

La Turbie is dominated by the 'Trophée des Alpes' (above)

LA TURBIE

Travellers on the A8 between Menton and Monaco can glimpse the 'Trophy of the Alps'. This triumphant monument, erected by Augustus to celebrate victories in the area, was used as a fortress in the 14th century and later blown up by Louis XIV. Renovation carried out this century has restored the monument to something approaching its original form, and a museum on the site has a model to show how it would have looked when it was first constructed.

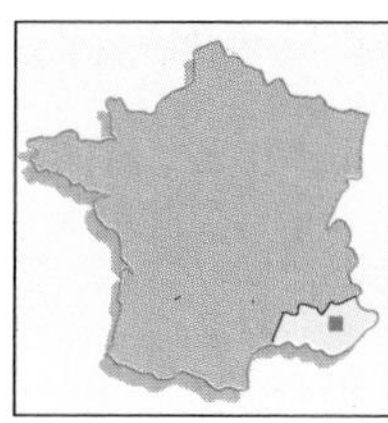

THE VERDON GORGE

THE RIVER VERDON is a long tributary of the Durance, and would be pleasing but hardly remarkable were it not for the deep gorge it has cut into the limestone plateau of Haute-Provence between the villages of Castellane and Moustiers-Ste-Marie. The Grand Canyon du Verdon is one of the natural wonders of Europe, and is scattered with spectacular viewpoints.

Comité Départemental du Tourisme et des Loisirs des Alpes de Haute-Provence
42, Boulevard Victor-Hugo - BP 170
04005 Digne-les-Bains Cedex
Tel: 92 31 57 29

Touring:
use Michelin sheet map 245, Provence/ Côte d'Azur

Opinions differ, but it is believed that the remarkable Grand Canyon du Verdon – 20km long and 800m deep in places – was cut either while the limestone plateau was being raised or while the local sea level was falling

Aiguines

This tiny village, at the start of the road known as the Corniche Sublime, is delightfully set among cypresses and has a 17th-century château. There is also a small but excellent craft museum.

Bargème

Bargème is a typical Provençal village and can only be visited on foot. Visitors should park below the village and enter it through a gate. There is a Romanesque church, and excellent views can be had from the ruins of the medieval castle.

Castellane

When he landed close to Antibes from Elba on 1 March 1815, Napoleon Bonaparte knew he would not receive a universal welcome from the French. He was disappointed, however, to be rejected by the garrison at Antibes, and, learning that he could expect no better treatment in the Rhône valley, he decided to strike inland, intending to reach the Durance valley and to use that to penetrate the French heartland. He and his followers headed towards Grasse, continuing on a difficult path to Séranon. To cross the River Verdon they made for the village of Castellane. Support grew, and when Napoleon reached Grenoble on 7 March he was met by shouts of 'Long live the Emperor'.

In Castellane Napoleon stopped for lunch at 34 Rue Nationale, the road that forms, with Place Marcel Sauvaire, the centre of this charming old village. Close by is the picturesque 14th-century clock tower set above one of the ancient gateways into the village. To the north there remains a section of the old ramparts.

Dominating Castellane is a huge cuboid limestone block topped by the chapel of Notre-Dame-du-Roc, a viewpoint which is reached by a steep, narrow track marked by the Stations of the Cross.

THE SENTIER MARTEL

The Verdon Gorge was first explored by the renowned French speleologist Édouard-Alfred Martel (1859-1938), and a footpath through it has been named in his honour: the Sentier Martel. The ends of this path are reached by others that go down the steep rock face at the Point Sublime, or at the Chalet de la Maline on the Route des Crêtes. Walking the path will take not less than six or seven hours, and because of the stops that will almost certainly be made, it is best to set aside a whole day.

Walkers on the route will find seven tunnels but *only the first two reached from the Point Sublime should be entered.* All the tunnels were made as part of an aborted scheme to dam the Gorge and the remainder are partially collapsed and very dangerous. The walker must also keep to the marked path: the level of the Verdon can rise suddenly and swiftly as upstream sluices are operated, and if you are caught off the path at an awkward point it could be very dangerous.

Walkers must be well equipped: warm and waterproof gear should be carried, boots with ankle support worn, and a head torch is essential. There is no drinking water along the route (despite the river's proximity) so water as well as food must be carried. Walkers should also obtain a map or guide, both of which are available locally, before setting out on this long and challenging route.

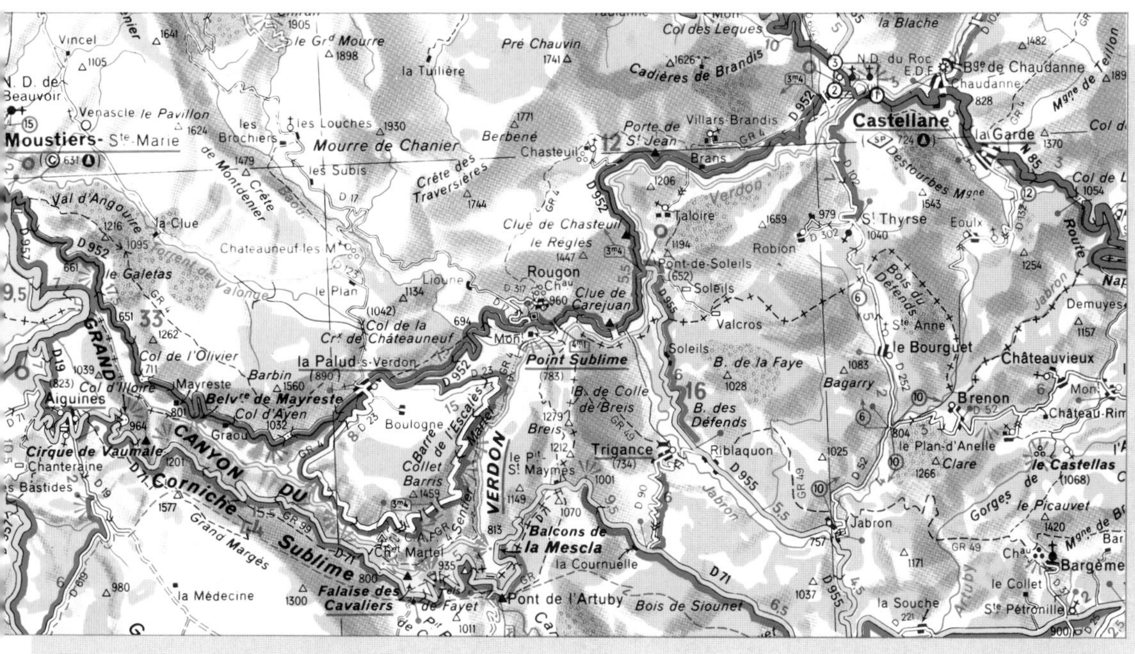

Grand Canyon du Verdon

Though Europe cannot match Arizona's Grand Canyon, the Verdon Gorge, which shares the name, is spectacular in its own right. Over millions of years the River Verdon has carved down into the limestone plateau. In principle the method of channelling is straightforward, yet the production of such a deep, clean-cut gorge is not fully understood, and experts disagree, because it requires a process that is both very rapid – on a geological rather than human timescale – and very corrosive.

Two roads run along the rim of the Canyon, each with numerous viewpoints. The southern route leaves the D952 a few kilometres south of Moustiers-Ste-Marie and goes down to the Lac de Ste Croix, an artificial lake feeding a hydro-electric power station, before rising to the rim of the Canyon. The road is called the Corniche Sublime and passes several tiny stopping points before reaching the attractively situated Restaurant des Cavaliers. Ahead now are the spectacular Tunnels de Fayet and a bridge over the River Artuby, before the high spot, the Balcons de la Mescla, is reached. 'Mescla' refers to the mixing of the two rivers, the Artuby flowing into the Verdon hundreds of metres below.

To reach the Castellane road (at Pont-de-Soleils) the visitor can either take the longer route via Comps-sur-Artuby, or the short cut through Trigance. On the southern edge of the Canyon, going now from Castellane to Moustiers-Ste-Marie, the road first reaches the Point Sublime, which is considered to give the finest view. Park at the inn here and walk to the edge of the 180-m cliffs.

Further on, the Route des Crêtes leaves the D952, clinging closer to the rim and reaching the belvedere at Barre de l'Escalès, which is another famous viewpoint. The D952 is joined again at La Palud-sur-Verdon, several more excellent viewpoints being passed before Moustiers-Ste-Marie is eventually reached.

Moustiers-Ste-Marie has long been famed for its glazed pottery. Visitors can see a museum devoted to the craft and choose from a wide range of items of local pottery on sale in the village

Moustiers-Ste-Marie

The most surprising thing about Moustiers-Ste-Marie is the star hanging from a rusty chain that spans the gorge above the village. This was put up by a local knight to celebrate his release from captivity during the Crusades. The village beneath the star is noted for its pottery, which became famous in medieval times when a monk from Faenza in Italy brought the secret of the glaze with him to the monastery here. By the 18th century, and despite its earlier fame, the potteries had ceased production, but the tradition was revived this century.

HILL VILLAGES

In the high hills of Haute-Provence there is a series of villages as characteristic of the area as the resort towns are of the Côte d'Azur. These are the *villages perchés* (perched villages), sometimes called *nids d'aigle* (eagles' nests). The villages performed the same function as the walled towns of the plains and valleys, or even of the hill-forts of an earlier age, being refuges from marauders. Some of the villages are so close to the coast that they may even have been used as a refuge from seaborne pirates. Many of the villages are piled up in a remarkable but very picturesque way. In the main, however, problems connected with access and water made them less favoured by the inhabitants than by visitors, and many of the least accessible gradually

fell into disrepair. Recently there has been a revival in their fortunes, with craftsmen and city-dwellers restoring the houses and revitalising the communities. Bargème and Trigance (above), near the Grand Canyon du Verdon, are typical hill villages.

VAR AND THE MASSIF DES MAURES

SANDWICHED BETWEEN the *départements* of Alpes Maritimes and Bouches-du-Rhône lies Var. Its coastline includes the extremes of Toulon, a heavily industrialised port, and glamorous St Tropez. There is much of interest to be found between the two, and the coast is backed for much of its length by the Massif des Maures, an extensive range of tree-covered hills.

Bormes-les-Mimosas

Drive east on the N98 from Hyères to Le Lavandou as the sun is rising or setting and you will see Bormes-les-Mimosas at its best, picked out by low-angled light. This charming hill village, alive with mimosa and camomile, offers excellent views from the ruined castle and has an 18th-century church built in the Romanesque style and a museum of local art.

Comité Départemental du Tourisme du Var
Conseil Général du Var
1, Boulevard Foch - BP 99
83003 Draguignan Cedex
Tel: 94 68 58 33

Touring:
use Michelin sheet map 916, Francia

Fréjus/St Raphaël

The two towns form a single conurbation, with Fréjus offering the inland, historical aspects and St Raphaël the beach resort. Fréjus was a Roman port and many sections of the Roman city can still be seen, but the harbour silted up after it was neglected, and efforts to revive the port were finally abandoned. The town's later history includes the construction of a fortified complex that takes in a small cathedral, cloisters, baptistery and a bishop's palace. The baptistery dates from the 4th or 5th century, and is therefore one of the oldest buildings in France.

St Raphaël is a sedate beach resort, a pleasant change, some might say, from St Tropez and the livelier resorts to the east. Its clear waters make it a popular centre for scuba diving.

Hyères

Hyères claims to be the oldest resort on the Côte d'Azur, and indeed in the 16th century Catherine de Medici considered building a royal villa here. Three hundred years later Queen Victoria visited the town, but ultimately its exposed winter position caused it to lose out to resorts further east. Tropical gardens are Hyères' pride: the Parc St-Bernard has a great number of tropical plants, as have the Jardins Olbius-Riquier, where there is also a fine collection of cacti. Even the wide, airy streets of the town are lined with plants.

The pretty village of Bormes-les-Mimosas benefits from a pleasant hillside setting with the sea in front and forest behind. Its three sandy bathing beaches and good-sized marina make it an attractive holiday resort

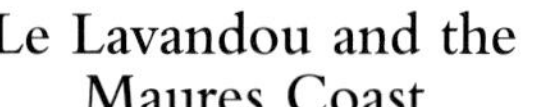

Le Lavandou and the Maures Coast

Le Lavandou is one of the discoveries of the Var coast, a Provençal fishing port that is still just that, despite an increase in tourism further east towards St Tropez. East of Le Lavandou there are several more charming spots, many with excellent beaches: St Clair, Cavalière, Le Rayol-Canadel-sur-Mer and Cavalaire-sur-Mer.

Massif des Maures

The heavily forested Maures – the name derives from the Provençal word for a dark forest – are a rocky range of mountains created in the same geological upheaval that formed Corsica. Today there are vineyards in the lush hill valleys, and cork oaks are grown to provide the corks for the bottles. The range can be explored by a series of narrow,

Cork oaks abound in the densely wooded Massif des Maures, which stretches from Hyères to St Raphaël

The Port-Cros National Park

Most of France's Parcs Nationaux are set in high, unspoilt country – the Cévennes, Vercors and so on. One exception is Port-Cros, which embraces several small islands and a marine nature reserve. The Ile de Port-Cros can be reached by boat from Hyères, Port-de-Miramar (east of Hyères) or from the nearby Ile de Porquerolles. The Park was created in 1963 and protects a sub-sea forest of seaweeds and kelp, inhabited by sea urchins, octopus and a large number of different species of fish. An underwater path is marked out for visiting divers.

On the island itself the vegetation can be divided into four distinct, and equally interesting, areas: the coast, the mountain slopes, the valleys and the high peak – not very high at 194m, but burned out by the sea and wind. The island is also famous for its reptiles, amphibians and butterflies.

The neighbouring Ile du Levant to the east and Ile de Porquerolles to the west, can also be explored. Levant has a single village, Héliopolis, which is used nowadays by naturists.

Ile de Porquerolles, the largest island, has a small holiday village. There are good walks from here to the lighthouse and the signal station, each of which gives a superb view. (Please note that no vehicles are allowed on the islands.)

The very name of St Tropez evokes the luxurious lifestyle associated with the Côte d'Azur as a whole. But alongside the glamorous resort an ordinary little fishing port gets on with its daily business

difficult roads with sudden viewpoints, reaching picturesque villages such as Collobrières, where the river is crossed by a humpback bridge.

Ste Maxime

Across the bay from St Tropez lies Ste Maxime, a lively resort well sheltered from the *mistral*. There are fine beaches, shops, cafés and restaurants, enough entertainment at night to keep the most discerning visitor happy and an extraordinary museum of mechanical music, with old gramophones, music boxes and barrel organs.

St Maximin-la-Ste Baume

For 13 years after the Crucifixion, it is said, Mary Magdalene lived with the Virgin Mary. Then, with several others, she was set adrift on the Mediterranean in an open boat. The party survived the journey and came ashore at Stes Maries-de-la-Mer, and went their separate ways. Mary Magdalene found and occupied a cave high on the mountain-side of St Pilon, on the Massif de la Ste Baume. There she lived for 30 years until, sensing her end, she came down to a village at the foot of the mountain to be blessed by St Maximin, Bishop of Aix.

A Provençal legend of long standing, the story goes on to tell that after Mary's death a church was raised over her sarcophagus, and that which contained the remains of St Maximin. Following a Saracen raid the remains were lost, but were rediscovered in the 13th century. The fine basilica in the town was then built to house the original sarcophagus and the bronze reliquary containing Mary's skull.

St Tropez

It is difficult to separate the real St Tropez from the myth that surrounds it. Yet once the yachts, the topless stars-in-waiting and the dream-seeking crowds have all left, it is revealed as a charming little town, bathed in the pure light that attracted Matisse, Braque and others to the area in the days before its notoriety. Some of their work can be seen in the Musée de Peinture de l'Annonciade. but most visitors come to see the port, the little squares and the view across the bay.

Toulon

France's second naval port was heavily bombed during World War II, its reconstruction creating a modern city, ideal for the shopper but with less to offer the committed tourist. The Tour Royale on the eastern harbour arm was built by Louis XII in the 16th century and has walls over 6m thick. It houses exhibits for which there was not room in the naval museum on the harbour's west side.

Toulon is a good starting-point for a visit to Mont Faron, reached by funivia or road from the north end of the town.

Toulon's naval connections are evident all over the city, whose fine harbour is overlooked by hilltop forts

THE CÔTE D'AZUR AND TOURISM

EVEN BEFORE THE REVOLUTION and the Napoleonic Wars people travelled in the South of France. The English novelist Tobias Smollett, travelling in 1763, wrote of one such journey. The difficulties he described – the section of his journey from Paris to Nice required many days and many means of transport, each slower and more uncomfortable than the one before – would have been enough to keep others away, even without the troubles that effectively closed the area from 1790 until the early 1820s.

Nevertheless, by the time of the Revolution about 100 British families spent their winters on the coast, mostly in Nice. The earliest British inhabitants of the city built the road that now bears their name, the Promenade des Anglais, and were the forerunners of a community that brought the area its earliest commercial success. Later, Russian aristocrats and then American writers and artists discovered the area's charms, making it truly cosmopolitan.

A postcard (above) shows the elegance of Monte Carlo in 1910

Queen Victoria (right) poses in the grounds of the Grand Hôtel in Grasse in 1891, on one of her many holidays on the Côte d'Azur

Cannes (below) was as popular in the 1930s as it is now

THE 19TH CENTURY AND THE BRITISH

In 1863 the railway arrived in Cannes, a year later it was in Nice and by 1868 it had pushed on to Monaco and Menton. The effect was dramatic: what had been an epic multi-day journey from the Channel coast to Nice became a pleasant two-day interlude. Almost at once the number of tourists went up, as did their social standing: Czar Alexander II came to Nice for the first time in the year the railway was opened.

Sixty years after the railway arrived the 'Blue Train' became famous, a train of blue and gold sleeping carriages that whisked the traveller from Calais to the Côte d'Azur in style. The earliest travellers had no such luxury, overnight stops being taken in hotels along the way until the arrival of the first, basic, wagons-lits in the 1880s. But the inconvenience of the night stops was only minor, and the coast from Menton to Cannes soon boasted a thriving British community in winter. There was an English-language newspaper for them, a cricket club was founded in Cannes in 1887 and hotels and shops sprang up that recreated English life.

The making of the Côte d'Azur, usually referred to by the British as the Riviera, as part of the social scene, was the arrival of Queen Victoria in 1882. Usually she stayed at Cimiez – though her first visit was to Menton and later she stayed at Grasse – and repeated her visits every year until 1898.

While in residence, Queen Victoria received in monarchical fashion visitors such as Russian dukes and other assorted European royalty, and on one occasion even the President of France himself.

Such was the impact of the Queen's visit that Menton raised a statue to her. Later members of her family kept up the tradition: Edward VII visited Menton while his mother was still alive, but lived on *Britannia*, moored offshore, to avoid her; and Edward VIII stayed there both before and after he had met Mrs Simpson. Gradually, however, the Côte d'Azur was attracting a greater diversity of visitors.

Russian visits had begun with Czar Alexander II, but it was later the Russian nobility, most specifically a collection of counts and grand dukes with glorious titles, who were to enliven the scene, bringing a boost to the economy as even the British had not, and an eccentricity that even they could not match.

At the start of the 20th century the Russian nobility was joined by the flower of Russian Art, particularly its composers and dancers. Stravinsky, Pavlova and Nijinsky all came, chiefly to join Diaghilev, making Monaco a world centre for ballet.

The 1920s and the Americans

Until the 1920s the season on the Côte d'Azur was a winter one. There were several reasons for this: it was believed that the hot Mediterranean summers were bad for health, the mosquitoes were awful and food did not keep well. But things were changing: refrigerators helped with the food, while DDT eliminated the mosquitoes. It took the Americans to recognise the benefits of the summer. Frank Jay Gould arrived in the early 1920s and realised the potential immediately, converting the tiny village of Juan-les-Pins, near Antibes, into a playground for those who wished to do little but soak up the sun. At about the same time Gerald and Sara Murphy, having been introduced to the area by Cole Porter, bought a villa at Antibes and turned it into a mecca for American artists. The Côte d'Azur had been popular with writers for some years – D H Lawrence is buried at Vence, for instance – but it was the arrival of Scott and Zelda Fitzgerald, Ernest Hemingway, Isadora Duncan, Gertrude Stein and Dorothy Parker that brought it pre-eminence. Of these it is the Fitzgeralds who have become synonymous with the area, which Scott immortalised in *Tender is the Night*.

Anything goes in St Tropez, now a playground for all rather than just for the rich and famous

The villa scene that formed around the Fitzgeralds outlived their final departure in 1929, though it was a short-lived survival, for World War II drew a veil over the Côte d'Azur for almost a decade.

When peace returned the old order had gone. The French now owned the Côte d'Azur, having reclaimed it from the impoverished English and absent Americans. Since the 1960s, however, it has once again become an international playground.

The Monte Carlo Casino

As early as 1856 the Prince of Monaco had granted a licence for the running of a casino within the principality, though it was not until the coming of the railway that the venture really took off. By then the licence was held by François Blanc, who made a great deal of money for himself as well as the prince. The locals soon had a saying that on the roulette wheel the win might sometimes be *rouge*, and sometimes *noir*, but it was always *Blanc*. The later history of the building was one of both increasing social importance and influence. The British Prime Minister was declined admittance when he could not show his passport. A local priest changed his church's hymns after one punter had put his life's savings on the last number on the hymn list – and won.

Monte Carlo's Casino (above)

Menton is an attractive resort framed by mountains (left)

The Casino was even able to make capital, so to speak, from the myth of its bank being broken. It range a bell and sent someone out for more cash if a player had seven consecutive wins, or a win over a certain limit, and this gave rise to great excitement and publicity.

Today the Casino is a fine building, sumptuously decorated, that looks especially good when it and the fountains outside are floodlit. Inside a passport is still needed by those who play in the big gaming rooms.

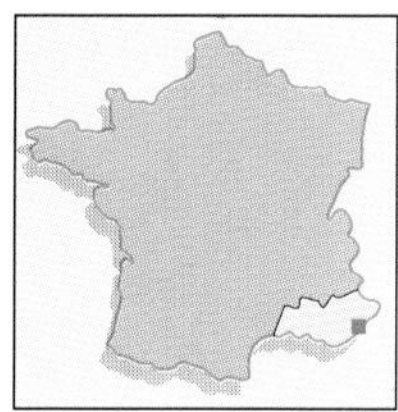

THE WESTERN CÔTE D'AZUR

THE NAME 'CÔTE D'AZUR' was coined in 1887 in a poem by Stephen Liégeard. Strictly speaking, it applies to the whole coastline between La Napoule in the west and Menton, near the Italian border, in the east. While nowadays the name is used more commonly of the stretch of coast east of Nice, the luminous blue water of the western section is equally deserving of the name.

The grandest of Cannes' many fine hotels are to be found along the elegant palm-tree-lined Boulevard de la Croisette

Cannes hosts the world's top film festival, a tradition which is celebrated here by the handprint of the American star Meryl Streep

Antibes/Juan-les-Pins

Antibes has an important place in French history, for Napoleon Bonaparte was placed in charge of it early in his career in 1794, and landed here when he returned from exile on Elba. The great man was snubbed by his old garrison at Antibes, and marched to Paris via Cannes. Ironically, there is a fine maritime museum, the Musée Naval et Napoléonien, on Cap d'Antibes.

Today the town is more famous as a holiday centre, particularly the adjoining village of Juan-les-Pins, which lies on the Cap. This delightful spot, with pines growing right down to the beach, is a centre for café society during the day and night-clubbers after dark.

Cannes

Now world-famous for its international film festival, Cannes grew up when the importance of the bay, the Golfe de la Napoule, was recognised. The bay is sheltered not only by the headlands of La Croisette, but by the offshore Iles de Lérins, and both the Celts and the Romans built settlements where Cannes now stands.

It was given its name, which derives from *cannes*, the reeds that grew in the harbour, in the 10th century when a pirates' watch-tower was erected on Mont Chevalier, where the Tour Suquet still stands. Local monks organised the defences, with one holy order taking care of the watch and another concerning itself with the ransoming of important prisoners taken in skirmishes. Though the 12th-century tower is only 22m high, it is a good vantage point. Le Suquet, the old quarter of Cannes, is spread out below; perhaps not quite as picturesque as Nice's equivalent section, but a welcome contrast to the bustle of the newer town.

To best enjoy the town, take a stroll along the elegant Boulevard de la Croisette. This starts at the marina, with its colourful collection of yachts, all seeming to spend more time at anchor than at sea, and continues between the town, to the left, and the beach, to the right. Cannes remains prosperous, boasting many sophisticated hotels, shops and restaurants.

ART AND THE CÔTE D'AZUR

The brilliant light, the clarity of the air and the benign climate have long attracted artists to the Côte d'Azur, but it is for its association with painters of the 20th century that the area is most renowned. Pablo Picasso lived in the South of France from 1946 until his death in 1973, the final years of his self-imposed exile from his native Spain. Much of that time he spent on the coast and the Musée Picasso in the Château Grimaldi at Antibes reflects the influence of the area on his work. There are numerous works in the museum, but one complete section, known as the 'Antibes paintings', is concerned with the Mediterranean and the folklore of the Côte d'Azur. Elsewhere in the museum there are drawings and lithographs, as well as ceramics.

Other works by the Spanish master can be seen in the Musée National Pablo-Picasso at Vallauris. The museum is housed in the chapel of the town's Renaissance château, and its centrepiece is *War and Peace*, a huge

Comité Regional du Tourisme de Riviera
55, Promenade des Anglais - BP 602
06011 Nice
Tel: 93 44 50 59

Touring:
use Michelin sheet map 245, Provence/Côte d'Azur

mural that took Picasso seven years to complete. The château also houses the Musée Municipale, which holds a bequest of work by the modern artist Magnelli, who lived in Grasse. The poster below was produced by Picasso in 1966 for the city of Cannes.

The twin towns of St Paul and Vence also reflect the growth of 20th-century art in the area. Vence has a chapel decorated by Henri Matisse over a five-year period around 1950. Matisse was delighted with the work. It had its imperfections, he said, but it was also his masterpiece, the culmination of a 'lifetime devoted to the search for truth'.

At St Paul is the Fondation Maeght, which houses works by Braque, who lived at Le Cannet, Chagall, who was stimulated by the light of Vence, Kandinsky, who was based in La Napoule, and Fernand Léger from Biot, as well as works by Miró and other modern artists. Léger has his own museum at Biot.

The Musée Renoir at Cagnes-sur-Mer fills the house where the Impressionist painter spect his last years.

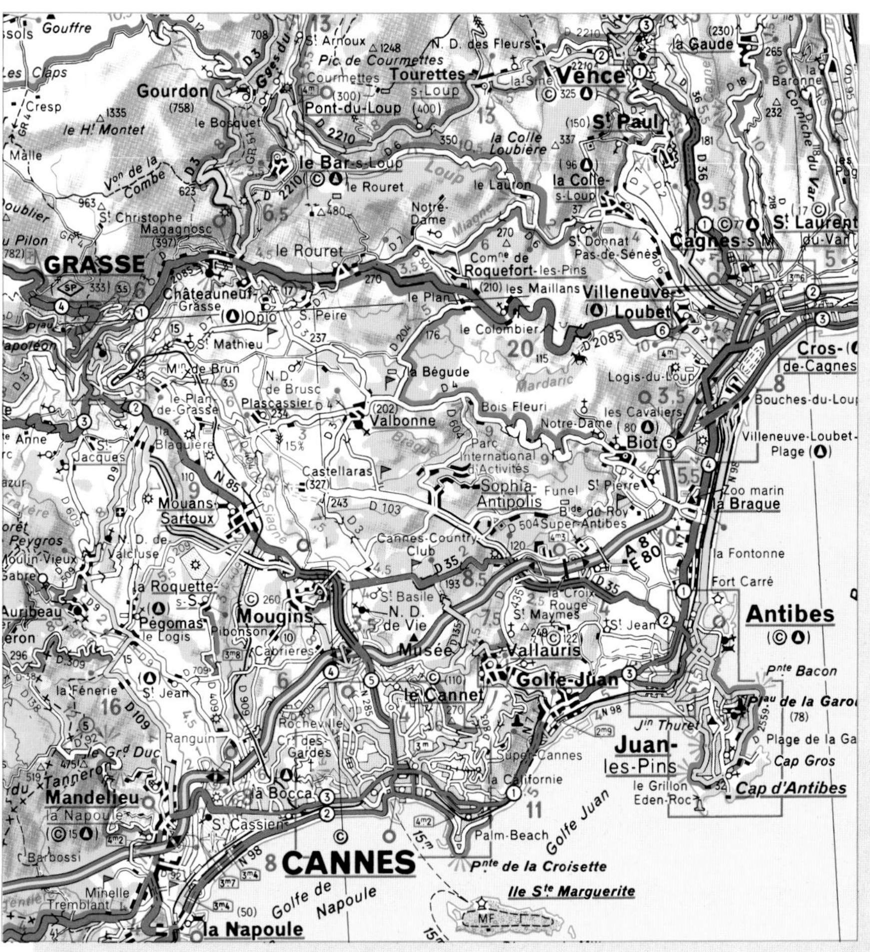

Gourdon

Just north of Grasse is the Gorges du Loup, a wonderful narrow gorge that is explored by a twisting road. The entrance to the gorge was once controlled by a castle on a spur of rock, and that castle survives as the centre-piece of the charming hill village of Gourdon. The earliest castle was built by the Saracens, but what is now seen dates from the 13th century. The castle holds a varied collection of arms and armour. From Gourdon a lovely drive follows the River Loup to Cagnes-sur-Mer.

Grasse

The centre of the important local perfume industry, Grasse was a republic in the 12th century. Here, in 1732, Jean-Honoré Fragonard was born, one of the most important artists at the time of the Revolution. His work can be seen in the Musée Fragonard.

Grasse is a charming place and those not visiting it for the perfumeries will still find much of interest. Relax with a coffee in the open-air cafés of Place aux Aires and admire the elaborate fountain, or stroll through the Jardin de la Princesse Pauline.

Mougins

Visitors who follow the A8 from Nice to Cannes will be surprised to find, in a service area north of Le Cannet, the entrance to a car museum. But is there really any better way to enter such a museum, with over 200 old cars, than from a motor-way? The address of the museum is Mougins, though it is a little farther on to this hill-top village with its splendid views and photography museum.

St Paul/Vence

These twin towns are perhaps most famous for their artistic associations (see box). But both, surrounded by perfume-flower fields, have further attractions. St Paul sits behind its still largely intact medieval walls and has a fine Gothic church, while Vence, also walled, has an impressive Romanesque cathedral. Be sure, if you visit Vence, to see Place du Peyra, which occupies the site of the old Roman forum and is the centre of the old town. With its fountain and trees, this is a cool and tranquil place.

The Perfume Industry

The world-famous perfume industry that is based around Grasse started in the 16th century, when the town was a centre for leatherwork, chiefly glove making. The Parisian taste for perfumed gloves led to the development of a small local industry that grew considerably in the 18th and 19th-centuries, and is now one of the most important sources of local employment.

The basic ingredients are grown around Grasse, so that a drive through the lanes near the town can be a heady experience. The fields are multi-coloured, the air filled with the heavy, almost sickly scent of lavender, jasmine, orange, cherry, eucalyptus, mimosa and many other varieties of flower. And yet Grasse is not the

home of perfume making, for the final blending is carried out, in secret, by the famous perfume houses in Paris. At Grasse the flowers are dissolved to extract their scent. The solvent is then distilled to produce the scent in a concentrated form, and it is this concentrate that is sent to Paris.

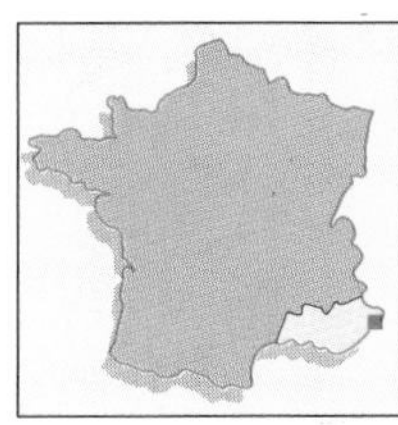

NICE TO MENTON

WHEN THE BRILLIANT BLUE OF THE MEDITERRANEAN is seen from the high *corniches* that follow the coast between Nice and Menton, it is easy to understand why this stretch of coast, perhaps more than that to the west, is thought of as the heart of the Côte d'Azur. This is a busy, densely populated coastline, a vibrant and colourful area that invigorates all the senses.

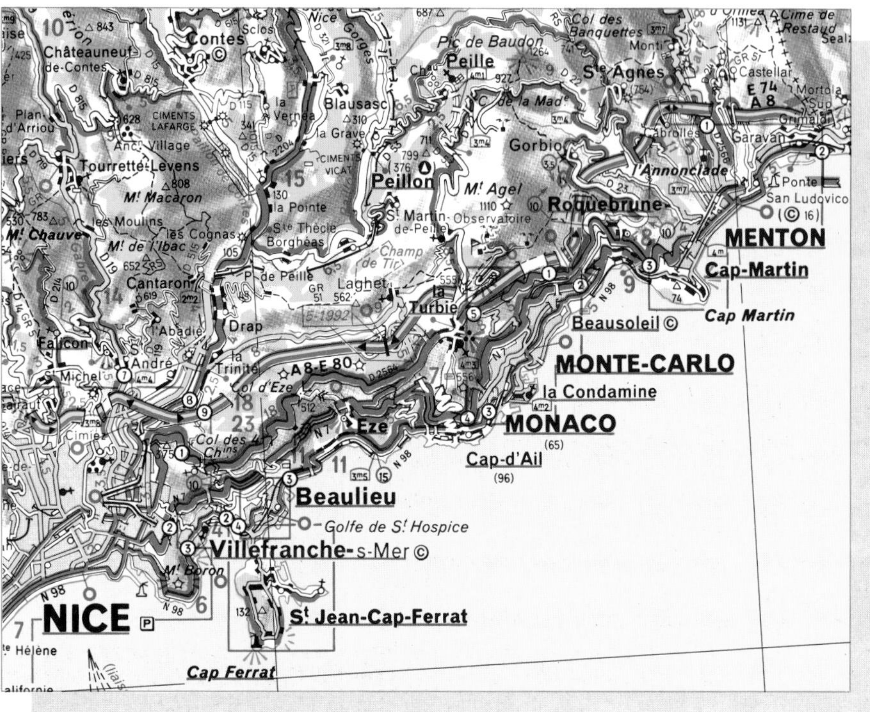

Menton

Menton, which claims to be the warmest town on the Côte d'Azur and boasts citrus orchards that reinforce the claim, is a typically Italian town set down in France. Despite its piled-up, cluttered look when seen from the sea, Menton is surprisingly spacious. The Jardin Biovès, at the western end of the Promenade du Soleil, is fringed with palm and lemon trees, while at the other end of the town the Colombières gardens have a splendid collection of Mediterranean shrubs and flowers.

Within the town itself the Musée Jean-Cocteau, at the southern corner of the port, has a good collection of the artist's work. Admirers of Cocteau should also visit the town hall to see the Salle des Mariages, which he decorated with murals depicting, among other things, a traditional Menton fisherman and a girl in a Nice bonnet. Across the port from the Cocteau museum is the Jetée Impératrice Eugénie, with its fine statue by Volti.

Comité Regional du Tourisme de Riviera
55, Promenade des Anglais - BP 602
06011 Nice
Tel: 93 44 50 59

Touring:
use Michelin sheet map 245, Provence/Côte d'Azur

Beaulieu

Cap Ferrat is reached across a narrow neck of land, on the inland side of which is Beaulieu, a resort town grouped around the sheltered Baie des Fourmis. Overlooking the bay is the Villa Kerylos, a faithful 20th-century reconstruction of a Greek villa.

Cap Ferrat

Beyond the Mont Boron headland, Cap Ferrat thrusts out into the Mediterranean. At its southern point – Cap Ferrat itself, though that name is now more commonly applied to the whole peninsula – is a lighthouse where a climb up 164 steps reveals an awesome panorama.

On the Cap there is a zoo and the old fishing village of St Jean-Cap-Ferrat. No visitor should miss the Musée Ile de France, an Italianate villa which displays Flemish tapestries, Chinese porcelain and Impressionist paintings, including works by Monet and Renoir.

Monaco

Completely surrounded by France, the Prinicipality of Monaco is a sovereign state of less than 200 hectares and with fewer than 25,000 inhabitants. Of these only about 4000 are genuine Monégasques, a population who preserve their own language, Monégasco, a French dialect. Monaco has its own car licence plates, stamps and money (though the latter is tied to the French franc, which is legal tender) and everything the tourist needs.

Hilly Menton gently echoes the mountains that lie behind it. The vantage point of the Jetée Impératrice Eugénie gives a good view of both the town and the peaks. Near by is Cap-Martin, another splendid viewpoint

Villefranche-sur-Mer is a fishing port with the added attraction of the fine Citadelle, now a museum

The Principality comprises three separate 'towns': Monaco itself, with the Palais du Prince; La Condamine, the commercial centre; and Monte Carlo, with its casino, marina and exclusive hotels, shops and restaurants. For many it is Monte Carlo that is the draw, a fabled, glittering town. But it comes as a surprise to learn that the Casino – a sumptuous building that looks even better when floodlit – now provides only 3 per cent of Monaco's income. The memory of past glories remains strong, however. But to appreciate Monte Carlo it is not necessary to be a big spender. The parks and gardens are beautiful, the seafront and views outstanding, while beyond the Grand Prix's hairpin bend the Galéa collection of dolls and automata is thought by many to be the world's best.

The Changing of the Guard outside Monaco's Palais du Prince preserves an ancient tradition much loved by visitors

Monaco is more staid, though no less glamorous. The palace of the Grimaldi family – who have ruled the Principality since the 14th century – is both ornate and imposing. Visitors walk past the distinctive guards and below the fish-tailed battlements on a guided tour. Close by is the superb Jardin Exotique, with thousands of varieties of cacti and other succulents, and breathtaking views across to Monte Carlo. But no less fascinating is the Musée Océanographique, holding over 4000 species of fish from all over the world.

Nice

Nice is regarded by many, and certainly the city itself, as the capital of the Côte d'Azur. It enjoys a beautiful setting, sheltered on its landward side by a ring of low hills and on its seaward side by the headlands that enclose a semicircular section of the Baie des Anges. Travellers arriving by air will be treated to breathtaking views of the coast on landing, and will be astonished by how close they are to the city, for the airport is right by the seafront.

The seafront road is the Promenade des Anglais. Its name recalls the efforts of the 19th-century British community, who built the earliest road, in order to provide better access to the water.

Nice is divided into two by the River Paillon, though for much of its journey through the city this flows beneath the buildings. To the east of the river is the old quarter. Until 1860 Nice was Italian – Garibaldi, the hero of the Italian Risorgimento, was born here – and that ancestry is reflected in the buildings close to the old port. The port, and the older, Italianate, quarter are overlooked by the 'castle', which is no more than a wide, flat-topped hill once occupied by a fortress that was demolished in the early 18th century. In the old quarter below is the Palais Lascaris, built in Genoese style by a 17th-century Count of Ventimiglia, and furnished in the grand Italian tradition. Nearby is the Malacology Museum, which houses a large shell collection, while in Rue de la Loge is the newly opened Galerie Municipale Renoir, which, unexpectedly, exhibits works by contemporary artists rather than those of Renoir.

Villefranche-sur-Mer

Nestling on the island flank of Mont Boron, and protected by Cap Ferrat, is Villefranche-sur-Mer, a delightful old fishing and trading port. The port was guarded by the Citadelle, built in the mid-16th century by a Duke of Savoy. The castle was built after the Congress of Nice, held in 1538 in an effort to bring peace between Charles V, Emperor of the Holy Roman Empire, and François I of France.

Nice Carnival

Exactly when the first Carnival took place in Nice is debatable. Certainly it was held in the 14th century, and there is evidence for its having taken place at least two centuries earlier. Probably it was a pagan springtime rite even earlier still. After the Restoration, in 1814, the Carnival fell into decline and would probably have disappeared altogether had not Nice's Russian community shown an interest in reviving it 50 years later. Then, in 1873, the Nice painter, Alexis Massa, restored the Carnival to its present form. The Carnival, or Mardi Gras, occupies the two weeks before Lent.

The Russian Orthodox Cathedral in Nice was consecrated in 1912. This magnificent building is constructed of red brick faced with grey marble and is topped by six onion domes

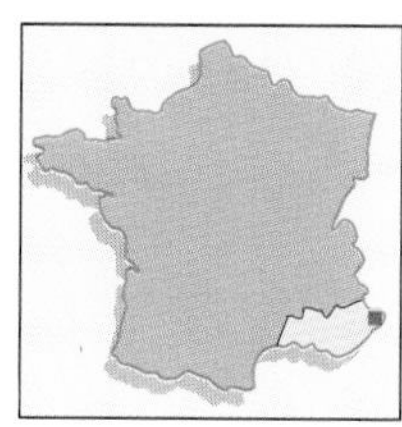

THE ROYA VALLEY AND THE MERCANTOUR NATIONAL PARK

NORTH OF MENTON, and reached most easily by crossing into and then out of Italy, is the Roya valley, at the head of which the traveller crosses back into Italy again. The Roya is a delight: narrow sections of gorge, hill villages seemingly hanging over the valley and several fine valley towns. To the west is the most historically interesting section of the Parc National du Mercantour.

Apart from having about half of the species of wild flowers native to France, and some 40 unique to the area, the Parc National du Mercantour boasts abundant wildlife, including rare birds, chamois, ibex and marmots, and many species of butterflies and other insects

Comité Regional du Tourisme de Riviera
55, Promenade des Anglais - BP 602
06011 Nice
Tel: 93 44 50 59

Touring:
use Michelin sheet map 245, Provence/Côte d'Azur

Col de Turini

Set on the opposite side of the Parc National du Mercantour from the Roya valley, Col de Turini is a high pass on the route from Sospel to St Martin-Vésubie. North-east of the pass the Pointe des Trois Communes offers a superb view of the Mercantour and south towards Nice. Here too is a monument to the battles fought in the area in 1793, when the Roya became French, and in 1944-5, when it was liberated from Axis control.

Madone del Poggio

Within easy walking distance of Saorge lies the chapel of the Madone del Poggio. Its name and architecture – it is pure 16th-century Romanesque – betray its Italian origins. The bell tower is decorated in Lombard style, and there are fine frescos inside. The several altarpieces in the chapel include a *pietà*.

Close by and set among olive trees, is a Franciscan convent built in the 17th century; later abandoned, it was only re-occupied within the past 25 years.

Parc National du Mercantour

Created in 1979, this is the most recent of the Parcs Nationaux. It covers parts of both the Alpes Maritimes and Haute-Provence and adjoins Italy's Argentera National Park. The Park consists of high rocky peaks and lush valleys, but was created chiefly to protect the rock engravings around Mont Bégo (see box).

The Park's flora is especially interesting, as it includes both alpine species such as saxifrage and Mediterranean species such as the olive. In all, around half of France's native flowers can be found growing in the Park, and about 40 species are unique to the area. A variety of insects feed on these flowers, including a large number of Europe's more exotic species of butterfly.

The bird life is excellent, the royal eagle and Tengmalm's owl being of particular interest to ornithologists. Animals that inhabit the area include chamois and ibex, but the most noticeable and unusual creature is the marmot, a big cuddly rodent.

MONT BÉGO

Mont Bégo is set at a point where the hot Mediterranean air moving north meets the cool Alpine air moving south. Where these air masses meet there are frequent thunderstorms, though this occurs commonly enough in a mountainous area. The difference in this case is that Mont Bégo is a ferritic mountain, so it attracts lightning. The sight of constant lightning strikes on the peak is believed to have convinced the Bronze Age folk who lived below it that gods inhabited the sparking mountain and communicated with the gods of the heavens by way of lightning. The people therefore climbed to the remote Merveilles and Fontanalbe valleys below the summit and inscribed offerings on the exposed rocks, which had been worn smooth by the glaciers of the last Ice Age.

The engravers chose rocks that allowed them to make inscriptions that could either be seen by the gods in the mountain, or that allowed them to see the peak as they worked. They carved using a stipple technique, the drawings comprising closely grouped dots

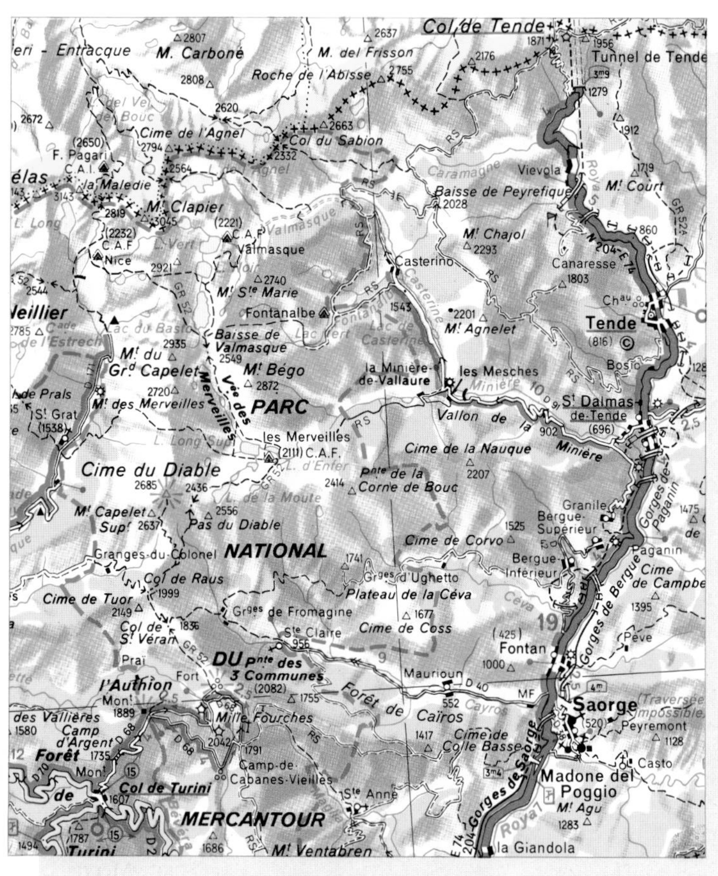

made by striking a sharp tool – an antler perhaps – with a stone or hammer. The engravings themselves fall into distinct groups: there is a plough pulled by bulls (represented only by their heads); there are axes and geometric patterns that are believed to represent fields and houses; and there is a small group of unique engravings. Of the latter the most significant are a Christ-like head, a sorcerer, and one called the 'Chief of the Tribe', a figure with hands outstretched but feet turned inwards.

In all, more than 100,000 engravings have been found. It is believed that the great majority of these date from the Bronze Age, though it is possible that some are later. The Merveilles guides' office in Tende can give advice about visiting the engravings.

More often heard than seen, the marmot whistles when alarmed, giving a piercing call that carries for a considerable distance. All visitors who leave their cars and walk in the Park are likely to hear marmots, though patience and a little luck will be needed to catch a glimpse of the whistler.

Saorge

Travelling up the Roya valley from its southern end the visitor reaches the narrow Gorges de Saorge, and the first sight of the village itself. Saorge sits in a natural amphitheatre high on the right wall of the gorge, apparently hanging above the river. It was claimed in medieval times that the site, a possession of the Grimaldis of Monaco, was impregnable, but it was taken by the French in 1794.

Cars cannot enter Saorge, and visitors walk through on foot the narrow, twisting streets, going under arches and past houses reached by spiralling, stepped paths. From a balcony on the valley side of the village the view of the gorge is particularly impressive. At the back of the village stands the fine 15th-century church of St-Sauveur, which has some fine altarpieces and paintings. The murals in the church were completed by artists of the Roya valley school of painting, which was active in the 17th and 18th centuries.

Tende

Tende is the home of the Merveilles guides, a group of official guides of the Parc National du Mercantour who escort visitors around the engravings of Mont Bégo (see box). It is an interesting town, with a labyrinth of narrow, tortuous streets between piled-up houses, and all in the shadow of the ruins of a medieval castle.

Vallée du Roya

Until the end of the 18th century this valley was involved in tangled political struggles with Italy. In the French expansion eastward of 1794, following the Revolution and Napoleon's rise to power, the valley was placed firmly in France, along with Nice. In 1814, when Napoleon abdicated and went into exile, both Nice and the valley were returned to the kingdom of Sardinia.

Ancient Saorge was a Ligurian and then a Roman settlement. This village of narrow, winding streets seems to hang from the hillside and can only be explored on foot, because cars are prohibited from entering

Finally, in 1860 with the reunification of Italy, the area around Nice was once more transferred to France – much to the disgust of the Italian hero Garibaldi, who was born in that city in 1807. Much of the architecture of the valley settlements is Italian and, since the head of the valley is defended by a fort of Mussolini and other buildings of Il Duce also exist, a drive up the valley can feel like a drive through Italy.

INDEX

Place names preceded by Le, La or Les are listed under their second component
Page numbers in italic refer to captions

A

B

C

R

S

T

U

V

Y

ACKNOWLEDGEMENTS

The Automobile Association would like to thank the following photographers, libraries and associations for their assistance in the preparation of this book.

J ALLAN CASH PHOTOLIBRARY 21 Vitré Castle, Combourg Castle, 27 Dinard, St. Malo, 79 Chenonceaux, 135 Pilat Dunes, 155 View from Puy de Sancy, 155 Riom Virgin & Bird, 178 Grand Port, Aix-les-Bains, 203 Les Eyzies skeleton, 216/7 Basque countryside, 216 Basque houses, 220 Cirque de Gavarnie.

ANCIENT ART & ARCHITECTURE COLLECTION 202 Cave paintings Les Eyzies, Grotte de Font-de-Gaume paintings, 209 Grotte du Peche-Merle Cave painting.

ARCTIC CAMERA 250 Parc National du Mercantour.

P ATTERBURY 51 Vimy.

BRIDGEMAN ART LIBRARY 237 Montagne Ste-Victoire, 246 Picasso's Cannes.

CHAMONIX TOURIST BOARD 185 Mont Blanc.

J CRUTTENDEN 99 Royal Palace seats.

E T ARCHIVE 103 Monet painting.

FRENCH GOVERNMENT TOURIST OFFICE 55 Giant.

FRENCH PICTURE LIBRARY (BARRIE SMITH) 101 Lido entertainer, 183 Chamonix, 195 Fishing, 226 Train, Cerdagne, 228 St Martin du Canigou, St Michel-de-Cuxa, 229 Corneilla-de-Conflent.

HAUTE SAVOIE 170 River Drance – Canoeist, 181 Lac d'Annecy.

LE STRADE AVEN ARMAND 167 Le Palmier.

J LLOYD 22 Roscoff, 130 Cascades du Hérisson, 140 Marais Poitevin, 164 Cévennes, 172 Lyon, Silk weaving, 173 Tournon, Vivarais railway, 174 Aven d'Orgnac, 175 Belvédère de la Madeleine, 220 Climbers, 221 Luz-St Sauveur.

MARY EVANS PICTURE LIBRARY 106 Louis XIV, 116 Medieval Cloisters, 185 Voegeli climbs Pic du Toedi, 199 Cyrano de Bergerac, 244 Monte Carlo, Queen Victoria at Grasse, Cannes.

J MILLAR 156 Parc Régional des Volcans d'Auvergne, 186 L'Ecot, 187 Vallée d'Avérole.

NATIONAL TRUST 104 Sèvres china.

NATURE PHOTOGRAPHERS LTD 83 Scarce swallowtail butterfly (K J Carlson), 141 Mussels (P R Sterry), 180 Alpine flowers (B. Burbidge), 226 Alpine meadows (C. Wilson).

OFFICE DÉPARTEMENTAL DE TOURISME DU DORDOGNE 196 Lascaux II Caves.

PICTURES COLOUR LIBRARY 182 The Cerdagne, Llo carvings.

R SALE 250 Merveilles Chief of Tribe.

SCOPE 169 Roquefort cheese, 222 Bourisp Fresco-Les Péchés Capitaux, 223 Guchan, Champ de Parots, St Lary-Soulan.

SPECTRUM COLOUR LIBRARY 21 Fougères Fortress, 93 Les Invalides, 100 Bäteau-mouches, 101 Folies Bergère, 112 Balloon festival, 163 Le Puy-en-Velay, 166 Grottes des Demoiselles, 247 Lavender fields.

TONY STONE WORLDWIDE 2/3 Farmhouse.

THE PHOTOGRAPHERS LIBRARY 156 Salers, 180 Annecy & town.

VLOO 53 Amiens cathedral, 114 Farm in the Morvan, 117 La Charité-sur-Loire, 158 St Gervais-d'Auvergne, Mozac church, 159 Pelissier Cathedral de Clermont-Ferrand, 179 Lac du Bourget, 185 Alpine sport.

WALT DISNEY CO © 104 Mad Hatter's Tea Cups, Euro Disney.

WORLD PICTURES LTD 68 Strasbourg old town, 84 Blois Château, 179 Chambéry, Fontaine des Eléphants, 181 View across L'Annecy, 183 Mer de Glace.

ZEFA PICTURE LIBRARY (UK) LTD 13 Carnac standing stones, Finistère, 14 Carnac, 15 Quiberon, 16 Quimper cathedral, 19 Crozon Coast, 57 Reims Cathedral, 69 Colmar, 94 Place du Tertre, Paris 163 Le Puy Cathedral.

All remaining pictures are held in the Association's own library **(AA PHOTOLIBRARY)** with contributions from:

P Bennett, J Edmunson, P Enticknap, P Kenward, D Noble, T Oliver, D Robertson, C Sawyer, M Short, B Smith, A Souter, R Strange, R Victor.

The publishers would like to acknowledge the facilities and assistance provided to the authors by the following:

Aunis Nord Tourisme
Brittany Ferries
Toby Oliver of Brittany Ferries
Departmental Tourist Offices
The Ford Motor Company Limited
The French Government Tourist Office
Novatel
P & O Ferries
Véronique Seban of the Côte d'Azur tourist office